Human physiology

M S. 1868-1934 Pembrey

THE PORTSMOUTH GRAMMAR SCHOOL

PRAEMIA VIRTUTIS HONORES

Prize Giving 2018

Serena White

Combined Cadet Force Cups:

Wessex Cup: Army

Dr A Cotton - Head

MACMILLAN AND CO., Limited
LONDON · BOMBAY · CALCUTTA
MELBOURNE

THE MACMILLAN COMPANY
NEW YORK · BOSTON · CHICAGO
ATLANTA · SAN FRANCISCO

THE MACMILLAN CO. OF CANADA, Ltd.

HUMAN PHYSIOLOGY

BY

PROFESSOR LUIGI LUCIANI

DIRECTOR OF THE PHYSIOLOGICAL INSTITUTE OF THE ROYAL UNIVERSITY OF ROME

TRANSLATED BY

FRANCES A. WELBY

EDITED BY

DR. M. CAMIS

INSTITUTE OF PHYSIOLOGY, UNIVERSITY OF PISA

WITH A PREFACE BY

J. N. LANGLEY, F.R.S.

PROFESSOR OF PHYSIOLOGY IN THE UNIVERSITY OF CAMBRIDGE

IN FOUR VOLUMES

VOL. I.—CIRCULATION AND RESPIRATION

MACMILLAN AND CO., LIMITED
ST. MARTIN'S STREET, LONDON

1911

PREFACE

"GOOD wine needs no bush," but it will perhaps not be an infringement of this maxim to introduce, in a few words, Professor
Luciani's excellent *Text-Book of Physiology* to the English-reading
public. The Italian Text-book is now in its third edition, the
final pages being in the Press. One or other of the earlier editions
has been translated into French, German, and Russian, and it is
a matter for surprise that we have had to wait so long for an
English version.

In the making of physiological text-books, we are at the
parting of the ways. The physiologists of the past generation
were brought up to know with familiarity all that had been
recently done in physiological research, whether in vertebrates or
invertebrates, in animals or in plants. The facts were not so
numerous that they could not be stored in the memory without
cumbering the judgment, and Physiologists could in some sort
be first-hand authorities on all branches of the subject. That
condition has been gradually passing away, and it is hardly
possible for any one who is not of the old school to write an
advanced text-book covering the whole ground of Physiology.
Thus the text-book of single authorship is giving way to the
text-book of multiple authorship. The latter, whatever its merits,
has not the unity of view and the sense of proportion which
belong to the former—qualities very important in a book intended
for students.

Professor Luciani's book, whilst describing phenomena with
considerable detail, treats lucidly the broad principles to be
deduced from them. It stands midway between the text-book
which confines itself to summing up the results of physiological
investigation, and that which gives also a minute historical
account of the progress of investigation. It deals with the main

--

outlines of the history of each branch of the subject, but does not allow this to interfere with the even flow of narration.

It is natural that writers of Text-books should make frequent reference to the work that has been done by their own country-men. Italian work is less widely known than it deserves, and one of the advantages of this book for English-speaking folk is that Italian workers receive their meed of notice. It will, how-ever, be a shock to many English readers to find that Professor Luciani allots the discovery of the systemic circulation of the blood to his countryman, Cesalpinus. That the circulation of the blood was described and demonstrated by Harvey, no one doubts. That there were a number of forerunners of Harvey who under-stood this or that important fact connected with the circulation is equally undoubted. In considering the place to be assigned to each of those who helped to solve the problem, two separate questions arise. First. How far are the facts and views original and not obtained from unacknowledged sources? and secondly, What was the exact degree of understanding of the subject possessed by each writer? It may seem that the former question only would be difficult to solve. In fact, the difficulty of the latter is no less, or at any rate differences of opinion with regard to it have not been less ardent; and so we find that whilst most authorities regard Cesalpinus as having but imperfectly compre-hended the systemic circulation, and to have seen it " darkly through Galenical glasses," some, as Professor Luciani, consider that his comprehension was whole and without flaw.

Finally, it may be noted that the Editor, Dr. Camis, has added at the end of each chapter a selected list of English-written Monographs and Papers, and thus has put the student who knows no other language than English in the way of obtaining a fuller knowledge of any branch of Physiology in which he may be interested.

J. N. LANGLEY.

TRANSLATOR'S NOTE

I BEG to offer my sincere thanks to Dr. Aders-Plimmer for his kind help in the translation of the chemical section of this volume: and to Mr. W. L. Symes for assistance in many other technical difficulties.

FRANCES A. WELBY.

CONTENTS

INTRODUCTION 1

1. Threefold division of biological science. 2. Special objects of physiology. 3. Materialism, neo-vitalism, Ostwald's energetic monism, Mach's psychical monism, pragmatic pluralism. 4. Physiology of the cell; general and comparative physiology; human physiology. Bibliography.

CHAPTER I

LIVING MATTER: ITS CHEMICAL AND PHYSICAL BASIS . . 11

1. The cell-theory. 2. Morphology of the cell. 3. Structure of protoplasm. 4. Structure of nucleus. 5. Chemical elements of the cell. 6. Proteins basis of living matter. 7. Classification of proteins. 8. Chemical constitution of proteins. 9. Enzymes or ferments. 10. Classification. 11. Other nitrogenous organic substances, fats, carbohydrates or saccharides, inorganic substances. 12. Chemical structure of living matter. Bibliography.

CHAPTER II

LIVING MATTER: ITS FUNDAMENTAL PROPERTIES . . . 42

1. Vital metabolism, and phenomena of nutrition and reproduction. 2. Vital metabolism and phenomena of excitability and sensibility. 3. Laws of stability and variability of living species. Critical examination of Theory of Evolution: Darwinism, and Neo-Lamarckism. 4. Evolutionary theories of Nægeli, Weismann, De Vries. 5. Distinctive characters of plants and animals: a Doctrine of Linnaeus; b doctrine of Cuvier; c doctrine of J. R. Mayer, Dumas, Liebig. 6. Different forms of plant and animal metabolism: a Nitrifying bacteria; b green plants; c a-chlorophyllous plants; d herbivorous and carnivorous plants. Bibliography.

CHAPTER III

PAGE

LIVING MATTER: CONDITIONS BY WHICH IT IS DETERMINED   .   64

1. Nutrition the necessary external condition of vital metabolism. Phenomena of inanition. 2. Importance of water. Latent life and anabiosis. 3. Importance of oxygen. Aerobic and anaerobic life. 4. External temperature indispensable to life. 5. Total pressure of air and water, and partial pressure of oxygen and carbonic acid. 6. External stimuli. 7. Chemical stimuli. Chemotaxis. 8. Mechanical stimuli. Barotaxis. 9. Thermal stimuli: thermotaxis. 10. Photic stimuli. Phototaxis and Heliotaxis. 11. Electrical stimuli. Galvanotaxis. 12. The various biological zones of ocean life *Plankton's*. 13. Internal conditions and stimuli of metabolism. Theory of automatism. 14. Hypotheses to explain the intimate mechanism of living matter. Bibliography.

CHAPTER IV

THE BLOOD: FORMED CONSTITUENTS   91

1. Arrangement of human physiology, and classification of functions. 2. Importance of the blood as centre of the vegetative system and agent of general metabolism. 3. Historical development of haematology. 4. General physico-chemical characters of the blood. 5. Estimation of total quantity. 6. Physical and morphological characters of erythrocytes, and estimation of their relative quantity. 7. Chemical composition. Properties of haemoglobin and its derivatives. 8. Character, composition, and physiological properties of leucocytes. 9. Blood platelets, and elementary granulation of the blood. Bibliography.

CHAPTER V

THE BLOOD: PLASMA   123

1. Different methods for separation of blood plasma from corpuscles. 2. Histogenic substances or proteins of plasma: fibrinogen, serum globulin, serum albumin, sero-mucoid. 3. Nitrogenous histolytic products of plasma. 4. Fatty substances. Carbohydrates and their derivatives. 5. Inorganic substances. Blood gases. 6. Theory of Coagulation: (*a*) Conditions of blood coagulation; (*b*) disintegration of corpuscles as cause of coagulation; (*c*) fibrinogen as fibrin generator; (*d*) analogies between blood coagulation and curdling of milk; (*e*) importance of time in coagulation; (*f*) thrombin and nucleins as coagulating substances; (*g*) histone and cytoglobulin as anti-coagulating substances. 7. Osmotic pressure, molecular concentration, electrical conductivity and viscosity of blood and serum. 8. Functions of the blood: (*a*) effects of bleeding; (*b*) effects of transfusion of homo- and heterogeneous blood; (*c*) bactericidal and immunising properties of blood and serum. Bibliography.

CHAPTER VI

THE CIRCULATION OF THE BLOOD: DISCOVERY . . . 157

PAGE

1. Physiological necessity for the circulation of the blood. Schema of cardio-vascular system. 2. Theory of Galen. 3. Discovery of the lesser circulation. Question of the priority of Columbus, Servetus, and Vesalius. 4. Discovery of the general circulation by Cesalpinus. 5. Completion of the work by Harvey. 6. Discovery of the lymph circulation by Eustachius, Aselli, Pecquet, Rudbeck, Bartholin. 7. Discovery of the capillary system, and direct observation of the circulation by Malpighi. 8. Microscopic observations of the phenomena of circulation. Spallanzani, Poiseuille, R. Wagner, etc. 9. Discovery of diapedesis of blood-corpuscles and migration of leucocytes: Waller, Addison, Recklinghausen, Cohnheim. Bibliography.

CHAPTER VII

MECHANICS OF THE HEART 180

1. Description of cardiac cycle or revolution. 2. Changes of external form, of the internal cavity, of the position and volume of the heart in the different phases of its activity. 3. Mechanism of semilunar valves. 4. Mechanism of auriculo-ventricular valves. 5. Theory of so-called heart-sounds. 6. Variations of pressure within the auricles and ventricles during the cardiac cycle. 7. The diastolic aspiration: various explanatory hypotheses. 8. Cardiac plethysmograms; theory of active diastole. 9. Cardiograms; theory of heart-beats or impulse. 10. Other mechanical effects of cardiac activity. 11. Work done by the heart. Bibliography.

CHAPTER VIII

THE BLOOD-STREAM: MOVEMENT IN THE VESSELS . . . 232

1. Fundamental laws of hydrodynamics for passage of fluid through rigid tubes. 2. Application of these laws to haemodynamics. 3. Mechanical effects of elasticity of vessel-walls and intermittence of flow of blood from heart; laws of wave motion. 4. Method of measuring and automatically registering variations in blood pressure. 5. Principal results obtained. 6. Methods of measuring velocity of circulation; experimental results. 7. Sphygmography and sphygmograms representing pulsatory oscillations in pressure. 8. Comparison of cardiograms and sphygmograms registered simultaneously, indicating duration of the principal phases of cardiac cycle in man. 9. Comparison of several sphygmograms registered simultaneously from arteries at different distances from the heart, indicating rate of transmission of primary and of dicrotic wave. 10. Tachymetry and tachygrams representing pulsatory variations in current velocity. 11. Plethysmography and

plethysmograms representing pulsatory oscillations in the volume of the arteries. 12. Schema of mechanical conditions of the circulation in the three great vascular systems; determination of duration of the entire circulation. Bibliography.

CHAPTER IX

PHYSIOLOGY OF CARDIAC MUSCLE AND NERVES . . . 285

1. Intrinsic processes by which cardiac rhythm is determined and regulated. 2. Extrinsic chemical conditions of cardiac activity. 3. Effects of ligation and section on different parts of the heart. 4. Automatic or reflex activity of heart. 5. Myogenic or neurogenic origin of cardiac rhythm. 6. Evidence for these conflicting theories. 7. Special mode in which cardiac muscle reacts to external stimuli. 8. Regulation of cardiac rhythm by nervous system: inhibitory or diastolic nerves. 9. Accelerator or systolic nerves. 10. Theory of anabolic action of diastolic nerves and katabolic action of systolic nerves. 11. Afferent nerves of heart or other parts of the body, which influence cardiac rhythm. 12. Nerve centres for cardiac nerves; their tonic excitability, and theory of regulation of cardiac rhythm. Bibliography.

CHAPTER X

PHYSIOLOGY OF VASCULAR MUSCLE AND NERVES . . . 341

1. Discovery of vasomotor nerves. 2. Vascular tone and its rhythmic and arhythmical variations, as depending essentially upon the automatic and reflex excitability of the smooth muscle cells. 3. Theory of vaso-constrictor nerves. 4. Theory of vaso-dilator nerves. 5. Vascular reflexes. 6. Bulbar vaso constrictor centre. 7. Spinal and cerebral centres for vaso-constrictor nerves. 8. Centres for vaso-dilator nerves. Bibliography.

CHAPTER XI

CHEMISTRY AND PHYSICS OF RESPIRATORY EXCHANGE . . . 369

1. Early notions of the importance of respiration (Aristotle, Galen, Leonardo da Vinci, van Helmont, Boyle, Hook, Fracassati, Lower, Mayow). 2. Modern doctrines (Black, Bergmann, Priestley, Lavoisier). 3. Theory of gas exchanges in the lungs and tissues (Lagrange and Spallanzani, W. Edwards). 4. Extraction of gases from the blood (Magnus, L. Meyer, Hoppe-Seyler, Ludwig, Pflüger). 5. Varying content of arterial, venous, and asphyxial blood. 6. State of the oxygen in the blood. 7. State of the carbonic acid in the blood. 8. Tension of gases in venous and arterial blood and in inspired and expired air; theory of pulmonary gas exchange by diffusion and by secretory processes. 9. Theory of gas exchanges in the tissues. 10. The respiratory quotient and its variations. Bibliography.

CHAPTER XII

PAGE

MECHANICS OF RESPIRATION 402

1. Historical. 2. Glandular structure of the lungs. 3. Conditions of the lungs and other viscera within the thorax; passive movements due to variations in the negative thoracic pressure. 4. The thoracic cavity; changes of form and dimensions with inspiratory and expiratory movements. 5. Muscular mechanism of inspiratory and expiratory movements. 6. Normal and forced respiration. 7. Accessory or concomitant respiratory movements. 8. Ventilation or renewal of pulmonary air spirometry, and respiratory pressure in the air-passage pneumatometry. 9. Respiratory displacement of the lungs, and acoustic phenomena of percussion and auscultation. 10. Respiratory variations of intrathoracic and intra-abdominal pressure. 11. Respiratory variations of pressure in the vena cava. 12. Respiratory variations of aortic pressure. 13. Effect of respiratory mechanics on the circulation of the blood. 14. Special forms of respiratory movements. Bibliography.

CHAPTER XIII

THE NERVOUS CONTROL OF RESPIRATORY RHYTHM . . 440

1. Motor nerves to respiratory muscles and smooth muscle cells of bronchi. 2. Bulbar respiratory centres and their localisation. 3. Spinal respiratory centres. 4. Cerebral respiratory centres. 5. Each of these centres results from the association of an inspiratory and an expiratory centre, which function rhythmically and alternately. 6. Automatic regulation of normal respiratory rhythm by afferent pulmonary fibres of vagus. 7. Influence exerted on respiratory rhythm by the cerebral tracts and sensory nerves in general. 8. Phenomena consequent on the separation of the bulb from the brain and spinal cord. 9. Dyspnœa and its different forms. 10. Eupnœa or normal quiet respiration. 11. Experimental apnœa from artificial respiration with the bellows. 12. Fœtal apnœa and the analogous forms of experimental apnœa that can be produced in the adult. 13. Voluntary, as compared with experimental apnœa. 14. Apnœa produced by continuous ventilation in birds. 15. Periodic respiration, or Cheyne-Stokes phenomenon. 16. Physiological theory of respiratory rhythm. Bibliography.

CHAPTER XIV

THE LYMPH, AND INTERCHANGES BETWEEN THE BLOOD AND THE TISSUES 505

1. Structure of lymphatic vascular system, lymph-spaces, sinuses and cavities. 2. Origin; physical, morphological and chemical characteristics; qualitative and quantitative variations of lymph. 3. Lymphatic circulation, and the various mechanical factors by which it is

determined. 4. Formation of lymph from the blood capillaries, and the so-called lymphagogues. 5. Secretory theory of Heidenhain, and transudation theory of Cohnheim. 6. Formation and modification of lymph by the tissues. 7. Lymphoid tissue, follicles and lymphatic glands. 8. Bone marrow. 9. The thymus. 10. The spleen. Bibliography.

INDEX OF SUBJECTS 561

INDEX OF AUTHORS 573

INTRODUCTION

1. Threefold division of biological science.   2. Special objects of physiology. 3. Materialism, neo-vitalism, Ostwald's energetic monism, Mach's psychical monism, pragmatic pluralism.   4. Physiology of the cell ; general and comparative physiology ; human physiology.   Bibliography.

THE remarkable development of Physiology during the nineteenth century justifies us in regarding it as one of the most modern sciences ; yet its origin is very ancient, and may be traced back to the first flashes of philosophic thought.   Throughout the classical world, however, with few exceptions, the term **Physiology** (according to its etymological signification) connotes the philosophic study of Nature in general, *i.e.* it includes the phenomena, not merely of living nature, but of inanimate nature as well.

During the Middle Ages, again, until the Renaissance, the Science of Life is confounded with Philosophy, with Natural History, with Medicine in general, and in particular with Anatomy.

In the second half of the eighteenth century the immense progress made in the vast field of Natural History (so-called) involved a corresponding division of labour.   Intimate relations obtain between mineralogy, geology, and physical geography. These are complementary and reciprocal subjects, which are all included among the inorganic natural sciences.   Most intimate, too, are the links connecting botany and zoology : "Between plants and animals," as was happily said by Buffon, "there are more common properties than real differences."   Between dead and living nature, however, the gap is far wider, the differences more essential, and the study of the one may be undertaken independent of the other.

At the commencement of the last century two eminent naturalists, Lamarck in France, and Treviranus in Germany, created the word **Biology**, and applied it in the first instance to designate the complex of closely related sciences which covers the phenomena observed in living beings in general, *i.e.* in plants, animals, and man.

But if Biology is to include the complete study of life in all its manifestations, it represents a field too vast to admit of comprehension by any single mind in all its details. Hence the necessity arises for a further division of labour.

1. If at any given moment of its existence we set out to consider the mode of life and action of any living being, we can at once distinguish the morphological characteristics, depending on anatomical and histological structure, from the functional or physiological features, which are dependent on its cytological, physical, and chemical constitution. If in living beings we consider the development, the perpetual becoming, in other words the morphological and physiological changes they undergo from beginning to end of their existence, we have the story of Evolution, which enables us to a certain point, both for the individual and the species, to follow the different phases of development as these fulfil themselves according to the great laws of heredity and variation.

The complete study of life, to which the term Biology has thus been applied, is appropriately divided into three branches:—

(a) **Morphology**, which covers the forms of living beings, i.e. the cellular elements from which the tissues are built up, the connections of the tissues whence the organs develop, the structure of the organs and systems.

(b) **Physiology**, which covers the functions or activities of living beings, and the various cytological, physical, and chemical factors from which these arise: in other words, the storage and dispersal of the energies of which organisms are the seat, and the phenomena or external manifestations by which they are revealed to us.

(c) **Biogenesis**, i.e. the story of evolution, morphological as well as functional, whether ontogenetic, for the individual, or phylogenetic, for the race.

The intimate connections of these three great branches of biological science are obvious. Since organic form is the necessary matrix of function, the study of Physiology perforce includes that of Morphology, or Anatomy—as the latter is commonly but loosely termed. These two branches are really offshoots of the same trunk, inasmuch as they constituted in bygone times a single science professed by a single teacher, when the (vastly predominating) study of the morphological signs of life was identified in various ways with that of its physiological properties. But as the study of *form* has methods of research and problems which are separate and quite distinct from those relating to *function*, anatomy has gradually detached itself from physiology, pursuing its own independent development. The History of Evolution or Biogenesis, again, which covers a vast field of researches in embryology, comparative anatomy, and palaeontology, is evidently an offshoot from the common trunk of Morphology and Physiology. In so far as it studies the development of forms it is intimately related to morphology; inasmuch as it investigates the development of functions it is united by the closest bonds with physiology.

This threefold development of biology rests on no profound scientific postulate, but merely arises from the convenience of a division of labour, whether in fulfilment of a didactic necessity or in order more rapidly to approach the ideal of a comprehensive knowledge of living phenomena. We may reasonably anticipate that in proportion as the task assigned to each department approaches its completion, and the corresponding methods of investigation are exhausted, the relations will become more intimate, and the intercourse between the workers in the three several fields more frequent, till finally the great Science of Life, completed by all the achievements of morphology, physiology, psychology, and natural science, is reconstituted in its initial unity, as was predicted by Lazzaro Spallanzani and Johannes Müller.

Of late years the special province of Physiology has become so vast that a considerable area of it is now set apart under the name of Chemical Physiology, and it may seem as though we were still very far from the synthetic reconstitution of Biology as a unitary and well-organised science—an ideal image of the living organism. Owing, however, to the aforesaid division of labour, or to the undeniable exhaustion of certain superannuated methods in other directions, General or Comparative Physiology, an important department which was too much neglected in the past, has been developed and perfected; this comprises the collective study of elementary organisms, in which Cytology and Proto-Morphology present to morphologists and physiologists a common field of research.

II. In the study of the living organism, the physiologist sets himself three main tasks: to define, to localise, and to interpret the phenomena of life. He aims at

(*a*) **Definition of vital phenomena**: by describing them exactly, forming, if possible, a graphic image that shall be accurate, not merely in its outlines, but also in its minutest details.

(*b*) **Localisation of the different vital phenomena in the several substrata**: by determining the specific energies developed by the various elements, tissues, organs, and systems of which the body is composed.

(*c*) **Explanation or interpretation of vital phenomena**: by inquiry into their genesis and inner mechanism, investigation of the external or internal conditions on which they depend, determination of the qualitative and quantitative changes they undergo in the play of the said conditions.

These three tasks represent three different grades of physiological science. The first is purely descriptive; the second, descriptive and experimental; the third, descriptive, experimental, and speculative. For the first, direct or indirect observation, *i.e.* the exact perception of vital phenomena, suffices—whether by the normal use of the senses only or by the help of instruments designed to reinforce them. For the second, observation is not enough, experiment also is required, *i.e.* premeditated observation, in which the external and internal conditions of the living phenomena can be varied. In the third, besides observation and experiment, an energetic criticism is imperative, *i.e.* the logical elaboration by the physiologist of the collected analytical data, in order to interpret and synthetise them. This, in the majority of cases, resolves itself into the arrangement of vital facts in order of co-existence and succession, or of co-ordination and sub-ordination.

In the first grade of physiological science we have an accumulation of loose facts, more or less unorganised, but adapted to call up a picture of the various and manifold energies of which the living organism is the seat. In the second, we arrive at an ordering and systematisation of the said energies, which enables us more or less clearly to conceive what Galen called the "*usus partium*," *i.e.* the topography of the vital functions. The third aims at harmonising the same energies, in order, by our knowledge of the influences exerted by each element or organ upon the other elements or organs of which the body consists, to form an idea as to how that individual unity is built up, which is revealed to us subjectively as the *ego*, objectively as the complete harmony of functions that characterises the state of perfect health.

The first and second grades of physiological science have a positive, immanent value, which time can only develop and perfect, while the third has seldom more than a hypothetical value, which is for the most part temporary, and therefore varies with time. It follows that facts, if well observed, and experimental data well harvested, are and will for ever be true in the progress of science, while the interpretation of facts, and their logical order, may vary greatly, and even alter fundamentally, with the advent of new data or new discoveries.

III. In the **interpretation of vital phenomena**, the physiologist seeks to apply the known laws of physics and chemistry, starting from the obvious position that organised bodies cannot lie beyond the scope of the laws of Nature. The interpretation of these laws is entirely based on the atomistic hypothesis of matter, with its corollary that the indivisible elements of which matter is composed are in themselves indestructible and invariable in their fundamental properties, having, *i.e.*, the same specific weight, the same valency or saturation capacity, the same affinity. The energy of which the atoms are the seat may be potential or kinetic. The former is transformed into the latter, and *vice versa*, either without change of the atomic groups (physical phenomena), or with changes in the same (chemical phenomena).

These great empirical laws of the Conservation of Matter (Lavoisier, 1789) and the Conservation of Energy (J. R. Mayer, 1842; Helmholtz, 1847) dominate living as well as non-living Nature. A living being objectively considered may be conceived as a machine transforming the matter and energy it derives from the external world. As a physico-chemical science of life, physiology will have fulfilled its task when it is able to provide an adequate mechanical representation of the inner processes which underlie the vital somatic phenomena, that is, when it succeeds in giving a satisfactory explanation of these phenomena, and in describing the processes on which they depend as links in the causal chain of the grand Procession of Nature.

The immense value of atomic and molecular mechanics, considered as the basis of vital phenomena (*i.e.* Physiological Materialism in the modern and scientific sense), is best appreciated in reviewing the vast and rapid progress made by physiology, since it has applied the positive methods of physics and chemistry to the study of life, and has abjured the vain abstract speculations used and abused at the beginning of the last century by the so-called " natural philosophers."

At the same time no sincere worker in the positive or scientific direction can deny that the specifically vital somatic phenomena, *i.e.* those by which living beings are differentiated from inorganic bodies, are inexplicable by the known laws of chemistry and physics, and that the psychical phenomena (of sensibility and consciousness), which for each individual constitute the culminating point of life, are altogether remote from any mechanical explanation: they cannot in any way be regarded as necessary links in the chain of cause and effect in the natural processes of Nature.

It is probable that not a few of the still unexplained physiological phenomena will become intelligible in the further progress of physics and chemistry; but even so, such phenomena as are specifically *vital*, and *psychical* phenomena, will remain refractory to any mechanical explanation.

The dynamic finality proper to living beings (which is essentially distinct from the static finality of the cognate parts of a machine created by human industry); the capacity for reproduction, reintegration, adaptation; the innate tendency to evolve, to progress, to become perfect, with relative independence of environmental conditions,—these and other specific phenomena of living beings must, to all who are emancipated from theoretical dogmatism, appear irreducible to a simple play of physical and chemical energies, irreconcilable with the iron necessity of mechanical laws. This is the position assumed by Neo-vitalism, which starts from this affirmation and transcends the earlier

Vitalism, inasmuch as it recognises the experimental method as the exclusive means of scientific progress.

When, on the other hand, we consider *psychical phenomena* (sensibility and consciousness), the impossibility of reducing these to physical and chemical processes becomes even more apparent.

Ostwald (1902) has recently attempted to formulate a unitary conception of the world by excluding the materialistic postulates of natural science, *i.e.* by eliminating the chemical concept of the atoms and substituting the physical concept of energy, psychical processes being regarded as special manifestations of energy. This Energetic Monism of Ostwald is, however, illusory. It is a new and degenerate presentation of the old Idealistic Monism of Hegel, in which the word energy is substituted for the empty word "idea," although equally devoid of definite content. In what, then, does the essential difference between the various forms of physical and that of the supposed psychical energy consist? In that the former are perceptible solely by the mediation of the senses, the latter by introspection alone—the first being objective, the second subjective phenomena? It is, however, precisely in this antithesis that the vulgar dualistic doctrine of the corporeal as distinct from the spiritual world arises. This theory, which was adumbrated by primitive man from his observations of *death* (as appears from ethnological and prehistoric studies), became, in the course of centuries, deeply embedded in the mind of the whole civilised world, resisting like a granite block the most potent and repeated attempts of scientific and philosophical critics to dislodge it. Du Bois-Reymond says in this connection: "It is fundamentally impossible to explain by any mechanical means why the note of a König's tuning-fork gives me pleasure, while contact with red-hot iron gives me pain" (1872).

A more profound (but in our opinion no less illusory) attempt to arrive at a monistic conception is that put forward by Mach in his well-known *Analysis of the Sensations, and the Relations of the Physical and Psychical* (3rd ed., 1902). According to Mach the dualism between body and soul exists in appearance only, and results from a superficial observation of reality. More profound reflection shows that the ultimate elements of reality are nothing but *sensations*. The entire corporeal world, organic or inorganic, is for us nothing but an aggregate of sensations; the whole of our thought is similarly constituted of a more or less complex combination of sensations. Hence there is no reason to postulate an essential difference, still less an antagonism, between the physical fact and the psychical fact: the one like the other, in last resort, results from homogeneous elements. The disparities are in appearance only, and depend upon the different construction of the aggregates, while the elements of these are quantitatively identical.

It is obvious that if this mode of philosophising (which recalls the mystical phenomenalism of Berkeley with his "*esse est percipi*") is to give us a monistic representation free from all hypothesis, not only the chemical concept of atoms, but also the physical concept of energy must be given up, the psychical concept of sensations alone being retained as the ultimate homogeneous and irreducible element of reality. To be strictly logical, we must cancel the entire doctrine of physics and chemistry, as based upon mere hypothesis, and throw ourselves into the arms of pure psychology, which alone enjoys the privilege of having for its content the aggregates of the homogeneous elements of reality! But how can we understand the manifold *qualitative differences* in these aggregates, if once we admit them to arise from *qualitatively identical* elements? How conceive of physical facts, and what in common parlance is called the "external world," as a *complex of sensations*, if we make an abstraction of the internal world, by means of which alone these are to arise as such in consciousness? How can the physiologist imagine a sensation as divorced from the law of causality and independent of the stimulus that excites it? Is it not absurd to admit an essential identity between the *esse* and the *nosse*, the *esse* and the *posse*? How are we to reconcile Mach's view, according to which the psychical fact is presented as something *less real* than — almost (as it were) a *shadow* of—the physical fact, with his general doctrine, according to which the physical and the psychical are said to be identical in their nature?

If we inquire from the followers of Mach what pragmatic value can attach to Psychical Monism (or Phenomenalism, or Empirical Criticism, as it is termed by others) they admit that it is *nil* when we are concerned with scientific work in the various fields of research. "Here all remains as before" (writes Max Verworn, 1905), "methods, symbols, facts, relations are all untouched. Scientific work pursues its course unchecked." This is equivalent to an admission that both the atomistic and the energetic hypotheses (which constitute *Materialism*), and the hypothesis of vital or psychical force (which constitutes *Neo-vitalism*), must continue to function as indispensable instruments, as poles or presumptions necessary to future discoveries and to the progress of science in general. In order to build up science we are constrained to descend from the rarefied regions of abstraction, and to live in the world of concrete facts, grappling with the vital processes in their varied and complex phenomenology, whether mechanical or psychical; in other words, *Monism* must be completed by *Pluralism*, according to our immediate experience.

Each new physiological experiment, each new scientific conquest, appears as a more or less important integration of the science of the living; it always signifies a process that either tends to apply the mechanical explanation to a supposed vital phenomenon, or brings out the essentially vital character of a supposed physico-chemical phenomenon.

The evolutionary process of physiological science has always been in the past, and will always be in the future, a continuous and fruitful struggle between the two opposite tendencies of Materialism and Vitalism. It is a mistake to suppose that either the one or the other will ever win the final victory. Both are one-sided; both reflect one face only of reality. Life, in its more highly evolved forms, results from their interpenetration and fusion. Seen from without, it is *body*; felt from within, it is *soul*: this is the great mystery that Art for ever celebrates—a mystery Science, with every possible and conceivable progress in physics and chemistry, with all the experimental methods that it may or might employ, will never be in a position to solve.

IV. As the physico-chemical science of living beings, Physiology includes the comparative study of the vital phenomena of plants, animals, and man.

Some vital phenomena are common to all living beings, without distinction of species, genera, classes, or kingdoms. These are fundamental phenomena, that is, they are the simplest and most elementary in life. Their material substratum is the **Cell**, *i.e.* the simplest morphological unit, which Brücke calls the elementary organism, whether living its independent life, or living in association with other cells to form cell aggregates or complex organisms.

The physiology of the cell lies at the foundation of all physiology, because the functions of the tissues, organs, and systems can ultimately be reduced to the vital activity of the various cells from which they evolve. Plant physiology, as well as animal and human physiology, derive the fundamental data relating to elementary functions from the physiology of the cell, and employ it as a basis in their study of the complex and special functions of the several tissues, organs, and systems.

The science of physiology calls for a different arrangement and development, and may assume a different aspect and even content, according as it is approached from a scientific, a philosophical, or a medical and practical standpoint. From the first two it assumes the form and content of general and comparative physiology, which is the necessary complement of general and comparative morphology; both are directed to the high aim of illustrating, tabulating, and developing the grand doctrine of Evolution or Descent, which from Darwin onwards has been undergoing constant transformation and integration. From the third it assumes the form and content of human physiology, taking Man as the goal of its investigations; it harvests the experimental data directly obtained from the higher animals; it utilises the data derived from pathological observations, which not seldom have a value comparable with that of experiments on animals; and it dwells with special insistence on such theories as have received or may receive an application to hygiene or preventive medicine, and to clinical or curative medicine.

Such essentially practical objects are dealt with in this Textbook, which aims at bringing the latest advances in science within reach of all who are working at medicine and at physical and psychological science,—and seeks at the same time to equip the younger students, as adequately as may be, with that knowledge of Physiology which lies at the foundation of all scientific culture and education.

BIBLIOGRAPHY

The following list comprises only such classical Treatises on Physiology as will be of most use to students in following the historical development of any given physiological question :—

CLAUDIUS GALENUS. De usu partium corporis humani. Lib. xvii.

A DE HALLER. Elementa physiologiae corporis humani, 1757-66. Auctarium, 1780.

JOH. MÜLLER. Handbuch d. Physiologie des Menschen. 4th ed. Coblenz, 1844. (French translation with Littré's note. Paris, 1857.)

H. MILNE-EDWARDS. Leçons sur la physiologie et l'anatomie comparée. Paris, 1857-86.

F. A. LONGET. Traité de physiologie. Leipzig, 1879-81.

L. HERMANN. Handbuch d. Physiologie. Leipzig, 1879-81.

E. A. SCHAFER. Text-book of Physiology. Edinburgh and London, 1898-1900.

W. NAGEL. Handbuch d. Physiologie des Menschen. Brunswick (in course of publication).

H. BEAUNIS and V. APUCCO. Elementi di fisiologia umana, comprendenti i principii di fisiologia comparata e di fisiologia generale. Turin (in course of publication).

CHAPTER I

LIVING MATTER: ITS CHEMICAL AND PHYSICAL BASIS

CONTENTS.—1. The cell-theory. 2. Morphology of the cell. 3. Structure of protoplasm. 4. Structure of nucleus. 5. Chemical elements of the cell. 6. Protein basis of living matter. 7. Classification of proteins. 8. Chemical constitution of proteins. 9. Enzymes or ferments. 10. Classification. 11. Other nitrogenous organic substances, fats, carbohydrates or saccharides, inorganic substances. 12. Chemical structure of living matter. Bibliography.

In Nature no phenomena can be independent of a material substratum: all are the external manifestation of the energies immanent in matter. Every vital phenomenon that comes under the observation of the physiologist is intimately connected with the living organism, and is the expression of internal causes, *i.e.* of the different forms of energy inherent within that organism.

Whoever, then, approaches the threshold of Physiology in order to study the Manifestations of Life, will feel it essential to have some knowledge of the material substratum out of which the living phenomena have been evolved.

I. Both in plants and animals the material substratum of vital phenomena, the physical basis of life, consists of a substance of highly complicated structure and constitution, soft or gelatinous in consistency, to which Hugo Mohl (1846) gave the name of protoplasm. In living beings this does not appear as a simple mass, without form or boundaries; but it is divided into minute particles, or separate entities, known as cells. Each cell comes from a pre-existing cell, just as every living being comes from the ovum, which is the primitive cell. The so-called *Protista*, which are the most primitive form of life (and probably constitute the common stock whence plants and animals have developed) are throughout their whole life represented by a single cell, which assumes various forms and dimensions. In the *Metazoa*, on the contrary, the primitive cell, or ovum, gives rise to other similar cells, and these to other cells in turn, which are gradually differentiated, transformed, and adapted to the several physiological offices which they serve.

In the *Protista* each cell is a distinct and independent physiological individual; in the *Metazoa* each cell or cell-derivative is still a distinct individual, but it is no longer independent, since the life of each is more or less bound up with the life of the others with which it is associated. The individuality of the social aggregate, or that of the organism as a whole, is but an individuality of a higher order, *i.e.* it is the sum of the life of each elementary organism. This is essentially the Cell Theory, formulated by Schleiden (1838) and Schwann (1839), reinforced and developed by Virchow (1855), and fully confirmed by later observers.

Yet among living physiologists there are not wanting some who believe that we must recognise a more radical difference between the independent unicellular organisms and the cells of which complex organisms are built up. The latter, it is said, since they are incapable of living apart from the body of which they form a part, do not constitute a real individual, so that the name of elementary organisms given them by Brücke is inappropriate. Since the several physiological functions essential to life are very unequally divided among the various cells of which the complex organism consists, they must each represent a physiologically simpler unit, and are not therefore comparable with the cells that constitute a true individual, and which are capable of living independent of other cells (E. Schenk and J. Loeb).

There is a certain amount of truth in this observation, but the conclusions deduced from it, *i.e.* the negation of the cell theory, are somewhat far-fetched. In the first place it should be noted that incapacity to live independent of other cells cannot be predicated of all the cells of which multicellular organisms are composed; it rises gradually with the zoological scale (cf. Chap. III. 12). It should further be observed that the life of every organism is invariably conditioned by its special environment, so that it perishes when transported into other media too unlike those in which it normally exists. In unicellular organisms the environment is represented by the sum of the nutritive materials and the stimuli which reach them from the external world; in the cells of which multicellular organisms are built up the medium is represented by the sum of the nutritive matters and the stimuli which reach them, either from the external world or from the other cells with which they live in association. Lastly, in the first as in the second kind of cell a different grade or trend of development may be observed for each of their vital functions.

For the rest, the cell theory, which affirms a certain functional autonomy of the morphological elements of which the organism as a whole consists, is founded on a synthesis of experimental facts that can be easily verified.

(*a*) The survival for a certain time of parts detached from a living organism.

(*b*) The non-synchronous death of the several tissues or organs of which the organism is composed.

(*c*) The localisation of the effects of toxins and pathogenic causes.

(*d*) The possibility of transplanting and grafting tissues and organs.

(*e*) The possibility of multiplying not only plants, but also many of the lower multicellular animals, for instance the fresh-water *Hydra* by merotomy, or division into segments.

II. The organisation of a perfect cell, capable of living and reproducing itself, requires not merely a simple lump of proto-plasm, as was originally maintained by M. Schultze (1863) and subse-quently by E. Haeckel (1870), but the interior of the protoplasmic mass must also contain a nucleus, a con-stituent already described by previous observers as an essential part of elementary organisms. The later work of Gruber (1888) on *Rhizopoda* and of Bütschli (1890) on *Bacteria*, has shown that these also consist of two characteristically differentiated parts, corresponding to the cell proto-plasm or cytoplasm, and the nucleus of the perfect cell. The membrane which envelops the protoplasm cannot be regarded as an essential part of the cell, because while rarely absent in plants, it is almost always lacking in the animal cell. The centrosome described by van Beneden and Boveri (1887), and considered by them to be the third element of the cell,

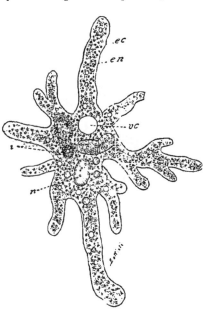

FIG. 1.—*Amoeba proteus*. (Hertwig.) *n*, nucleus; *vc*, contractile vacuole; *i*, ingesta; *en*, granular endoplasm or granuloplasm; *ec*, hyaline ectoplasm or hyaloplasm.

appears from the more recent work of Hertwig (1891) and Brauer (1893) to be part of the nuclear substance, which is generally extruded into the cytoplasm during the activity of the nucleus, to incite germination and cell division. The morpho-logical concept of the cell is accordingly very simple: it is funda-mentally a lump of protoplasm which includes a more or less distinct nucleus.

The importance of the nucleus to the life of the cytoplasm can be demonstrated experimentally, as also the importance of the cytoplasm to the life of the nucleus.

The first experiment consists in bisecting a unicellular animal, *e.g.* an *Amoeba* (Fig. 1), in such a way that one half contains the nucleus and the other is deprived of it: and then observing under the microscope the behaviour and final modifications of the half provided with, and that destitute of nucleus. When the operation is effected with as little injury as possible, the edges of the cut soon unite again, and each half of the amoeba contracts, assuming a globular form. After a few seconds each of these two globules begins to move, changing its shape and creeping along, as is the normal habit of intact amoebae. Later on, however, a difference between the two halves is perceptible, and while the new nucleated amoeba continues to live and grow, and behaves as a normal individual, the half without a nucleus slackens its movements, takes no more food, retracts its pseudopodia, and, according to the best results obtained by Hofer, dies in ten or twelve days. This proves the vital importance of the nucleus.

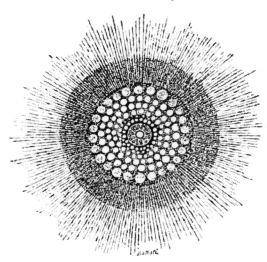

Fig. 2. — *Thalassicolla nucleata*. (Verworn.) From without, inwards : radiating corona of pseudo-podia; gelatinous layer; layer of vacuoles; pigmented sheath to central capsule; central capsule with nucleus.

The second experiment, designed to show the vital importance of the cytoplasm, was carried out by Verworn on a species of *Radiolaria ; Thalassicolla* (Fig. 2). In this animal it is possible to shell out the nucleus, separating it from the ray-shaped mass of the protoplasm, and to observe the effects of isolation. Even when the operation succeeds without any perceptible nuclear lesion, the nucleus inevitably dies without showing any sign of regeneration.

A third experiment consists in bisecting a unicellular organism, in such a way that each half contains a portion of the nucleus and a portion of protoplasm. This succeeds readily in a trumpet-shaped Infusorian called *Stentor*, in which both protoplasm and nucleus are elongated (Fig. 3). When bisected each half continues to live, and regenerates gradually into a perfect Stentor, although of smaller dimensions. This fact cannot be adduced against the theory which considers the cell as the lowest step in the scale of living individuality, because each half of the divided Stentor has the value of a cell containing the two essential constituents, nucleus and cytoplasm. It merely shows that the living matter in the said cellular constituents may vary quantitatively to a considerable extent, without forfeiting the conditions necessary to the constitution of a complete individual.

Just as a half-cell may live and regenerate into a complete

cell, so, on the other hand, a number of cells fusing their protoplasm into a single mass may compose a single multinuclear cellular individual (Fig. 4). Multinuclear cells are fairly common, whether as a living species or as the complex elements of higher organisms. They represent transitional forms between the simple mononuclear cell and a tissue, which is an aggregate of similar but individually distinct cells. In some of the lower creatures, known as *Myxomycetes*, the multinuclear protoplasmic mass assumes externally the aspect of a network which may cover an area of several decimetres (plasmodium). This reproduces

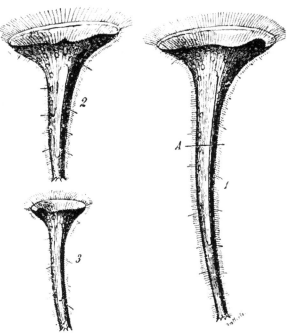

FIG. 3. — *Stentor Roeselii.* (Verworn.) 1, Complete individual, trumpet-shaped, showing in the body-axis a very elongated nucleus of lighter appearance. When bisected at *A*, each segment regenerates into a smaller, complete individual, the upper half being represented by 2, the lower by 3.

by spores, and from each spore there develops an amoeboid cell of distinct outlines. Eventually the outlines of the cells disappear, and they resume the form of a reticulated plasmodium (Strasburger). This fusion of many cells into a simple multinuclear protoplasmic mass is termed a *syncytium* (Fig. 5).

The external form of the cell may vary greatly both in organisms which consist of a single morphological element, and in multicellular organisms. A primary distinction must be made between cells of variable, and those of fixed form. The former are termed amoeboid,

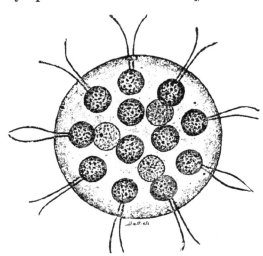

FIG. 4. — *Eudorina elegans.* (Verworn.) Complex individual (colony) resulting from fusion of a number of flagellated individuals into a common globular mass of gelatinous substance.

because they change their shape like the *Amoebae* (Fig. 1), which are little naked protoplasmic bodies with no enclosing membrane, having often a distinct nucleus. These put out in all directions projections of their body-substance, or *pseudopodia*, which are continually changing in shape. The majority of cells, however, possess a constant form, whether the protoplasm be enclosed in

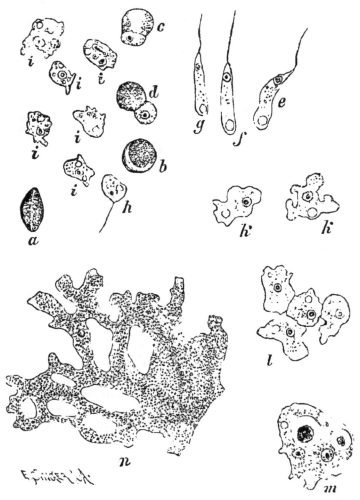

FIG. 5.—*Chondrioderma difforme*, life phases. (Strasburger.) *a*, dry spore; *b*, turgid spore; *c*, *d*, dehiscence of spore-membrane and escape of cell-contents; *c*, *f*, *g*, transformation of primitive spore into piriform and flagellate zoospore; *h*, zoospore passing into state of myxamoeba; *i*, *i*, young myxamoebae; *k*, *k*, adult myxamoeba; *l*, adherent myxamoebae ready to fuse; *m*, young plasmodium; *n*, portion of adult reticulated plasmodium.

a membrane or not. Many permanent forms repeat the temporary shapes assumed by the amoeboid cells.

The size of the cells, again, varies greatly, though they are almost always of microscopic dimensions. The smallest Bacteria measure only a few thousandths of a millimetre, while the largest Amoebae exceed a tenth of a millimetre. The cells of the higher organisms, Man included, are rarely more than eight hundredths of a millimetre in their largest diameter. Muscle fibres, indeed, both plain and striated, may measure more than a decimetre, and the nerve processes of the ganglion cells more than a metre. Still the amount of living matter contained within a cell is always, comparatively speaking, very small. In a bird's egg, which is a single colossal cell, the active, living protoplasm consists only of one very delicate layer, the whole of the rest being inactive yolk, which is destined to feed the germ during its embryonic development.

III. Both in animal and in plant cells, protoplasm has the same common properties: it appears as a semi-fluid, almost always colourless substance, with no apparent morphological structure, although it contains a variable quantity of small punctiform gran-ules: it is readily permeable by water, which swells it up without dissolving it; impenetrable as a rule to colouring matters during life, it stains readily after death. When at rest it has an alka-line reaction, which may become neutral or even acid during activity. The hya-line, non-granulated protoplasm often forms in the cell a more or less dense external layer, known

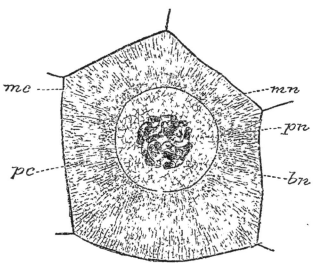

FIG. 6.— Epithelial cell from intestine of insect larva. (Carnoy.) *mc*, cell membrane: *pc*, cell protoplasm in form of net-work with granulations; *mn*, nuclear membrane; *pn*, nuclear protoplasm with achromatic, reticulated substance; *bn*, skein of chromatic substance in centre of nucleus.

as ectoplasm or hyaloplasm, to distinguish it from the internal granular portion that surrounds the nucleus, the so-called endo-plasm or granuloplasm (Fig. 1).

Under the high power of the microscope, this apparently homogeneous protoplasm shows a very complicated structure. Remak (1844) and M. Schultze (1871) affirmed that there was a fine fibrillar structure in the protoplasm of the ganglion cells of the nervous system, a theory subsequently extended to epithelial, glandular, and other cells. Fromman (1865) and Heitzmann (1873) modified this statement, and assumed a finely reticulated structure, in which the granules would be the nodal points of the protoplasmic network. Carnoy (1883), while admitting the theory of a reticulum, affirmed that the granulation represented not the network but the fluid contained in its meshes, to which he gave the name of *enchylema* (Fig. 6). Finally, Bütschli (1892) showed

that the reticulum existed in appearance only, and was merely the
optical expression of the finest vesicles in close apposition. Protoplasm thus consists of a foam-like ground-substance, constructed

FIG. 7.—Alveolar structure of protoplasm. (Bütschli.) *a*, Delicate foam of alveolar structure
obtained by prolonged whipping of olive oil and cane-sugar; *b*, alveolar structure of intra-
capsular protoplasm from *Thalassicolla nucleata*, as in Fig. 2.

in the form of delicate polyhedric vesicles or alveoli, closely pressed
together. The protoplasmic granules lie in greater or less numbers at the corners of the foam-bubbles, never in the liquid of the
alveoli themselves (Fig. 7).

FIG. 8.—Cell from staminal
hair of *Tradescantia
virginica.* (Strasburger.)
The nucleus is surrounded
by a spongy network with
wide meshes.

Even under the low power, apparently
homogeneous protoplasm not infrequently
exhibits drops of fluid, or *vacuoles*, as they
are somewhat infelicitously termed. Such
accidental vacuoles must be distinguished
from the permanent ones, which are so
numerous and conspicuous in certain plant
cells as to give a spongy appearance to the
protoplasm (Fig. 8). Rhythmically pulsating
vacuoles may sometimes be observed; these
empty themselves on contracting, and refill
with fluid on dilating. This is especially the
case in certain kinds of Amoebae, and is very
frequent among the ciliated Infusoria. In
these cases the vacuoles function as a centre
of circulation for the protoplasmic fluid.

Besides the vacuoles, there are in vegetable protoplasm granules of chlorophyll,
starch, and aleuron: in animal protoplasm,
fat globules, accumulations of glycogen, and
granules known as "vitellin." The chlorophyll corpuscles are of capital importance
to the plant cell, since the most characteristic
part of its vital processes depends on them; viz. the reduction of
carbonic acid, and fixation of carbon. The granules of starch,
aleuron, fat, glycogen, and vitellin are nutritive materials, products
of protoplasmic activity, stored up within the cell.

Lastly, it should be noted that the unicellular animals which have no membranes, such as amoebae, leucocytes, infusoria, and other cells, often contain food-stuffs or other solid bodies which they have ingested, *e.g.* diatoms, small algae, bacteria, etc. (Metschnikoff), which are gradually digested, and appear as solid inclusions in the protoplasm (see Fig. 1).

IV. Many of the peculiarities which we have noted in the constitution or structure of the cytoplasm are characteristic of the nucleus also. This is usually a vesicular body, surrounded by a membrane; at other times it may assume various forms, and may lose the enveloping membrane which divides it from the cytoplasm.

Under a high magnification Bütschli detected an alveolar structure similar to that of the cytoplasm, which presents the appearance of a reticulum. The vesicles contain the nuclear fluid: the substance which forms them is termed a-chromatic, since it does not stain with carmine, haematoxylin, or other dyes. Another substance, peculiar to the nucleus, which does stain with dyes, and is termed chromatic, can also be distinguished. This appears in the form of small granules or filaments, threads diffused at the nodal points of the a-chromatic substance, or collected in a heap or kind of central skein (see Fig. 6).

V. Chemical analysis of animal and vegetable organisms has shown that the elements which enter most constantly and abundantly into the composition of the cell are :—

Name.						Symbol.	Atomic Weight.
Carbon .	.	.	.	.	.	C	12·00
Nitrogen	.	.	.	.	.	N	14·04
Sulphur	.	.	.	.	.	S	32·07
Hydrogen	.	.	.	.	.	H	1·00
Oxygen .	.	.	.	.	.	O	16·00
Phosphorus	.	.	.	.	.	P	31·00
Chlorine	.	.	.	.	.	Cl	35·46
Potassium	.	.	.	.	.	K	39·14
Sodium .	.	.	.	.	.	Na	23·04
Magnesium	.	.	.	.	.	Mg	24·00
Calcium	.	.	.	.	.	Ca	40·00
Iron	.	.	.	.	.	Fe	56·00

In addition to these twelve principal elements, other elements occur, but in relatively smaller quantities; they are not present in every cell, but only in certain special plants and animals. These are :—

Name.						Symbol.	Atomic Weight.
Silicon .	.	.	.	.	.	Si	28·19
Fluorine	.	.	.	.	.	F	18·98
Bromine	.	.	.	.	.	Br	79·76
Iodine .	.	.	.	.	.	I	126·55
Aluminium	.	.	.	.	.	Al	27·00
Manganese	.	.	.	.	.	Mn	53·90
Lithium	.	.	.	.	.	Li	7·00

	Name.					Symbol.	Atomic Weight.
Copper	.	.	.	.	.	Cu	63·17
Lead	.	.	.	.	.	Pb	206·47
Zinc	.	.	.	.	.	Zn	64·90

With the exception of silicon, which is widely distributed in both kingdoms, fluorine, which in small but constant quantities enters into the chemical composition of the enamel of the teeth, and iodine, which has lately been found in one of the constituents of the thyroid gland, it is probable that all these elements are without physiological significance to the cell-body in which they are found, and that they enter accidentally, like many other extraneous elements, e.g. drugs, toxins, or such as are merely indifferent bodies.

It is worth noting that the twelve principal elements that enter constantly into the composition of cells have all a low atomic weight. Nine of them, in fact, belong to the first three series of Mendelejeff's Periodic System, and only three (potassium, calcium, iron) belong to the fourth series of the system. Further, these are all found either in the state of elements or as very simple inorganic combinations, which are widely diffused in the air, in water, and in the upper layers of the soil—the only habitat of flora and fauna.

VI. The chemical compounds of which the cell is built up may be divided into organic and inorganic. Organic substances are distinguished as nitrogenous and non-nitrogenous : the former include the Proteins and their derivatives, the latter the Fats and Carbohydrates.

Proteins are the most important organic substances, and are indispensable in the constitution of living protoplasm. They are essentially distinct from carbohydrates and fats in their elementary composition, for in addition to carbon, hydrogen, and oxygen they contain nitrogen and sulphur. Their molecular structure, and the exact number of atoms of the several elements which enter into their constitution, are still unknown to us. There is, however, no doubt that the molecular structure of these substances is highly complex : more so, perhaps, than that of any other chemical substance, since the ratio of the number of the various atoms reaches a very considerable figure.

It should be noted that the five elements above mentioned are found in the different proteins in much the same proportions, as appears from the following table, which gives the limits between which the percentages of the various elements of protein oscillate :—

				mean		
C	50	−55	„	52	per cent.	
H	9·5	−7·3	„	7	„	
N	15	−17·6	„	16	„	
O	19	−24	„	23	„	
S	0·3	−2·4	„	2	„	

These figures, of course, throw no light on the grouping of the respective elements; *i.e.* the chemical structure of the protein molecule. They show, however, that the different proteins form a well-defined class of chemical compounds, having a strict relation among themselves, as is further apparent from the physico-chemical properties common to the several members, as follows :—

(*a*) Non-diffusibility through the pores of animal or vegetable membranes and of artificial parchment; they belong, therefore, to the class of bodies which Graham termed colloids. They are obtained in a crystalline form with difficulty, and only by special methods. If the colloid is fluid it is termed *sol*; if solid, *gel*. Liquid and solid gelatin are examples of these two states. When water is the medium in which the colloid is dispersed the terms *hydrosol* and *hydrogel* are used respectively. Besides the proteins, many inorganic substances can exist in a colloidal form, *e.g.* colloidal metals, silicic acid, etc. There has been much recent discussion as to the state in which the colloids exist in a solvent (which in the case of the proteins of the living body is exclusively represented by water). According to the latest conclusions, we are here concerned not with true *solutions*—having the well-known properties of solutions, due to the mixing of the soluble crystalloids, salts, urea, glucose, etc., with water—but rather with very fine *emulsions* or *suspensions*, *i.e.* the particles of the colloid substance can be seen in a separate state, suspended in the liquid, and do not enter into those intimate relations with the solvent on which depend the physico-chemical characters of true solutions (osmotic pressures, homogeneity under high magnification, etc.). In fact, these colloidal solutions scarcely lower the freezing-point of the solvent, and under the ultra-microscope are seen to consist of various-sized granules moving in the body of the fluid.

(*b*) All proteins have, further, very definite chemical properties, by which they are sharply differentiated from all other known chemical aggregates, crystalloids or colloids. Their aqueous solutions are optically active, since they deflect the plane of polarised light to the left. Heat, the addition of small quantities of mineral acid, salts of the heavy metals, as also absolute alcohol, solutions of tannin, phosphotungstic acid, picric acid, etc., precipitate and often coagulate them (albumins and globulins). In this case the protein molecule undergoes profound changes, for after removal of the precipitating agent the initial state of colloid cannot be restored; the protein is said to be *de-natured*. Proteins are further precipitated by saturation of the solvent with salts of the alkalies or alkaline earths (sodium chloride, magnesium sulphate, ammonium sulphate). It is important in the chemistry of the proteins to note that in the precipitation determined by these salts the proteins are not de-natured, or at any rate become so very much more slowly—for they re-dissolve on removal of the salts by which they were precipitated.

All proteins give specific colour reactions. The best known are the following :—

Millon's Reaction.—On adding a solution of mercuric and mercurous nitrate and nitrite in nitric acid (Millon's reagent) and heating, the white precipitate first formed turns red.

Xanthoproteic Reaction.—On heating with nitric acid the solution of protein turns yellow, and then, on the addition of ammonia, orange.

Molisch's Reaction.—On adding a few drops of α-naphthol and running in concentrated sulphuric acid, under the solution, a violet ring appears at the junction of the two fluids. If alcohol, ether, or potash be now added it turns yellow. The substitution of thymol for α-naphthol gives a fine rose carmine, which gradually becomes green.

Biuret Reaction.—A few drops of 2 per cent copper sulphate added to a solution of protein made alkaline with caustic potash or soda, produces a clear violet colour in the cold. Proteoses and peptones, which are the primary decomposition products of the more complex proteins formed by the action of proteolytic ferments (*infra*), give a pure pink colour.

Sulphur Reaction.—On warming with potash and a little lead acetate, the white precipitate which first appears (lead hydroxide) turns brown and then black, owing to the formation of lead sulphide.

These colour tests for proteins are important, not merely as showing the presence of protein, but because they prove the existence in the complex molecule of certain definite chemical compounds to which the several reactions are due. The sulphur test, *e.g.*, indicates the presence of cystine which contains this element; Millon's test, of the tyrosine group; the xanthoproteic test, of aromatic groups; Molisch's reaction, of a carbohydrate: and so on. In fact, these chemical aggregates respectively always give these identical reactions, which are accordingly known as "constitutional tests." The biuret reaction is the most general test for proteins, since it is given by all the proteins and their most immediate derivatives (the proteoses and peptones). It is given by biuret and other compounds which contain $CO.NH$ groups. It is also given by some of the less complex derivatives (polypeptides), but not by the ultimate products of their decomposition (amino-acids).

VII. Owing to our inadequate knowledge of the exact chemical constitution of the different proteins their **classification** is still based principally upon their physical or physico-chemical properties, *e.g.* solubility in water or in certain salt solutions, the temperature at which they coagulate, etc. The Chemical and

Physiological Societies of Great Britain adopted the following scheme of classification in 1907 [1] :—

    I. Protamines, *e.g.* salmine, sturine.
    II. Histones, *e.g.* thymus histone.
    III. Albumins, *e.g.* ovalbumin, serum albumin, various vegetable albumins.
    IV. Globulins, *e.g.* serum globulin, fibrinogen and fibrin, myosinogen and myosin. Vegetable globulins.
    V. Glutelins, *e.g.* wheat glutelin ⎫
    VI. Gliadins, *e.g.* wheat gliadin ⎭ present only in cereals.
    VII. Phosphoproteins,[2] *e.g.* caseinogen, vitellin, ichthulin.
    VIII. Scleroproteins,[3] *e.g.* collagen and gelatin, keratin, elastin, fibroin, spongin, amyloid, albumoid, pigments.
    IX. Conjugated proteins. These are combinations of protein with other compounds.
        (*a*) Nucleoproteins.
        (*b*) Chromoproteins, *e.g.* haemoglobin.
        (*c*) Glucoproteins.
    X. Derivatives of proteins. These are formed from members of the other groups by the action of acids and alkalies, or enzymes.
        (*a*) Metaprotein ⎰ acid albumin.
                     ⎱ alkali albumin.
        (*b*) Proteoses : albumose, globulose, caseose, gelatose, etc.
        (*c*) Peptones, *e.g.* fibrin peptone, caseo-peptone, etc.
        (*d*) Polypeptides, *e.g.* glycyl-l-tyrosine, d-alanyl-glycine, l-leucyl-d-glutamic acid, d-alanyl-l-leucine, etc. The majority are synthetical compounds. Several have now been isolated from proteins.

Albumins are coagulable proteins, soluble in distilled water, in dilute salt solutions, in acids and bases, and they are not precipitated by saturating the solutions with neutral sodium chloride or magnesium sulphate when the solution is neutral, but they are precipitated by these salts when the solution is acid. They are precipitated by saturating the solution with ammonium sulphate.

Globulins are coagulable proteins, insoluble in distilled water and dilute acids, soluble on the other hand in solutions of neutral salts and dilute bases. They are precipitated on saturation with magnesium sulphate and to a certain extent with sodium chloride ; with ammonium sulphate they are precipitated at a lower degree of concentration ($= \frac{1}{2}$ saturation) than that required to precipitate albumin.

The vegetable globulins differ in many respects from the animal globulins ; they have a great tendency to crystallise, and have been prepared in large quantities in a crystalline form (Osborne).

Fibrinogen and myosin will be discussed in the chapters on Blood Plasma and Muscle.

Phosphoproteins are characterised by the fact that phosphorus enters into their composition, so that formerly they were erroneously classed with the nucleoproteins. They are distinct from these

---

[1] Substituted by translator for O. Cohnheim's 1904 scheme.
[2] Formerly nucleoalbumins.   [3] Formerly albuminoids.

inasmuch as they contain no xanthine or purine bases, which are characteristic of nucleoproteins. They differ from nucleoproteins also in that the phosphorus is completely removed, as inorganic phosphoric acid, by treatment with 1 per cent caustic soda at 37° C. for 24 hours (Plimmer and Scott). The phosphoproteins have the properties of acids: they turn blue litmus paper red, and are soluble in distilled water only in the form of their alkaline salts, from which solutions they can be precipitated by the addition of stronger acids. Solutions of their salts do not coagulate with heat.

Histones, on the contrary, have the character of weak bases, their solutions being precipitated by alkalies.

The protamines form a very definite group, differentiated in not a few particulars from the rest of the proteins: they do not contain sulphur, and are richer in nitrogen and poorer in carbon than the other proteins. They are distinctly basic in character, more so than the histones. They have been isolated from the spermatozoa of many fishes (salmine, clupine, scombrine, sturine, etc.).

We shall deal with the derivatives of the proteins, more particularly with the proteoses and peptones, which result from the action of the proteolytic ferments on the more complex proteins, in the chapter on Digestion.

The conjugated proteins are combinations of a protein with a chemical aggregate, which is not a protein, and which Hoppe-Seyler termed a "prosthetic group." In the *nucleoproteins* discovered by Miescher and Bloss (1871) in cell-nuclei, this prosthetic group is represented by nucleic acid: nucleoprotein therefore results from a combination of protein and nucleic acid. The nucleic acids are organic acids which contain phosphorus and nitrogen, but no sulphur, their chemical constitution being unknown. Their decomposition products, on the contrary, are known to us: these are phosphoric acid, purine bases (adenine, guanine, hypoxanthine, and xanthine), pyrimidine bases (thymine, uracil, cytosine), pentoses (laevulinic acid).

Of the various proteins which are able to unite with the nucleic acids to form nucleoprotein, the protamines and histones are the principal. These enter into the molecules of the nucleoproteins of fishes' testicles. Nucleic acid is also combined with histone in the leucocytes of the thymus and the nucleated red corpuscles.

Nucleoproteins have distinct acid properties: they are soluble in water and in saline solutions, still more in alkaline fluids; they are precipitated on the addition of acids, but are redissolved by excess of mineral acid.

Haemoglobin (to which we shall return in discussing Blood) results from the combination of a histone (globin) and a complex chemical aggregate containing iron (haematin).

Glucoproteins are conjugated proteins, consisting of a carbo-hydrate radicle combined with protein. The nature and consti-tution of this carbohydrate group is unknown. It appears to be a polysaccharide, since it does not reduce: it contains an amino group (NH_2), for when boiled with acids, it usually yields gluco-samine.

The group of proteins known as the scleroproteins includes a series of substances which have few physical properties in common with the preceding groups, but share many other characters with them. They never form part of the animal cell, but compose the skeletal or supporting substance for the cells and organs of the body: they belong to the histological group of the connective tissues in the widest sense of that term. There are no sclero-proteins in the tissue fluids of animals' blood, lymph, etc. The concept scleroprotein is essentially morphological, and from a chemical point of view includes most various bodies.

As proteins, the scleroproteins have many properties in common with the other groups. By the action of acids or of proteolytic ferments they are split into proteoses, peptones, and amino-acids; they form salts; and they have the same percentage composition and give the same colour reactions.

Of the various scleroproteins enumerated in the table, we may say that collagen is the general substance of bone, cartilage, and connective fibres; on boiling, it takes up water and is transformed into gelatin. Keratin, the ground substance of the cornea, is an elaboration product of the epidermic cells of the cutis. Elastin, a component of the fibres of elastic tissue and the ligamentum nuchae, is a product of connective tissue cells. Fibroin, the principal component of silk, is an elaboration product of the spinning gland of the silkworm. Spongin is the organic support-ing substance of the bath sponge. Conchiolin is the organic matrix of the snail and other molluscs. Amyloid, lastly, is a substance which is absent in the healthy organism, but accumulates in enormous quantities under the influence of various pathological degenerative processes.

Albumoid is the name which has been given to many different substances found in various organisms, *e.g.* the membrana propria of certain glands, the vitreous membrane, sarcolemma, the solid constituents of the lens, scales of fishes, etc. These are also scleroproteins.

Lastly, the group of pigments, or melanins, includes all those various pigments, brown, black, chestnut, etc., which determine the characteristic hue of hair, fur, and choroid, and which are found in the so-called melanotic tumours.

VIII. The analytical and experimental work on the chemical structure and constitution of proteins, as recently carried out by such distinguished physiological chemists as Kossel, Hofmeister, and more particularly Fischer and his school, has led within the last few years to important results. While these do not as yet account fully for all the different chemical units which build up the complex protein molecule, they represent a great advance in this direction. A brief review of this work, which has profoundly modified most of the theories previously held by physiologists, is essential.

The analytical method is invariably employed in investigating the chemical structure of highly complex bodies. The complex substance must be decomposed and split up into its simpler constituents, *i.e.* into the units of which it is built up. For proteins, hydrolytic cleavage is the method of artificial decomposition that gives the best results, *i.e.* decomposition with absorption of molecules of water. This hydrolytic cleavage or hydrolysis of proteins may take place by the prolonged action—

(*a*) Of mineral acids, by boiling the protein with concentrated hydrochloric acid or 25 per cent sulphuric acid for twelve to fifteen hours (method proposed by Fischer, and generally used in his laboratory);

(*b*) Of alkalies; and

(*c*) Of proteolytic ferments.

The most important result of all the researches into hydrolytic cleavage up to the present time is that even the most unlike proteins have, among themselves, a very similar constitution, judging from the end products. These are invariably the same, no matter what process of hydrolytic decomposition is employed. It was formerly believed that one essential difference only existed between hydrolysis by the proteolytic ferments and that by acids and alkalies: the disintegrating action of the ferments was supposed to be more gradual, since before reaching the final products of cleavage, which no longer yield the biuret reaction, those intermediate cleavage products were obtained which are known by the name of proteoses and peptones (of which we shall treat fully in the physiology of Digestion). These products were supposed not to appear in the cleavage effected by strong acids and bases, but complex products with similar properties have now been isolated and studied by Fischer and Abderhalden. Some of the final products of cleavage are still unknown; most of them, however, have been isolated and identified. They are the organic compounds known as *amino-acids,* or organic acids, in the molecule of which an amino-group (NH_2) is substituted for one or more atoms of hydrogen; our knowledge of the various amino-acids that arise from proteins by cleavage is mainly due to Fischer, who has devised new methods for their isolation and recognition. The number and variety of the amino-acids at present isolated is shown in the following table of Abderhalden :—

I. *Aliphatic or Fatty Series.*

1. Mono-amino-mono-carboxylic acids : glycine
                                      alanine
                                      valine
                                      leucine
                                      isoleucine.
2. Mono-amino-oxy-mono-carboxylic acids : serine.
3. Mono-amino-thio-mono-carboxylic acids : cysteine and cystine.
4. Mono-amino-di-carboxylic acids : aspartic acid
                                      glutamic acid.
5. Di-amino-mono-carboxylic acids : lysine
                                      arginine.
6. Di-amino-oxy-mono-carboxylic acids : di-amino-tri-oxy-dodecanic acid.

II. *Aromatic Series.*

1. Mono-amino-mono-carboxylic acids : phenylalanine.
2. Mono-amino-oxy-mono-carboxylic acids : tyrosine.

III. *Heterocyclic Compounds.*

1. Mono-amino-mono-carboxylic acids: proline (α-pyrrolidine-carboxylic acid)
                                      tryptophane (indole - α - amino - propionic acid)
                                      histidine (imidazole - α - amino - propionic acid).
2. Mono-amino-oxy-mono-carboxylic acids : oxy-proline (oxy-pyrrolidine-carboxylic acid).

Some chemists further regard the carbohydrate (glucosamine) group as a cleavage product of proteins : this group, however, occupies a special position, inasmuch as it is absent in many proteins, while in others its presence is doubtful, and, moreover, those which contain large amounts of it are by many considered to be compound proteins (gluco-proteins). We may suppose that as all proteins contain units which exhibit great affinity to the molecule of a carbohydrate, since they contain six carbon atoms, there is a possible transition from this group to the carbohydrate molecule. Lysine, *e.g.*, which is an amino-acid invariably present among the cleavage products of all proteins, has a formula very like that of glucosamine and glucose, as will be seen from the following table :—

$CH_2(OH)$	CH_2OH	$CH_2(NH_2)$
$CH(OH)$	$CH(OH)$	CH_2
$CH(OH)$	$CH(OH)$	CH_2
$CH(OH)$	$CH(OH)$	CH_2
$CH(OH)$	$CH(NH_2)$	$CH(NH_2)$
$CH : O$	$CH : O$	$COOH$
Glucose	Glucosamine	Lysine

Returning to the various amino-acids which represent the products of the hydrolytic cleavage of proteins, we must note the important fact that, with the exception of the protamines, all proteins hitherto decomposed contain the same units. One or other of the amino-acids, e.g. glycine in egg albumin and serum albumin, may be wanting, but these are rare exceptions.

What differentiates the several proteins among themselves is, on the other hand, the varying quantitative relations of the different amino-acids which compose the protein molecule. In some proteins, certain special amino-acids, e.g. leucine and more particularly glutamic acid, occur in enormous quantities, as in the proteins of plant seeds. There are great differences, again, in the relative proportions of the mono- and di-amino acids; the latter are found in large quantities in the protamines, while they are almost absent in some of the scleroproteins.

The histones occupy an intermediate position between the protamines and the coagulable proteins (albumins and globulins).

From these facts it may be anticipated that we shall before long be able to classify the various groups of proteins on the basis of similar end products. Indeed, from the fact that the same units enter into their constitution, although in different proportions for the different substances, we can even now to a certain extent perceive how the several alimentary proteins may be converted into the other definite proteins of the animal body.

It has been objected that the ultimate cleavage products of the artificial hydrolysis of proteins are not really pre-formed as so many units in the protein molecule: but the various data recently acquired meet this objection. The following may be briefly noted :—

(a) In whatever way the hydrolytic cleavage of any protein is effected, whether by acids, by alkalies, or by proteolytic ferments, the final products are approximately the same in quality and quantity. Tryptophane is the sole exception, since it is largely destroyed on hydrolysis by acids.

(b) Fischer has succeeded in artificially combining two or more molecules of amino-acid, and has thus obtained synthetically the chemical compounds which he terms polypeptides, which in a number of properties have affinity with the natural proteins. The type on which this synthesis has been successfully carried out is represented by the simplest dipeptide, which is known as glycyl-glycine, and which results from the coupling together of two molecules of glycine (or glycocoll) according to the following equation :—

$$NH_2.CH_2.COOH + HNH.CH_2.COOH =$$
glycine   glycine

$$NH_2.CH_2.CO.NH.CH_2.COOH + H_2O.$$
glycyl-glycine

Here the basic group (NH_2) of one molecule of glycine is united with the acid group (COOH) of the second, with loss of a molecule of water—a true polymerisation. It is clear that by the same process another molecule of glycine may be united with this compound (dipeptide), thus making a tripeptide, and so on. If we remember that all other amino-acids are capable like glycine of similar combination between themselves and with the molecules of other amino-acids, it is evidently possible to obtain a very numerous series of different and more or less highly complex compounds.

Fischer and his school have already succeeded in producing synthetically some seventy similar compounds; the most complex is an octadecapeptide, which consists of eighteen molecules of amino-acid united together in this manner.

It is important to note that many of these polypeptides, particularly the more complex, give the biuret reaction, which, as we have said, is the most characteristic test of protein, and that some of them are digested by pancreatic juice, which disintegrates them into the amino-acid components, as is the case with natural proteins.

IX. Enzymes and ferments must further be included in the protein group, and belong in all probability to the nucleoproteins, or, according to others, the scleroproteins. These, being elaboration products of the living cell, represent, according to the latest view (Hofmeister, 1901), the chemical instruments by means of which all chemical changes of the different substances which form the material substratum of living matter take place. These chemical changes result in the disintegration of the complex molecule into simpler compounds (cleavage by analytical ferments), either by rendering it suitable in form and quality for assimilation, as in the case of the various digestive ferments of the alimentary canal in animals, or by setting free the potential energy which is manifested in the form of heat or movement. To this large class of *analytic* ferments another class of ferments is opposed, whose work consists not in the chemical cleavage of substances with large molecules, but in *synthetic* processes, in which simple molecules unite to form more complex molecules, as occurs in the so-called anabolic phase of metabolism in living organisms. The theoretical existence of these supposed synthetic ferments has so far not received any decisive proof. We will therefore content ourselves with a rapid survey of the class of analytic ferments, of which much has been learnt by recent work.

The fermentative processes of decomposition were, until recently, divided into two great classes which were very distinct from one another. In the one class were placed all the *non-organised ferments* or *enzymes*, which were regarded as the elaboration products of the various secreting glands, capable of being isolated,.

and of acting as pure chemical agents, independent of the living elements which produced them. The several digestive enzymes of the gastro-intestinal tract in animals were considered as examples of these non-organised ferments.

The second class comprised the so-called *organised ferments*, or *ferments* proper, represented by micro-organisms (fungi, bacteria, etc.), the action of which was then held to be in direct dependence upon the vitality of the latter, and to cease on their death or disorganisation. *Saccharomyces cerevisiae*, which determines the alcoholic fermentation of glucose (Pasteur), was regarded as the prototype of such organised ferments.

Now, however, in consequence of Buchner's work (1899), this distinction can no longer be maintained. Buchner has demonstrated experimentally that it is possible to extract from the cells of beer-yeast, when exposed to enormous pressure, a substance rich in protein, which is free from living elements, and is able to set up the alcoholic fermentation of solutions of glucose. The property by which yeast cells ferment glucose is therefore due, not to a true vital process, but to the action of an enzyme or *zymase*, produced by the cell. Specific enzymes of other micro-organisms formerly held to be organised ferments (the bacilli of lactic fermentation, of acetic fermentation, etc.) have also been isolated.

All enzymes are now regarded as organic substances (most probably of the nature of proteins) which are elaboration products of the living cells, from which they can be separated and extracted by various methods without losing their activity. Generally speaking they can be extracted from the cells and the tissues, on treating these with water or glycerin. The latter solvent, in particular, yields solutions that remain active for a considerable time, and has been largely employed in practice to extract these enzymes.

It should be stated that the enzymes are frequently not found pre-formed within the cells which produce them, but are as it were in a potential state. The complete development of their specific enzyme activity necessitates the further action of oxygen and other chemical compounds known as *kinases*. The mother-substances from which the enzymes are derived are called *zymogens* or *pro-enzymes*. We shall discuss these at length in speaking of the digestive ferments, since there is in the intestine a substance which activates the pancreatic enzymes (*entero-kinase*).

No characteristic chemical reactions are common to all enzymes; generally speaking, they are precipitated from their colloidal solutions by alcohol, and are destroyed by high temperatures from $+80°$ to $+100°$ C. In order to recognise them, it is necessary to observe the properties which characterise their mode of action. In the first place enzymes, in consequence of their peculiar chemical action, do not form stable combinations with the substances on which they act, or with the decomposition products arising from their activity. An infinitesimal quantity of enzyme is able to act upon a relatively enormous quantity of fermentable substance. It has been found, *e.g.*, that one part of invertase is capable of splitting up 100,000 parts of saccharose, and one part of chymosin or rennet of coagulating 400,000 parts of caseinogen.

A second property of enzymes is the specific character of their action, inasmuch as any one enzyme acts only upon a definite substance, or upon a restricted group of allied substances. Enzyme action is always in strict relation with the configuration and constitution of the atomic grouping of the relative molecules, to which the enzyme is as rigorously adapted as the key to the wards of a lock—to repeat once more the picturesque expression of E. Fischer. This specific action is, in fact, so conspicuous as to serve as a method of distinguishing isomeric chemical compounds from one another.

Enzyme action is further influenced by various external conditions, *e.g.* the reaction of the liquid: some ferments are active only in an acid medium, others—and far the greater number —in a neutral or faintly alkaline medium.

Temperature has a marked influence on the course of enzyme activity, which usually increases with the rise of temperature to a certain point representing the optimum, after which a further rise of temperature diminishes the enzyme action until it disappears.

The accumulation of cleavage products has a marked inhibitory influence on the development of enzyme activity; the inhibition ceases so soon as these products are removed.

How is it possible to explain the action of enzymes?

Certain inorganic substances exhibit properties highly similar to those of the analytical enzymes we have been considering, since they are capable of producing cleavage processes which do not essentially differ from processes of fermentation. These substances, which have been known for some time to chemists, are the so-called catalysers, and determine the process of catalysis (Ostwald). A classical example of catalytic action is that represented by the decomposition of hydrogen peroxide (H_2O_2) into oxygen (O) and water (H_2O) by platinum black. A trace of this substance will decompose an enormous amount of hydrogen peroxide without any loss of activity.

Bredig (1899) has recently enlarged the class of catalysers by showing that all metals in a colloidal state, to which he gives the name of inorganic ferments, belong to it. Moreover, he has brought out so many interesting coincidences between the action of these catalysers and that of enzymes as to render the hypothesis highly probable that both classes of substances act in virtue of the same principle.

To Ostwald is due the special distinction of having effectively contributed to our knowledge of the mode of action of catalysers. According to him, every catalytic process consists essentially of a change of velocity in a chemical process, which occurs spontaneously. " A catalyser is a body which, without appearing in the end product of a chemical reaction, alters its velocity by accelerating or by retarding it."

This theory is especially applicable to the example cited of hydrogen peroxide and platinum black : we know, in fact, that the hydrogen peroxide slowly decomposes by itself into water and oxygen, to such an extent that after a few days there is no longer any trace of the hydrogen peroxide in an open vessel containing it. The platinum black merely accelerates the spontaneous process of scission. The same thing must occur in the case of enzymes and the substances which they split up.

This is not the place for discussion of the various theories put forward to explain the action of catalysers and of ferments : it need only be said that nowadays everything points to the conclusion that this action is effected not directly, but by the formation of intermediate products (which do not, however, appear in the end products of cleavage), and that according to Euler enzymes and catalysers act as collectors of ions.

X. In the present state of physiology the only possible basis for a classification of the different enzymes is the changes which they effect.

According to Hammarsten, the enzymes which have more especially been made the subject of experimental research may be subdivided into two great classes, *i.e.* *hydrolytic* and *oxidative*.

The class of hydrolytic ferments, *i.e.* those which split up complex chemical aggregates into simpler molecules by the absorption of molecules of water, comprises all the several digestive ferments, which, as we shall see, fulfil the office of disintegrating complex proteins, polysaccharides and alimentary fats into simpler compounds. The latter are better adapted for absorption by the intestinal epithelium, where they are either finally split up, or elaborated into new and more complex chemical compounds by the metabolic activity of the tissues. They are :—

(a) *Proteolytic* or *proteoclastic enzymes*, which split up proteins, and of which we have already spoken. In the animal body there are two (according to some authors, three) different types of proteolytic ferments—pepsin, trypsin, and to these, according to some modern workers (O. Cohnheim), erepsin must be added. We shall deal fully with these enzymes in the chapter on Digestion. Vegetable proteolytic ferments (*e.g.* papain) are also known.

(b) *Amylolytic enzymes or amylases*, which split the poly-saccharides (starch, etc.) into di- or mono-saccharides. To these belong the various diastases of the animal and plant kingdom (ptyalin, amylopsin). The so-called *invertases* which split di-saccharides into mono-saccharides are in close relation with these; *e.g.* maltase which splits maltose into two molecules of glucose; invertase, which splits saccharose into one molecule of fructose and one of glucose; lactase, which splits lactose into one molecule of glucose and one of galactose.

(c) *Lipolytic enzymes or lipases*, which split neutral fats into their components, *i.e.* glycerin and fatty acids. To these belongs the so-called steapsin of the pancreatic juice to which, according to the latest investigations, must be added another lipase, formed by the gastric mucosa.

The class of hydrolytic ferments further includes a number of other ferments recently discovered in the tissues and organs of animals and plants, such as arginase, which splits arginine into urea and ornithine; adenase and guanase, which split up adenine and guanine respectively into ammonia and hypoxanthine or xanthine; urease, which splits urea into ammonia, water, carbonic acid, etc.

A special position (which has been little noticed) is occupied by the so-called *coagulating enzymes*, such as the rennin or chymosin of the digestive tube, which forms casein from the caseinogen of milk, and thrombin or thrombase, which determines the clotting of blood by transforming fibrinogen into fibrin, as we shall see in treating of blood plasma.

The class of oxidising ferments contains all those ferments which determine the disintegration of complex substances by oxidising them, by a process highly similar to that which occurs in inorganic nature in the various forms of combustion, *e.g.* of carbon, which burns, combining with the oxygen of the air.

These ferments, too, are analytic, *i.e.* they break down the complex chemical compounds into simpler compounds, making them richer in oxygen derived from the atmosphere or other sources—and thereby liberating a certain quantity of potential chemical energy. Great importance is ascribed to these oxidising ferments, as they are the agents of the various processes of oxidation, which occur, as we shall frequently find, within the living organism: and it has been possible, by modern methods of research, to isolate a large number of enzymes belonging to this class from animal and vegetable tissues.

Direct *oxidases* (the name given to the oxidising ferments) must be distinguished from the indirect, which are known as *peroxidases*. The former are capable of causing oxygen to act directly; the latter can only oxidise in the presence of peroxides (hydrogen peroxide). Oxidases give a blue reaction directly with tincture of guaiacum, peroxidases only in presence of a peroxide.

Some consider as a third group of the oxidising ferments the so-called *catalases*, which split up hydrogen peroxide into oxygen and water, but never give a blue reaction with tincture of guaiacum.

The alcoholic fermentation of glucose by means of beer yeast, or the ferment known as *zymase*, which was first isolated by Buchner from the cells of that micro-organism, is not a true and proper oxidation in which free oxygen is absorbed by the sugar— as may be deduced from the fact that such fermentation takes place anaërobically, and according to the equation :—

$$C_6H_{12}O_6 = 2C_2H_5OH + 2CO_2.$$
Glucose   Alcohol   Carbonic
                                    acid

It should rather be considered as an internal or intra-molecular oxidation, by which part of the molecule of glucose is oxidised, and burns at the expense of the other part, till it finally splits up into alcohol and carbonic acid. According to recent investigation, we have here the co-operation of two separate and distinct enzymes, one of which, lactolase, or lactacidase, converts sugar into lactic acid, while the other, zymase, or alcoholase, splits the lactic acid into alcohol and carbonic acid.

According to some authors (whose conclusions have, however, been warmly disputed), a similar anaërobic fermentative process of glycolysis takes place in animal tissues.

In conclusion we must mention another class of ferments, of which we know at present even less than those already discussed —the so-called reducing ferments, reductases or hydrogenases.

Another classification of enzymes is based upon the difference of place in which they normally occur. Thus, to the ferments known as *extracellular* or secretory, because normally found in the liquids secreted by the various glands or cells, are opposed the *intracellular* ferments or endo-enzymes, which are found within the cell, and represent the chemical agents by which the cells are able to split up or fabricate the several chemical components of their substance. To this class of endo-enzymes belong Buchner's zymase, many of the oxidases, and also a series of hydrolytic, proteoclastic enzymes, which according to Vernon are of the type of O. Cohnheim's erepsin.

To these intracellular proteolytic ferments are due the phenomena of post-mortem *autodigestion* or *autolysis*, described for the first time by Salkowski (1900), which occurs in the organs or organic fluids, when isolated from the body, and kept free of bacterial or extraneous enzymatic contamination. After a certain lapse of time it can be shown that protein cleavage has taken place in the tissues or fluids, accompanied by a similar cleavage of fats and carbohydrates.

The phenomena of *post-mortem* autolysis have been the subject of numerous recent researches, in the hope of throwing some light upon *intra vitam*, intracellular, fermentative processes, which we must assume to be of great importance in the metabolism of the tissues and of the living cells. The results so far obtained are not, however, decisive enough to serve as the basis of any definite conclusion.

XI. The proteins of living matter are always accompanied by a large amount of simpler substances, nitrogenous or non-nitrogenous, which represent products of decomposition or of retrogressive changes in these substances, or in nutrient substances from outside, which have been more or less elaborated by the activity of the cell. The name *deutoplasm* has been given to these substances as a whole, that of cytoplasm being reserved for the living substance generically known as protoplasm.

The nitrogenous products of the retrogressive metamorphoses of protein form a series of well-defined chemical substances, many of which are eliminated with the urine in very varying amounts in the higher animals. The largest in quantity and in nitrogen content is urea, next come uric acid, hippuric acid, creatine and creatinine. The purine bases form a distinct group already referred to, xanthine, hypoxanthine or sarkine, adenine, guanine, and they are the decomposition products of nuclein. These substances cannot all be extracted from the tissues, owing to the minimal quantity in which they are present. Another group of nitrogenous and phosphorised substances, the lecithins, occur, according to Hoppe-Seyler, in every plant and animal cell, and in particularly large quantities in the elements of nerve, the blood corpuscles and in yolk of egg. In its chemical characters (solubility in ether and alcohol, insolubility in water) lecithin shows great similarity to fats. It resembles nuclein inasmuch as it contains phosphorus, and is capable of forming unstable combinations with albumin and other substances. The yolk of egg contains a combination of lecithin with vitellin. Protagon, extracted by Liebreich (1865) from the brain, is the combination of a lecithin with cerebrin, a nitrogenous substance free from phosphorus, similar to the glucosides.

The non-nitrogenous organic products which enter into the chemical constitution of the cell are represented by the *fats* and *carbohydrates*. These originate partly in the consumption of proteins, partly from external food-stuffs, or their transformations as effected by the cell-enzymes.

Chemically considered, the fats represent combinations of glycerin (triatomic alcohol) with the acids of the fatty series (stearic, palmitic, butyric, valerianic, caproic, as also with oleic acid, which does not belong to the normal fatty series.

Cholesterin resembles the fats in certain of its characteristics, though absolutely unlike them in its chemical constitution : it is regularly found in every animal and plant cell, particularly in the brain and liver. Since it is a secretion from the skin of man and other animals, it is found in the epidermal structures (hair, fur, feathers, nails, etc.), for which it forms a kind of protective grease. Cholesterin is a monatomic alcohol of unknown constitution, which crystallises from alcoholic solution in laminae like mother-of-pearl. Like glycerin, it forms with fatty acids compounds which correspond to the fats.

From a chemical point of view the carbohydrates are aldehydic or ketonic derivatives of polyhydric alcohols. They may be divided into three groups: (*a*) monosaccharides, (*b*) di-saccharides, (*c*) polysaccharides.

(*a*) Among the *monosaccharides* are more particularly grape sugar (glucose or dextrose) and fruit sugar (fructose or laevulose), which are abundant in plant juices; the first also occurs in animal tissues. They turn the plane of polarised light to the right or left. They are readily oxidised; they are fermented by yeast, and converted into alcohol and carbonic acid :—

$$C_6H_{12}O_6 = 2C_2H_5OH + 2CO_2.$$

They have the property of readily abstracting oxygen from the surrounding medium, and behave as reducing agents to oxidised compounds. This property is utilised in detecting the presence of sugars, and also in estimating them. The tests most used are Trommer's and Böttger's. In the former the sugar solution, rendered alkaline with caustic potash or soda, on adding a few drops of dilute copper sulphate, and heating, reduces the copper oxide to cuprous oxide, a suboxide which forms a reddish-yellow precipitate. In the second test a few drops of bismuth subnitrate are added to the alkaline solution of sugar, which is turned black by the reduction of the bismuth salt to the metallic state.

Besides these two tests, which, since they are based on the reducing property of glucose, are not, strictly speaking, specific to this compound, but are common to all the reducing substances, three other specific tests are known for glucose, namely Moore's test, the phenyl-hydrazine test, and that of alcoholic fermentation (biological test).

In the first the solution of glucose is warmed, after diluting it with about a quarter of its volume of caustic soda or potash. The mixture first turns yellow, and then successively (according to the content of sugar) orange, brown, dark brown, giving off the characteristic odour of burnt sugar or caramel, which becomes more intense on acidification.

The second test consists in warming the glucose solution with acetate of phenyl-hydrazine; characteristic yellow crystals (needles of phenyl-glucosazone are formed (E. Fischer).

The biological test is based on the fact that beer yeast is able to provoke alcoholic fermentation in a solution of glucose.

We shall give the quantitative tests for glucose in dealing with urine.

(*b*) *Di-saccharides* have the formula $C_{12}H_{22}O_{11}$, which represents the combination of two molecules of a monosaccharide with elimination of a molecule of water. The most important are cane sugar (saccharose) and milk sugar (lactose). On warming with dilute mineral acids, and under the action of certain bacteria, the di-saccharides are inverted, *i.e.* transformed into monosaccharides. Under the fermentative action of the *Bacterium lacticum* these last are transformed into lactic acid ($C_6H_{12}O_6 = 2C_3H_6O_3$). With *Bacillus butyricus* lactic acid undergoes further decomposition, giving rise to butyric acid, carbonic acid, and hydrogen :—

$$2C_3H_6O_3 = C_4H_8O_2 + 2CO_2 + 4H.$$

(*c*) *Polysaccharides* are also anhydrides of monosaccharides, and result from the combination of several molecules; they therefore have a high molecular weight, which differs in different compounds of the group. Their general formula is $nC_6H_{10}O_5$. They do not taste sweet, are generally amorphous, are partly soluble, partly insoluble in water, and are convertible into monosaccharides by various means. They include a series of bodies widely distributed in both plant and animal cells. The most important are starch, which in the form of stratified corpuscles is found in the protoplasm of many plant cells; glycogen or animal starch, which occurs in almost all animal tissues, but particularly in the amorphous granules of the hepatic cells, as also in muscle fibre, embryonic tissue, and proliferating cells in general : animal and vegetable gums; cellulose, which is the principal component of the cellular membranes of plants, and is also found in the animal kingdom in the mantle of *Tunicata* and the chitinous skeleton of insects.

Polysaccharides behave variously to solutions of iodine. The starches turn blue, glycogen brown : cellulose does not stain at all with iodine, and only assumes a bluish tint on treatment with sulphuric acid.

In addition to free carbohydrates, living protoplasm contains other compounds such as mucin and chitin, as is shown in their derivatives and decomposition products (dextrin, sugar, lactic acid, butyric acid, etc.).

The inorganic substance of elementary organisms consists of water, salts, and gases.

Water is indispensable to the activity of living matter, since it dissolves the single particles, and renders them capable of being transported. It is present partly in chemical combination, partly as solvent for the various substances of the cell-contents. The amount by weight of water in the tissues is on an average over 50 per cent. According to von Bezold, the total content of water in the human body is about 59 per cent. Bone contains 22 per cent water, liver 69 per cent, muscle 75 per cent, the kidneys 82 per cent.

The water holds in solution a number of salts, which are never wanting in living substance. Chlorides largely predominate ; next come the carbonates, sulphates, phosphates of the alkalies and alkaline earths. Such are the chlorides of sodium, potassium, and ammonium ; the carbonates, sulphates, and phosphates of sodium, potassium, calcium, magnesium, and ammonium. A considerable part of these salts is probably in chemical combination with the organic substances.

The gases, oxygen, carbonic acid, and nitrogen, when not chemically combined, are simply dissolved in the water : very occasionally they occur in the form of gaseous vesicles, as in certain unicellular Rhizopods.

XII. After this bird's-eye review of the vast province of the chemistry of elementary organisms, undertaken solely with the object of classifying into groups and subgroups the several bodies that compose the substratum of the phenomena of life, it must again be emphasised that we are far from any adequate knowledge of the chemical structure of living matter. It is impossible to investigate this living matter without first killing it, *i.e.* destroying its vitality. The chemical compounds, organic and inorganic, which we have seen to exist in plants and animals, are only the products of this destruction, *i.e.* they represent the chemical aggregates, which can be recognised and isolated from the dead body. They certainly exist in the cell ; but we are entirely ignorant of the mode in which they are associated and combined among themselves, so as to compose the living matter. Nor should this surprise us, when we reflect that with the ordinary methods of chemical analysis we have no means of ascertaining the exact chemical nature of the individual salts contained, *e.g.* in a mineral water. We can only determine the quality and quantity of the acids and bases contained in it : as to what these salts are, and how they are mixed together, we know nothing. Any statements in regard to this are mere guesswork.

The physiologist needs to be very circumspect and cautious in applying the data thus derived from the chemistry of dead matter to the phenomena of living substance, in which the chemical relations of the several molecular aggregates are very different, and the molecules themselves are highly complex and excessively unstable.

Immense progress has been made of late years in the knowledge of the finer morphological structure of the cell, which must help in determining the chemical differences between the protoplasm and the nucleus, respectively. The first advances in this direction are due to the methods of Micro-Chemistry.

Kossel's work (1891) has shown that in the nucleus, compounds of protein with substances containing phosphorus largely predominate, while the cytoplasm consists principally of simple proteins and their compounds with combinations which contain no phosphorus. Miescher had previously demonstrated (1874) that the nucleins which he discovered resist the digestive action of gastric juice, and that on placing cells of various kinds in this juice the cytoplasm of the cell dissolves, while the nuclei remain, although of smaller size. Malfatti (1892) next showed that it is the chromatic substance and the nucleolus of the nuclei which do not digest, while the nuclear fluid and a-chromatic substance dissolve. This proves the chromatic substance and the nucleolus of the nuclei to consist essentially of nucleins or their combinations, while the cell protoplasm consists of other proteins. Lastly, Lilienfeld and Monti (1892) showed that ammonium molybdate is a microchemical reagent for phosphorus-containing substances, in the presence of which phospho-molybdic acid is formed, which stains brown on the addition of pyrogallol. By means of this reagent it has been ascertained that the compounds of phosphorus, in the most dissimilar cells, are almost exclusively contained in the nucleus.[1]

Carbohydrates and fats, on the other hand, are almost exclusively localised in the cytoplasm and limiting cell membrane.

Nothing is known in regard to the localisation of the inorganic compounds; except that, according to Vahlen, potassium compounds are absent from the nuclei of cells.

BIBLIOGRAPHY

F. HOPPE-SEYLER. Physiologische Chemie, I. Teil, Allg. Biol. Berlin, 1877.
O. HERTWIG. Die Zelle u. die Gewebe. Jena, 1893-1898. (English translation, The Cell, Campbell, 1895.)
M. VERWORN. Allgemeine Physiologie. 4th ed. Jena, 1906. (English translation, General Physiology, by F. S. Lee. Macmillan, 1899.)
R. NEUMEISTER. Lehrbuch d. physiologischen Chemie. Jena, 2nd ed., 1892.
F. BOTTAZZI. Trattato di chimica fisiologica. Milan, 1898.
O. HAMMARSTEN. Lehrbuch d. physiologischen Chemie. Wiesbaden, 6th ed., 1907.
E. ABDERHALDEN. Lehrbuch d. physiologischen Chemie. Berlin and Vienna, 1906.
E. FISCHER. Untersuchungen über Amino-säuren, Polypeptide, u. Proteine. Berlin, 1896.

---

[1] Scott has shown that it is only the inorganic phosphates which react with this reagent. Organic phosphorus compounds do not react, especially those of the nuclein type, which are not readily hydrolysed into phosphoric acid.—PLIMMER and SCOTT.

C. OPPENHEIMER. Die Fermente u. ihre Wirkungen. Leipzig, Vogel, 1903.
C. BREDIG. Die Elemente d. chemischen Kinetik, mit besonderer Berück-
sichtigung des Katalyse u. der Ferment-Wirkung. Ergebnisse d. Phy-iol., I.
Part I., 1901.

Recent English literature of the subject :—

F. G. HOPKINS and S. W. COLE. A Contribution to the Chemistry of Proteids,
Part I. Journ. of Physiol., 1901-2, xxvii. 418.
P. A. LEVENE and L. B. MENDEL. Some Decomposition Products of the
Crystallized Vegetable Proteid *edestin*. Amer. Journ. of Physiol., 1902, vi.
48.
A. N. RICHARDS and W. J. GIES. Chemical Studies of Elastin, Mucoid, and other
Proteids in Elastic Tissue, with some Notes on Ligament Extractives.
Amer. Journ. of Physiol., 1902, vii. 93.
W. W. LESEM and W. J. GIES. Notes on the Protagon of the Brain. Amer.
Journ. of Physiol., 1903, viii. 183.
F. G. HOPKINS and S. W. COLE. A Contribution to the Chemistry of Proteids,
Part II. Journ. of Physiol., 1903, xxix. 451.
W. CRAMER. On Protagon, Cholin, and Neurin. Journ. of Physiol., 1904, xxxi.
30.
C. SEIFERT and W. J. GIES. On the Distribution of Osseo-mucoid. Amer.
Journ. of Physiol., 1904, x. 146.
H. NEILSON. The Hydrolysis and Synthesis of Fats by Platinum Black. Amer.
Journ. of Physiol., 1904, x. 191.
H. G. WELLS. On the Relation of Autolysis to Proteid Metabolism. Amer.
Journ. of Physiol., 1904, xi. 351.
E. R. POSNER. Do the Mucoids combine with other Proteids ? Amer. Journ. of
Physiol., 1904, xi. 404.
P. A. LEVENE. The Autolysis of Animal Organs. Amer. Journ. of Physiol.,
1904, xi. 437 and xii. 276.
T. B. OSBORNE and I. F. HARRIS. The Precipitation Limits with Ammonium
Sulphate of some Vegetable Proteins. Amer. Journ. of Physiol., 1905, xiii.
436.
T. B. OSBORNE and I. F. HARRIS. The Solubility of Globulin in Salt Solution.
Amer. Journ. of Physiol., 1905, xiv. 151.
H. C. HASLAM. The Separation of Proteids. Journ. of Physiol., 1905, xxxii.
267.
R. H. A. PLIMMER. The Formation of Prussic Acid by the Oxidation of Albumins.
Journ. of Physiol., 1904, xxxi. 65 ; and 1905, xxxii. 51.
P. A. LEVENE. The Cleavage Products of Proteoses. Journ. of Biolog. Chem.,
1905-6, i. 45.
E. R. POSNER and W. J. GIES. Is Protagon a Mechanical Mixture of Substances,
or a definite Chemical Compound ? Journ. of Biolog. Chem., 1905-6, i. 59.
H. D. DAKIN. The Oxidation of Amido-acids with the Production of Substances
of Biological Importance. Journ. of Biolog. Chem., 1905-6, i. 171.
A. E. TAYLOR. On the Synthesis of Protein through the Action of Trypsin.
Journ. of Biolog. Chem., 1907, iii. 87.
T. B. ROBERTSON. Note on the Synthesis of Protein through the Action of
Trypsin. Journ. of Biolog. Chem., 1907, iii. 87.
C. H. NEILSON. Further Evidence on the Similarity between Catalysis and
Enzyme Action. Amer. Journ. of Physiol., 1905-6, xv. 148.
C. H. NEILSON. The Inversion of Starch by Platinum Black. Amer. Journ.
of Physiol., 1905-6, xv. 412.
W. B. HARDY. Colloidal Solution. The Globulins. Journ. of Physiol., 1905-6,
xxxiii. 251.
R. H. A. PLIMMER and W. M. BAYLISS. The Separation of Phosphorus from
Caseinogen by the Action of Enzymes and Alkali. Journ. of Physiol., 1905-6,
xxxiii. 439.
F. G. HOPKINS and E. G. WILLCOCK. The Importance of Individual Amino-acids
in Metabolism. Journ. of Physiol., 1906-7, xxxv. 88.
W. M. BAYLISS. Researches on the Nature of Enzyme Action. Journ. of Physio.,
1907-8, xxxvi. 221.

W. M. Bayliss. The Nature of Enzyme Action. London, 1908.

P. Hartley. On the Nature of the Fat contained in the Liver, Kidney, and Heart. Journ. of Physiol., 1907-8, xxxvi. 17.

O. Rosenheim and M. C. Tebb. The Non-existence of "Protagon" as a definite Chemical Compound. Journ. of Physiol, 1907-8, xxxvi. 1.

H. D. Dakin. Comparative Studies of the Mode of Oxidation of Phenyl Derivatives of Fatty Acids by the Animal Organism and by Hydrogen Peroxide. Journ. of Biolog. Chem., 1908, iv. 419 ; and 1908-9, v. 173, 303.

R. H. A. Plimmer and F. H. Scott. The Distribution of Phospho-proteins in Tissues. Trans. Chem. Soc., 1908, xciii. 1699.

A. E. Taylor. On the Synthesis of Protamin through Ferment Action. Journ. of Biolog. Chem., 1908-9, v. 381.

A. E. Taylor. On the Composition and Derivation of Protamin. Journ. of Biolog. Chem., 1908-9, v. 389.

T. B. Robertson. On the Synthesis of Paranuclein through the Agency of Pepsin, etc., etc. Journ. of Biolog. Chem., 1908-9, v. 493.

R. H. A. Plimmer and F. H. Scott. The Transformations in the Phosphorus Compounds in the Hen's Egg during Development. Journ. of Physiol., 1909, xxxviii. 247.

T. B. Osborne, Leavenworth and Brautlecht. The Different Forms of Nitrogen in Proteins. Amer. Journ. of Physiol., 1908-9, xxiii. 180.

R. H. A. Plimmer and R. Kaya. The Distribution of Phospho-proteins in Tissues, Part II. Journ. of Physiol., 1909-10, xxxix. 45.

E. V. McCollum. Nuclein Synthesis in the Animal Body. Amer. Journ. of Physiol., 1909-10, xxv. 120.

CHAPTER II

LIVING MATTER: ITS FUNDAMENTAL PROPERTIES

CONTENTS.—Vital metabolism and phenomena of nutrition and reproduction. 2. Vital metabolism and phenomena of excitability and sensibility. 3. Laws of stability and variability of living species. Critical examination of Theory of Evolution; Darwinism, and Neo-Lamarckism. 4. Evolutionary theories of Nägeli, Weismann, De Vries. 5. Distinctive characters of plants and animals: (a) Doctrine of Linnaeus; (b) doctrine of Cuvier: (c) doctrine of J. R. Mayer, Dumas, Liebig. 6. Different forms of plant and animal metabolism: (a) Nitrifying bacteria; (b) green plants; (c) a-chlorophyllous plants; (d) herbivorous and carnivorous plants. Bibliography.

THE fine morphological organisation and highly complex chemico-physical structure of elementary organisms, while sufficiently distinctive in character to differentiate non-living matter from living bodies, are not adequate to distinguish the living body from the dead, or from the products elaborated by the living. As a matter of fact, our knowledge of cytological structure depends mainly, and the data we possess in regard to the chemical composition of the cell depend entirely, upon observations made on the dead organism.

Yet it is upon the cytological and physico-chemical structure of the cell that the physiological activity and functions common to all living beings are founded, and it is by these that they are characteristically distinguished from non-living matter.

General Physiology has of late undergone a remarkable development in the direction of philosophical interpretation. We must here confine ourselves to summarising the most definitely ascertained conclusions—passing over the many hypotheses by which it is attempted to fill the unbridged gaps, and keeping strictly to what may serve as the foundation of scientific culture, and preparation to the study of human physiology.

I. Life is essentially characterised by instability and movement, by the constant transformation of matter, with a corresponding evolution and accumulation of energy, which is exhibited in unicellular as in multicellular organisms, in plants as in animals. The name Metabolism ($\mu\epsilon\tau\alpha\beta\circ\lambda\acute{\eta}$, change) has been given to these physico-chemical changes of living protoplasm as a whole. It is

42

the result of two opposite processes, which are continually super-posed and succeed each other : a synthetic, assimilative, and con-structive process, known as *anabolism*, and an analytical, dissimila-tive, and destructive process, known as *katabolism*.

In the anabolic process, the cell forms or elaborates organic matter from the nutrient materials, by the aid of energies derived from the environment or developed by oxidation of its own substance ; it takes up this organic matter by intussusception, transforms it into living protoplasm, or stores it as reserve material.

In the katabolic process, the cell breaks up and uses the reserve materials, disintegrates its own protoplasm, and returns to the environment the products of decomposition, combustion, and activity.

While the two opposite processes which constitute metabolism, or the exchanges of matter and energy, are intimately connected, they are differently distributed in the two principal phases of life, the progressive and the retrogressive. During the first phase the organism grows and develops, and is active in its functions; during the second, it dwindles and degenerates, and its functions are abated. The characteristic phenomena of nutrition, growth, and development in the organism are the natural consequences of metabolism, where the assimilatory or anabolic processes prepon-derate ; so, too, atrophy, senility, and death result from predomin-ance of the dissimilatory or katabolic processes, when life is on the wane.

Between the progressive and retrogressive phases of life, between youth and age, there lies a long intermediate period, during which the two opposite processes, anabolic and katabolic, are practically in equilibrium. This is the phase of maturity, characterised by the full and vigorous exercise of all the vital functions, more particularly of the reproductive capacity.

It is only when growth and ontogenic development are com-plete that the organism is able to reproduce itself. In other words, only when the factors or hereditary tendencies accumulated within the germ from which the organism has arisen, have become per-fectly developed and active, is it capable of forming by itself or by intercourse with an individual of the opposite sex, new germs, *i.e.* new aggregates of hereditary elements adapted for reproduction and conservation of the species.

Metabolism is the invariable physiological basis of these marvellous phenomena : when the anabolic process predominates, the hereditary tendencies contained in the germ develop and become active ; when the evolution of the individual is com-plete, the metabolic process is turned to preparing the hereditary material of new organisms.

II. Metabolism as the exchange of matter between organism

and environment is intimately connected with metabolism as exchange of energy. Each living organism contains within itself at any given moment of its life a sum of potential energy, drawn from the sun's rays, and from the food-stuffs which it has accumulated or assimilated; and this energy is always ready to discharge itself, or explode by transformation into kinetic energy, in consequence either of internal impulses or of external stimuli. The most striking form assumed by the energy developed in a living organism is the movement of masses, the power of surmounting resistance, *i.e.* of doing mechanical work. When these movements or changes of form or position in space depend upon internal stimuli they appear to be spontaneous or automatic, and are the most common and obvious objective sign that the organism that accomplishes them is living. When they are provoked by external stimuli they appear as reflex movements, *i.e.* as the effects of internal reactions to external stimuli; in that case there is a striking disproportion between action and reaction, although this is not a distinctive sign of life, since the same may be observed in many chemical combinations—the so-called explosives. What does, however, differentiate the latter from living substances, is that the chemical activity of explosives exhausts itself in the explosion, while the organism becomes fatigued with work, and recuperates in repose, *i.e.* at each reaction it only discharges part of its energy, and during the functional pauses it recovers by the anabolic process the quantity of potential energy that has been consumed.

This peculiar capacity for developing, spending, and reaccumulating energy, which characterises living beings, has received the name of *Excitability*, and is distinguished as *reflex* or *automatic*, according as the reactions or excitations are provoked by internal tendencies or impulses, or by external stimuli, or excitations extrinsic to the organism.

That there must be a marked analogy between the internal conditions of automatic, and those of reflex excitability, appears from the fact that it is often very difficult to differentiate objectively between automatic movements and reflexes; on the other hand, many movements originally automatic become reflex by a simple morphological evolution of the elementary organism that produces them, while many originally reflex movements become automatic by long exercise and habit.

These phenomena of excitability, which can be observed under various forms in all living organisms, are intimately connected with another group of phenomena, that can be directly observed upon ourselves alone, since they are accessible only to immediate internal observation or introspection. These last are the psychical phenomena, which as a whole constitute the content of consciousness.

The most rudimentary forms of consciousness, and as such the most widely dispersed (common, it may be, to all living beings), are represented by the phenomena of *Sensibility*, taken in the true psychological and not in the metaphorical sense—which is invariably intended by physicists in speaking, *e.g.* of the sensibility of the balance, galvanometer, or thermopile.

Certain physiologists, including Claude Bernard, have considered *sensibility* to be the highest form, or evolutionary product, of *excitability*, *i.e.* of the physiological property common to all, even elementary, organisms of reacting to stimuli according to their nature. This, however, is either to disallow the psychical import of the word sensibility, or to admit as a fact that which is wholly inconceivable, *i.e.* the emergence of any psychical phenomenon—even in the form of vague internal sensations—from simple molecular movements. According to our physiological concepts, sensibility and excitability do but express the same thing from two different standpoints. "*Excitability* is for us *sensibility* expressed in a verbal symbol suggested by external observation ; *sensibility* is the same *excitability* expressed in a verbal symbol derived from introspection. If we denote by excitation and sensation the effects corresponding, respectively, to excitability and sensibility, then excitation is the objective or material aspect of sensation ; sensation is the subjective or psychical aspect of excitation " (Luciani, 1892).

This is merely a formal statement of the fundamental hypothesis of psychophysics, viz. that psychical phenomena are the correlatives of physiological phenomena, and express the aspects under which the latter surge up in consciousness, and form its content. From the objective standpoint, psychical phenomena also must be regarded as so many forms of excitation, determined by the metabolism of the protoplasm, which is the common physiological basis of all vital phenomena.

III. In fulfilling the functions of nutrition, reproduction, excitability, and sensibility, all plant and animal organisms are subject to two laws, which to a certain extent are antagonistic, the Law of Heredity, and the Law of Variation. The first represents the principle of Stability, the second the principle of Evolution. Neither the one nor the other are to be understood in an absolute sense, since they are mutually exclusive, but it is extremely difficult to fix the precise limit between stability and variability, as appears from the history of biological science.

Until some half-century ago the mind of most naturalists was dominated by the law of stability, Fixity of Species being a dogma, solemnly proclaimed by Linnaeus in his famous aphorism " Species tot sunt quot diversas formas ab initio produxit infinitum Ens " (*Philosophia botanica*, 1751).

A little more than a century later, in 1859, the publication of

Darwin's book *On the Origin of Species by Means of Natural Selection* caused a radical change in the ideas of the naturalists, and led to the almost unconditional triumph of the law of evolution, to the detriment of the law of stability. The evolutionists fell into excesses, even denying the existence of biological species. We have recently entered upon a period of acute criticism of old and new theories of the Origin of Species, and at present the conviction is gaining ground that none of these theories has an absolute demonstrative value, all having rather the significance of hypotheses that are of great use to the biologist in orientating himself in his positive researches.

The idea of evolution has till now been the only conception imagined by the naturalists to account for the evident affinity exhibited among themselves by the different plants and animals which are grouped into species, genera, families, orders, classes. In all these groups a certain conformity of morphological type is apparent.

According to the Evolutionary Theory, this unity of type is the expression of a unity of origin (monophyletic origin), from which the various families, genera, and species, animal and vegetable, have been derived by successive differentiations. Comparative anatomy, embryology, palaeontology, botanical and zoological geography, offer numerous facts that accord perfectly with the theory of evolution. With the progress of biological science, however, other data have gradually emerged that are difficult to reconcile with the concept of simple, continuous, monophyletic evolution.

Many of the resemblances, analogies, and homologies admitted by comparative anatomists up to a few years ago are no longer valid in face of a more profound and exact knowledge of the true structure and function of certain organs that were previously imperfectly known. For embryologists, the value of the so-called "great biogenic law" that was held by certain naturalists to be one of the fundamental proofs of evolution, has depreciated owing to the many exceptions which it presents. Further, the analogy between the development of the individual (ontogenesis) and the development of the species (phylogenesis) is essentially different, since the cell-ovum from which the individuals of the evolved species originate differs entirely from the ovum of the *Protista*, and must in itself (by a still incomprehensible mystery) contain the whole of the determinants of the complex final development, determinants that are obviously wanting in the ovum of *Protista*, or are contained there in a far less degree.

Nor, again, have recent palaeontological data provided all the arguments in favour of the theory of evolution that were claimed a few years ago. Nowadays we can no longer invoke insufficiency of material to explain the great lacunae found in the development of fossil plants or animals.   Species, genera, families are seen to disappear incontinently, and other species, other genera, other families are substituted for them, with no evidence of that continuity and regularity of development which is demanded by the theory of evolution.   Even when continuity of development is observed for any given organ (*e.g.* the foot of Solidungula), it is more apparent than real, since it has been arrived at by observing a single organ apart from all the other organs which constitute the species under consideration.

Finally, it should not be forgotten that the fundamental basis for a complete and satisfactory theory of the evolution of the entire organic world, in virtue merely of the elements and forces of the inorganic world (as the pure evolutionists maintain with Spencer), is still wanting, viz. the demonstration of the spontaneous generation of life from inorganic matter and force. The greater the progress made by science, the more do the organisms believed to be simple appear complex, and the more improbable is spontaneous generation.

Notwithstanding this and other serious difficulties, it must be admitted that the hypothesis of evolution has proved in practice to be a tool of remarkable utility.   It has enabled us to gather up under one concept an infinite variety of scattered facts which would otherwise have escaped the researches and analysis of modern science, and thanks to which our positive knowledge has made extraordinary progress.

Even if all biologists agree in admitting the theory of Evolution, this harmony ceases when we attempt to determine its mechanism, *i.e.* its real causes and factors.

The Darwinians and the so-called neo-Darwinians consider natural selection to be the principal, if not the sole factor in evolution, while the Lamarckians and the neo-Lamarckians almost entirely deny the value of selection, and assert on the contrary that transformation of species is the result of direct adaptation to the variable conditions of environment.

Darwin and all his modern followers, while they defend the principle of selection to the hilt, are forced to admit an innate tendency to variation within the species, without being able to indicate its causes.   If the said variation is slow, continuous, gradual and indefinite, as supposed by Darwin, this does not explain how the appearance of a variation can turn to the advantage of the species, and give opportunity for selection, in such a way as to favour the individual or individuals in which the new variation originates, in the struggle for existence, to the prejudice of the other individuals deprived of the same minimal variation.

On the other hand, the concept of variability of species, both in plants and animals, has made considerable progress.   In the time of Darwin a pure speculation, it is now a positive experimental fact; and the new biometric methods have led to the discovery of facts and laws of capital importance which throw fresh light on the problem of the origin of species, showing it to be far more complex and difficult than had been supposed.

These laws demonstrate the necessity of carefully distinguishing between variation and variation.

Some variations are merely quantitative and fluctuating, and when studied by the statistical method are found to be subject to the so-called Law of Quetelet. Such variations are in strict relation with the nutritive conditions, or with the environmental conditions in general, and when these change, the values of the said variations change also, since they are not in themselves hereditary; but the individuals that exhibit them return to the normal type whenever the conditions of the environment again become normal. It is clear that such variations can have no importance in determining a transmutation of species.

Other variations, on the contrary, are qualitative and non-fluctuating, and are not subject to the Law of Quetelet. They are fixed, independent of the condition of the environment, and should in reality be termed not variations, but typical hereditary forms, or again *elementary species* (or *races*). Each of the classical Linnaean species comprises a greater or less number of such elementary species, which in the first instance were confused with the fundamental typical species, and were erroneously held to be simple variations of the same. The majority of our plants and domestic animals are examples of these elementary species. Selection, as practised artificially by man, or effected by Nature in the struggle for existence, is of great importance in the sifting of such elementary species as are more suited to the needs of man, or better adapted to the environmental conditions. It would, however, be a great mistake to think that these elementary species were created and formed by means of selection. In reality selection did nothing more than seal and set in evidence what already existed in a mixed and confused state in the fundamental species, and it created nothing new. Hence the majority of the examples cited by Darwin from plants and domestic animals are of no value as evidence of the agency of selection in the formation of new species. It is on this account that many speak to-day of a crisis in Darwinism, when this means the theory of selection in a restricted sense, and is not a synonym of evolution.

The falling-off in the supporters of Darwinism (in this limited sense) has reinforced the adherents of Lamarckism, who attribute the origin of species directly to the environment, to the action of external causes, climate, soil, nutrition, etc. According to Lamarck's original idea (1809), it is the want that creates the organ, which then becomes gradually perfected by use, while with disuse the organ atrophies and disappears. This idea presupposes a teleological principle, regulating the transmutation and adaptability of the new organ, a principle in sharp contrast with the canons of the materialistic doctrine, which seeks for the mechanical causes of phenomena, and excludes all mystical, transcendental interpretations. The neo-Lamarckians renounce the teleological principle, on the strength of recently acquired data as to the determining action of certain external agents, *e.g.* light, heat, water, gravity, chemical substances, action of parasites, mechanical action (photomorphosis, thermomorphosis, hydromorphosis, geomorphosis, chemomorphosis, biomorphosis, mechanomorphosis, etc.). This field of research, as cultivated especially by the modern botanist, is one of the most fruitful to the progress of biological science.

At the same time it must be remembered that the external agent, *e.g.* light or heat, which determines a modification in the structure and conformation of an organ, is not the true cause of such a modification, but is rather the external stimulus adapted to develop a variation which already existed potentially in that organ. The determining agent, therefore, creates nothing new, it only stimulates the species to the expression of those properties which it already possesses potentially. This conclusion, which is inevitable in the present state of our knowledge, must obviously limit to a great extent (some even say reduce to zero) the value of the direct action of external agents in the formation and transformation of species.

But further: in order that the influence of the environment in the production of new characters in a species shall be efficacious and enduring, it is necessary to presuppose that the newly acquired characters are hereditary. Does any such heredity really exist?

This is one of the problems most keenly discussed among modern biologists. It is obvious that a decidedly negative reply would cause the whole edifice of the Lamarckian and neo-Lamarckian theory to crumble. But no one is yet in a position to give a definite answer. The majority of the facts that were at one time cited in proof of the heredity of acquired characters have been triumphantly refuted by Weismann. Some few data relating to the lower organisms (*Bacteria* and *Saccharomyces*) remain, in which the heredity of newly acquired characters seems to be demonstrated; but how far these data are of value in the solution of the general problem with which modern biologists are so engrossed, is a matter for discussion.

For the present it must be confessed that with the exception of these few cases among the inferior organisms, all the attempts hitherto made to obtain new forms of plants and animals by the effect of one or several external causes have given negative results.

IV. Starting from a profound criticism of Darwinism and Lamarckism, Nägeli (1887) founded a new theory of evolution, according to which the origin of species depends upon the intimate constitution of the germinal matter (or *idioplasm*), inasmuch as this possesses an inherent tendency to perfect itself and to progress, developing by a slow and continuous evolution new and more complex forms, which are independent to a certain degree either of the variations of the environment or of the struggle for existence.

It is undeniable that all the branches of the zoological trunk exhibit a progression from the lower forms to the higher, and always in a sufficiently cognate form, although the animals may be subjected to very different external conditions of existence and development. We see, for instance, that the eye, which in the rudimentary species of animals is represented by a simple spot of pigment, is provided in worms, in arthropods, in molluscs, in vertebrates, with accessory apparatus, such as the lens, the vitreous body, iris, choroid, etc. This tendency towards perfection, whether of single organs and apparatus, or of the individual as a whole, which is revealed everywhere in the organic world, must, according to Nägeli (since it is comparatively independent of extrinsic vital conditions), find its explanation in the very being of the living substance.

Unlike Darwinism and Lamarckism, which accord a predominating importance to external causes in phylogenic evolution, Nägelism assigns the maximal importance to internal causes. Nägeli's phylogenesis harmonises perfectly with his ontogenesis. The internal causes of the transformation are perfectly analogous to those by which the germ, or fertilised ovum, develops into the perfect individual, and the mutilated individual is capable of regenerating a missing member (*e.g.* a pollarded tree can recover all its branches, a lizard can reproduce its lost tail, a decapitated snail can reproduce its head). It is certainly within the intimate physico-chemical structure of the idioplasm of the egg, or mutilated individual, and not in the environment, that we must seek the determining cause of the individual development or reintegration. So likewise the determining causes of the mutability of species, and of the slow formation of new and ever more perfect species, must lie not in the environment, but in the intimate structure of the idioplasm.

As in ontogenic evolution the environment, in addition to nutritive matters, provides a sum of stimuli favourable to the development of hereditary tendencies; so in phylogenic evolution the environment provides impulses favourable to the development of creative tendencies, and in measure as these develop, moulds and modifies them, adapting them to the circumstances.

It is not our task to follow Nägeli in the development of his theory. From the standpoint of general physiology, it suffices to show that it harmonises perfectly with the principle we have formulated in regard to the elementary vital activities, which are all centred in metabolism. Both the reproductive capacity, by which the hereditary tendencies are rapidly completed, and the evolutionary capacity, by which the creative tendencies slowly develop, are founded upon the metabolic processes of living protoplasm.

The same difference that we have seen to exist between automatic activity as depending essentially on internal impulses and tendencies, and reflex activity as due to external stimuli, exists between Nägelism and neo-Lamarckism.

Starting from the psycho-physical theorem that conscious psychical phenomena are the introspective aspect of correlative physiological excitations, it is not too bold to assume that unconscious physiological phenomena likewise have a psychical aspect which is not clearly revealed to introspection, although it helps to build up the content of consciousness. With this premise, it seems reasonable to admit with Hering that ontogenic phenomena are the correlatives of an unconscious memory inherent in the protoplasm ; just as phylogenic phenomena might be considered the correlatives of an unconscious formative imagination.

Weismann (in 1892) attempted a sort of reconciliation between Darwinism, Lamarckism, and Nägelism by assuming that the action of external causes might be fixed in the species, and become hereditary, if the said action were exercised on the plasma of the germinal cells. The modifications suffered by these would manifest themselves in the embryo and the adult individual, and would be transmitted to the descendants. In this way what Weismann calls germinal selection would become possible, in which the action of external agents, combined with natural selection, would determine the origin of new species.

These, however, are merely ingenious abstract speculations, which more or less successfully disguise our impotence to determine in any precise and accurate manner the relation between the action of external causes and the reaction of internal causes, manifested in the development of a morphological process.

De Vries (1901) thought to escape from the many and insuperable difficulties of the hypotheses we have been examining by his Theory of Mutations, according to which new species originate not in a continuous variation, but in discontinuous variations, by sudden leaps which he termed mutations. In certain moments of the life of the species, under special conditions, some individuals may unexpectedly assume a series of new characters, differing from those possessed by their progenitors, and these characters might be hereditary.

Many well-known facts in the history of plants and domestic animals seem to prove the sudden origin of new forms, as supposed by the theory of De Vries. The majority of the new varieties cultivated in the fields, orchards, and gardens, when not obtained by hybridising, appear to have originated in such unexpected mutations.

These facts were illustrated and described, even before De Vries, by Korschinski, who gave the phenomena the name of *heterogenesis*.

De Vries in his famous experiments at the Botanical Garden of Amsterdam saw several distinct species originate in a few years from *Oenothera Lamarckiana* — *Oenothera gigas*, *O. albida*, *O. rubrinervis*, *O. nanella*, etc., species which are said to give rise on direct fertilisation to products of a constant character. This would be the first experimental instance on record of neo-genesis in species belonging to the higher organisms. Not all biologists, however, are inclined to accept the conclusion of De Vries. Many (among them Bateson, and Cuboni in Italy) maintain that the so-called new species have no constant characters of descent, and that the new forms observed by the illustrious botanist of Amsterdam represent merely special cases of polyhybridism, in which the dominant and recessive elements of the progenital forms separate out according to Mendel's Law. In favour of this supposition we have the fact that some of the pollen grains of *Oenothera Lamarckiana* are deformed and sterile, as always occurs with hybrids.

If we admit that the mutations observed by De Vries are no more than a return to the parent species, the fundamental basis of his theory loses all evidential value. Further, it is undeniable that many facts of systematic botany, and above all of palaeontology, can be more readily interpreted on the generally accepted theory of continuous variations. And lastly, it should be noted that De Vries himself recognises that the all-essential point, *i.e.* the internal causes of mutation, still remains an impenetrable mystery to human investigation.

Whatever the future of the different theories relating to the mechanism by which the various living forms have developed one from another, whatever the nature of the internal causes determining the formation of new species, it must never be forgotten that the Law of Descent, *i.e.* the general Theory of Evolution, which by means of Darwinism dominated the minds of scientific men for half a century, has been marvellously fecund, and has incited a vast series of researches, leading to the acquisition of new truths, which without that theory might never have been gathered up. It therefore remains the corner-stone of biological research; even more than as a hypothesis we are constrained to admit it as a necessary postulate, because its negation would logically include the negation of a unitary biological science.

From the foregoing observations on the vital activities common to all living beings, we may formulate the following general propositions :—

(*a*) All vital activity is founded on the metabolism of living matter.

(*b*) As a material exchange, metabolism expresses itself in anabolic and katabolic processes.

(*c*) As a dynamic exchange, metabolism manifests itself by the accumulation and discharge of energy.

(*d*) The anabolic and katabolic processes express themselves in the phenomena of nutrition (consumption and repair) and reproduction (formation and evolution of germs).

(*e*) The accumulation and transformation of energy is exhibited in the phenomena of rest and excitation (automatic or reflex in character).

(*f*) All the processes of vital metabolism conform to the conservative laws of heredity, and to the evolutionary laws of variability.

(*g*) Vital metabolism is exhibited under a double aspect: to external observation it manifests itself in somatic phenomena; to introspection it reveals itself in psychical phenomena, conscious and unconscious.

V. On penetrating deeper into the study of common vital activities, we must inquire whether, from the standpoint of general physiology, it is possible to differentiate sharply between the two great kingdoms of living nature—plants, and animals.

In comparing what are relatively the highest representatives of the two kingdoms, nothing seems more simple and natural than the distinction between a plant and an animal. Many erroneous opinions have, nevertheless, been promulgated in the attempt to define their differential characters. Of these the principal are as follows :—

According to Linnaeus, the lack of sensibility and capacity for active movement in plants is sufficient to distinguish them from animals. But the case of *Mimosa pudica* (Fig. 9), *Dionea muscipula* (Fig. 10), and other sensitive plants, whose leaves move at the slightest contact with an insect, show that excitation in the form of active movement, the external sign of sensibility, is demonstrable in plants also. Claude Bernard (1878) showed that anaesthetics (ether and chloroform) act in the same way on animals and on sensitive plants.

Cuvier was of opinion that the existence in animals of a distinct digestive apparatus with the accompanying digestive function, of which no trace exists in plants, was a sufficient sign of distinction between the former and the latter. To-day, however, we know that an immense number of the lower animals have no digestive tube, while on the other hand the so-called insectivorous plants, described by Darwin, possess organs capable of subjecting animal substances to a real digestion. Papain, an enzyme which has the same properties as pepsin, has been extracted from *Carica*

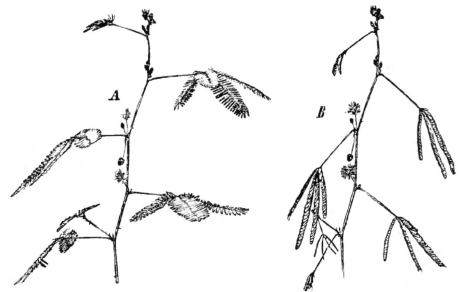

FIG. 9.—*Mimosa pudica.* During the day the leaves are extended, as in *A*; when stimulated by shaking or touching, they close up, drooping backwards, as in *B*. After chloroform narcosis this reaction does not take place.

papaja. The juices of the leaves of *Nepenthes*, *Drosera*, and *Dionea* (Figs. 11 and 12) digest meat to the great advantage of the plant. We know further that plants, like animals, accumulate sugar, starch, oil, and proteins as reserve nutritive materials, and, for nutritive purposes and to bring them into circulation, submit them to a regular digestion by the action of certain enzymes, such as diastase, invertin, emulsin, and the peptic or hydrolytic ferments.

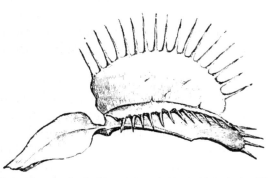

FIG. 10.—Leaf of *Dionæa muscipula.* (Darwin.) The upper surface of the leaf shows the bristles that react on the slightest contact with an insect, provoking immediate closure of the two halves of the leaf, and capture of the insect, which is then digested by the secretion from the glands upon the surface of the leaf.

After Lavoisier (1777) had demonstrated that animals absorb oxygen and exhale carbonic acid, and the Dutch Ingenhousz, and almost contemporaneously the Genevans Sénébier and Th. de Saussure (1800), had discovered that green plants reduce the carbonic acid of the air by assimilating carbon and emitting oxygen, a theory was involved which predicated a functional antagonism between plants and animals. By storing up the

energy of the sun's rays, as observed by J. R. Mayer (1845), plants
reduce carbonic acid and form organic sub-
stances, which serve as fuel for the animals
that constantly devour the plants and disperse
the energy stored up in them.   The plant is
accordingly an apparatus for reduction, the
animal an apparatus for oxidation.

   This theory was more particularly developed in France by Dumas and Boussingault,
in Germany by Liebig.   There is between
plants and animals a constant circulation of
matter and exchange of energy.   The animal,
by means of the oxygen of the air, transforms
into heat, electricity, or motion the potential
energy contained in the food-stuffs obtained
directly (herbivores) or indirectly (carnivores)
from plants, and produces water, carbonic acid,
ammonia and salts.   The plant draws these
ultimate products from the air and soil, and
by means of solar radiation builds them up
into carbohydrates, fats, and proteins.   Animal

life as a
whole is
thus sub-
ordinated
to the pre-
existence
and co-ex-
istence of

Fig. 11.—Ascidium of leaf
of *Nepenthes*.   At the
bottom of the pitcher-
shaped receptacle is seen
the fluid *F*, secreted by the
glands, in which the ani-
malcules that fall in can
be digested.   This figure
is somewhat reduced.

plant life, the latter being wholly
independent of the former.

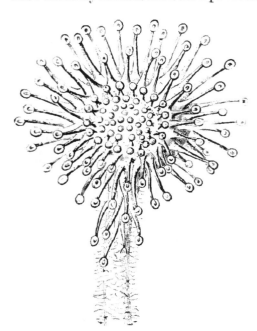

Fig. 12.—Leaf of *Drosera rotundifolia*.   (Darwin.)
The leaf shows numerous pedunculated
glands, each having at its extremity a drop
of secretion which serves to catch and digest
the insect.

   This doctrine of vital antagonism between plants and
animals is no less false than the
teaching of Linnaeus and Cuvier,
as was readily demonstrated by
Pflüger in 1875.   It is a fallacy
to assume any radical difference
of function between plant and
animal protoplasm.   In the last
chapter we saw that both kinds
of protoplasm differentiate into
cells or elementary organisms
endowed with an essentially
analogous structure and com-
position.   In considering the vital characters common to all
living beings we recognised both in plant and in animal metabolism

a double process, anabolic and katabolic : the first synthetic, re-ducing, assimilatory ; the second analytic, oxidising, disintegrative.

The antagonism apparent at the extreme limits of function between the higher plants and animals becomes less and less in proportion as we descend the scale of the two groups of living beings. On comparing the simplest animal and plant organisms, it is impossible to trace a sharp line of demarcation between the two kingdoms. This fact demonstrates their common origin, according to the Unitary Theory of Life, by which plants and animals must be regarded as two divergent stems arising from a common trunk represented by the simplest, or primitive, living forms, to which Haeckel gave the name of *Protista*.

The fallacy of this supposed antagonism between the functions of plants and animals lies in a confusion between the katabolic, re-spiratory function, chemically represented by processes of oxidation, which is common to all living beings, and the anabolic, chloro-phyllic function which is peculiar to the green parts of plants. Vegetable protoplasm, including that provided with chlorophyll, breathes like animal protoplasm, *i.e.* it absorbs oxygen and gives off carbonic acid, when removed from the action of the sun's rays. Under the influence of these rays, it breathes in the reverse sense, *i.e.* it absorbs carbonic acid and gives off oxygen, because the reducing function of the chlorophyll, which is actively aroused by the solar radiation, exceeds in its activity the respiration proper, and masks its effects.

It has long been known that the presence of oxygen is almost always essential to plant as to animal life. As early as 1822, De Saussure was aware that the most vigorous plants, such as the Cactus, die quickly when brought into an atmosphere deprived of oxygen. P. Bert found that wheat germinated less freely in proportion as the oxygen tension of the air in which it was kept was lowered.

So, too, when tension of carbon dioxide reaches an excessive degree it is as harmful to plant as to animal life. It was, again, De Saussure who demonstrated that plants brought into an atmosphere of CO_2 perished. An atmosphere containing $\frac{1}{5}$ of carbonic acid is sufficient to check the germination of most plants ; accordingly, respiration as an oxidative process is a function as indispensable to the life of plants as to animals.

The antagonism that is sometimes proposed between plants and animals is therefore fallacious, and derives from the fact that the former accumulate the energy elaborated from the sun's rays, while the latter consume it, or transform it into special forms of heat and motion.

It is in general true that plants cool the surrounding atmo-sphere, while animals raise the temperature ; but this is due to the fact that respiration is not usually very intense in plants, and is associated with a considerable transpiration of water, by which a large amount of heat is rendered latent, so that the plants as a rule become cooler than their environment. But when transpiration is checked, or when plants which are breathing actively are observed, they are found to develop as much heat as animals. For instance, on bringing together a mass of germinating peas, a rise of temperature of some 2° C. above the surrounding atmosphere can be detected ; a rise of 15° C. was measured in the large flowers of the *Victoria Regia*.

Lastly, it should be noted that if all animals live directly, or indirectly, on the elements provided by the vegetable kingdom, it is not, on the other hand, true that all plants live on the inorganic substances provided exclusively by the soil, air, and water. A great number of plants, lacking in chlorophyll, live saprophytically at the expense of the organic substances of plant residues and dead animals, or parasitically at the cost of other living things. Such are the *Schizomycetes* and *Fungi*, properly so-called. As the life of animals is subordinated to that of plants, so the life of this innumerable vegetable host is subordinated to that of animals or other plants.

VI. Since antagonism between the vital activities of plants and animals is excluded, it follows logically that the functional differences which exist between the two great kingdoms of living Nature, and which are very apparent in the higher classes, must consist in the different manifestations in the two kingdoms of *Metabolism*, which underlies all vital phenomena. It is evident that the anabolic processes are predominantly developed in plants, the katabolic processes in animals.

The fact above emphasised, that all animals require for their nutrition organic matters (proteins, fats, and carbohydrates) already formed by other animals or plants, shows that their anabolic capacities do not extend to synthesis of these substances from inorganic materials. The majority of plants, on the contrary, can live and flourish on exclusively inorganic matter, showing that their anabolic capacity is strong enough to enable them to make this synthesis.

The anabolic capacity seems to be most highly developed in the group of the so-called *nitrifying* bacteria, which in recent years have aroused great interest among physiologists. Devoid of chlorophyll, they are none the less able, independent of the action of the sun's rays, to form by synthesis all the organic substances which they require for their development and reproduction, given the inorganic materials provided by the soil and the air. More wonderful still, some of them, on closer observation, are found to be capable of synthetically forming organic nitrogenous matter by absorption of free nitrogen from the air and soil. Among these is *Clostridium pasteurianum*, studied by Winogradsky, which utilises carbonic acid or the carbonates of the soil to form carbohydrates, and free nitrogen to form proteins. No less interesting are the various forms of *Rhizobium leguminosarum*, studied by Hellziegel, Nobbe, Beyerinck, Franck and others, which penetrate the root-hairs of the common *Leguminosae* (beans, peas, lupins, trefoils, etc.), and produce hypertrophy in the form of nodules or tubercles

containing a fungoid mass, consisting of bacteria for the most part of exceptional size, with a less number of normal form and proportions (Fig. 13). According to the said authors, the rhizobium lives in symbiosis with the leguminous plant. The latter provides the bacterium with carbohydrate; and the bacterium, by conversion of the free nitrogen into an organic form, provides the leguminous plant with the nitrogenous compounds required for the synthetic formation of proteins, thus promoting the general welfare of the plant.

In the greater number of cases, however, the assimilation of carbon is an anabolic function of green plants, which are capable of reducing the carbonic acid of the air by means of chlorophyll, under the influence of the luminous rays of the sun (particularly of the less refrangible red and yellow rays); and the assimilation of nitrogen is, generally speaking, due in plants to reduction of the nitrates contained in the humus, and not to intake of free nitrogen. The clearest demonstration of this fact is

Fig. 13. Root of *Vicia faba.* (Noll.) Shows root-hairs copiously provided with nodules—the rhizobium.

afforded by the cultivation of green plants in artificial solutions which, with the exception of carbon, contain all the chemical elements that participate in the formation of living matter, in the form of combinations of salts. The formula given by Sachs for this artificial nutrient fluid is as follows:—

	gr.
Water	1000·0
Potassium nitrate	1·5
Sodium chloride	0·5
Potassium sulphate	0·5
Magnesium sulphate	0·5
Calcium phosphate	0·5
Ferrous sulphate	0·005

If a grain of maize is placed in this solution to germinate, the experiment being carried out in a glass jar (as shown in Fig. 14), the plant, under the influence of light, will develop normally, flower, and bear fruit. If the iron sulphate is wanting in the solution, the plant may live for some time, but its leaves will be colourless, and under the microscope show absence of chlorophyll; if the other salts are wanting, the plant will not germinate, or perishes as soon as it develops.

This experiment proves that all the carbon assimilated by the plant is derived from the carbonic acid of the air—the grand discovery of Ingenhousz; further, it shows that the assimilation of carbon is conditioned by chlorophyll, the molecules of which contain iron : lastly, the assimilation of nitrogen is due to the reduction of nitrates, and the assimilation of sulphur and phosphorus to the reduction of sulphates and phosphates.

The intimate processes by which the plant succeeds, by the assimilation of all these elements, in synthetically forming organic substances are for the most part unknown. Thanks, however, to the work of Sachs, we know something of the process of starch formation in the

Fig. 14.—*Zea mais* in culture solution. *Mg.*, grain of maize; *Sn.*, Sachs' nutrient solution; *s*, cork to support plant in vertical position.

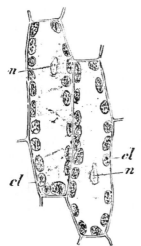

Fig. 15.—Two leaf-cells of *Funaria hygrometrica*. *cl*, chloroblasts; *n*, nucleus. Magnification, 300 diameters.

green parts, which may be taken as the starting-point for all other synthetic processes in plants. In the adult cell, chlorophyll is contained within special ellipsoidal corpuscles known as chloroplasts, which are for the most part found in great numbers heaped against the parietal protoplasm (Fig. 15). After a green plant has been exposed for a few minutes to full sunlight, starch granules are seen to appear in the middle or edge of the chloroplasts, which gradually increase in size until their volume exceeds that of the chloroplasts. During the night, when starch formation is suspended, this accumulation is dissolved by the action of diastatic ferments, and conveyed under the form of sugar to the parts in which it can be utilised as food material.

Starch represents the principal nutritive reserve material that accumulates in a solid form in the plant cells in which it is formed.

Many monocotyledons normally exhibit no formation of starch, but produce sugar in solution; it is only when this is in excess that starch in the solid form is manufactured.

The other organic matters, fats and proteins, are formed by gradual chemical change from the carbohydrates, starch and sugar. The formation of oil from starch may be directly observed in the seeds of certain plants. Paeony seeds, for instance, so long as they are immature, contain only carbohydrates and scarcely any fat. When placed in moist air, it is found after a time that all the starch has disappeared by conversion into oil. In many of the lower plants, e.g. Algae, the first visible product in the cell is not starch but oil.

Far more complex is the synthesis of proteins and nucleoproteins effected by the roots from the carbohydrates and derivatives

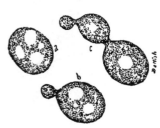

FIG. 16. – Cells of Beer Yeast (Saccharomyces cerevisiae): a, resting; b, c, gemmating.

of the nitrates, sulphates, and phosphates of the soil. We know nothing about this marvellous synthesis, indispensable as it is to the nutrition and development of living protoplasm. It is only known that oxalic acid ($C_2H_2O_4$) is frequently formed as a secondary product, which, in itself toxic, combines, as it is formed, with lime into an insoluble innocuous salt that collects in the form of a crystalline powder round those parts of the plant in which the formation of proteins and nucleins takes place. It also seems probable that asparagine ($C_4H_8N_2O_3$), a soluble and diffusible amino-body, is an intermediate product in protein synthesis.

From the green plants one must, in virtue of their metabolism, distinguish all those plants which are lacking in chlorophyll, and live as saprophytes, or parasites, or again as parasites and saprophytes according to circumstances. The innumerable host of fungi and bacteria come under this category. They have the singular property of consuming in their nutrition and reproduction only the minimal part of the organic matters which form their food, and of destroying all the rest by processes of fermentation and putrefaction, effected by enzymes contained within the cell or secreted from without.

A classical example of this mode of metabolism is afforded by *Saccharomyces cerevisiae* (Fig. 16), which produces alcoholic fermentation of glucose according to the equation:

$$C_6H_{12}O_6 = 2CO_2 + 2C_2H_6O.$$

When a certain quantity of yeast is introduced into grape juice, there is formed along with the development of carbonic acid and the production of alcohol a small amount of glycerin, of

succinic acid, and of various ethers, which eventually inhibit
fermentation and bring it to a standstill.   The quantity of yeast
which is then deposited at the bottom of the vessel is conspicuously
augmented, showing that the cells of the Saccharomyces have
abundantly reproduced themselves; but the organic nutritive
matters contained in the grape juice would, if they had not been
decomposed by the fermentative process, have sufficed for the
nutrition and multiplication of an incomparably larger amount of
yeast.

Many pathogenic or non-pathogenic bacteria are able to dissolve gelatin or coagulated albumin for their nutrition and multiplication, and effect a putrid decomposition of the various culture
fluids or media, with development of carbonic acid, sulphuretted
hydrogen, ammonium sulphate, ammonia, and a simultaneous formation of new substances which generally have a toxic action, and are
the cause of virulent disease.

In general those plants that contain no chlorophyll, and require
for their nutriment the organic matters already formed by other
plants or animals, utilise these substances merely as the raw
material of nutrition, submitting them further to special chemical
transformations.   Fungi and bacteria, indeed, can adapt previously
inadequate substances to their nutrition.   By means of invertase
they transform saccharose into glucose, by diastase starch is turned
into sugar, with the trypsin and pepsin ferments albumin is converted into albumoses and peptone.   Fungi have been proved to
flourish in very different culture media, and are capable, with the
help of the organic compounds of carbon, and nitrogenous mineral
salts, of building up synthetically all the highly complex products
essential to the formation of protoplasm.   They represent, accordingly, in their metabolism an intermediate group between the
chlorophyll-containing plants and animals.

The anabolic capacity of all animals, without exception, is
limited to the elaboration of the three principal groups of organic
substances, and their conversion into living protoplasm, with the
further synthetic formation of new substances which do not exist
in the plant world.   They are incapable of reducing fully oxidised
organic substances so as to produce carbohydrates, fats, and
proteins; but they have the power (as we shall be able to
demonstrate fully) of transforming carbohydrates into fats, albumoses and peptones into true proteins.

Within the animal kingdom again we can distinguish different
groups, according to their nutritive requirements and corresponding metabolism.   Herbivores and frugivores more particularly
need to supplement the proteins with the carbohydrates in which
vegetable food is superabundant : insectivores and carnivores, on the
contrary, profit by the many fats which abound in animal food.
Neither fats nor carbohydrates, however, are absolutely indis-

pensable to life. Some animals have adapted themselves to a purely protein diet, and, further, to a single form of the same. Thus, *e.g.*, the clothes-moth lives exclusively on the keratin of which the hairs of the wool or fur consist, and from which it derives all that is necessary for the construction of its protoplasm. Again, as we shall see, it is possible to keep a dog alive, and in its normal state, on a purely flesh diet, while this is found impossible on an exclusive diet of fats and carbohydrates, no matter how abundant.

The chief part of the mineral substances which enter into the chemical composition of animals cannot be assimilated as such, but only when they are present in organic combinations, as, *e.g.*, the calcium phosphate of milk casein, the potassium salts of muscle protein. If mice are fed on casein from which the greater part of the salts contained in the organic combinations of milk have been previously washed out, and if sugar be added, as well as all the salts contained in the ashes of milk in a non-organic form, the mice perish slowly during this diet, and succumb after about forty days (Lunin). This and similar experiments on artificial feeding in other animals, show that they are only capable to a small extent of assimilating inorganic substances, *i.e.* of binding them synthetically into the protein molecule on which the living protoplasm is nourished.

BIBLIOGRAPHY

The following may be consulted for the literature of the Theory of Evolution :

LAMARCK. Philosophie zoologique. Paris, 1809.

CHARLES DARWIN. On the Origin of Species by Means of Natural Selection. London, 1859.

C. VON NÄGELI. Mechanisch-physiologische Theorie der Abstammungslehre. 1884.

WEISMANN. Das Keimplasme : eine Theorie d. Vererbung. Jena, 1892.

H. DE VRIES. Die Mutationstheorie. Leipzig, 1901, 1903.

YVES DELAGE. L'Hérédité et les grands problèmes de la biologie générale. Paris, 1903.

DETTO. Die Theorie d. direkten Anpassung. Jena, 1904.

PAULY. Darwinismus und Lamarckismus. Munich, 1905.

LOTSY. Vorlesungen über Deszendenztheorien. Jena, 1906.

SCHNEIDER. Einführung in die Deszendenztheorie. Jena, 1906.

RIGNANO. Sur la transmissibilité des caractères acquis. Paris, 1906.

The two following text-books may be consulted for the general physiology of plants, and their characteristics as distinct from animals :—

E. STRASBURGER, F. NOLL, H. SCHENCK, A. F. W. SCHIMPER. Lehrbuch d. Botanik. Jena. G. Fischer, 5th ed., 1902.

W. PFEFFER. Lehrbuch d. Pflanzenphysiologie. Leipzig, 1897-1901.

Recent English Literature of the subject :—

W. PFEFFER. The Nature and Significance of Functional Metabolism in the Plant. Proc. Roy. Soc., London, 1898, lxiii. 93.

K. PEARSON. Data for the Problem of Evolution in Man. Proc. Roy. Soc., London, 1900, lxvi. 23, 316.

K. PEARSON. Mathematical Contributions to the Theory of Evolution. Proc. Roy. Soc., London, 1900, lxvii. 140.

W. BATESON. Heredity, Differentiation, and other Conceptions of Biology. Proc. Roy. Soc., 1901, lxix. 193.

T. M. BALDWIN. Development and Evolution. London & New York, 1902.

A. K. MARSHALL, E. B. POULTON, etc. Five Years' Observations and Experiments (1896-1901) on the Bionomics of South Africa Insects. Trans. Entom. Soc., London, 1902, p. 287.

K. PEARSON. Mathematical Contributions to the Theory of Evolution. Proc. Roy. Soc., London, 1902, lxix. 330 ; 1903, lxxi. 288.

A. R. WALLACE. Darwinism : Exposition of the Theory of Natural Selection with some of its Applications. London, Macmillan. 1902.

W. F. R. WELDON. Professor de Vries on the Origin of Species. Biometrika, 1902, i. 365.

TH. M. MORGAN. Evolution and Adaptation. New York, 1903.

W. BATESON. Opening Address at the British Association (Zoology). Nature, 1904, lxx. 406, 539.

A. D. DARBISHIRE. On the bearing of Mendelian Principles of Heredity on Current Theories on the Origin of Species. Manchester Lit. Phil. Soc., 1904, xlviii.

A. S. PACKARD. The Origin of the Markings of Organisms (poecilogenesis) due to the Physical rather than to the Biological Environment ; with criticism of the Bates-Müller hypotheses. Proc. Amer. Phil. Soc., 1904, xl. 393.

R. C. PUNNETT. Merism and Sex in spinax niger. Biometrika, 1904, iii. Part IV., p. 313.

A. E. BROWN. The Utility Principle in Relation to Specific Characters. Proc. Ac. Nat. Sc., Philad., 1905, lvii. 206.

E. S. CONKLIN. The Mutation Theory from the Standpoint of Cytology. Sc., N.S., 1905, xxi. 525.

H. E. CRAMPTON. On a General Theory of Adaptation and Selection. Journ. of Exper. Zool., 1905, ii. 425.

C. B. DAVENPORT. Evolution without Mutation. Journ. of Exper. Zool., 1905 ii. 137.

W. S. HARWOOD. New Creations in Plant Life : an Account of the Life and Work of Luther Burbank. New York, 1905.

N. DE VRIES. Species and Varieties. Chicago, Open Court, 1905.

R. H. LOCK. Recent Progress in the Study of Variation, Heredity, and Evolution. London, 1906, xv. 299 pp.

C. U. MERRIAM. Is Mutation a Factor in the Evolution of the High Vertebrates ? Science, 1906, p. 241.

CHAPTER III

LIVING MATTER: CONDITIONS BY WHICH IT IS DETERMINED

CONTENTS.—1. Nutrition the necessary external condition of vital metabolism. Phenomena of inanition. 2. Importance of water. Latent life and anabiosis. 3. Importance of oxygen. Aërobic and anaërobic life. 4. External temperature indispensable to life. 5. Total pressure of air and water, and partial pressure of oxygen and carbonic acid. 6. External stimuli. 7. Chemical stimuli. Chemotaxis. 8. Mechanical stimuli. Barotaxis. 9. Thermal stimuli : thermotaxis. 10. Photic stimuli. Phototaxis and Heliotaxis. 11. Electrical stimuli. Galvanotaxis. 12. The various biological zones of ocean life (*Plankton*). 13. Internal conditions and stimuli of metabolism. Theory of automatism. 14. Hypotheses to explain the intimate mechanism of living matter. Bibliography.

Two orders of conditions, external and internal, are essential to the maintenance of metabolism. Both the one and the other may act directly or indirectly. The former cannot fail without cessation of life, nor the latter without modifications and disturbances of vital phenomena. If we were acquainted with all the internal and external conditions of life, the task of Physiology would be terminated ; the " conditioned," *i.e.* Life, would be perfectly known to us.

Not all the vital conditions are essential in the same degree to every living being. Each organism has special requirements in virtue of which it lives and flourishes. Each living species, therefore, demands special treatment. From the standpoint of general physiology we have only to consider in broad outlines the most universal and best known of the vital conditions.

1. The first and most general external condition of metabolism is Nutrition, *i.e.* the sum of the chemical materials essential to the building-up of living protoplasm.

We saw in the last chapter how various were the chemical forms of the foods necessary to different groups of living beings—to nitrifying bacteria, green plants, saprophytic and parasitic fungi, herbivorous and carnivorous animals. To this we may add that in accordance with the chemical composition of the nutritive medium, the various elementary organisms react very differently. Some can only live in fresh water ; others in salt water. All die more or less rapidly when brought into distilled water. Every simple or complex organism, indeed, exhibits a certain capacity of adapting itself to an environment and nutrition different from those to which it has been accustomed, provided only that the change is effected very slowly and gradually. In consequence of this adaptation, temporary modifications of the specific characters ensue. According, however, to certain experiments of Nägeli, these are not persistent, but quickly disappear when the organism is brought back to its original environment and alimentation.

In order to form an adequate concept of the adaptability of various organisms to unusual conditions in respect of nutrition, we may refer to certain bacteria, recently investigated by Winogradsky, which he calls sulphur or iron bacteria. The sulphur bacteria are represented by a family of microbes, which can only live in the water of bogs or marshes, where, owing to the decomposition of vegetable and animal matters, there is a great development of hydrogen sulphide. This they absorb, oxidising it, and setting free the sulphur, which they accumulate in the body of their cells in the form of highly refractive granules. On subsequent oxidation, these granules give rise to a formation of sulphuric acid, which is excreted as such. The iron bacteria live in marshy water, where ferrous carbonate is found in solution; this they take up, and convert it into ferric carbonate, which readily decomposes on excretion, and the precipitate of iron oxide forms the ochre-like deposit known as meadow-ore.

Both sulphur and iron bacteria perish when brought into spring water, which contains no hydrogen sulphide or ferrous carbonate, while these compounds act as poisons to all other living beings. They must, therefore, have undergone a permanent adaptation to a quite exceptional form of environment and nutrition.

Whatever the nature of the food-stuffs appropriate to the various organisms, they are indispensable to the maintenance of life. Absolute or relative deprivation of food produces a state of inanition, during which the organism primarily consumes the reserve materials stored up in the body of the cell, and then absorbs its own protoplasm, shrinking more and more, until it finally perishes when the protoplasm has no longer enough potential energy to maintain the balance of metabolism (Fig. 17).

Fig. 17. — *Colpidium colpoda* — a ciliated infusorium. (Jensen.) *a*, under normal conditions; *b*, in state of inanition, in which it is shrunken, transparent, and deprived of granules. Magnification, 260 diameters.

The individual living elements of which the tissues and organs of the higher animals are composed draw all their nourishment from a common fluid, the lymph, which circulates in the interstices of the tissues.

During inanition, the total consumption of the organism is not equally distributed among the different tissues: a sort of struggle for existence goes on between them, some being consumed and liquefied for the benefit of others, which continue to exist as parasites, and are even able to reproduce themselves (Luciani). The process of inanition in the higher animals and man will, however, be treated in detail later on.

II. Another condition no less indispensable to metabolism is water, which infiltrates the living protoplasm in large quantities, rendering it soft or semi-fluid. In order to realise the importance of water to the vital functions, we need only consider the consequences of natural or artificial desiccation in unicellular organisms. Within certain limits the intensity of metabolism increases or decreases with the increase or decrease of the water content of the living matter, while beyond those limits vital activity ceases altogether. In the great majority of plants, natural dryness of environment is sufficient to cause death. Many mosses, lichens and algae, however, which live on naked rocks are able to support the drought of summer without injury. Seeds and spores, in particular, when removed from the plant, may be kept in a dry state without losing their capacity for germination. It was formerly stated that the wheat found with the Egyptian mummies retained its power of germinating after more than two thousand years; but this fact was disproved by the famous Egyptologist Mariette. It has, however, been demonstrated that spores of mosses and the seeds of *Mimosae*, kept in a dry state for over sixty years in a herbarium, were perfectly capable of germination ; other seeds, on the contrary, lose their vitality after one year, others again after a few days, while others will not tolerate any desiccation, *e.g.* the seeds of *Salix*.

Some groups of animals can be kept for years in a desiccated state without losing the faculty of awakening to life a few moments after they are moistened again (Preyer's anabiosis). Among these are the so-called *Rotiferae*, small crustaceans, and the *Tardegrada*, arachnoids resembling mites, which live in the moss and dust of roofs, as discovered by Leeuwenhoek (1719), who first described this remarkable phenomenon. Also the *Anguillulae* of mildewed wheat, on which Spallanzani (1776) made many curious experiments of repeated anabiosis. Lastly, the greater part of the bacteria, particularly in the spore state, come under the same category.

It is not easy in any of these cases of apparent death to determine whether there is absolute suspension of metabolism a true latent or potential life. or a metabolism reduced to the lowest terms, *i.e.* to the state which Spallanzani was the first to characterise as minimal life. To decide the question, it is necessary to determine whether these organisms in a state of apparent death exhibit any trace of respiratory exchange, *i.e.* of absorption of oxygen and excretion of CO_2. W. Kochs 1892) used for this purpose a large quantity of perfectly dry seeds of plants, which he placed in large glass tubes from which the air had been pumped out, and which were then hermetically sealed. After many months, a minute analysis of the contents of the tubes failed to detect any trace of carbonic acid; and yet the seeds perfectly retained their capacity for germination. This experiment proves that it is possible to establish a state of true potential life in the seeds of certain plants.

The results of a number of experiments undertaken by the author in collaboration with Piutti (1888) on silk-worm eggs were somewhat different. Without artificial desiccation these did not entirely cease to breathe when kept for a long while at a temperature of 0 C., and even at that temperature they could not survive prolonged exposure to an atmosphere of pure nitrogen. When kept for 139 days in conical flasks in which the air was maintained constantly dry by means of concentrated sulphuric acid, they perished entirely if the temperature was 9-14 C., and partly if it was 0 C. It is therefore clear that under these conditions the silk-worm eggs are reduced to a state of *vita minima*. When placed in glass flasks, in which a perfect vacuum was produced by the mercury pump, after which they were sealed up and kept at 0 C., more than half the eggs after 83 days were alive, and capable of development when brought under normal conditions of incubation. Here we have evidently a state of minimal life approximating to that of latent life. Lastly, the silk-worm eggs were placed under a glass bell-jar, hermetically sealed to a plate and containing a desiccator with concentrated sulphuric acid; when after 128 days the enclosed eggs (which had shrunk in an extraordinary way from the desiccation) hatched out, a very copious but incomplete brood of caterpillars was produced, which were smaller and less lively than the normal. From these results it seems probable that insect eggs, like plant seeds, can be artificially brought by desiccation into the state of latent or potential life. According to Preyer's ingenious comparison, this state is comparable to that of a clock wound up, but with the pendulum arrested ; the state of death, on the contrary, is like a clock which can no longer go because its wheels are broken.

III. We saw in the last chapter that plants breathe like animals, *i.e.* they take in oxygen, in order by a slow process of combustion to form carbonic acid and water. The presence of oxygen is, accordingly, one of the most fundamental conditions in the active upkeep of metabolism.

This does not mean that the presence of oxygen as such is indispensable to the maintenance of life. In order to understand its importance we must start with certain general considerations.

Every assimilatory or anabolic process results in an accumulation of energy, and necessarily implies a source of kinetic, which can be transformed into potential, energy. Each dissimilatory or katabolic process, on the other hand, results in a dispersion of energy, and presupposes a store of potential, to be transformed into kinetic, energy. This is why the two opposite processes are simultaneous, or constantly and rapidly alternating, during life, while the two together constitute metabolism, which—as we have seen—is the physiological basis of all the phenomena of life.

Since in green plants anabolic largely predominate over katabolic processes, the energy which they develop by oxidation is inadequate for the synthetic formation of their highly complex organic substances, and the intervention of the energy derived from the sun's rays becomes necessary.

In animals, on the contrary, in which katabolic processes largely predominate, the energy which they develop by the oxidation of organic substances is not only enough to yield mechanical work, and to keep the temperature of the body above that of the environment, but also suffices to secure the anabolic processes, or new organic syntheses, by elaboration of the foodstuffs drawn from plants.

The destruction of the organic molecules by the katabolic processes does not take place all at once, so as immediately to turn combustible substances into final products; but it is effected gradually and successively, the more complex being converted into other less complex molecules, and these into the end-products rejected by the body.

The presence of oxygen is not essential to all these regressive metamorphoses. In the absence of free oxygen, protoplasm is able for a certain time to obtain oxygen from the combinations in which it is held loosely or firmly, and thus to develop kinetic energy. The great plasmodia of the *Myxomycetes, e.g.*, if placed in a medium deprived of oxygen, will continue their movements for three hours; ciliated epithelia can live even longer without oxygen (Engelmann); excised frog's muscle placed in an atmosphere of pure hydrogen will give off carbonic acid for many hours before it becomes inexcitable (Hermann). Many organisms of the lowest orders, particularly in the numerous groups of bacteria, have the faculty of living permanently without oxygen. Pasteur, who was the first to call attention to this most important phenomenon, gave the name of anaërobic to the organisms which live in the absence of oxygen, in contradistinction from the aërobic, which can only live in presence of this gas. According to Tarozzi (1905), the incapacity of anaërobic bacteria to develop in culture media in the presence of oxygen, is due not to a toxic action of the oxygen on these microbes (as has been stated by many authors) but rather to chemical modifications of the proteins in the broth used for the culture. These modifications consist essentially in processes of oxidation, and the anaërobes appear to be incapable of utilising highly oxidised proteins in their assimilation. Accordingly, they can only develop when these substances are once more reduced, which is effected either by artificially removing the oxygen, or (after Tarozzi) by adding to the broth a scrap of fresh organ aseptically prepared, which acts as a reducer, in virtue of the chemical processes of which it is the seat, and favours the development of the anaërobes. In this case it is not necessary to remove the oxygen before the bacteria can develop. This explains how such development takes place naturally when these bacteria are in the presence of tissues of animals that have just died, or, generally speaking, whenever they find protein matters at their disposal which have not suffered profound oxidative changes. And this is why all anaërobes belong exclusively to the class of putrefaction microbes (saprophytes).

According to the work of Duclaux, Gautier, and Ehrlich, anaërobic metabolism may be recognised not only in a great number of microbes, but in a still greater number of plant and animal cells.

Many decompositions of organic molecules due to enzyme action within the cell, or in external secretions, are produced without intervention of atmospheric oxygen, and are accompanied by a development of energy which is partly utilised by the cells for their constructions or organic syntheses. Thus, e.g., the katabolic action of beer yeast, in the absence of oxygen, breaks up glucose into alcohol and carbonic acid, with evolution of heat which is partly employed in the multiplication of the cells of the ferment. In a well-aërated medium the same beer yeast, on the contrary, effects complete oxidation of the molecule of glucose, converting it into water and carbonic acid, and in this case there is a greater development of heat and a far larger multiplication of *Saccharomyces*. Pasteur's interpretation of these phenomena is very illuminating : Saccharomyces, in order to nourish and reproduce itself, makes great use of the energy developed in the oxidation of sugar, when it is in an oxygenated medium. When oxygen is scarce, it utilises the inferior amount of energy which it is able to develop by abstracting oxygen from the fermentable material, i.e. from the same sugar, by a kind of internal oxidation.

Accordingly, it is not oxygen as such that is essential to life, but the energy that is developed by any kind of oxidation. Green plants have less need of oxygen than animals, because they obtain from the sun's rays a great part of the energy which they require in fixing the carbon. If the majority of living beings positively demand free oxygen, it is because much heat is developed in its combinations, which can be utilised in a variety of ways.

In proof of the extent to which oxygen is essential to the life of the various tissues of the higher animals, we may refer to a remarkable experiment of Pflüger's on the frog. He placed two of these animals in an atmosphere at 0° C. which had scrupulously been deprived of every trace of oxygen. After a quarter of an hour they exhibited considerable dyspnoea, which, however, was unaccompanied with convulsions. After five hours the frogs were quiet and flaccid, but reacted to stimulation with a wire. After nineteen hours they lay as if dead, and no longer reacted to the strongest cutaneous stimuli, or showed any trace of respiratory movement. After twenty hours, they were taken out of their prison into the fresh air, but no sign of life could be elicited in spite of repeated insufflation of air through the trachea. On opening the thorax of one of the frogs, Pflüger was astonished to see the heart still beating with great energy, while the arteries contained bright red blood. But it was not till two hours after the animal had been brought into the oxygenated atmosphere that spontaneous muscular movements were exhibited, followed by reflex movements and spontaneous respiration. The more complicated voluntary movements, however, which depend upon the higher nervous system never came back.

To explain this long survival in an atmosphere wholly deprived of oxygen, it must be admitted for vertebrates also that the living protoplasm of the various tissues has the property (in different degrees) of utilising the oxygen which is bound up in the organic molecules. The cells of the central nervous system are the most sensitive to deprivation of free oxygen; other cells, on the contrary, can live for a long while in a medium destitute of oxygen, because they have the power of taking it from organic combinations, and utilising the potential energy.

The most interesting phenomenon, from the point of view of anaërobic metabolism, is afforded by the group of bacteria which are not only capable of living in the absence of oxygen, but die in a medium that contains it, e.g. Tetanus and Anthrax bacilli. Interesting phenomena, too, are exhibited by other bacteria, e.g. the comma bacillus of Cholera, which is greedy of oxygen, and is at the same time capable of living and multiplying enormously in the intestine, where there is no trace of free oxygen, so that it must necessarily utilise the combined oxygen of the alkaline salts.

IV. In addition to food-stuffs, water and oxygen, which penetrate into the body, and directly condition metabolism, other conditions of a dynamic character are indispensable in order that the vital functions may be accomplished. The external temperature exercises a predominant influence on elementary organisms. Each cell demands a temperature oscillating between given limits, beyond which the cell must die. For the majority of plant and animal cells, the maximal limit of endurable temperature lies between 40 and 47° C. Kühne found that the contractile protoplasm of Amoebae coagulated sometimes at 40 C., sometimes at 45 C. For plant cells, Max Schultze found that the fatal temperature could be raised to 47 C. Other elementary organisms, indeed, support much higher temperatures, which would seem incredible if they were not substantiated by direct measurement. In the hot baths of Casamicciola, *e.g.*, certain Algae flourish at a temperature of 63° C., while, according to Ehrenberg, some of the ciliated Infusoria (*Oscillaria* or *Rotifera*) can live at a temperature of 81 - 85° C. More surprising still, the spores of Anthrax, according to Koch, Brefeld and others, can support a temperature of over 100° C., and only lose their vitality completely after three hours' dry heat at 140° C. It must be remembered in explanation that the protoplasm of these organisms consists of proteins combined in such a way that they do not coagulate nor decompose at these high temperatures.

The minimum temperature compatible with life is equally surprising. While as a rule the poikilothermic animals and plants die when the temperature falls to such a point that the water imbibed by the protoplasm freezes, Raoul Pictet's latest experiments show that a temperature of less than 0° C. is not necessarily fatal to certain organisms. In fact he ascertained positively that fishes frozen at a temperature of − 15° C. can recover their vitality, provided the thawing is effected with great caution. If, however, the fall in temperature amounts to − 20 C., they inevitably perish. Frogs, on the contrary, tolerate a temperature of − 28 C., centipedes one of − 50 C., while, lastly, bacteria can survive exposure to − 100° C.

Here we reach the vexed question whether frozen animals, capable of recovering their vitality on thawing, are in a state of minimal or of absolute latent vitality. Although the latter possibility is not excluded, Pictet's experiments do not seem to favour this hypothesis. If these frozen fishes were in a condition of latent vitality, it is difficult to see why they should not be indifferent to a fall of temperature below − 15 C., which they can survive. It seems more rational to admit that at this temperature metabolic exchanges are still maintained, although reduced to the lowest terms, and that death ensues when metabolism ceases altogether.

V. The pressure of the air and water in which these organisms live must also be considered among the general conditions of life. It is indeed evident *a priori* that pressure must act against the thermal vibrations of the atoms; when therefore there is a marked rise of pressure obstructing the thermal vibrations, this favours the appearance of chemical combinations, while a marked diminution, by increasing the amplitude of the said vibrations, must weaken the mutual attraction of the atoms and dissociate the unstable chemical combinations.

Very little work has been done on the determination of the limits between which the total pressure of the air and water, and the partial pressure of the oxygen and carbonic acid which these contain, condition the life of the organisms which inhabit them.

The experiments of Paul Bert (1873) bring out the interesting fact that pure oxygen under a pressure of three atmospheres is fatal to warm-blooded animals, while ordinary air only produces the same effect at a pressure of 15-20 atmospheres. The same fatal effect ensues when the partial pressure of the oxygen of the air is reduced below a certain limit.

In order to determine how great a fall in the barometric pressure is compatible with life, we may utilise certain data furnished not so much by ascents of the highest mountains as from aerostatic ascents, in which the effects of fall of barometric pressure are not complicated by muscular fatigue. The famous ascent by Croce-Spinelli, Sivel, and Tissandier in 1875 was fatal to the two former. When the balloon reached 8000 metres Tissandier, the sole survivor, lost consciousness, and only came to his senses when the balloon had dropped to 7059 metres.

We know hardly anything of the effect of aqueous pressures upon sea animals. Contrary to former conceptions, it has within the last few decades been ascertained that there exists a special flora and fauna at the lowest depths of the ocean, in regions where there is a pressure of several hundred atmospheres, and where no light can ever penetrate. The fishes caught at the greatest depths are, when first brought to the surface, so distended in consequence of the sudden reduction of pressure, which allows the gases in their bladder to expand, that the viscera protrude from their mouths and the scales stand up (Keller).

In regard to the pressure exerted by water upon marine animals, the fact must be insisted on that it exercises a great influence only upon such organs as, like the fish's swim-bladder, contain gas in the gaseous state, and do not communicate with the exterior. The tissues of these animals, which may be considered as liquids, only feel the effects of the high pressure in a negligible degree, since, as we know from physics, several hundredths of atmospheric pressure are necessary in order to obtain any marked diminution in volume of fluids—these being practically incompressible. This is confirmed by the fact that marine animals, such as Echinoderms, Molluscs, Crabs, and Selachians or Teleosteans, which have no swim-bladder, and normally live at a great pelagic depth, can be transported to the surface without any danger, and continue to live for a long time in ordinary aquaria when the pressure of the water is from ½-1 metre.

VI. With the exception of those above enumerated, none of the general external conditions are essential to life. Other external physical or chemical factors may indeed influence vital metabolism to such a marked degree so as to render them indispensable to the life of given groups of organisms, *e.g.* light in the case of green plants. These special external conditions are usually known as stimuli, since they exert a direct influence on the excitability of the protoplasm as expressed in the various forms of excitation.

In the previous chapter we distinguished between automatic and reflex excitation; the former being determined by internal, the latter by external stimuli. This must not be understood to mean that the excitations which have the character of spontaneity, as opposed to the reflexes provoked from without, are independent of all external determining factors. The first, like the second, are effected under the constant influence of the general and normal external conditions of life; but while automatic excitations have for their immediate and determining cause a stimulus or impulse proceeding from the living matter itself, reflex excitations have for their immediate and determining cause either a sudden change in the normal external conditions, or the abrupt and unexpected intervention of other special external agents.

The external agents that commonly function as stimuli are represented by different chemical actions, by various mechanical shocks, by light, heat, and electricity.

The changes in metabolism determined by the action of stimulating agents may be predominatingly anabolic or katabolic in character. In the first case there is development of kinetic energy, and the phenomena are those of excitation properly so-called; in the second, there is an accumulation of potential energy, and the phenomena are said to be assimilatory, or trophic, or inhibitory, according to the most conspicuous characteristic which they present under observation.

When the action of the stimuli is too prolonged, or too frequently repeated, or exceeds the physiological limits in its intensity, there may result not an increase but a depression, suspension, or abolition of metabolism, as exhibited in the phenomena of fatigue, paralysis, or death of the protoplasm.

We must now briefly summarise the most universal and best ascertained conclusions in each of these categories of phenomena.

VII. Innumerable chemical compounds function as stimuli when brought into relation with living matter, *i.e.* they provoke phenomena of excitation. The mode in which they act has, however, been experimentally studied only in a very few cases. We must therefore confine ourselves to recording certain typical phenomena which are particularly worthy of attention.

Max Schultze (1863) and Kühne (1864) made classical researches on the effect of chemical stimuli upon the amoeboid movements of masses of naked protoplasm, such as the *Rhizopoda* (*Amoebae, Myxomycetes, Polythalamidae,* etc.). The effect most generally observed was contraction, *i.e.* retraction of the pseudopodia. The most various chemical substances are capable of producing this effect: 1-2 per cent solution of sodium chloride, dilute hydrochloric acid 0·1 per cent, caustic potash 1 per cent, weak solutions of other acids, alkalies, or salts.

The Rhizopods treated with these solutions assume a globular form on retracting their pseudopodia, owing to the concentric contraction of the protoplasm (Fig. 18). Ciliated cells, on the contrary, when treated with the same stimuli, increase their vibratile movements—sometimes to a very marked extent. Smooth and striated muscles contract, and sometimes exhibit a rhythm of contraction that they do not normally possess, recalling the rhythmical movements of the vibratile cilia.

Besides the contractile effects of chemical stimulation, it is

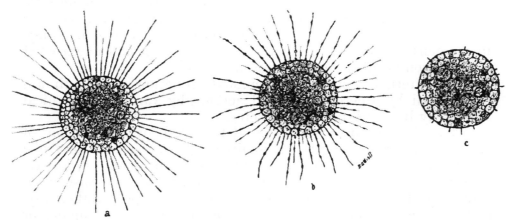

Fig. 18.—*Actinosphaerium Eichhornii.* (Verworn.) *a*, under normal conditions; *b*, at commencement of chemical excitation, the filiform pseudopodia are contracted and varicose; *c*, after prolonged chemical excitation, the pseudopodia are completely retracted.

possible also to observe expansive effects, *i.e.* active elongation of the pseudopodia in *Amoebae*, *Myxomycetes*, etc., effects which in the first instance were studied by Kühne. On placing an amoeba, for instance, in a gas chamber in which oxygen has been substituted for hydrogen, the movements are suspended after a short time. On again admitting oxygen, the amoebae, after twenty-four hours of inactivity, at once begin to expand their pseudopodia with normal vivacity.

Even more important than this direct excitation are the phenomena of the directive action of chemical stimuli upon the movements of elementary organisms, phenomena known as chemotactic or chemotropic. *Chemotaxis*, as first discovered by Engelmann on Bacteria, observed by Stahl on Myxomycetes, and studied on a large scale by the botanist Pfeffer in 1887, has assumed a great importance.

Positive must be distinguished from negative chemotaxis. The former consists in the active approach of the micro-organisms to the source of the chemical stimulus, as if attracted by it; the second consists in the opposite phenomenon, *i.e.* active withdrawal from the seat of the stimulus, as if it exerted some repulsive action.

A given solution may be an energetic chemotactic stimulus for one organism, and weak for another. The efficiency of the stimulus depends on its chemical constitution: potash, *e.g.*, is active in combination with one acid and not with another. Certain poisons (sodium salicylate, morphia) in weak solutions exert an attractive action, in concentrated forms a repulsive action. Some substances (alcohol, alkalies, free acids) always have a repellent action, *i.e.* they exert negative chemotaxis.

The method adopted by Pfeffer in studying chemotaxis is very simple: he merely immerses in the water which contains the microbes a capillary glass tube filled with the solution to be investigated, and closed at one end. If the microbes penetrate into the tube, there is positive chemotaxis; if they move away, there is negative chemotaxis. If, *e.g.*, a 0·05 per cent solution of malic acid is introduced into the capillary tube, the open end of which dips into a drop of fluid containing the spermatozoids of Ferns, the malic acid will scarcely have begun to diffuse in the drop when the spermatozoids move towards the entrance of the tube and crowd into it. The same thing may be seen with a much weaker solution (0·001 per cent) of malic acid. The movements of the spermatozoids must be directed by the difference in concentration of the acid which is in contact with the different parts of their body. When the concentration of the acid diffused in the drop becomes the same at every point, it can no longer exercise any directive action upon the movements of the spermatozoids.

Leber, Massart and Bordet, Metschnikoff and others discovered

Fig. 19. — Positive chemotaxis of leucocytes in presence of *Staphylococcus pyogenes albus.* (Massart.) Capillary glass tube (magnified under the microscope), closed at one end, and filled with a culture of Staphylococcus, towards which the leucocytes are streaming through the open end of the tube. The observation is made after the capillary tube has been introduced into the peritoneal cavity of the frog, or beneath the skin of a rabbit, and kept there 10-12 hours.

chemotactic activity in the leucocytes of vertebrate blood. The products of the metabolism of pathogenic bacteria exert a marked chemotactic action upon them (Fig. 19), a fact which is of great importance in the interpretation of the inflammatory phenomena of infective diseases, as we shall see in discussing Blood.

VIII. Mechanical stimuli (blow, contact, puncture, shake, pressure, etc.) are the simplest means of provoking excitation in living matter. The least shake of the object-carrier on which the movements of an amoeba are being watched under the microscope is sufficient to produce temporary standstill, and if the impact is strong enough a partial retraction of the pseudopodia. If the shock is repeated at frequent intervals the effects induced by each stimulus summate, resulting after a minute or two in a true mechanical tetanus, during which there is a concentric contraction of the whole of the protoplasm, which causes the amoeba to assume a globular form.

In addition to general mechanical stimulation, the effects of local stimulation have been experimentally studied, by touching or stabbing the amoeba with a blunt body or with very fine needles. In this case, when a reaction appears, it is at first confined to the point stimulated, whence it is slowly transmitted to the rest of the body.

The mechanical excitations of the living matter consist for the most part in a modification of the pressure relations under which it exists. In every case in which there is a difference of pressure at two different parts of the body of any organism, phenomena of excitation are manifested, which, since they are produced by a unilateral pressure, are known as barotactic. Several forms of *barotaxis* may be distinguished according to the kind of pressure, while it also can be positive or negative, according as the organism turns towards the side of greater or less pressure.

Verworn groups under the name of *thigmotaxis* the tendencies exhibited by many organisms, both animal and vegetable, to adhere to the surface of more solid bodies, or to penetrate through their pores, even in defiance of gravity.

Stahl defines as *rheotaxis* the peculiarity certain organisms exhibit of moving in the direction contrary to a current of water. Since this movement is determined by pressure acting in a particular way, rheotaxis is merely a special form of positive barotaxis. Thus far the phenomenon has been studied only in the plasmodia of Myxomycetes and in a few plants; but it is highly probable that the rise of the spermatozoa in animals and man from the vagina to the uterus, and thence to the oviduct to meet the ovum, is a rheotactic phenomenon, since this movement is accomplished in a direction contrary to that of the current of mucous fluid set up by the cilia of the epithelial cells which line the surface of the uterus, and which vibrate in a direction contrary to the movements of the spermatozoa.

A third form of barotaxis is *geotaxis*, or the well-known property of plants to place themselves with their median axis in a definite direction toward the centre of the earth. The stimulus in this case is afforded by minimal differences of pressure acting on points at different heights of the organism. The stems of trees grow away from the centre of the earth, and are, therefore, negatively geotactic; the roots grow toward the centre of the earth, and are, therefore, positively geotactic; further, the leaves, and not seldom the branches, grow in a direction tangential to the earth's surface, and thus exhibit transverse geotaxis.

Loeb (1888) discovered that geotaxis is a phenomenon widely diffused among animals also. It is possible to convert animals that exhibit negative, into animals exhibiting positive, geotaxis, and *vice versa*.

Many infusoria and bacteria exhibit geotactic phenomena. They frequently collect on the surface of the water in which they live (negative geotaxis, Fig. 20); at other times they sink down and crowd together at the bottom (positive geotaxis).

Fig. 20.—Glass tube containing Paramoecia. (Jensen.) In consequence of negative geotaxis, the infusoria have collected at the top of the tube, although they are specifically heavier than the fluid.

Knight (1809) showed that geotactic phenomena are determined by differences in pressure acting like gravity on the different points of the vegetable organism. He employed wheels turning in a vertical plane, to which he attached plants in various positions, as well as germinating seeds. He found that all the stems grew in towards the centre of the wheel, while the roots grew away from it. Jensen practically repeated the same experiments on infusoria living at the surface of the water, by rotating the test tubes which contained them in the centrifuge. Provided this were not driven too quickly, so as to make the infusoria, which are specifically heavier bodies, drop to the bottom of the test tube, they remained at the top, where pressure is lowest during rotation.

IX. Heat rarely exerts any direct stimulating action on living matter. In the higher animals, however, the special terminal organs of certain centripetal nerve-fibres are excited by heat. Kühne was the first to observe thermal tetanus in Amoebae when the temperature was raised to 35° C. On cooling the atmosphere again, the amoeboid movements were slowly restored: heating to 40-45° C. kills the animal by coagulation of its protoplasm.

When the heat acts on one part only of the amoeba, the

stimulus is found capable not merely of exciting protoplasmic movements, but even of determining their direction up to a certain point. Verworn observed that amoebae always move in a direction opposite to the thermal stimulus, *i.e.* they exhibit negative thermotaxis. Mendelssohn studied on a ciliated infusorium, *Paramoecium*, the thermotactic influence of different grades of temperature. When one end of a vessel full of liquid, and swarming with Paramoecia, is heated to 24-28 C., the creatures move to the cooler end of the vessel; when, on the contrary, one end of the vessel is cooled below the said degrees, the infusoria move towards the warmer end. Thus there may be positive or negative *thermotaxis* according to the degree of temperature.

In this case, as in chemo- and barotaxis, the movements are determined by the difference of temperature at the two poles of the Paramoecium, differences which can be estimated at about 0·01 C.

X. Light rays, like heat rays, act as a direct stimulus on comparatively few elementary organisms. In the higher animals they only affect the nervous elements of the retina, and great intensity is required to stimulate the cutaneous endings of the thermal nerves as well. The skin of invertebrates is also excitable to light.

Many observations have been made in order to determine the nature of the action of light upon *Protista*, and to ascertain whether excitability to light is a general property of protoplasm, or first appears during the phylogenic evolution of living beings. The results with amoebae were purely negative. Other Rhizopoda, however, were seen to contract on sudden illumination.

E. Oehl (1886-91) saw that the leucocytes of the blood both of man and frog, when exposed to bright sunshine under the microscope, reacted by active migratory and amoeboid movements, which were not present previous to the photic stimulation.

The work of Strasburger and others shows that intensity of light exerts a great influence on bacteria and diatoms, so that up to a certain point of intensity they exhibit positive *phototaxis*, and approach the source of light; with greater intensity they move farther off, and exhibit negative phototaxis; at a mid-point they show themselves wholly indifferent. The wave-length of the light rays is also of great importance. Engelmann has shown that the *Bacterium photometricum* (observed in the microspectroscope) swarms into the region of the ultra-red rays, and to a less extent into that of the orange and yellow rays, *i.e.* towards Frauenhofer's D-line (Fig. 21).

The term *heliotaxis* has long been employed to denote the common property of plants to turn on their axis in the direction of the sun's rays. The phenomenon is particularly conspicuous in plants grown inside the house. Both stems and petioles curve towards the light that comes in at the windows (positive heliotaxis), while the surfaces of the leaves spread out perpendicularly in the direction of the light rays (transverse heliotaxis). In plants with aerial roots these turn and grow towards the darkest part of the room (negative heliotaxis).

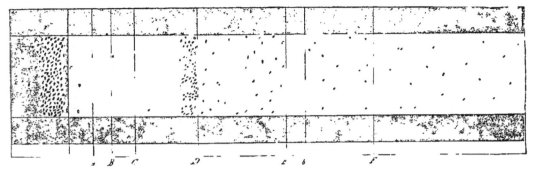

Fig. 21.—Petroleum (?) bacteria, in micro-spectroscope. (Engelmann.) The bacteria are collected in the region of the ultra-red and yellow rays.

Heliotactic movements are especially favoured by the blue and violet rays; red and yellow rays are practically inactive (Fig. 22).

Loeb (1888) described phenomena of heliotaxis in many animals, which are perfectly comparable with those observed on plants: they are also determined by the most refrangible rays of the spectrum. The mechanical explanation of the phenomenon is, according to Loeb, that the symmetrical points of an organism

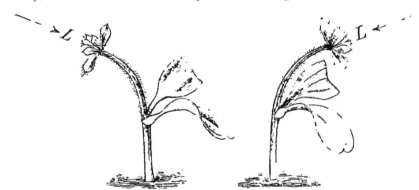

Fig. 22. *Galium aparine* showing heliotaxis. (Noll.) The plant curves left or right, to the source of light, as indicated by the arrow *L*. The leaves exhibit transverse heliotaxis.

possess equal excitability, and the unsymmetrical points unequal excitability: the points nearest the buccal pole possess an excitability greater than, or different in form from, that of the points nearest the opposite pole. By this is meant that with unilateral illumination the muscles of the excited side are thrown into a tension which is relatively greater or less than that of the muscles of the opposite side, so that the animal deviates in the direction of its movements, in the sense of positive or negative heliotaxis. In some animals it is possible to transform positive into negative heliotaxis, and *vice versa*.

XI. Electrical stimuli are those most frequently adopted by physiologists for the excitation of living matter. Their action on muscle and nerve will be treated at length in another connection. Here we must confine ourselves to the effects of electrical excitation on unicellular organisms.

Kühne and Engelmann were the first who investigated this subject. They both found that after weak induction shocks the amoebae suspended their locomotor movements; with stronger shocks the pseudopodia assume a globular form; if the shocks were still further strengthened, electrical tetanus resulted, followed by a kind of coagulation of the protoplasm, which was shared by the nucleus. Galvanic currents also, in proportion with their intensity,

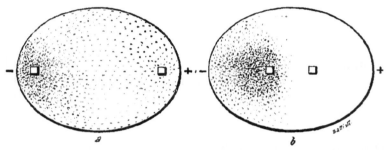

Fig. 23.—Kathodic galvanotaxis in a drop of water with paramoecia. (Verworn.) *a*, on closure of current, the paramoecia swim in curved lines to approach the kathode; *b*, paramoecia collected round the kathode.

produced a partial or total contraction of the protoplasm of amoebae.

Verworn discovered a directive action of the galvanic current analogous to that produced by other stimuli, which he terms *galvanotaxis*. He particularly investigated certain species of ciliated infusoria, *e.g. Paramoecia*. When immersed in a drop of water through which current is passing, these infusoria flock to the kathode in wavy movements which are more pronounced in proportion as the current is weaker. On breaking the circuit the Paramoecia scatter themselves again uniformly through the drop of water (Fig. 23). This is not a case of kataphoric action, *i.e.* of mechanical transport in the direction of the current, such as might occur with non-living particles, because the infusoria would then swim in a straight line, and move more rapidly, with no orientation of the principal axis of the body. Moreover, chloroform or ether paralyse these movements, which would not occur if they did not represent physiological phenomena in living beings. Budgett and Loeb noted that these same Paramoecia moved to the anode if the water which contains them is replaced by a 0·4-0·7 per cent solution of sodium chloride.

Dineur found that the leucocytes of the blood also exhibit galvanotactic properties with a marked preference for the anode.

A different form of kathodic and anodic galvanotaxis was observed at the end of 1885 by Hermann. When a galvanic current is passed through a vessel containing tadpoles or fish embryos, these animalcules orientate themselves with their long axes in the direction of the lines of current so that the head faces the anode and the tail the kathode. They remain in this position as long as current is passing; if its direction be reversed, they face to the opposite direction, like soldiers at the word of command.

Verworn recognised another form of galvanotaxis in a ciliated infusorium, *Spirostomum ambiguum*, which, when traversed by the galvanic current, turns so that the principal axis of its body is at right angles to the direction of the current. This he terms transverse galvanotaxis.

XII. The directive action of stimuli, particularly of those due to light and temperature, is of special importance for marine organisms. Scientific data in regard to the fauna and flora of the ocean are at present scanty in comparison with our knowledge of the terrestrial fauna and flora, but there seems reason to believe that the variety and magnitude of the animal and vegetable kingdoms of the ocean are incomparably greater than of those upon the earth. The paucity of data in regard to life in the deep sea is obviously due to the difficulty of securing such beings as live at a depth of several thousand metres below the surface.

Many expeditions have been organised for the purpose of studying marine biology; these are equipped with ponderous dredges, and are intended to remain several months at sea in order to collect with different kinds of apparatus, at various seasons of the year, the organisms that exist at different levels or at the bottom of the ocean. The most important have been the *Challenger* Expedition, conducted by Murray and Thompson (1884), and the *Valdivia*, conducted by Chun (1898-99), in different seas. In the Mediterranean, Krupp, on the *Maia* and the *Puritan*, investigated the pelagic fishes, the scientific results of this expedition having been illustrated and published by S. Lo Bianco (1901-3).

The distribution of organisms in the different strata of water (bathymetric distribution, either in the vertical or the horizontal direction) has been determined with a fair amount of accuracy by the use of special contrivances, constructed *ad hoc*. Such are the nets fitted with an apparatus enabling them to be closed at any required depth (measured by the soundings), so that they cannot, when pulled up through the supernatant strata of water, enclose any animals from these higher levels. Some are draw-nets weighted with heavy rings of iron or other metal, which fall to the bottom and are pushed along, gathering up the living organisms from the ocean bed. By this method a certain amount of exact knowledge has been obtained in regard to the fauna and flora of the seas. As regards the vertical distribution of these pelagic organisms, it is interesting to note that the forms which live at different heights in the same region of the sea vary enormously among themselves, so that we ought to speak of so many special biological zones in relation to the different depths of water.

The main factor which determines this diversity in the forms of life at various depths, is *light*; then come *temperature,* and *movement of the water*, which are of secondary importance; while *pressure* of water is, save for the *Teleosteans* provided with a swim-bladder, of no importance, as we have already pointed out.

In regard to *light,* the following zones can be distinguished in a vertical section of the water of the ocean :—

(*a*) A first zone, highly illuminated, which extends from the surface to about 30 metres down.

(*b*) The shaded zone, from about 30 metres below the surface to the farthest limits to which light penetrates (some 500 metres deep).

(*e*) The dark zone, which commences at 500 metres, and extends to the greatest depth known to be inhabited, *i.e.* some thousands of metres (in the Mediterranean the *Puritan* dredged to a depth of some 1500 metres).

It agrees with this, and with the fact that light is an indispensable condition of plant life (chlorophyll function), that no vegetable organisms (algae) have so far been dredged at a lower level than the shaded zone, *i.e.* below 500 metres. On the other hand, numerous animal organisms have been found, and described, below this level, in accordance with the fact that light is not an indispensable vital condition to animals. It is, however, interesting in those animals which live entirely in the dark, to observe the morphological changes in the sense organs destined to receive luminous stimuli (eyes). In some they atrophy completely, as in terrestrial creatures living in caves; in others, on the contrary, they develop enormously; while in order to furnish the stimuli required to make them perform their functions, they develop numerous and powerful luminous organs in different parts of the body.

Hensen was the first to propose the collective name of *Plankton* (πλαγκτός, wandering), which is now universally accepted, to indicate the world of living organisms (fauna and flora) in mid-ocean; while the name of *Benthos* (βένθος, bottom) is applied to the aquatic organisms that live at the bottom of the sea.

Lo Bianco (1903), on the strength of the facts already discussed, to the effect that light is the factor determining the varying distribution of plankton, proposed to term the biological stratum which corresponds with the first of the above zones *phao-plankton,* the organisms living in the second, shaded zone, *knepho-plankton*, and those living in the third, dark zone, *scoto-plankton*.

Since, beside these, there are many organisms which live indifferently on the surface or at the greatest depths, he proposes to collect the four classes together under the collective name of *pante-plankton*.

This is not the place in which to enumerate the forms and species of the organisms that constitute, respectively, these four great classes of marine life. We will only state that phao-plankton consists principally of ova that find in this zone the best condition for their evolution, and of the larvae or young forms of organisms, which in the adult state live either at the bottom (benthonic forms) or in the deeper strata of the sea. Besides the phao-plankton, certain species of *Crustacea* (copepods) are abundant The temperature of the water in this zone oscillates from 13° C. in winter to 26° C. in summer. The more or less copious contents of the phao-plankton varies with the seasons; it is particularly abundant in the spring because reproduction is most active at that season. A striking characteristic of most components of phao-plankton is their minute dimensions. It is a remarkable fact that many pelagic forms are larger in proportion with the depths at which they live.

The temperature of the second (shaded) zone varies from 13° to 24° C. in its superficial stratum, and by a couple of degrees only in the deeper parts, becoming constant (13° C. in the Mediterranean) below that. The plankton which inhabits this region (*knepho-plankton*) is the richest of all. " This zone," writes Lo Bianco, " since it is sheltered from the direct rays of the sun and movements of the waves, is the *habitat* most favourable to pelagic organisms : these physical conditions make it the richest and most varied in both plant and animal forms."

Many varieties of *scoto-plankton* are brilliant in colour, *e.g.* most kinds of Crustacea have very red bodies.

XIII. After discussing the general conditions and *external* stimuli of cell life, we ought, in another chapter, to consider the general conditions and *internal* stimuli, *i.e.* such as arise within the organism itself, and which govern all the vital phenomena that appear to be spontaneous or automatic—whether these originate in predominatingly katabolic processes (protoplasmic movements, sensory phenomena, development of heat, electricity, and light), or are due to predominatingly anabolic processes (phenomena of nutrition, reproduction, evolution). Our concrete knowledge of these internal conditions and stimuli is, however, at present so fragmentary that a few paragraphs will contain such general notions as have been determined in relation to them.

The constitution of a complete elementary organism, capable, *i.e.*, of every kind of essential vital activity, requires that the protoplasm shall have attained a certain degree of organisation, whether chemico-physical or morphological, so as not to be homogeneous in any individual particle. We saw in Chapter I. that the minimal degree of organisation necessary to constitute a complete organism is in all probability represented by its differentiation into cytoplasm and nucleus. A homogeneous bit of living matter detached from an elementary organism, either of cytoplasm or of nucleus, is incapable of prolonged existence; on the other hand, a minute particle of heterogeneous protoplasm, *i.e.* a fragment of nucleus and cytoplasm combined (p. 13), is capable of nutrition, integration, and reproduction. Vital metabolism cannot continue without the natural union of these two essential parts of the cell, showing that there exist between them reciprocal exchanges of matter and energy—the universal internal condition of cell life.

The same applies to complex or multicellular organisms. In the lowest grades of organisation, it is possible to divide a multicellular individual into one or more segments without fear of killing it; each segment continues to live, to show signs of sensibility, to grow and regenerate into a new individual like that of which it was originally a part. The classical example of this marvellous phenomenon was given for the first time on animals, in 1774, by the Genevese naturalist Trembley, with fresh-water polyps. The interpretation now accepted is that the cells of which the polyp is built up are not too highly differentiated in structure and function to be capable of mutual substitution; each cell, *i.e.*, represents the germ of the entire polyp, and can therefore reconstruct it.

In the higher grades of organisation, on the contrary, where there is a more or less advanced differentiation, both morphological and functional, of the parts that constitute the organism as a whole, it is no longer possible to multiply the individual by sections, because the life of each part is conditioned by that of the others, and they all represent integrating factors of more or less importance to the life of the aggregate. In the higher vertebrates also it is possible to amputate a limb or an organ, or even several limbs or organs, without necessarily causing death. This is either because the function of the lost parts can be replaced by others, or because there is not between the missing parts and those which remain a reciprocal exchange of matter and energy sufficient to make them indispensable to the life of the entire aggregate, in the way that the nucleus is necessary to the life of the cytoplasm and the cytoplasm to the life of the nucleus.

We know nothing positive in regard to the conditions, the internal stimuli, and the intimate mechanism of the phenomena of the nutrition and growth of protoplasm, and of cellular reproduction or neo-formation. All our ideas on this subject are exclusively morphological and are treated at length in text-books of histology, to which the reader should refer.

Very undetermined also, and far from concrete, is our knowledge of the internal conditions and stimuli of all those vital acts of which protoplasm is capable, even when it is as far as possible protected from every external agent that can function as a stimulus, by deviating from the general external conditions.

Some hold that the stimulus to movement and other automatic acts arises in the waste products that develop and accumulate in the cell, in consequence of its metabolism. In this case it is evident that both automatic excitations and reflexes are the effect of stimuli extrinsic to the protoplasm; but in the former these are generated by the activity of the organism itself, in the latter they come from without.

The intrinsic fallacy of this doctrine is easily appreciated when we consider that, on its showing, all the phenomena of excitation, paralysis, or of fatigue that are seen in the different forms of auto-intoxication must be regarded as automatic phenomena, because the agents by which they are determined (*e.g.* carbonic acid, as in asphyxia from suffocation, urinary products, as in uraemia, muscular toxins, as in fatigue or exhaustion consequent on excessive and prolonged muscular exertion) all originate in the metabolic activity of the different tissues of the body.

The true concept of automaticity is very different: either we must demonstrate that there are no automatic phenomena, properly speaking, or we must hold that the stimulus, or, more generically, the determining cause of the phenomena, is intrinsic to the elementary organism which exhibits them, and consists in an oscillation (rhythmical or irregular) of its metabolism or its excitability, by which it finds within itself the conditions for the development of the energy it has stored up (Luciani, 1873). The chemical and molecular transmutations of protoplasmic metabolism are usually conceived as something continuous and monotonous, which can only be changed or modified by external influences; but nothing forbids us to imagine a more vital process, which without invoking external factors may become disturbed of itself, or in consequence of the particular structure of the protoplasm, or the facility with which the particles of which it is composed are able to change their relations.

XIV. Various hypotheses and theories have been put forward as to the nature of the intimate processes that go on in living matter, and by which the several vital phenomena, thus briefly summarised, are determined. The starting-point and fundamental concept from which these different speculations have for the most part been evolved is invariably the same, starting from the oft-accentuated hypothesis that *chemical energy* is to be regarded as the sole and ultimate cause of all the manifestations exhibited by living organisms —which chemical energy, introduced into the animal body in the potential form by the different complex food-stuffs, becomes free or kinetic, owing to the activity of the living protoplasm.

From this it may be deduced that the living organism is distinguished from the dead in virtue of the incessant metabolism, or exchange of materials, which is taking place, even when it is apparently in the state of most complete repose. These material exchanges are, of course, associated with exchanges of energy.

Pflüger, in his classical essay on Physiological Combustion in Living Organisms (*Pflügers Arch.* x. 1875), recognised on the strength of many different experimental data that the essential characteristic of living matter consists in its being highly unstable, splitting up and regenerating itself incessantly.

"The fact," he writes, "which every biologist encounters on all sides, is the amazing instability (*Zersetzbarkeit*) of almost all living matter. . . . This instability is the cause of excitability. Does not the infinitesimal vital force of a ray of light evoke the most potent effects in brain and retina? I think no one will deny that living matter is not merely highly unstable (*zersetzbar*), but also that it is continually breaking up (*zersetzend*)." The ultimate cause of these chemical transmutations, and of the continuous atomic and molecular transformations of living matter, lies in the intra-molecular heat which comes into play in virtue of the specific nature of living matter.

In summing up his theory Pflüger concludes: "The vital process is the intra-molecular heat of the highly unstable (*zersetzbarer*) molecules of protein present in the cell-substance, which split up (*zersetzender*) by dissociation —with formation of carbonic acid, water, and starch compounds—and which, on the other hand, are perpetually regenerated, and also increase by polymerisation."

We saw in the last chapter that Metabolism may be regarded as the result of two opposite antagonistic processes: the ana-bolic, synthetic, restorative process, and the katabolic, analytic, disintegrative process. E. Hering (1888) gave to the former the name of Assimilation, to the latter that of Dissimilation, and laid down certain important considerations in regard to the theory of the intimate processes of living matter.

He starts from the indisputable fact that living matter at any given moment is the seat of two opposite processes which arise and proceed simultaneously, even when no external stimulus is acting on the living matter. He gave the name of *autonomous assimila-tion* (A) and *autonomous dissimilation* (D) to those processes which take place in living matter, when no external stimulus intervenes. If these two opposite processes are equal, so that neither the one nor the other predominates, then the substance alters neither quantitatively nor qualitatively; we have what Hering terms *autonomous equilibrium*.

But, as we have seen, external stimuli are continually acting upon living matter and modifying the state of its metabolism. Hering distinguishes two kinds of stimuli, which differ essentially *inter se*, inasmuch as the one kind excite the dissimilatory phase (*dissimilatory stimuli*)—and these are more usually noticed-- while the other kind act by exciting or augmenting the phase of assimilation (*assimilatory stimuli*).

Assuming, then, the action of a dissimilatory stimulus, dissimilation will be increased, and is termed by Hering *allono- mous dissimilation*: the living substance changes in its quality and quantity, and has a lower energy value (is "below par"). Hering assumes that in proportion as the living matter, under the influence of this stimulus, is excited to increased dissimila- tion, its inherent tendency to the dissimilatory phase diminishes while its inherent tendency to the assimilatory phase increases. Owing to this property, which he terms the internal automatic regulation of living matter, at the close of the dissimilatory stimulus the opposite process of assimilation sets in more vigorously than usual, so that after a certain time the living matter regains the mean energy value of equilibrium (*i.e.* is "at par") towards which it strives—the more incessantly, and with so much the greater energy, the farther it is removed from the said equilibrium in the one direction or the other, by the action of external stimuli.

It may, however, happen that the dissimilatory stimulus does not cease, but persists for an indefinite time; then in consequence of the diminished dissimilatory activity, and the simultaneous increase in autonomous assimilation, a new state of equilibrium is finally arrived at, which Hering terms *allonomous equilibrium*, and which prevails so long as the dissimilatory stimulus is acting. The living matter has *adapted* itself to the prolonged action of the stimulus.

The same reasoning holds for the action of the assimilatory stimuli, which provoke an increase in the assimilatory process.

Verworn, in his *General Physiology* (1895), has developed Hering's doctrine, while he takes Pflüger's theory also into consideration.

"Pflüger's assumption of living protein, which distinguishes living cell-substances from dead, and in the loose constitution of which lies the essence of life, is necessitated. But this substance must be of essentially different composition from dead protein, although, as follows from the character of its decomposition- products, certain characteristic atomic groups of the proteins are contained in it. The great lability that distinguishes it from other proteins, can be conditioned only by an essentially different constitution. In order to distinguish this body, there-fore, from dead protein, and to indicate its high significance in the occurrence of vital phenomena, it appears fitting to replace the term 'living protein' with that of *biogen*. The expressions 'plasma molecule,' 'plasson molecule,' 'plastidule,' etc., which Elsberg and Haeckel have employed, and the conceptions of which are comprised approximately in the expression 'biogen molecule,' are less fitting in so far as they easily give the impression that protoplasm is a chemically unitary body, which consists of wholly similar molecules; such a view must be ex-pressly rejected. Protoplasm is a morphological, not a chemical conception."

Verworn gives the name of *Biotonus* to the ratio between the assimilatory and dissimilatory processes, which Hering, as we have seen, regards as the theoretical foundation of the processes that go on in living matter.

"If we consider," he goes on, "the quantitative relation of assimilation to dissimilation in a considerable mass of living substance, such, for example, as is contained in a cell, we find it very variable, and even without the influence of stimuli it changes within wide limits. This relation of the two processes in the unit of time, which can be expressed by the fraction $\frac{A}{D}$ and will be termed, in brief, *biotonus*, is of fundamental importance for the various phenomena of life. The variations in the value of the fraction effect all changes in the vital manifestations of every organism.

"The fraction $\frac{A}{D}$ is merely a general form of the expression of biotonus. In reality, assimilation and dissimilation are not simple processes; on the contrary, the events that lead to the construction of the biogen molecule, and the formation of the decomposition-products, are very complex and consist of processes closely interwoven. Hence if we would express biotonus in a specialised way, we must give the fraction the form

$$\frac{a + a_1 + a_2 + a_3 +}{d + d_1 + d_2 + d_3 +},$$

in which a, a_1, a_2, a_3, etc., and d, d_1, d_2, d_3, etc., represent the partial processes that combine to form the whole."

With our present limited knowledge of the more special transformations that take place in living substance, it is impossible approximately to gauge the significance of the individual com-ponents of the biotonous quotient. Verworn, therefore, refers only to considerations arising from the general formula $\frac{A}{D}$.

Where assimilation and dissimilation are equal in the unit of time, the fraction $\frac{A}{D} = 1$, Hering's metabolic equilibrium. In this state, the sum of the excreted substances of every kind is equal to the sum of the ingested substances.

"If the individual members of series A increase in a constant relation to one another, while the members of series D remain equal or decrease, so that in the unit of time the sum of the members of A is greater than that of the members of D, then the metabolic quotient $\frac{A}{D} > 1$.

"This case is realised in growth, where the formation of living substance surpasses its destruction.

"If, *vice versa*, the members of series D grow proportionately to one another, while those of series A remain unchanged, or become smaller, biotonus $\frac{A}{D} > 1$. This condition is the basis of atrophy, and leads finally to death."

In a later work (1903) Verworn developed this theory more fully, giving it the name of *Biogen hypothesis* and enumerating the various indirect arguments, of early or recent date, which tell in its favour, and show how by its application we may arrive at a unitary explanation of the action of the several stimuli upon living matter.

"In my opinion" (he concludes) "the principal value of the biogen hypothesis lies in the fact that it enables us to gather up all the vital phenomena under a single, very definite and simple point of view, without contradicting any of the facts hitherto noted. This hypothesis provides us with a clear idea of the phenomena fundamental to the whole of life, and is thus of singular utility in facilitating the interpretation of many complex and controverted problems."

"Still" (he adds) "it must once more be pointed out that this is merely a working hypothesis, and that it would be quite fallacious to attribute to it any other value. Whether it be a faithful representation of the real facts, or whether it be inadequate, matters little : as a working hypothesis it keeps its value so long as it is useful and fecund in the progress of science. The history of science is richer in fallacies than in truth ; but in the development of the human mind a fertile error is of infinitely greater value than a sterile fact."

BIBLIOGRAPHY

In addition to the general treatises on animal and plant physiology cited above see :

PFLÜGER. Pflügers Arch. x. 1875.

Cl. BERNARD. Leçons sur les phénomènes de la vie commune aux animaux et aux végétaux. Paris, 1878-79.

E. HERING. Vorgänge d. lebender Materie, "Lotos," ix. 1888. English translation. Theory of the Functions of Living Matter, by F. A. Welby. Brain, xx. 1897.)

J. ROSENTHAL. Lehrbuch d. allg. Physiologie. Leipzig, 1901.

S. Lo BIANCO. Mitteilungen aus d. zoolog Station zu Neapel, xvi. 1903.

M. VERWORN. Allgemeine Physiologie. Jena. G. Fischer. 4th ed., 1903. (English translation by Dr. F. S. Lee. Macmillan.

M. VERWORN. Die Biogenhypothese. Jena. Fischer, 1903.

J. LOEB. Studies in General Physiology. Chicago, 1905.

Recent English Literature :

E. W. TOWLE. A Study in the Heliotropism of Cypridopsis. Amer. Journ. of Physiol., 1900, iii. 345.

J. LOEB. On Ion-proteid Compounds and their rôle in the Mechanics of Life Phenomena. Part I. Amer. Journ. of Physiol., 1900, iii. 327.

R. M. YERKES. Reaction of Entomostraca to Stimulation by Light. I. Amer. Journ. of Physiol., 1900, iii. 157.

R. M. YERKES. Reaction of Entomostraca to Stimulation by Light. II. Amer. Journ. of Physiol., 1901, iv. 405.

R. PEARL. Studies on Electrotaxis. I. Amer. Journ. of Physiol., 1901, iv. 96.

R. PEARL. Studies on the Effects of Electricity on Organisms. II. Amer. Journ. of Physiol., 1901, v. 301.

E. B. HOLT and F. S. LEE. The Theory of Phototactic Response. Amer. Journ. of Physiol., 1901, iv. 460.

H. H. DALE. Galvanotaxis and Chemotaxis of Ciliate Infusoria. Part I. Journ. of Physiol., 1900-1, xxvi. 291.

W. M. FLETCHER. The Relation of Oxygen to the Survival Metabolism of Muscle. Journ. of Physiol., 1902, xxviii. 474.

R. S. LILLIE. On Differences in the Direction of the Electrical Convection of certain Free Cells and Nuclei. Amer. Journ. of Physiol., 1903, viii. 273.

G. P. ADAMS. On the Negative and Positive Phototropism of the Earthworm *Allolobophora foetida*, as determined by Light of Different Intensities. Amer. Journ. of Physiol., 1903, ix. 26.

A. MOORE. Some Facts concerning Geotropic Gatherings of Paramoecia. Amer. Journ. of Physiol., 1903, ix. 238.

E. TORELLE. The Response of the Frog to the Light. Amer. Journ. of Physiol., 1903, ix. 466.

E. P. LYON. On Rheotropism. I. Rheotropism in Fishes. Amer. Journ. of Physiol., 1904, xii. 149.

E. P. LYON. On Rheotropism. Part II. Amer. Journ. of Physiol., 1909, xxiv. 244.

G. SMITH. The Effect of Pigment-Migration on the Phototropism of *Gammarus annulatus*, S. I. Smith. Amer. Journ. of Physiol., 1905, xiii. 205.

E. P. LYON. On the Theory of Geotropism in Paramoecium. Amer. Journ. of Physiol., 1905, xiv. 421.

E. P. LYON. An Outline of a Theory of the Genesis of Protoplasmic Motion and Excitation. Trans. Roy. Soc. of South Australia, 1905, xxix. 7.

T. B. ROBERTSON. Investigations on the Reactions of Infusoria to Chemical and Osmotic Stimuli. Journ. of Biolog. Chem., 1905-6, i. 185.

O. P. TERRY. Galvanotropism of *Volvox*. Amer. Journ. of Physiol., 1905-6, xv. 235.

J. W. BANCROFT. On the Influence of the Relative Concentration of Calcium Ions on the Reversal of the Polar Effects of the Galvanic Current in Paramoecium. Journ. of Physiol., 1906, xxxiv. 444.

P. B. HADLEY. The Relation of Optical Stimuli to Rheotaxis in the American Lobster *Homarus americanus*. Amer. Journ. of Physiol., 1906-7, xvii. 326.

P. B. HADLEY. Galvanotaxis in Larvae of the American Lobster *Homarus americanus*. Amer. Journ. of Physiol., 1907, xix. 39.

J. R. MILLER. Galvanotropismus in the Crayfish. Journ. of Physiol., 1906-7, xxxv. 215.

CHAPTER IV

THE BLOOD: FORMED CONSTITUENTS

SUMMARY. — 1. Arrangement of human physiology, and classification of functions. 2. Importance of the blood as centre of the vegetative system and agent of general metabolism. 3. Historical development of haematology. 4. General physico-chemical characters of the blood. 5. Estimation of total quantity. 6. Physical and morphological characters of erythrocytes, and estimation of their relative quantity. 7. Chemical composition. Properties of haemoglobin and its derivatives. 8. Character, composition, and physiological properties of leucocytes. 9. Blood platelets, and elementary granulation of the blood. Bibliography.

JUST as no absolute difference can be admitted between the vital activities of plants and animals, so no absolute difference can be recognised between the functions of the individual living cells, tissues, organs, and systems of which the higher organisms, including man, consist. It is nevertheless to be observed that in all complex organisms, whether animals or plants, there is *pari passu* with the morphological differentiation of the primitive cell, which occurs during ontogenic development, a functional differentiation, resulting in a division of labour, *i.e.* in the greater or less specialisation of the capacities or functions of the different parts. As in the great industries an ever-increasing development and perfection of industrial products is obtained with the progressive division of the work assigned to the various groups of workmen, so the increasing perfection observed in the scale of living beings is essentially the result of progressive morphological differentiation and functional specialisation in the cells of which the organism is composed (Milne Edwards, 1827). It is evident that the arrangement of the special physiology of man, and the rational classification of his functions, must rest upon this specialisation of the different organs and systems in the higher animals.

I. At the commencement of the nineteenth century Xavier Bichat, in his inspired book *Sur la vie et la mort*, made a sharp distinction between two orders of functions in the higher organisms, which he designated as the functions of organic (or vegetative) life and the functions of animal life respectively.

By means of the former, says Bichat in effect, these organisms are constantly transforming into their own substance the materials which they receive from outside, while they continually eliminate the useless products of consumption; by means of the latter, they feel and perceive the external world, express their sensations, perform voluntary movements under the influence of these, and are able to express their desires and fears, their pains and pleasures.

Although modern science has established the unitary conception of life, and has refuted the supposed antagonism between the functions of plants and of animals, Bichat's general distinction holds good as the basis of a rational classification. It is a fact that the cardinal function of plants, taken as a whole, is the synthetic building-up of organic matter, while that of animals is its disintegration.

On the other hand, it is undeniable that the higher animals possess a system of organs and apparatus which essentially serve the internal life of the body, by preparing and constantly renewing the *pabulum* common to all the living elements of which it consists: while there is a second system which especially serves the external life, by developing the potential energy of the living matter. The first system recalls the predominance of anabolism in plants, as compared with animals; the second the predominance of katabolism in animals, as compared with plants.

Yet, if we attempt to determine exactly which organs and apparatus compose the *vegetative* system, in distinction to those of which the *animal* system consists, we encounter difficulties. The embryological criterion, so often invoked in this connection, *i.e.* the derivation of the different parts from one or other of the three germinal layers, leads to no satisfactory result, since it is now well established that tissues and organs are developed from the external, and yet more from the middle, layer, which obviously belong some to one system and some to the other. Clearly these two systems do not represent two distinct and superposed organisms, but rather two that are intimately connected and interdependent, to be distinguished only by artificial means, contingent to a certain extent on individual judgment and appreciation.

It is the obvious function of the *vegetative* system, as a whole, to keep constant the quantity and quality of the mass of blood, from which is formed the lymph or plasma constituting the common internal medium indispensable to the life of each vital element. This system consists necessarily of the blood, of the cardio-vascular apparatus by means of which it circulates, and of the whole of the glandular organs and apparatus designed for its constant renewal, elaboration, and cleansing.

On the other hand, the function of the *animal* system is to bring the animal through its sense organs into relation with the external world, and to modify these relations in various ways by means of the organs of motion. It consists accordingly of the central and peripheral nervous system, *i.e.* the sensory and conducting organs, and of the muscular and skeletal system, *i.e.* the active and passive apparatus of movement.

The blood is the centre and objective of all the functions of the vegetative system : the brain is the central seat and focus of the functions of the animal system.

A third order of physiological processes must further be distinguished from the special functions of the vegetative and animal systems, in which both these and, in a certain sense, the entire organism participate. These are the physiological phenomena of general metabolism and the regulation of the balance of output and intake ; thermogenesis and the regulation of the heat balance ; sexual and reproductive functions ; the physiology of the embryo, and of the different stages of uterine life.

II. As centre of the vegetative system, the blood contains all the histogenic substances destined to nourish and renew the tissues, and all the histolytic products of consumption, useless or noxious residues, to be eliminated. The first, which filter through the living walls of the capillaries, pass in the form of lymph into the interstitial plasma-spaces of the tissues for which they provide aliment ; the second, secreted by the tissue cells, pass into the blood by way of the lymph vessels, and are thence eliminated by the kidneys, lungs, skin, and liver.

From the histological standpoint the blood may be regarded as a tissue. It contains a number of formed elements, represented by the corpuscles, and an intercellular substance, the plasma, which is essentially a product elaborated and secreted by all the cells which take part in haematopoiesis and haematolysis. The blood is distinguished from the other tissues by the fact that it is fluid and that it circulates, and is therefore capable of exerting its action on all the fixed tissues, bringing them into relation and binding them together. It thus functions as the centre of the vegetative system, and is the agent of metabolism, *i.e.* of the material exchanges of the whole body.

III. To compress within a few lines the historical development of our physiological knowledge of the blood would be a work of difficulty. In this field there is no one great discovery to be recorded, only the gradual acquisition of separate facts due to the labours of a vast number of observers. We shall confine ourselves to enumerating a few of the principal dates and names as landmarks.

The Italian Malpighi (1661) was the first who saw the red corpuscles, while the Dutch Leeuwenhoek (1673) first described them accurately. In England Hewson (1770) also observed the leucocytes, found that many salts delayed or inhibited coagulation,

and foresaw many of the theories that are now generally accepted.
A few years later (1794) J. Hunter published an extensive work
on the blood, which contained not a few new observations and
ingenious experiments. Just as the history of the physics and
morphology of the blood begins only in the seventeenth century
with the discovery of the microscope, so the history of its
chemistry only assumes notable proportions at the commencement
of the nineteenth century, after Priestley (1775) and Lavoisier
(1784) had laid the first methodical principles of modern
chemistry. As the precursors of our present science of haematology, we may name Berzelius (1808), Prévost and Dumas (1821),
Chevreul (1824), Nasse (1842), Simon (1842), Mulder (1849),
Lehmann (1850) and many others.

IV. If we consider the most striking characters of the blood,
it is found to be a red fluid (arterial blood, scarlet: venous blood,
dichroic, i.e. dark red in reflected, greenish in refracted, light),
somewhat viscous, opaque even in thin layers, faintly salt and
sweetish in taste, with a characteristic odour. It is a little
heavier than water: the specific gravity of a man's blood varies
between 1·057 and 1·066, that of a woman from 1·053 to 1·061.
The reaction of the blood circulating in the vessels is alkaline in
the normal state: extracted from the vessels, it becomes neutral
and then slightly acid. It must, however, be noted that in all blood
reactions, and, generally speaking, in all the fluids of the body, we
have to distinguish between the *actual* or *true* reaction and the
potential reaction.

Recent researches in physical chemistry have brought out the
fundamental fact that the degree of acidity or alkalinity of a
solution is determined by its content of H + ions and OH − ions
respectively. Since the actual reaction of a liquid is that which
represents its content of free H + or OH − ions, it is necessary
in determining it to make use of means which do not alter the
numbers of these ions. The potential reaction is that which
represents the degree of acidity or alkalinity of a liquid when
the electrolytes which it contains are all fully dissociated into
their ions.

The determination of these two kinds of reaction leads in the
case of the blood to very different results. While according to
the potential reaction the alkalinity of the blood corresponds
to a soda solution of 0·2 · 0·4 per cent, according to the actual
or true reaction it would be that of $\frac{1\cdot3}{10,000,000}$ N of soda, which is
practically neutral (Farkas).

The *Pycnometric Method* is certainly the most exact for determining the
specific gravity of blood in animals, and also in man when there is a sufficient
quantity of blood to work with. A glass pycnometer is used, which carries a
thermometer in its stopper so that the temperature at which the experiment

is carried on can be recorded (Fig. 24). After carefully cleaning and drying the pycnometer, it is weighed, first empty, then when filled with distilled water. It is then washed out with alcohol and ether, dried again, and weighed once more when filled with the blood to be examined. The weighing must be accurate to $\frac{1}{10}$ mgrm. The weight of distilled water at 15 C. being equal to 1, it is easy to calculate that of blood at the same temperature. The *areometric method*, also used in physiology, is more rapid, but is less exact than the pycnometric, because it determines the specific gravity of the plasma rather than that of the blood *in toto*. When only small quantities of blood are available, as in clinical researches, the capillary pycnometer of Schmalz is employed, which consists of a capillary tube some 12 cm. long by $1\frac{1}{2}$ mm. wide, in which distilled water and blood are aspirated and weighed in succession. The weighing and calculating are carried out as in the first case.

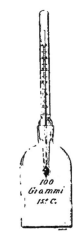

Besides these direct methods of ascertaining specific gravity for small quantities of blood, there are other indirect ways which are all based on the principle of obtaining from a more dense and a less dense substance a mixture of the same density as the drop of blood to be examined. This is ascertained when, on introducing the drop of blood into the mixture with a pipette, the drop neither sinks nor rises to the surface. The density of the mixture is then determined with the areometer, and will be that of the blood. The various indirect methods differ among themselves according to the quality of the substances used for the mixture. Fano employs a solution of gum, Roy a solution of glycerin. It should be noted that these indirect methods rather determine the specific gravity of the corpuscles than that of the blood *in toto*.

When care is taken to employ liquids in which the components of blood are the least soluble (for example chloroform and benzol, Hammerschlag's method), these methods can be used with approximate accuracy, and they may also be employed for the separate determination of the specific gravity of serum (1028) and of the red corpuscles (1088).

The following methods are used in determining the chemical reaction of the blood :—

1. *Kühne's Method.*—The drops of blood to be examined are placed in a small dialyser, made of moist parchment, shaped by pressure over a hemispherical mould. The drops of blood are introduced into the resulting hollow, and the whole placed in a watch-glass containing distilled water, to dialyse. After a certain time the reaction of this water is tested with litmus-paper.

2. *Liebreich's Method.*—A drop of the blood to be examined is put on a slab of chalk or plaster, previously saturated with a neutral litmus solution. After a given time the slab is washed with a vigorous spray of distilled water, and the spot where the blood-drop lay is found to be more or less blue in correspondence with its alkalinity.

3. *Zuntz' Method.*—Glazed strips of neutral litmus-paper are used, which are saturated with a solution of sodium chloride or sodium sulphate. After bringing these into contact with the blood to be examined, they are washed rapidly with a fine spray of distilled water.

The *Titration Methods*, which consist in determining the quantity of an acid or alkaline solution of a given strength to be added to the liquid under examination, in order to modify the colour of an indicator, merely give the potential, and not the actual, reaction of the fluid. Apart from errors due to the nature of the indicator, it must be remembered that not only the quantity of free H + and OH ions remaining in the fluid, but, further, the quantity of H + and OH − set free in consequence of the modifications of chemical equilibrium between non-dissociated and associated molecules, are determined.

The titration methods most commonly employed to estimate the alkalinity of the blood are as follows :—

1. Zuntz neutralised the alkalinity of the blood by a titrated solution of phosphoric acid, 1 c.c. of which corresponds to 0·005 grm. of sodium carbonate. Litmus-paper is used as the indicator. Lassar, on the other hand, employs a decinormal solution of tartaric acid (7·5 grms. of acid per litre).

2. Landois adopts the decinormal solution of tartaric acid, and a perfectly neutral, saturated solution of sodium sulphate. As indicator he uses the finest litmus-paper. With these two solutions ten mixtures are made in the following proportions :—

I. 10 parts $\frac{N}{10}$ tartaric acid to 100 parts saturated sol. $NaSO_4$.

II. 20 ,, ,, 90 ,, ,,

X. 100 ,, ,, 10 ,, ,,

The first mixture is then aspirated to a distance of 8 mm. along a graduated pipette made of a glass tube 1 mm. in diameter, and the blood to a distance of 16 mm., i.e. 8 mm. of each fluid. This mixture is emptied into a watch-glass and the reaction tested. Each successive mixture is employed in the same way until the alkaline solution becomes acid. The degree of alkalinity corresponding to the several mixtures is as follows :

I. = 0·036 per cent NaOH.	VI. = 0·216 per cent NaOH.
II. = 0·072 ,, ,,	VII. = 0·252 ,, ,,
III. = 0·108 ,, ,,	VIII. = 0·288 ,, ,,
IV. = 0·144 ,, ,,	IX. = 0·324 ,, ,,
V. = 0·180 ,, ,,	X. = 0·360 ,, ,,

Jaksch has modified Landois' method in practice as follows. He too employs a solution of $\frac{N}{10}$ tartaric acid and a concentrated solution of sodium sulphate. He dilutes the first solution 10 and 100 times, making solutions of $\frac{N}{100}$ and $\frac{N}{1000}$ tartaric acid respectively. These solutions are mixed with the solution of sodium sulphate in eighteen mixtures, which contain :—

I. 0·9 c.c. $\frac{N}{100}$ acid with 0·1 c.c. of $NaSO_4$.

II. 0·8 ,, ,, 0·2 ,,

IX. 0·1 ,, ,, 0·9 ,,

X. 0·9 c.c. $\frac{N}{1000}$,, 0·1 ,,

XI. 0·8 ,, ,, 0·2 ,,

0·1 c.c. of blood is dropped into each watch-glass, stirred up, and the reaction tested with litmus-paper. The solutions correspond to the following degree of alkalinity of the blood :—

I. 0·360 NaOH in 100 grms. of blood.

II. 0·320 ,, ,,

III. 0·250 ,, ,,

IX. 0·040 ,, ,,

X. 0·036 ,, ,,

XVIII. 0·004 ,, ,,

The actual reaction of the blood is measured by the Electrometric Method concentration cell. Particulars will be found in any modern text-book of

The blood has the highly important property of coagulating spontaneously. In a few moments (3-12 minutes for human blood) after it has been taken from the blood-vessels it is transformed into a gelatinous mass, which assumes the shape of the vessel that receives it. It is the formation of this clot which checks the continuation of haemorrhage in small injured vessels which would otherwise lead to the death of the animal. Clotting depends on the formation and separation of a protein from the plasma, *i.e. fibrin* (which, as we shall see, does not pre-exist as such) in the form of a fibrillar reticulum of such excessive fineness, that it encloses in its meshes not merely the whole of the corpuscles, but also the entire liquid portion of the blood. This fact appears the more marvellous when we consider that the amount of fibrin formed during coagulation never exceeds 1 per cent of the mass of blood, but is more often represented by a fraction, 0·4 per cent, of this, and may even fall to the minimum of 0·1 per cent. The separation of the fibrin from the mass of blood can be effected by prolonged washing of the clot (Malpighi, 1666), or by whipping the freshly-extracted blood (Ruysch, 1707). In this last case the fibrin clings to the rod used for whipping as a fibrous, elastic, whitish mass; and blood thus defibrinated is incapable of clotting.

From the clot containing the whole mass of blood a yellowish fluid gradually separates out in consequence of the physical retraction of the fibrous reticulum, the so-called *serum*, which represents that part of the plasma that remains liquid after coagulation. When all or nearly all this serum has separated out from the clot, the latter is seen to be considerably diminished in volume, though it still keeps the form of the vessel. The clot thus reduced by the separation of the plasma is sometimes termed the *crassamentum*.

In blood which has been rendered incoagulable by defibrination, the red corpuscles, being heavier than the serum, tend to fall to the bottom of the vessel, so that an almost transparent upper layer is formed by degrees, consisting principally of serum, with an opaque lower layer formed almost exclusively of the mass of corpuscles. The separation of the serum from the corpuscles is effected with maximal speed and perfection by the Centrifuge, which can be performed with the elegant little model represented in Fig. 25.

If coagulation is delayed in blood newly drawn from the veins (as is often observed in human blood during inflammatory diseases, and normally in horses' blood) there is again a partial separation of the plasma from the red corpuscles, and the clot subsequently formed presents a greyish superficial layer of greater or less density, known as the buffy coat, or *crusta phlogistica*, which consists of coagulated plasma mixed with leucocytes, without any red corpuscles.

V. The estimation of the total quantity of the blood, or its relations with the weight of the animal, presents great practical difficulties. The older anatomists held very exaggerated views on the quantity of blood in man, estimating it erroneously by the amount of injection mass that can be forced into the blood-vessels of a dead body. Far too low values, on the other hand, were obtained at a later period by the method of completely bleeding the animal (Herbst, 1822), since this does not sufficiently take into account the quantity of blood left in the vessels, which may vary considerably in different cases.

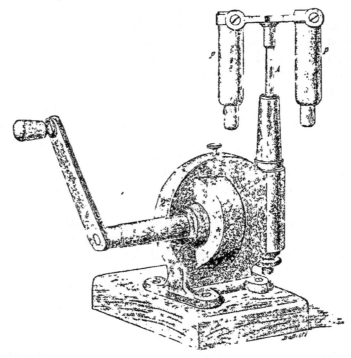

FIG. 25.—Hedin's small centrifuge. By means of three cogged wheels enclosed within 1, 2, 3, each turn of the handle is multiplied 100 times from the axis A, the apex of which carries a cross-piece, with the test-tube holders pp, which are kept horizontal during the rotation.

A better method is that carried out by Lehmann and Ed. Weber on two criminals (1853). They weighed the individuals before and after decapitation, and from the difference in weight estimated the mass of blood lost by bleeding. They took a sample of this blood. They then injected water through the arteries of the trunk and head, until it flowed almost colourless from the veins, and lastly determined the weight of the solids contained in the blood and in the washings. From these determinations they calculated the quantity of blood left in the body after decapitation.

It is obvious that this method must give too high a result. The introduction of water into the vessels must extract not only the fixed constituents of the blood remaining in the system, but also such as have penetrated by the lymphatic system and by diffusion from the tissues, during and soon after the bleeding. In one of the criminals, who weighed 60,540 grms., the mass of the blood weighed 7520 grms., *i.e.* one-eighth of the body-weight.

More exact results were obtained with the chromometric method, which is based on the colouring properties of the blood pigment (haemoglobin). It was first employed by Welcker (1854) and was perfected later by Gscheidlen (1873). A little normal blood is first drawn from the animal and weighed; the whole of the blood that can be extracted by bleeding is then collected; that left behind is subsequently washed out of the system by irrigating with a stream of isotonic (0·60-0·55 per cent) salt solution; then, after removing the contents of the gastro-intestinal canal, gall bladder and urinary bladder, the viscera are minced up and soaked for several hours in the saline fluid used for washing; lastly, the washings are mixed with the mass of blood obtained by bleeding. The blood-content is calculated from the coloured liquid obtained, after determining the quantity of saline that must be added to the weighed specimen of blood in order to obtain the same degree of colour. To make the experiment more exact it is advisable to saturate the haemoglobin with carbon monoxide, in order to secure the same degree of colour in both mixtures.

The calculation for determining the quantity of blood contained in the body is very simple:—If a is the quantity of blood extracted in the first bleeding, x the quantity of blood left in the body, b the quantity of physiological saline employed to wash out the vascular system and organs of the animal, c the quantity of physiological saline necessary to make the colour of the blood a equal to that of the blood x, *plus* the fluid b (a quantity which is known to us, and which we may, to simplify matters, denote as d); it is easy to calculate the quantity of blood x according to the following equation:

$$a : c : a :: d : x$$

and therefore $x \dfrac{a \cdot d}{a + c}$.

Having thus determined the value x, we can at once arrive at the total volume of the blood by adding the first portion a extracted in the preliminary bleeding to x: if we then multiply the volume of blood by its specific weight, we obtain the absolute weight of blood, the relation of which to the total body-weight of the animal has finally to be calculated.

Welcker came to the conclusion that the mass of the blood varies in dogs from 7 to 9 per cent of the body-weight, in rabbits from 5 to 9 per cent. Bischoff (1855), who applied these methods to the bodies of two criminals, obtained results which approximated closely to those obtained by Welcker for dogs (7·1 to 7·7 per cent). Assuming that in man the blood averages $\frac{1}{13}$ of the body-weight, there would be 5 kilograms of blood in an individual of 65 kilograms body-weight.

It goes without saying that the quantity of blood must vary with the constitution, sex, age, state of nutrition, and with many other functional or purely individual factors. Clearly, lymphatic individuals and those whose fatty tissues (which are poorest in blood) are strongly developed, must have a considerably less quantity of blood than other individuals in whom muscular tissues which are richly irrigated with blood predominate. The former may be relatively termed anaemic, the latter plethoric.

VI. The morphological study of the blood is founded on microscopical observations, which show the presence of three distinct elements—Red Corpuscles (Erythrocytes or Haemacytes), White Corpuscles (Leucocytes), and Platelets (Hayem's Haematoblasts).

The Erythrocytes are in the form of biconcave discs, non-nucleated and round in all mammals (save the camel and the llama,

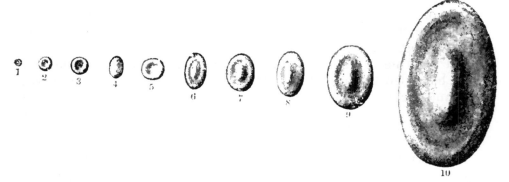

FIG. 26.—Form and relative size of erythrocytes of different animals, viewed from the surface. 1. Erythrocyte of musk-deer; 2, goat; 3, marmot; 4, llama; 5, man; 6, pigeon; 7, tench; 8, lizard; 9, frog; 10, proteus.

in which they are elliptical); nucleated and elliptical in birds, reptiles, amphibia and fishes (Fig. 26). The red corpuscles of man have a diameter of 7-8 μ and a depth of 1·7 μ; in other mammalian animals they are even smaller; in birds and the lower vertebrates they are much bigger (21 μ in frog, 29 μ in Triton, 58 μ in Proteus). Viewed from above, and isolated, they are greenish-yellow in colour; seen from the side as a rouleau of discs, they are red (Fig. 27); to them the blood owes its characteristic colour, and they render it opaque. They are soft, almost gelatinous in consistency—hence they easily change their shape; but they are perfectly elastic, and recover their original form directly the contracting force ceases to act on them.

Red corpuscles may be divided, according to their affinity for staining, into orthochromatic and polychromatic (Ehrlich). The orthochromatic are the most numerous, and stain with aurantia and eosin. The polychromatic, which are much less frequent, take up fuchsin when they are stained with tri-acid; with eosin-methylene-blue they stain violet, etc. Red corpuscles are classified according to their form and size (distinctions which concern the pathologist) into normal erythrocytes, micro- and macrocytes, and poikilocytes (pear-shaped, rod-shaped, etc.). Again there are red corpuscles which exhibit granules of different sizes and shapes in their protoplasm, and which will stain with all the basic dyes (basophile granulation). On changing the stains, the figures produced assume quite different forms: this shows that the figures that we see do not correspond exactly with the pre-existing arrangement of the chromatic substance, but depend on the different physico-chemical actions exercised by each individual colouring substance (Cesaris Demel). The significance of these granules is uncertain; by some they are considered to be the remains of nuclei, according to others they are protoplasmic formations.

Fig. 27.—Red blood-corpuscles of man. (Magnification, 650 diameters.), Some are seen flat, others in profile, the majority are disposed in rouleaux.

Although Schultze has described active movements of the protoplasm in the nucleated erythrocytes of the chick, it is very doubtful whether the red corpuscles of mammalia are capable of expanding and contracting in the medium in which they normally live. When, however, they are taken out of the vessels, and cooled or warmed, or excited by induction shocks; when the degree of concentration of the plasma in which they float is altered by the addition of water or of saline solutions; when they are brought in contact with extraneous chemicals,—they readily change their shape, assuming a mulberry-like or even prickly (crenate) appearance, and extending or retracting different segments of their protoplasm, as if undergoing amoeboid movements. The former changes are the effect of altered osmotic conditions, the latter are probably to be regarded as active movements (Figs. 28 and 29).

The capacity of erythrocytes for active movements in certain special abnormal conditions is confirmed by the observations of A. Cavazzani. He noticed that when blood was collected in an isotonic or hypotonic solution of sodium chloride, to which potassium ferrocyanide or a highly dilute solution of potassium sulpho-cyanide had been added in the proportion of about 1 per 1000, and then examined under the microscope at a temperature of 35-37° C., the erythrocytes of man and other mammalia (not of birds and batracians) put out delicate prolongations like cilia, the rapid vibratory movements of which enable the corpuscles to oscillate, rotate, or move forward. These cilia-like pseudopodia

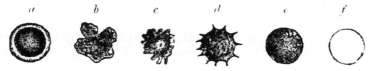

FIG. 28.—Successive effects upon erythrocytes of discharge from a Leyden jar. (Rollett.) *a*, normal erythrocyte; *b*, rosette form; *c*, mulberry form; *d*, prickly form; *e*, rounded and swollen erythrocyte; *f*, ghost.

rise from the smooth surface of the erythrocytes, and vary in length and number. Their movements of expansion and retraction are slow and limited. If a drop of solution of cocaine hydrochloride is added to the preparation, the erythrocytes resume their former shape in a few moments. If washed free of the cocaine, and treated afresh with the ferrocyanide, they may resume their ciliated aspect.

Since, according to the researches of Albertoni, cocaine paralyses protoplasm, it follows that the changes of form exhibited by the erythrocytes under the influence of potassium ferrocyanide must be considered as active movements of the protoplasm. Erythrocytes have a fairly tenacious vitality. When taken out of the blood-vessels and reinjected, they survive after as much as 4-5 days, but only provided they are kept in ice. If heated to 52° C., they die and break up when reintroduced into the circulation. If transfused into animals of

FIG. 29.—*a*, Successive effects upon erythrocytes of water (Schafer); *b*, action of a solution of salt; *c*, action of tannic acid.

a different kind they do not survive, but degenerate and disintegrate more or less rapidly, owing to the heterogeneous plasma with which they are brought in contact.

The direct enumeration of the corpuscles contained in a given quantity of blood (1 c.mm.) was correctly performed for the first time by Vierordt and Welcker (1854), the results they obtained having been confirmed by more recent observers. The method and apparatus have been perfected, and are now practical and easily applicable for clinical purposes. We must here confine ourselves to naming those of Malassez, Hayem, and Thoma-Zeiss.

Haemacytometer of Thoma-Zeiss. In order to count blood-corpuscles with the Thoma-Zeiss apparatus, the point of the capillary glass pipette (Fig. 30, I) is dipped into the drop of blood to be examined, which is obtained by pricking the finger with a needle. A column of blood is aspirated by means of the rubber tube to division 0·5 or 1 of the pipette, and after quickly drying the lower end, the bulb of the pipette is filled up to the figure 101 (which expresses its capacity in c.mm.) with 3 per cent salt solution, or with Pacini's fluid as modified by Hayem and Gram (corrosive sublimate 0·5 grm., sodium sulphate 5 grms., sodium chloride 2 grms., distilled water 200 grms.). It is then sufficient to shake the pipette for a few moments in order that the glass ball (*a*), which is loose inside the bulb, may mix the blood with the salt solution, and make the fluid homogeneous. As the division 0·5 corresponds exactly to $\frac{1}{200}$ of the total capacity of the bulb, and the figure 1 exactly to $\frac{1}{100}$, we know that the mixture obtained is in the ratio of 1:200 or 1:100.

The counting is done upon a carrier (II) of thick glass with a groove (*b*), the bottom of which is divided by lines cut with a diamond into 400 minute squares (as is shown in III). Into this groove, the capacity of which is 0·1 c.mm., a drop of the blood solution contained in the bulb of the pipette is introduced, care being taken to drive out the liquid contained in the capillary portion, which has not been mixed with the blood. When the drop is placed in the groove, a cover glass (*a*) is quickly applied, and after letting the preparation rest for a few minutes upon a perfectly horizontal surface, in order that the red corpuscles may be spread evenly upon the floor of the groove, the counting is undertaken under a magnification of 200

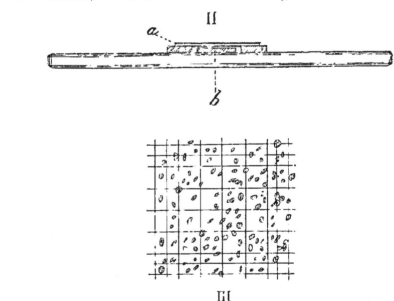

Fig. 30.—Thoma-Zeiss Haemacytometer. I, Graduated pipette (Potain's mixer); II, cell for counting corpuscles, side view; III, squared divisions of bottom of haemacytometer.

diameters. The number of the corpuscles counted is divided by the number of squares examined, which should never be less than 200; thus obtaining the average of the red corpuscles contained in each square, which represents $\frac{1}{4000}$ c.mm. Hence, if we wish to know the number of corpuscles in c.mm. it is only necessary to multiply the number found first by 4000, and then by 100 or 200, according as the blood has been diluted 100 or 200 times. To take a practical example:— If 1225 corpuscles are counted in 250 squares, and the blood has been diluted 200 times, 1 c.mm. of blood will contain $\frac{1225}{250} \times 4000 \times 200 = 3,920,000$ red corpuscles.

The white blood-corpuscles can be counted at the same time; but if a separate enumeration is desired for the sake of accuracy, the blood must be agitated with a 0·3 per cent solution of acetic acid, in which the red corpuscles will dissolve while the white remain intact.

Hedin's *Haematocrit* is an apparatus for determining the total volume of red corpuscles in 100 parts of blood. It consists of a small centrifuge (Fig. 25, p. 98) and of two graduated tubes (*a*, *a'*, Fig. 31). The determination is carried out as follows: A small quantity of Müller's fluid (sodium sulphate 1 grm., bichromate of potash 2 grms., distilled water 100 grms.) is taken up with a pipette, and dropped into a small porcelain dish. The finger is then pricked with a lancet so as to obtain a large drop of blood. With the same pipette a quantity of blood equal to the quantity of Müller's fluid is taken up, and emptied into the same dish. The two fluids are then thoroughly mixed with a glass rod, with the double object of retarding the coagulation of the blood (the mixture will not clot under half an hour) and of fixing the red corpuscles in their natural size. The graduated tube is then filled with the mixture thus obtained, by taking up the fluid from the dish directly into the tube,

Fig. 31.—Hedin's Haematocrit—substitute for test-tube holder of Fig. 25, p. 98. *a*, *a'*, Graduated tubes, kept in the hollows prepared for them by the presence of two elastic springs; *b*, *b'*, small metal rods that compress the spirals in loosening or tightening the tubes.

which has previously been fitted with a rubber tube furnished with a mouth-piece. The tubes have a calibre of 1 sq. mm., and are divided into 50 parts. The filled tubes are then fixed to a horizontal holder (shown in Fig. 30), which replaces the test-tube holders, *pp*, of the centrifuge (Fig. 25), care being taken not to lose any of the fluid. They are now centrifuged for five to seven minutes with a velocity of 80 turns per minute of the handle of the apparatus, which corresponds to 8000 revolutions of the tubes, until the red corpuscles separate out into a compact and well-marked column, the volume of which will not shrink further. Since the tubes have very thick walls, and the graduation is cut on the surface, errors may occur in the reading which are due to the different positions of the reading eye. The inventor of the apparatus has calculated this error as equal to 0·2 degree of the scale, and to avoid it suggests that the reading be carried out by looking along a glass plate held at right angles to the tube. From the volume found, the volume of corpuscles in 100 parts of blood can be determined by multiplying the volume of the column of blood-corpuscles by 4. As two determinations of the volume of the erythrocytes are made at the same time, these form a reciprocal control.

Since the total volume of the mass of corpuscles is proportional to the relative number of the erythrocytes, this method can be substituted for that of Thoma-Zeiss, which takes much longer to carry out.

Many series of determinations on the relative mass of corpuscles have been worked out, on man as well as animals, in order to ascertain the variations due to age, sex, constitution, functional state of the body, various morbid conditions of the blood, and so on. As an average it may be taken that 1 c.mm. contains 5,000,000 red corpuscles in a man, 4,500,000 in a woman: that they are more abundant in venous than in arterial blood; less abundant in adolescents than in adults, more numerous in new-born infants than in the mother; that all the influences that induce a marked loss of water in the body increase their number, while a high intake of water diminishes them; that they multiply with every improvement in the external and internal conditions of life, while poor food and a vast number of morbid conditions tend to reduce them.

It is remarkable that the lowering of atmospheric pressure on high mountains produces a considerable increase in the number of erythrocytes (Viault). The same effect has been observed in mice on rubbing their skin with croton oil, and on prolonged exposure to strong electric light (Kronecker). It should also be noted that not merely scanty nutrition, but even an absolute fast of thirty days, produces no marked variation in the number of the erythrocytes (Luciani). Obviously the relative quantity of corpuscles, which depends upon the degree of concentration and amount of water contained in the blood, can rarely yield a safe conclusion as to the absolute quantity to be found in the total mass of blood.

The volume and surface of the erythrocytes have been approximately determined, by using models of enormous magnification; 5,000,000 corpuscles are found to have a volume of about $\frac{1}{3}$ c.mm. and a surface of 610 sq. mm.

The specific gravity of erythrocytes is, as already stated, greater than that of plasma and serum (1·088-1·105). The weight of the corpuscles contained in 100 grms. of defibrinated blood is not far short of that of the serum, averaging a weight of 48 grms. in man and 35 grms. in woman. Given a man of 78 kilograms, whose blood amounts to $\frac{1}{13}$ of his body-weight, the total weight of the erythrocytes would be about 2 kgrm., with a total surface of some 3840 sq. metres.

VII. The pigment which colours the erythrocytes is a compound of highly complex chemical structure, known as *Haemoglobin*. Under physiological conditions it is entirely absent from the plasma, and exclusively saturates the colourless spongy mass of the corpuscle, termed by Rollet the *stroma*. This fact suggests that it may be in chemical combination with one of the constituents of the stroma, perhaps with the lecithin (Hoppe-Seyler). But the most certain and most important property of the pigment, and that on which the capital function of the erythrocytes depends, is its affinity for oxygen, with which it combines as soon as the partial pressure of the gas reaches a certain value, forming oxyhaemoglobin, which with a fall of the partial pressure is again reduced to haemoglobin. It prevails in the form of oxyhaemoglobin in arterial, as haemoglobin and oxyhaemoglobin in venous, exclusively as haemoglobin in asphyxial blood.

There are many physical and chemical means by which the pigment is easily separated from the stroma of the corpuscles and dissolved in the plasma. Among the physical methods are warming of the blood to 50-60 C., repeated freezing and thawing, the discharges of a Leyden jar, induced or galvanic currents; among the chemical methods, simple dilution with water, addition of ether, chloroform, dilute alcohol, acid or alkaline solutions, bile, heterogeneous serum, etc. By using sodium chloride solutions of various concentrations, different degrees of diffusibility of pigment can be detected in different corpuscles and different individuals.

According to Winter's researches (1896), the isotonic solution, *i.e.* that which has the same degree of molecular concentration as the corpuscles (and therefore produces no disturbance of osmotic relations and no diffusion of haemoglobin in the plasma), is represented by a solution of about 0·91 per cent NaCl in distilled water.

In proportion as the pigment separates out from the stroma, the corpuscles grow pale, and finally change into roundish, colourless, almost transparent bodies which have been termed ghosts (*Blutschatten*), because they are almost invisible. They stain brown with iodine and can thus be detected.

In order to study the chemical composition of the stroma of the erythrocytes a large mass of blood corpuscles must be collected, separated from the plasma, washed with dilute solution of sodium chloride, and completely freed from haemoglobin by the addition of 5-6 volumes of distilled water. By this treatment all is removed save the stroma, which forms a gelatinous mass and can be separated by filtration from the watery solution.

The small amount of matter remaining on the filter dissolves in dilute salt solution, and gives all the reactions of globulin. But the stromata separated from the erythrocytes of birds contain, in addition to globulin, a considerable quantity of nuclein, derived from the nuclei of these corpuscles (Plosz, Hoppe-Seyler). Kossel, with dilute hydrochloric acid, also extracted a substance belonging to the albumose group, to which he gave the name of histone

If further chemical researches prove that the erythrocytes of mammals contain no nuclein, this would be an additional proof that they really are non-nucleated, which has been denied by some observers.

An ethereal extract of a mass of stromata yields the other organic components of protoplasm, *lecithin* and *cholesterin*.

The inorganic substances of the stroma consist of potassium

phosphate and potassium chloride; in man, and a few other animals only, there is also a small amount of sodium chloride.

The water content of the erythrocytes is very low as compared with other organs. In man it reaches only 57·7 per cent, while in the muscles and glands it amounts to 75 per cent (Hoppe-Seyler).

The dry substance of the erythrocytes consists principally of haemoglobin (87-95 per cent), so that the stroma is a very small amount (13·5 per cent). For the total quantity of the blood, about 13·8 per cent haemoglobin has been calculated for man, and about 12·6 per cent for woman.

Hoppe - Seyler was the first to investigate the chemical properties of haemoglobin (1866-71) and to recognise that although it is a colloid body, it is capable of crystallising in different forms in different animals, all, however, belonging to the rhombic system (with the exception of squirrel's blood, which crystallises in hexagonal plates: Fig. 32). To obtain crystals of pure haemoglobin, they must first be dissolved in the blood by freezing and gradual melting; the blood in a layer 2 mm. deep is then allowed to evaporate slowly in a flat, wide-bottomed capsule.

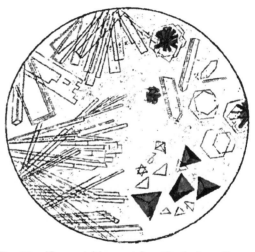

Fig. 32.—Haemoglobin crystals. (Funke.) *a*, From man; *b*, guinea-pig; *c*, squirrel.

The different forms of oxyhaemoglobin crystals, the different quantities of water of crystallisation which they contain, their different solubilities and different resistance to decomposing agents, in short the varying results of elementary analysis, all point to the conclusion that oxyhaemoglobin is not identical in different animals. It is a highly complex, iron-containing protein, the formula of which was determined by Hüfner from analysis of the haemoglobin of dogs' blood. Each molecule of haemoglobin combines with a molecule of oxygen to form oxyhaemoglobin.

Haemoglobin has a greater affinity for carbonic oxide than for oxygen, and forms with it *carboxyhaemoglobin*, which, unlike oxyhaemoglobin, does not reduce with deoxidising agents. While carbonic oxide turns out oxygen, the latter has difficulty in driving carbonic oxide out of its combination with haemoglobin. To this fact is due (in part, if not wholly) the toxic action of carbon monoxide.

With a series of oxidising agents, particularly with nitrites, permanganate of potash, potassium ferricyanide, active oxygen, hydrogen peroxide, etc., haemoglobin is converted into *methaemoglobin*, which is an isomer of oxyhaemoglobin, but in which the oxygen is more closely combined, so that it cannot be driven out by the unaided vacuum. Methaemoglobin can also be formed in circulating blood by the excessive use of chlorate of potash and other substances used in medicine in recent years as antipyretics.

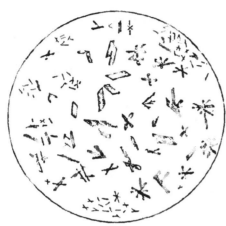

FIG. 33.—Haemin crystals. (Preyer.)

Haemoglobin undergoes spontaneous decomposition slowly under the influence of air and water, rapidly as the effect of acids or alkalies, or of heating. Another iron-containing pigment is thus formed, *haemochromogen*, which oxidises readily in the presence of oxygen and is converted into *haematin*, which gives a brownish colour to the solution. Along with haemochromogen and haematin, the decomposition of haemoglobin gives rise to considerable quantities of acid or alkali albumin, according as acids or alkalies are used to break up the blood pigment. From these facts Hoppe-Seyler regards haemoglobin as a protein, which consists of an albumin, associated with an iron-containing pigment, haemochromogen. One hundred parts of haemoglobin contain ninety-six parts albumin and four parts pigment. *Haemin* must be noted among the decomposition products of blood pigment on account of its great practical importance ; it crystallises in the form of small rhombic plates or rods, of a shining brown colour (Fig. 33). Haemin crystals are of great importance in forensic medicine, in the detection of blood-stains. A trace of dried

FIG. 34.—Haematoidin crystals. (V. Frey.)

blood suffices to obtain them. A grain of sodium chloride is added, dissolved in a few drops of glacial acetic acid, and cautiously heated over a spirit lamp until gas bubbles are formed.

Haemin is haematin hydrochloride, and to obtain pure haematin it is necessary to start from this combination. It is a sulphur-free compound, but is richer in iron than haemoglobin. When treated with sulphuric acid, the haematin loses its iron and takes up water, turning into *haematoporphyrin*, an iron-free pigment somewhat resembling haemoglobin in colour.

Another iron-free derivative of haemoglobin, which forms spontaneously in a crystalline form in the corpora lutea and in old haemorrhagic foci, is *haematoidin* (Virchow), now regarded by chemists as identical with *bilirubin*, one of the principal bile-pigments (Fig. 34).

It seems clear that all the colouring matters of bile and urine are derived from successive transformations of blood pigment; but with the exception of bilirubin, which forms spontaneously, only one of the urinary pigments, *urobilin*, has at present been produced artificially from haemoglobin or haematin.

Many of the pigment substances above recorded, haemoglobin, oxyhaemoglobin, carboxyhaemoglobin, methaemoglobin, haemochromogen, haematin, haematoporphyrin, urobilin, possess the important property, when examined in layers of known thickness and concentration, of absorbing well-determined and distinct zones of the spectrum in aqueous solutions, acid or alkaline, as shown in Fig. 35. It is important to note that while haemoglobin shows a single absorption band between the Fraunhofer D- and E-lines, oxyhaemoglobin and carboxyhaemoglobin show two bands that almost coincide in the two cases, lying practically within the same region of the spectrum. Apart from the different tint exhibited by oxy- and carboxyhaemoglobin, the former being the pinker, they can, however, readily be distinguished by adding a reducing substance, *e.g.* carbon disulphide, to the two solutions, when the spectrum of oxyhaemoglobin is speedily transformed into that of haemoglobin, while the spectrum of carboxyhaemoglobin undergoes no modification.

To determine the relative quantity of haemoglobin contained in a given quantity of blood, several instruments have been adopted. The simplest and most convenient Haemoglobinometer is Gowers' apparatus, provided with a standard solution of CO-haemoglobin. The method, as accurately described by Haldane,[1] gives extremely good results.

For more accurate quantitative determination, either of the haemoglobin or of the pigments derived from it, the Spectro-Photometric Method must be employed.

This method is based on the law that the coefficient of extinction of any coloured solution is (for any given zone of the spectrum) directly proportional to its concentration, *i.e.* $C : E = C'' : E'$, when C and C' indicate the corresponding coefficient of extinction. By coefficient of extinction of a fluid is meant the negative logarithm of that intensity of light which remains after it has traversed a liquid stratum of the depth of 1 c.c. (Krüss, *Kolorimetrie u. quantit. Spectralanalyse*, 1891).

From the above equation it follows that $\dfrac{HC}{E} = \dfrac{V'}{E}$; this ratio, known as that of absorption, is a constant for the same colouring substance. Now, if

---

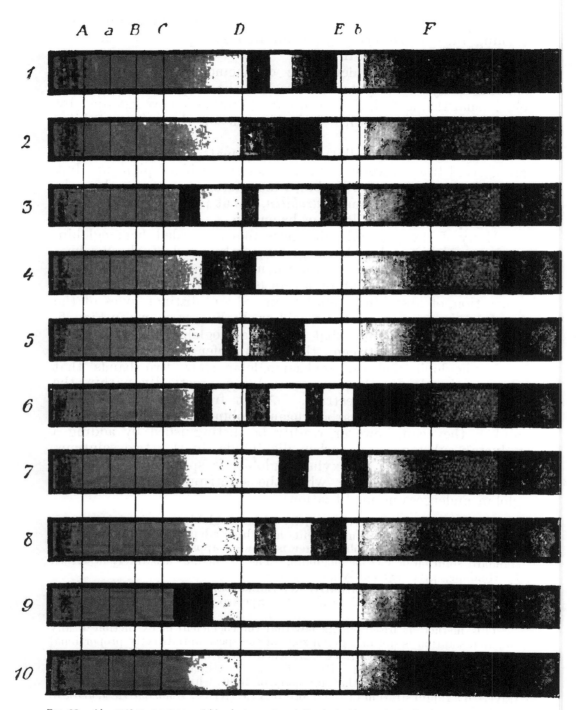

Fig. 35.—Absorption-spectrum of blood-pigment and its derivatives. 1, Oxyhaemoglobin; 2, haemoglobin; 3, methaemoglobin and haematin in acid solution; 4, haematin in alkaline solution; 5, haematoporphyrin

the absorption ratio be represented by A, the coefficient of extinction by E, and the content of colouring matter in 1 c.c. (calculated in grams) by C, it follows that C will be equal to A × E.

The most exact of the various instruments constructed for the determination of coefficients of extinction is that of Krüss. This (as shown by Fig. 36) resembles an ordinary spectroscope and differs from the spectro-photometers of Vierordt, Hüfner and others, in that the two slits *f f'* (Fig. 38) which give the two spectra, one above the other, enlarge and contract in both directions with a single movement of the screws V and V'.

To use this apparatus, fill a small pipette of capillary bore with blood to a

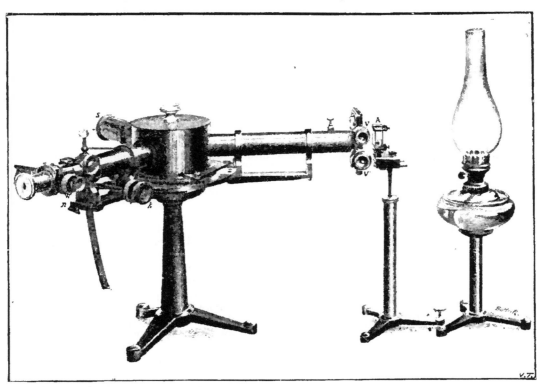

Fig. 36.—Spectro-photometer of Krüss viewed as a whole. The extreme end of the eye-piece is shown in Fig. 37. The extreme end of the objective is shown in detail in Fig. 38. The lettering corresponds. The absorption-chamber containing the solution of the pigment to be examined is shown in Fig. 39. The third branch *s*, illuminated by a gas flame, projects the millimetre scale on to the spectrum.

given capacity, say 20 c.mm. This blood must be rapidly expelled into a small beaker in which a measured quantity of distilled water has first been placed, so that the blood is diluted in known measure. The degree of dilution varies with the greater or less colouring power of the blood to be tested, but as a rule the ratio of 1-200 is preferred. The pipette which held the blood should be washed out several times with the water used for dilution, and the liquid must be agitated till it is homogeneous in colour. The absorption chamber (Fig. 39), which is a crystal cell with parallel faces, is then filled, and a cube of glass, D, of the exact diameter of 1 cm., introduced, to which the name of Schultz' cube is given. The two absorption spectra are those of two strata of the same fluid differing by 1 cm. in depth.

The extinction coefficients for human oxyhaemoglobin have been determined in two different regions of the spectrum, *i.e.*

$$D\ 32\ E - D\ 54\ E\ \text{and}\ D\ 63\ E - D\ 24\ E:$$

in which Hufner has determined the absorption ratios or constants for, viz.:
0,001330 and 0,001000 respectively.

The limits of these spectral positions, which are comprised between the
Fraunhofer D- and E-lines, may be expressed in wave-lengths by means

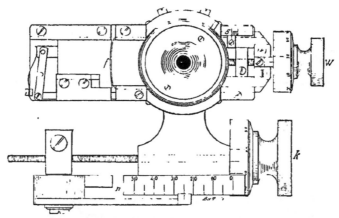

Fig. 37. *W*, Micrometer screw, divided into hundredths, each turn of which displaces the index of
the scale *S* by one division. This serves to regulate and measure the width of the slit *f*, which
can be carried by a horizontal movement to the centre of the eye-piece. *k*, Micrometer screw
divided into hundredths, each turn of which displaces the index of a scale *n* by one division.
This moves the eye-piece by an angular development to carry it to any given region of the
spectrum.

of the table published by Krüss (as above cited). In practice they can be
obtained by finding on the illuminated scale of the spectrum (Fig. 36, *s*)
the values corresponding to the two wave-lengths calculated, and limiting

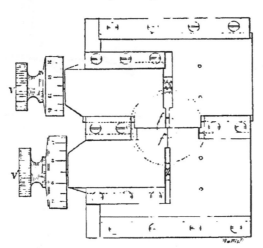

Fig. 38. — *I'*, *I"*, Micrometer screw divided into
hundredths, serves to widen or narrow the slit *f, f'*,
by simultaneous displacement of the two plates
that confine it.

the spectral region which these
comprise by the horizontal screw
of the telescope (Fig. 37), and that
marked W, which controls the
slit *f* of the eye-piece. The absorption chamber A is then placed
on its support between the plane
of the spectrum and the source of
light, taking care that the upper
surface of the cube D corresponds
exactly with the line of division
between the first and second slit,
and that the aperture of these
corresponds to a complete turn of
the screw: a turn divided into
100 parts, as shown on the scale
affixed to the screws *v* and *v'* in
Fig. 38.

On then looking through the
instrument, two positions of the
spectrum will be visible, one below
the other: one is brighter, corresponding to the cube of Schultz,
the other obscured by the absorption due to the solution of oxyhaemoglobin.

The slit corresponding to the brighter part of the spectrum is then
narrowed until it assumes the same tone of light as the other, and the
scale on the screw read to show how many turns were required to produce
uniform obscurity. From this number, which indicates the intensity of the

light remaining after the luminous rays have traversed the colouring matter of the blood, the negative logarithm that represents the extinction co-efficient can be calculated, and this must be multiplied first by the constant of the spectral tone obtained, and then by the degree of dilution of the blood. Thus it is calculated how many grams of haemoglobin are contained in 1 c.c. of blood.

Practical Example.—Let the blood under examination have been diluted 200 times, and the first spectral region be that in which the constant is 0·001330, the intensity of the remaining light will be found to be 0·255 ; to calculate the amount of oxyhaemoglobin contained in 1 c.c. of the blood, multiply 0·001330 by 200, and then by the negative logarithm of 0·255, i.e. by 0·5935. In this case the oxyhaemoglobin of 1 c.c. of blood will be equal to 0·1578 grm.

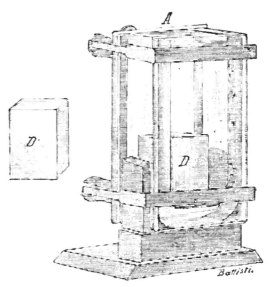

FIG. 29.   A, Absorption-chamber with parallel faces : D, Schultz' cube, made of glass 1 c.c. in depth, introduced into the chamber.

VIII. The White Blood Corpuscles or Leucocytes are true and complete cells, consisting of naked granular protoplasm, with one or more nuclei, which are not easy to dis-

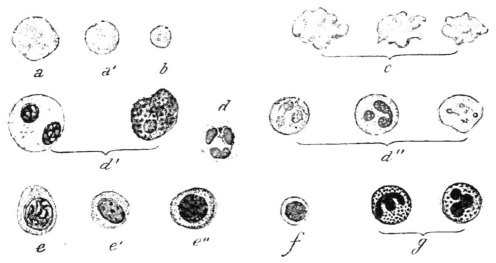

FIG. 40.—Different kinds of human leucocytes examined either in the fresh state, or after fixation with various reagents, magnification about 1000 diameters (partly from Kanthack and Hardy). a, a', b, Fresh leucocytes of three different sizes, in the resting state ; c, the same in amoeboid state ; d, polynuclear acidophile leucocytes with large (d') and fine (d'') granulation ; e, e', e'', hyaline leucocytes, destitute of granules ; f, lymphocytes ; g, leucocytes with basophile granulation.

tinguish in the fresh state, but may become very conspicuous on adding a drop of acetic acid to the microscopic preparation.

The varying character of the protoplasm and nucleus make it possible to distinguish several kinds of leucocytes. From their size, and probably from their various grades of development, Schultze recognised three varieties; the smallest attain at most a diameter of $5\,\mu$ and possess a large nucleus, the medium have an average of $7\,\mu$, the largest of $9\,\mu$; the latter are often multinuclear and of irregular external shape. In the foetus of less than four months there are still larger ones which may reach $15\text{-}19\,\mu$ (Fig. 40).

According to a more rational classification proposed by Ehrlich and Engel, leucocytes are divided into two classes: those with and those without granules. The leucocytes with granules are distinguished as mononuclear and polynuclear, and by their staining affinity, as acidophile, neutrophile, and basophile.

Mononuclear leucocytes with granules are extremely rare, or entirely absent, in normal circulating blood; according to many authors they represent the transition forms to polynuclear correspondents. Polynuclear neutrophile leucocytes constitute the greater part of the white corpuscles (from $\frac{2}{3}$ to $\frac{3}{4}$); they have a diameter of $9\text{-}10\,\mu$, exhibit lively amoeboid movements, and perform the function of phagocytosis. Polynuclear leucocytes with fine or coarse acidophile granulations are very scarce (from 2 per cent to 4 per cent). Still rarer in the circulating blood are those with basophile granulations (0·5 per cent); they are found almost exclusively in the tissues of the haematopoietic organs.

The non-granular leucocytes are distinguished as lymphocytes, large lymphocytes, large mononuclear cells and inflammatory forms. The lymphocytes are the size of normal erythrocytes, with a reticular nucleus which occupies nearly the whole cell. They represent about $\frac{1}{4}$ the total number of white corpuscles: their number varies not merely in certain physiological conditions, as for instance in digestion, but also in pathological states.

The large lymphocytes, large mononuclear cells, and inflammatory forms have precisely similar characters to the preceding: they are differentiated by the volume of their protoplasm. These cells are comparatively rare in normal blood, and are more interesting to the pathologist than to the physiologist.

Many clinical, anatomical, and experimental researches have been directed to the object of establishing the relations existing in last resort between the lymphocytes and the granular leucocytes with polymorphous nuclei, as well as the general relations between the various white morphological elements of the blood. Here we must only say that while Ehrlich's theory admits a sharp distinction between the cells derived from the lymphatic system and those derived from bone-marrow, there is another opposing theory, according to which the lymphocytes are the young cells which give rise to all other elements of the blood (Ouskoff).

Notwithstanding these different theories and conflicting arguments, Ehrlich's view is that generally supported.

In the circulating blood the white corpuscles are almost always round, and since their specific gravity is somewhat lower than that of the erythrocytes, they leave the more rapid axial current of the vessels and follow the slower peripheral stream, keeping in perpetual contact with the internal walls of the vessels and constantly rotating along them (cycloid movement). When observed in an isolated drop of blood, the object-carrier of the microscope being warmed to 35-40° C., it is easy to recognise their mobility, which exactly resembles that of the *Amoeba*, so that Lierberkühn (1854), who was the first to study and describe them exactly, regarded leucocytes as peculiar parasitic amoebae. It is more interesting to watch the amoeboid movements of the leucocytes within the blood-stream. Cohnheim (1869) was the first to demonstrate the fact that leucocytes, by their amoeboid properties, are capable of perforating the internal walls of the smallest veins by a pseudopodium and of passing their whole body, little by little, through the temporary wound thus formed, as through a mesh, emigrating in this way from the blood torrent into the interstices or plasma canals of the tissues. This emigration may become tumultuous in tissues that have suffered inflammatory irritation (natural or experimental). The pathological doctrine of suppuration and formation of abscesses is definitely co-ordinated with this fact. The more recent researches of Thomas, Recklinghausen and others have demonstrated that corpuscular diapedesis must be regarded not as a passive extravasation, but as an active emigration due (as was Cohnheim's original idea) to the amoeboid mobility of the leucocytes.

The discovery of *Phagocytosis*, founded more particularly on the elegant researches of Metschnikoff (1892), added new and interesting arguments for the close approximation between leucocytes and amoebae. Even when removed from the blood, and observed with the microscope, leucocytes, like amoebae, are seen to be capable of ingesting many foreign bodies, by surrounding them with protoplasm, whether these are inorganic particles (such as carmine granules and other colouring matters), fat drops, dead cells or fragments of cells, or living cells and microbes (*e.g.* erythrocytes and bacteria) of various pathogenic or non-pathogenic species.

Leucocytes, like amoebae, are capable of digesting dead bodies, and of chemically killing and dissolving the living cells and microbes which they have ingested. The red corpuscles thus dissolve slowly in the interior of the phagocytes (large leucocytes), leaving a residue of pigment. They exercise a similar dissolving action upon pus granules (dead or dying leucocytes), on the fibrin of inflammatory exudates, and on muscle fibres in cases of acute atrophy of the muscular tissue. Lastly, the phenomenon of the digestion of the microbes englobed by leucocytes (anthrax bacilli, spirilli of recurrent fever, vibrios of septicaemia, streptococci of erysipelas) have been directly observed in various phases. These facts are much in favour of Metchnikoff's view that the protoplasm of leucocytes contains enzymes which are more active than the secretions of the digestive glands of higher animals (pepsin and trypsin), since the latter fail to kill the same microbes.

According to Leber, Massart, Bordet and other observers, the migratory and phagocytic faculties of the white corpuscles are phenomena of *chemotaxis* (*i.e.* the property of being attracted or repelled by certain chemical compounds, even at a distance). It is a fact that leucocytes do not devour all the species of microbes which they encounter in their wanderings, but are capable (at least up to a certain point) of selecting the prey on which they feed. In the body the physiological function of the leucocytes depends essentially, as we shall see below, upon their phagocytic capacity.

The number of leucocytes varies conspicuously, even under physiological conditions. This may partially at least—be explained by the fact that they are continually (in different degrees, according to the functional state of the viscera) emigrating from the lymphatic system, in which they originate, to the vascular system, and thence again by diapedesis into the lymphatic system.

The method for counting leucocytes is fundamentally the same as for the enumeration of erythrocytes. In normal blood their number is much lower than that of the erythrocytes. According to Grancher, there are in healthy young people of twenty to thirty, 3000 to 9000 leucocytes in 1 c.mm. at different hours of the day. The ordinary ratio between these and the erythrocytes would be from 1:1200 to 1:1500, but it may increase to a maximum of 1:900. According to Malassez, on the other hand, there are 4000-7000 leucocytes per c.mm. in healthy persons; and the ratio with the erythrocytes is from 1:1250 to 1:1650. It must always be remembered that the number of leucocytes varies according to the vascular region from which the blood is drawn, and with age, season, state of nutrition, in menstruation, pregnancy, etc. Disease has the greatest influence on the number of leucocytes; during suppuration, but especially in certain morbid states (leucaemia), their numbers may be enormously increased, and their ratio with the red corpuscles may rise to 1:15 or even higher. On the other hand, it should be noted that the opposite occurs during the first week of an absolute fast, when there is marked and progressive diminution of the leucocytes (Luciani).

It has not hitherto been found possible to examine the chemical composition of the leucocytes of the blood, owing to the difficulty of separating them from the plasma without admixture of other elements. The first observations on this subject were based on the researches, first of Miescher and subsequently of Hoppe-Seyler, on the composition of *pus*. Pus cells, however, are essentially composed of extravasated leucocytes which have lost their vitality in great measure, or are on the way to dissolution. They cannot, therefore, have the same chemical composition as young and normal leucocytes.

Lilienfeld has recently studied the chemical composition of the leucocytes of the lymph (lymphocytes)—which are richly distributed in the reticulum of the lymphatic glands—with interesting results.

When a considerable quantity of lymph nodules previously freed from fat and blood-vessels is put under pressure, a turbid juice is yielded containing many well-preserved leucocytes, which can be separated from the liquid by centrifuging. These readily dissolve in water, and it is possible with magnesium sulphate to obtain two globulins from the filtrate of the watery extract, one of which coagulates at 73-75° C., the other, on the contrary, at 48° C. If dilute acetic acid be added to the filtrate of the watery extract, a phosphorus-containing substance belonging to the group of nucleo-proteins, which Lilienfeld terms nucleo-histone, is precipitated, and this is the principal constituent of the nucleus, not only in leucocytes, but in other cells also.

Nucleo-histone (which can be obtained pure, in the form of a white powder, soluble in water) breaks up, on treatment with baryta, or with dilute hydrochloric acid, or boiling water, into its two component groups: a nuclein, which Lilienfeld calls leuco-nuclein, and an albumose, which, as we have seen, was in the first instance extracted by Kossel from the nuclei of birds' erythrocytes, and which he called histone.

On making an alcoholic extract from the mass of leucocytes (obtained as above) it is found to contain protagon, lecithin, cholesterin, inosit, and potassium phosphate. Fat is exhibited by an ethereal extract.

Besides these substances, leucocytes contain a small, constant amount of glycogen (Hoppe-Seyler).

According to Lilienfeld, the quantitative per cent composition of leucocytes is as follows :—

Protein substances	1·76
Leuconuclein	68·78
Histone	8·67
Lecithin	7·51
Fat	4·02
Cholesterin	4·40
Glycogen	0·80
Nuclein bases (weighed as silver compounds)	15·17

IX. The Blood-Platelets, which Bizzozero (1880) regarded as the third formed element of the blood, had been previously described by Hayem under the name of haematoblasts, because they were erroneously considered to be the precursors, or early stages of development, of the erythrocytes (Fig. 41). They are in the form of circular flat discs and consist of a finely granulated, highly refrangible substance, colourless (hence entirely destitute of haemoglobin), and staining fairly intensely with aniline dyes. They are two to three times smaller than the erythrocytes 2-3 μ: see

Fig. 41). Their number varies from 200,000 to 500,000 per c.mm. The numerical relation of the leucocytes to the platelets is about 1:40, and of the platelets to the erythrocytes about 1:25. Their surface is highly viscous, and in stagnant blood they agglutin-

FIG. 41. Blood-platelets viewed from the surface and laterally : highly magnified. In the centre is an erythrocyte for comparison of size.

ate, forming granulated heaps which readily break up and dissolve in the plasma.

Löwit is of opinion that the platelets are formed by disintegration of the leucocytes, and are not pre-existent in the blood before it is extracted from the vessels. Bizzozero, however, proved that they can easily be seen in the mesenteric vessels of guinea-pigs, and in the wings of bats, on retarding the circulation. Osler, in investigating the mesentery of the mouse (Fig. 42), confirmed this observation. But the fact that they are found in living, circulating blood does not seem a sufficient argument for regarding them as distinct morphological and physiological individuals. Lilienfeld's later researches proved that the platelets contain nuclein in the form of nucleo-albumin, the micro-chemical reactions of which are similar to those of the nuclei of the leucocytes. It seems not improbable that they are derived from the latter, owing to disintegration of

FIG. 42. — Erythrocytes and blood-platelets in small mesenteric vein of mouse. (Osler.)

cellular protoplasm. Besides blood-platelets, the older observers detected granules and irregular protoplasmic fragments of various dimensions (and quite distinct from the fat drops that dissolve in ether) in the blood, which evidently originate in the disintegration of the protoplasm of the lymphatic cells or leucocytes; on this they founded the hypothesis that the platelets too are derived from the disintegration of leucocytes.

In accordance with this theory, Fano has demonstrated that there are scarcely any platelets in dog's lymph. Probably this is due to the fact that the younger lymphatic cells predominate in lymph, and that their protoplasm disintegrates less readily. It should also be added that blood-platelets of characteristic form do not exist in blood that has been whipped and defibrinated, and that they disappear from the blood of dogs that have been repeatedly bled, with subsequent infusions of the same blood after it has been defibrinated. In such animals nothing otherwise abnormal can be detected, and the blood-platelets gradually reappear, and are present in their usual number after a few days (Gad). On the theory that the platelets originate in the decomposition of leucocytes, the explanation of these facts may be that the young leucocytes, supplied to the blood by the lymphatic system, require a certain time to develop, become adult, grow old, and disintegrate, when their nuclei give rise to the formation of new platelets.

On the other hand, not a few of the recent workers in this field incline from many standpoints to the view that the platelets originate from the red corpuscles.

Köppe, Hirschfeld, and Pappenheim observed that a certain number of erythrocytes are spherical in form, without depressions, within which are masses that stain pink with tri-acid, and faint turquoise with methylene blue, and which when isolated differ in no respect from blood-platelets; while blood-platelets can often be distinguished among the erythrocytes. Other observers hold that the erythrocyte consists of two parts—a central, and a peripheral stratum. The peripheral layer contains the haemoglobin (Foa): beneath this lies the true protoplasm.

It must also be remembered that according to Engel, every non-nucleated blood-corpuscle has at one time or other been one of those nucleated corpuscles of which the mantle contains haemoglobin and is aurantiophile, its chromatin consisting of nuclein, and its achromatic acidophile substance containing protein. When, under normal conditions, the nuclei of the red nucleated corpuscles apparently disappear in kariolysis, the nuclei lose their shape, but the chemical substances of which they are composed persist under other forms. One form of these nuclear rests is the basophile granulation of the erythrocytes (see below); the other, more common, form is represented by the almost amorphous blood platelets. On this theory it may be said that every red corpuscle of the depressed form has already lost its platelets, while erythrocytes from which the platelets are on the point of issuing, or in which they are still confined within the corpuscle, are the more nearly spherical.

This mode of origin of the blood-platelets would account for the appearance they sometimes present of escaping, even where detachment is not complete. The body thus detached may, even if rarely, resemble a nucleus surrounded by protoplasm.

Foa has recently (on repeating with modern methods of fixing and staining the experiments he made in 1889, in collaboration with Carbone) confirmed the existence of platelets in the spleen which are identical with those circulating in the blood; these, he maintains, are not simply deposited there, but originate *in situ*. According to Foa the platelets are autonomous elements, and since they are composed of protoplasm and nuclear substance, are real cells *sui generis*, capable of multiplying by direct division in the circulating blood.

In view of the importance assigned to the platelets in respect of blood coagulation, we shall return to them after considering the chemical constitution of blood plasma.

The microscopic examination of the blood can be made with fresh or fixed preparations. It is essential to use slides and cover-glasses that have been scrupulously cleaned (first in alcohol containing HCl, and then in ordinary alcohol) and well dried with a linen cloth. The blood required is obtained by pricking the ball of the finger or lobe of the ear with a needle (better, a lancet), so that the blood wells out in drops without employing compression. In order to examine fresh preparations microscopically, it is only necessary to take up a drop of blood on the cover-glass and lay this on the slide with the drop downwards. If the glasses are clean, the blood spreads uniformly between them, and the preparation only needs a gentle tap on the cover-glass to distribute the morphological elements in an even layer and make it ready for observation.

In order to keep the formed constituents of the blood alive for prolonged observation, a drop of blood must be gently compressed between two cover-glasses, which are then separated by drawing one across the other. One of these films is laid over the central depression of a special slide, such as is used for the observation of bacteria in hanging drops. The margin of this depression is previously filled with vaseline to prevent the intrusion of air, which would cause the preparation to dry up—making a minute moist chamber. The preparation is then placed on Schultze's warm carrier and kept at the required temperature.

The fixing of the blood for microscopic study is performed in two different ways, by the wet or the dry method. To fix it by the wet method the blood is collected in a watch-glass and the various fixing solutions added. Such are solutions of osmic acid, corrosive sublimate, palladium chloride, Kleinenberg's picro-sulphuric acid, Flemming's osmic-chrom-acetic mixture, etc. When completely fixed, the solution is removed, and the preparation can be examined immediately or after staining. Fixing by the dry method is effected by warming the film preparation. It must be dried in the air, and then passed 6-10 times through the flame of a spirit lamp, care being taken not to scorch it; or it may be laid for about an hour on a copper plate, warmed to 120. Fixation is also effected by placing the air-dried blood film for an hour in a mixture of equal parts of absolute alcohol and ether.

Excellent results are obtained by warming, and then dipping into alcohol and ether.

Staining is necessary in studying the detailed structure of the formed elements of the blood. To stain fresh preparations, weak solutions of iodine, methyl-violet, methylene-blue, eosin, etc., must be used. For staining dry preparations, countless methods are described in special text-books, but we must here confine ourselves to the most ordinary, which are also the most practical for the doctor. The film-preparations are passed 6-10 times through the flame of a lamp, and then placed for about half-an-hour in equal parts of absolute alcohol and ether. They are then dried again in the air, and stained in a watch-glass with Ehrlich's acid haematoxylin (haematoxylin 2 grms., absolute alcohol 60 grms.). To this first solution is added the following mixture, which has previously been saturated with alum : glycerin 60 grms., distilled water 60 grms., acetic acid 3 grms. In 5-10 minutes the cover-glasses are taken out of the haematoxylin, washed in water, and stained for the second time by dipping them for a few moments into a 1 per cent solution of eosin. They are then washed again in distilled water, wiped at the edges with filter-paper, dried over the flame, and mounted on the slide with a drop of Canada balsam dissolved in xylol.

The nuclei and blood-platelets stain blue with the haematoxylin, the protoplasm pink with the eosin.

A copious literature has recently sprung up in regard to *osmotic phenomena*, and the resistance of the erythrocytes to yielding their haemoglobin, when brought into salt solutions of different concentrations. Since, however, this subject is intimately connected with the physico-chemical structure of the blood plasma, we shall consider it in the next chapter.

The important question of the origin, formation, and destruction of Erythrocytes and Leucocytes will be discussed in treating of the function of the haematopoietic and haematolytic organs.

BIBLIOGRAPHY

WELCKER. Zeitschr. f. rat. Med., 1858.
PREYER. Die Blutkrystalle. Jena, 1871.
A. ROLLETT. Hermann's Handbuch d. Physiol., 4, 1880.
C. BIZZOZERO. Arch. It. Biol., 1882, 1883.
HAYEM. Arch. de physiol., 1883. Gaz. méd., 1883.
HEDIN. Strass. Arch. f. Physiol., 1890.
E. A. SCHÄFER and A. GAMGEE. Schäfer's Text-Book of Physiology, i. 1898.
H. F. HAMBURGER. Osmotischer Druck u. Ionenlehre. Wiesbaden, 1901-5.
R. HÖBER. Phys. Chemie der Zelle u. der Gewebe, 2nd ed. Leipzig. 1906.
F. WEIDENREICH. Die roten Blutkörperchen-Ergebnisse. Merkel and Bonnet, 1903-4.
GRAWITZ. Klin. Path. des Blutes, 1902.
ENGEL. Leitfaden z. klin. Unters. des Blutes, 1902.
FOA. Arch. d. scienze med. Turin, 1906.

Recent English Literature :—

W. MYERS. The Causes of the Shape of Non-nucleated Red Blood Corpuscles. Journ. of Anat., xxxiv. 3, p. 351.
A. GAMGEE. On the Behaviour of Oxyhaemoglobin, etc., etc., in the Magnetic Field. Proc. Roy. Soc., lxviii. 450, p. 503.
J. HALDANE. The Colorimetric Determination of Haemoglobin. Journ. of Physiol., 1900-1, xxvi. 497.
G. N. STEWART. The Conditions that underlie the Peculiarities in the Behaviour of the Coloured Blood Corpuscles to certain Substances. Journ. of Physiol., 1900-1, xxvi. 470.
S. PESKIND. Notes on the Action of Acids and Acid Salts on Blood Corpuscles and some other Cells. Amer. Journ. of Physiol., 1903, viii. 99 and 404.
G. N. STEWART. The Behaviour of Nucleated Blood Corpuscles to certain Haemolytic Agents. Amer. Journ. of Physiol., 1903, viii. 103.
G. T. KEMP. Relation of Blood Plates to the Increase in the Number of Red Corpuscles at High Altitudes. Proc. of the Amer. Physiol. Soc. (Amer. Journ. of Physiol.), 1902, vi. p. xi.
G. T. KEMP and O. O. STANLEY. Some New Observations on Blood Plates. Proc. of the Amer. Physiol. Soc. (Amer. Journ. of Physiol.), 1902, vi. p. xi.
C. C. GUTHRIE. The Laking of Dried Red Blood Corpuscles. Amer. Journ. of Physiol., 1903, viii. 441.
G. N. STEWART. The Influence of Cold on the Action of some Haemolytic Agents. Amer. Journ. of Physiol., 1903, ix. 72.

E. T. REICHERT. Quick Methods for Crystallising Oxyhaemoglobin. Amer. Journ. of Physiol., 1903, ix. 97.

P. B. HAWK. On the Morphological Changes in the Blood after Muscular Exercise. Amer. Journ. of Physiol., 1904, x. 384.

P. P. LAIDLAW. Some Observations on Blood Pigments. Journ. of Physiol., 1904, xxxi. 464.

C. E. HAM and H. BALEAN. The Effects of Acids upon Blood. Journ. of Physiol., 1905, xxxii. 312.

S. PESKIND. Ether-laking : A Contribution to the Study of Laking Agents that Dissolve Lecithin and Cholesterin. Amer. Journ. of Physiol., 1905, xii. 184.

C. G. DOUGLAS. A Method for the Determination of the Volume of Blood in Animals. Journ. of Physiol., 1905-6, xxxiii. 493.

E. W. REID. Osmotic Pressure of Solutions of Haemoglobin. Journ. of Physiol., 1905-6, xxxiii. 12.

T. W. CLARKE and W. H. HURTLEY. On Sulph-haemoglobin. Journ. of Physiol., 1907-8, xxxvi. 62.

H. C. ROSS. On the Death of Leucocytes. Journ. of Physiol., 1908, xxxvii. 327.

H. C. ROSS. On the Vacuolation of Leucocytes and the Liquefaction of their Cytoplasm. Journ. of Physiol., 1908, xxxvii. 312.

CHAPTER V

THE BLOOD: PLASMA

CONTENTS. - 1. Different methods for separation of blood plasma from corpuscles. 2. Histogenic substances or proteins of plasma: fibrinogen, serum globulin, serum albumin, sero-mucoid. 3. Nitrogenous histolytic products of plasma. 4. Fatty substances. Carbohydrates and their derivatives. 5. Inorganic substances. Blood gases. 6. Theory of Coagulation: (a) conditions of blood coagulation; (b) disintegration of corpuscles as cause of coagulation; c) fibrinogen as fibrin generator; (d) analogies between blood coagulation and curdling of milk; (e) importance of time in coagulation; f) thrombin and nucleins as coagulating substances; (g) histone and cytoglobulin as anti-coagulating substances. 7. Osmotic pressure, molecular concentration, electrical conductivity and viscosity of blood and serum. 8. Functions of the blood: (a) effects of bleeding; (b) effects of transfusion of homo- and heterogeneous blood; (c) bactericidal and immunising properties of blood and serum. Bibliography.

I. THE property by which the blood coagulates spontaneously a few moments after it has been drawn from the veins, and the instability of the corpuscles, which renders them liable to injury from the slightest causes, owing to modification of their osmotic and secretory properties, make it difficult and almost impossible to separate the plasma from the total mass of corpuscles, or formed elements, in the identical amount and composition in which it circulates in the vessels.

To effect this as perfectly as possible, horse's blood must be employed, since this, as has been said, coagulates slowly, and gives time for the red corpuscles (which have a higher specific gravity) to separate partially from the plasma and sink towards the bottom of the vessel. If the blood streaming from the veins is cooled to about 0 C. by receiving it in a tall narrow cylindrical vessel, surrounded with ice, coagulation can be retarded so long that after about an hour the transparent plasma, free from erythrocytes, and containing only a small admixture of leucocytes, floats on the corpuscles, and can be removed with a previously cooled pipette (Brücke). It is, however, impossible by this method, even with all the precautions suggested by experience, to avoid a certain diffusion of haemoglobin from the corpuscles to the plasma, which then becomes more or less tinted and shows the characteristic spectrum of oxyhaemoglobin.

If the plasma thus obtained by simple cooling of horse's blood is warmed to the temperature of the atmosphere, it coagulates, like the blood *in toto*, and an incoagulable fluid separates out, which is pure serum. If the clot is squeezed and washed out, the purest fibrin is obtained. Serum is, therefore, nothing but plasma in which the protein which gives rise to the formation of fibrin, and was therefore termed fibrinogen, is wanting. Besides this cardinal difference, however, we shall see that other secondary differences that can be demonstrated between plasma and serum are the result of the coagulation process.

Since the plasma of horse's blood can coagulate, it is not suitable for the examination of the true proteins which it normally contains. In order to obtain a purer plasma, as free as possible from corpuscles and haemoglobin, and at the same time incoagulable, the blood of a dog, into whose veins a certain quantity of albumoses (pro-peptones) has been injected intravenously a few minutes before the bleeding (Schmidt-Mühlheim, Albertoni, Fano), is employed. The *peptonised* blood obtained in this way has lost its faculty of spontaneous coagulation, so that it is easy by prolonged centrifuging to separate the plasma completely from the mass of corpuscles. The same effect is arrived at by intra-venous injection of leech-extract (Haycraft). Apparently all blood-sucking animals, independent of their zoological position, and merely in relation to the nature of their food and their mode of obtaining it, possess substances in their buccal secretions which impede coagulation: such are the leech (Haycraft), the tick (Sabbatani), and the mosquito (Grassi).

The plasma obtained from peptonised blood is a transparent, light yellow fluid, absolutely free from haemoglobin: under the microscope it is found to contain no erythrocytes, and only a few leucocytes and blood-platelets. It does not coagulate spontaneously; but when diluted with an equal volume of water, or when a stream of carbonic acid gas is passed through it for a couple of minutes, it is soon converted into a quivering, gelatinous mass, from which the serum, in which floats the snow-white cake of pure fibrin, separates out (Fano).

Incoagulable plasma can also be obtained by receiving the blood that issues from the veins in a vessel which contains a certain quantity of salt solution, since, with hardly any exceptions, all salts render the blood incoagulable in greater or less degree owing to various physical and chemical reasons (Buglia and Gardella). The solutions most frequently employed in the chemical physiology of the blood are sodium sulphate, sodium chloride, and magnesium sulphate. Twenty-four hours after extraction, or sooner if the centrifuge is used, the mass of the corpuscles separates from the plasma. One inconvenience of this method is that the corpuscles are deformed, and a considerable amount of hæmoglobin diffuses out and stains the plasma. The separation of the proteins of the blood in a pure state was, however, effected by A. Schmidt and Hammarsten, mainly with salted plasma. To-day we are acquainted with various less active saline solutions, which when properly used do not rupture the erythrocytes, and yield a perfectly colourless plasma; among these are sodium oxalate and metaphosphate.

Lastly, it should be noted that plasma can be rendered incoagulable by adding sodium oxalate to the amount of 0·06-0·10 per cent to the fresh blood issuing from the vein. We shall return to these facts in discussing the theory of coagulation.

Still greater difficulties arise when we attempt not merely to obtain more or less genuine plasma, but also to determine the quantitative ratio between the normal mass of corpuscles and the plasma. The methods employed with this object by Hoppe-Seyler and Bunge give very different values, not only for different animals, but also for different animals of the same species. Without citing the results of the various series of observations, we may say that in man the amount of plasma is slightly in excess of that of the corpuscles, in the wet state: average, 52 per cent plasma and 48 per cent corpuscles (Arronet). In the horse, on the contrary, the opposite result is obtained: average, 47 per cent plasma and 53 per cent corpuscles (Bunge).

II. According to recent analysis, blood plasma contains on an average 91·8 per cent water and 8·2 per cent solid substances; 6·9 per cent of this consists of proteins, so that all the other constituents of plasma are reduced to 1·3 per cent, of which about 0·46 per cent are organic extractives, 0·84 per cent inorganic.

In all the higher animals the proteins of blood plasma consist mainly of globulins (metaglobulin and paraglobulin), and to a less degree of serum albumin.

The most important is *metaglobulin*, commonly called *fibrinogen*, because it gives rise during coagulation to fibrin formation. It is therefore entirely absent from serum, and to prepare it in a pure state salted plasma must be used, or the morbid transudations of the pericardium (hydropericardial fluid), or the tunica vaginalis testis (hydrocele fluid), which always contain it. It can be separated out from salted plasma by utilising the property which causes fibrinogen to precipitate from its solutions so soon as these contain 16 per cent of sodium chloride, when none of the other globulins have lost their solubility, since they are precipitated only when their solutions are saturated with sodium chloride. To precipitate metaglobulin from the transudates, it is only necessary to add sodium chloride in the solid form.

If a solution of pure fibrinogen is warmed to 56-60 C., it splits up into two other globulins, of which we shall speak later, and an insoluble coagulum is formed.

Paraglobulin is also known as *serum globulin*, because it remains unchanged in the serum after spontaneous blood coagulation. It can be readily separated in the pure state by diluting the serum with at least ten volumes of water, and then leading a stream of carbonic acid through it, or by slightly acidifying it with dilute acetic acid, or by saturating it with magnesium sulphate.

Serum globulin dissolved in a 10 per cent solution of common salt coagulates at 75° C.

Serum albumin or *serin* is separated from globulins of the serum by salting the latter with magnesium sulphate at 30° C., filtering it at the same temperature, and adding to the saturated filtrate dilute acetic acid, or ammonium or sodium sulphate to saturation. This precipitates the serum albumin: the precipitate is separated by centrifuging, and purified by dialysis.

Pure serum albumin dissolved in distilled water coagulates rapidly at about 50° C.; but on adding salts its heat-coagulability is considerably lowered. In solutions of 5 per cent sodium chloride, coagulation first occurs at 72-75° C.

Serum albumin is not identical with *or-albumin*, as appears from certain chemical properties, and more particularly from the physiological characteristic by which the latter, when injected into the veins, is not retained in the blood, but is at once excreted by the kidneys and passes unchanged into the urine.

After Mörner had isolated a protein of the *mucinoid* group from white of egg, to which he gave the name of *oro-mucoid*, Zanetti, in Ciamician's laboratory, by a happy inspiration sought to ascertain whether the same or some other analogous substance were not also contained in blood serum, which shows a certain similarity to egg-white in its composition. His experiments with ox serum were crowned with success. The new substance *sero-mucoid*, which he discovered, exhibits physical and chemical properties highly similar to those of ovo-mucoid.

The four proteins named above are all that have at present been definitely demonstrated in blood plasma. When exposed to the action of freely diluted acids or alkalies, and warmed, they turn into alkaline or acid albumins, the former being similar to the casein of milk, the latter to syntonin. But there is no evidence for the presence of these in normal blood plasma.

The quantitative relation between fibrinogen, serum globulin, and serum albumin is not easy to determine. It appears probable that the relative quantity of these three proteins is very variable, and that all three function as tissue-forming substances, the albumin representing the true form, and the two globulins two different modifications produced by cell metabolism. Miescher and Burckhardt have actually shown that the globulins of the blood increase during hunger, while the albumin decreases.

The same facts and the explanation of them have been

confirmed by many experiments carried out by Fano and his pupils Ducceschi and di Frassineto, who studied the blood in anaemia, in the two sexes, after thyroidectomy, etc.

The serum of mammalian blood contains a saccharifying ferment, as was pointed out by Magendie, Cl. Bernard and others. Bial found that the blood of man (obtained by bleeding, or taken from the placenta) also contained the power, although in a lesser degree, of converting starch paste into glucose and dextrin, and is further capable of converting maltose into dextrose. In the newborn, in man as in other animals, the saccharifying property is very low, and may be entirely absent: it increases with age, and with its increase there is an apparent diminution in the glycogen-content of the muscles.

E. Cavazzani found that the quantity of haemo-diastase is not alike throughout the vascular system; the blood of the portal veins contains more than the blood of the hepatic veins, the jugulars, and the carotid arteries. This leads to the conjecture that it originates in the digestive organs, and that its presence in the blood is to a certain extent fortuitous, and dependent on digestive processes.

According to recent researches, blood serum contains various other enzymes.

Claude Bernard (in his observations on the amount of glycogen in normal dog's blood) found it necessary to test for glycogen immediately after the blood had been drawn from the vessels of the animal, because in a longer or shorter period, according to the surrounding temperature, it was destroyed by a fermentative process.

A similar disappearance of glycogen (as also of laevulose, maltose, and galactose) occurs on adding sugar artificially to the blood in vitro, and it was more particularly after the researches of Lépine and Barral that this disappearance of sugar in the blood was attributed to the action of a special glycolytic enzyme, which, according to these authors, originated in the white corpuscles. This glycolysis is effected, according to Nasse, Röhmann and others, by an oxidative process, and more precisely by the agency of an oxidising ferment (oxidase), while according to Stoklasa it is due to a process analogous to alcoholic fermentation, to the agency, that is, of a special zymase.

In addition to these two amylo- and glycolytic enzymes there exists in the serum, according to Hanriot, a lipolytic ferment (lipase), which, according to most authors, acts only on mono-butyrin, and is incapable of splitting up olein and other neutral fats (Arthus, Doyen and others).

Along with this restricted lipolytic property of serum, the blood, according to Connstein and Michaelis and Weigert, has also a property of transforming fats into certain soluble substances, the composition of which is not known.

Nor does this complete the enumeration of all the enzymes in blood. According to the most recent researches, it further contains oxidases, catalases, and proteolytic enzymes (chymosin and trypsin): nor are the corresponding anti-enzymes or anti-ferments lacking: according to Delezenne there is also an anti-kinase.

Quantitative Estimation of Fibrinogen.—The quantitative estimation of the fibrinogen or metaglobulin of salted plasma, which also contains paraglobulin, is based on the different solubilities of these two substances in salt solutions. Hammarsten (*Pflüger Arch.* xvii., xviii., xix.) has shown that paraglobulin remains in solution in water containing 16-18 per cent NaCl, while fibrinogen, on the contrary, is completely precipitated, and remains soluble only at a lower concentration. If a sufficient quantity of saturated salt solution is added to a vessel containing salted plasma, a flocculent precipitate of fibrinogen is obtained on stirring the fluid briskly with a glass rod. In order to purify this, it is again dissolved, after filtering, in an 8 per cent solution of NaCl, and reprecipitated with concentrated solution as before. This operation is repeated three or four times, and the last precipitate, which is quite white, and held in a filter previously dried at 115° C., and weighed, is placed in a warm chamber at 115° C. to coagulate. The filter is then replaced on the stand; the coagulated fibrinogen is washed with warm water, to remove the salts, and then with alcohol and ether. The filter and precipitate are then dried again, and weighed repeatedly at long intervals, till a constant weight is obtained. It is now easy from the known quantity of blood employed to calculate the fibrinogen content of 100 or 1000 c.c.

Estimation of Fibrin Ferment.—Carbone's is the only known method of estimating the fibrin ferment contained in blood-serum; it yields comparative, not absolute results. This method is based on the fact that leech extract acts in regard to the ferment in a manner analogous to that of anti-toxin towards toxin. Carbone mixed a constant quantity of fibrinogen dissolved in 0·8 per cent NaCl, in a series of test-tubes, with a constant quantity of the serum in which the ferment was to be titrated. He then added to the different test-tubes an increasing quantity of leech extract, and eventually made the volume of liquid equal in all by adding 0·8 per cent NaCl. After twenty-four to forty-eight hours he examined the test-tubes and the clot, which only formed where there was little leech extract. He estimated the quantity of ferment by the quantity of extract necessary to neutralise its coagulating action.

Estimation of Paraglobulin.—Magnesium sulphate is added to saturation to a measured quantity of blood serum. The fluid is vigorously shaken, the precipitate in the form of a white paste, finely granulated, is collected on a filter and washed with saturated solution of $MgSO_4$, to remove the albumin. If the precipitate left on the filter is coloured, it is dissolved in a dilute solution of $MgSO_4$ or NaCl, and reprecipitated as before. This operation is repeated several times, and then completed in the manner described for the estimation of fibrinogen.

Estimation of Serum Albumin.—The serum saturated with magnesium sulphate, from which the paraglobulin has been removed by filtering, can be used again for the quantitative estimation of serum albumin. This can be precipitated by the addition of a small amount of 0·5-1 per cent of acetic acid. To purify it, dissolve again in water, and reprecipitate with solution of ammonium sulphate. The further treatment is the same as that described above for fibrinogen. Serin is, however, more frequently calculated by difference, as follows: In one portion of serum the paraglobulin is estimated by the preceding method, and in a second portion, equal to the first, the total weight of the proteins coagulated by alcohol or by heat. The percentage amount of serum albumin can be calculated from the difference between the two values.

Estimation of Sero-mucoid.—I. To prepare and simultaneously estimate sero-mucoid, Zanetti used the same method Mörner employed for ovo-mucoid. The proteins are first precipitated from a given amount of blood serum diluted with two volumes of 10 per cent NaCl solution, by coagulation, after previous acidification with acetic acid. The filtrate is evaporated on the water bath to a reduced volume, and is then treated with alcohol. To purify the precipitate obtained, which consists of sero-mucoid, it is again dissolved in water, and reprecipitated with alcohol. This operation is repeated five or six times, till a very slightly coloured precipitate is obtained, which can be collected on a filter that has been previously dried and weighed. After repeated washing with ether, the substance is dried *in vacuo* over sulphuric acid till the weight is constant. The sero-mucoid appears as a light straw-coloured powder. It is somewhat hygroscopic, dissolves in warm water, and gives all the reactions of mucoid substances. Its property of reducing Fehling's solution after previous boiling with hydrochloric acid, led Zanetti to term it gluco-protein.

III. The various proteins differ little in their percentage composition, and are probably derived from the molecular complex into which the different nuclei or groups of atoms have entered in different relations. In fact, when broken up by steam at high pressure, or by prolonged boiling with dilute alkali or mineral acids, they invariably yield the same products, viz. ammonia, hydrogen sulphide, and a series of amino-acids, among which tyrosine, leucine, and asparaginic acid are always present. Since tyrosine is a compound of the aromatic series, and leucine and asparaginic acid are two bodies of the fatty series, we may conclude that atomic groups of both series enter into the protein molecule.

Within the body, however, in consequence of the metabolic activity of the living elements of the tissues, the proteins give rise to a large number of decomposition products, which are either simple waste products, destined as such to be eliminated by the various excretory organs, or products of internal secretion, destined to fulfil other functions and to undergo further transformations before they are eliminated. For the most part these consist of the constituents of urine, which are excreted by the kidneys, among the most important being creatine, creatinine, uric acid, hippuric acid, carbamic acid, and urea. All these are nitrogenous compounds, and are therefore derived from retrogressive or katabolic metamorphoses of the proteins.

As these waste products are promptly eliminated as fast as they reach the blood plasma, they can obviously exist there only in very minute quantities. As a matter of fact, urea and ammonia are the sole constituents of urine that can be isolated from blood serum, urea only in an amount of which the maximum does not exceed 0·05 per cent (l. Munk), ammonia in an average amount of 0·79 mgrm. to each 100 grms. of blood (Beccari). Creatine and uric acid are found in much smaller quantities; hippuric acid least of all, since, as will be shown later on, the greater part at any rate is formed by a synthetic process in the kidneys. Under pathological conditions, however, when the renal function is profoundly affected or abolished (uraemia), as also in grave alterations of the blood (leucaemia), besides these nitrogenous products others, which are normally present in the urine in exceedingly small quantities, *e.g.* the xanthine bases (Scherer), can be demonstrated in the serum.

IV. Besides the nitrogenous compounds, neutral fats are found in the blood serum, emulsified to minute drops which can readily be extracted with ether. The amount, which under normal conditions does not exceed 0·1-0·2 per cent, increases conspicuously after a fatty meal, giving a milky appearance to the serum, and it may reach or exceed 1 per cent of the total quantity of blood (Röhrig); whereas in the fasting state only minute traces remain (Pfeiffer). It is thus obvious that the fats of the blood are derived principally from the fatty substances taken in with the food. In certain morbid conditions, however (alcoholism, diabetes, diseases of the bone marrow), the amount of fat in the blood plasma may increase so much that the serum assumes a milky aspect (lipaemia) as after a meal that has been rich in fats. It is therefore probable that the fat of the blood is, even under normal conditions, derived to a lesser extent from what is eliminated or liquefied from the adipose tissues.

In addition to neutral fats, blood serum contains soaps, lecithin, and cholesterin (Hoppe-Seyler). These form part of the products of pancreatic digestion, hence they also come in part from the digestive canal.

A third group of organic substances also found in serum are conventionally comprised under the term carbohydrates: glucose, glycogen, lactic acid. There is yet another reducing substance, which is not fermentable: it contains phosphorus, is capable of extraction with ether, and gives all the reactions of jecorin (Jacobson). Lastly, there is a small quantity of animal gum (Freund).

The most important of all these substances is certainly glucose, which originates partly direct from the food, partly from the digestive transformation of alimentary starch, partly from the glycogen of the liver and muscles. The quantity of glucose in the blood is independent of the nature of the food, because, as we shall see later, nearly all the glucose absorbed from the intestine is stored up in the liver in the form of glycogen (liver starch). The amount of glucose found in normal human blood varies from 0·10 to 0·15 per cent (Otto): but under abnormal conditions it may reach 0·3 per cent or more. It is at a maximum during post-digestive absorption in the blood of the portal veins, while during inanition it is most abundant in the blood of the hepatic veins.

The small amount of glycogen that can be demonstrated in blood serum (Pavy) probably derives from the disintegration of the leucocytes, which, as stated, contain a certain amount of it.

The constant presence of lactic acid in blood serum is independent of the ingestion of carbohydrates, while it is, on the contrary, partly dependent on the flesh food. The amount of lactic acid found in the blood of dogs during absorption after a full meat meal, may amount to 0·3-0·5 per cent, while after forty-eight hours' starvation it diminishes to 0·17 per cent (Gaglio). Lactic acid, as we shall see, is one of the decomposition products of proteins, elaborated either by the blood corpuscles or by the living elements of the various tissues.

V. The mineral constituents of blood plasma occur partly in the form of free salts, partly in combination with the proteins, from which they cannot be separated by simple dialysis. What the true physical and chemical conditions within the plasma—the reciprocal relations and the fixed or labile bonds between the various mineral constituents on the one hand, and the various proteins on the other—may be, is one of the most difficult problems in the chemical physiology of to-day, and its solution is the aim of various physico-chemical researches, of which this is not the place to speak.

If combustion is employed to isolate the inorganic matters from the dry residue of serum, the ash will be found to contain a large amount of sulphates, derived from the combustion of the sulphur of the proteins, which are not among the mineral constituents of true plasma. In the same way, if care be not taken before the serum is incinerated to remove the lecithin by ether, there will, owing to combustion of its phosphates, be an excessive increase in the phosphates of the ash.

Setting aside for these reasons the sulphates and phosphates found in the ash of serum, the results of the different analyses made for man and for the other mammals harmonise perfectly for the rest of the constituents, as appears from the following table :—

In 1000 parts of serum.

	Human Blood (C. Schmidt).	Pig's Blood (Bunge).	Calf's Blood (Bunge).	Average of the three analyses.
K_2O	0·394	0·273	0 234	0·300
Na_2O	4·290	4·272	4·351	4·304
Cl	3·612	3·611	3·717	3·646
CaO	0·155	0·136	0·126	0·139
MgO	0·101	0·038	0·045	0·06·
	8·552	8·330	8·473	8·450

These figures show that sodium chloride is by far the most abundant constituent of the ash of serum. It is held in simple solution in the plasma or in the form of highly unstable compounds, for when serum is dialysed in distilled water, osmotic equilibrium between the two fluids is soon arrived at in regard to the chlorine.

The greater part of the sodium of the ash exists in the form of bicarbonate (Gürber) in the plasma, a lesser amount being combined with phosphoric acid in the form of di-sodic phosphate.

It should be noted that potassium salts predominate in the corpuscles, sodium salts in the plasma.

The osmotic pressure of plasma depends largely upon the sum of the inorganic matters which it contains; it is, as we shall see, of great importance in the metabolic exchanges between corpuscles and plasma, and between plasma and tissues.

The blood gases, as a whole, represent a very small part of the weight of the blood (0·10-0·15 per cent). They are oxygen, carbonic acid, nitrogen, and also argon. The two first occur principally in combination, the two last in simple solutions. Nitrogen and argon are not known to fulfil any function in the animal economy; on the other hand (as we shall find in discussing the Chemistry of Respiration), oxygen and carbonic acid are of capital importance. Here we must confine ourselves to stating that the combinations which they form of oxygen with haemoglobin, and of carbonic acid with haemoglobin and the alkalies, are very unstable, so that it is possible with the vacuum to separate and estimate volumetrically the whole of the gases contained in the blood.

VI. After ascertaining the several constituents of the blood corpuscles and blood plasma, it is easier to marshal the data referring to the solution of the problem of Blood Coagulation, a problem which is indeed one of the most difficult in physiological chemistry.

Although this problem has of late years been treated with extraordinary acumen by a number of observers (e.g. A. Schmidt in particular), we cannot at present claim to have established any theory that is universally acceptable in all its details.

In studying the phenomena of coagulation it is well to treat the different questions and problems involved as if each were separate and distinct in itself.

(a) The first problem that presents itself is why, i.e. under what conditions, the blood, which remains fluid so long as it circulates within the vessels, coagulates spontaneously soon after it leaves them. This question was attacked by Hewson in the eighteenth century, while Brücke solved it more completely in 1857.

Clotting does not depend upon the cooling of the blood, for when frozen before coagulation, it is found on thawing still to be fluid, and clots soon after in the usual manner. Cooling, therefore.

retards coagulation; as shown by the fact that when the shed blood is warmed to the ordinary temperature of the animal (37°-38° C.) it clots more rapidly (Hewson).

Coagulation does not depend on the quiescence of the blood drawn from the vein, for some of the blood in the dog's heart 13 hours after death (Hewson), and the whole of a dog's blood $6\frac{1}{2}$-$7\frac{1}{2}$ hours after death by asphyxia, is found to be fluid. Again, the blood in a tortoise heart that has been ligatured or excised, and kept at a temperature of approximately zero, is found to be fluid 7-8 days after (Brücke).

Nor, again, does coagulation depend on contact with the air or its oxygen, for the blood received under a bell-jar filled with mercury coagulates, and the blood of a tortoise does not clot after injection of a considerable quantity of air into its vessels (Brücke).

Contact with the normal, living walls of the vessels inhibits coagulation of the circulating blood, while the injury or death of the vascular endothelium, or the introduction of any foreign body into the vessels (e.g. a needle pushed through the heart of a living tortoise), make the blood coagulate (Brücke).

When the blood is received directly into a vessel greased with vaselin, or under oil, it neither adheres to it nor clots, nor does it on stirring with a well-greased glass rod. On the other hand, it coagulates readily when stirred with a rod that has not been greased, or when any foreign body is introduced which the blood can adhere to. It is therefore highly probable that the circulating blood remains fluid because its morphological elements do not adhere to the normal endothelium of the vessels, and that a thrombus is formed whenever such adhesion becomes possible by degeneration of the endothelium (Durante) or other morbid lesions of the internal walls of the vessels and heart, as, e.g., in phlebitis, endocarditis, endarteritis, atheromatosis (Freund, 1886).

(b) The second question to be solved is the determination of the immediate cause of coagulation, i.e. why the simple adhesion of certain elements of the blood to foreign bodies, or to the injured endothelium, should give rise to the formation of fibrin.

In this connection we have a series of striking observations, which show plainly that the formation of the fibrin clot is intimately bound up with the functional alteration or destruction of the formed elements of the blood, more particularly of the leucocytes, which, as we have seen, are very unstable, and easily damaged by every imaginable external physical influence. Simple contact with foreign bodies, to which they may adhere, is sufficient to provoke secretion in the plasma of substances able to produce clotting.

This theory, proposed by Addison (1841) and Beale (1864), was clearly demonstrated for the first time by Mantegazza (1876). Wherever a thrombus is produced within the vessels or the heart, the fibrinous clot is seen under the microscope to be infiltrated with more or less altered leucocytes.

If a silk thread is introduced into the interior of a large vein, and carefully drawn out after some time and investigated under the microscope, a fine coagulum will be seen to have formed round the thread, which is denser in the places where the leucocytes enclosed among the filaments are most numerous (Mantegazza).

When the coagulation of a small drop of blood plasma is watched under the microscope, the fibrin threads of which it is constituted are often seen to spread out like rays from a centre. which is formed by a leucocyte or a collection of disintegrated platelets (Ranvier, Hayem, Bizzozero).

On separating the plasma of horse's blood by cooling, and filtering it through a triple layer of filter-paper, it can be obtained entirely free of formed elements. In this case it will be seen that the plasma left at the temperature of the environment may remain fluid even after twenty-four hours. But if even a nominal amount of a watery extract of leucocytes, or a little blood serum containing leucocytes, be added, clotting at once occurs (A. Schmidt).

Certain morbid pathological transudations behave exactly like the cell-free plasma, *e.g.* hydrocele, or pericardial fluid, which are free from formed constituents, and are of a similar composition to plasma. Left to themselves, they remain fluid for an unlimited time, but coagulate so soon as a little blood clot or serum is added (Buchanan, 1835).

When entirely freed from corpuscles by prolonged and energetic centrifuging, the plasma separated from peptonised blood not only does not coagulate spontaneously, but will not do so on the addition of water, or when a stream of carbonic acid is passed through, as is the case with peptonised plasma not wholly deprived of leucocytes. But if a little clump of leucocytes and platelets obtained by centrifuging be added, coagulation at once occurs (Fano).

The theory of Hayem and Bizzozero to the effect that coagulation depends essentially on injury or destruction of the blood-platelets, does not contradict the preceding theory, by which it is associated with the injury or destruction of leucocytes. Assuming (as seems probable from the researches of Lilienfeld, referred to in the last chapter) that blood-platelets are derived from leucocytes and represent the mass of their nuclei, the two points of view are quite in harmony. and may be combined and enlarged into a single theory.

A. Petrone has recently discovered that the blood coagulates firmly and rapidly in the early stages of pyrogallic acid poisoning (1 per cent solution introduced *per rectum* for dogs and rabbits. while the platelets are not injured, and even appear to increase. the erythrocytes only suffering marked deterioration. The analytical investigation of this complex intoxication has, however been too incomplete to make it the basis of a theory so opposed to observations and experiments conducted on simpler and, therefore, more convincing lines.   Lymph contains neither erythrocytes nor platelets, as shown by Fano, and yet it coagulates.

(c) The third point in the theory of coagulation is to determine on which or what chemical constituents of the blood the formation of fibrin depends, since it is insoluble and cannot, therefore, pre-exist as such in the blood.

It was pointed out by Hewson (1770) and by G. Müller (1832) that the mother-substance of fibrin is derived, not from the corpuscles, but from the constituents of the blood plasma. Hewson was the first to obtain salted plasma comparatively free from corpuscles, and noted that it formed a white clot on the simple addition of water. Joh. Müller succeeded in filtering frog's blood, in which coagulation had been retarded with a sugar solution, thus separating the corpuscles that remained on the filter from the colourless plasma of the filtrate, and obtained in the latter a clot of pure fibrin. The first, however, to demonstrate that coagulation is a change of chemical state in a substance of the plasma which he termed *fibrinogen* (which is found isolated in the transudates already referred to, and mixed with serum globulin and serum albumin in the plasma), was A. Schmidt.

He assumed that two elements enter into the composition of fibrin: *fibrinogen* (the fibrinogenic substance), and *paraglobulin* (fibrinoplastic substance), explaining by this the observations of Buchanan, as cited above. Subsequently, however, it was shown by Hammarsten (1875), and confirmed by others, that paraglobulin takes no part in the formation of the clot, since the blood contains an equal amount both before and after coagulation, and since a solution of pure fibrinogen obtained from salt plasma can yield a fibrinous clot on adding a little watery extract of serum, which is quite free from paraglobulin.

(d) A fourth problem: granted that fibrinogen is able to produce fibrin by a change in its chemical state, it must be determined in what this change consists.

This question is attacked in the later work of Hammarsten, Arthus, Lilienfeld, Carbone and others.

Some hold the coagulation of blood to be a phenomenon analogous to the curdling of milk. The substance derived from the corpuscles which excites coagulation splits up the fibrinogen into two new globulins—thrombosin, which is insoluble, and changes into fibrin: and fibrinoglobulin, which remains in solution in the plasma. During this splitting of the fibrinogen, *i.e. hydration*, the chemical association of water with the proteins occurs. A. Schmidt has recently shown that pure horse's plasma, dried before coagulation, weighs about 2 per cent less than an equal amount of the same plasma dried after coagulation.

The presence of a certain amount of soluble and readily ionisable lime salts in the plasma seems essential to coagulation, or to the transformation of the soluble thrombosin into fibrin, which precipitates as a clot. The reason why oxalates and sodium fluoride, even in small doses, render plasma incoagulable lies in the fact that they precipitate the calcium salts dissolved in the plasma, and thus hinder the conversion of thrombosin into fibrin by combination with the lime salts. Fibrin accordingly would be a compound of calcium with thrombosin, and comparable as such with the soluble curd which is a calcium compound of paracasein. Just as milk casein splits under the action of the rennet ferment into paracasein and a special albumose, so fibrinogen splits up during blood coagulation, two-thirds of it forming thrombosin and one-third fibrinoglobulin. As paracasein in combination with lime forms curd, so thrombosin in the same combination produces fibrin (Arthus, Lilienfeld).

To this ingenious parallel between the clotting of blood and that of milk, the objection has been raised that even if fibrin always contains lime, it is no richer in lime than is the fibrinogen; hence it cannot be assumed that fibrinogen takes up lime from the plasma in its transformations into fibrin.

Others on the contrary affirm, perhaps more reasonably, that coagulation is produced by a simple splitting of the fibrinogen into a less soluble body that precipitates (fibrin), and another that is soluble (fibrin globulin) which remains in the serum; the presence of lime seems indispensable, not to this reaction directly, but to the production or the activity of the fibrin ferment.

In any case it is undeniable that *the presence of calcium in plasma is essential to coagulation*, even if its precise action is still undetermined.

(e) Another question to be solved relates to the chemical form of the calcium when it participates as an indispensable factor in coagulation.

Some hold that it intervenes as a phosphate, more correctly as a tricalcic phosphate, and think that as it is insoluble in water, it remains dissolved in the plasma in combination with the proteins; Arthus, however, demonstrated that insoluble lime salts are useless, and that the presence of soluble salts is essential. Sabbatani further demonstrated that it is not merely the soluble salts, but also the ionisable salts of calcium that are always present in plasma, which are indispensable.

It therefore appears probable that calcium intervenes in coagulation in virtue of its characters and chemical properties as a kat-ion, combining with those elements that have the function of an-ions, perhaps with the *leuconuclein* of Lilienfeld, which we shall discuss later.

The quantity of calcium ions adequate to produce blood

coagulation, unlike that required in milk coagulation, is minimal, but under uniform experimental conditions it is constant; we thus have a critical value for the concentration of Ca-ions, below which the blood remains indefinitely liquid.

On the one hand, accordingly, all physical or chemical agents that lower the concentration of the Ca-ions of the blood below the critical value provoke incoagulability; on the other, all those agents which raise it above the said value favour coagulation. Among the former are cold, high molecular concentration, small doses of reagents which form almost insoluble salts with calcium (oxalates, fluorides, soaps, carbonates, alkaline pyrophosphates), moderate doses of reagents which with lime form simple salts that are sparingly soluble (di-sodic sulphate and phosphate, sodium bicarbonate), small doses of reagents which with lime form compounds that are little ionisable (tri-sodic citrate, sodic metaphosphate); among the latter are heat, dilution with water, addition of small quantities of ionisable lime salts, addition of reagents that liberate the calcium from its insoluble or little dissociable compounds.

On the other hand, the addition of small quantities of calcium to normal blood invariably diminishes coagulability (Sabbatani, Regoli), and it was only the inexact interpretation of certain experiments of Dastre and Hammarsten that led people for some time to believe that it was increased by the same; the addition of a moderate quantity much delays coagulation: large doses entirely prevent it (Horne).

From all these results it appears, in regard to the concentration of Ca-ions in the blood, that we must assume an optimum value for coagulation (lying between the limits of the physiological variations which calcium presents in normal blood), and two critical values, minimal and maximal, above and below which the blood no longer coagulates.

The addition of lime increases coagulation only when the blood is deficient in it.

(ƒ) Next comes the question of determining by what process the injury or dissociation of blood corpuscles leads to the breaking-up of fibrinogen into fibrin and fibrin-globulin.

A. Schmidt and his school (Dorpat) treat blood coagulation as a process determined by an enzyme which they call *thrombin*, which is derived from the blood corpuscles, particularly from the leucocytes and platelets. In the normal state these contain, not the ferment, but a zymogenic substance, *pro-thrombin*, which on injury or destruction of the corpuscles gives rise to the ferment proper, *thrombin*. This can be extracted either from defibrinated blood or from blood serum, by absolute alcohol, which precipitates the protein matters with the ferment. The ferment can be extracted from the mass of the well-dried and pulverised clot by making a watery extract.

The watery extract containing thrombin quickly produces fibrinous coagulation, either from solutions of pure fibrinogen, containing a small amount of lime salts in solution, or from the fluid transudate of hydrocele.   When injected rapidly in moderate doses into the vascular system of an animal, instantaneous death may be produced by diffused thrombosis, which inhibits the circulation of the blood (Edelberg).

That there is in circulating blood no thrombin proper, but only pro-thrombin, is proved by the fact that the watery extract has no coagulative action when it is obtained (as above) not from defibrinated blood or serum, but from fresh blood received direct from the vein into absolute alcohol (Jakowicki).   The perfect ferment, or thrombin, is only formed when the blood-corpuscles have been injured or disintegrated.

Thrombin in a watery solution is not attacked by antiseptics; on warming to 75 C. it loses all its enzyme action; it exhibits the general properties of the globulins, and is a phosphorus-free protein.

Thrombin is not, however, the only substance derived from leucocytes which is able to determine coagulation by the transformation of fibrin.   Besides these enzymes there are other substances (particularly in the nuclei of leucocytes and the protoplasm of blood-platelets) which can produce the same effect, as has recently been established by the experiments of Lilienfeld.

We have seen that the fundamental substance of the nuclei of leucocytes is a highly complex structure, which is termed *nucleohistone* because it results from the association of two groups, one an acid phosphorus containing leuconuclein, the other basic, with the properties of albumoses.   Now Lilienfeld has demonstrated that not only leuconuclein but also its derivative, nucleic acid, are capable of decomposing fibrinogen and of producing fibrinous clotting under all conditions in which Schmidt's thrombin has the same action.   Histone, on the other hand, not only does not excite clotting, but, like other albumoses, has anti-coagulative properties, both for circulating and for shed blood.

From the blood that is rendered incoagulable by histone it is possible to separate a histonised plasma that is highly resistant, and only coagulates on the addition of nucleic substances.   The anti-coagulating substance obtained by A. Schmidt from the alcoholic extract of lymph glands, which he called *cytoglobulin*, corresponds essentially with histone.

Lilienfeld's results thus tend to prove that coagulation can occur without fibrin ferment, through the action of the nuclein substances of the leucocytes and platelets; yet, as Carbone shows, there is a considerable analogy in respect to the production of fibrin ferment between the theory of Schmidt and that of Lilienfeld.

According to Schmidt, we have a zymogen, pro-thrombin, which in splitting gives rise to the ferment and to a substance, the nature of which he does not define, which arrests the splitting of the pro-thrombin: according to Lilienfeld, we have nucleo-histone, which divides into leuconuclein with a coagulating action, and histone with an anti-coagulating action. It seems probable enough, one may almost say certain, from the researches of Pekelharing, that the ferment and the zymogen are nucleo-proteins. Finally, according to Schmidt, the pro-thrombin is transformed into thrombin (ferment) solely by the action of unknown substances which he terms zymoplastic; according to Pekelharing zymogen is transformed into ferment solely by the action of lime salts, and Lilienfeld's leuconuclein becomes active as a ferment only in the presence of calcium.

To sum up, it is admitted that the exciting agent of coagulation (fibrin-ferment, thrombin) is a derivative of nucleohistone, a derivative of acid character, which becomes active solely in the presence of calcium-ions; we may therefore represent the formation of the ferment by the following scheme:—

Nucleohistone
(paralyses the coagulating action of leuconuclein)

Leuconuclein.	*Histone.*
(In presence of Ca-ions becomes a coagulating ferment.)	(Arrests splitting of nucleohistone and paralyses action of leuco-nuclein.)

The predominance of one or other of these three substances gives rise to various normal or abnormal states of the blood, which can be tested after the injection of albumose, or substances with similar action.

The latest researches of Morawitz and others have led to a more exact acquaintance with the so-called zymoplastic substances, *i.e.* substances capable of accelerating the process of coagulation. Delezenne had already observed with birds' plasma that various extracts of organs or tissues have a similar action. Morawitz has indicated the active principle of these extracts by the name of *thrombo-kinase*, which he considers indispensable, in addition to the calcium salts, for the transformation of pro-thrombin into thrombin. The production of thrombokinase is thus a general property of protoplasm, while more particularly characterising the leucocytes of birds and the blood-platelets of mammals.

(*g*) Lastly, one further question has to be explained. As under normal conditions the old blood-corpuscles are continually breaking up, and young, new cells substituted for those which perish, how is it that thrombosis does not occur in circulating blood, since both fibrin ferment and coagulative nucleic substances must be poured into the plasma on the disintegration of the corpuscles?

This question has not at present been adequately considered.

Fano, on the strength of certain ingenious experiments, suggested that peptonised blood does not coagulate because it contains an anti-coagulating substance of uncertain nature, which comes, not from the formed elements of the blood, but from the other tissues—seeing that the addition of peptone to freshly-drawn blood does not inhibit its coagulation. A. Schmidt, in pursuance of this theory, subsequently extracted his *cytoglobulin*, which has a pure anti-coagulative action (and is probably identical with *histone*), from the lymph glands and other tissues—as above stated. On the ground of many experiments, he maintains that the liquid state of circulating blood must be regarded as a function of the living cells of the fixed tissues, with which the blood is in continual exchange. These receive the nutrient matters from the blood, and return to it the products of their metabolism, including the globulins (the mother substance of fibrin) and cytoglobulin, which obstructs the coagulative action of the ferment that constantly diffuses in the blood owing to the disintegration of the nuclei of the leucocytes. When the blood is extracted from the vessels, cytoglobulin no longer pours in, while thrombin, owing to the rapid alteration of the leucocytes, is abundantly present, and coagulation takes place.

The latest experiments of Lilienfeld show the ease with which *nucleohistone*, when introduced into the circulation, breaks up by a process of which we are wholly ignorant, into its two components, the coagulating *leuconuclein*, and the anti-coagulating *histone*, which last is found in a free state in blood drawn off immediately after the injection, and according to Wright is present in urine also. Lilienfeld, however, makes no definite suggestion as to why, under normal conditions of circulating blood, the anti-coagulative action of the histone always outweighs the coagulative action both of the nucleic substances and of the ferment, even when the latter is present in great quantities in the plasma, as occurs with the innocuous transfusion of defibrinated blood or of simple serum.

In regard to this and other phenomena, which call for more adequate explanation, we cannot at present feel satisfied with the work that has been done, or the theories proposed, in reference to blood coagulation.

The latest attempts to discover why the blood does not clot within the vessels, admit the presence of an *anti-thrombin*, or substance which neutralises the action of the small amount of thrombin present in normal blood.

According to the observations of Nolf and others, the incoagulability of peptonised blood depends on the fact that under the action of albumoses the leucocytes and endothelial vessels produce a substance which gives rise in the liver to a large secretion of anti-thrombin, which is subsequently poured out into the circulatory torrent.

VII. The blood plasma, of which we have enumerated the principal constituents, presents as a whole a solution of organic and mineral substances, which are partly in chemical combination, partly a simple mixture in which the corpuscles are suspended. After the physico-chemical theory of solutions had been established by the work of Pfeffer, H. de Vries, Raoult, Van't Hoff and Arrhenius, the method was, later on, applied to physiology. The determination of molecular concentration, osmotic pressure, electrical conductivity and viscosity in the blood serum and other tissue fluids of the body, is now of some importance, since it has brought out certain striking facts which are the starting-point of a new chapter on the *physical properties of blood plasma.*

Let us commence with certain theoretical considerations.

By the *molecular concentration* of a solution we mean the number of dissolved molecules (irrespective of their chemical nature) in relation to a given weight of solvent, which in the case of the organic fluids is always represented by water.

Such a solution, introduced into the graduated tube of a Dutrochet's endosmometer, in connection with a mercury manometer, and separated from the solvent by a semi-permeable membrane (*i.e.* one which permits the passage of the solvent, but not of the substances dissolved`, sets up a current through the membrane by which the solution is more and more diluted, so that the manometer column rises to a certain height, after which it remains stationary. The pressure then recorded by the manometer represents the osmotic pressure of the given solution.

Pfeffer showed experimentally that the osmotic pressure is in direct ratio with the molecular concentration. Given this relation, it follows that when the osmotic pressure of a certain solution is known, its molecular concentration is known also, and *vice versa.*

Perfect osmotic equilibrium between two solutions is obtained each time that the solutions, separated by a semi-permeable membrane, contain the same number of molecules in the same volume of water, even if they are of different chemical constitution. Suppose, for instance, a solution of urea and one of sugar to be separated by a membrane that is permeable to water but not to the dissolved substances. So long as one of the two solutions contains a larger number of molecules dissolved in the same volume of water than the other, there will be a diffusion of water from the more dilute to the more concentrated solution. This diffusion ceases as soon as the number of molecules in the two solutions, in respect of the same volume of water, becomes equal for the two fluids, although their chemical constitution remains unlike, since the one contains only urea and the other sugar.

Solutions which are of equal molecular concentration, and are therefore called equi-molecular, have also the same osmotic pressure and are termed *isotonic* (from ἴσος, equal, and τόνος, tension). In fact, when separated by a semi-permeable membrane they are found to be in osmotic equilibrium.

According to a law discovered by Raoult (1882), each molecule of any substance dissolved in a given quantity of water lowers the freezing-point of the water by a certain and always constant degree, so that the lowering of the freezing-point depends on the number of molecules dissolved, and not upon their weight or their chemical constitution. The determination of the freezing-point of different solutions is termed Cryoscopy, and the difference between the freezing-point of the solution and that of the pure solvent is indicated by the symbol Δ.

The cryoscopic method serves indirectly, by an easy technique, to determine the molecular concentration and the osmotic pressure of any given solution.

The salts in general are an exception to Raoult's Law, since their solutions indicate a higher osmotic pressure than that which, according to the law, should be exerted by the number of their molecules. The molecules of these salts behave as if a portion of them were split up. This led to Arrhenius' hypothesis of the electrolytic dissociation, or ionisation, of dissolved saline molecules —a phenomenon which is in strict relation with the electrical conductivity of the solutions of salts, acids and bases, which are called electrolytes, as distinguished from the solutions of non-ionisable molecules which do not conduct electricity well, and are known as anelectrolytes. This ionisation again is in relation with the electrolysis which can be verified in these solutions on the passage of a galvanic current. The dissociation of the molecules of salts increases with dilution of their solutions.

Such in a few words is the modern physico-chemical theory of solutions. We must now go on to examine some of the most important results obtained by this method in regard to the osmotic pressure and molecular concentration of blood serum.

These investigations were initiated in Holland by Hamburger, and continued by others.

Hamburger's method is founded upon the resistance offered by erythrocytes to diffusion of their haemoglobin when they are immersed in a *hypotonic* solution, *i.e.* one in which the concentration is less than isotonic. He sought to alter the molecular concentration of the circulating blood plasma, in order then to study its effects on the serum collected from a small quantity of shed blood.

On introducing into the veins of a horse seven litres of a *hypertonic* solution (solution of higher concentration than an isotonic) of 5 per cent sodic sulphate, he saw that the salt was immediately eliminated by the excretory organs, the hypertony of the blood serum lasting only for a few moments after the injection, although analysis of the same serum, when once more isotonic, proved it still to contain a very abnormal quantity of sodium sulphate.

Again, he found that the serum recovered its normal osmotic pressure in a very short time after the intravascular injection of a hypotonic solution of 0·5 per cent sodic sulphate.

He further found that the rise of osmotic pressure in the serum, caused by the anhydraemia produced artificially by the subcutaneous injection of pilocarpin and eserin (which cause marked loss of water by exaggerated secretions of sweat and saliva), lasts only a short time as also the hydraemia occasioned by copious bleeding.

Hamburger concluded from these facts that the vascular system has the property of maintaining constant the osmotic pressure of the plasma, notwithstanding the most varying changes in the chemical composition of the blood.

He explained this fact on the hypothesis of a secretory property of the vascular endothelium, which, when stimulated by the increase or decrease of the osmotic pressure of the blood, reacts by a rapid reinstatement of isotony. The secretory capacity of the capillary endothelium was, as we shall see, experimentally confirmed by Heidenhain.

Starting from these results, Winter made other experiments with the cryoscopic method. He found that the freezing-point of blood serum in the mammalia which he investigated was practically constant. Freezing nearly always took place at - 0·55° C., which point corresponds to that of a solution of 0·91 per cent NaCl in distilled water. According to him, therefore, the osmotic pressure of the blood, being independent of species and individual, must in all probability depend, like temperature, on the general conditions of the mammalian environment.

The 0·91 per cent NaCl is not hypertonic for erythrocytes as some believe, but is much nearer their isotonic value than the solution at 0·61 per cent, which rather represents the minimal limit of concentration compatible with a rough anatomical integrity of the erythrocytes apart, that is, from the changes in shape which they undergo. In fact, it is shown by the observations of Hamburger, Malassez and others that the lowest concentration of a solution of NaCl at which the erythrocytes resist diffusion of their haemoglobin is 0·61 per cent. Even the solution of NaCl at 0·75 per cent which for a long time was considered physiological, is hypotonic. For man we must take the 0·90 per cent solution to be isotonic; and although Winter found the chlorides contained in serum to be, when expressed in terms of NaCl, a little in excess of this figure—which represents the extreme limit of corpuscular resistance (0·62-0·72 per cent)—it must be remembered that the osmotic pressure of the blood is due, not only to the chlorides, but, in a minor degree, to other salts and organic molecules, so that the result is considerably higher than it would be for the chlorides alone. On the other hand Winter himself demonstrated, by means of cryoscopy, that on dilution of the serum the molecular concentration is clearly higher than that previously expected from the dilution, which he attributes to dissociation of the molecules of NaCl. From these observations, that is, from the rich sodium chloride content of blood serum, and from the ready ionisation of its molecules, Winter was led to consider this salt as the compensating factor in disorders of the osmotic conditions of the blood and tissue fluids generally.

These results of Winter, in so far as they concern the relative constancy of the freezing-point of blood serum in mammalia, are unsatisfactory inasmuch as they disagree with the data previously obtained by Hamburger and Gryns, and more recently by Bugarszky and Tangl, and Bottazzi and Ducceschi. Here are some of the data obtained by these authors:—

Hamburger.

Serum of horse	.	.	$\triangle$ = 0·596
,,	,,	.	,, 0·585
,,	,,	.	,, 0·620
,,	,,	.	,, 0·568
,,	ox	.	,, 0·647
,,	pig	.	,, 0·621
,,	dog	.	,, 0·605

Gryns.

Serum of horse	.	.	$\triangle$ = 0·549
,,	,,	.	,, 0·561
,,	,,	.	,, 0·520
,,	fowl	.	,, 0·619
,,	,,	.	,, 0·624
,,	,,	.	,, 0·620
,,	,,	.	,, 0·600

Bugarszky and Tangl.

Serum of horse	.	.	$\therefore$ = 0·527
,,	,,	.	,, 0·531
,,	,,	.	,, 0·532
,,	,,	.	,, 0·570
,,	,,	.	,, 0·605
,,	,,	.	,, 0·585
,,	cat	.	,, 0·601
,,	,,	.	,, 0·633
,,	sheep	.	,, 0·613
,,	,,	.	,, 0·588

Bottazzi and Ducceschi.

Serum of frog	.	.	— = 0·563
,,	toad	.	,, 0·761
,,	tortoise	.	,, 0·463
,,	,,	.	,, 0·485
,,	cock	.	,, 0·623
,,	hare	.	,, 0·564
,,	dog	.	,, 0·576

Fano and Bottazzi found in a series of cryoscopic observations that the osmotic pressure of dog's serum presents only slight variations from a mean value (higher than that found by Winter), even when the animal has been subjected to the most various organic injuries, such as splenectomy, asphyxia, inanition, anaemia from repeated bleeding, peptone injection, ligation of thoracic duct, section of medulla oblongata.

These results exclude the hypothesis of a special regulatory apparatus of the physical conditions of the blood, since they are independent of the nutrition of the body, and the functional conditions of the circulatory apparatus and nerve centres. It is logical to assume that the practical constancy of the osmotic pressure of the blood depends on the mutability of the physicochemical grouping of atoms, whether intra- or extra-cellular (in the tissue fluids), through which adjustment to the disturbances of osmotic equilibrium, and compensation, are readily effected. Besides the ionisation of the molecules of sodium chloride as demonstrated by Winter, we may, according to Fano, hold that the associations and dissociations of the salts with the proteins, and the polymerisations and depolymerisations, come into play in the rapid compensation of the abundant rise or fall of the osmotic blood pressure.

Bottazzi's latest observations on the osmotic pressure of marine animals prove that the value of the osmotic pressure of the blood is more or less related to the general environmental conditions of the organism. The blood, both of marine invertebrates and also of the cartilaginous fishes, shows an osmotic pressure approximately equal to that of sea-water $\triangle = 2\cdot2 - 2\cdot3$. In Teleosteans the independence of the osmotic conditions of the tissue fluids from the external environment of the organism begins to appear. Their blood shows an osmotic pressure which is about half that of sea-water, and intermediate between that of the cartilaginous fishes and of the higher vertebrates, which, although they live in the sea, make use of aerial respiration. The blood of these last exhibits an osmotic pressure differing little from that of the higher terrestrial vertebrates.

The special conditions which determine these differences have still to be ascertained experimentally.

Bottazzi and Ducceschi in other interesting experiments endeavoured to determine the relations between the resistance of the erythrocytes to diffusion of their haemoglobin, the osmotic pressure of serum, and the alkalinity of plasma in the different classes of vertebrates. Their chief conclusion is that in the blood of mammalia a certain ratio and mutual dependence between all three factors can be observed, but that this ratio or correspondence disappears in animals with nucleated red corpuscles. It therefore seems probable that the presence of a nucleus makes the erythrocytes to a certain degree independent of the physico-chemical factors of the fluid in which they live, which from a teleological standpoint may tend to maintain their integrity, particularly in the poikilothermic animals, which are subject to perpetual changes of external environment. A mechanical explanation of the greater resistance of nucleated erythrocytes to the diffusion of their haemoglobin, even in very dilute solutions of sodium chloride, may, according to these authors, consist in the fact either that the nucleus of the cell exerts a positive chemotactic influence on the haemoglobin of the stroma, or that the haemoglobin makes a more stable combination with the lecithin of the stroma. In any case, it is clear from these results that the resistance of the nucleated corpuscles is neither an expression nor a measure of intracorpuscular osmotic pressure.

In a series of publications (1895-97) Manca (experimenting always with the red blood-corpuscles of mammalia, i.e. with non-nucleated erythrocytes sought to determine the relations in these between vitality and osmotic pressure, in order to distinguish the physiological from the purely physical factors in the phenomena of their resistance and osmotic exchanges with the plasma He set out from the conclusions of Hamburger, Limbeck, and other physiologists and pathologists, who, in considering the variations of resistance offered by the erythrocytes to various physiological and pathological conditions, interpret these phenomena as dependent on changes in their vital conditions, and affirm that only living erythrocytes obey the laws of osmosis and of isotonic coefficients. The problem, attacked by Manca from various aspects, led to a consensus of results, which may be summarised in a few words.

In experiments made with the venous blood of dogs, both before and after prolonged muscular exertion, he found that the resistance of the erythrocytes (determined by Hamburger's method, underwent a slight but constant increase.

Erythrocytes treated in vitro with strong doses of cocaine hydrochlorate, strychnine sulphate, atropine sulphate, morphine hydrochlorate, showed less resistance than the normal, but perfectly obeyed the same laws that govern the osmotic exchanges of normal blood-corpuscles.

The resistance of the corpuscles left to themselves outside the body, with no aseptic precautions, also diminishes gradually ; but after 3-10 days (when, according to Hamburger, they must be considered as dead) they react to solutions of NaCl and KCl like normal erythrocytes, and obey the same laws of osmosis. The erythrocytes behave towards dilute solutions of the same salts in such a way that it must be assumed that the molecules of NaCl and KCl are equally dissociated or ionised, and that the erythrocytes are either impermeable to them or permeable to the same small extent.

The erythrocytes of the blood when treated in vitro with even the strongest doses of chloroform, and those from the blood of animals killed with chloroform, show a lower resistance than the normal, but perfectly obey the same laws that govern the osmotic relations of normal blood-corpuscles.

In a series of experiments which Manca undertook with the haematocrite method, using solutions of NaCl, KCl, LiCl, he confirmed the previous results obtained with the colorimetric, or Hamburger's method, even when the blood had been preserved for two or three months, with or without aseptic measures, or even after saturation with CO. From an average of seven experiments with the haematocrite, undertaken to determine the degree of concentration of NaCl isotonic with the serum and erythrocytes of fresh defibrinated ox blood, he found that it corresponded with a value of 0·82 per cent, a figure somewhat lower than that determined by the cryoscopic estimations of Winter, Fano, and Bottazzi.

From the sum of Manca's results, it seems legitimate to conclude that the so-called phenomena of resistance of the erythrocytes (at any rate of those that are non-nucleated) and their osmotic properties, are independent of their vitality, and that the red corpuscles behave like simple, inorganic, artificial Traube's cells, which consist of semi-permeable membranes.

The above are the most interesting results obtained by the experimental analysis of the osmotic properties of the plasma and blood-corpuscles. From these few indications it would appear that we cannot as yet form a definite physiological opinion on this important subject: it did not, however, seem proper to omit the matter completely, since it must obviously be of cardinal importance in a not distant future.

Three methods in particular are to be recommended for the determination of the osmotic pressure of blood-serum and erythrocytes that of Hamburger, founded on the resistance of the erythrocytes; the cryoscopic, or Raoult's method, founded on the lowering of the freezing-point; and that of Hedin and Koppe, founded on the determination of the volume of the erythrocytes by means of the haematocrite.

Hamburger's method for determining the osmotic pressure of blood serum is based on the examination of that solution of NaCl with which it is isotonic. The erythrocytes of mammalia will only part with their haemoglobin when the serum in which they are immersed is diluted with 50-60 per cent distilled water. Thus, to find the value of the solution which gives the exact osmotic pressure, it is only necessary to prepare some specimens of the serum diluted to the required extent. Take six numbered test-tubes, 5 c.c. of serum being added to each. To the first add 3·1 c.c. distilled water, to the second 3 c.c., to the third 2·9 c.c., to the fourth 2·8 c.c., to the fifth 2·7 c.c., and to the sixth 2·6 c.c. Then let three drops of defibrinated blood fall into each test-tube, agitate the mixtures and centrifuge.

It is known experimentally that the NaCl solution isotonic with mammalian blood, thus diluted, fluctuates between 0·55 and 0·65 per cent. Pour about 8 c.c. of the following solutions of NaCl into six more test-tubes similarly numbered—0·62, 0·61, 0·60, 0·59, 0·58, and 0·57 per cent. Then, as in the first series, let three drops of defibrinated blood fall into each tube, and shake.

After two hours the erythrocytes will have sunk to the bottom in all the test-tubes. In the first series the fluid will be red in some, colourless in others.

When, e.g., they are red in the test-tubes to which 3·1, 3·0, and 2·9 c.c. of water have been added, and colourless in the rest, the result works out as follows: The mixture of 5 c.c. serum + 2·9 c.c. water shows diffusion of blood pigment, while the mixture of 5 c.c. serum + 2·8 c.c. water remains colourless. On examining the second set of test-tubes, the fluid is seen to be tinted in a saline solution of 0·58 per cent and in the weaker solutions, while the contents of the tubes with the stronger solutions, 0·59, 0·60 per cent, etc., remain untinged.

The mixture of 5 c.c. serum $\frac{2\cdot9 + 2\cdot8}{2}$ water is therefore isotonic with a solution of NaCl at $\frac{0\cdot59 + 0\cdot58}{2} = 0\cdot585$ per cent.

Accordingly in calculating the NaCl solution isotonic with the normal non-diluted serum, the following equation may be employed:

$$5 : 5 + 2\cdot85 = 0\cdot585 : x$$

whence it follows that: $x = \frac{5 \cdot 2\cdot85 \cdot 0\cdot585}{5} = 0\cdot92 \text{ per cent}$

In this case the blood serum is isotonic with a NaCl solution of 0·92 per cent.

Raoult's Method. The determination of osmotic pressure by this method is more easily carried out. The apparatus commonly adopted is that of Beckmann (Fig. 43). It consists essentially of a glass vessel C, which is filled with a freezing mixture (crushed ice and salt), a test-tube B introduced to a certain depth in the vessel C, and a longer tube A fitted with a lateral tube, which also dips into the tube B. The tube A is closed with a cork, through the centre of which passes the special Beckmann thermometer D (or an ordinary thermometer with a scale divided into hundredths of a degree) and platinum wire F, which is bent into a loop at its lower end. This platinum wire, which is intended to stir the fluid contained in the glass tube A, is automatically set in motion by a little motor driven by water or electricity or other power. In using the apparatus the vessel C is first filled with the freezing mixture, then a few c.c. of serum are poured into the tube A till the bulb of the thermometer is covered, when the stirrer F is set in motion. The mercury column of the thermometer must be watched until, after sinking, it rises again, and then remains for a few seconds at the temperature attained, which is the freezing-point of the liquid.

In practice, it is usual to assist the freezing and rise of the thermometer by dropping a small crystal of ice into the liquid through the lateral tube E.

When the freezing-point, which Raoult indicates by δ, has thus been obtained, it is easy in the case of blood serum to calculate the solution of NaCl with which it is isotonic. If, e.g., with ox serum, $\delta = 0\cdot55$, when the 1 per cent solution is found to freeze at $-0\cdot588$, it can easily be calculated that the NaCl solution isotonic with the serum under examination is equal to 0·90 per cent.

Haematocrit Method. This method adopted by Hedin, Gärtner, Daland, Koppe, Eykman, Gryns, Manca is founded on the property possessed by the red corpuscles of varying their volume with the variations of the solutions with which they are in contact. On studying the action of solutions of different concentration of the same substance (provided there is no destructive action on the erythrocytes), these become smaller in more concentrated solutions, larger in more dilute solutions; their volume is constant only in a solution which is weaker than that which crenates the corpuscles, and stronger than others which make them swell out. On experimenting the volume of the corpuscles remains unchanged. These solutions, taken as isotonic, correspond exactly with those found by the methods of Hamburger and Raoult.

The apparatus employed is practically the same as that described on p. 104, Fig. 31, save that the capillary tube (haematocrite), 7 cm. long, is divided into 100 parts, finished at one end by a funnel-shaped swelling.

To ascertain the solution of NaCl that is isotonic with that of mammalian blood serum, the first step is to aspirate into different haematocrites a quantity as equal as possible, and containing about 0·02 c.c. of blood corpuscles. The haematocrites are placed in the horizontal supports represented in the said figure, and centrifuged till the column of erythrocytes becomes regular and constant, while the height they reach is simultaneously noted. Next, to the free portion in each haematocrite is added, by means of a Pravaz' syringe or a measuring pipette graduated in hundredths of c.c., a given quantity (0·2 c.c.) of the various solutions of serum, diluted in the same way as those employed in examination of the osmotic pressure of the serum according to Hamburger's method. The erythrocytes are mixed with the solution by means of a fine needle, care being taken to close the capillary end of the haematocrite with the finger, and they are then again centrifuged for an hour and a half, until the level of the stratum of corpuscles remains constant. This is easily ascertained when, on reading the height of the stratum of erythrocytes, at intervals of a few minutes' centrifuging, they show the same figure. On then examining with a lens the several columns of fluid corpuscles, that solution is to be taken as isotonic in which the column in the haematocrite is level with the original. If none of the columns are exactly in this condition, the isotonic solution is intermediate between the tube in which the corpuscles are either just shrunk or just swollen, i.e. the first is just hypertonic, the second is just hypotonic.

Method of Electrical Conductivity.—The cryoscopic method enables us to study the molecular concentration of the blood and the serum, that of electrical conductivity permits us to study the electrolytes they contain. According to Arrhenius, electrical conductivity is due to the dissociated portion of the electrolytes, to the positive and negative ions (kations and anions), their number and their velocity in the fluid. It varies with everything that causes the concentration and mobility of the ions to vary, such as the chemical nature of the electrolytes, their molecular concentration, the presence of anelectrolytes and colloids, the temperature.

The electrical conductivity (K) of a solution is the reciprocal of the resistance (r), measured in ohms, which it offers to the passage of the electrical current.

Resistance is measured by Kohlrausch's method with the apparatus shown

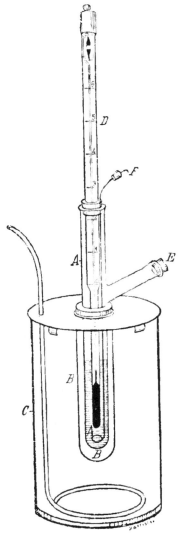

Fig. 43.—Beckmann's Cryoscope.

in the schema of Fig. 44. Here I is the source of the induced current, r the resistance of the liquid to be determined, R a resistance expressed in ohms, T a telephone, x a contact that slides along a metal wire pq, which is kept tense and parallel with a scale divided into 1000 parts and one metre in length.

This arrangement constitutes the so-called Wheatstone Bridge, and no electrical current passes through the telephone T, *i.e.* it remains silent, when the contact x divides the wire pq into two parts, px and xq, such that the resistances of px, xq, r and R are related thus :—

$$r : R = px : xq.$$

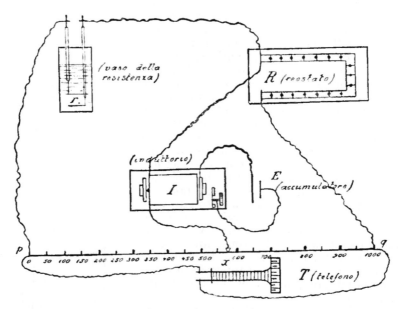

FIG. 44. —Diagram of apparatus used for determining the electrical conductivity of fluids.

It is easy to find this point x by holding the telephone to the ear and sliding the contact along the wire pq, the above ratio enabling us to calculate the required resistance, as $2 = R\frac{px}{xq}$, and noting that $px + xq = 1000$:—

$$2 = R\frac{px}{1000 - px}.$$

The resistance capacity (C) of the cell containing the fluid to be examined is found by determining the resistance (2) which it offers with a given solution of known conductivity (x), *e.g.* KCl $\frac{N}{10}$, and calculating $C = x2$. In all other fluids to be examined in the same cell the specific electrical conductivity is calculated on the basis of this value, $x = \frac{C}{2}$. The conductivity at 25 of the serum of healthy human blood (Viola) calculated in ohms ($x \times 10^5$) oscillates between **1128** and **1232**. That of the blood is much less, and at the moment of clotting it presents a rapid diminution (Galeotti).

Besides osmosis and electrical conductivity, we must briefly consider the physiological importance of another physical property, the viscosity of blood plasma, to which no one had called attention previous to the interesting work of Albanese, *On the Influence of the Composition of Nutritive Fluids on the Activity of the Isolated Frog's Heart* (1893).

Let it be said in the first place that the *viscosity* of a homogeneous fluid, such as plasma or blood serum, is due to the internal friction between its molecules and those of the solvent (water), and of the bodies in solution or in pseudo-solution (colloids), whether or no these are electrolytes, dissociated or non-dissociated; and that in heterogeneous fluids, such as the blood, entire or defibrinated, the viscosity is largely augmented by the presence of the corpuscular elements.

It varies considerably with temperature, and is measured by special instruments called viscometers. The measurement is based on the time which a known volume of fluid takes to pass along a capillary tube. When the pressure under which the fluid passes, and the dimensions of the capillary tube, are known, it is possible to obtain absolute values (ρ) of viscosity; but often it suffices to obtain the relative value (η) by comparison with that of another fluid, *e.g.* distilled water.

Hürthle suggested another method by which it is possible to determine the viscosity of circulating blood in the living animal; but better results are obtained experimentally *in vitro* and with blood serum.

Bottazzi found the value η at 15° C. for dog's serum = 2·0233-2·0486, and at 39° C. = 1·84-1·87: Mayer at 40° C. for mammalia obtained values that oscillated between 1·41 and 1·95. In the dog the viscosity of serum and defibrinated blood is as 1:5 (Bottazzi).

The viscosity of blood determined by Albanese with Ostwald's viscometer (v. *Grundriss der allgemeinen Chemie*, Leipzig, 1890) is approximately equal to that of a 2-3 per cent solution of gum arabic. He believes in a certain constant ratio between isotonicity and isoviscosity; but this seems improbable, since the fluids within the body are isotonic but not isoviscous.

The physiological importance of viscosity depends principally on the great resistance which it entails on the blood passing through the capillaries, and on the corresponding effort that must be made by the heart. But it is probable that the high viscosity of the blood and the presence of colloids influence some chemical reactions in a way that does not obtain in pure water or in fluids of less viscosity; and this notwithstanding that the diffusion of crystalloids in colloid solutions is effected with the same rapidity as in water. From this it appears that a fluid, in order to be completely physiological, that is to say, indifferent and innocuous to the living tissues, must, besides being *isotonic* and *isoconductive*, be also *isoviscous*, *i.e.* it must possess a degree of viscosity equal to that of blood plasma.

VIII. In order to appreciate the importance of the functions of the blood in the animal economy, it will be well to examine briefly the most important consequences of haemorrhage and transfusion of blood.

(a) Loss of blood, however produced, results in a weakening of the body in correspondence with the amount of blood lost. A haemorrhage of 30 grms. is dangerous or deadly in the new-born infant, of 180-200 grms. in a child of one year old, of half the blood (2000-2500 grms.) in the adult. Women appear to stand loss of blood relatively better than men, because they have the power, being subject to periodical haemorrhages (menstruation), of reforming it more quickly. In consequence of the relative speed at which blood forms again it is possible to obtain a greater volume of blood by repeated bleeding than was originally present in the animal, without causing its death.

Vierordt (1854) was one of the first to investigate the effect of bleeding upon the number of red corpuscles, and he found that they diminished continuously with successive bleeding, and that death occurred when the relative quantity of blood corpuscles fell below a certain limit, which differs for different individuals. If the loss of blood is not pushed so far as to kill the animal there will be an increased influx of lymph into the blood, by which more water, with its contained salts and proteins, is taken up from the tissues. The neo-formation of erythrocytes takes longer. A condition of *hydraemia* then obtains, associated with *oligocythaemia* and *leucocytosis*, due to the increased passage into the blood of lymph which carries a greater number of leucocytes with it. All these facts (and others which we shall discuss in speaking of haematopoiesis) have been substantially confirmed by recent observers (Hayem, Bizzozero, Golgi).

(b) The effects of transfusion of blood are more important. We must distinguish between direct transfusion, from vein to vein, and indirect, viz. the injection of extracted and defibrinated blood, between homogeneous transfusion of the blood of the same species and heterogeneous transfusion of the blood of animals of other species.

Direct homogeneous transfusion is readily tolerated. According to the observations of Worm-Müller the normal quantity of serum in an animal can be increased to 83 per cent, in consequence of the great adaptability of the vascular system, without serious symptoms. But if the increase of blood is carried too far, so that its quantity is doubled, alarming symptoms occur, and when the increase is raised to 145 per cent the animal dies from interstitial haemorrhage, in consequence of vascular laceration.

If a certain quantity of blood is transfused, there will be a rapid return to the normal, owing to increased elimination from the kidneys. The proteins of the plasma are also reduced (if less rapidly) to the normal quantity, owing to their conversion into nitrogenous waste products. A marked increase of urea in urine is actually observed during the first (2-5) days after transfusion (Worm-Müller, Landois). The erythrocytes diminish far more slowly, so that the blood for about a month is richer in corpuscles (*polycythaemia*) and haemoglobin (Panum, Lesser, Worm-Müller). The diminution of the corpuscles is due to the breaking-up of their constituents, as manifested in a moderate increase in the urea excreted daily by the kidneys, and the bile pigments secreted by the liver (Landois).

It is remarkable that a rapid consumption of transfused blood is observed even during inanition. In a dog that has been subjected to a prolonged fast, periodical transfusion does not hinder progressive wasting of the body (Luciani).

Indirect, as well as direct, homogeneous transfusion is tolerated (provided the amount be not excessive), although defibrinated blood contains a considerable quantity of thrombin and of co-agulative nuclein-containing substances. Panum succeeded in replacing almost the whole of a dog's blood by other homogeneous, defibrinated blood, without injury to the animal. In this case, no plethora is produced: the transfused blood is supported well by the new individual, and shows no abnormal tendency to degenerate. This indicates homogeneous transfusion as a rational measure to avoid the danger of death in severe haemorrhage. Since, however, in many cases death ensues not from deficiency of the nutritive matters of the blood, but because the necessary mechanical conditions of the circulation are wanting, it is simpler in practice to replace transfusion of blood by intravenous injection of physiological saline (0·9 per cent), as suggested by Kronecker. The salt water is of itself capable of maintaining the circulation, giving time for new blood to form, and thus averting the danger of death from haemorrhage.

Transfusion of heterogeneous blood is dangerous to the life of the animal even when it is administered in moderate doses. It provokes fever with haemoglobinuria (Ponfik), due to dissolution of erythrocytes (Landois); capillary embolism, due to agglutination of foreign blood-corpuscles (Albertoni); fibrinous clotting, extravasation of blood, diarrhoea, cholaemia, and bile pigments in urine, etc., all effects of the destruction of blood-corpuscles.

This toxic and specifically haemolytic action of the blood of an animal in regard to the blood of another animal of a different species is exhibited regularly, but in varying degrees, in the different species. Thus the blood of certain fishes, *e.g.* of the eel and lamprey, is excessively toxic to mammals (A. Mosso). In order to kill a rabbit, it suffices to inject 0·5 grm. of eel's blood for each kgrm. of the rabbit's, into the circulation or peritoneal cavity; while to produce the same effect with duck's blood, 7 grms. are required; with dog's blood 40 grms. per kgrm. (Héricourt and Richet).

The haemolytic or globulicidal toxic action of heterogeneous blood depends rather upon the plasma than on the blood-corpuscles. Approximately the same effect is produced by injection of heterogeneous serum (Landois).

(e) The capacity of the blood, or serum, to destroy the foreign cellular elements that penetrate it, is intimately connected with another, and, from the medical point of view, far more important of its properties—viz. destruction of certain pathogenic bacteria; this constitutes a natural defence of the body against special infectious diseases, and is even more important than the phagocytosis attributed to the leucocytes.

Fodor (1887) and then Nuttall and Flugge (1888) were the first to demonstrate the bactericidal properties of the blood of living healthy animals. H. Buchner (1889) showed that these depend on the very unstable proteins of the plasma, which derive from the metabolic activity of the leucocytes or other cells, and which he designated by the name of *alexins* (from ἀλέξησις, defence). He found that the serum lost its bactericidal property on simple dialysis with water, but not with physiological salt solution.

By this treatment the serum only loses its salts; yet after the restoration of its original molecular concentration it does not recover its bactericidal activity. This is perhaps due to the fact that the salts before dialysis are in some way bound up with the proteins, which association, on account of its great instability, cannot be reinstated when once disturbed by dialysis. The serum also loses its bactericidal effect on warming to 55° C. for an hour or to 52° C. for six hours, a fresh proof of the great lability of the alexins.

The bactericidal action of one kind of blood is not common to all other species, nor does it extend to all bacteria, only to certain of them. Thus, *e.g.*, the serum of human blood contains alexins against the bacteria of typhoid and cholera, while it has less effect upon *Staphylococcus pyogenes*, and none on streptococci and the diphtheria bacilli and anthrax; the serum of the rabbit and dog will kill typhoid bacilli, while the serum of the calf and horse have not this power (Buchner); the serum of the rat kills anthrax bacilli, while the serum of mouse, guinea-pig, rabbit and sheep has no bactericidal effect upon them (Behring).

Yet more wonderful is the fact, which has been recognised for some time, that recovery from certain infectious diseases is followed by immunity to them. Behring and Kitasato (1890) discovered the cause of this phenomenon to be that the said infections develop as an after-effect (in the blood of those persons who survive them) a previously non-existent property of rendering the bacterial toxins innocuous. They further showed that if the serum of an individual who has become immune to any given infection be injected into other individuals in sufficient doses, it is capable of transmitting to those persons immunity to that same disease, to which they would previously have been liable. These facts cannot be understood without admitting that in such cases the infective agent sets up a formation of special protective substances or antitoxins in the body, which are then poured into the blood, and which apparently consist in certain special modifications in the proteins of the plasma. We cannot, however, enter at length upon this interesting subject without transgressing the limits of a Text-book of Physiology.

BIBLIOGRAPHY

For Classical Bibliography of the Blood, see--

H. NASSE. Blut. Wagner's Handwörterbuch d. Physiologie, pp. 75-220. Brunswick, 1842.

For Modern Literature, besides recent books on Chemical Physiology (see p. 39 *et sq.*, the two following monographs may profitably be consulted :—

A. SCHMIDT. Zur Blutlehre, Leipzig, 1892. Weitere Beiträge zur Blutlehre, Wiesbaden, 1895.

R. v. LIMBECK. Klinische Pathologie des Blutes, Jena, 1896.

For Physico-Chemical Theory of Solutions, Molecular Weight, and Osmotic Pressure, see :—

R. NASINI. Analogia tra la materia allo stato gassoso e quella allo stato di soluzione diluita. Gazz. chimica It. xx. 1890.

T. GARELLI. Pesi molecolari. Enc. chim. Unione tip.-editr. torinese, 1894-95.

H. J. HAMBURGER. Die osmotische Spannkraft in den medicinischen Wissenschaften. Virchow's Arch. 140, 1895. Osmotischer Druck u. Ionenlehre. Wiesbaden, J. F. Bergmann, 1901.

For Bibliography of Concentration and Osmotic Pressure of Blood Plasma and Resistance of Corpuscles, see—

H. KÖPPE. Über den Quellungsgrad der rothen Blutscheiben durch äquimoleculare Salzlösungen, und über den osmotischen Druck des Blutplasmas. Du Bois-Reymond's Arch., 1895.

J. WINTER. De la concentration moléculaire des liquides de l'organisme. Arch. de physiol. de Brown-Séquard, tome viii. 1896.

G. FANO e F. BOTTAZZI. Sur la pression osmotique du sérum du sang, et de la lymphe en différentes conditions de l'organisme. Archives ital. de biologie, tome xxvi., 1896.

G. MANCA. La Legge dei coefficienti isotonici nei globuli rossi del sangue conservato fuori dell' organismo. Archivio di Bizzozero, vol. xx., 1896.

T. CARBONE. Contributo allo studio della coagulazione del sangue. Memorie della R. Accademia di Scienze, Lettere ed Arti in Modena, Sezione Scienze, serie III. vol. iii., 1900.

L. SABBATANI. Funzione biologica del calcio. Parte seconda: Il Calcio-ione nella coagulazione del sangue. Memorie della R. Acc. delle Sc. di Torino, serie II. tomo lii., 1902, pag. 213-257.

E. GARDELLA. Azione anticoagulante degli anioni in rapporto alla diluzione del sangue. Archivio di fisiologia, vol. ii., 1905.

G. BUGLIA. Azione anticoagulante dei cationi in rapporto alla diluzione del sangue. Archivio di fisiologia, vol. iii., 1906.

G. GALEOTTI. Ricerche sulla conduttività elettrica dei tessuti animali. Lo Sperimentale, anno lv., 1901.

G. VIOLA. Ricerche elettro-chimiche e crioscopiche sopra alcuni sieri umani normali e patologici. Rivista veneta di sc. med., anno xviii., 1901.

F. BOTTAZZI. Ricerche sull' attrito interno (viscosità) di alcuni liquidi organici e di alcune soluzioni acquose di sostanze proteiche. Archivio ital. di biol., tome xxix. (1898), Principii di Fisiologia, vol. i. Elementi di chimica fisica, Milano, Società editrice libraria, 1906.

P. Morawitz. Ergebnisse d. Physiol., 4. Jahrg, 1905. (This synthetic review of the Chemistry of Blood Coagulation comprises 490 references to papers.)

Recent English Literature :

T. G. Brodie. The Immediate Action of an Intravenous Injection of Blood Serum. Journ. of Physiol., 1900-1, xxvi. 48.

A. E. Wright. On a Method of measuring the Bactericidal Power of the Blood for Clinical and Experimental Uses. The Lancet, 1900, No. 4031, 1556.

A. E. Wright. On the Measurement of the Bactericidal Power of Small Samples of Blood under Aerobic and Anaerobic Conditions, etc. etc. Proc. Roy. Soc. lxxi. 54.

A. E. Wright. The Action exerted on the Coagulability of the Blood by an Admixture of Lymph. Journ. of Physiol., 1902, xxviii. 514.

J. Barcroft. The Estimation of Urea in Blood. Journ. of Physiol., 1903, xxix. 181.

E. P. Baumann. The Effect of Haemorrhage upon the Composition of the Normal Blood, etc., etc. Journ. of Physiol., 1903, xxix. 18.

S. G. Hedin. On the Presence of a Proteolytic Enzyme in the Normal Serum of the Ox. Journ. of Physiol., 1904, xxx. 195.

R. Burton-Opitz. The Changes in the Viscosity of the Blood produced by Alcohol. Journ. of Physiol., 1905, xxxii. 8.

R. Burton-Opitz. The Changes in the Viscosity of the Blood during Narcosis. Journ. of Physiol., 1905, xxxii. 385.

G. N. Stewart. The Influence of the Stromata and Liquid of Laked Corpuscles on the Production of Haemolysins and Agglutinins. Amer. Journ. of Physiol., 1904, xi. 250 ; and 1905, xii. 363.

R. T. Frank. A Note on the Electric Conductivity of Blood during Coagulation. Amer. Journ. of Physiol., 1905, xiv. 866.

J. Mellanby. The Physical Properties of Horse Serum. Journ. of Physiol., 1906-7, xxxv. 473.

W. H. Howell. The Proteids of the Blood with Especial Reference to the Existence of Non-Coagulable Proteids. Amer. Journ. of Physiol., 1906-7, xvii. 280.

L. J. Rettger. The Coagulation of Blood. Amer. Journ. of Physiol., 1909, xxiv. 406.

J. Mellanby. The Coagulation of Blood. Journ. of Physiol., 1909, xxxviii. 28.

J. Mellanby. The Coagulation of Blood, Part II. The Actions of Snake Venoms. Journ. of Physiol., 1909, xxxviii. 441.

H. E. Roaf. The Osmotic Pressure of Haemoglobin. Proc. Physiol. Soc.,
Journ. of Physiol. xxxviii. 1.

CHAPTER VI

THE CIRCULATION OF THE BLOOD: ITS DISCOVERY

CONTENTS.—I. Physiological necessity for the circulation of the blood. Schema of cardio-vascular system. 2. Theory of Galen. 3. Discovery of the lesser circulation: question of the priority of Columbus, Servetus, and Vesalius. 4. Discovery of the general circulation by Cesalpinus. 5. Completion of the work by Harvey. 6. Discovery of the lymph circulation by Eustachius, Aselli, Pecquet, Rudbeck, Bartholin. 7. Discovery of the capillary system, and direct observation of the circulation by Malpighi. 8. Microscopic observations of the phenomena of circulation: Spallanzani, Poiseuille, R. Wagner, etc. 9. Discovery of diapedesis of blood-corpuscles and migration of leucocytes: Waller, Addison, Recklinghausen, Cohnheim. Bibliography.

THE Blood, in order to fulfil its physiological task as centre and agent of the metabolic exchanges of the whole body, must be in perpetual motion within the vascular system which contains it. If the blood remained stagnant, that portion of it which lay within the capillaries of the pulmonary system might indeed become saturated with oxygen, but would be unable to conduct it to the parts where it is required, i.e. to the parenchyma of the organs; on the other hand, the portion contained in the capillaries of the aortic system would become charged with carbonic acid which could not be exhaled from the body. The blood of the capillaries leading to the portal veins would become charged with the nutritive materials taken up from without, but would be unable to reach the organs that require feeding; while the products of consumption, again, would accumulate in these organs, since they could not reach the organs of excretion.

I. Owing to the intensity of metabolism necessary to the maintenance of the principal vital functions, especially in the higher animals, the arrest of the movements of the blood leads in a few moments to death from asphyxia of all the tissues. The vascular system is therefore provided with a pumping apparatus, which serves to keep the blood in continuous rapid movement in all parts of the body.

If we reduce the cardio-vascular system to a schema (Fig. 15), we may distinguish anatomically a central organ, and the arterial, venous, and capillary systems: physiologically, a right or venous,

157

and a left or arterial heart, connected by a system of vessels running centrifugally and another running centripetally, which are closed, and communicate by a capillary system. The system of the lesser, or pulmonary, circulation unites the ventricle of the right with the auricle of the left heart; the system of the great, or aortic, circulation connects the ventricle of the left heart with the auricle of the right. The auriculo-ventricular orifices and the orifices of the two big arteries which arise from the ventricles are provided with valves; the orifices of the great veins, which open into the auricles, have no valves, although on the other hand valves are plentiful along the course of the veins.

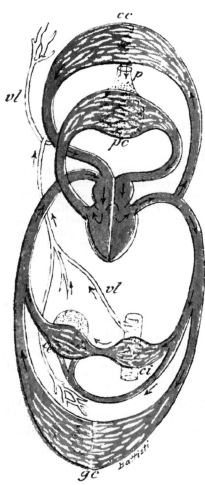

Fig. 45.—Diagram of cardio-vascular system. Red indicates the vessels connected with the left heart, in which the arterial blood circulates. Blue indicates the vessels connected with the right heart, in which circulates the venous blood. Yellow indicates the lymphatic system. *pc*, Lesser, or pulmonary circulation; *p*, lung; *gc*, great or systemic circulation, formed by all the vessels of the aortic arterial system, and the venous system of the venae cava; *ci*, portal system; *cv*, hepatic system; *cc*, cephalic circulation; *cl*. lymph vessels.

The importance of the several parts of the circulatory system is very different. Only the capillary portion serves the physiological uses of the blood. The arteries and veins are only paths to conduct the blood to the seat of its activity, whence it is again returned to the heart. The heart is the motor, a perfect pumping machine to circulate the blood, emptying its contents into the arteries during systole, filling itself again with blood from the veins during diastole.

The discovery of the Circulation of the Blood is certainly the most important event recorded in the history of physiology. By it nearly the whole system of physiological and medical knowledge, as handed down from antiquity, received a violent wrench, and underwent a fundamental reconstruction. With it begins the modern science of physiology, founded on the ruins of the ancient doctrine.

It is indispensable that any one who aspires to physiological culture should be acquainted at least in its main points with the history of this great discovery (which has been misrepresented in many text-books and monographs), and should know the names of the men who have participated in its preparation or fulfilment. In reviewing this interesting history we shall have an opportunity of bringing forward those fundamental principles relating to the Circulation, which must necessarily precede a more detailed treatment of the subject.

II. The story of the discovery of the circulation begins with Galen (125-201 A.D.), who in his vivisections perceived the error of the Alexandrian school. Headed by Erasistratus (300 B.C.), they taught that the left heart and arteries are empty of blood, and connected with the small bronchi by means of the *arteria aspera* (trachea), which serve to carry the vital spirits (*pneuma*) to the different parts of the body, to animate them; hence the veins alone would contain the blood destined to provide the whole body with nutriment.

Galen showed that on puncturing any artery or the left heart in a living being, the blood gushes forth, and, unlike that of the veins, is pure, thin, and vaporous, due, that is, to a mixture of blood with the air obtained through the lungs, " mixtum quid ex ambobus."

According to Galen, the arterial centre is the left heart, which drives the blood endowed with vital spirits (*sanguis spiritosus*) through all the organs to invigorate them. The centre for the veins, on the other hand, is the liver, from which the nutritive blood (*sanguis nutritivus*) is conducted by a kind of attractive and selective force to every part of the body. The blood of the right heart, supplied by the *rena cava inferior*, passes mainly through the pores of the septum (which Galen accepts, although he declares them invisible), becomes spirituous by admixture with the pneuma, and is then distributed by the aorta throughout the body. A lesser portion of the blood contained in the right ventricle passes, however, through the *rena arteriosa* (pulmonary artery) and returns by way of the *arteria venosa* (pulmonary vein) to the left ventricle.

Thus Galen had an idea, however rudimentary, of the pulmonary circulation, and knew that the venous vessels anastomose with the arterial, since he had observed that an animal could bleed to death from one artery. One point, indeed, in his doctrine led certain critics astray in their interpretation of the text. Galen assumed that the blood of the *arteria venosa* (pulmonary vein) flowed back to the lungs at each systole (by a sort of physiological insufficiency of the mitral valve), in order to expel by expiration the fuliginous vapours formed in the blood. He thus allotted to the pulmonary vein a double and opposite task, *i.e.* that of first carrying the arterial blood from the lungs to the heart, and then returning a portion of the same with the vapours from the heart to the lungs. Galen also assigned a double function to the portal vein, and assumed that during digestion it carried the chyle to the liver, and then when the intestine was empty carried the blood from the liver back to the gut. These two errors of the porosity of the septum, and the systolic reflux, have not a little weakened the lustre of Galen's theory of the *lesser circulation*; it cannot, however, be denied that he was the first to have any idea of it, as was recognised (long before G. Ceradini once more pointed it out) by competent interpreters, such as Harvey, Maurocordato, Douglas, Haller and Senac, more particularly on the strength of a passage in Cap. 10, Book VI. *De usu partium.*

Who, then, was the first to rectify and complete the Galenic doctrine, by denying the permeability of the cardiac septum, and determining that not merely part, but the *whole* of the blood expelled from the right ventricle returns to the left by the anastomosis of the pulmonary vessels?

III. In the year 1553 the Spanish physician and theologian, Servetus,[1] published his book *Christianismi restitutio*, which led, at the instigation of Calvin, to his death at the stake, by which he perished in Geneva in the autumn of the same year. Only two copies of this book, which was a theological treatise, are extant, the greater number having been burned, some at Vienna in Dauphiné, with the author's effigy, and the rest in Geneva, with the author himself. It contains a passage in which Servetus describes the lesser circulation, denying the communication between the ventricles by the septum, and affirming that the blood passes from the right ventricle into the lungs, where " flavus efficitur et a vena arteriosa (pulmonary artery) in arteriam venosam (pulmonary vein) transfunditur."

In 1559, some six years later, Realdus Columbus of Cremona, for fifteen years prosector, and then successor to Vesalius in the Chair of Anatomy at Padua, published his work *De re anatomica libri XV.* at Venice, in which on page 177 there is a description of the lesser circulation, and statement of the impermeability of the septum. The author lays great stress upon this discovery, and claims priority for it: " Nam sanguis per arteriosam venam ad pulmonem fertur, ibique attenuatur : deinde eum aëre una per arteriam venalem ad sinistrum cordis ventriculum defertur : quod nemo hactenus aut animadvertit, aut scriptum reliquit."

It is undeniable, if we examine the date of the two publications, that priority of discovery belongs to Servetus; and if it could be proved (as was attempted by Tollin and Preyer in Germany, and by Willis in England) that Columbus had read the *Christianismi restitutio* of Servetus, the Cremonese anatomist could not be held guiltless of plagiarism. Against this assumption, however, must

---

[1] Mosheim's opinion that "Servetus" or "Serveto" was the anagram of Reves seems to be definitely confuted by Comenge, author of a memoir *La Circulacion de la sangre* (1887), where it is proved that the full name of the Spanish doctor and theologian was Michele Servet y Reves, and that he was a native of Villanueva li Sinena (Aragona), where his father was a notary.

be placed certain indisputable facts, which have been collected with great acumen by G. Ceradini (1876-77).

Ceradini points out that Valverde, a Spanish pupil of Columbus, ascribes the impermeability of the septum to his master in an anatomical treatise, which appeared in Rome in 1556. To this there is a preface dated 1554, in which the author states that he had already prepared the numerous plates that were to illustrate his book, which must have taken him at least twelve months. This takes us back to 1553, the year in which Servetus published the book that cost him his life. It is, further, only reasonable to suppose that Columbus had developed his theory from his Chair some years before publishing it in his treatise.

We know that the physiological passages of *Christianismi restitutio* were first discovered at the end of the seventeenth century. Ceradini shows that in 1571, G. Günther, who had taught Servetus and Vesalius in Paris, described the lesser circulation in the words of Columbus, praising him without allusion to his pupil Servetus—a proof that he was unacquainted with the *Christianismi restitutio*. In all probability it was unknown in Italy, as it is not upon the *Index librorum prohibitorum*, drawn up by the Council of Trent, and published in Rome by Pius IV. in 1564, which contains the two other heretical works of Servetus, *De Trinitatis erroribus*.

Lastly, by comparing the two theories, Ceradini produced cogent evidence that Columbus was no plagiarist from Servetus.

Columbus completely and unconditionally denied the permeability of the cardiac septum ; he affirmed that not merely the *vena arteriosa*, but also the *arteria venosa*, were of a conspicuous size ; he further contradicted (incorrectly) Galen's respiratory function, that is the formation of smoky fumes in the blood, and their expulsion by means of expiration. Servetus, on the contrary, while denying the presence of openings in the septum, admitted that "aliquid resudare possit" through the same, and maintained Galen's doctrine by his assertion that the blood "in ipsa arteria venosa inspirato aere miscetur, et exspiratione a fuligine expurgatur."

Without going so far as to support Ceradini's hypothesis that Servetus learned the theory of the lesser circulation from Columbus, and attempted to bring it into harmony with the older doctrines of Galen, we cannot doubt that the Cremonese anatomist had expounded his theory some time before the Spanish physician and theologian published his.

Roth, too, whom Tigerstedt calls the most learned anatomist of the sixteenth century, attributes the discovery of the pulmonary circulation to Columbus, and he expressly adds that there was nothing in favour of the opinion that Servetus had contributed to it. It is interesting to follow Roth's arguments. He insists on the fact that we have no direct means of estimating the anatomical knowledge of Servetus.

He had indeed been dissector for Günther: but the latter was a man of no originality, and his *Institutiones* of the year 1539 showed no advance on the 1538 edition of the anatomical works of Vesalius, but was rather a retrogression.

Another argument is derived from analysis of the anatomical passages of the works of Servetus. His theory of the communications between the nerves and vessels, as conjectured by Praxagoras, was confuted by Galen and Vesalius. The impermeability of the ventricular cardiac septum belongs, as we have seen, to Columbus, and the capacity of the pulmonary artery to an observation of Vesalius. Added to this, Servetus never properly verified the new anatomical observations, which he vaguely adopted; and never attempted criticism of arguments contrary to his own views; nor did he bring forward any valid anatomical demonstrations in support of his position. From all this but one conclusion is possible. Servetus worked from books, and not from the subject: he was a compiler, not a practical anatomist.

He pieced together the doctrine of Galen, certain ideas of Praxagoras, and the observations of Vesalius; with the discovery of the latter he perfected and completed Galen's rudimentary views on the pulmonary circulation; but by quoting from Praxagoras, he made a step backwards, not merely behind Vesalius, but behind Galen also. In short, Servetus, animated by his desire to conciliate science with the Bible, promulgated a speculative, not a real anatomy, an *anatomia imaginabilis*, not an *anatomia sensibilis*.

Roth, therefore, confirms Ceradini's statements as to the priority of Columbus over Servetus, in regard to the lesser circulation.

It is interesting, again, to determine the part taken in this great discovery by the Belgian Vesalius, the founder of modern anatomy, to whom Flourens (1857) ascribed priority in the theory of the impermeability of the septum, while the theologian Tollin (1884) accused him of plagiarising from Servetus, an opinion also maintained by Tigerstedt (1893).

In the first edition of his great work, *De humani corporis fabrica* (1543), Vesalius says that he finds himself "driven to wonder at the handiwork of the Almighty, by means of which the blood sweats from the right into the left ventricle through passages which escape human vision." In the second edition of this work, published in 1555, he omits the expression of admiration for the Creator, and declares himself unable to understand how "per septi illius substantiam ex dextro ventriculo in sinistram ne minimum quid sanguinis assumi possit." According to Tollin, Vesalius must have derived this more accurate mode of thinking from the *Christianismi restitutio*, which had been published two years previously, in 1553, by Servetus.

Foster, on the contrary, maintains that the passage quoted from the first edition of Vesalius was an expression of irony on the part of the author, who frequently made use of this means when his personal opinions were in too forcible contrast with the doctrine of Galen. In the second edition, when his own fame was established, and the revival of anatomy had advanced with giant strides, he suppressed the greater portion of these veiled doubts, and openly expressed his own opinions. This hypothesis of Foster, however, seems arbitrary and untenable, when we take into account the temperament of Vesalius, and his critical, not to say aggressive, attitude towards the doctrine of Galen, on account of which Silvio gave him the nickname of "Vesanus."

On the other hand, Ceradini, by an elaborate comparison of the contents and dates of some of the lesser publications of Vesalius (which would take us too far afield if we entered upon it), showed that he had learned the impermeability of the septum from his prosector Columbus at Padua in 1542, and had defended this doctrine at Pisa in 1543, without, however, explicitly deducing its physiological corollary, the theory of the lesser circulation, which implied, as already recognised by Galen, an anastomosis between the *vena arteriosa* and the *arteria venosa*. Vesalius grudged any praise of Columbus, whom he never forgave for having, as it seems, excited the students of Padua to animosity against him.

Without belittling the great services rendered by Vesalius in the reform of anatomy, it may be held proved that he had no direct share in the discovery of the circulation. Indirectly, however, he contributed to the refutation of not a few of Galen's fallacies, more particularly in regard to the theory of hepatic haematopoiesis. The fact that the lumen of the *vena cava* is larger in the proximity of the heart than it is nearer the liver, in his eyes justified the return to Aristotle's theory of cardiac haematopoiesis, and the admission that not only the arteries but the veins also are dependent on the heart.

IV. When in the year 1543 Vesalius, in obedience to a wish expressed by Cosimo I. dei Medici, who had appointed him Professor at Pisa, addressed himself to giving a short course of "amministrationes anatomicae" upon the fallacies of Galen, it is probable that his hearers included Andreas Cesalpinus of Arezzo, who was at that time barely nineteen years old, and to whom belongs the great honour of having first recognised and demonstrated the general circulation of the blood.

In 1571 the Aretine physician and philosopher published his *Peripateticarum questionum libri quinque*, in which he assumes a constant and physiological transit of the blood from the arteries to the veins, through the anastomosis, which he termed the " vasa in capillamenta resoluta," to every part of the body ; this perpetual forward movement of the blood from the vena cavae to the right heart, thence to the lungs, from the lungs to the left heart, and from the left heart to the arteries was termed by him *Circulatio*. He was the first to recognise the arterial structure of the pulsating vessel, which arises in the right ventricle, and was designated by Galen the *rena arteriosa*, and the venous structure of the non-pulsating vessels, which had been known as the *arteria venosa*. He also recognised that the blood in the arteries stands at far higher pressure than that in the veins, and that in its passage from the one to the other the capillary anastomoses offer greater or less resistance according to the degree of their contraction or dilatation.

Again, in his books *De plantis*, which appeared twelve years after the *Questiones peripateticae*, and would alone suffice to bring him undying fame as a forerunner of Linnaeus, Cesalpinus affirmed that the blood " per venas duci ad cor, et per arterias in universum corpus distribui."

In 1593 Cesalpinus published his *Questionum medicarum libri II.*, giving the experimental evidence for his theories. He observed that when in a living animal a vein was exposed, ligatured, and soon after cut below the ligature in the direction of the capillaries, the blood which first flowed out was darker in colour, and that which followed lighter. From this observation he deduced with great acumen the physiological function of the anastomoses that occur in almost every organ between the veins and arteries, maintaining " venas cum arteriis adeo copulari osculis, ut, vena secta, primum exeat sanguis venalis nigrior, deinde succedat arterialis flavior, ut plerumque contingit."

He founded a second experimental proof of the circulation on the fact that in any part of the body the ligatured vein swells between the ligature and its capillary origin, and not between the heart and the ligature, as would be the case according to Galen's notion, " intercepto enim meatu, non ultra datur progressus ; tumor igitur venarum citra vinculum debuisset fieri."

Notwithstanding this brilliant experimental evidence for the doctrine of the circulation, as first brought forward by Cesalpinus, certain writers, among them the celebrated Haller, maintained that while the Aretine philosopher was undoubtedly acquainted with the circulation, he recognised it solely for the sleeping, and not for the waking state. This is founded on a quite erroneous interpretation of a passage in which Cesalpinus admits a certain regurgitation of blood from the arteries towards the heart during the waking state. Ceradini, with convincing logic, has shown the absurdity of Haller's contention, to be explained perhaps by the fact that as a member of the Royal Society of London he might have some interest in debasing the merit of the Aretine, in order to exalt that of Harvey. It is unfortunate that Ch. Richet, in his *Dictionnaire de physiologie* now in course of publication, should repeat Haller's mistake in regard to Cesalpinus, since it has been contradicted by Ceradini, whose historical studies he has evidently not consulted.

A further and very convincing proof of the circulation of the blood is the presence of the valves, which occur abundantly along the course of the veins, and are so contrived that only the centripetal passage of the blood is permitted, while the centrifugal is impeded (Fig. 46).

This evidence was not, however, adduced by Cesalpinus, for which he has been criticised by Sprengel, a medical historian. As a matter of fact, although Cannanus of Ferrara described certain valves of the azygos vein in 1547, and showed that their concavity was directed towards the heart, Fabricius of Acquapendente, a few years later, found and demonstrated to his students analogous valves in all the veins that contribute to the vena cavae. This discovery was first published in *De venarum ostiolis* in 1603, some ten years after the publication of Cesalpinus' *Questiones peripateticae*.

On the other hand, it must be stated that Fabricius, who first described the valves of the entire venous system, did not recognise their function, which is to check the reflux of the blood in a centrifugal direction, and promote it in the centripetal, by muscular force; he assumed that they were there to retard the current of blood from the heart to the periphery of the veins. Who, then, was the first to establish the theory of the circulation upon the function of the venous valves?

Ceradini deserves much credit for bringing forward a series of important documents, which lead us to the logical conclusion that the first to discover the function of the valves of the veins was the famous Petrus Paulus Sarpi, theologian and canonist of the Venetian Republic, the friend and pupil of Fabricius. It is a fact that some contemporary authors ascribed the discovery of the

FIG. 46.- External iliac vein, slit down, and pinned out to show the numerous valves, in the shape of swallows' nests, placed singly or two to three together, along its course. (Calori.) *a*, Tunica interna, stripped off and turned over at *b*; *c*, valves; *d*, tunic. externa; *e*, orifices of branch veins; *f*, branching veins cut through.

circulation to Sarpi. Frate Micanzio, Bartholin, Vesling, Gassendi, Walaeus, all hail him as the discoverer. Voss (1685) wrote that the circulation was discovered by Cesalpinus in Italy, *Paulo Sarpio Veneto in primis placuit*. Vesling communicated to Bartholin that after Sarpi's death he had seen one of his autograph manuscripts in the hands of the Bros. Micanzio, in which the circulation of the blood was described. The famous Dutch physician Walaeus wrote in 1640: " Paulus Servita Venetus valvularum in venis fabricam observavit accuratius . . . ex valvularum constitutione aliisque experimentis, sanguinis motum deduxit egregioque scripto asseruit." Unfortunately, however, the manuscripts of Sarpi, which were preserved in the Servite Library at Venice, were destroyed by fire, with a great portion of the convent, in September 1769, only one fragment from a letter cited by Griselini in his book *Del genio di Fra Paolo Sarpi* (Venice 1785) remaining, in which Sarpi alludes to matters by him " observed and described in regard to the course of the blood in the vessels of the animal body, *and to the structure and function of their valves.*"

V. What, then, was the real merit of William Harvey, the supposed discoverer of the circulation of the blood, after Columbus, after Cesalpinus, after Sarpi? Assuredly he was not the first to correct Galen's error as to the permeability of the septum, and to affirm that the whole of the blood passes from the right heart to the left through the pulmonary vessels; this was the discovery of Columbus. Nor was he the first to recognise the presence of arterio-venous anastomoses, the passage of blood through the same, and the centripetal direction of the blood-stream in all the veins: this was the great discovery of Cesalpinus. Nor, again, was he the first to describe the valves of the veins, for they were known to Cannanus, and were accurately described by his pupil Fabricius of Acquapendente; nor to discover their physiological office in the circulation—this was the discovery of Paulus Sarpi. Nevertheless, Harvey's merit was immense; it consisted in a wider and stronger development of the doctrine communicated by his predecessors, to which he gave a solid basis by means of countless vivisections and ingenious experiments. He committed a grave injustice, however, in claiming the whole merit of the discovery, inasmuch as he ignored the work, and omitted to mention the names, of Cesalpinus and Sarpi.

After the critical studies of Ceradini and also of Tollin (which coincide in this matter) it would be absurd to pretend that Harvey was not fully acquainted with the works of Cesalpinus, which were published in Venice in 1593, some five years before Harvey settled at Padua, where he remained for four years (1598-1602) as the pupil of Fabricius of Acquapendente. His silence, when accused of plagiarism by his contemporaries Micanzio, Vesling, Walaeus,

Riolan, Bartholin, and others indicates that he prudently avoided a dispute in which he had much to lose and nothing to gain. Willis, in order to explain Harvey's action, has recently advanced the view that he was a freethinker, and anti-Trinitarian like Servetus and Cesalpinus, whose works he certainly knew, and with whose views he fully sympathised. As court physician to Charles I., the severe persecutor of Anabaptists and anti-Trinitarians, he could not own to these tendencies without grave danger. Hence, being indisposed to martyrdom, he kept silence. It is obvious, however, that while this might explain his attitude towards Servetus, it could not apply in any way to Cesalpinus, who was the Pope's chief physician, and is known to have performed the necropsy of Filippo Neri, in describing which his orthodoxy is only too apparent.

Nevertheless, Harvey's little book of 72 pages which came out at Frankfurt in 1628, *Exercitatio anatomica de motu cordis et sanguinis in animalibus*, is unmistakably the masterpiece of a man of genius.

Even now, after more than two and a half centuries of scientific discovery, this *opusculum aureum*, as Haller termed it, arouses the admiration of the reader by its lucid ideas, and the logical arrangement of its observations, which were all founded on vivisection. With the exception of a few inaccuracies and errors everything it contains is well observed and reasoned, and it may still serve as the introduction to a deeper study of this interesting subject.

After exposing the cardiac region in the living animal, Harvey noted that the heart is alternately in a state of motion and of rest. During systole it rises and strikes the thoracic wall with its apex; it contracts in all its parts, more particularly in the lateral portions; it hardens, like the muscles of the upper arm when they contract: and in cold-blooded animals it becomes pale when the blood is emptied out of its cavity. The diastole or pulse of the arteries coincides with the heart's systole. When the heart stops, the arteries cease to pulsate. On opening an artery the blood gushes out at every systole. Hence at the moment of systole the blood is forced into the arteries, and cannot flow back, because the valves hinder the reflux.

The auricles contract and relax together like the ventricles, but before them. The movement appears to start from the auricles and then reaches the ventricles. When the heart dies the left ventricle is the first to stand still, then follows the left auricle, then the right ventricle, the *ultimum moriens* being, as noted by Galen, the right auricle. If the apex of the heart be cut when the right auricle alone is contracting, the blood is seen to gush out at every beat. The blood, therefore, reaches the ventricles in consequence of the contraction of the auricles, and not by aspiration due to distension of the ventricles.

The office of the heart in its movements is to drive the blood from the veins to the arteries, and distribute it throughout the body. Since the ventricular septum is impermeable, the whole of the blood must, as recognised by Columbus, traverse the lungs by the arterial vein and the venous artery, in order to pass from the right to the left ventricle. None of this is fundamentally new : it is only the correction of certain fallacies of Galen in regard to the movements of the heart.

The concept of the general circulation is expressed clearly by Harvey in the following words : " Patet sanguinem in quodcumque membrum per arterias ingredi, et per venas remeare : et arterias vasa esse deferentia sanguinem a corde, et venas vasa et vias esse regrediendi sanguinis ad cor ipsum ; et in membris et extremitatibus sanguinem (vel per anastomosin immediate, vel mediate per carnis porositates, vel utroquoque modo) transire ab arteriis in venas ; sicut ante in corde et thorace a venis in arterias : unde in circuitum moveri, illinc huc et hinc illuc, e centro in extrema scilicet, et ab extremis rursus ad centrum, manifestum fit."

To establish his theories he gives experimental evidence of the three following propositions :—

1. The blood expelled by the contractions of the heart passes incessantly from the vena cava to the arteries in such quantity " ut ab assumptis suppeditari non possit, et adeo ut tota massa brevi tempore illinc pertranseat."

2. The blood driven forward by the arterial pulses penetrates continuously to every member or part of the body, " majori copia multo, quam nutritioni necessarium sit, vel tota massa suppeditari possit."

3. " Ab uno quoque membro, ipsas venas hunc sanguinem perpetuo retroducere ad cordis locum."

The experimental proof of the first proposition is the most original part of Harvey's work. Starting from the capacity of the right ventricle in man (which contains a little over 3 oz. of blood) he pointed out that a considerable quantity of blood must be driven into the arteries at each systole, owing to the width of the orifices and the force of contraction. Whatever this quantity, it must be in relation with the difference in the capacity of the contracted and the dilated ventricle. If the heart of man or other animals expels only one dram of blood in one contraction, and if it contracts a thousand times in half an hour, then in this short time it must drive ten pounds and five ounces of blood into the arteries, a quantity far too large to be derived from the nutritive elements taken into the system, unless the blood returns by the same path. On opening, not the aorta, but any small artery, the whole of the blood in the body escapes in less than half an hour, as was noted by Galen.

The evidence for the second statement is merely an extension of the experiments and ideas of Cesalpinus. When the arm is tightly ligatured, as for an amputation, the arterial pulse disappears at the periphery, while centrally the arteries pulsate more strongly and swell up. The hand and arm become cold after a time. When the arm is ligatured loosely, as for blood-letting, the arm swells below the ligature, and the veins become prominent and varicose. Above the ligature, on the other hand, they are invisible. Tight ligatures impede the flow of blood through the arteries, a loose one only blocks it in the veins. The blood, therefore, passes from the arteries into the veins. In this Harvey, in slightly

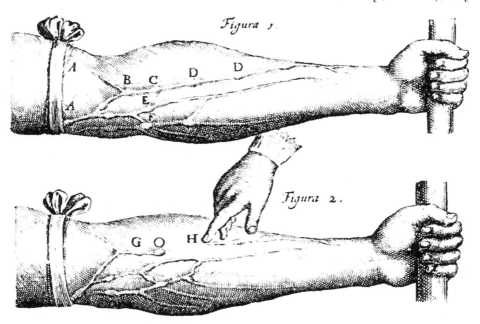

FIG. 47.—Reproduction of two first figures in Harvey's work (edition, 1639, *ex officina Joannis Maire, Ludguni Batavorum*). Fig. 1 is an exact imitation of the figure in the *De venarum ostiolis* of Fabricius. The arm is bandaged at *AA*, as for bleeding. The turgid veins are seen, with swellings at *B, C, D, E, F*, caused by the valves. These occur not merely at the points of bifurcation (*E, F*), but elsewhere (*C, D*). Fig. 2 represents the same arm, from which the blood has been expelled by pressure with the finger from *O* to *H*. The vein between *H* and *O* is now obliterated, because at the point *O* there is a valve, which prevents the blood from flowing back to *H*, and at *H* the compression of the finger impedes the passage of the blood from the peripheral veins.

different words, repeats the conclusions of Cesalpinus: "Apparet qua de causa in phlebotomia . . . supra sectionem ligamus, non infra." The conclusion that the blood flows to the several organs in much larger quantity "quam nutritioni sufficiens sit," is again taken from Cesalpinus, who described as "alimentum nutritivum" what is brought by the blood to nourish the organs, as "alimentum auctivum" what returns to the heart, after passing from the arteries to the veins by the capillaries.

The demonstration of the third point is founded entirely on the physiological function of the valves of the veins. Harvey treats this point with great subtlety, since his chief concern is to convince the unbelieving, and he gives four figures of ligatured arms (one of which is an exact reproduction of the "Figura I., Tabulae II. brachii vivi ad sanguinis missionem ligati" from the treatise of his master Fabricius, *De venarum ostiolis*) which demonstrate the varicose and congested veins at points corresponding with the position of the valves (Fig. 47). The valves are not intended to hinder the accumulation of blood in the lower parts of the body, for they are found also in the jugular veins, which run down from above, in the renal and mesenteric veins, etc. These impede the flow of blood from the greater to the lesser veins, to prevent their becoming lacerated and varicose; they show that the blood in the veins flows, not from the centre to the extremities, but from the extremities to the centre. Injections from the greater to the lesser veins are often arrested by the resistance of the valves, while no difficulty arises in injecting from the small to the great veins.

If the blood in a vein is compressed with the finger in the ligatured arm, it will be seen that the blood which has passed beyond the swelling (formed by a valve) cannot regurgitate, and the portion of the vein between the swelling and the finger seems to be obliterated. The function of the venous valves is therefore the same as that of the semilunar valves of the aorta and the vena arteriosa (pulmonary artery), which close the ostium and hinder the blood from flowing backward.

VI. It might be thought that the Theory of the Circulation of the Blood as demonstrated by Cesalpinus, and completed by Harvey, would have won its recognition in science, and have been universally accepted and adopted.

Opponents, however, were not wanting, among the most important and stiff-necked being Jean Riolan, the famous Parisian anatomist, and Kaspar Hoffmann, a celebrated German scientist of the day, who, like Harvey, had been a disciple of Fabricius of Acquapendente. They recognised that the new doctrine undermined the foundations of the medical science of their day, and all means seemed to them lawful to avert what they held to be a serious danger. Needless to say, this opposition (although it showed up certain defects and fallacies in the work of Harvey) only succeeded in spreading the new doctrine more widely, and making it better appreciated. Ceradini's observation is very apt, to the effect that " Harvey owed his fame to the Parisian anatomist who, after the death of Fabricius, was reckoned the first authority in Europe: and the error of the English partisans lies in the parallel they established between the impression produced on the scientific world of his day by his writings and those of Cesalpinus. Had Cesalpinus in his lifetime encountered a Riolan, to accuse him of plagiarism, of absurdity, and of heresy; had he not for more than thirty years developed peacefully from his professorial chair, first at Pisa and then in Rome, his ideas on the circulation, without laying stress on their possible consequences and eventual applications, no one would have contested with him the glory of the discovery." Harvey, for the rest, was so far from suspecting the wide-reaching consequences of the theory of the circulation, as he had learned it from the Aretine, that it only occurred to him to put it into print after publicly discoursing of it to his pupils for nine years, when he was compelled to this course by the fact that the doctrine had brought him on the one hand friends and disciples, on the other enemies and opponents, and that these last were making a mighty disturbance. And even after its publication in 1649, the physiological importance of the theory appeared to him so problematical, that in his reply to Riolan, who refuted it, because he saw in it "neque efficientem, neque finalem causam," he could find nothing better to say than " Prius in confesso esse debet quod sit antequam propter quid inquirendum. . . . Quod sunt in physiologia, pathologia et therapeia recepta, quorum causas non novimus, esse tamen nullus dubitat ? "

Obviously, so long as the Aristotelian doctrine, as resuscitated by Cesalpinus and Harvey, flourished,—to the effect that the function of the lungs consists in reviving the blood, and that these organs, in which the blood becomes once more spirituous and subtle, are nourished by the crude blood flowing back from all the other organs ; so long, especially, as the laboratory for the blood, and the paths by which the products of food digestion reached the circulation, remained unrecognised—for so long did the theory of the circulation of the blood fall short of its true significance, and appear to be merely a physiological curiosity.

Certain passages of Galen indicate that Herophilus and Erasistratus, the heads of the Alexandrian School (3000 B.C.) observed the chyle vessels in the mesentery of sheep. At the end of the seventeenth century Portal, and more than a century previously Fracassato, pointed out that the celebrated Roman anatomist Eustachius (*Opuscula anatomica*, Venetiis, 1564) in studying the course of the azygos vein in the horse had recognised the thoracic duct, and even detected some of its valves. It is certain, however, that save for a vague tradition, all trace of these fortuitous and isolated observations had been lost when the Cremonese Gaspare Aselli, Professor of Anatomy at Pavia, found the chyle vessels, which he termed lacteals, in the dog's mesentery, in 1622. So fortunate did he esteem himself, as he relates, in having found what he was seeking, that "conversus ad eos qui aderant : εὕρηκα inquam cum Archimede." But he had no inkling of the true function and physiological importance of these vessels.

In the year 1648 Pecquet, a young physician of Dieppe, who was studying at Montpellier, noted that the lacteals carried their contents not to the liver, as had been supposed by Aselli, but to a large vessel which he rediscovered after Eustachius, the thoracic duct, which empties itself into the subclavian vein. Two years later, the lymphatics of the liver were discovered by a Swede, Rudbeck, who recognised that they, too, emptied their contents into the thoracic duct. Finally, in 1652, the celebrated Danish anatomist, T. Bartholin, discovered the same vessels in every part of the body, and found that they all flowed, with the chyliferae, into the thoracic duct. In order to extend the theory of the circulation, which he attributed to Harvey, he brought out a new edition of his Anatomy, *ad sanguinis circulationem reformata*, in the legitimate conviction that he had found a new and invaluable argument, even though an indirect one, in its favour.

"Riolan," adds Ceradini, "Riolan himself, the adherent of every old tenet and opponent of all that was new, on this occasion held back the darts of his criticism, that he might not blunt them against the weight of facts. Harvey alone rejected chyle as well as lymph vessels, together with the function of the thoracic duct, and died, without retracting his views, in 1658, six years after Bartholin."

VII. One last decisive step was wanting to complete the new doctrine and bring it into prominence — the discovery of the capillary vessels and direct observation of the circulation through these from the arteries to the veins. "Supererat," as said Haller, " ut ipsis oculis circuitus sanguinis subjiceretur."

Galen, as already stated, was the first to postulate a direct connection of the arterial and venous blood in the organs, figuring it as a direct anastomosis or conjunction of the two sets of vessels. This did not correspond with the notion of Cesalpinus, who certainly admitted that the communications were made by " per vasa non desinentia, ulterius trasmeantia " or " per vasa in capillamenta resoluta" (which Harvey translated into "per carnis porositates"), thus divining the existence of that new order of vessels, joining the arteries with the veins, which were subsequently termed capillaries.

Marcello Malpighi, in 1661, was the first to see the movement of the blood in the capillaries of the frog's lung under the microscope. He exclaims, " Talia mihi videre contingit, ut non immerito illud Homeri usurpare possim ad rem praesentem melius : magnum certum opus oculis video" (Fig. 48)

After Malpighi, Leuwenhoek, Cooper and Haller tried in vain to repeat this observation on warm-blooded animals. The first who succeeded was Lazzaro Spallanzani, who bethought himself of using the hen's egg during the development of the embryo. The enthusiastic words in which the great physiologist records his discovery are pleasant reading : " Long have I been burning with curiosity to discover the circulation in warm-blooded animals, and to grasp it as completely as in the case of the cold-blooded; hence these vessels" (umbilicals of the chick) "attracted my observation more than any others, and invited my consideration, because they belonged to the said animals. Since the room in which I found myself was insufficiently lighted, and I was determined at all costs to satisfy my curiosity, I decided to examine the egg in the open, under direct sunlight. After fixing it in the apparatus of Lyonet" (a small microscope used by Spallanzani) "I turned the lens upon it, and, notwithstanding the strong light that surrounded me, was enabled by focussing my eyes, to see plainly how the blood flowed in the entire circuit of the arterial and venous umbilical vessels. Thrilled with this

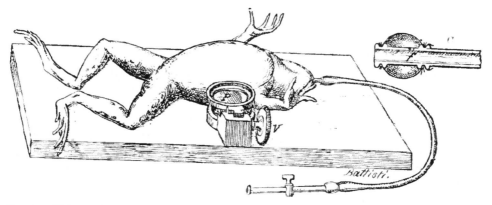

Fig. 48.—Holmgren's Apparatus (improvement on Malpighi's method) for observing the pulmonary circulation in a curarised frog. *V*, screw to regulate position of glass plate, *P*, which is intended to keep the surface of the frog's lung flat; *C*, cannula closed at the end by an elastic membrane, which, when introduced into the glottis and blown up, closes the opening, so that the lung cannot distend.

unexpected joy, I felt that I, too, might exclaim, 'I have found it! I have found it!' I made this discovery in May 1771, and employed myself in the summer vacation of that year with its development."

These observations of Malpighi and of Spallanzani, a century apart, constitute one of the most striking incidents in the history of medicine; no one has ever contested with Italy the honour of having initiated the direct observation of the circulation. Modern scientists, with more perfect microscopes and a more elaborate technique, have only succeeded in completing the description of the phenomena of the circulation, as visible under the microscope. These must now be briefly described, since they contain some interesting data that should precede the study of haemodynamics.

VIII. In direct observation of the transparent parts of the living animal under the microscope the blood is seen to circulate in a closed system of capillary canals, which unite the arteries with the veins by a network, and form a continuous circuit. That was the true discovery of Malpighi.

In all the vessels a sharp delimitation can be seen under the microscope, in the form of two parallel dark lines, which represent the walls of the vessels. In the most transparent and superficial parts, the structure of the vessel walls can also be made out to a certain extent below the tissues that cover them.

The movement of the blood within the vessels, which is visible by means of the transported corpuscles, is continuous, and is always in the same direction, save in a few branches of the capillary network, in which a temporary block, due to the accumulation of blood-corpuscles or a transitory reversal of the current, can occasionally be detected (Spallanzani).

In certain vessels the current is centrifugal, that is, it sets from the greater trunks to the lesser ramifications. In others it is centripetal, i.e. from the lesser ramifications to the greater trunks. The former are evidently arterial vessels, the latter venous.

In the arteries the current is continuous, with rhythmical accelerations; in the veins it is continuous and uniform; in the capillary network it is irregular, subject to impediments, arrests, deviations, or accelerations, according as the blood corpuscles are dispersed or accumulated.

In the medium vessels, arterial as well as venous, a more rapid axial, and a far slower peripheral current can be distinguished (Poiseuille, 1834). The erythrocytes move compactly along the axial stream, and between them and the vessel walls on both sides a thin streak of clear plasma is plainly visible, in which the leucocytes move at irregular distances from each other, ten to twelve times slower than the erythrocytes. The diameter of this clear layer, which is occupied by plasma and leucocytes, and its relation to the diameter of the axial current, varies considerably in the different vessels, even in those of equal cross-section.

R. Wagner described as characteristic of the blood-stream in the lungs and gills, a complete absence or excessive tenuity of the parietal stratum, and lack of separation between leucocytes and the erythrocytes — the time required for such separation being cut short, owing to the greater current velocity and less extensive path of the lesser circulation.

Poiseuille designated the parietal layer as the *stratum adhesirum*, and considered it to be immobile or capable only of very slow motion. From the theoretical standpoint, however, it is only the thinnest stratum of plasma immediately bathing the internal walls of the vessels that can be termed immobile. There can be no doubt that the separation of the slower peripheral from the more rapid axial current is a phenomenon of adhesion and of internal friction caused by the viscosity of the blood plasma. Hydrodynamic observations on the nature of the movement of fluids in tubes have determined that the velocity of motion is increased for the axial portion of the current, and decreases gradually from the central to the peripheral fluid cylinders, being lowest or *nil* in those immediately adhering to the walls of the tube.

This decrease of velocity of movement from axis to periphery of the fluid cylinder, as represented by the blood, fully explains the rotation of the leucocytes in the plasmatic layer round an axis perpendicular to the direction of the current. The necessity of this rotation is obvious, when we consider that the leucocytes nearest the axis of the vessels are under the influence of a more rapid current than those nearest the walls.

The explanation of the fact that the leucocytes are nearly always in contact with the walls of the vessel while the erythrocytes move along the axial stream, is not (as many think) that some viscosity of their surface makes them adhere to the walls, but lies in the difference between their specific gravity and that of the erythrocytes.   It can be demonstrated in the microscope that granules of graphite, carmine, and colophonium suspended in water, and made to circulate in capillary glass tubes, behave like the red and white corpuscles in respect to parietal and axial currents.   The granules of graphite, being specifically heavier, swim in the axial current; the particles of carmine, which are specifically lighter, follow the marginal stream.   On the other hand, these last occupy the axial current, when they are made to circulate with grains of colophonium, since the specific gravity of the latter is lower than that of carmine.   It has also been determined experimentally that the leucocytes leave the parietal current and follow the axial, when they are made to circulate, not with erythrocytes, but with drops of milk, which are specifically lighter (Funke).

IX. The phenomenon of diapedesis of blood-corpuscles, alluded to in Chap. IV., which may be observed in the microscope, deserves special mention on account of its great importance.

Cohnheim, in 1867, was the first who directed the attention of biologists to the fact of the active emigration of leucocytes from the blood-stream through the uninjured vessel walls.   He founded on this fact a new theory of inflammation and suppuration which is a complete antithesis to that of his celebrated teacher Virchow. The same facts, however, had been observed and described in 1846 by Waller, who was the first to recognise the identity of the leucocytes and pus corpuscles, but regarded the migration of the blood-corpuscles as a phenomenon of filtration.

In 1849 W. Addison formally expressed the concept of an active emigration of the leucocytes, and distinguished various stages in the course of the phenomenon.

In 1864, v. Recklinghausen discovered and described the movements of the leucocytes through the spaces of the connective tissue and the lymphatic canaliculi of such tissues as the cornea, which have no blood-vessels, distinguishing between the fixed and the movable or migratory cells.   He did not investigate the origin of the migratory cells, but his work was obviously (as stated by P. Heger) "the true introduction to that associated three years later with the name of Cohnheim."

We must now briefly describe the facts that can be observed without difficulty either in the mesentery or the tongue of the frog, after it has been paralysed with curare, or its spinal cord destroyed, when a certain amount of neuro-paralytic dilatation of the small arteries is produced.

When the peritoneum is exposed to air, the circulation in the peritoneal vessels exhibits a marked retardation after about an hour, so that (with a magnification of 200 to 300 diameters) the corpuscles can not only be seen distinctly circulating in the capillaries and veins, but also in quicker motion within the small arteries.

This delay has no sooner begun than a partial block and

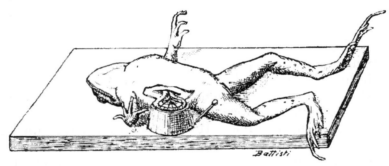

Fig. 49.—Cohnheim's apparatus for studying the course of the circulatory phenomena in inflammation of frog's peritoneum.

accumulation of corpuscles will be observed in the capillaries, which gradually disappears in some places to reappear in others.

In the small veins the most conspicuous feature is the immobilisation of the leucocytes on the internal walls of the vessels.

As they leave the capillary network, they advance with a rotary motion along the wall of the vein, and become fixed in contact with those that are already immobilised. Little by little they cover the entire internal surface of the small veins, forming a hollow cylinder of motionless leucocytes surrounding the cylinder of moving erythrocytes.

On continuing to observe the leucocytes clinging to the walls of the small veins and capillaries, it is possible in about two hours from the beginning of the experiment to catch the corpuscles *in flagrante*, in the very act of traversing the vessel walls to penetrate into the meshes of the connective tissue or into a lymph sheath, or the surface of the serosa. Here and there on the outside of the vessel an irregular lump of protoplasm is seen, which forms a sort of hernia, and is continuous with the intravascular portion of the protoplasm of the corpuscles. The external portion of the corpuscle becomes gradually larger, while the intravascular portion—still keeping its round shape—continuously diminishes in volume, till at last it appears only as a mere shining point, and eventually disappears altogether. The extravasated leucocyte is then seen completely free from the vessel; it resumes its circular shape, and remains motionless.

The direct observation of diapedesis can be facilitated by staining the leucocytes of the blood with methylene blue or other colouring matters introduced into the dorsal lymph-sac of the frog—the method of Cohnheim.

Recent researches have left no doubt that the diapedesis of leucocytes is an active phenomenon, intimately connected with their amoeboid mobility. The extravasation of red corpuscles (the true *haemorrhagia per diapedesin*, as divined by the ancients) is, on the contrary, a passive process, depending either on rise of intravascular pressure or on nutritional disturbances and lowered resistance of the capillary walls.

In the frog's peritoneum the extravasation of the erythrocytes (from the capillaries rather than from the veins) is first noticed after several hours, and becomes conspicuous only twenty-four hours after the beginning of the experiment, in the capillary network where the circulation is at a standstill and the block of corpuscles is greatest.

This observation led Cohnheim to the opinion that the leucocytes penetrate through tiny pre-formed stomata in the vessel wall, by which the erythrocytes can escape only when the openings are abnormally enlarged by the active work of the leucocytes. The opinion that prevails at present, however, is that no pre-formed stomata exist, and that the emigration proceeds by temporary openings, excavated by the pseudopodia of the leucocytes at the junction of the histological elements of the venous walls or capillary endothelia. The erythrocytes, owing to the softness and elasticity of their protoplasm, pass readily (perhaps even passively) through the openings excavated by the leucocytes, as through a network.

It is still doubtful if corpuscular extravasation (whether active, as for the leucocytes, or passive, for the erythrocytes) is to be regarded as a *physiological* phenomenon, exaggerated under abnormal conditions of inflammatory irritation, or as an emphatically *pathological* phenomenon.

E. Hering adopted the former opinion, on the strength of the following experiment. He injected a finely pulverised aniline pigment into the blood of an animal, and after some time examined the hepatic lymph, when he found numerous leucocytes as well as erythrocytes impregnated with pigment, but no free granules of pigment in the lymph plasma. From this he concluded that under normal conditions also certain leucocytes (and possibly erythrocytes as well) migrate from the vascular system by diapedesis, and penetrate through the lacunae of the plasma into the lymphatic system.

Be this as it may, it is certain that diapedesis proceeds tumultuously during inflammatory irritation, and gives rise to the phenomenon of suppuration at the focus of inflammation.

In order to complete the theory of corpuscular diapedesis we must further inquire why the leucocytes become stationary and adherent at the origin of the veins, and migrate from the vascular system. A satisfactory answer to this question can only be obtained from the interesting studies of Pfeffer on *Chemotaxis*, which were alluded to in Chap. III. (pp. 74-76).

Leber was the first to regard the migration of leucocytes as a chemotactic phenomenon, caused by an attractive or directive action exerted by the chemical products of the pyogenic or pus-producing microbes on the leucocytes. He extracted from the culture of *Staphylococcus pyogenes aureus* a crystallisable substance, which he termed phlogosin, and observed that some time after the introduction of a capillary tube filled with a solution of this substance into the anterior chamber of the rabbit's eye, a mass of leucocytes migrated from the pericorneal vessels.

Lubarsch was able to show that living bacteria had a greater attraction for frog's leucocytes than those previously killed by heat.

Massart and Bordet succeeded in showing that the same leucocytes are attracted by liquid cultures of different microbes (v. Fig. 19, p. 75, *Staphylococcus pyogenes albus*), by inflammatory exudates, and by certain nitrogenous or phosphorus-containing waste products, *e.g.* leucin. They also discovered another important fact: if the leucocytes are narcotised in the total narcosis of the animal by paraldehyde or chloroform, they are checked like amoebae in their active movements, and all emigration that might be going on from the vessels ceases entirely. This confirms the idea that the migration of the leucocytes is a process dependent on their excitability or amoeboid sensibility.

In microscopic observations of the circulation in small vessels and capillaries, the transparency of the richly vascular organs of certain animals can be made use of. This is excellently seen in the frog's lung, by Holmgren's method (v. Fig. 48, p. 173). After curarising the animal by the subcutaneous injection of a few drops of 1 per cent curare (sufficient to paralyse it) a lateral incision is made through the whole depth of the body wall, a little below the anterior limb. The lung inflated with air will usually protrude of itself from the opening. To avoid emptying the lung, which is useless for observation in the collapsed state, Holmgren employed a small cannula, which is introduced through the glottis, and attached by a ligature to the lower jaw. The end of the cannula has two circular grooves in which is tied a bit of frog's intestine into which the cannula had been introduced. Between the two grooves are two openings, into which air is blown so as to distend the intestine drawn over it. This dilates, and serves as a tampon, preventing the air of the lung from escaping through the space between the cannula and the glottis. A small rubber tube is fixed to the cannula, carrying at the other end a clip which is closed so soon as the lung has reached the desired state of extension. To obviate the inconvenience due to the convex surface of the organ, Holmgren invented a little apparatus, which consists of a special frog-holder, on which the animal can lie. It has an opening closed by a glass plate, above which a second glass plate is fixed in a metal frame, which can be raised or lowered by a screw. The lung, suitably inflated, is brought between these two plates, its convex surface being flattened and adapted for observation by gentle pressure of the upper plate.

Another admirable subject for the observation of the circulation, which was used more particularly by Cohnheim in his classical work on inflammation, is the frog's mesentery (c. Fig. 49, p. 176). The experiment is carried out as follows: The curarised frog is laid on a cork plate, with a hole in its centre to correspond with the aperture in the stage of the microscope, to which the cork plate is fixed by clamps. Above the hole in the cork plate a ring, also cut out of cork, is fixed by pins, the upper edge of which has a depression that serves to hold the bit of intestine fixed so as to stretch the mesentery.

A lateral incision now has to be made in the frog's abdomen, avoiding the lateral vein, when a loop of intestine is carefully drawn out with forceps, and laid in the depression of the cork ring, so that the stretched mesentery lies taut over the aperture of the ring. This brings the part under examination to a higher level than the abdominal wound, otherwise it would become charged with blood and serum escaping from the wound.

The above ring is not required for observing the circulation in the interdigital membrane or tongue of the frog, or in the tadpole's tail, etc., as these can be simply fixed to the cork plate by pins. When the observation is to be prolonged for any length of time, it is necessary to prevent the parts from drying up, which is done by placing over them little strips of filter-paper soaked in physiological salt solution. The same method, with greater precautions in regard to moisture and temperature, will serve for examining the capillary circulation in warm-blooded animals, using, e.g., the mesentery of mouse, guinea-pig, etc.

BIBLIOGRAPHY

For the history of discovery of the Circulation of the Blood, the reader is referred to the two following monographs, which comprise an enormous amount of research in original texts, and a clear and impartial criticism of ancient and modern contributions to the literature of this vexed question :—

G. CERADINI. Ricerche storico-critiche intorno alla scoperta della circulazione del sangue. Milan, Fratilli Richiedei, 1876 (333 pp.). Difesa della mia Memoria intorno alla scoperta della circulazione del sangue, contro l'assalto dei signori H. Tollin teologo in Magdeburg, e W. Preyer fisiologo in Iena. Con qualche nuovo appunto circa la storia della scoperta medesima. Genoa, 1876.

SIR MICHAEL FOSTER. History of Physiology. Cambridge, 1901.

R. WILLIS. Preface to Sydenham Edition of Harvey's Works. London, 1878.

M. ROTH. Andreas Vesalius Bruxelliensis. Berlin, 1902.

For discovery of Lymph Circulation the fine article in Lipsius may be consulted :—

W. HIS. Über die Entdeckung des Lymphsystems. Zeitschr. f. Anat. u. Entwickelungsgeschichte, 1875.

For discovery of Corpuscular Diapedesis, a complete account will be found in the following memoir :—

P. HEGER. Étude critique et exp. sur l'émigration des globules de sang, envisagée dans ses rapports avec l'inflammation. Brussels, H. Manceaux, 1878 (116 pp.).

For Phagocytosis and Chemotropism of Leucocytes see :—

E. METSCHNIKOW. Leçons sur la pathologie comparée de l'inflammation. Paris, 1892.

CHAPTER VII

MECHANICS OF THE HEART

CONTENTS.—1. Description of cardiac cycle or revolution. 2. Changes of external form, of the internal cavity, of the position and volume of the heart in the different phases of its activity. 3. Mechanism of semilunar valves. 4. Mechanism of auriculo-ventricular valves. 5. Theory of so-called heart-sounds. 6. Variations of pressure within the auricles and ventricles during the cardiac cycle. 7. The diastolic aspiration; various explanatory hypotheses. 8. Cardiac plethysmograms; theory of active diastole. 9. Cardiograms; theory of heart-beats or impulses. 10. Other mechanical effects of cardiac activity. 11. Work done by the heart. Bibliography.

THE continuous circulation of the blood from the arteries to the veins through the capillaries demands, as its first indispensable condition, a mechanism by means of which blood pressure is maintained high in the arteries and low in the veins, so that there is a considerable difference of pressure between the two parts of the vascular system. This mechanism is represented by the heart, which in its rhythmical movements drives as much blood through the aorta and pulmonary artery during systole, as it receives from the venae cavae and pulmonary veins during diastole.

I. When the movements of the exposed heart are observed in the living animal, a series of phenomena, which are repeated at regular intervals, is witnessed. Each such cycle of movements is known as the cardiac cycle, or revolution. The duration of each cycle is exactly equal to the time interval between any two recognisable arterial pulses.

This interval may be divided into three periods: in the first is the (normally synchronous) systole of the two auricles; in the second, the (normally synchronous) systole of the two ventricles: in the third, the pause or rest of the whole heart. For simplicity's sake, the first may be termed pre-systole; the second, systole: the third, peri-systole. The diastole of the auricles coincides with the commencement of systole, the diastole of the ventricles with the commencement of perisystole.

The words συστολή and διαστολη from συ-στέλλειν, contrahere, and δια-στέλλειν, distrahere, were first used by Galen. The term peri-systole for the resting period of the heart as a whole was introduced by Riolan (Encheiridium *anatomicum,* 1649), that of *pre-systole* by Spring, 1860, who, however, intended to describe an imaginary active dilatation of the ventricle, immediately preceding systole.

Normally the duration of presystole is much shorter than that of systole. With accelerated cardiac rhythm, *i.e.* when the period of the cardiac cycle decreases, perisystole, more particularly, shortens, and shows a tendency to disappear altogether; the duration of systole, on the other hand, is either unchanged (Ludwig), or shortens only when there is an exaggerated acceleration of rhythm (Donders).

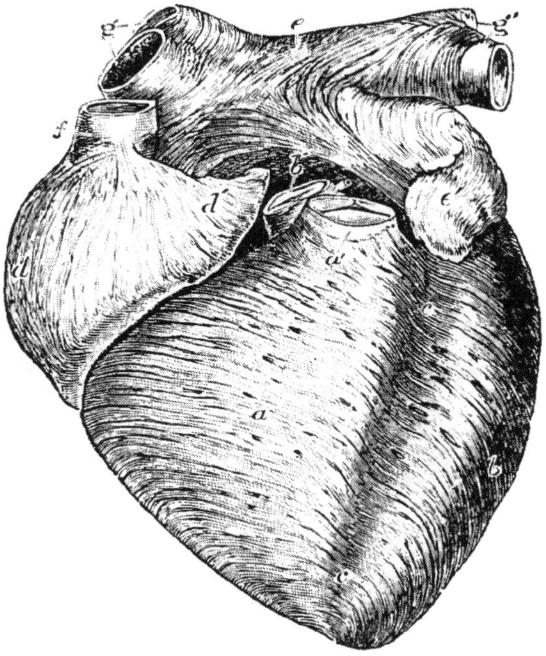

Presystole consists in a contraction of the muscular walls of the auricles, seen with the unaided eye to be peristaltic: this peristalsis starts from the extreme end of the veins which open into the auricle, is propagated in the auricle from above downwards, and extends as far as the auriculo-ventricular groove. The presystolic contraction diminishes the cavity of the auricles in every diameter, least, however, in the longitudinal direction (Kürschner).

The striated muscle fibres with which the veins are provided in the vicinity of their openings into the auricle, and the arrangement of the muscular fibres of which the walls of the auricles consist (Figs. 50, 51), account for the changes in diameter exhibited in presystole.

FIG. 50.—Human heart dissected after boiling, to show superficial muscular fibres, seen anteriorly. (Allen Thomson.) *a'*, Aorta; *b'*, pulmonary artery cut short close to semilunar valves, to show anterior fibres of auricles; *a*, superficial layer of fibres of right ventricle; *b*, that of left; *c, c*, anterior interventricular groove; *d*, right auricle; *d'*, its appendix, both showing chiefly perpendicular fibres; *e*, upper part of left auricle; between *e* and *b* the transverse fibres, which, behind the aorta, pass across both auricles; *e'*, appendix of left auricle; *f*, superior vena cava round which, near the auricle, circular fibres are seen; *g, g'*, right and left pulmonary veins with circular bands of fibres surrounding them

In systole, the ventricles seem on simple inspection to contract simultaneously at every point. Yet more delicate observation shows that the contraction here also is peristaltic, commencing at the auriculo-ventricular groove, when the presystolic movement has reached its maximum, and spreading thence to the apex with such velocity that the eye cannot follow it. Systole is accordingly only a continuation of the presystolic contraction wave, which suffers a brief delay on reaching the auriculo-ventricular groove, and is then propagated with extreme rapidity from base to apex of the ventricles.

II. The changes exhibited in the three principal diameters of the ventricles, and the modifications of the internal conformation of the heart during systole, can be estimated by direct observation (Harvey), by approximate measurements (Ludwig), and by recording apparatus (Roy and Adami). Not only the transverse diameter— which no one contests—but the longitudinal diameter also, shorten during systole : the sagittal or antero-posterior diameter seems on the other hand to lengthen a little—although this is contradicted by some observers. It is certain that during systole the elliptical base of the heart becomes almost circular, and the apex, which in rest is tilted to the left, becomes perpendicular to the centre of the base, advancing towards the thoracic wall. The ventricles simultaneously undergo a twist from left to right, by which a portion of the left ventricle wall becomes visible, which during rest is covered by the wall of the left lung.

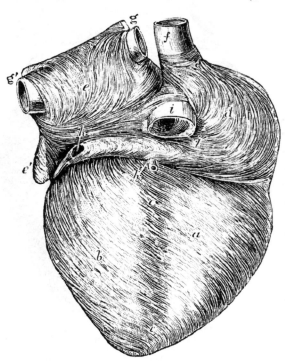

FIG. 51.—Posterior view of same preparation as in preceding figure. (Allen Thomson.) *a*, Left ventricle ; *b*, left ventricle ; *c, c'*, posterior interventricular groove ; *d*, right auricle ; *e*, left auricle ; *f*, superior vena cava ; *g, g'*, pulmonary veins cut short ; *h*, sinus of great coronary vein covered by muscular fibres ; *h'*, middle cardiac vein joining coronary sinus ; *i*, inferior vena cava ; *i'*, Eustachian valve.

That these changes of form in the ventricles during systole depend essentially, like those of the auricles during presystole, upon the specific structure of the myocardium, is shown by the fact that the same changes of form and diameter can be observed in the mammalian heart, when excised and placed upon a flat surface (Ludwig).

The structure of the myocardium is so complicated that it only lends itself to schematic representation, and not to exact description. The more recent studies of Hesse and Krehl, following on those of Ludwig and Henle, have, however, cleared up the points of greatest physiological interest, which may now be briefly summarised.

The external muscular layer of the myocardium is common
to both ventricles
(Figs. 50, 51, 52).
Its fibres take origin
in the fibrous ring
at the base of the
ventricle; they de-
scend obliquely from
above downwards,
and after rejoining
the apex of the
heart most of them
form a vortex, sink-
ing deeper and fur-
nishing almost the
whole of the inner
layer of the left
ventricle, papillary
muscles, columnae
carneae and muscu-
lar fascia of the
greater chordae ten-
dineae of the mitral
valves, as first de-
scribed by Oehl.

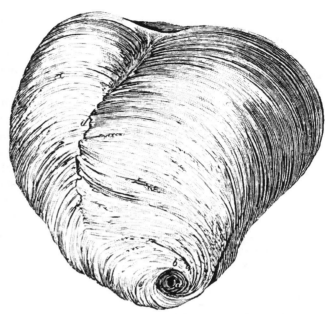

FIG. 52.—Surface fibres of ventricles of human heart from the front
and below. (Reid.) *a*, Vortex of apex; *b*, bundle of fibres emerging from exterior of left ventricle at vortex *a*, and crossing lower
part of septum uninterruptedly. At *d* the surface fibres are
somewhat interrupted.

The fibres of the internal muscular layer of the
right ventricle, on the
contrary, originate in
the upper border of the
interventricular sep-
tum, and form numer-
ous reticulated, almost
transverse, trabeculae.
At different heights of
the ventricular cavity,
innumerable little
muscle bundles and
tendon fibres unite the
septum with the walls
of the ventricle, while
other separate bundles
ascend as papillary
muscles, to unite by
the chordae tendineae
with the tricuspid valve
(Fig. 53).

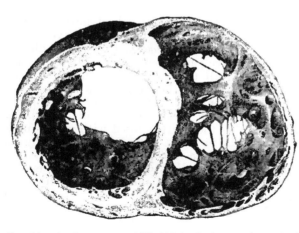

FIG. 53.—Section across middle third of a human heart fixed
in diastole. Seen in perspective. (Krehl.) The cavity of
the right ventricle shows a number of trabeculae, muscle
bundles and tendinous filaments, which connect the walls
of the ventricle in every direction with the interventricular
septum. The cavity of the left ventricle is much simpler.
The figure also gives a clear idea of the difference in thickness of the walls of the two ventricles.

In the cavity, both of the left and of the right ventricle, two
parts of the internal wall can be distinguished, which are termed

coni arteriosi (lying beneath the orifices of the aorta and pulmonary arteries); these present a smooth surface, destitute of reticular trabeculae, and provided with stout bundles of longitudinal muscles.

The far greater bulk of the walls of the left ventricle, in comparison with those of the right, is especially due to the presence of a third layer of muscle fibres, which can be isolated with nitric acid; this dissolves the tendinous and connective tissues, making it possible to separate the inner and outer coats of muscle fibres. In this way an intermediate layer of fibres can be isolated which are almost circular in direction and form a somewhat conical mass; these do not end in tendons, but wind round upon themselves, and belong exclusively to the left ventricle (Krehl: Fig. 54).

FIG. 54. Middle layer of muscular fibres, destitute of tendons, from left ventricle of human heart, after removing internal and external layers. The form of the heart is schematically indicated. ½ the natural size. (Krehl.)

No less interesting than the changes of external form are the systolic changes within the ventricular cavities. To form an adequate notion of these, it is necessary to fix and harden two human hearts, one in a state of total systole, the other, as nearly as possible of the same size, in a state of maximum diastole (Krehl's method).

To obtain the dead heart fixed in diastole, it must either not have entered the state of *rigor mortis*, or must already have passed out of it. After carefully removing the heart from the thorax, all the great vessels must be made water-tight (by means of corks introduced into their lumen), with the exception of the pulmonary vein and the vena cava superior, into which two glass tubes of the same calibre as that of the vessels must be introduced, and fixed by ligatures. Through these tubes the heart is filled with water under a hydrostatic pressure of 50-100 mm. of mercury. The water enters by the great veins into the auricles, and by the aorta into the coronary arteries, out of which it filters slowly through the cardiac walls. The heart is thus thrown into acute diastole, which is more pronounced than in life, and is left 6-8 hours in this state. It is then fixed with 96 per cent alcohol, which is passed through it for 3 to 4 hours under the same pressure as that used for the water. To complete the hardening, absolute is substituted for the dilute alcohol, without any further pressure.

Fixation in systole is effected by Hesse's heat method. The freshly extracted heart is placed for an hour in a solution of potassium bichromate at 52° C., which throws it into a state of pronounced systole.

Total systole of the human heart can only be demonstrated on the heart of a subject who has died suddenly, at the maximum of *rigor mortis*.

Dissociation of the cardiac fibres is easy after treatment with ordinary nitric acid. This acid, however, shortens the muscle fibres, and throws the heart into more or less complete systole. In order to dissect out the heart in diastole, it is necessary to prepare it with the acid under a pressure of 60 mm. mercury. This may be a complete success, but often fails, owing to the easy rupture of the heart, more particularly of the auricles. After submitting it to the action of the acid for about three hours, the heart is laid for several days in water, in which the connective tissue, softened by the acid, partly dissolves, and the rest can be readily separated from the muscular tissue. The muscle fibres can then be teased out without difficulty.

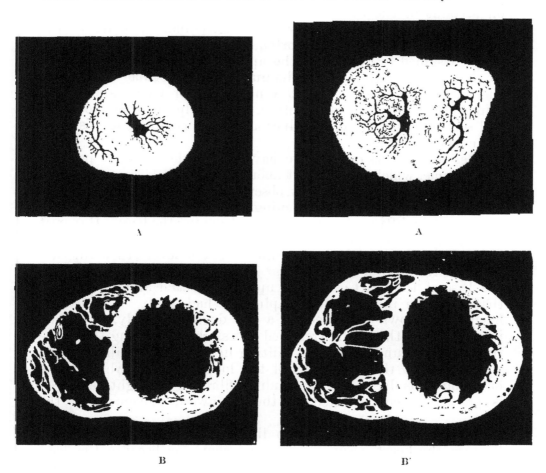

Fig. 55.—A, Section through heart of a criminal, fixed in systole, at limit of lower third of ventricles. A′, Section through same heart, at limit of upper third. B, Section through heart of approximately the same size as the preceding, fixed in diastole, at same level as A. B′, Section of same heart, at level of A′. All four figures are diminished by half. (Krehl.)

The cavity of the left ventricle, seen in section, appears in systole as an irregular, somewhat star-shaped fissure, the centre of which corresponds with the conus arteriosus. This proves that the left ventricle is unable to empty itself completely, even in maximal contraction, so that a small quantity of blood is left in it, more especially in the space immediately behind the semilunar valves of the aorta. Its driving power depends mainly on the middle layer, contraction of which must produce a lengthening of the longitudinal diameter of the ventricle: this is, however, checked by the contraction of the external and internal coats, which compress the middle coat from above downwards. The longitudinal diameter of the left ventricle thus remains almost unaltered (Krehl).

The cavity of the right ventricle is reduced in the maximal systole to a narrow space, which is curved towards the left ventricle on account of the convexity of the septum (Fig. 55). Owing to the absence of a middle layer, the longitudinal diameter of the right ventricle is bound to shorten, and contributes to the conical shape assumed by the heart, the apex becoming almost ventrical to the centre of the base. The numerous trabeculae with which the inner layer of the right ventricle is provided, and which connect its walls with the septum, must help to bring ventricle and septum together, and produce an almost complete occlusion of the cavity.

Besides changes of form we have to consider those of position and volume, which are brought about in systole.

It is easy to see by direct observation of the exposed living heart that the systolic shortening of its longitudinal diameter occurs not by lifting the apex, but by dropping the base. Haycraft (1891) demonstrated this on the closed thorax of cat and rabbit by pushing needles into the heart, which acted as levers, their fulcrum being in the wall of the thorax. The end of the needle fixed in the base of the heart oscillated upwards at each systole, showing that the base in which it was plunged had sunk. The needles fixed lower down oscillated in a less degree. Lastly, if pushed into the apex, the needle trembled but slightly, showing this to be the point that undergoes least shifting in systole from above downwards, so that the shortening of the long diameter (which, as we have shown, is due to the longitudinal fibres of the right ventricle) is practically compensated by the downward movement of the base.

The apex, however, presses a little on the thoracic wall, either because the heart assumes a conical shape, or because the base not only sinks during the emptying of the ventricle but is also tilted a little more obliquely from the back forwards (Carlile and Ludwig).

Along with the mechanical effects of the cardiac cycle it is necessary, lastly, to consider the changes of volume produced in the heart during this revolution. From what has already been said it is evident that the volume of the heart diminishes during systolic evacuation, and increases during perisystolic filling. It is further apparent that the state of maximum evacuation and minimum volume (which Ceradini proposes to call *meiocardia*) coincides with the termination of systole, and that the moment of maximal filling and maximal volume (*auxocardia*) coincides with

III. The active mechanical functions of the cardiac muscles are intimately connected with the passive mechanical functions of the semilunar and intracardiac valves, with which the arterial and auriculo-ventricular orifices are respectively provided.

The semilunar valves are fibrous membranes, forming pockets attached to the edges of the arterial orifices, their concavity being turned upwards, and their curved free borders nearly always provided with a nodule (corpus Arantii). These valves are regularly arranged so that one segment corresponds with the posterior wall of the aorta, and one with the anterior wall of the pulmonary artery : the remaining two closing with the former and converging towards the anterior wall of the aorta, and the posterior wall of the pulmonary artery.

Each segment at the place where it is attached to the arterial orifice abuts on a dilatation in the artery, which is known as the sinus Valsalvae.

Above the three reunited sinuses is the dilatation of the first section of the two arteries, which is known as the bulbus arteriosus. The aorta accordingly possesses one posterior and two anterior lateral sinuses, a right and a left : from each of these arises a coronary artery, right and left. In the pulmonary artery we have, on the contrary, one anterior and two posterior sinuses, from which no arteries arise.

Acquaintance with the anatomical form of these valves suffices to show that their physiological function can be no other than to inhibit or moderate the reflux of blood from the arteries to the ventricles in diastole, while they readily permit the efflux from ventricles to arteries during systole. From Galen to Vesalius, and from Vesalius to our own day, it has been held that the opening of the semilunar valves was the effect of the torrent of blood rushing from the ventricles at systole, and that their closing was due to the regurgitation of blood from the artery to the ventricle at the commencement of diastole ; "nam obstaculum ne quid penitus regurgitaret effingere fuit impossibile" (Vesalius). Supposing that in systole the semilunar valves are completely raised, so that they are applied to the walls of the sinus Valsalvae and occlude the openings of the coronary arteries (Thebesius, Brücke), or that they assume the half-open position (Hamburger, Rüdinger, Hyrtl), then at the beginning of diastole a greater or less reflux of blood must be postulated, to bring the valves back from the open, or half-open, position to that of complete closure. Ceradini (1871 was the first who demonstrated that the office of the semilunar valves was not to moderate, but entirely to inhibit the diastolic reflux.

He repeated and perfected certain experiments of Rüdinger in direct observation of the valves, by applying a sort of *speculum cordis* to the cadaveric heart, while imitating the cardiac systole and diastole, and was able to show :—

1. That the position of elastic equilibrium of the semilunar valves corresponds not with closure but with half-opening (Fig. 56).

2. That during the systolic efflux the three sinuses of Valsalva and the bulbus arteriosus dilate, and the semilunars assume and maintain a half-opened position, with vibration of their free borders, which therefore become blurred and give rise to a muffled sound.

3. That at the cessation of systole (systolic dead point) the valves close rapidly and then reopen, if systole is not followed by diastole.

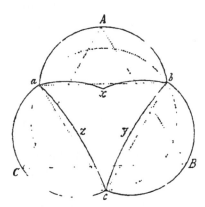

FIG. 56. Diagrammatic section, life size, across sinus of art. pulmonaris of pig; constructed by Ceradini from average of five measurements. The figure shows the position of equilibrium of the free borders of the semilunar valves. *A, B, C*, and *a, b, c*, represent the largest and the least equilateral triangle that can be described by the three outlines (*aCc, cBb, bAa*) of the sinuses of Valsalva. The circle surrounding the smallest triangle represents the projection of the constriction of the artery which divides the sinoid from the bulbar portion. The valve *x*, which corresponds to the anterior surface of the heart, has a different equilibrium from that of the two lateral valves, *y*.

4. That when diastole follows systole, the valves (which were already closed at the systolic dead point) extend towards the conus arteriosus of the ventricle, forming with their surfaces a tetrahedron, with the point directed upwards, and emit a short sound which is of higher pitch than the preceding.

From these results it is obvious that the closing of the semilunars is the effect not of commencing diastole, but of the close of systole. It is easy to see that no reflux is possible under these conditions, since the valves are already closed at the beginning of diastole, and when thrown into elastic tension do but keep up this position of closure.

When, according to Ceradini's method, diastole is imitated by starting with the half-open position of the valves, their closure is obtained by a reflux, and the amount of fluid which under these conditions regurgitates from artery to ventricle can be measured. According to Ceradini, this would be considerable, amounting to a seventh part of the flow that leaves the ventricle at systole. This proves the importance of the pre-diastolic closure of the semilunar valves, which normally prevents the loss of a considerable part of the useful effect of the cardiac cycle.

In repeating the experiment, with Ceradini's apparatus, we found several inconveniences, which we attempted to eliminate by modifications indispensable to the demonstration of the play of the valves before any large audience. Fig. 57 shows this improved apparatus.

The theoretical explanation of the mechanism of the valves

as elucidated by Ceradini, is founded on simple laws of hydro-dynamics. The engineer Darcy (1857) demonstrated that fluids passing through a tube are not under the same pressure, nor do they move with the same velocity, in the different lines into which the fluid cylinder can theoretically be analysed. The velocity is greatest, the pressure lowest, in the axial threads; in the peripheral lines the velocity is lowest and the pres-sure greatest. This law was confirmed a year later by the re-searches of Ludwig, who employed new and ingenious meth-ods. In order to esti-mate the different velocities of the lines of current, he em-ployed opaque gran-ules of lycopodium powder, suspended in water running through a glass tube. To esti-mate the difference in pressure, he observed the direction of the current in a bent tube, introduced into the main tube in such a way that one aperture was just inside the wall of that tube, whilst the other pro-jected farther towards the axis of the current.

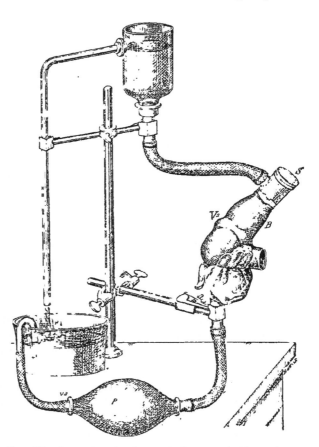

Ceradini further showed that when a piston was pushed in-to a cylindrical glass tube, held in the ver-

FIG. 57.—Apparatus for demonstrating mechanism of semi-lunar valves. B, Bulb of art. pulmonaris from heart of recently killed pig; Vs, sinus of Valsalva; S, Rüdinger's speculum, closed at one end by a simple glass plate; P, elastic rubber syringe, with which systole and diastole can be imitated by hand; vd, valve by which water can be aspirated in diastole from a receiver, and then raised, during systole, to the constant level of an upper vessel fixed at a height which corresponds to the mean blood pressure of the pulmonary artery in the living animal.

tical position, and half filled with water in which lycopodium seeds are suspended, a centripetal eddy may be observed at the base of the fluid cylinder depressed by the piston, and a centri-fugal eddy at the other end. When the movement of the piston ceases, the water cylinder breaks up momentarily into an inner cylinder, which continues to move forward, and an outer ring, which moves backward, united by a centripetal eddy.

When water containing a lycopodium suspension is made to circulate through a glass tube of small bore, which after a short distance continues as one three or four times larger in diameter, it is easy with a lens to see that there is a centripetal eddy at the point where the tube suddenly widens, at which the lycopodium granules at the base of the dilatation become central instead of peripheral in position, and move towards the axis of the current, where their velocity is greatly accelerated.

This experiment, which we have demonstrated for over forty years, is well adapted to explain the mechanism of the semilunar valves. Hesse and Krehl showed that in systole the arterial orifices are reduced by the contraction of the longitudinal fibres, which invest the inner wall of the coni arteriosi, to narrow fissures, above which is the marked dilatation formed by the sinus Valsalvae and the bulbi arteriosi. It is clear that the systolic current that flows out during systole and passes the contracting orifices must make a centripetal vortex in the sinus Valsalvae, which hinders the semilunar valves from opening completely, by tending to throw them into the closed position. So long as the systolic efflux continues, they can only vibrate round the half-opened position; but as soon as the efflux ceases, the centripetal vortex continues, owing to the force acquired from the blood, and immediately flings the valves into the position of closure. This closure, which would only be temporary, becomes permanent from the fact that the column of blood in the artery presses hard against the valves directly diastole commences.

This mechanism of the opening and closing of the semilunar valves furnishes the best and most rational explanation of the many which have come under discussion. Tigerstedt has explicitly adopted it in a recent synthetic review (1902). But he erroneously attributes the theory to Krehl, forgetting that it was clearly formulated, and fully developed and illustrated, by Ceradini, in a memoir republished in the German language as early as 1872.

IV. The mechanism of the auriculo-ventricular valves is essentially similar in type to that of the semilunars: but contains in addition other secondary features, which reinforce, and at the same time complicate, the physiological function of the valves.

The auriculo-ventricular valves (tricuspid and mitral) consist of tubular membranes, which take origin in the fibrous rings at the base of the ventricles, and divide into three tricuspid) or two bicuspid or mitral) flaps (Fig. 58).

These flaps are united by tendinous cords (chordae tendineae) —which are attached partially to the free border, partially to the inferior surface of the valvular cusps—with the pillars formed by the larger papillary muscles, or the columnae as they emerge from the walls of the ventricle. The mitral valves are more solidly

constructed than the tricuspid, to meet the greater force they have
to encounter.

Kürschner (1844) was the first to show that not a few of the
muscular fibres descend from the auricle to the superior or internal
surface of the valvular fibres.   Oehl (1861) described small muscle
bundles which accompany the larger cords of the mitral valves.

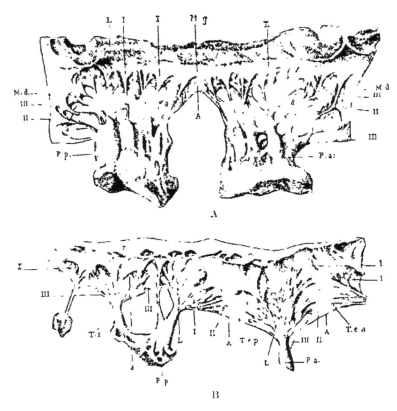

Fig. 58.—A, Mitral valve of man, seen from below.   The whole valvular ring has been spread out
in one plane, by a section through the median line of the great flap.   B, Tricuspid valve of
man, seen from below.   The valvular ring has been cut at the junction of the antero-external
and the internal flaps.   *P.a*, Anterior papillary muscles ; *P.p*, posterior papillary muscles ;
M.d, right flap of mitral valve ; *M.g*, left flap of mitral ; *T.e.a*, exterior and anterior flaps of
tricuspid ; *T.e.p*, exterior and posterior flaps of tricuspid ; *T.i*, interior flap of tricuspid ; *I, I*,
accessory tongue of valves ; *A*, great arch of free border of valves ; *a, a*, small arch of free
border of valves.   I, Tendinous cords of first order ; II, tendinous cords of second order ; III,
tendinous cords of third order.   (Marc Sée.)

Paladino (1876) described muscle fibres that are continued from
the base of the ventricle to the lower or internal surface of the
valves.

It is certain that without these valves, with which the auriculo-
ventricular orifices are provided, not a single drop of blood could
pass from the ventricles to the arteries during systole ; it would
all be forced back into the auricles and veins, where the pressure is
very low.

Many theories are current about the function of these valves, and are correct up to a certain point, but are all more or less incomplete and inadequate. A complete theory can only be obtained by weaving the several partial hypotheses together.

Prior to Lower (1679) there was no well-founded theory of the mechanism of the auriculo-ventricular valves.

He formulated a theory of the passive systolic closure of these valves by regurgitation of the blood, which had a great success. Vieussens, Winslow, Haller, Senac, Magendie and others adopted much the same opinion.

Meckel (1825) and Parchappe (1848) brought forward a very different theory, and admitted an active systolic closure of the auriculo-ventricular orifice by approximation of the folds of the valves, which are kept tense by the papillary muscles connected with them. This theory, too, found its followers, including Bérard, Surmay, and Sée, the last of whom (reasoning from the position of the valves in the hardened human heart) modified it in several particulars, while retaining the main idea of an active systolic closure. This theory, like the preceding, assumed a certain reflux of blood from ventricle to auricle. The difference is, that while on the former it was the reflux that closed the valves, on the latter it is the movement of active closure of the valve that drives back some at least of the blood contained in the conus valvularis into the auricles.

Kürschner (1840) was the first to ascribe an active function in the expulsion of the blood to the cuspid valves. He admitted, even if obscurely, that there must be a presystolic closure of the valves, brought about more particularly by the contraction of the auriculo-valvular fibres, which he described. At the beginning of systole the valves are tense, and the chordae tendineae prevent their reversal into the auricular cavity; with the progress of systole, however, they are drawn down by the contraction of the papillary muscles, and thus assist in emptying the ventricles in the direction of the arteries.

Baumgarten (1843) and Weber (1848) adopted these theories: and, in order to give a more satisfactory explanation of the pre-systolic closure of the auriculo-ventricular orifices, they included in their considerations the low specific gravity of the valves, in consequence of which they open with a light pressure, as well as the elastic tension into which the ventricles are thrown as the effect of the presystolic wave. The same explanation was adopted by Ludwig, Friedreich, Vierordt, and others in Germany.

In France, Küss, with the intention of further developing and completing Kürschner's theory, proposed a new hypothesis. He assumed that a hollow cone was formed during systole, in consequence of the contraction of the papillary muscles, which, as it descends into the ventricular cavity, tends to bring the segments of the valves into close proximity with the walls of the ventricle, which is simultaneously brought nearer the valves by the efflux of blood from the arteries. The effect of this mechanism would be a negative pressure in the auricle during systole. But the idea that the valves, when the heart is functioning *normally*, can form a sort of hollow cone during systole, which presses into the cavity of the ventricles like a stamp, is contradicted by the observations of Krehl, as already cited.

In order to form a correct notion of the mechanism of the auriculo-ventricular valves, it is indispensable to determine their position during the entire period of perisystole, presystole, and systole.

1. During perisystole, a centrifugal eddy of regurgitation must be produced at the base of the ventricles by the kinetic energy of the blood which is rushing from the auricles to the ventricles. This vortex, directed from apex to base of the ventricle, is capable of maintaining the folds of the valves (which are easily floated in consequence of their light weight) in the half-open position.

2. During presystole, ventricular pressure is slightly increased, owing to the wave of blood that is driven from auricle to ventricle. The walls of the ventricle dilate passively, and are thrown into elastic tension, while the wave of regurgitation from the centrifugal vortex increases, and the borders of the valvular folds tend to approach, and take up a position approximating to closure. The auriculo-valvular fibres of Kürschner contract simultaneously, which tends to shorten the valves and maintain them in the upright position.

3. At the presystolic dead point there is a cessation of the flow from auricle to ventricle, while the centrifugal vortex persists, in consequence of the dynamic force acquired by the blood; this causes the valves to close with perfect apposition, not merely of their borders, but also of a considerable portion of their internal or superior surfaces.

4. At the commencement of systole the valves which are already closed expand and vibrate, in consequence of the sudden rise of ventricular pressure, and form an irregularly curved arch at the level of the auriculo-ventricular orifice. This can be detected in larger animals by passing the finger through an opening made in the auricular appendix, as far as the auriculo-ventricular orifice (Chauveau), and results from the varying lengths of the chordae tendineae affixed to the inferior surface of the valvular folds (Krehl, Fig. 59).

5. During the systolic evacuation of the ventricle, the auriculo-ventricular orifice becomes more and more restricted until it almost entirely closes. At the same time the valvular folds are drawn forcibly onwards by the contraction of the papillary muscles, so that increasingly larger portions of their inner or upper surface are brought fully into contact, and deflected so as to become vertical.

The synchronous contraction of the ventriculo-valvular fibres augments their expulsive efficiency.

In this complex theory of the mechanism of the auriculo-ventricular valves (which we have insisted on for thirty years), the fact which is usually less generally accepted is that of the presystolic closure of the venous orifices, which we hold to be an indispensable condition of the normal exclusion from the systole of all trace of reflux from ventricles to auricles. Chauveau, while maintaining the theory of Kürschner, says expressly that "les valvules auriculo-ventriculaires sont pendantes à la fin de la systole auriculaire" (1876); without considering that if this phenomenon (which in his experiments is obviously the result of weakened functions in the exposed heart of the horse, injured, moreover, by the introduction of the finger into the auricle) were normal, there would, under physiological conditions, be a pronounced reflux of blood into the auricle at the beginning of systole, synchronously with the sharp rise of the valves. For it is clear that at systole the pressure increases not only in the blood that is beneath the valves, but also in that which lies along the axis of the ostium, and which can flow back freely so long as the valves are not closed.

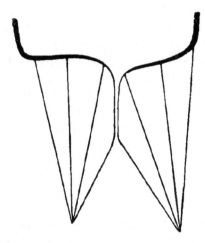

Fig. 59.—Diagram showing position of auriculo-ventricular flaps of valves at commencement of systole, owing to pull of chordae tendinae. (Krehl.)

The mechanism of valvular closure at the systolic dead point is demonstrated by the following experiment upon the excised heart of man, pig, or other large mammal. The cardiac cavity must be washed free of clot, and corks fixed in the aorta and pulmonary artery, which are cut off short; the two auricular cavities are then opened freely from above, and the margins of the openings attached to an iron ring upon a support (Fig. 60) without tearing or deforming the base of the ventricles. When the valves are normal, and *rigor mortis* has passed off, it is only necessary to fill the two ventricles and the funnel-shaped cavity formed by the walls of the auricles with water, in order to see how the valves float up and assume the half-open position. If presystole be now imitated, by injecting a few c.c. of water with a powerful syringe, the nozzle of which is directed towards the centre of the (right or left) auriculo-ventricular ostium, a marked rise of the valvular flaps will be seen, with such approximation of the borders that the orifice is converted into a narrow slit, in consequence of the centrifugal vortex and subsequent wave of regurgitation, which drives the valves upward, and tends to close them.   So soon as the

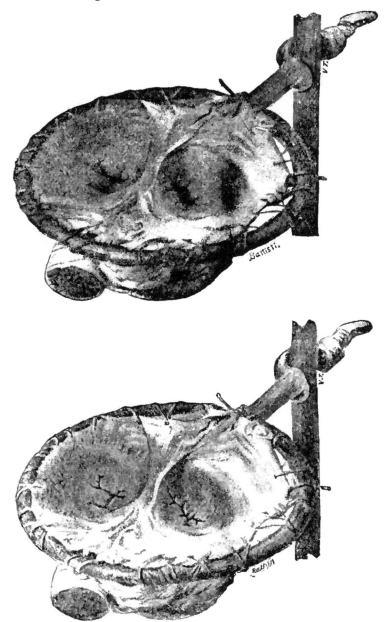

Fig. 60.—Apparatus to demonstrate presystolic closure of auriculo-ventricular valves. The two figures represent the same normal heart of a young subject. The two arteries, aorta and pulmonary, are divided near the orifices, and ligatured to corks. The walls of the auricle are opened above and stitched to an iron ring clamped to a support. On filling the cavity of the heart with water, the auriculo-ventricular valves are seen to float into the semi-open position (upper figure).   After injection of a few c.c. of water in the direction of the axes of both orifices, the valves temporarily assume the position of perfect closure (lower figure).

injection ceases, the flaps of the valves suddenly come together, closing the ostium completely for the space of a few seconds.

This shows that the persistence of the centrifugal vortex produced by the kinetic energy of the injected fluid, is *of itself* an adequate mechanical condition to secure the perfect function of the valvular apparatus, without the slightest regurgitation from ventricle to auricle—even if we admitted that presystole is not immediately succeeded by systole, but that a period of intersystole constantly intervenes, as has been proposed by Chauveau (*infra*, p. 201).

V. The acoustic phenomena which accompany the cycle or cardiac revolution are intimately connected with the valvular mechanism.

When the heart of a healthy person is auscultated directly with the ear or with the stethoscope, two distinct murmurs are heard, known to physicians as the *cardiac sounds*.

No one prior to Laennec (1819) had grasped the diagnostic importance of these sounds. Harvey, whose panegyrists claim that he was the first to describe them, confines himself to stating that at the moment when the pulse is perceptible, a murmur can simultaneously be heard in the chest. That is, he merely detected the systolic sound, and rightly named it a murmur, since it has all the properties of the latter, and can with difficulty be determined as a musical tone.

Nothing is easier under physiological conditions than to distinguish the first from the second sound: the first is longer, deeper, duller; the second is shorter, sharper, clearer. The second sound is followed by a long pause, while between the first and second there is a lesser pause.

Since the first sound is systolic, *i.e.* it persists throughout almost the entire systole, Laennec assumed that the first was the effect of the systolic efflux from ventricles to arteries, the second, of the diastolic afflux from auricles to ventricles, due to the auricular systole or presystole.

It was easy for Turner (1829) to refute the second part of this theory, by showing that the second or short sound, since it succeeds immediately to the first or long sound, coincides with the commencement only of ventricular diastole (or perisystole), and cannot therefore be the result of the auricular systole (or presystole).

Still more erroneous is Magendie's theory (1835), which assumed that the first sound was the effect of the impact of the apex of the heart against the thoracic wall in systole, and the second of the impact of the base during presystole. The sounds persist even after the thoracic cavity has been opened, and the heart exposed.

The so-called *valvular theory* of cardiac sounds was first formulated by Carswell and Rouanet (1832). Starting from the correct observation that the first sound is more acute in the region of the ventricles, and the second in that of the arterial orifices, they admitted that the first depended on the vibrations of the venous auriculo-ventricular valves, the second on the vibration of the arterial or semilunar. They also succeeded in producing an artificial sound in an excised aorta, by throwing the valves into sudden tension.

Williams and the Dublin Committee of the British Association (1835) undertook to test this theory, and confirmed by ingenious experiments the part which referred to the second sound. They noted that the second sound was abolished when the play of the semilunar valves was impeded, as when the apex was cut, and the blood prevented from issuing by the arteries. They, however, found the valvular theory to be incorrect as regards the first sound, observing that it persisted even when the heart was void of blood and excised from the animal. Accordingly they postulated a purely *muscular* origin for the first sound—a theory that was taken up later on by Ludwig and Dogiel 1868, and confirmed by numerous experiments.

Wollaston had already shown in 1810 that the contraction of a muscle can produce a bruit. Ludwig further showed that the muscles of the ventricle, which are interwoven in various intricate ways, and form two cavities with trabeculated inner surface, must be better able than skeletal muscles to generate a bruit when suddenly thrown into tension.

The demonstration of the muscular theory does not, however, exclude there being some truth in the valvular theory of the first sound. Wintrich 1875, by means of Helmholtz' resonators, succeeded in analysing the first sound, and recognised it to be the result of two components: a deep sound (or rumble of a muscular character, and one or more sharp tones, depending not merely upon the vibrations of the auriculo-ventricular, but also upon those of the semilunar valves, demonstrated, as above, by Ceradini.

Even with these additions, however, the theory of the sounds of the heart was incomplete. Talma (1880) examined the valvular theory from the standpoint of the laws of acoustic vibrations, and objected that since the valves are immersed in a fluid of lower specific gravity than themselves, the sounds that are generated when they are thrown into sudden tension must essentially depend upon the vibrations of the blood, rather than on those of the valves.

Webster (1882), however, showed that Talma had overlooked one fact, namely, that both the first and second sounds can be resolved into several components, by the help of a resonator. He attempted to prove that the effects of the vibrations of the semilunars and also of the walls of the bulbi arteriosi, can be distinguished from the effects of the vibrations of the blood in the second sound. To this we would add that the valvular vibrations that contribute to the formation of the second sound, coincide, not with the *closing* of the valves, as is stated in every text-book, but with the *tension* into which they are thrown after closure, when the ventricular diastole commences.

In conclusion, we may admit the following points as established :—

1. The systolic sound is essentially a muscular bruit, with which higher tones are associated that depend on the vibrations of the auriculo-ventricular valves, the semilunars, and the mass of the blood.

2. The post-systolic sound is the result of higher tones depending on the vibration either of the semilunars and the bulbi arteriosi when thrown into tension, or of the mass of the blood.

The importance of the heart-sounds, from a physiological stand-point, consists in recognising them as the external signs of the duration of the phases of the cardiac cycle, since there is good reason for assuming that the commencement of the first sound coincides with the commencement of systole, the commencement of the second sound with the commencement of diastole ; and that the interval between the first and second sounds represents the duration of systole, the interval between the second and first, the duration of perisystole *plus* presystole. We shall see how Edgren has applied these criteria.

It is not the physiologist's task to make any profound examination of the pathological changes in the heart's sounds, or to go into their great significance from the diagnostic and clinical standpoint. But in so far as these changes are a proof, and a further illustration, of physiological theory, the most general aspects of them may be summed up in a few words.

Cardiac sounds under pathological conditions may be reinforced or weakened, according as the heart's action is stronger or weaker than in the normal state. The first may be a sign of hypertrophy, the second of degeneration, of the myocardium.

In auricular hypertrophy there may be a presystolic murmur, immediately preceding the systolic, giving the effect of a duplication or abnormal lengthening of the first sound. On the other hand there may be a real doubling of the second sound, when the tension of the aortic semilunar valves (which normally have to bear a greater pressure) precedes that of the semilunars of the pulmonary (which normally sustain less pressure) in marked degree.

In stenosis of the orifices and in valvular insufficiency the sounds are replaced by "blowing" murmurs, which are produced by the vibrations of the blood as it passes through the narrowed orifices or imperfectly closed valves.

In these can be distinguished :—

(*a*) Post-systolic murmurs, the diagnostic sign of insufficiency of aortic or pulmonary semilunars, according as they are more audible in the region of the origin of the aorta (right sternal

border between the first costal and second intercostal space) or in
that of the pulmonary artery (left sternal border, at the level of
the second intercostal space).   (Fig. 61, *Ad* and *As*.)

(*b*) Presystolic murmurs, the diagnostic sign of stenosis of the
right or left auriculo-ventricular orifice, according as it is more or
less audible in the region of the right ventricle (external border
of sternum at the level of the fourth intercostal space), or in the

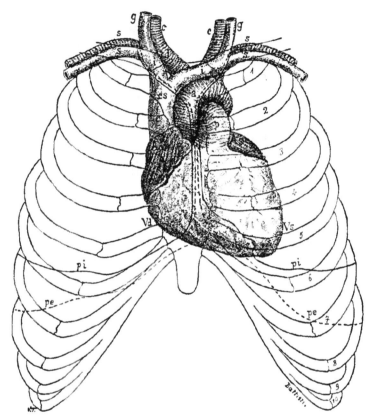

Fig. 61.—Semi-diagrammatic figure of topography of the heart and its relations with the lungs
and thorax. *Vd*, Auscultation point of right ventricle ; *Vs*, auscultation point of left
ventricle ; *Ad*, auscultation point of aorta ; *As*, auscultation point of pulmonary ; *A*, aorta ;
P, pulmonary artery ; *cs*, vena cava superior ; *i, i*, innominate artery and vein ; *s, s*, subclavian
artery and vein ; *c, c*, carotid arteries ; *g, g*, jugular veins ; *pe*, dotted line to show limit of
lungs in inspiration ; *pi*, continuous line showing limit of lungs in expiration ; 1-10, 1st to
10th ribs.

region of the left ventricle (left mamillary line in the fourth or
fifth intercostal space).   (Fig. 61, *Vd* and *Vs*.)

(*c*) Systolic murmurs, the diagnostic sign either of insufficiency
of the venous valves (bicuspid or tricuspid), or of stenosis of
the arterial orifices (aortic or pulmonary), according as it is
more conspicuous at one or other of these four points. Systolic
murmurs are distinguished from the preceding by their greater
accentuation, since they are produced by stronger vibrations, and
by the fact that the thoracic walls vibrate along with them

(*fremitus*), as can be perceived on laying the hand upon the precordial region.

The mechanical deficiencies of the heart can be compensated

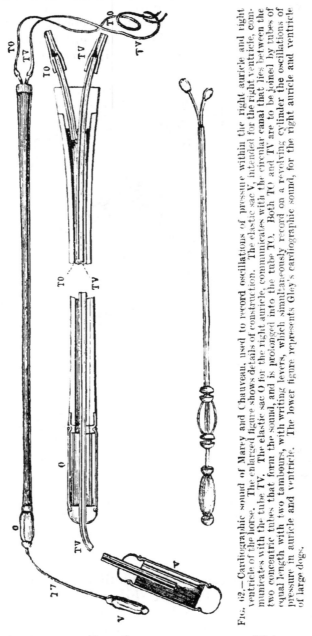

FIG. 62.—Cardiographic sound of Marey and Chauveau, used to record oscillations of pressure within the right auricle and right ventricle of the horse. The enlarged figure shows details of construction. The elastic sac V, intended for the right ventricle, communicates with the tube TV. The elastic sac O for the right auricle, communicates with the circular canal that lies between the two concentric tubes that form the sound, and is prolonged into the tube TO. Both TO and TV are to be joined by tubes of equal length with two tambours, with writing levers, which simultaneously record on a revolving cylinder the oscillations of pressure in auricle and ventricle. The lower figure represents Gley's cardiographic sound, for the right auricle and ventricle of large dogs.

so that patients may live for many years. This compensation depends essentially upon hypertrophy of the myocardium: more particularly upon hypertrophy of the ventricles, in cases of valvular insufficiency—upon hypertrophy of the auricles in arterial

VI. In order to comprehend the nature of the evacuation and refilling of the heart, it is important to make an experimental study of the oscillations of pressure within the auricles and the ventricles, in presystole, systole, and perisystole.

These observations were first made by Chauveau and Marey (1861) on the horse, by means of the so-called *cardiographic sound*, in conjunction with a tambour and lever writing upon a rotating cylinder (Figs. 62 and 63). The modifications in instrument and method made by Fick, von Frey, Hürthle, Roy, Fredericq, Bayliss and Starling, and Porter, have led to results which differ in certain important points from those of the two French investigators.

In the original researches of Chauveau and Marey, the tracings of the oscillations of pressure in the right auricle were very imperfect, owing possibly to insufficient sensibility of the elastic ampulla introduced into the said cavity. At the Rome Congress (1894), Chauveau corrected certain errors of Marey, on the strength of new cardiographic curves, obtained from the horse by means of more perfect exploratory sounds.

These observations were published in a series of memoirs (1899-1900), which seem to us

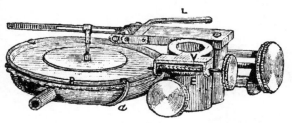

Fig. 63. — Marey's tambour with writing lever (Verdin's perfected type). *a*, Metal capsule closed by rubber membrane, attached without tension to metal ring B. The aluminium disc fixed to the centre of the membrane carries a writing lever. Special contrivances make the instrument more or less sensitive by adjusting the initial position of the lever, and bringing the writing point nearer to or farther from the surface of the moving drum.

rather to indicate the unreliability of results obtained with the cardiac sound, than to add to the known data of cardiac mechanism.

Let us examine the most important of these memoirs, that entitled *L'Intersystole du cœur* (1900). This Chauveau calls a phase of his cardiographic tracings, interpolated between presystole and systole.

If the interpretation which he gives of this period, interposed between the systole of the auricles and that of the ventricles, were correct, it would involve a complete revolution in the fundamental concepts of cardiac mechanism. To prove this, it is only necessary to bear in mind the conclusions above stated in regard to the function of the auriculo-ventricular valves.

These close at the end of presystole, so that they are already shut at the beginning of systole. If, however, we admit an intersystolic phase, then the said valves, not being kept in the position of closure by rise of ventricular pressure, would reopen, and thus render useless the entire apparatus described above for closing them.

Chauveau, disregarding the conclusions of Ceradini (whom he does not mention), maintains on the ground of obscure experiments and complicated arguments, that the contraction of the papillary muscles of the ventricles occurs during his "intersystole," with the object of disposing the flaps of the auriculo-ventricular valves in such a manner that the systolic rise in ventricular pressure (which, according to him, brings about the valvular closure) may impinge principally not upon the axial but upon the parietal face of the valves.

No long argument is required to demonstrate the impossibility of this hypothetical doctrine. We know that the auriculo-ventricular valves close at the termination of presystole. The

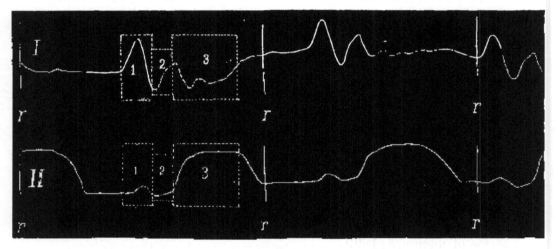

FIG. 64.—Tracings obtained by Chauveau from the horse, by his perfected cardiographic sound. I, Oscillations of pressure in right auricle; II, Oscillations of pressure in right ventricle; r, return to abscissa; 1, period of auricular beat (contraction and relaxation); 2, period of intersystole; 3, period of ventricular beat (contraction only). This is succeeded by the period of ventricular diastole, which Chauveau does not indicate.

supposed intersystolic contraction of the papillary muscles, causing them to reopen, could not, even if it placed them in a position unfavourable to the systolic reflux, entirely prevent it. On the other hand, the researches of Roy (1890) show that the papillary muscles do not contract before the muscular walls of the heart, but enter into tardy contraction, thus facilitating the almost complete evacuation of the ventricles in systole.

Tigerstedt's interpretation of Chauveau's intersystole, in the fourth edition of his *Physiologie des Menschen*, seems no less impossible. He thinks it depends on the elastic reaction of the walls of the ventricles, which are passively distended in auricular systole, and which occurs only in cases in which the termination of the latter and the commencement of the ventricular systole are separated by a considerable time interval. It is, in fact, sufficient to look at one of Chauveau's curves, especially that of the internal pressure of the auricle and right ventricle, which he gives as typical (Fig. 64), to see that the intersystole does not follow immediately upon simple systole, but on the complete pulsation of the auricle (auricular systole and diastole).

Since, however, the intersystole coincides with a sharp rise of pressure in the auricle, and since the presence of a sound introduced between the flaps of the valves may give rise to a slight reflux of blood from ventricle to auricle, it seems probable that the intersystole depends precisely upon this slight reflux, coincident with the initiation of ventricular systole.

It is evident from these data that the "intersystolic phase" of Chauveau's tracings represents no real fact, occurring during the normal cycle of cardiac movement, but is in all probability an artefact, coincident with the period of latent systole, artificially prolonged by the presence of the exploring sound in the auriculo-ventricular orifice.

But if this point in Chauveau's tracings is difficult to interpret, another feature offers far more insuperable obstacles, i.e. that part of the pressure curve in the auricle which corresponds to the ventricular diastole, which Chauveau passes over, keeping silence on the subject.

At that period there is in Chauveau's curves an incomprehensible rise of auricular pressure. Now the observations of all other experimenters, carried out by different methods, more reliable than the sound, have, without exception, resulted in showing a negative pressure in the ventricle during the primary phase of diastole. Since in diastole, when the cuspid valves are open, the auricle and ventricle form a single cavity, it is evident that the negative pressure existing in the ventricle must be propagated to the auricle also.

More interesting and more probable, on account of their simplicity, are the researches carried out by numerous experimenters on the venous pulse of the cava and jugular veins, either in man or in animals, which throw light on the mode in which the right heart is filled and emptied.

Among the authors who have more recently been engaged on this subject are Mackenzie (1902), Beccari (1903), Wenckebach (1906), Fredericq (1907). They have recorded tracings of the venous pulse (phlebogram) with a simultaneous record of the cardiac pulse (cardiogram), or of the radial artery (radiogram).

In nearly all healthy people, in the horizontal supine position, with head and neck a little lower than the body, it is possible to detect with the eye the pulsation at the base of the neck, and to take a tracing of it, by means of a sufficiently sensitive exploring tympanum. In the stage of convalescence from diseases, accompanied, as in jaundice, by weakening of the heart-beat, it is easy to obtain fairly clear phlebograms, which in their elevations and depressions faithfully reflect the phases of activity of the right heart.

The phlebograms made by Wenckebach present three elevations and three depressions as shown in Fig. 65.

Elevation (*a*) coincides with presystole, and expresses the temporary arrest of the venous current (perhaps its partial reflux also) during the contraction of the right auricle. The second rise (*c*) corresponds with systole and depends, according to Mackenzie and Wenckebach, on the mechanical transmission of the carotid pulse beneath the vein that is being explored. This is rightly

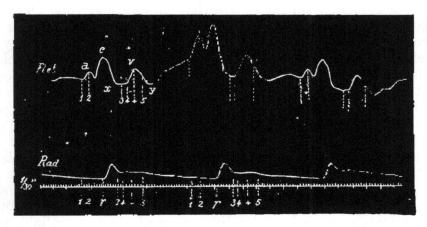

FIG. 65. Tracings of oscillations of pressure in jugular vein (phlebograms) recorded with a fairly sensitive exploring tambour, applied to the base of the neck in a youth of 25, recovering from catarrhal jaundice (Wenckebach). Sphygmograms from radial artery simultaneously recorded with the phlebograms. Time marked in ⅕". The points of return marked on the tracings divide the period of pulsation into the five intervals described in the text.

contested by Fredericq, on the strength of his researches on dogs, from which he proved that the rise (*c*) which accompanies the beginning of systole is due to the closure movement of the tricuspid valve. (Better expressed as, due to the projection towards the auricle of the said valve, already closed at the termination of presystole.) The third rise (*r*) coincides with the tension of the semilunar valves already closed at the termination of systole, and probably depends upon the impulse received by the right auricle in the dilatation of the ostium and arterial bulb in consequence of the wave of rebound which occurs at the commencement of diastole.

The depressions of the phlebograms are more interesting to consider, *i.e.* the two negative phases of the venous pressure. The first (*x*), from the apex of (*c*) to the base of (*v*), coincides with the phase of systolic emptying of the ventricles, and is due to the sinking of the base of the ventricle by which the auricular cavity becomes filled, and exercises a marked aspiration upon the veins. The second negative phase (*y*) coincides with diastole, and depends, according to Wenckebach, on the fact that during ventricular relaxation the blood can flow freely from the vein to the auricle, from the auricle to the ventricle, by the negative pressure or aspiration which this exerts during the said phase.

L. Fredericq, in his studies on dogs (in relation to cardiography of the heart and the venous pulse, 1890-1907), insisted on the virtual identity of the phlebograms with the tracings of the variations of blood pressure within the right auricle, which he obtained with open thorax, on putting this cavity into direct communication with a sensitive sphygmoscope (Fig. 66).

Fig. 66.—Marey's sphygmoscope, which acts as an elastic manometer in connection with a tambour. It consists of a cylindrical glass tube, closed at both ends by rubber stoppers with a hole through the centre of which come two glass tubes. An elastic cap is slipped over the right-hand stopper, filled with an anticoagulant solution, and connected with a blood-vessel. The cap reacts to each rise and fall of pressure, by expanding or contracting. The tube on the left-hand side conveys these movements to the tambour.

To obtain an idea of the individual phases of the cardiac cycle and the oscillations of pressure within the auricles, ventricles, and large arteries, we may avail

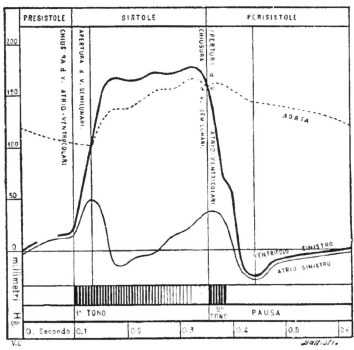

Fig. 67.—Diagram of cardiac cycle or revolution. The three curves reproduce the tracings of oscillations of pressure obtained simultaneously from the left auricle, left ventricle, and aorta of the dog, by Fredericq's method. The duration of the different phases of the cycle, and the time at which the heart-sounds are perceptible, are marked on the abscissæ; the intracardiac and aortic pressures in mm. Hg, upon the ordinates.

ourselves of a diagram constructed from the data provided by the work of Fredericq, which agree fundamentally with those admitted by all competent physiologists who have occupied themselves with the mechanics of the heart (Fig. 67).

The diagram is so clear that a detailed description is superfluous. As appears in the figure, during presystole (which lasts for about the sixth part of the time of the internal revolution) there is a slight rise in auricular pressure which is transmitted to the ventricle also, and which, as we shall see, effects the perfect closure of the venous valve at the presystolic dead point.

In systole (which lasts two and a half times longer than presystole) two periods must be distinguished; the first, which is short, termed the period of tension or latent systole; the second, somewhat longer, that of efflux, or systolic evacuation.

The first corresponds to the time necessary for the ventricular pressure to reach and exceed the level of aortic pressure, in order to determine the opening of the semilunars.

With the sharp rise of ventricular pressure, there is a simultaneous rise of auricular pressure, determined by the tension and upward propulsion of the cuspid valves.

The duration of this period in the horse is, according to Marey, 0·1″; Hürthle, on the contrary, finds it to be for dog 0·02-0·04″, and Fredericq confirms this last figure. For man the data vary considerably. Marey, Rive, Landois, Edgren give figures oscillating between 0·1″ and 0·073″, Grunmach indicates a value of 0·07″, Keyt 0·054″. Hürthle, on the ground of his researches on the dog, calculates the period of tension as equal to 0·03″ for man, a figure which is certainly too high.

The second systolic period coincides with the rise of aortic pressure (arterial pulse), the final elevation of ventricular pressure which is then arrested in a kind of *plateau*, and a sudden drop of auricular pressure, until it falls below zero, after which there is again a slow but progressive rise.

Physiologists have long disputed over that portion of the curve of intra-ventricular pressure which is known as the *systolic plateau*, and corresponds to the ventricular efflux. While the tracings obtained by Chauveau and Marey in 1863 on the horse, and all the subsequent publications of Chauveau, show an almost horizontal tract between the rapidly ascending (systolic), and the corresponding and rapidly descending (diastolic), portions, many authors maintain that the curve which represents the internal pressure of the ventricle is composed solely of a rapidly rising, followed by a correspondingly rapidly falling portion; they deny the existence of the systolic plateau. This point has recently been taken up again by various authors, both English and American, among whom are Bayliss, Starling, and Porter. They have introduced important technical alterations in the method, which tend to exclude instrumental inertia.

Bayliss and Starling employed a manometer containing a solution of magnesium sulphate, one arm of which is open, and connected with the cavity of the ventricle by means of an open sound, while the other arm consists of a capillary tube sealed in the flame and containing air. This small volume of air becomes more or less compressed by the liquid in the manometer, owing to the pressure transmitted to it from the ventricle. The degree of compression of the air column is registered by the displacement of the shadow of the meniscus of the liquid column, which is projected on to a rotating cylinder covered with sensitive paper.

Porter invented a method with the same object, but too complicated to be given here. Both his results and those of Bayliss and Starling confirm the statement that the curve of intraventricular pressure presents a true systolic plateau during the efflux of blood from the heart. This important feature of the cardiac function seems, therefore, to be definitely established.

In perisystole, too, it is possible to distinguish two periods ; the one shorter, of active diastole, the other more prolonged, of passive diastole or rest of the whole heart. During the former, pressure falls suddenly both in ventricle and auricle, and becomes negative, thus permitting the active refilling of the heart by aspiration of blood from the veins. During the second, the negative pressure rises again slowly in the ventricle and auricle, until at the beginning of presystole it approximates to the zero line : this represents the period of passive filling of the heart, caused by the *vis a tergo* of the venous blood stream, and the negative pressure in the thoracic cavity, when the experiment is conducted with the closed thorax.

The elastic ampullae and sphygmoscopes of Chauveau and Marey are instruments well adapted for obtaining tracings of the form of the rapid oscillations of pressure that occur within the cavities during the cardiac cycle, but they are inadequate to determine the absolute value of the intracardiac pressure. The best method for determining the maximum to which the pressure

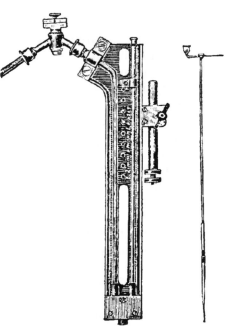

Fig. 68.—Ludwig's mercury manometer (Zimmermann's type). The float seen on the right consists of a fine steel rod terminating at the lower extremity in a pointed ivory cone, which dips into the column of mercury, and at the upper extremity in a glass pen filled with ink, which traces the variations of pressure upon the paper of the revolving drum.

in the cavities may rise, and the minimum to which it may fall, is that of Goltz and Gaule (1878), which was also employed by De Jager (1883), and consists in fitting to the recording mercury manometer (Fig. 68) a valvular apparatus which closes when the pressure falls, and opens again when it rises, or *vice versa*, so that the manometer serves as a maximum or minimum manometer. When connected with a cavity of the dog's heart by means of an open sound, the column of the manometer will rise at each systole to a given maximal height, after which it traces a horizontal line (maximum manometer) : or falls at each diastole to a certain minimum, after which it remains stationary (minimum manometer).

The highest figures for cardiac pressure were obtained by De Jager, who employed a maximum manometer and a sound of wide calibre, on large dogs. He found in three experimental series :—

	I.	II.	III.
In left ventricle	235	174	111 mm. Hg
In aorta	212	162	158 ,,
In right ventricle	28	44	72 ,,

These values are probably below the normal, since it cannot be supposed that the introduction of a sound into the cavity of the heart produces no disturbance of the systolic function.

It would be more interesting to determine the exact relation between the maximal pressure of the right and that of the left ventricle, since these must harmonise with the different strengths of the muscular walls of both ventricles, and with the different resistances which the two vascular systems (aortic and pulmonary) present. The experimental data so far obtained have not, however, led to any concordant results. On an average it may be assumed that the pressure in the right ventricle and pulmonary artery is to that of the left ventricle and aorta as $1:2.5$, or $1:3$ (Goltz and Gaule, Colin, Beutner).

VII. The absolute values of negative intracardiac pressure obtained with the minimum manometer are linked with the question so much discussed in the last quarter of last century, *i.e.* the determination of the mechanical factors by which the filling of the ventricle during diastole is effected.

The theory supported by Harvey and Haller, to the effect that the diastolic filling of the heart occurs quite passively, from the wave of blood which rushes from auricle to ventricle in presystole, was for a long while accepted almost unanimously by physiologists. The opposite theory, by which the heart acts as an aspirating pump in diastole and as a pressure pump in systole, is, however, still older, since it was formulated by Erisistratus and Galen, and maintained at a later period by Vesalius, Bichat, Sprengel, and Magendie, without indeed finding any large number of adherents.

In 1871 we revived the *theory of diastolic activity*, on the strength of certain rudimentary experiments. which may be described as follows :—

(*a*) When in a dog with opened thorax a trocar is introduced through the apex into the interior of one of the ventricles, and a horizontal glass tube, open at the end, is attached to the cannula, a jet of blood can be seen in the tube at each systole. which recedes at each diastole.

(*b*) If the pressor effect of the presystole is impeded by seizing the walls of the auricle with a forceps, the diastolic aspiration increases conspicuously.

(*c*) If in consequence of vagus excitation, the heart's movements are retarded, the diastolic aspiration increases so much that the tube connected with the ventricle is emptied.

(d) If the hollow of the pericardial chamber is filled with milk, and connected with a horizontal glass tube, containing a fluid to serve as index, the total volume of the heart will be found to increase during diastole, while with gentle stimulation of the vagus this diastolic increase of volume is still further augmented. This phenomenon is not necessarily connected with slowing of the heart's action, since the same thing can be seen in the frog with no appreciable changes in systolic frequency. (Coats.)

The conclusions we deduced from this and other facts had the rare fortune of being confirmed by more complete and decisive experiments. A. Fick (1873) showed by means of the metal manometer, which he connected up with the right or left ventricle of the dog (by a sound introduced through the jugular vein or carotid), that pressure sinks below the zero line during diastole. Goltz and Gaule (1878) endeavoured with their minimum manometer to determine the absolute value of the negative diastolic pressure with open thorax, and found that it may amount to − 320 mm. of water in the left, and − 25 mm. in the right ventricle, and diminishes progressively with the weakening of systole, *i.e.* in proportion as the systolic evacuation becomes less complete. The values obtained by De Jager by the same methods were higher : he found a negative pressure that may amount to − 38 mm. Hg. in the left, and − 6 mm. Hg. in the right ventricle. Values approximating very closely to these were obtained by other workers, *e.g.* Rolleston, v. Frey, and Krehl (1890), with the elastic manometer, both with closed and with open thorax.

It was Stefani, however, who directly undertook the task of experimentally checking, one by one, the propositions which we had formulated in 1871, and repeated with certain alterations in 1874 and 1876. In a series of interesting memoirs (1877-1891) he placed on a firm experimental basis that same doctrine of the activity of cardiac diastole which we had preached for many years with ever-growing conviction, adding many new arguments in its favour.

It is essential to the comprehension of this theory to premise that the thesis of active diastole may be considered from two different points of view. The diastole may be considered *active* in a purely mechanical sense, viz. that the refilling of the ventricles during the first period of perisystole is the effect not of the *vis a tergo* of the blood descending from the auricles into the ventricles, but of the aspiration developed by the latter during that interval. The expression *active* can, however, also be employed in a strict physiological sense, viz. that the diastole is controlled and regulated the action of the vagus. Let us first consider the mechanical aspect.

We have already seen that two periods can be detected in the course of a cardiac revolution, during which the heart develops a negative pressure and exercises aspiration upon the blood issuing from the veins: there is a moment of systolic and a moment of diastolic aspiration (see Fig. 67). The former is confined to the auricles: the latter extends both to auricles and ventricles.

When systolic aspiration (as in Fredericq's experiments cited above) takes place with the opened thorax, it must depend on the sudden sinking of the base of the heart in the first period of systolic efflux, which increases the capacity of the diastolic auricle. This is the explanation given by Purkinje (1843), by Nega (1851), and more recently by Chauveau and Lefèvre, as well as Fredericq. This aspiration of the auricles has nothing to do with diastolic activity; it is caused by the systole of the ventricle, which works simultaneously as a pressure pump against the arteries, and as an aspirating pump against the auricles and veins.

The diastolic aspiration, on the contrary, which coincides with the first period of perisystole, and spreads from the ventricles to the auricles and adjacent veins, does really represent energy developed by the ventricles during diastole. The mechanical effect of diastole is indeed very small as compared with the mechanical effect of systole: but in any case it is sufficient to defend the opinion that the ventricles are active in the first period of perisystole, and dilate by aspiration, not by the *vis a tergo* of the blood rushing in from the auricles. The little frog heart is capable in its diastolic distension of overcoming a resistance equal to 15-20 mm. of water (Mosso and Pagliani); the heart of a dog can dilate, even when pressure is put upon its outer surface, in excess by 20-30 cm. of water of that to which its inner surface is submitted (Stefani).

Various hypotheses have been put forward to explain the diastolic aspiration, which may be rapidly summarised:—

(*a*) The pressure within the thoracic cavity is negative even in the expiratory position of the lungs, and becomes more strongly negative during inspiration.

As early as 1853 Donders pointed out the importance of this mechanical factor, which serves to facilitate the course of the blood in the intrathoracic veins and the diastolic filling of the heart by aspiration. Yet this does not adequately explain the diastolic aspiration, which can be demonstrated even with the open thorax. Nor does it explain the cardiac aspiration visible with closed thorax, since this is greater in the left than in the right ventricle, and in the latter again than in the auricles, where it should, in consequence of the ready extensibility of the auricular walls, be greatest.

(*b*) In 1855 Brücke revived the theory of the auto-regulation of the heart, basing it on the same arguments as already brought forward by Thebesius (1708). According to this theory the coronary arteries empty during systole and expand in diastole, either because in systole the orifices of the coronary vessels are closed by the raising of the semilunar valves and their application to the walls of the sinus Valsalvae, or because the finer ramifications and capillaries of the coronary vessels are closed or drawn together by the contraction of the myocardium.

The first argument was refuted by Lancisi (1728) in opposition to Thebesius, and again, with more cogent reasoning, by Hyrtl against Brücke, and it is, in the light of all that is known about the mechanism of the semilunar valves, entirely erroneous. Neither Hyrtl nor Ceradini, however, found any valid objection to the second argument, which is to-day regarded as established by the experiments of Klug and Rebatel, and the more recent work of Porter and Hyde. Klug succeeded in the living animal in ligaturing one heart in systole and another in diastole. On microscopic examination he found that the superficial vessels were full of blood in the first heart, while the deeper ones were almost empty: in the second, all the coronary vessels were turgid. Rebatel, using Chauveau's haemodromograph (see next chapter), succeeded in obtaining a tracing of the pressure and velocity of flow in the coronary arteries of the horse. He found that pressure and velocity increase in the first period of systole; that at a second period, pressure increases and velocity decreases until it becomes negative (arrest and recession of blood into the coronary vessels); finally, that at the beginning of diastole there is acceleration of velocity without increase of pressure. Porter was able to convince himself by an admirable method, in the dog, that the intramuscular branches of the coronary vessels were compressed and emptied by the contraction of the myocardium, and that this systolic evacuation assisted the streaming of the blood through the walls of the heart when the myocardium relaxed, owing to the diminished resistance offered by the slack and empty vessels to the blood-stream. Lastly, Hyde studied the effects of the various distensions of the ventricular cavities on the isolated cat's heart, by suffusing blood through the coronary vessels at constant pressure. He determined that whether the heart was at rest or beating, the flow of blood diminished when the heart was more extended, i.e. when circulation in the coronary arteries was impeded.

But even if the automatic regulation of the heart, in so far as systole impedes the circulation in the coronary arteries by compressing them, while diastole facilitates the filling of the coronaries, be accepted, it does not necessarily follow, as assumed by Brücke, that there is in diastole a kind of erection of the cardiac walls which tends to produce a negative pressure in the cavity, and to facilitate its filling. It is true that Donders and Albini claim, with the help of a manometer communicating with a cavity in the dead heart, to have observed a diminution of pressure, so soon as they injected the walls of the heart from the coronary artery; but Oehl, on repeating the experiment, found exactly the contrary, i.e. increase of pressure within the heart, so soon as the pressure was strongly augmented in the coronary vessels.

This contradiction between the results of such experienced experimenters shows, without reference to other arguments that might be brought forward, and have been adduced by Oehl, that Brücke's theory is quite inadequate to explain diastolic aspiration.

(c) Gaule (1886) suggested that the negative pressure in the ventricle, which he determined with Goltz by means of a minimum manometer, depended on the dilatation of the aortic orifice after closure of the semilunar valves at the commencement of diastole. Since the aorta is connected with the fibrous ring from which the muscle fibres of the ventricle originate, it follows that the ventricular cavity must dilate at the moment when the ring becomes distended, producing a negative pressure. Both Minck (1890) and Krehl (1891) proposed this hypothesis.

But even if it is undeniable that when the aortic orifice dilates, the conus arteriosus which lies below, and is in a certain sense one with it, dilates also, it does not follow that this condition occurs at the beginning of diastole, and can explain the diastolic aspiration. The maximum of pressure and dilatation in the bulbus aortae must obviously be reached during the systolic efflux, and not at the commencement of diastole. "At the first outpouring of the systolic stream," as Ceradini says, "the bulbous portion of the artery (aorta or pulmonary) dilates, so that each of its diameters increases by about one-fifth: the walls of the sinus Valsalvae are better able to resist the impact, yet they, too, show a very considerable dilatation, owing to the distension of the valvular membranes, whose free borders become straight at the first onset."

At the commencement of diastole, on the other hand, the valves are already closed and bulge towards the conus arteriosus, so as to diminish its capacity, presenting with their united margins the figure of the sides of a tetrahedron, the apex of which, built up of the three coincident corpora Arantii, falls on its vertical axis, and is inverted downward towards the hollow of the conus arteriosus. "The insertion of the valvular borders," says Ceradini, "are externally recognisable at the points of contact of the ellipsoid formed by the sinus Valsalvae, by a conspicuous depression, which is visible at the arterial wall at the first onset of diastole, in consequence of the sudden distension of the semilunar membranes."

Gaule's explanation accordingly fails to explain the diastolic aspiration.

(d) The oldest hypothesis in explanation of the active diastole is that of Galen, who distinguished in the heart predominatingly transverse, and predominatingly longitudinal fibres. In systole the former contract, and the cavities of the heart are restricted; in diastole the latter contract, and the cavities are dilated. Vesalius assumed much the same position, which had many adherents both before and after Harvey, who denied that there was diastolic activity. In 1861 it was revived (with slight modifications) by Spring. He supposed that the more or less longitudinal fibres of the heart contracted somewhat before the transverse, thus producing an active dilatation of the ventricular cavities before the commencement of systole proper. This theory is, however, put out of court by the fact that aspiration is determined not at the pre-systolic but at the post-systolic moment.

Brachet (1815) maintained that active diastole depended on hypothetical radial fibres, coursing from endocardium to pericardium, which he believed himself able to demonstrate on the heart of man, horse, and ox. According to this author, the walls of the heart exhibit a considerable thickening in systole; in diastole the radial transverse fibres contract and reduce the diameter of the walls of the heart, thus augmenting its capacity. Most French writers of the first half of last century, e.g. Filhos (1855), Choriol (1841), upheld this view, which, however, was strongly disputed by Parchappe and Bérard. In order to prove this position it would be necessary to show that the two kinds of fibres in cardiac muscle contracted successively and not simultaneously, as we must assume.

In a corrected and amended form the hypothesis of Galen, of Brachet, and of Spring was revived by Krehl (1891). He assumes an unequal i.e. a non-sychronous relaxation of the different muscular layers of the heart, and held that the expulsor muscle (intermediate layer of the left ventricle) relaxed earlier than the longitudinal fibres of the internal layer, so that the latter, being no longer compressed, enabled the walls of the ventricle to move apart. He founds his position upon the experiment of Roy (1890), who succeeded in obtaining simultaneous tracings of the contraction of the walls of the heart, and of the papillary muscles, and demonstrated that these last contract later and relax earlier. This fact, however, contradicts Krehl's view, according to which the papillary muscles relax later than the walls of the ventricle. Among Krehl's various hypotheses this appears to us the least acceptable.

(c) The most universally accepted view of diastolic aspiration is that it depends on the elastic reaction of the myocardium, thrown into tension at systole. This is the theory which was clearly expressed in 1838 by Magendie, when he compared diastole to the dilatation of a rubber tube when released from compression. L. Fick (1849) was the first to prove this on the dead heart in which he imitated systole by compressing it with his hand, and diastole by simply releasing it. On sinking the heart in a vessel of water, he was able at each compression to drive a jet of fluid through the arteries, a proof that, after releasing the ventricles, the internal cavity distended and filled with water. It was objected to this experiment that the phenomenon might be due to cadaveric rigidity of the heart: Goltz and Gaule, however, regarded the elastic reaction of the heart at the commencement of diastole as proved by their experiments with the minimum manometer.

The same view was taken by De Jager, who met every conceivable objection to the theory that the filling of the heart at the commencement of diastole depended not on the *vis a tergo* of the blood, but on the elastic reaction of the heart's walls, by the fact that, after opening the thorax, pressure is at zero in the cavity of the right auricle and adjacent vein. This one fact is sufficient to establish the doctrine of diastolic activity in the mechanical sense.

But in this connection arises the question of the origin of this elastic reaction at the commencement of diastole. Is it dependent on cardiac muscle properly so-called, or on the elastic tissue implanted in the walls of the heart? Certain authors subscribe in virtue of quite independent arguments to the former of these theories, admitting a possibility of an active lengthening of the muscular fibres of the myocardium. The first to express this view was the English physiologist Carpenter, who, at the end of 1855, maintained that the active force which causes the heart to dilate must originate in the myocardium proper. He propounded the hypothesis that just as active muscular contraction, which causes the muscle to shorten, depends on the attraction of the particles of which that muscle is formed, so the reciprocal repulsion of those same particles must produce the active elongation of the muscle fibre.

In 1871, not being aware of Carpenter's hypothesis, we brought forward another, essentially similar to it, but differently expressed. We suggested that the contraction and subsequent expansion of the myocardium might be determined by two antagonistic physiological processes, so that the cardiac diastole would, like the systole, be an active movement. At a later time this hypothesis was taken up and elaborated by Stefani (*infra*).

Lastly, mention must be made of Albrecht, who has recently (1903) published a valuable study on the myocardium. He, too, considers diastole to be an active physiological process, on the ground of Verworn's theory of the general physiology of muscle. According to Verworn the expansive phase of the mechanical response of muscle is active, and is determined by the tendency of the anisotropous substance, saturated during the contractive phase by the katabolic products, to assimilate oxygen and nutrient juices from the environment. For this purpose the anisotropous substance seeks to acquire the largest possible superficies, *i.e.* it expands. Verworn does not deny that this expansive movement (*i.e.* relaxation) is assisted by numerous extrinsic factors, *e.g.* the tension of tendons and fascia, etc., but he still attributes a not inconsiderable function to the expansive activity proper of the muscle fibres. Albrecht extended to the heart the idea which Verworn had formulated for muscles in general. He accordingly defines diastolic activity as a functional necessity of recuperation.

Other authors, on the contrary, ascribe the active character of diastole to the elastic tissue contained in the myocardium. Krehl appears to have adopted this hypothesis. He holds that there are many elastic fibres beneath the endocardium, surrounding the muscle bundles of the internal layers, which may be thrown into tension during systole, and react in diastole by dilating the cavities of the heart. The elastic lamellae which extend from the semilunar valves passing under the origin of the aorta into the interior of the muscles may produce the same effect. Lastly, he believes that the root of the aorta, deeply implanted, and always distended under high pressure during the energetic systolic diminution of the base of the heart, must be deformed; so that at the commencement of diastole, when it recovers its position of equilibrium, the pressure must involve a distension of the soft muscles. This last idea is a new form of Gaule's hypothesis, as already refuted. In any case, Krehl's propositions, as a whole, leave us uncertain whether the dilator reaction of the heart, at the commencement of diastole, is to be ascribed to the elastic tissue or to the cardiac muscle. The former is, however, absolutely put out of court by certain very important facts adduced by Stefani, which go to determine the physiological character of the active diastole.

VIII. In a previous paragraph we referred to the changes in total volume of the heart, during the several periods of its activity. We said that it diminished during systole, at the termination of which *meiocardia* occurs, *i.e.* the maximal diminution of the heart's volume; and that it increases during perisystole until it attains the maximal volume, or *auxocardia*, at the commencement of presystole.

After our first experiments in 1871 (in which, to estimate the changes in volume of the heart, we employed the pericardial cavity filled with milk) Franck and Stefani (1877) were the first who adopted the method of the pericardial fistula for curarised dogs, kept alive by artificial respiration—tracings of the oscillations of the total volume of the heart (cardiac plethysmogram) being recorded on a rotating drum. This is easy enough with simple air transmission, *i.e.* by connecting up the cannula applied to the pericardium with a tambour and writing lever, artificial respiration being temporarily suspended.

.The plethysmograms obtained by this method give an approximate picture of the quantity of blood with which the

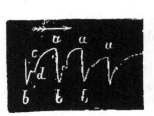

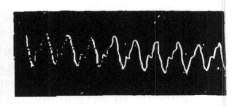

Fig. 69.—Cardiac plethysmograms. (Stefani.) *a*, *b*, Descending portion. coinciding with systolic outflow ; *b*, *c*, rapidly ascending portion, coinciding with active diastolic influx ; *c*, *a*, slowly ascending portion, coinciding with passive diastolic influx ; *d*, notches, which nearly always occur on the ascending shoulder.

heart is charged, or which it discharges at the different periods of its cycle, and consequently of the systolic diminution, and perisystolic amplitude of the ventricular cavity.

As appears from the tracings in Fig. 69 we can distinguish :—

(*a*) A rapidly descending line which coincides with the period of systolic evacuation.

(*b*) A rapidly ascending line (in which there is invariably a notch) corresponding with the period of active diastole.

(*c*) A slowly ascending line (sometimes horizontal or even slightly descending as shown in Fig. 70), which corresponds to the time of passive diastole and presystole.

It is obvious that neither the period of presystole nor the succeeding interval of tension or latent systole, during which the total volume of the heart undergoes no important modification, can be distinctly shown in cardiac plethysmograms. Since in the

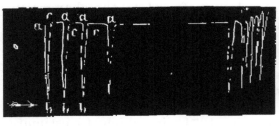

Fig. 70.—Cardiac plethysmograms, in which the line *c*, *a* of passive refill is descending or almost horizontal.

third period of the plethysmogram there may be a slight augmentation of cardiac volume, or it may be stationary, or diminish, the deduction of Stefani seems valid, to the effect that " the venous current (in consequence particularly of presystole) must in the first case suffer a simple retardation, in the second an arrest, in

the third a reflux." The most important results which Stefani
obtained from analysis of cardiac plethysmograms are as follows:

(*a*) Their magnitude varies considerably not merely in different
animals, but also in the same animal, showing that the heart,

Fig. 71. A, Plethysmogram obtained under normal conditions; B. Plethysmogram from same
dog, during dyspnoeic excitation of vagus.

under different circumstances, is able more or less completely to
fill and empty itself of blood, "so that it may assume a volume
considerably greater than that attained in the preceding cycles,
independent of any modification in the frequency of the beat."
(This comes out clearly in Figs. 69, 70, 71.)

(*b*) There is no perceptible difference in the duration and form
of the two first periods of the plethysmogram (line of systolic

Fig. 72. Plethysmogram showing augmentation of cardiac volume during excitation
of left vagus.

evacuation and active diastolic refill) with changes in frequency
of the heart's beat. It is only the third period (of slow passive
refilling) that varies in duration and form with the acceleration
or retardation of the cycle. (This is demonstrated in the tracings
of Figs. 71, 72, 73.)

From this Stefani draws the logical conclusion that both the
first and second periods of the plethysmogram are the effect of
physiological activity—while only the third can be regarded as the
effect of repose of the heart.

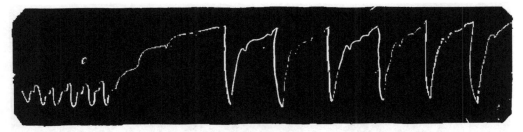

FIG. 73.—Plethysmogram showing that stimulation of one vagus by strong induction currents
has no effect on systolic evacuation, but conspicuously increases the period of passive refill.

(c) If the vagus be excited, either directly or by cessation of
artificial respiration (which has the effect of increasing the venosity
of the blood), profound changes appear in the cardiac plethysmograms, varying in form according to the degree of excitation
and the excitability of the nerve, but all having this in common
that the ascending line of the diastolic refill has a considerable
upward lift, which signifies that the heart acquires a greater
volume. (Tracings of Figs. 71, 72, 73, 74, 75.)

This phenomenon cannot be dependent on the slowing or
suspension of the beats of the heart, because on the one hand the
increase of volume occurs rapidly and in a degree which far exceeds
the normal, and on the other there is a marked demarcation
between that part of the line of refill which corresponds with active
and that which corresponds with passive diastole; and finally
because the heart is able on excitation of the vagus to attain its
maximum volume before the venous pressure has had time to rise
to any considerable
extent (Fig. 76).

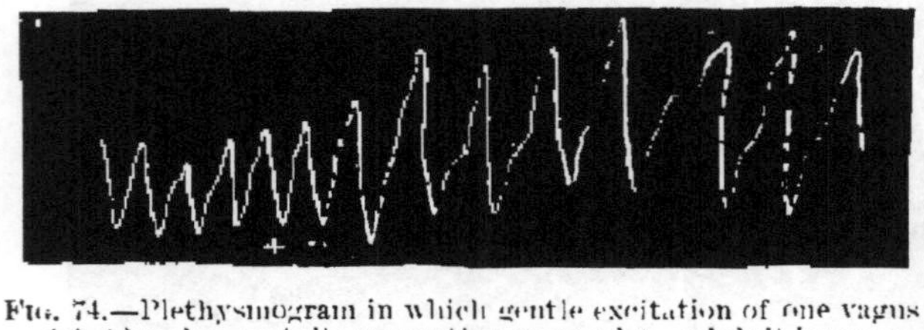

Stefani considers
that these facts con-
firm the doctrine
we have maintained
since 1871, to the
effect that the vagus
is a diastolic nerve,
in the sense that
"it actively provokes increase of volume in the heart, by modifying the physiological condition of the cardiac muscles."

FIG. 74.—Plethysmogram in which gentle excitation of one vagus
(at +) makes systolic evacuation incomplete while it increases
diastolic refill.

This same theory of the mode of action of the vagus upon the
heart (to be discussed in detail in the next chapter) was successively
put forward by Rossbach (1882), Heidenhain (1882), Williams
(1887), Tigerstedt and Johannssohn (1889), and also by François-

Franck (1891), who in 1877 had pronounced in precisely the opposite sense.

It thus became necessary to determine more exactly the nature of the action of the vagus, in so far as it is a diastolic nerve, capable, i.e., of modifying the internal physiological state of the cardiac muscles. With this object, Stefani undertook to measure the pressure that must be exerted on the outer surface of the heart in order to arrest the circulation of the blood. This he compared with the pressure simultaneously exerted upon its internal surface, and noted the

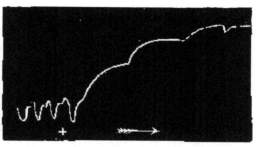

FIG. 75. Plethysmogram showing that strong excitation of one vagus (at +) exaggerates effect shown in preceding figure.

changes in the difference between the two pressures, according as the vagus was excited or paralysed. From this ingenious and original research Stefani obtained most important results, which we may summarise in a few words.

A pericardial fistula was made on a dog, the cavity being connected by a T-shaped tube, on the one hand with a pressure bottle filled with 1 per cent solution of NaCl, on the other with a mercury manometer. When the fluid is made to descend into the cavity of the pericardium, the manometer measures the pressure exerted on the outside of the heart. Another manometer, in which

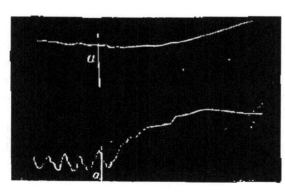

FIG. 76. The upper curve represents the venous pressure, the lower the plethysmogram. At a, a (the corresponding points on either curve) one vagus was strongly excited. The two curves show that the augmentation of cardiac volume corresponds to a slight fall of venous blood pressure.

an alkaline, anti-coagulant solution is substituted for mercury, is connected with a glass tube introduced into the vena cava superior, in order to measure the venous pressure acting upon the internal surface of the heart. A third mercury manometer can be connected with the carotid in order to measure the arterial pressure.

In proportion with the increase of pericardial pressure, the venous pressure increases owing to the obstruction of the flow to the heart, while arterial pressure diminishes owing to the diminished output from the heart. When the pericardial pressure is so high that it completely inhibits the flow of blood to the heart and circulation is arrested, the arterial pressure rises to 15-20 mm. Hg and the venous pressure to 12-18 cm. H_2O. If one vagus is stimulated by an induction current at the moment at which circulation ceases, the interesting phenomenon of a rise in arterial pressure may be observed, and cannot be explained otherwise than by admitting with Stefani that the heart is capable, under vagus stimulation, of charging itself with blood, even against the pericardial pressure, which previously impeded this loading. The vagus is thus able to excite active dilatation of the heart.

Stefani applied the term diastolic pressure to that exerted by the heart in diastole upon the surrounding fluid of the pericardium, by which it overcomes the resistance, distends its cavities, and permits the blood to penetrate it. He measured this diastolic pressure in eight dogs, determining the difference between the pressure in the pericardial cavity and in the vena cava. The results are as follows:—

No. of Animal.	At the moment of Arrested Circulation.		
	Pressure in Pericardium.	Pressure in Vena Cava.	Diastolic Pressure.
1	35 cm. H_2O	10 cm. H_2O	25 cm. H_2O
2	20 ,, ,,	6 ,, ,,	14 ,, ,,
3	40 ,, ,,	8 ,, ,,	32 ,, ,,
4	27 ,, ,,	13 ,, ,,	14 ,, ,,
5	27 ,, ,,	8 ,, ,,	19 ,, ,,
6	27 ,, ,,	13 ,, ,,	14 ,, ,,
7	25 ,, ,,	14 ,, ,,	11 ,, ,,
8	26 ,, ,,	12 ,, ,,	14 ,, ,,

It appears from these figures that in ordinary diastole the heart develops a pressure upon the pericardial fluid which is capable on an average of supporting a column of water of 19 cm. This result harmonises well with that obtained by the minimum manometer of Goltz and Gaule as described above.

On measuring the pericardial pressure capable of arresting the circulation, before and comparatively soon after section of the vagi, Stefani obtained the following results on five dogs:—

No. of Animal.	Pericardial Pressure able to Arrest Circulation.		Difference.
	Before Section of Vagi.	After Section of Vagi.	
1	35 cm. H_2O	20 cm. H_2O	15 cm. H_2O
2	26 ,, ,,	16 ,, ,,	10 ,, ,,
3	21 ,, ,,	12 ,, ,,	9 ,, ,,
4	24 ,, ,,	13 ,, ,,	11 ,, ,,
5	23 ,, ,,	13 ,, ,,	10 ,, ,,

Diastolic pressure is accordingly reduced after division of the vagi to an average of 11 cm. H₂O, *i.e.* to a value little more than half of that developed with intact vagi, which confirms the diastolic or dilator action of the vagi upon cardiac muscle.

If the vagus is excited after bringing the circulation to a standstill by pericardial pressure, the manometer in connection with the pericardial cavity shows a rise of pressure which soon falls again when stimulation ceases. If these oscillations of the manometer be recorded on a rotating cylinder, the following tracing (Fig. 77) is obtained, which is a new and direct proof that the degree of diastolic dilatation is regulated by the vagus.

Lastly, in order better to control the theory of diastolic activity, Stefani successfully employed certain poisons (atropine, digitaline, and strychnine), measuring the diastolic pressure before and after injection of the drug, and before and after section of the vagi. He came, in a few words, to the following conclusions: that

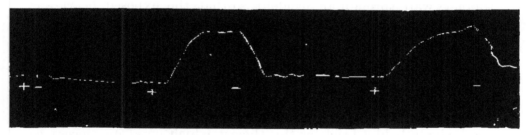

FIG. 77.—The recording mercury manometer is connected with the pericardial cavity. Show disappearance of plethysmographic oscillations in the heart, in consequence of hydrostatic pressure exerted within pericardium. The vagus was stimulated in the neck at —. slightly at first, afterwards more strongly.   marks close of excitation. During stimulation the heart dilates, and resumes its original volume at the close of excitation. (Stefani.)

atropine lowers the diastolic pressure because it paralyses the dilator action of the vagi, and that digitaline and strychnine increase the diastolic pressure because they act directly upon the cardiac muscle, and render it capable of active dilatation in excess of the normal.

Until these important facts determined by Stefani are contradicted or shown to be fallacies, we shall continue to regard the theory of diastolic activity (which we formulated in 1871) to be well founded, both from a purely mechanical and from a physiological point of view.

In the ninth chapter we shall discuss certain experimental data which enable us to determine, up to a certain point, the nature of the internal process by which the vagus develops and regulates the activity of the diastole.

IX. After developing the mechanism of the systolic evacuation and diastolic refill of the heart it is easy to deal with the question of the cardiac beat or pulse, which, like the heart-sounds, constitutes an important external sign in the investigation of this organ in man and in intact animals. It consists in a rhythmical elevation of the intercostal spaces corresponding with the pericardial region to the left of the sternum. The impact is generally supposed to be greatest at the level of the fifth intercostal space, a little within the mamillary line, where the apex of the heart lies normally; but from a series of careful investigations by Mariannini and Namias (1882) it appears, on the contrary, that the point at which the beat of the heart is normally strongest corresponds more frequently (in 67 per cent) with the fourth than with the fifth intercostal space, in the supine horizontal position. It is usually perceived by palpation, but in thin persons with large intercostal spaces it is visible to the eye.

Harvey was the first to point out that the cardiac beat occurred during systole. His theory is the more valuable, inasmuch as he had the opportunity of directly observing the beats of the heart on Viscount Montgomery, who had lost part of his thoracic wall through an accident, so that the exposed heart was visible (*Exercitatio de generatione animalium*, lii.).

This generally accepted doctrine, which has received ample confirmation from modern researches with the graphic method, was at one time contradicted, on the strength of fallacious observations in which the *ictus cordis* was regarded as the effect of the sudden dilatation of the ventricles at the moment of presystole. Corrigan, Stokes, Pigeaux, Burdach (1832), Beau (1835), Baccelli (1859), successively held a brief for this theory, which owed its success, as Marey remarked, "à ce qu'elle était simple et logiquement déduite."

The first promoters of this theory, Corrigan and Stokes, admitted their error, and that it is still perpetuated by the Italian clinician Baccelli is doubtless the result of an ambiguity. At the Rome Congress in 1894 he maintained that the impact of the heart coincides with the moment immediately preceding systole. It is obvious that by systole he means the period of evacuation or ventricular efflux, as was always understood by physiologists as well as clinicians, prior to the introduction of the graphic method. But since it is now well established that the efflux is preceded by a period of tension or of latent systole, which lasts from 0·10 to 0·08″, it is clear that this must be the moment with which, according to Baccelli, the impact of the heart coincides. We are completely at one with this opinion, provided it be understood in the sense that the displacement of the thoracic wall reaches its greatest height during that period. It agrees, in fact, perfectly with what we learn from the cardiogram.

The method now generally adopted by physiologists and clinicians in recording the tracings of the cardiac beat (cardiogram) is that of tambours with an elastic membrane and air transmission. Hürthle, in 1892, made an interesting control research with the different models of cardiographs as *a priori*, expect a certain number of the various characteristics found by different authors in the cardiograms of healthy individuals, to be due to the method or rather to the instruments employed. Hürthle performed a double series of experiments. In the first place, with the tambours of Marey, Knoll, and Grunmach, he recorded an identical impulse, mechanically produced. Then with the same tambours he successively recorded the cardiograms of one healthy individual. The result of his experiments showed that while Marey's tambour was not wholly free from error it recorded the impulses in such a way as to reproduce their characteristics accurately. The cardiographs invented by Knoll and Grunmach, on the other hand, were very fallacious.

The following tracing (Fig. 78), obtained by François-Franck from a woman suffering from *ectopia cordis congenita*, is convincing since in this case the heart, having dropped down through an abnormal opening in the diaphragm, beat beneath the skin in the linea alba of the epigastrium. It is clear that the rhythmical elevation determined by the ventricular systole commences exactly at the close of presystole.

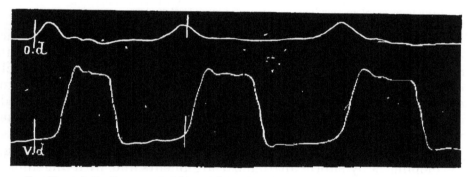

FIG. 78. *o.d*, Cardiograms of right auricle ; *v.d*, cardiograms of right ventricle, recorded simultaneously by two separate explorers with writing levers. (François-Franck.)

No less convincing are the cardiograms obtained from man under normal topographical conditions of the heart, which are recorded simultaneously by an electric signal at the precise moment at which the first and second sounds are first heard. We have shown that the first sound is concomitant with systole, and any one who questions whether it begins at the moment of tension, *i.e.* prior to the ventricular efflux, need only study the tracing obtained by Marey from the horse with a cardiographic sound introduced into the right ventricle (Fig. 79).

Starting from this well-established fact, the cardiograms of the heart-beat (Fig. 80) which Edgren obtained from his cardiograph, used simultaneously with the stethoscope, have the same value and lead to the same conclusions as the foregoing tracings of François-Franck.

Since the cardiac pulse is proved to be initiated in the rapidly ascending movement before the intraventricular tension has succeeded in opening the semilunar valves, all those hypotheses are necessarily discredited which seek to explain this phenomenon as the effect of the systolic outflow of the blood into the arteries.

Carlile (1833) and Ludwig (1848), in order to explain the cardiac pulse, took into special consideration the conical form assumed by the ventricular mass in systole, and the forward

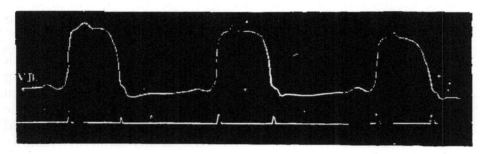

Fig. 79. Oscillations of pressure in right ventricle (V.D.) of horse, transmitted through cardiac sound to recording tympanum. (Marcy.) The times at which the first and second heart-sounds begin to be heard are simultaneously recorded by an electric signal.

inclination observed in the base of the ventricle, which causes the apex of the heart to impinge on the wall of the thorax. But since this change of form and movement of the heart is the effect of systolic evacuation, it is obvious that it cannot be adduced to explain the sudden rise seen in the cardiograms during the period of tension, *i.e.* before the blood begins to stream out of the ventricles.

In a recent work Keith (1904) has taken up the idea of Ludwig, developing it by subtle anatomical arguments and with ingenious experimental methods for which we refer the reader to the original memoir. Keith maintains that the base of the ventricle

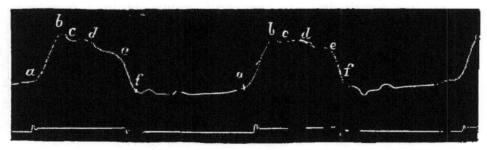

Fig. 80.—Cardiogram transmitted to cardiograph from fifth left intercostal space in man. (Edgren.) The times at which the first and second heart-sounds begin to be heard are simultaneously recorded by an electric signal.

rises slightly during presystole. This displacement depends more particularly on the peculiar disposition of the pectinate muscles. In consequence of this rise of the base of the ventricle, it almost meets the blood which is driven towards it. When, on the contrary, systole sets in, upon which the ventricle is restrained in every dimension, its base is pushed out in the opposite direction.

It follows that the apex of the heart does not approach the base, but on the contrary the base approaches the apex, so that the latter is energetically thrust against the thoracic wall and produces the cardiac beat. It may, however, be objected to this ingenious experiment that the sharp lift produced by the cardiac impulse takes place not during the period of efflux, but in that of tension.

The same reason invalidates the doctrine of the recoil (*recul balastique*) supported particularly by Skoda 1842 and Hiffelsheim (1854), which in so far as it assumes locomotion of the heart resembles the preceding. It is also contrary to the fact that the cardiac pulse is not confined to the region of the apex in the fifth intercostal space, but (as we have seen) is even more frequently accentuated in the fourth intercostal space.

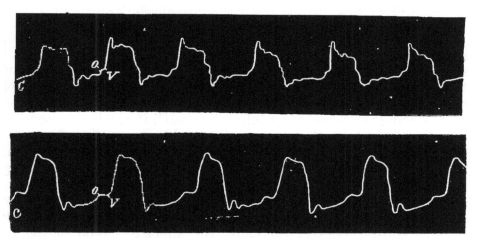

Fig. 81.—The upper tracing is an artificial cardiogram obtained from a perfected model. The lower tracing is a cardiogram taken on man. In both tracings the rise O represents the effect of presystole; the rise V, the effect of systole. (Marey.)

Still more inadequate is the theory maintained by Senac (1749), Bahr (1862) and others, which derives the cardiac pulse from the downward impulse of the apex in consequence of the distension of the arterial arches (aortic and pulmonary) determined by the pressure produced in these by each wave of blood that surges from the heart. We have seen that the apex is the least mobile point of the heart in the longitudinal direction, because the elongation of the arterial arches almost exactly compensates for the systolic shortening.

All these mechanical factors intervene as accessory and complementary data in the production of the *ictus*, during the period of systolic evacuation : but the essential and fundamental cause of the phenomenon is the tension and hardening of the heart during the whole period of systole. The heart is in perpetual contact with the internal wall of the thorax and the external parts of the lungs,

which cover it to a great extent : but during the period of passive
diastole or repose, its walls are soft and easily compressible, while
in the systolic period they become hard and tense, and this is
enough to determine the phenomenon of *ictus*. This theory,
adumbrated by Harvey, was clearly set forth by Kiwisch (1846),
and upheld more recently by Bamberger, and by Chauveau and
Faivre (1856) ; but Marey (1863-76) was the first to give convincing
proof of its accuracy by his ingenious schemata of the movements
of the heart. He succeeded with these in producing artificial
cardiograms, which exhibit all the most important features of the
cardiograms obtained on man, as shown in the two tracings of
Fig. 81.

The analytical study of these features is of great scientific and
practical interest, but we must consider them together with the
waves exhibited by the arterial pulse and the sphygmograms, with
which they are intimately connected by their origin.

X. The systolic movements of the heart in the period of tension
must, since they determine a sudden elevation of the intercostal
spaces of the precordial region, produce a rhythmical dilatation of
the thoracic cavity, in proportion with the energy and rapidity of
the impact. Further, the diminution of the total volume of the
heart during the period of systolic efflux until it reaches meiocardia
is commensurate with the quantity of blood expelled from the
arteries. Half this blood, passing through the pulmonary system,
does not leave the thoracic cavity ; but the other half, passing
through the aortic system, issues rapidly from the thorax, producing a comparative vacuum, which cannot be compensated by
the blood that simultaneously enters the thorax by the venae
cavae. During systole, therefore, the thoracic cavity must, in
virtue of distinct mechanical conditions which succeed each other,
develop an aspiration, capable of being felt in the intercostal
spaces not in contact with the heart—in the lungs, the diaphragm
and the veins adjacent to the thorax.

In thin persons it is, in fact, easy to see coincidently with
systole, a depression of the intercostal spaces, to which the name of
negative cardiac pulse has been given (to distinguish it from the
positive pulse that can be observed in the region of the apex of
the heart and its vicinity). At the same moment there is also a
negative pulmonary pulse, *i.e.* a gentle inspiratory movement of
the lungs which, when the glottis is open, may produce a systolic
diminution in the pressure of the air contained in the buccal cavity
or nasal fossae. It is also possible to detect a negative pulse of
the abdominal wall in the epigastric region, which is the effect of
an aspiration exerted by the thoracic cavity on the diaphragm.
Lastly, it is possible also to observe a negative systolic pulse in the
jugular veins due to the same cause, although here it is probable
that other mechanical factors co-operate, which are independent of

the changes of intrathoracic pressure, and depend on variations of pressure within the right auricle.

Many physiologists have exercised their critical and technical abilities upon these phenomena of *negative pulsation*, the indirect effects of the positive cardiac pulse and of meiocardia. Buisson (1861) was the first to describe the negative thoracic pulse, and the negative pulmonary pulse: Voit (1865) again observed the

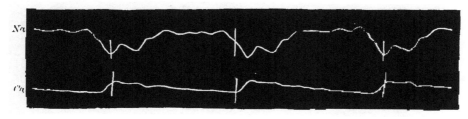

Fig. 82.—*Na*, Pneumogram taken from the nostrils; *Ca*, sphygmogram from the carotids, recorded simultaneously with open glottis. (Mosso.) It will be seen that the inspiratory movement precedes the carotid pulse.

rhythmical systolic inspirations, and held them to be the effect of the diminution in the heart's volume: Ceradini (1869) clearly perceived the mechanical consequences of meiocardia and auxocardia, but made no experimental study of them; Paul Bert (1870), among the oscillations of air-pressure within the trachea of a dog, included those dependent on cardiac movements; Lovén (1870) took tracings of the negative thoracic, and the positive pulse of the radial artery, and observed them to be simultaneous: Landois (1876) obtained tracings of the cardiac oscillations of air-pressure of the nasal cavities (which he termed cardio-pneumatic curves),

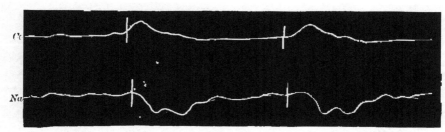

Fig. 83.—*Ca*, Cardiogram taken on man at fifth intercostal space; *Na*, pneumogram taken from nostrils. Simultaneously recorded with open glottis. (Mosso.)

and was the first to distinguish the negative pulse which can be verified at each systole when the glottis is open, from the positive pulse which occurs when the glottis is closed, and the nasal cavities function as a space distinct from those of the pulmonary passages, in which there is diminished pressure with each wave of blood that inundates the arterial vessels.

Mosso (1878) was, however, the first who grasped this subject fully, and employed an exact experimental *technique*. In his cardio-pneumatic curves obtained with an ordinary Marey's tambour

connected with the nasal cavities, he was able to distinguish a first
inspiratory depression, due to the systolic lift of the intercostal
spaces of the precordial region, from a second, later depression due
to meiocardia. This is plain in the two tracings (Figs. 82 and 83),
in the first of which the negative pneumogram of the nasal fossae
is recorded simultaneously with the sphygmogram of the carotid,

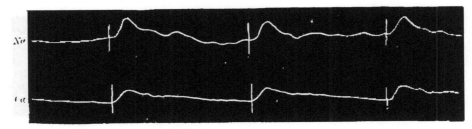

FIG. 84.— Na, Positive pneumogram taken from nostrils with open glottis ; Ca, carotid
sphygmogram, recorded simultaneously. (Mosso.)

and in the second with the thoracic cardiogram. Repeating the
experiment with closed glottis, the negative pneumogram is transformed into the positive (as shown on Fig. 84). All who, like the
author, are incapable of holding their breath without closing the
glottis, obtain, on the repetition of Mosso's experiment, positive
pneumograms only. This was the case (as Mosso points out) with
Terné van der Heul (1867), who, on making these experiments
under the guidance of Donders, invariably obtained results that
contradicted the above theory.

If a sound is introduced into the oesophagus, covered at the

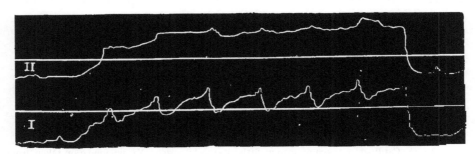

FIG. 85.—1, Cardiac sphygmogram from dog, transmitted from oesophageal explorer to recording
tambour during long expiratory pause ; II, effects of cardiac beats transmitted from rectal
explorer, recorded simultaneously. (Luciani.)

end by a very fine rubber membrane like the finger of a glove,
the canal is transformed into an intrathoracic cavity communicating with the exterior in such a way that (on connecting up
the external opening of the sound with a tambour and
writing lever) the vibrations produced within the thorax can
all be traced on the rotating cylinder. The negative oscillations are recorded by descending, the positive by ascending
lines. We were the first, in 1877, to introduce this method into

physiological technique, and to recognise in the tracings, not merely the large oscillations dependent on the respiratory movements, but also the lesser variations due to the movements of the heart.

We found the cardiac sphygmograms obtained by the oesophageal method to be of very complex form, varying greatly,

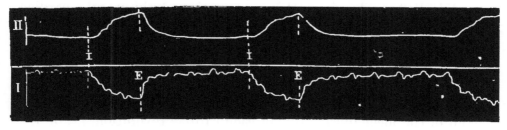

Fig. 86.—From same dog as preceding figure, after section of cervical cord between fifth and sixth vertebrae. (Luciani.) It will be seen that diaphragmatic respiration alone persists. I, Inspirations; E, expirations. The cardiac sphygmograms are reduced to minute oscillations, and are only visible on the oesophageal tracing.

particularly in their dimensions, with the condition of the animal (Figs. 85 and 86). We also found that they could not be dependent exclusively on the effects of meiocardia and auxocardia, but were influenced also by the nature of the relations of contact between the heart and the oesophagus, since on opening the thoracic cavity they do not entirely disappear, but are considerably modified (Fig. 87).

Léon Fredericq (1888) took up this point again in order to make a more detailed analysis of the oesophageal sphygmograms, and obtained complex forms of oscillations which closely resembled the very interesting oscillations which he observed in the cavity of

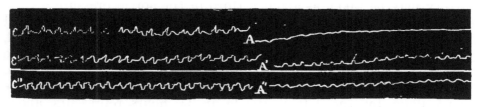

Fig. 87.—Cardiac sphygmograms transmitted from oesophageal explorer during apnoea of forced artificial respiration in anaesthetised dog. (Luciani.) C. With closed thorax; A, with opened thorax; C', A', the same on another anaesthetised dog; C'', A'', the same on a third curarised dog.

the auricles (see Fig. 68, p. 207). From this he concluded that they were dependent on a direct transmission to the oesophagus of the active and passive movements of the left auricle, pointing out the intricate anatomical relations between these two organs. He denied that they were in any way dependent on the effects of meiocardia or auxocardia, because they are not abolished by the opening of the thorax. This last conclusion, however, does not take into account the fact, which we discovered twelve years earlier, that the pulsations in the oesophagus are considerably changed and simplified after opening of the thorax.

Martius (1888), on the other hand, while almost contemporary with Fredericq, considered only the effects of meiocardia and auxocardia in interpreting the oesophageal pulsations, and thus came to a one-sided conclusion in the opposite direction.

XI. Before leaving this interesting subject of cardiac mechanism, it is necessary to form some approximate conception of the work that is usually performed by the heart in a unit of time.

The work of the heart is equal in the time unit to the weight of the blood it is capable of moving, multiplied by the height of the pressure to which the said weight is lifted. To determine this work it is necessary to form a proper appreciation on the one hand of the mechanical value of each cardiac revolution, i.e. of the quantity of blood that passes from veins to arteries in the said unit of time; on the other, of the height of pressure in the arteries nearest to the heart.

The weight of blood driven into the arteries at each systole depends both on the degree of diastolic filling (auxocardia), and on the degree of systolic evacuation (meiocardia). It is very difficult to arrive at an exact determination of this weight, since it varies with varying conditions. The values of 185·5 and of 180 grms. cited by Volkmann and Vierordt in calculating the work of the heart are certainly exaggerated. The values adopted by Fick (50-75 grms.), by Tigerstedt (50 grms.), and by Zuntz (60 grms.) are probably nearest to the truth.

On the other hand, the mean pressure of the aorta may be taken as approximately equal to 150 mm. Hg, i.e. in round figures to a column of blood 2 metres high, and the pressure in the pulmonary artery may be taken as about a third of the aortic pressure.

Assuming that the left ventricle drives some 60 grms. of blood into the aorta at each systole under a pressure of 2 m. of blood, and, allowing for the velocity acquired by the same, which is a negligible quantity, we obtain a yield of 120 grammetres at every revolution. Given 72 revolutions per minute, it is easy to calculate that the work done by the left ventricle in 24 hours represents about 12,450 kilogrammetres. If a third of this, i.e. 4150 kilogrammetres, be added as the approximate work of the right ventricle, the total work of the heart in 24 hours may be reckoned as 16,600 kilogrammetres.

The friction to which the blood is submitted in its passage through the closed vascular system transforms the entire work of the heart into heat. Starting from the fact that 425 kilogrammetres are necessary for the development of 1 calorie, the 16,600 kilogrammetres of the heart's daily work represent some 39 calories, corresponding with the heat developed by the combustion of less than 5 grms. of carbon.

BIBLIOGRAPHY

G. KIRSCHNER. Herzthätigkeit. Wagner's Handwörterbuch der Physiol., Zweiter Band, S. 30-107. Braunschweig, 1844.

C. LUDWIG. Lehrbuch der Physiologie des Menschen. Zweite Auflage, Zweiter Band. Leipzig und Heidelberg, 1861.

R. TIGERSTEDT. Lehrbuch der Physiologie des Kreislaufes. Leipzig, 1863.

CHAUVEAU e ARLOING. Cœur (Physiologie, Dictionnaire encycloped. des sciences médicales, tome xviii. pp. 314-382. Paris, 1876.

MAREY. La Circulation du sang à l'état physiologique et dans les maladies. Paris, 1881.

L. LUCIANI. Dell' attività della diastole cardiaca. Rivista clinica. Bologna, 1871, 1874, 1876.

A. STEFANI. Cardiovolume, pressione pericardica e attività della diastole. Memoria letta all' Accademia medico-chirurgica di Ferrara il 5 agosto 1891.

G. CERADINI. Il Meccanismo delle valvole semilunari del cuore. Gazzetta medica italiana-lombarda. Milano, 1871.

G. PALADINO. Contribuzione all' anatomia, istologia e fisiologia del cuore. Movimento medico-chirurgico. Napoli, 1876.

L. LUCIANI. Delle oscillazioni della pressione intratoracica e intraddominale. Archivio di Bizzozero, anno II. Torino, 1877.

A. MOSSO. Sul polso negativo. Archivio di Bizzozero, anno II. Torino, 1878.

L. FREDERICQ. La Pulsation du cœur chez le chien. Travaux du laboratoire, tome ii. 1887-88.—Arch. internationales de physiol., vol. v. 1907.

J. G. EDGREN. Cardiographische und sphygmographische Studien. Skandinavisches Archiv für Physiologie, Erster Band, S. 66-151. Leipzig, 1889.

L. KREHL. Beiträge zur Kenntnis der Füllung und Entleerung des Herzens. Aus dem physiologischen Institut zu Leipzig. xvii. Band der Abhandlungen der K. Sächs. Gesell. d. Wissenschaften. Leipzig, 1891.

TIGERSTEDT. Intrakardialer Druck und Herzstoss. Ergebnisse der Physiologie, 1902. (60 works are cited in this article.)

E. EBSTEIN. Die Diastole des Herzens. Ergebnisse der Physiologie, 1906. (187 works are cited in this article.)

Recent English Literature.

W. P. LOMBARD and W. B. PILLSBURY. Secondary Rhythms of the Normal Human Heart. Amer. Journ. of Physiol., 1900, iii. 201.

A. R. CUSHNY. On Periodic Variations in the Contractions of the Mammalian Heart. Journ. of Physiol., 1899-1900, xxv. 49.

J. A. MACWILLIAM. Rigor Mortis in the Heart and the State of the Cardiac Cavities after Death. Journ. of Physiol., 1901-2, xxvii. 336.

D. J. LINGLE. Restorers of the Cardiac Rhythm. Amer. Journ. of Physiol., 1905, xiv. 433.

Y. HENDERSON. The Volume Curve of the Ventricles of the Mammalian Heart, and the Significance of this Curve in Respect to the Mechanics of the Heart-Beat and the filling of the Ventricles. Amer. Journ. of Physiol., 1906, xvi. 325.

T. LEWIS and A. S. MACNALTY. A Note on the Simultaneous Occurrence of Sinus and Ventricular Rhythm in Man. Journ. of Physiol., 1908, xxxvii. 445.

CHAPTER VIII

THE BLOOD-STREAM: MOVEMENT IN THE VESSELS

SUMMARY.—1. Fundamental laws of hydrodynamics for passage of fluid through rigid tubes. 2. Application of these laws to haemodynamics. 3. Mechanical effects of elasticity of vessel walls and intermittence of flow of blood from heart; laws of wave motion. 4. Method of measuring and automatically registering variations in blood pressure. 5. Principal results obtained. 6. Methods of measuring velocity of circulation; experimental results. 7. Sphygmography and sphygmograms representing pulsatory oscillations in pressure. 8. Comparison of cardiograms and sphygmograms registered simultaneously, indicating duration of principal phases of cardiac cycle in man. 9. Comparison of several sphygmograms registered simultaneously from arteries at different distances from the heart, indicating rate of transmission of primary and of dicrotic wave. 10. Tachymetry and tachygrams representing pulsatory variations in current velocity. 11. Plethysmography and plethysmograms representing pulsatory oscillations in the volume of the arteries. 12. Schema of mechanical conditions of the circulation in the three great vascular systems; determination of duration of the entire circulation. Bibliography.

WHEN the circulation is observed under the microscope (see Chap. VI., 8) it is easy to detect a phenomenon which is among the most fundamental in Haemodynamics: the movement of blood in the vessels is continuous: continuous and rhythmically accelerated in the arteries, continuous and constant in the veins. The analysis of this complex phenomenon in its details and in its elements, the determination of the mechanical conditions on which it depends, and the laws by which it is governed, form the contents of this chapter.

1. The movement of the blood from the heart through the vessels is regulated and determined, like the movement of water driven rhythmically through a tube from a pump, by two antagonistic influences: the energy developed from the heart, or pump, which drives the fluid through the vessels; and the resistance represented by the internal walls of the vessels, owing to the adhesion of the fluid, and its viscosity. The velocity of each molecule of fluid is proportional to the difference between the impulses felt by each *a tergo* and *a fronte*. The more the driving force overcomes the sum of the resistances, the faster will be the flow of a fluid through the system. In order, however, to form a more exact and concrete idea of the mechanism of the movement of fluids, it will be well to review certain principles

of hydrodynamics, which are intimately connected with haemo-dynamics.

(*a*) Let us take the simplest case of a fluid contained in a vessel having an outlet in its base. As soon as this is opened, the resistance offered to the hydrostatic pressure over the outlet vanishes, and the fluid pours out through the opening. According to Torricelli's theorem (1643), the velocity (*r*) with which a fluid escapes is (apart from the resistance it encounters) exactly equal to that which a body would acquire in falling free through the height of the column of fluid to the orifice. It is therefore independent of the nature of the fluid, and depends on the pressure, *i.e.* on the height (H) of the column of fluid, and is proportional to the square root of this height, *i.e.* it increases as 1, 2, or 3, when the increment of height is as 1, 4, 9. If the acceleration due to gravity at each second (which = 9·8 m.) is represented as *g*, we have :—

$$r = \sqrt{2gH}.$$

(*b*) When a rigid horizontal tube is joined to the orifice of the same vessel (in which a column of fluid is maintained at equal height and constant diameter throughout its length) the velocity of outflow, and therefore the amount of fluid escaping from the end of that tube, will be less than in the previous case, because a portion of the available hydrostatic pressure will be applied to overcoming the new resistance which the fluid encounters in its passage through the tube, and cannot therefore add to the velocity of the escaping fluid.

The resistances are represented by the internal friction between the molecules of fluid, which are forced, partly by the adhesion of the external layer of fluid to the walls of the tube, partly by viscosity (see p. 151), to glide one over the other. As we have seen elsewhere (p. 189) the velocity of the single-current threads, into which we may consider the cylinder of fluid driven through the tube to be broken up, increases from the periphery to the axis of the cylinder, where it is maximal. The mean velocity corresponds with half the maximal velocity observed in the axis.

Since liquids are incompressible, *i.e.* can neither be compressed nor the reverse in their passage through tubes, it follows that their average velocity must be equal at every section of the same, also that the amount passing every section in the unit of time must be equal.

Owing to internal friction the fluid exerts a lateral pressure on the walls of the tube, which can be measured by fixing manometer tubes, or *piezometers*, perpendicular to the axis (Fig. 88). The height to which the fluid ascends in the piezometers decreases regularly from that in the tube nearest the orifice by which it enters to that nearest the outflow, so that the highest points of the columns of fluid in all the piezometers can be joined by a straight line. This straight line, which represents the gradual fall of lateral pressure along the tube, is more or less steep in proportion to the velocity of outflow.

As shown in the diagram, the total force represented by the height II of the column of fluid contained in the vessel falls into two parts: that employed in overcoming the resistance offered to the free passage of the fluid through the tube h', and that employed in driving the fluid through the tube h. The first is termed lateral pressure or resistance-head, the second velocity-head.

(*c*) When the tube connected with the vessel varies in diameter

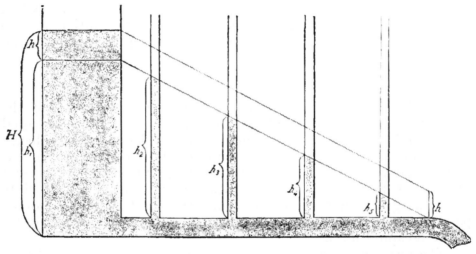

Fig. 88.—Schema to demonstrate the laws which regulate the flow of a liquid, at constant pressure, through a conducting tube with rigid walls and uniform diameter.

in its different parts, the same fundamental law applies as has been laid down for tubes of constant bore. Since fluid is incompressible, an equal amount must flow through every section of the tube, independent of its diameter in the time-unit.

In consequence of this law, the velocity of the current in sections of tubes that vary in diameter stands in inverse proportion to the sectional area.

Since the resistance in the wider parts of the tube is less than in the narrower sections, it follows that the fluid requires less force to propel it through the former than it does to pass through the latter. The lateral pressure accordingly sinks more slowly in the former and more rapidly in the latter, as shown in Fig. 89. At points where a wider section of the tube passes into a narrower, velocity rises, and there is considerable diminution of pressure, owing to the greater resistance which the fluid encounters; where, on the contrary, a wider section follows a narrower, velocity falls, while pressure on the contrary increases or remains unchanged, or

falls. This paradoxical fact was explained by Donders as the
result of the formation of vortices, at the base of the dilatation
already referred to (Chap. VII. p. 190). It is certain that the
vortices consume a certain amount of force. When this consumption is considerable, pressure falls: when, on the other hand,
it is inconsiderable, pressure either remains unaltered, or increases,
as must always occur in consequence of the diminution of velocity.

It is obvious that where the dilatations and constrictions of the
tube occur gradually instead of suddenly, the alterations of velocity
and pressure in its different sections must obey the same laws, with
the simple difference that they are produced slowly, so that their

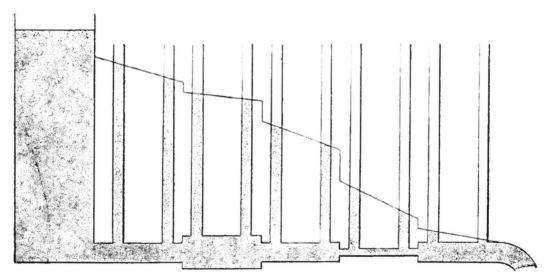

Fig. 89.—Schema similar to that of preceding figure. The rigid conducting tube of equal diameter
is here replaced by a tube of unequal diameter in its various parts. (Rollett.)

course is represented by a curved rather than by a straight gradient,
as in the preceding case.

(*d*) When the tube connected with the vessel branches into two
or more smaller tubes so that the bed of the current is widened,
i.e. the sum of the sectional area of the branches presents a
larger diameter than the original tube, the result is complicated.
Since the sectional area of the current is enlarged, the sum of the
resistances should be diminished; on the other hand, the branching
of the tube must introduce new resistances, which increase with
the size of the angle made by the branches. These two opposite
conditions are to a certain extent compensatory. Jacobson's
experiments (1860), however, show that the preponderating influence is always the widening of the bed, by which the amount of
fluid passing through each cross-section of the system in the
time-unit is increased.

(*e*) If the tube after branching so as to widen the bed of the current, unites again into a single outflow tube in which the sectional area is once more reduced, we obtain a system of canals which schematically represents the circulatory system. Under these complex conditions the same fundamental laws hold good that we have been discussing for the preceding simple cases.

The rate of flow to the different parts of the system is inversely proportional to the sum of the cross-sections, *i.e.* to the width of the current bed. Since the same amount of fluid enters the system by the inflow tube, and leaves the system by the outflow tube, in the time-unit, so the same amount of fluid must pass through every section of the system in the same time, with a correspondingly greater velocity where the sectional area is narrower, with less velocity where it is wider.

The pressure at every point of the system must be proportional to the sum of the resistances which the fluid has to overcome before reaching the outflow. Since the section of each tube decreases as the system branches, while the total sectional area increases, so the sum of the resistances must increase with the former and decrease with the latter. Which of these two conditions has the preponderating influence? Experience shows that when the branching of the system goes as far as the production of capillary tubes, the sum of the resistances increases in these to such an extent that it cannot be compensated by the widening, however great, of the bed of the stream. In a system of capillary vessels the velocity of outflow is, according to Poiseuille, proportional, not, as in tubes of larger diameter, to the square, but to the fourth power of the radius.

II. All these laws, in so far as they concern pressure, velocity, and outflow, are perfectly applicable to the vascular blood system, since this consists of canals which ramify until they are reduced into a capillary network with a vast extension of the bed of the current, and then gradually form into canals again, each of which has individually a wider cross-section, but which as a whole make up a narrower channel. Setting aside for the moment the differences between the circulatory system and the system of conducting tubes which we have just been considering, it is possible to formulate three general laws which are at the base of the circulatory phenomena.

(*a Laws of Current.*—Under normal circulatory conditions, the amount of blood that flows out of the heart through the arteries in the time-unit is exactly equal to that which flows into the heart by the veins; the amount of blood which enters or leaves the right or left heart is exactly equal to that which leaves or enters the left or right heart; in more general terms, the amount of blood which passes through any total cross-section of the circulatory system is exactly equal to that which passes in the same time through any other total cross-section of the same system.

The validity of this law would be absolute if the blood, which—like all fluids—is incompressible, were circulating in a system of rigid tubes. But since the walls of the vessels are extensible and elastic, it is evident that there may be a temporary infraction of it without disturbing the fundamental conditions of the circulation. The mass of blood driven through the pulmonary arteries, *e.g.*, may for a few seconds be greater than that which simultaneously enters the left auricle through the four pulmonary veins: this must produce a certain degree of pulmonary congestion, compatible with life. If, however, this condition be maintained too long, and if the converse phenomenon does not immediately succeed it, so that normal circulatory conditions are restored, the congestion in the pulmonary vessels will obviously increase to such an extent in a short time that it presents an invincible obstacle to the flow of blood. Obviously, therefore, the above law has only a relative value, when the time-unit is taken as an interval of a few seconds: it has an absolute value where a longer period, *i.e.* of one or more minutes, is taken.

(b) *Law of Velocity.*—It follows as the necessary result of the law of outflow that the velocity is inversely proportional to the cross-section, in the different parts of the vascular system. In order to determine the proportion in which velocity alters in the different parts of the circulatory system it is enough to measure the total sectional area of the vessels in that part. This is only possible with the large arteries and veins nearest the heart, which is the centre of the system: it is necessary, however, to measure them not on the dead body, but on the living subject, under the most normal circulatory conditions possible, so as to obtain the sectional area under physiological tension and filling of the vessels. Since the total sectional area or current bed increases slowly on the one hand, from the large to the small arteries, and rapidly from these to the capillaries; and on the other hand, falls rapidly from the capillaries to the small veins, and slowly from these to the large veins, it may be stated in general terms that velocity alters in the inverse sense and same proportion. Since, further, the sectional area of the aorta is less than the sum of the sectional area of the two venae cavae, while, on the other hand, the sectional area of the pulmonary artery is larger than the sum of the sectional area of the four pulmonary veins, the velocity of the blood-stream in the systemic circulation will be maximal in the aorta, minimal in the aortic capillaries, medium in the venae cavae; while in the pulmonary system it will be maximal in the pulmonary veins, minimal in the capillaries, medium in the arteries.

The difference in mean velocity of the flow in the vessels of the pulmonary and aortic circulations can also be arrived at *a priori*, starting from the fact that the capacity of the first system is to that of the second as 2:11. It follows that the pulmonary circulation is completed at a mean velocity some five times greater than that of the aortic circulation (Jolyet, 1880).

(c) *Law of Pressure.*—Seeing that pressure in the individual parts of the system is determined by the sum of the resistances which the blood has to overcome in order to reach the centre of the circulation, *i.e.* the heart, it follows that it must diminish progressively in both the aortic and the pulmonary circulations, from arteries to capillaries, and from these to the veins, in which last, as we have seen, it falls to zero. Since the sum of the resistances, *caeteris paribus,* derives mainly from the friction surface, and this increases slowly from large to small arteries, rapidly from the latter to the capillaries, and then diminishes again slowly from capillaries to veins, it follows that pressure must fall slowly in the arteries, rapidly in the capillaries, and then slowly again in the veins.

Broadly speaking, it may be assumed that the sum of the resistances which the blood expelled from the right heart has to overcome in order to pass through the pulmonary system, in comparison with that overcome by the left heart in traversing the systemic system, is approximately proportional to the difference in capacity of the two systems, so that the mean pressure in the pulmonary circulation must be correspondingly less than that of the aortic. The dissimilar thickness of wall in the two ventricles is, as we have seen, an indicator of dissimilar work or force expended by the two systems.

III. The circulatory system differs from the artificial system of rigid tubes in two important particulars—the complete elasticity of its walls and the intermittent character of the impulse, and therefore of the output of blood from the heart.

If the driving force exerted on the blood by the heart were continuous and uniform, the elasticity of the system would have no effect other than to produce a greater or less degree of vascular dilatation, in proportion with the force of the prevailing pressure; but the blood-flow would remain stationary in every part, and be governed by the same laws as in the system of rigid tubes. If in the latter the driving force is not continuous but intermittent, the current through the tubes and the outflow at the end of the system are also intermittent. But when the impulsive force works intermittently in a system of elastic tubes, then, during the impulse, a portion only of that force will be employed in propelling the fluid along the tubes; while the other portion, by which the tubes are dilated, will be stored up in the form of elastic tension, and given back by the reaction at the close of the impulse. Owing to this elasticity, the current which is intermittent at the head of the system becomes remittent during its course, till at the outflow or extremity of the system it is continuous and uniform.

Marey's experimental schema is the best way of demonstrating the effect of the elasticity of the vessel walls in regulating the blood-flow and making it continuous. A large Mariotte flask raised to a certain height by a wooden block is employed, having an orifice at its base opening into a flexible lead tube, divided into two branches. One of these is attached by a short rubber junction to a long narrow glass tube, somewhat pointed at the end : the other branch is continued as a fine tube of elastic rubber of the same diameter as the glass tube, ending in a short glass mouthpiece with the same aperture of outflow as the other (Fig. 90). When the tap is opened and the water contained in the Mariotte flask is allowed to flow out through the two tubes, one having rigid, the other elastic walls, the amount of fluid escaping simultaneously

FIG. 90.—Mosso's apparatus for demonstrating the effect of an intermittent flow on two tubes, one having rigid, the other elastic, walls.

from the two tubes will be equal, since the two orifices are equal in diameter. This proves that when hydrostatic pressure is continuous and uniform, elastic tubes act like rigid tubes. But if the action of hydrostatic pressure is rendered intermittent by rhythmically opening and closing the compression lever carried by the apparatus, as shown in the figure, it will be seen that the glass tube expels the water intermittently from its mouth, while the elastic tube yields a continuous and regular flow. Uniformity of current is thus shown to be due to the elasticity of the tube.

The impulse imparted to the blood by the elastic reaction of the vessels is not a new force added to that developed by the heart during its systolic output : it is only the restitution of that part of the impulsive force of the heart which was applied to throwing the arteries into elastic tension (Bérard). Yet even if the elasticity of the arteries adds nothing to the sum of the driving force of the heart, it still diminishes the sum of the resistance opposed to the

entrance of the blood into the arteries. In this way a portion of
the mechanical work of the heart, which would otherwise be lost
in overcoming the great resistance which the blood would meet in
making its way into the arteries, if these were rigid tubes, is saved
and utilised. By the same experimental schema Marey was easily
able to demonstrate that the amount of fluid passing through an
elastic tube is considerably greater than that flowing in the same
time through a rigid pipe, when fluid is driven through both
intermittently.

Another invariable result of the intermittent character of the
driving force exerted by the heart on the arterial blood is the
production of a *positive* wave at each systole, *i.e.* a dilatation which
is rapidly propagated in a diminishing degree from the larger to
the smaller arteries, and usually dies out at the threshold of the
capillary network. This positive wave gives rise to the arterial
pulse, and is accordingly known as the *sphygmic* or *pulse wave*.
The rapid transmission of the pulse wave through the arteries
coincides with a momentary rise of blood pressure perceptible
to the touch, and a momentary acceleration of the blood-flow,
which, as we have seen, can be directly observed under the
microscope.

E. H. Weber (1850) was the first to make a thorough experimental study of the laws of wave movement. For our purpose it
will be sufficient to consider the fundamental principles on which
the complex and delicate mechanism of the production of this wave
depend. At each outflow of blood from the ventricles, the walls
of the first section of the arteries expand in consequence of the
sudden impact, and then by elastic reaction produce the dilatation
of the succeeding sections by exerting pressure on the blood with
which they are filled. This elastic transmission of the wave is
repeated in the next section, and so on. Thus, it is the blood
expelled from the heart which causes the wave-like dilatation of
the vessel walls, while the elastic reaction of the walls consequent
on this dilatation propagates the wave.

The gradual diminution of the wave in its course through the
arteries until it disappears at the capillary threshold is an effect
of the growing resistance which it encounters at each ramification
of the vessels. The amplitude of the wave decreases by the same
laws as the average pressure in the arteries.

The velocity of transmission of the wave depends on the specific
gravity of the fluid, on the diameter of the vessels, on the thickness
of the vessel walls, and on its elastic coefficient. According to
Moens, it is inversely proportional to the square root of the specific
gravity of the fluid and to the internal diameter of the vessel, and
directly proportional to the square root of the thickness of the
walls, and their coefficient of elasticity.

By means of the graphic method it is possible to study every detail of the propagation of the pulse-wave in elastic tubes. Besides the classical researches of E. H. Weber (1850), we have the observations of Donders (1859), Marey (1875), and Moens (1880). In rubber tubes the rate of propagation of the wave varies, according to different observations, from 10 to 18 m. per second.

In an elastic tube, thrown into tension by a fluid, and closed at both ends, it is possible to evoke negative as well as positive waves, generated not by the sudden rise, but by the sudden fall of pressure. It is only necessary to let a small quantity of fluid escape suddenly from one end, or, after compressing the tube at one point, suddenly to release the compression, in order to produce the transmission of a wave, represented not by a dilatation but by an undulatory depression. The velocity of propagation of the negative wave is practically the same as that of the positive wave, and essentially obeys the same law.

When the rubber tube in which the positive or negative wave is produced is not so unduly long that the wave has died out at the extreme end, the first wave propagated through the tube gives rise to a second reflex wave, which traverses the entire tube in the opposite direction and interferes with the primary wave, since it has the same velocity of transmission.

In elastic tubes which branch like the arterial system, the waves generated in the principal vessel extend to all the communicating branches, and at the points at which the vessels branch, where there is a sudden rise of resistance, there is invariably a formation of reflex waves. These reflex waves are, however, lost when they reach the main vessel, which in consequence of its capacity and the great elasticity of its walls acts as a kind of extinguisher to the small waves reflected from the secondary vessels. The aorta must act in this way in regard to the reflex waves from the bifurcation points of all the other arteries (Marey).

Having thus discussed the general laws of pressure, circulatory velocity, and pulse-wave in the arteries, we must next consider the most important data established by the study of these three complex phenomena.

IV. The idea of measuring the blood pressure in the arteries originated with Stephen Hales (1733). He connected the artery of a horse with a long glass tube in order to see the height to which the blood would rise. In this way he ascertained that the arterial pressure was equal to a column of blood of 8 to 9 feet. He further noted that the height of the column of blood in the tube oscillated with the cardiac systole. Poiseuille (1828) replaced Hales' piezometer by a U-shaped mercury manometer, which was a great advance in practical method. To this Ludwig (1847) added a float provided with a pen, which records every variation of the mercury column on a rotating cylinder. This is another immense advance, as the *recording manometer* was the first application of the automatic graphic method, which has since been employed in the most various directions, and has rendered signal service to physiology. (Fig. 91 ; and Fig. 68, p. 207.)

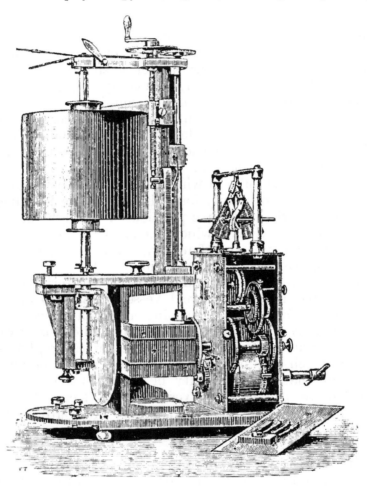

FIG. 91.—Ludwig's kymograph. (Baltzar's type.) The movements of the drum are rendered uniform by the clockwork of a Foucault regulator. The velocity of rotation is altered either by pushing the little wheel on the axis of the drum nearer to or farther from the centre of the vertical metal disc, which drives the drum by simple friction, or by adjusting the clockwork of the regulator.

Ludwig's writing manometer or *Kymograph* is the classic instrument by which the absolute value of the average blood pressure of any artery can be directly obtained under natural conditions. An anti-coagulant alkaline or peptone solution is introduced between the blood and the mercury. If the manometer is connected by a **T**-cannula with the artery, the flow of blood through the vessel is not interrupted, and the resulting value gives the lateral pressure obtaining in the branch vessel. For greater convenience, however, it is customary to join the artery to the manometer by a simple cannula, ligatured to the central side of the artery, so that the vessel is occluded. In this case the height of the manometer column of course expresses the lateral pressure in the arterial trunk from which the occluded vessel sprang. The cannula may also be introduced in a peripheral, instead of central, direction in the artery. In this case the manometer measures the pressure either in the capillary network or in the other arterial branches with which the artery, to which the cannula is peripherally connected, anastomoses. For instance, a manometer connected by a cannula with the central side of the dog's carotid measures the lateral pressure in the aorta; if, on the other hand, the cannula is connected with the peripheral side of the same artery, the pressure that obtains in the so-called Circle of Willis will be obtained. In the first case, the pressure, according to

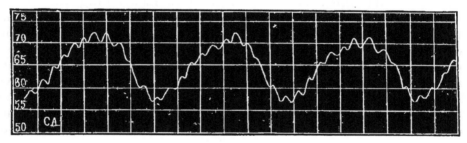

Fig. 92.—Tracing of arterial pressure in dog's carotid, recorded by Ludwig's kymograph. (Marey.)

Steiner, may reach a value of 214 mm. Hg: in the second, a pressure of only 154 mm. Hg results. The first value represents the lateral pressure that prevails in the trunk of the aorta at the origin of the carotid; the second, the pressure in the arterial Circle of Willis, which communicates directly with the peripheral trunk of the carotid.

As can be seen in Fig. 92, the tracings recorded with Ludwig's manometer exhibit small oscillations corresponding with the single cardiac systoles, and more ample and less steep oscillations which correspond to the respiratory movements.

The latter will be considered in relation to the mechanics of respiration; as regards the pulsatory oscillations it must be noted that the mercury, owing to inertia, is incapable of faithfully recording the rapid variations of arterial pressure produced by each wave of blood expelled from the heart, so that Ludwig's instrument is the least fitted for the study of the form of the pulse-wave. Since this instrument is intended to determine the value of the average blood pressure, the pulsatory oscillations are a superfluous complication which can easily be excluded by a constriction in the manometer at one point, as proposed by

Setschenow, which prevents the mercury from making any rapid movement. In the manometer represented in Fig. 68, p. 207, this is easily effected by adjusting the screw placed at its lower end to the required point. The mercury column is then practically immobile between the highest and lowest points of the pulsatory oscillations, and the apparatus merely records the average blood pressure.

In order to obtain as true a record as possible of even the most rapid oscillations of blood pressure, the *elastic manometer* or *tonometer* was invented, in which the mercury mass is replaced by a spring or other elastic body, having but a small mass, and being, therefore, more free from the errors due to inertia, and better adapted to follow accurately the finer details of the pulsatory oscillations of pressure. The history of the modifications and gradual perfecting of the elastic manometer are of merely technical interest. We must confine ourselves to mentioning the *hollow spring manometer* of A. Fick 1864, constructed on the same principle as Bourdon's metal manometer, employed in steam-engines, and the *metal manometer* of Marey, which is constructed on the principle of the aneroid barometer. In 1885 Fick invented another flat *spring manometer*, which is simpler and more sensitive than the preceding. The entire apparatus is reduced to a slender tube ending in a small capsule, closed by a rubber membrane capable of small excursions which are transmitted to a flat steel spring. By this method it is possible to reduce the movements of the column of fluid in the tube connected with the artery to a minimum, which facilitates the transmission of the more rapid oscillations, and avoids the inconvenience of coagulated blood at the point of the cannula. In order to magnify the oscillations of pressure transmitted to the spring, and to record them on a rotating drum, it is fitted with a long, light lever made from a straw. Hürthle perfected this manometer of Fick's by some accessory contrivances, which made its application easier and more certain, and confined the fluid between artery and manometer to the lowest possible minimum in order to transmit the variations of pressure more rapidly and faithfully. Of course both Fick's manometer and that of Hürthle must be empirically graduated by a mercury manometer in order to show absolute pressures.

Still better than a steel spring, however, for obtaining true curves of the pulsatory oscillations of pressure is the tonometer formed of elastic guttapercha, the simplest type of which is Marey and Chauveau's sphygmoscope Fig. 66, p. 205 in connection with their writing tambour Fig. 63, p. 201. In order to diminish the mass of fluid communicating with the artery, Hürthle reduced Marey's tambour to a small capsule, covered with a resistent rubber membrane : its excursions were magnified by a long and very light lever while the capsule, by omitting the sphygmoscope was placed in direct connection with the artery. This is Hürthle's *rubber manometer*. Since the rubber membrane easily perishes, Gad substituted for it a thin metal plate. Finally, v. Frey gave the most practical form and shape to the entire apparatus, combining the maximum of sensitiveness with stability and permanence. He called it a *metal tonograph* (Fig. 93).

More recently (1904) Ducceschi has described a still simpler method, by which the tracings of the normal blood pressure in the carotid of dogs and rabbits can be recorded. After isolating a sufficiently long tract of this artery in the neck, he divided it between two ligatures, putting the central end in direct communication with the isotonic lever of a myograph by means of an inextensible thread, and counterbalancing the tension with an adequate weight. In principle this method is the same as that employed by Engelmann to record the pulsations of the frog's heart (see next chapter), and its author gave it the name of method of *suspension of the artery*, just as Engelmann called his the method of *suspen-*

Fig. 93.—Von Frey's metal tonograph, in which the rubber membrane is replaced by a metal plate.

sion of the heart. It is evident that the pressure of the blood, exerted on the closed trunk of the carotid, must distend it in correspondence with the average pressure and the rhythmical oscillations due to the rhythmical beat of the heart (longitudinal locomotion and arterial pulse).

Since these methods all involve the opening of an artery, and introduction of a cannula, they are only practicable on man in certain surgical operations (amputations) and other conditions more or less removed from a physiological state. Methods have accordingly been invented by which it is possible to determine blood pressure without any surgical operation, and these can therefore be applied to man. Vierordt (1855) was the first who conceived the idea of measuring the blood pressure in an artery indirectly, by ascertaining the weight required to suppress the pulsations. Waldenburg, Potain, Talma, Roy and Brown attempted the solution of the same problem. The *sphygmomanometer* of v. Basch (1876) is a small instrument designed for this purpose, which has found wide acceptance with clinicians on account of its easy applicability. It consists of a rubber finger-stall filled with water, by which the radial or temporal artery is compressed. The finger-stall communicates by a rubber tube with a metal manometer, the indicator of which shows the pressure exercised on the artery. When the indicator no longer shows pulse-waves in the compressed artery, the internal pressure, according to v. Basch, must (at any rate approximately) be equal to the external compression. Tigerstedt rightly pointed out the untrustworthy character of the values obtained by this method. In spite of the improvements introduced by Rabinowitz (1881) and Potain (1889) in the apparatus, and adopted by von Basch in the latest model of his sphygmomanometer (1890), and notwithstanding the many control experiments carried out by various

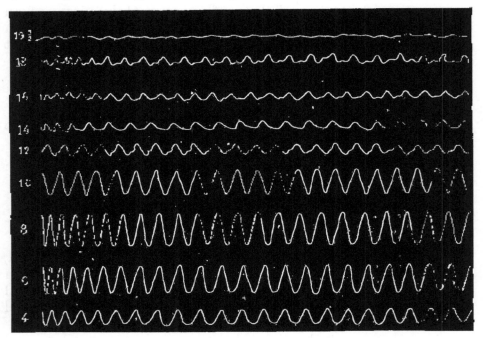

Fig. 94. — Tracings of pulsatory oscillations in volume of forearm, recorded with Marey's sphygmomanometer. Shows the variations under the influence of increasing external pressure, as indicated in cm. Hg at the side of each tracing. (Marey.)

authors upon animals (which show that while the pressure values obtained from this instrument are unreliable, they still yield results comparable *inter se* on the same individual), there are certain obvious drawbacks to its practical application to man which are not easily removed, and which render it untrustworthy. The results may vary considerably in different cases, according to the depth of the paniculus adiposus, the development of the muscles, the arrangement and normal or sclerotic state of the arterial walls, and in particular the tension of the aponeurotic fascia which cover the arteries investigated, and more or less hinder their compression.

The investigations initiated by Marey (1876), resumed in 1878, and continued in Italy in 1895 by Mosso, were more successful.

Marey's sphygmomanometric method consists in applying a variable external counter-pressure not to a limited point of an artery, but to the whole surface of a limb. He introduced the forearm into a cylindrical vessel closed by a rubber ring, which was filled under easily adjustable pressure with water, and connected with a recording manometer, and then took a tracing of the total pulsations of all the arteries of the forearm. He saw that with gradual increase of hydrostatic pressure within the cylinder, the pulsations increased during a first period, and then diminished in a second, till they ceased entirely. In the tracings of Fig. 94 it can be seen that the pulsations attain their maximal excursion when the counter-pressure on the forearm reaches 8 cm. Hg; they then gradually diminish, and almost entirely disappear at a counter-pressure of 19·5 cm. Hg.

In a second series of experiments Marey, in order to make his method more practicable, gave up the pressure on the whole forearm, and confined himself to one finger of the hand, as seen in the apparatus of Fig. 95. In order to make the pulsations of the

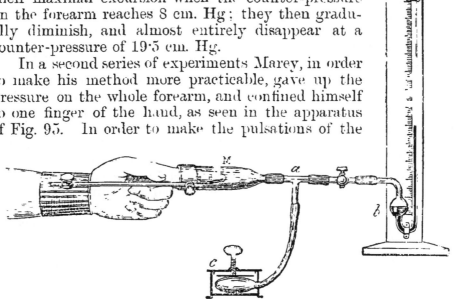

Fig. 95.—Marey's sphygmomanometer. It consists of a glass holder M, which is completely closed after introducing the fore-finger, and communicates on the one hand with a capillary mercury manometer b, on the other with a stout bag c, which is gradually compressed by a screw. The whole apparatus should be filled with water, care being taken to avoid air-bubbles.

digital arteries more conspicuous, he employed a mercury manometer of ⅓ mm. diameter, and limited himself to reading the maximal and minimal values of the pulsatory oscillations on the scale. This method again confirmed the preceding observation, to the effect that the pulsations, with increase of counter-pressure, are greater at first, and subsequently diminish and tend to die out. But he also found that it was very difficult to obliterate them completely, even when the counter-pressure reached a height of 28-30 cm. Hg, i.e. a value which is certainly higher than the pressure exerted by the blood on the arteries of the fingers. According to Marey, however, the value of his method lies in the determination of the counter-pressure with which the most ample oscillations of the mercury column are obtained. "At that moment," he says, " we learn theoretically that the vessels of the immersed limb are wholly relaxed, and that their walls fluctuate as it were indifferently between the internal pressure of the blood and the external pressure of the water. The pressure of the blood, therefore, acts as though it were exerted directly upon the manometer." This is as much as to say that we then obtain the true measure of the lateral pressure exerted by the blood upon the arteries of the finger. The arterial walls at that time must be in a state of elastic equilibrium, since the internal force which makes for their distension is completely counterbalanced by the external force which makes for their compression. If this criterion is applied to the results shown in Fig. 94, the average pressure of the arteries of the forearm in man is found equal to 8 cm. Hg, since the pulsations reach their maximal amplitude when a counter-pressure of 8 cm. Hg is put upon them.

Mosso continued and developed these investigations of Marey. His sphygmomanometer is a modification of that shown in the previous figure. He makes the counter-pressure act on four fingers instead of on one, in order to obtain the total pulsations of a larger number of arteries, and to record the tracings with a Ludwig's mercury manometer. The following tracings, obtained by Mosso and Colombo, are very instructive, the effects of various degrees of compression of the four fingers under normal conditions being compared with the tracings obtained from the same person after a warm bath (Fig. 96).

As might be expected, the average pressure sinks on account of the relaxation of the vessels due to the warm bath, and falls to 20 mm. Hg. At the same time the height of the pulsations after the bath increases considerably, showing that they do not depend on the internal pressure of the blood, but are in inverse ratio with the degree of tonic contraction of the vessels. Evidence for this is found in the fact that when the vessels of the fingers are strongly contracted (as often happens in winter), it is impossible to obtain the slightest sign of pulsation with Mosso's sphygmomanometer. This is a disadvantage which renders the instrument applicable only to a limited number of persons, and which is avoided by returning to the original method of Marey, i.e. that of applying compression to the whole forearm.

Starting from Marey's original method, Hürthle (1896) introduced some interesting modifications which deserve notice.

Both in Marey's and in Mosso's apparatus it is necessary in measuring the lateral pressure prevailing in the arteries of the part of the body examined, to increase or lower the external counter-pressure repeatedly, in order to discover at what strength of counter-pressure the maximal pulsations are obtained. With Hürthle's apparatus, on the contrary, the observation is continuous, and there is no need to vary the counter-pressure applied at the outset to the forearm.

He starts with the production of artificial anaemia by an

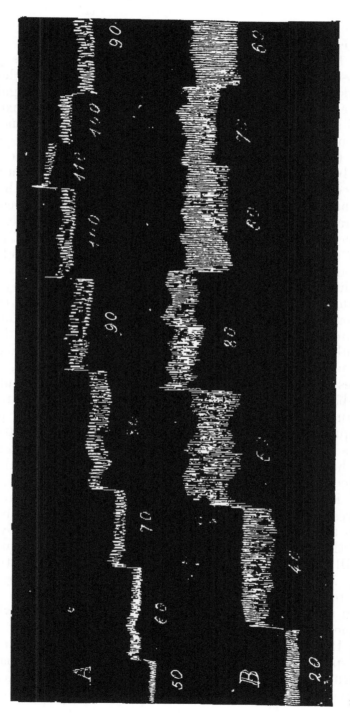

Fig. 96.— Blood-pressure tracings from Mosso's sphygmomanometer: A, Under normal conditions; B after a warm bath. (Mosso and Colombo.) In A the pulsations reach their maximal height when the compression exerted on the four fingers amounts to 80-90 mm. Hg.   In B the pulsations are, generally speaking, far more excursive, and are maximal at 60 mm. Hg.

Esmarch's bandage in the forearm and part of the upper arm, and ties a ligature round the latter.   He then introduces the anaemic extremity, as far as half the forearm, into a glass cylinder, connected on one side with a pressure bottle, on the other with his spring manometer. An ingenious apparatus that is absolutely air-tight fixes the end of the cylinder to the forearm. After the cylinder has been filled with water and the connection with the pressure bottle closed, the ligature is taken off; the blood from the artery then flows into the limb and drives some of the water against the manometer, which records a pressure equivalent to that exerted by the blood streaming into the artery. Since the spring manometer permits only small excursions, the quantity of blood entering the artery of that part of the arm which is enclosed in the cylinder will also be small. Hürthle takes it to be not more than 10 c.c., which is certainly not sufficient to restore circulation in the vessels of the limb. He therefore concludes that the values recorded by his apparatus represent, not the simple *lateral* pressure, but the *total arterial pressure (total head* which would obtain if the large artery of the forearm were opened, and directly connected with the manometer.

Hürthle has not, up to the present, published any control experiments that justify his conclusions, and there are good reasons for doubting whether he has really succeeded in completely obliterating all the vessels of the forearm, so as to interrupt the circulation in the vessels of the interosseous space. The external pressure is not readily transmitted to this space, since the two bones are connected by strong aponeuroses, which make this cavity a box with rigid walls that yield little to pressure greater even than that of the largest arteries. It is therefore probable, in consequence of the incomplete stoppage of the circulation, that Hürthle's apparatus does not register the *total head*, but merely a pressure head which is not of the same value as the lateral pressure of the blood normally circulating in the vessels of the forearm, but increases in proportion with the sudden restriction of current-bed in the greater part of the limb that is under investigation.

From the clinical standpoint these methods of Marey, Mosso, and Hürthle involve too complicated an apparatus, requiring no little skill on the part of operator as well as patient, to ensure success. Moreover, they only determine the lateral pressure in arteries too small and too remote from the heart to give the physician any adequate expression of the energy with which the heart is acting under various morbid conditions.

Riva-Rocci (1896 accordingly invented a simple and easily applied sphygmomanometer, which measures by the manometer the external counter-pressure required to block the progress of the pulse-wave in one of the larger branches of the aorta, *e.g.* in the brachial artery. The measurements obtained with this instrument, which express the total pressure head (*i.e.* the lateral pressure *plus* the velocity head) in the brachial artery, express the values of the lateral pressure that prevails in the aorta or innominate artery, according as the apparatus is applied to the left or to the right arm.

Riva-Rocci's sphygmomanometer is an ingenious modification of the method of v. Basch. The elastic finger-stall is replaced by a hollow rubber ring (made inextensible by a cloth cover) which fits round the arm and is connected with a mercury manometer (Fig. 97). Air is then blown into the hollow ring by an ordinary spray bellows, which becomes inflated and compresses all the vessels of the limb, while the mercury rises in the tube of the manometer. If more air is gradually forced in, so that the mercury rises evenly, there comes a moment at which the radial pulse disappears. The height of the mercury column at that moment represents the total head of pressure supported by the brachial artery during the interruption of the circulation in the arm, which value approximates to that of the lateral pressure in the aorta, as demonstrated by experiments with artificial circulation in rubber tubes, or in the brachial arteries of the dead body, as well as by experiments on the crural arteries of dogs and rabbits.

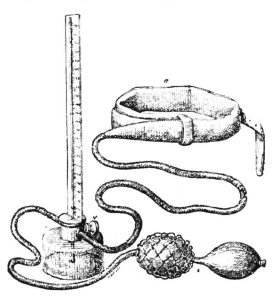

FIG. 97.—Riva-Rocci's sphygmomanometer. *a*, Hollow rubber ring covered with silk; *m*, mercury manometer with only one arm; *b*, double rubber bellows.

As the sphygmomanometer of Riva-Rocci is applied to the upper arm, which has only one central bone, the muscles, when fully relaxed, behave exactly like a fluid, and convey the pressure of the elastic ring perfectly to all the vessels of the upper arm, as was not the case when the apparatus was applied to the forearm. The chief defects of v. Basch's sphygmomanometer thus seem to be excluded.

In order to obtain utilisable values with the Riva-Rocci apparatus, it is essential that the subject whose pressure is to be measured should be absolutely quiescent. In this way only can the value of the individual minimal pressure be obtained, uninfluenced by the disturbances produced by emotional influences, which vary to a considerable extent in the same person, with the same stimulus. The armlet is fastened preferably to the middle of the right arm by means of the ligature attached from behind to the lower part of the arm, so that it is applied to it like a flat bandage.

The forearm is bent towards the upper arm, care being taken that all the muscles of the latter, especially the biceps, are entirely relaxed. With one hand the operator feels the brachial or radial pulse at the bend of the elbow joint, and with the other he slowly blows in air, until every trace of pulse is lost. If the manometer scale is now read for the exact point at which the pulse disappeared without reappearing during maintenance of the pressure, the desired pressure value will be obtained.

Another simple apparatus, easy to handle, which with certain modifications is making its way like the preceding into medical practice, is *Gärtner's tonometer* (1899). This apparatus (Fig. 98) to some extent combines the principles of the methods of Hürthle and of Riva-Rocci. It also consists of a hollow ring, with an internal wall of rubber, which can be gradually inflated by an elastic spray bellows, and communicates on the other hand with a mercury manometer, on the scale of which the pressure values may be read. It is fixed round one of the

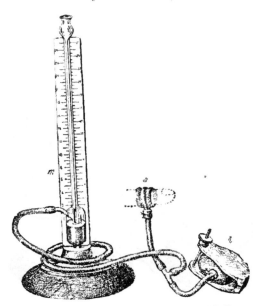

fingers, and measures the total pressure of the blood in the arteries of that finger. The method is as follows. First, as in Hürthle's method, the phalanx of the finger to be experimented on is made anaemic, by applying an elastic bandage to the finger or by slipping a rubber ring over it; or, on the principle of an Esmarch's bandage, rolling down from the point of the finger to the root, over the different joints in succession, a fine strip or tube of elastic rubber. The finger is then introduced into the pneumatic ring of the apparatus, so that the ring embraces the phalanx, and air is blown in from the elastic bag by turning the screw of the compressor until the pressure of the tonometer exceeds that of the blood. The bandage which produced anaemia is then removed, and the pressure within the tonometer slowly reduced by turning the screw that compresses the elastic bag in the opposite direction, until the internal pressure exceeds the external counter-pressure, and the blood re-enters the arteries of the finger as shown by the flushing of the pulp, or subjectively by the return of the pulse. The value read at that moment on the manometer scale is equal to the total pressure of the blood in the digital arteries.

FIG. 98.—Gärtner's tonometer. Consists of bellows (b) or screw compressor with an elastic bag, communicating on the one hand with a one-armed mercury manometer (m), on the other with a hollow ring (a) which slips over the second phalanx of the index-finger, after it has been made anaemic.

V. Volkmann concluded from the data which he collected in order to determine the variations of normal blood pressure in various species of animals, that the height of pressure is in no sort of ratio with the size of the animal. The lateral pressure in the dog's aorta, *e.g.*, fluctuates between 130 and 180 mm. Hg. in the rabbit between 100 and 130 mm. Hg, in the horse between 150 and 200 mm. Hg. This seems paradoxical at first sight, but is not so when we reflect that the work of the heart depends not only upon the magnitude of resistance or pressure, but also upon the volume of blood driven by the heart into the arteries at each systole. Even if blood pressure in the horse differs little from that of the rabbit, yet the horse's heart does far more work, because it throws a far greater quantity of blood into circulation.

The mean blood pressure in man cannot differ much from that of the larger mammals. We may think of it as varying approximately from 130 to 150 mm. Hg, values which come very near those which Faivre (1850) determined directly upon the femoral and brachial arteries in amputations.

The values obtained by Marey and Mosso by their sphygmomanometric methods reach no such high figures 80 to 90 mm. Hg : yet it must be remembered that they only represent the average total pressure of all the arteries, large and small, of the forearm. or of the fingers of the hand.

The mean arterial pressures, as determined by Riva - Rocci with his sphygmomanometer, oscillated in healthy individuals between 125 and 135 mm. Hg. They corresponded to the greatest total pressure obtained in the brachial artery of man when a simple cannula is introduced in a central direction, and connected with Ludwig's kymograph. As we have said, these values represent approximately that of the lateral pressure that prevails in the aorta.

The blood pressure sinks very little between the aorta and the larger branches of the arteries, in which it is possible to introduce a cannula connected with a manometer, because the resistance due to the friction surfaces increases very little. Volkmann gives the following data for dog and calf, which correspond essentially with those obtained by Bernard, Marey, and others :—

Carotid	of dog	172 mm. Hg.	Carotid	of calf	116 mm. Hg.
Femoral	,,	165 ,,	Femoral	,,	116 ,,
Metatarsal	,, =	155 ,,	Metatarsal	,,	88 ,,

On the other hand, pressure falls rapidly in the small branches of the arteries. where there are many ramifications, and in the capillaries, where the friction surfaces are greatest. The values obtained by v. Kries with Ludwig's method of counter-pressure can only be taken as approximate. Generally speaking, we may assume that pressure in the capillaries does not exceed $\frac{1}{4}$-$\frac{1}{7}$ of the aortic pressure about 20-38 mm. Hg.

In the trunks of the veins nearest the heart, as in the innominate, subclavian, and jugulars, there is on an average a negative pressure. which according to Jacobsen may attain a value of 0·1 mm. Hg, and is due to the aspiration exerted by the lungs in consequence of the elastic tension into which they are thrown during the expiratory phase. The pressure becomes positive in the veins farthest from the heart and thorax. According to Jacobsen it amounts to 0·3 mm. in the external facial vein of sheep, to 4·1 mm. in the brachial vein, and to 11·4 mm. Hg in the crural vein.

In the pulmonary circuit the pressure cannot be determined directly without opening the thorax, and giving artificial respiration which produces a condition very unlike the normal. Here we can only say that in the left branch of the pulmonary artery Ludwig found a pressure = 29·6 mm. Hg in the dog ; = 17·6 in the cat ; = 12 mm. Hg in the rabbit. The relation between the pressures in the pulmonary artery and the aorta can be deduced from the highest values which the pressure reaches during systole within the two ventricles. According to Goltz and Gaule the pressure in the pulmonary artery is to that in the aorta as something like 2 : 5.

Blood pressure may vary very considerably not only in different individuals of the same species, but also in the same individual under different conditions, notwithstanding the regulatory mechanism which tends to keep it constant. These variations depend on those of the three main factors by which pressure itself is normally determined :—

(a) The variations in the energy of the heart, i.e. in the amount of blood driven in the time - unit through the arterial system.

(b) The variations of resistance encountered by the blood in its passage through the vessels.

(c) The variations of the total mass of blood contained in the system.

The energy of the heart, and the work performed in the time-unit, depend both on the frequency of its revolutions, and the mechanical value of each of these. An increase in the frequency of cardiac rhythm can be compensated by a corresponding diminution in the mechanical value of each revolution, and vice versa. This mechanical value is dependent on the degree of systolic evacuation, and the degree of diastolic filling. In brief, whatever the determining conditions, an augmentation or diminution in the quantity of blood driven through from the heart to the arteries in the unit of time produces, ceteris paribus, a proportional increase or decrease in blood pressure.

Variations in the resistance of the vessels exert the same influence on blood pressure. Given the same energy of cardiac function, a greater or less proportion of the driving force will, on increase or decrease of vascular resistance, be expended on throwing the walls into tension, which produces a corresponding rise or fall of pressure.

Increased vascular resistance can, under physiological conditions, be determined only by augmentation of the tonic contraction of the muscle cells, with which (as we shall see in the next chapter) the middle layer of the vessel walls, particularly in the small arteries, is richly provided.   The increased resistance to the passage of the blood, provoked by the augmentation of vascular tone, depends both on the degree of this augmentation, and on its extension over a more or less extensive vascular area.

In like manner, the diminution of vascular resistance must, under physiological conditions, depend upon a more or less pronounced or diffuse paralysis or diminution of tone in the vessels.   In the next chapter we shall study the physiological adaptations for regulating cardiac and vascular activity, and the processes by which the central and peripheral variations of the circulation tend to become compensated.

In order to determine the dependence of blood pressure on the mass of blood contained in the system, it is obvious that the effects on blood pressure of transfusion and bleeding must be considered.   This subject was studied by Tappeiner, and in an exhaustive manner by Worm-Müller in 1873, in Ludwig's laboratory.   The results of the experiments show that in the dog during the increments in blood pressure produced by successive transfusions of homogeneous defibrinated blood, or the corresponding decrement produced by successive haemorrhages, the physiological limits vary very little, far less than would be expected from the amount of blood added to or taken from the system.   Further, such rise or fall in arterial pressure is of very brief duration, and therefore can only be influenced to a minimal extent by increase or diminution in transudations, and urinary secretions, through the capillaries. There must, therefore, be some compensatory mechanism, which tends rapidly to restore blood pressure to the normal, by producing a dilatation or constriction of the small arteries and capillaries, which adapts them even to very considerable alterations in the blood content.

Pawlow's researches (1878), which confirm Worm - Müller's observations by another method, must also be noted.   When a dog was fed on dry bread or meat he found that blood pressure fell 10 mm. Hg in an artery of the thigh, owing to the dilatation of the intestinal vessels and digestive secretions.   On giving the same dog a large quantity of broth he found no rise of blood pressure.   There must, therefore, be some mechanism which promptly reduces an increase or decrease in the amount of fluid contained in the body to its normal limits.

Pawlow further showed on dogs that, during complete rest and sensory inactivity, blood pressure from day to day does not alter. On the other hand, it increases slightly after meals, and sinks slightly in the morning.   It regularly becomes lower after a warm bath.   The abrupt upward or downward changes in arterial pressure are due to disturbances of vascular innervation (*infra*, Chapter X.).

The results of a series of experiments which Colombo carried out in Mosso's laboratory with a sphygmomanometer applied to the fingers of a healthy man are only partially in agreement with Pawlow's.

He found that when a man is removed from all external and internal influences liable to produce disturbance of the vasomotor functions, the lateral pressure of the digital arteries fluctuates constantly within 24 hours between a minimum of 65 and a maximum of 100 mm. Hg (average 80-85). The greatest decrease occurs after meal times, the greatest rise during hours most removed from meals. The daily curve of blood pressure must accordingly run an opposite course to that of pulse frequency and temperature. As a matter of fact the pulse is accelerated when arterial pressure falls, and becomes slower when it rises, which is apparently the expression of some compensatory mechanism.

The depressor effect of meals is certainly due to active vascular dilatation of the digestive organs, and possibly to the entrance of a small amount of peptones into the circulation. Colombo found that the highest fall of pressure (which may amount to 20 mm. Hg) is apparent two hours after meals, when the absorption of the products of digestion is beginning.

The introduction of a large quantity of milk, contrary to what might be expected, produces a rise in pressure, in consequence of the overloading of the circulation, which cannot apparently be compensated by depression of the vascular tone.

Alcohol, chloroform, opium, warm baths, sleep, lower the blood pressure; cold baths and coffee raise it.

Gymnastics and massage of the limbs and back produce a rise, massage of the abdomen a fall, in blood pressure, probably because they influence the vascular tone in a different degree and in different proportions.

The pressure in the veins, in consequence of their ready distension, is less subject to fluctuation than arterial pressure. Theoretically it may be assumed that all the circumstances that produce a rise or fall in arterial pressure, cause, or may cause, a change in venous pressure in the opposite direction. Venous pressure is specially affected by: —

      a Increment or decrement in amount of blood.

      b Respiratory movements (to be discussed later).

      c Position of the body (according to the laws of hydrostatics).

VI. Observations on the velocity of the circulation have been made in two opposite directions. On the one hand it has been attempted to determine the mean velocity with which the blood moves in any given artery; on the other, to establish the form of the pulsatory changes of velocity.

At present we must confine ourselves to the methods employed for ascertaining the first point.

By *mean* velocity of the blood in an artery is meant the length of the blood column that traverses the section of the said artery in the time-unit, usually 1″. It can easily be calculated when the sectional area of the artery and the amount of blood that traverses it in the time-unit are known.

The first to attempt the exact determination of this point was Volkmann (1846). His method was adopted by Ludwig (1867) who perfected *Volkmann's haemodromometer*. His instrument (the *Stromuhr*) permitted the repetition on the same animal, for an indefinite number of times, of the determination of the mean velocity of the circulation, so that its variations with changes of experimental conditions can be investigated.

Ludwig's Stromuhr or haemo-dromometer (Fig. 99) consists of two glass receivers of equal capacity (A, B), which com-municate above by a U-bend, in the centre of which there is a tube opening to the exterior. By means of this aperture the bulb A can be filled with oil, and bulb B with physiological saline, after which the aperture is closed by a stop-cock. The cannula *a* (which communicates with the bulb A) is then con-nected with the central end of the artery, and the cannula *b* (which communicates with the bulb B) with its distal end. As soon as the blood reaches the stromuhr, it penetrates A and drives the oil into B, when the salt solution contained in the

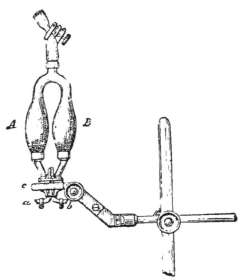

FIG. 99.   Ludwig's haemodromometer or *Stromuhr*. A, B, Glass bulbs of equal capacity ; *a*, *b*, can-nulae to be connected with central and periph-eral trunks of artery ; *c*, metal plate fixed on a support, on which the air-tight metal disc in which the two receivers end can rotate.

latter is driven into the peripheral part of the artery. When the blood has completely filled the bulb A, the two receivers which are reversible upon the metal plate *c* are changed by a rapid half-turn, so that A is now in connection with the cannula *b*, and B with cannula *a*. The bulb containing oil is now again filled with blood, and the oil once more driven into the bulb A, and so on. If the number of turns in a given time are counted, then with known capacity of the receivers it is easy to calculate the total quantity of blood flowing in that time through the artery, from which the quantity passing per second can be calculated.

Tigerstedt modified Ludwig's Stromuhr by substituting for the two receivers a single, accurately calibrated glass cylinder, along which runs a hollow metal ball. The pressure of the blood drives this ball from one end of the cylinder to the other : so soon as this occurs, the cylinder is reversed by a mechanism resembling that of Ludwig's Stromuhr, and the ball moves in the opposite direction, driving the blood before it.

We also invented a haemodromometer, which, with the utmost simplicity of construction, presents the advantage of being able to vary the capacity of the two receivers, which correspond to the bulbs of Ludwig's apparatus, by employing two elastic bags in a receiver full of water. The first two editions of this text-book gave the description and figure omitted here in favour of the new model constructed by Hürthle, which has the further advantage of automatically registering its movements.

Hürthle's haemodromometer (as shown in Fig. 100) consists essentially of an inverted U-tube, in one branch of which there is a cylindrical receiver containing a piston, which is easily movable from the top to the bottom and the bottom to the top. The blood-stream, which issues from the central end of the artery (carotid in the dog), ascends by a branch of the said tube, penetrates the cylindrical receiver, and, by lowering the piston, empties out the fluid (artificial serum with which it was filled at the outset) into the distal end of the artery.

When the ball reaches the extreme end of its course, the experimenter at once reverses the blood current through the cylinder by giving a half-turn to a disc beneath it by means of a screw. The blood current will then flow into the cylinder from below, driving the piston up, and turning the blood into the distal end of the artery.

The reversal of the current is repeated each time the ball reaches the top or bottom. The interval between one reversal and the other expresses the duration of each filling and emptying of the cylinder that measures the current. The excursions upward and downward of the ball are transmitted by a system of pulleys to a lever writing on the smoked paper of a rotating drum. A Deprèz signal simultaneously records the time on the same drum, while an elastic manometer (Hürthle) applied to the artery shows the pulsatory oscillations of the arterial pressure.

The tracings in Fig. 101 are reproduced from those obtained by Hürthle with his ingenious haemodromometer (reduced by one-third), which serves at the same time for a spring manometer recording the oscillatory pulsations in pressure and for an electric time-marker.

These haemodromometric methods are certainly not free from defects, and they give, not the normal absolute values of current velocity in any given artery, but values as much lower than the normal as the resistances artificially opposed to the passage of the blood through the measuring apparatus are greater. Since, however, these new resistances are a fixed and constant coefficient, they do not interfere with the value of the comparative results.

On the other hand, the method still occasionally adopted after

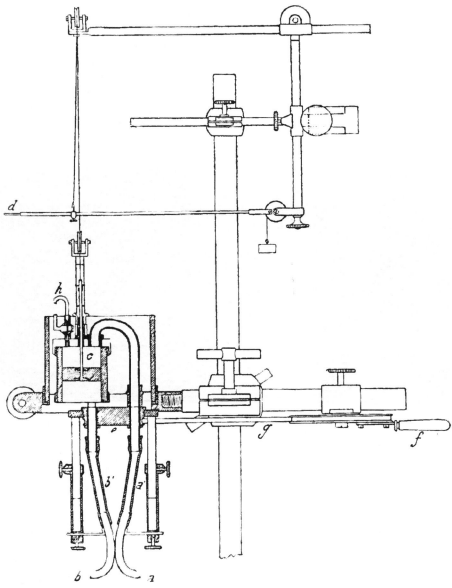

FIG. 100.—Hurthle's recording haemodromometer, partly schematic, partly in section. *a*, *b*, Cannulae connecting with central and peripheral ends of artery ; *c*, well-calibrated glass cylinder into which the blood flows, pushing the piston now from above downward, now from below upwards.   The piston is connected by a thread passing over two pulleys, to the lever *d*, which records on a rotating drum the movements of the piston, *i.e.* the filling or emptying of the cylinder.   Below the metal plate which supports the measuring cylinder is a movable disc *e*, with handle, *f*, connected with the metal band *g*, which turns the disc 180°, reversing the current and crossing the rubber tubes *a′ b′*.   Before applying the apparatus, the whole of the tubing *a*, *a′*, *b*, *b′*, *c* is filled with physiological saline.   This is effected by the tube *h* carrying a tap, which is shut off when the tubes are completely filled.

Harvey (who first employed it to measure the velocity of the circulation) is entirely fallacious, since it is based on the amount of blood which escapes in the unit of time from a divided artery. In this case all the peripheral resistances which the blood has to overcome under physiological conditions are artificially excluded. Even when the lumen of outflow is artificially constricted (*e.g.* by introducing a glass cannula of narrow bore) in order to build up a resistance similar to that which the blood normally encounters, it is impossible to obtain any correct values of current velocity, both because we do not know if the resistance added is of the same value as that subtracted, and because in any case the animal is losing the blood that flows out, which sets up quite abnormal conditions.

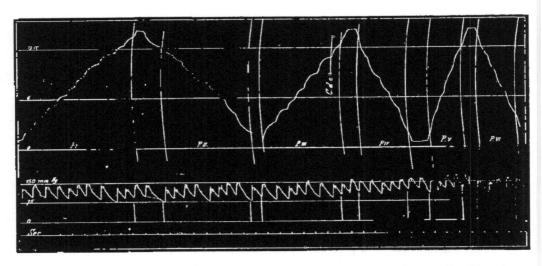

Fig. 101.—Curve of velocity and pressure of blood in left carotid of a dog of 13 kgrms. (Hürthle and Tschuewsky.) The upper tracing is divided along the abscissa into six periods (Pᵢ, Pᵢᵢ, etc.), at which the current in the measuring cylinder was reversed. The spaces comprised between the horizontal lines of the tracing correspond with 6 c.c. of blood. The curves of the second level represent the pulsatory oscillations of blood pressure in the central cannulae of the haemodromometer, and were recorded with a spring manometer. The bottom line gives the time in seconds. The vertical line C.d.c. of the third period gives the moment at which the right carotid was compressed, which produced an augmentation both of velocity and of pressure in the left carotid, as shown in the tracing.

The experimental results obtained by Dogiel and Nicolaïdes with Ludwig's stromuhr are somewhat meagre owing, no doubt, to the very variable conditions that affect the velocity of current in any given artery. They show that both in the carotid and the femoral of the dog or rabbit the velocity may alter greatly from one moment to another. Since the first determinations usually show a higher value than the subsequent, it was conjectured that this was due to a commencement of clotting at the insertion point of the cannula. This supposition was, however, excluded, inasmuch as the same fact was observed with blood that had been rendered incoagulable by peptone injection, viz. that velocity diminished as the experiment proceeded, more often in the carotid, less frequently in the crural artery.

The following are some of the data derived from Dogiel's researches :—

Animal.	Duration of Observation in seconds.	Velocity in mm	Weight of Animal in kgrms.
Rabbit	110	226-94	1·7
Dog	80	733-349	23·3
,, ...	127	520-243	12·1
,, ...	63	458-411	3·2
,, (division of vago-sympathetic) . . .	45	339-204	3·6

The velocity of the blood-flow, which is essentially a function of the resistances in that part of the circulation to which the haemodromometer is applied, must rise and fall with the increase and decrease of resistance. It is probable that the mere manipulation necessary for inserting the cannula in the artery is sufficient to produce relaxation of it and its principal branches, thereby determining an abormal rise of current velocity, which soon falls again in consequence of the recovery of normal vascular tone.

Dogiel further showed that there may be a compensatory rise in current velocity in the carotid on exciting the splanchnic nerve : this has no direct action on the carotid region, but since it provokes contraction of the vessels in the abdominal viscera, it increases resistance in a remote vascular region of considerable extent. He also observed, when using two stromuhrs on the same animal, that the velocity in the carotid and the femoral arteries may vary now in the same, now in the opposite sense. This shows the great adaptability of capacity in the various vascular regions, the mechanism of which will be studied in the next chapter.

Tschuewsky (1903), using Hürthle's recording stromuhr, has made a great many observations on dogs, upon the mean velocity of the blood in the different arteries, and under various experimental conditions. The following table gives the average of his results :—

Artery.	Experimental Conditions.	Average Weight of Body in kgrms.	Average Diameter of Vessel in mm.	Average Blood Pressure in mm. Hg.	Average Velocity in mm. per sec.
Crural .	Nerves of limb intact	13·7	2·5	77	128
,, .	,, ,, cut	14·6	2·8	88	275
Carotid .	Vagus and sympathetic intact .	14·1	3·27	92·6	241·2

From this table it appears that the velocity is normally much lower in the crural artery than in the carotid, and that after division of the nerves to the limb (paralytic vaso-dilatation) the diminution of resistance due to relaxation of vascular tone may cause current velocity to rise to more than double the normal.

Tetanic excitation of the nerve, on the contrary, increases resistance by increase of vascular tone (vaso-constriction) and compression of the vessels by muscular contraction, with consequent diminution of velocity, as shown in the following table :—

Experimental Conditions.	Weight of Dog in kgrms.	Diameter of Crural Artery, mm.	Average Pressure of Blood in Crural Artery, mm. Hg.	Average Velocity in Crural Artery, mm. per second.
Before excitation . .	11·2	2·45	83·0	201·7
During tetanisation of sciatic nerve with strong currents . .	...	..	84·8	96·6
After-effect of excitation	..	...	81·5	236·5

The results of experiments to determine the effect of temporary anaemia of different vascular regions due to compression of the arteries are also interesting.

The following are examples :—

Experimental Conditions.	Average Duration of Compression in seconds.	Average Pressure of Blood in carotid in mm. Hg.	Average Velocity in carotid in mm. per second.
I. Before compression . .		109·2	308·2
During compression of carotid of opposite side .	23·3	111·2	394·6
II. Before compression . .	...	120·1	293·3
After temporary compression of arteries on the side to which the haemo-dromometer has been applied	21·0	127·0	411·7

From this table we see (a) the marked compensatory rise of velocity on constriction of an adjacent area ; (b) the marked rise of velocity after temporary anaemia of the vascular area on the same side, owing to the diminution of peripheral resistance due to the resulting vaso-dilatation.

As regards the mean velocity of the blood-flow in the veins, we have already stated that it must be less than that in the corresponding arterial region, in proportion as the total area of the venous system is greater.

The velocity of blood-flow in the axes of the capillaries can be determined without difficulty under the microscope by measuring the time taken by a red corpuscle to traverse a certain distance, which can be measured by an ocular micrometer. The values obtained with this method by different observers are shown in the following table by Tigerstedt :—

Animal.	Velocity in mm. sec.	Observers.
Frog. abdominal muscle	0·28	Hales
Frog larva, tail	0·57	E. H. Weber
Frog, interdigital membrane	0·51	Valentin
,, ,, ,,	0·25	Vorkmann
Salamander larva, gill	0·36	Vierordt
Frog larva, tail	0·40	Volkmann
Fish, caudal fin	0·12	,,
Puppy, mesentery	0·80	,,

The velocity of the red corpuscles in the capillaries of the retina was ingeniously determined by Vierordt upon himself, by means of their entoptic images. If we look without accommodating the eye at a large clear surface, *e.g.* the sky, numerous shining points appear which move one after the other by tortuous paths: these are the blood-corpuscles seen entoptically, owing perhaps to concentration of light upon their concave discs. Vierordt projected these images upon a surface of 11-16 cm. from the eye, and there determined the space traversed by a single corpuscle in the time-unit. From this he deduced a velocity of 0·5-0·9 mm. per sec. The values of the velocity of blood-flow in the capillaries is of special interest, owing to the fact that it is possible from these to deduce the approximate extent of the total area of the capillary system. Since the velocity of the blood in the vascular system is inversely proportional to its total area, we can calculate from the area of the aorta and the velocity of the blood in the aorta and its capillaries the total area of these last, inasmuch as the area of the capillary system

$$= \frac{\text{area of aorta} \times \text{velocity in aorta}}{\text{velocity in capillaries}}$$

If we admit the value of 0·5-1 m. as the mean velocity in the aorta and that of 0·5-1 mm. in the capillaries per second, thus, with an aortic area of 4·4 cm.^{2}, we obtain the value of 8800-2200 cm.^{2} for the total area of the capillary system (Tigerstedt)

VII. We must now pass on to the methods devised in order to analyse the *pulsatory oscillations* of blood pressure, of current velocity, and of the volume of the vessels. All three phenomena are intimately related among themselves, and all depend on the fact that the flow of blood from the heart to the arteries is not continuous, but occurs in intermittent waves, which coincide with the cardiac systole. We will begin by reviewing, collectively, the

observations made on these three phenomena in order subsequently
to compare the results.

The so-called sphygmographic methods have yielded perfect
sphygmograms, which give an exact graphic representation of the
pulsatile oscillations of pressure.

Even the ancient physicians, more particularly Herophilus,
Erasistratus, and Galen, recognised by touch some of the chief
characteristics of the arterial pulse, and the alterations in frequency
(*pulsus frequens et rarus*), magnitude (*p. magnus et parvus*), rate
of dilatation (*p. celer et tardus*), hardness or compressibility
(*p. durus et mollis*), regularity or irregularity of rhythm (*p. inter-
mittens, alternans, intercurrens*), and lastly, in the form of the pulse
wave (*p. dicrotus seu bis feriens*). But all these and many other
distinctions of pulse, as laid down by Galen, are founded far too

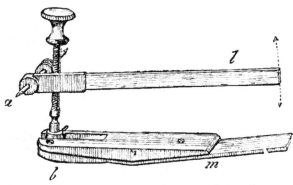

much on subjective
appreciation. Cusano
(1565) made a great
advance when he first
used a watch to count
the beats; still greater
progress was made by
Vierordt (1855) who
first demonstrated the
possibility of register-
ing the pulse auto-
matically, although his
sphygmograph did not
succeed in giving a
true picture of the
form of the pulse-wave

FIG. 102.—Marey's contrivance for transmitting the movements of the spring to the writing-lever of the sphygmograph. *m*, Steel spring; *b*, button compressing the artery,
connected above with a little rod, of which the screw bites
into the wheel of the axis *c*, which moves the lever *l* from
above downwards in the direction of the arrow.

or the pulsatile oscillations of arterial pressure.

The first sphygmograph which accurately recorded the form of
the pulse was that constructed by Marey in 1860, which found
ready acceptance among physicians owing to the elegance of the
method, and the exaggerated hopes of clinical advantage that were
founded on it. The essential part of Marey's sphygmograph was a
steel spring, pressed against the radial artery by a button, which
transmitted the pulsations to a long and very light lever, by which
they were recorded exactly, in a magnified form, upon a metal
plate covered with smoked paper, propelled at a uniform rate by
clockwork. Fig. 102 shows the mode of transmitting the movements of the spring to the lever according to the most recent
improvements, and Fig 103 shows the complete instrument applied
to the forearm. The sphygmograms obtained with Marey's
sphygmograph may vary considerably under different conditions of
health and disease; but all have one characteristic feature—a
rapidly ascending and slowly descending period can always be

distinguished. The former, produced by the pulse-wave which starts from the aorta, usually reaches its culminating point without interruption: the latter, on the contrary, shows several

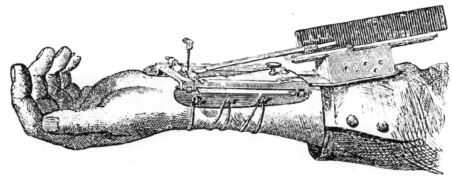

Fig. 103.—Marey's direct sphygmograph, applied to the radial artery.

oscillations, one of which (the second, expressed in a rise preceded by a slight depression) is rarely absent in pulse tracings. It is known as the dicrotic wave, and consists in a negative wave (dicrotic notch), immediately followed by a secondary positive wave.

It has been proved by innumerable control experiments of Buisson, Marey, Landois and others, that the sphygmograms thus obtained do really reproduce the form of the pulsatile oscillations of blood pressure, and that their constant dicrotism is no factitious product of the registering apparatus. Here we need only say that sphygmograms obtained with the sphygmoscope or other elastic manometers (Fig. 67, p. 205) present the same dicrotic form. Moreover, as Landois showed, it is possible to obtain autosphygmograms by dividing the artery of an animal, and directing the rhythmical jet of blood against a rotating drum covered with filter-paper (*haemautography*). As shown by Fig. 104, the form of the haemautogram agrees perfectly with

Fig. 104. — Auto-sphygmogram (Haemautogram) from posterior tibial artery of large dog. (Landois.) *p*, Primary wave; *d*, dicrotic wave.

those from the sphygmograph and sphygmoscope: while the dicrotic wave is even more apparent, this being the only really important feature of the pulse curve that we need consider.

Since the dicrotic wave persists, and is even more pronounced in autosphygmograms, it is proved to be the result of a positive wave of central origin and centrifugal course—which excludes the hypothesis still maintained by some, that it arises in a peripheral and centripetally reflected wave. This last hypothesis is also irreconcilable with the fact that the secondary positive wave is nearly always preceded by a negative wave which, as we shall see immediately, can only be of central origin.

Fig. 105. Sphygmograms from radial artery (Sr), and changes produced by inhalation of amyl nitrite (S'r'). (A. D. Waller.)

The long experience of nearly half a century, during which Marey's sphygmograph (or other sphygmographs which are only modifications of this instrument) has been employed clinically, has proved it to be of very little diagnostic value. We have for many years insisted on this fact, and for the following reasons.

Fig. 106. -Marey's transmission sphygmograph applied to radial artery. This only differs from the direct sphygmograph in that the movements of the button of the spring are not transmitted by a lever, but by a receiving tambour, which then transmits them to a second tambour writing upon the revolving drum of the kymograph.

It is quite true that the sphygmogram is the true expression of the form and magnitude of the pulsatile oscillations in pressure in the artery to which the instrument is attached, but it is far from representing their absolute values. Local arterial pressure is indeed dependent on many variable factors: on the tension of the spring, the elasticity and tone of the arterial walls, the amount and degree of torpor in the surrounding soft parts. From all these causes, the size of the pulse, i.e. the amplitude of the sphygmogram, is in no definite ratio either with the volume of blood driven from the heart to the arteries at every systole, nor with the height of pressure within the artery investigated; it is only proportional to the magnitude of the local oscillations of the pulse, which (as we saw on p. 248) are, *ceteris paribus*, in inverse ratio to the tension of the arterial walls. As a matter of fact, not only the primary, but also the secondary dicrotic wave is lower with greater, and higher with reduced arterial pressure. Not even this fact, however, can be taken as a general law, since the varying degree of contraction or relaxation in the artery explored has great influence upon the amplitude of the sphygmic undulations. In order to realise this,

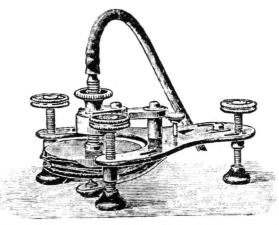

Fig. 107.—Burdon-Sanderson's cardiograph, which can also be used as a sphygmograph for the carotid, and a pneumograph (Zimmermann's type). The apparatus rests on three ebonite feet, which can be adjusted by screws. It is fixed by a band to the thorax or neck, so that the central button, which has a steel spring (the tension of which can be altered by a screw), presses against the spot at which the beat of the heart or carotid pulse is most perceptible. The transmission by air of the movements of the spring is effected through a receiving tambour, the position of which in regard to the spring can be regulated by a screw.

we have only to consider the marked changes that appear in the form and magnitude of the sphygmogram after inhalation of amyl nitrite, which immediately produces depression of arterial tone (Fig. 105). The beats of the heart become more frequent, and yet the amplitude of the primary as well as of the dicrotic wave increases.

Fig. 108.—Edgren's sphygmograph for carotid. Consists of a receiving tambour attached to a semicircular spring intended to fit round the neck. The pressure of the exploring button upon the artery is regulated by a plate applied to the neck, which stretches the spring more or less according to the position of the screw.

for the same artery.

Far more interesting and instructive, from the clinical point of view, is the comparison of the sphygmogram with the simultaneously recorded cardiogram, as also the comparison of two or more sphygmograms simultaneously recorded from different arteries. For this purpose, however, the direct sphygmograph is not suitable, and others with air transmission must be resorted to. These are essentially identical with cardiographs, but are different in form, since they are intended for use on the several arteries. One of these *transmission sphygmographs* is that of Marey (represented in Fig. 106), for the radial artery. A simpler model is that of Edgren Burdon-Sanderson's *cardiograph* (Fig. 107) can be used for the carotid, femoral, or other arteries, as also Edgren's sphygmograph, or any kind of tympanum with an elastic membrane kept stretched by a spiral spring, and provided with an exploring button in the centre, which can be pressed against the artery to be examined (Fig. 108).

VIII. The comparison of cardiograms and sphygmograms simultaneously recorded on the same revolving cylinder gives all the data necessary to establish the chief characteristics of the two tracings. Those of Fig. 109 were obtained by Edgren on a healthy youth of twenty-five. The various features of the cardiographic curve (a, b, c, d, e, f, g, h, i) are indicated by vertical lines. Since

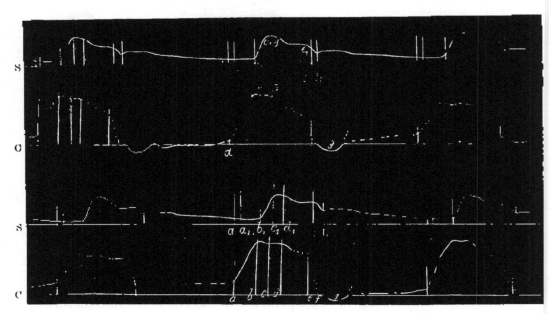

FIG. 109. Cardiograms (C) and sphygmograms (S) of carotid of a healthy subject of 25. (Edgren.) a, b, c, d, e, f of the cardiograms correspond with the a_1, b_1, c_1, d_1, e_1, f_1 of the sphygmograms.

these are obvious, they need no further description. After what was said in the previous chapter (Fig. 80, p. 224) we know that the point a corresponds with the onset of systole, when the first sound of the heart begins to be heard, and the point f with the onset of diastole, when the semilunar valves, which have already been closed at the systolic dead point, are thrown into tension, and the second sound develops. In the sphygmographic curve of the carotid the point coinciding with a shows no marked feature. The primary sphygmic wave which starts from the arterial orifice first reaches the carotid at the point b'. The interval ab', therefore, represents the time taken up by the transmission of the pulse wave from the arterial orifice to the carotid, *plus* the time of the latent systole, *i.e.* that between the commencement of the contraction of the myocardium and the moment of the opening of the semilunar valves (point b of the cardiographic curve). Since the points b, c, d, e, f of the cardiogram correspond to the same number of points on the sphygmogram at b', c', d', e', f', but all with a delay, equal approximately to the interval aa', it follows that this interval expresses the time occupied by the transmission of the primary wave from the arterial orifice to the carotid, and that the intervals ab, $a'b'$ represent the time of latent systole.

The interval bc, which can hardly be seen on the cardiogram as a slight drop in the curve, corresponds to the interval $b'c'$ marked by the sharply ascending curve of the primary wave. The interval cd, indicated by a slight rise of the cardiographic line, corresponds to the interval $c'd'$, indicated on the sphygmogram by a tract that is almost horizontal (the *plateau*). The interval de, corresponding to $d'e'$, both on the cardiogram and on the sphygmogram shows a slowly descending line; and the intervals ef and $e'f'$ correspond in both curves with rapidly descending lines.

Leaving aside the features c and d which are less conspicuous, and have only a dubious significance, it is evident, or at any rate extremely probable, that the entire interval be represents the period of systolic outflow or evacuation, during which the heart, in consequence of the diminution in its volume, exerts a constantly decreasing pressure on the intercostal space to which the cardiograph is applied. In the sphygmographic curve these periods are represented by the interval $b'c'$ in which the primary pulse wave is traversing the artery.

The small interval ef coincides with the beginning of active diastole, during which, owing to the diminished tension of the cardiac muscle, the intercostal space on which the button of the cardiograph rests, sinks in. This corresponds to the lines $e'f'$ of the sphygmogram, which represent a true negative wave that precedes the secondary or dicrotic wave.

To understand the origin of this dicrotic wave it is enough to consider that at the commencement of diastole an enormous difference between aortic and intraventricular pressure arises : this causes the blood column to gravitate towards the semilunar valves which are already closed, throwing them into vibration so that they develop the second sound, and set up the negative wave in the artery, owing to their distension towards the conus arteriosus. The sharp tension of the valves is succeeded by their elastic reaction, which produces the positive dicrotic wave that follows immediately on the negative wave. The great majority of physiologists, including Grashey, Edgren, Hoorweg, Hürthle, are unanimous in accepting this explanation of the dicrotic wave. To us its central origin appears conclusive, on account of the negative wave that precedes it and can only be caused by the rapid recession of the column of blood in the aortic bulb, which distends the valves and pushes them down towards the conus arteriosus :—not by the reflux of a certain amount of blood from artery to ventricle, to produce closure of the valves, as is arbitrarily assumed by Edgren.

The points *g*, *h*, *i*, which are distinguishable on the long descending shoulder of the cardiographic curve, of course find no analogue in the sphygmogram, because after closure of the semi-

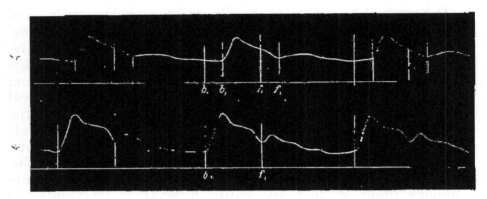

FIG. 110.—Comparison of synchronous sphygmograms of carotid (*Sc*) and of radial (*Sr*). (Edgren.)

lunar valves changes of pressure within the ventricle can no longer be transmitted to the arteries. Here we will only say that the point *g*, which marks the lowest depression of the cardiographic curve, very probably corresponds with the moment at which the negative pressure in the ventricle exerts the maximum of aspira-

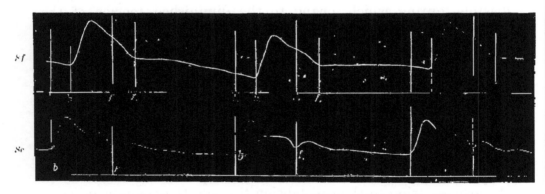

FIG. 111. Synchronous sphygmograms of carotid (*Sc*) and femoral (*Sf*). (Edgren.)

tion ; that the point *h* marks the moment at which active diastole ceases, and passive diastole or the true rest of the heart begins; and that finally the point *i* (which is usually, but not constantly, visible in cardiographic tracings) points to the moment at which presystole commences, causing a certain degree of passive dilatation of the ventricle, as perceived in a gentle rise of the cardiograph button.

When the rate at which the cylinder rotates is known, and the characteristics of the cardiographic and sphygmographic curves, as described above, are well marked, the length in millimetres, and corresponding period in fractions of a section, of the chief phases of the cardiac cycle in man can easily be determined. It is well to make these determinations from tracings obtained from one healthy individual, with constant experimental conditions during the research. The data thus obtained are of approximately absolute value for the individual under observation, and are certainly far more trustworthy than the average data derived from comparison of results yielded by various individuals under varying experimental conditions.

From the careful measurements taken by Edgren upon a

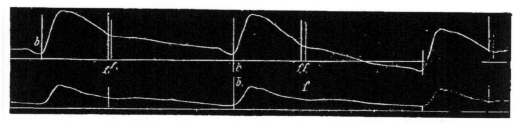

FIG. 112.—Synchronous sphygmograms of radial (Sr) and femoral (Sf).   (Edgren.)

healthy man of 25, whose pulse beat 70 times per minute, the following values were obtained, which may be taken as the average of ten successive cardiac revolutions :—

Period of tension	$ab =$ 4·67 mm.	= 0·0934 seconds
Period of efflux	be 11·71 ,,	0·2342 ,,
Total duration of systole	$= ae = 16·38$,,	= 0·3276 ,,
Active) diastole	$ef -$ 2·60 ,,	= 0·0520 ,,
Passive)	$fa - 24·14$,,	= 0·4828 ,,
Total duration of diastole	$= ea = 26·74$,,	= 0·5348 ,,
Total duration of cardiac revolution	$= aa$ 43·12 ,,	= 0·8624 ,,

IX. If the pulse of the carotid and radial, or the carotid and the femoral, or the femoral and radial are registered simultaneously as shown in Figs. 110, 111, 112, it is possible to determine with great accuracy the time occupied in the propagation of the primary wave b', or the dicrotic wave f', by deducing it from the delay between the appearance of the two waves in the arteries most remote from the heart. This delay is represented in the three figures by the intervals $b'b'$ and $f'f'$. If they are measured with a millimetre scale, it will be seen that their length alters with the difference between the two arteries of which the sphygmograms are compared. It will also be seen that the wave b' appears simultaneously in the femoral and the radial, while the wave f' appears with a measurable delay in the femoral.

Edgren obtained the following results as the average of a number of measurements of these intervals in sphygmograms taken

on two healthy individuals 25 years of age. The delay between
the radial pulse and the carotid for the wave $b' = 3.93$ mm. $= 0.0786$
seconds, for the wave $f' = 3.96$ mm. $= 0.0792$ seconds.

Since the distance from the semilunar valves to the point on
the carotid at which the sphygmograph was applied was 20 cm.
and to the corresponding point on the radial 80 cm., the time
difference found corresponded to a length of 60 cm. From these
data the time of transmission of the wave b' from heart to carotid
can be calculated :

$$3.93 : x = 60 : 20 ; \quad x = 1.31 \text{ mm.} = 0.0262 \text{ seconds} ;$$

and from heart to radial :

$$3.93 + 1.31 = 5.24 \text{ mm.} = 0.1048 \text{ seconds.}$$

By a similar calculation the propagation of the wave f' from
heart to carotid is found to be :

$$3.96 : x = 60 : 20 ; \quad x = 1.32 \text{ mm.} = 0.0264 \text{ seconds} :$$

and from heart to radial :

$$3.96 + 1.32 = 5.28 \text{ mm.} = 0.1056 \text{ seconds.}$$

Repeating the same measurements and calculations for the
single series of tracings obtained on the two young men, Edgren
obtained the results appended on the following table :—

Distance.	Time of Transmission			
	of Primary Wave b'.		of Dicrotic Wave f'.	
From heart to carotid I.	1·31 mm.	0·0262 sec.	1·32 mm.	0·0264 sec.
,, ,, II.	1·36 ,,	0·0272 ,,	1·36 ,,	0·0272 ,,
From heart to radial I.	5·24 ,,	0·1048 ,,	5·28 ,,	0·1056 ,,
,, ,, II.	6·32 ,,	0·1064 ..	5·32 ,.	0·1064 ,,
From heart to femoral I.	5·50 ,,	0·1100 ,.	6·35 .,	0·1270 ,,
,, ,, II.	5·31 ,,	0·1062 ,,	6·32 .,	0·1264 ,,

From these data Edgren found it easy to calculate the rate of
transmission of the two waves, i.e. the distance they traversed in
one second (the unit of time).

The results are given in the following table :—

Distance.	Velocity of Transmission	
	of Primary Wave.	of Dicrotic Wave.
From carotid to radial 60 cm.	7·63 m.	7·53 m.
,, ,, 58 ,,	7·32 ,,	7·32 ,,
From carotid to femoral = 52 ,,	6·20 ,,	5·20 ,,
,, ,, 52 ,,	6·59 ,,	5·40 ,,

These results agree well with those of previous authors, notably with those of Keyt. The differences depend principally on the respective degree of elasticity of the arteries explored, and the respective height of the mean blood pressure within them: the greater the elasticity of the arteries, the higher the blood pressure, and the greater will be the velocity of wave transmission (Moens, Grunmach, Keyt).

Edgren's results, like the earlier conclusions of Keyt, lead us to think that the velocity of the wave in the vessels is higher in the upper limbs than in the lower. Edgren further found by comparing the velocity of the primary and the dicrotic wave that it is less in the latter. The difference, which can hardly be detected between heart and radial artery, is conspicuous between the heart and the femoral artery, as appears from the above tables.

The wave-length can easily be calculated from the velocity of transmission of the waves and from their number, since it is in direct proportion to the rate of propagation (h) and inversely proportional to the number of vibrations (n), according to the equation $\lambda = \dfrac{h}{n}$. If with Edgren we reckon the time of systolic outflow = 0·23 seconds, the number of vibrations in one second will be equal to 5·75, and their velocity of propagation (taking the average of that calculated by Edgren for the primary wave) is equal to 6·93 m. per second. Accordingly the wave-length $\lambda = \dfrac{6·93}{5·75} = 1·20$ m. Since in an adult the distance from heart to small arteries of the foot is a little greater, these arterial tracts of the body are the only ones long enough to accommodate the entire length of the pulse wave, and the end of the wave usually passes the orifice of the aorta when the front of it has already reached the peripheral arteries (Tigerstedt), so that these pulsate during the whole of the systolic outflow.

We know experimentally how many influences react on the pulse-rate: e.g. the lowering of blood pressure and dilatation of the vessels produced by heat, by amyl nitrite, and by profound narcosis. The pulse is perceptibly slowed, as can be measured not merely in artificial narcosis on animals, but also in physiological sleep, and on man. Patrizi compared the velocity of the pulse wave in the waking state and in deep sleep, by means of experiments on a boy of 13, as also the pulsations of the brain (the boy had lost part of the bony substance of his cranium) and of the feet.

Velocity of propagation in waking state, 6·50 m. per second.

Velocity of propagation in sleep, 5·77 m. per second.

X. The pulsatile oscillations of pressure in the sphygmograms must be distinguished from the pulsatile oscillations of velocity, which are also determined by the rhythmical undulations of the heart. Vierordt (1858) was the first to construct an apparatus for the study of these oscillations. Vierordt's *haemotachometer* is based on the principle of the hydrostatic pendulum, used by

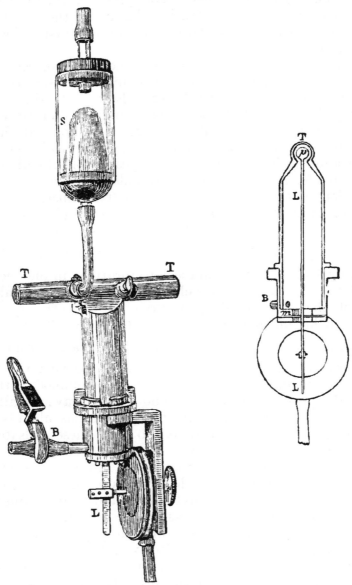

FIG. 113.—Chauveau's haemodrometer. Left-hand figure shows the instrument as a whole; right-hand, a vertical section of it. (Explanation in text.)

engineers to measure the rate of a stream of water. His method was perfected and developed by Chauveau (1860), who constructed a very ingenious recording apparatus on the same principle, which he termed a *haemodromograph*.

Fig. 113 shows this apparatus as a whole on the left, and in section on the right. The tube TT is intended for insertion in the carotid artery of a horse or other large animal; L represents the bar of the pendulum which ends in a very light plate or disc p, dipping into the axis of the blood-stream. The bar of the pendulum passes at m through a rubber membrane, which acts as a pivot to the pendulum, and is then prolonged externally till it joins a Marey's air tympanum. The tube TT has a narrow longitudinal cleft along which the terminal disc of the pendulum can move, in accordance with the oscillations of current velocity: these are reversed at the membrane of the receiving tambour, which again transmits them to a tambour with a writing lever. No blood can enter the groove in which the bar of the pendulum oscillates freely, because it is connected with an external space filled with an alkaline solution through the side tube B, and then closed with a clamp. The sphygmoscope S is applied at the side of the tube TT, and records the oscillations of pressure on a revolving cylinder by means of a second writing tambour which acts synchronously with the first.

Just as sphygmograms do not give absolute values of oscillations of blood pressure, so the tachygrams or dromograms recorded by Chauveau's haemodromograph yield only relative values of the oscillations of current velocity above and below the zero line, which is reached when there is no movement, because the disc of the pendulum is under equal pressure on both sides. In order to ascertain the absolute value of velocity and its oscillations, the apparatus must be graduated. Chauveau did this by sending a stream of water through it, of which the outflow was regulated until the deflections of the pendulum attained the maximal, minimal, and mean values obtained on applying the apparatus to the carotid of the horse. It is then easy to determine the velocity corresponding to these points, by calculating it from the diameter of the arteries, and from the respective amount of outflow, obtained with different degrees of deflections of the pendulum.

Chauveau and his pupils Bertolus and Leroyenne were able to determine that the velocity of the blood-flow amounted to 520 mm. per second in the carotid of the horse during systole, to 220 mm. during the dicrotic wave, and to 150 mm. during diastole.

When the carotid is ligatured on one side, a compensatory rise of velocity is visible in the other carotid. During the masticating movements also, in consequence of a dilatation of the vessels of the masticatory muscles and salivary glands, there is an increase of circulatory velocity in the carotid, which may become five or six times greater than the initial value. When any considerable vascular dilatation is produced by dividing the spinal cord, the rate of flow is considerably augmented during systole, but becomes extremely low during diastole. At the end of diastole the velocity is greater in the peripheral than in the central arteries;

at the commencement of systole, on the other hand, it increases more in the central than in the peripheral arteries.

It is no less interesting to examine the features presented by tachygrams as compared with sphygmograms simultaneously recorded. Fig. 114 gives an instructive example of these tracings as obtained by Lortet, another of Chauveau's pupils. Point 1 corresponds to the moment in which the primary systolic wave, on reaching the carotid, produces a simultaneous rise in pressure and in velocity. At point 2 the pressure reaches its maximum when the velocity has already begun to fall in accordance with the increase of elastic tension in the distended artery, by which the velocity of the movement of the blood is proportionately moderated

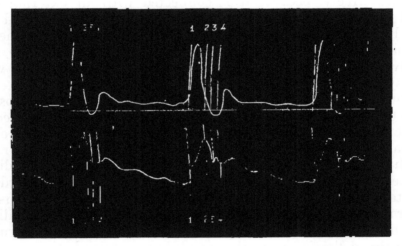

Fig. 114.—Tachygram (V) and sphygmogram (P) registered simultaneously on carotid artery of horse, with Chauveau's haemodromograph. (Lortet.)

and depressed. Point 3 probably corresponds to the moment at which the systolic efflux ceases and the closure of the semilunar valves ensues, and point 4 to the moment at which the latter are thrown into tension owing to the beginning of diastole, which makes the blood column gravitate and recede against the already closed semilunar valves, and in the sphygmogram determines the negative wave that precedes the positive dicrotic wave. This interpretation is in fact confirmed by the course of the tachygraphic curve, which at points 3 and 4 drops below the zero line indicating a backward movement of the current, followed rapidly by the dicrotic rise. In the entire interval from 4 to 1 (which corresponds approximately to the periods of peri- and pre-systole), the pressure curve shows a slowly falling line, which expresses the decrease of arterial pressure in proportion as the elastic reaction of the artery drives the blood into the capillaries and veins. Velocity also decreases at the same time, but more slowly.

XI. During the passage of the pulse wave through the arteries, it produces a transverse dilatation and elongation, which are in relation with the pulsatile oscillations of pressure. The lengthening of the arteries produces a movement of the vessels at each wave of blood that traverses them, as is clearly visible in arteries ligatured after amputation. Normally, however, since the arteries are not free to elongate in the longitudinal direction, they become laterally curved when rectilinear, and increase their curvature if (as in old people) they have a winding course; and when (as in the aortic and pulmonary area) they form a free arch with a short radius of curvature, the curvature tends at each systolic wave to change, and to assume a longer radius, by a mechanism similar to that of the metallic manometer of Bourdon.

The elongation of the arteries, since it is plainly visible, was known to the older surgeons: the transverse dilatation on the other hand is a less obvious phenomenon, so that in the eighteenth century some of the clinicians (De la Mure in particular) denied it altogether, and held that the arterial pulse perceptible to touch is the effect of simple vascular locomotion. Spallanzani (1773) was the first to demonstrate the pulsatile dilatation of the aorta in the salamander by an ingenious experiment. "The aorta" (he wrote) "pulsates in its entire length, and in pulsating it dilates, but not equally in all its parts. Where it arches, its diameter is increased by a third, but elsewhere it increases only about a twentieth. Although my eye informed me that in the pulsations the increase in diameter or bulging of the aorta occurred more or less at each point of the circumference, I employed the following method to illustrate it:—I passed the aorta through a small open metal ring which, when closed, was of slightly larger diameter than the aorta. When the aorta dilated in its pulsations, the empty space between it and the ring became smaller; when it was constricted the space became larger. I then diminished the capacity of the ring. Now, where the aorta bulged, that is where there was the greatest dilatation, the circular space was lost during the cardiac systole, being filled in every direction by the dilated vessel: this proved decisively that the aorta in pulsating dilated at all points of its circumference" (*Dei fenomeni della circolazione, Dissertazione terza*).

In proof of the same phenomenon, Poiseuille (1828) introduced a length of a large artery into a long chamber, having at both ends a circular hole of the same diameter as the artery it was to receive. The cover of the chamber (which could be closed so as to become water-tight) was pierced by a vertical glass tube provided with a millimetre scale. After the chamber containing the artery had been filled with fluid, the fluid could be seen to rise in the tube at each systolic wave, and to fall at each diastole. Poiseuille measured the increase in arterial diameter by the highest point of the rise.

This experiment of Poiseuille was the starting-point for the construction of the apparatus known as the plethysmograph, because it serves to register the content, *i.e.* the variations in volume, of any organ, owing to the dilatation and constriction of the vessels it contains. It is easy to see that where the different organs or parts of the body are highly vascular, the total movements of passive or active dilatation or constriction of all the arterial branches they contain must produce very considerable variations in volume.

In order to estimate these variations in volume, Piégu (1846) introduced a limb into a vessel filled with lukewarm water and closed completely, save at a point through which passed the vertical tube intended to show the changes in volume. He described the changes in volume depending on cardiac, as well as those depending on respiratory rhythm. Chelius (1850), who was not acquainted with the previous investigations of Piégu, investigated the changes in volume of a limb by the same method, and with the same results.

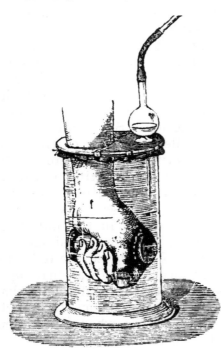

FIG. 115.—François-Franck's plethysmograph, for recording rapid changes of volume of the hand, which are transmitted to a tambour with highly sensitive lever.

Ch. Buisson (1862), who discovered the graphic method by means of air transmission to a writing tambour, subsequently perfected by Marey, was the first who applied it to the plethysmographs of Piégu and Chelius.

A. Fick (1868), with the same object, connected the water-tight chamber in which the forearm was enclosed with a recording water manometer, which directly recorded the pulsatile changes in volume of the investigated limb upon a revolving cylinder.

A. Mosso (1874-75) described another ingenious plethysmograph, with which he intended to record in absolute values the changes of volume in an isolated organ or a limb. Owing, however, to the sluggishness with which the recording apparatus functions, it is incapable of following the rapid *passive* changes due to the cardiac rhythm, while it is able to record the slow changes in volume due to the active contraction and dilatation of the vessels, which are entirely independent of cardiac rhythm. We shall return to this in Chapter X.

François-Franck (1876) made some useful modifications in the details of Buisson's apparatus, giving the apparatus the form of Fig. 115. The flask placed in front of the rubber tube, which joins the plethysmograph with the writing tambour, cuts out the oscillations of the fluid along the vertical tube. The method and instrument afterwards used by Mosso (1880) for recording the

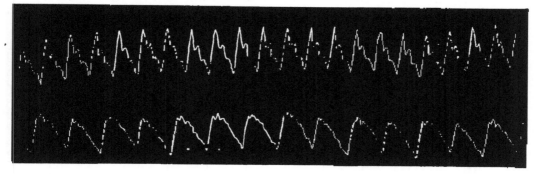

Fig. 116.—A', Plethysmogram of forearm in fasting state; A, the same, in same individual, after a meal. (Mosso.)

pulsatile changes in the volume of the forearm, to which he gave the name of hydrosphygmograph, is very similar.

Among the various results of more or less importance obtained by the plethysmographic method, we can here only refer to the form of the curves depending on the pulsatile oscillations in volume of the part explored, i.e. to vascular plethysmograms and their interpretation.

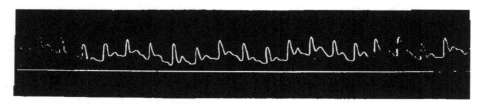

Fig. 117.—V, Plethysmogram of hand taken with apparatus of Fig. 115, the oscillations of the column of fluid being suppressed by the bulb interposed between the exploring apparatus and the recording tambour. (Fr.-Franck.)

Vascular plethysmograms are very similar to sphygmograms, and exhibit the same principal features, including dicrotism, as shown in Figs. 116 and 117. Still they cannot be identical since, as we have seen, sphygmograms are obtained with an apparatus which by means of a tense spring exerts pressure on the artery investigated, depressing its lumen to a greater or less extent: while plethysmograms, on the contrary, depend solely on the alterations in volume of the forearm or hand, all external pressure being as far as possible excluded. Since the flow of blood in the veins is continuous and uniform, it is clear that the changes of volume in the limb can only depend on variations in the blood-stream, or the velocity with which the blood flows into the arteries at different moments of the cardiac cycle. It is possible from the different inclinations of plethysmographic curves to the axis of the abscissa to construct the velocity curve (as Fick did), and thus to derive the tachygram from the plethysmogram.

To illustrate this conversion of volume curve into velocity curve, we enlarged the first plethysmogram of Fig. 117 by means of a projection apparatus, subsequently reducing the ordinates by half. This gave the curve represented by the fine line in Fig. 118, which has the same form as the plethysmogram of Fig. 117 would

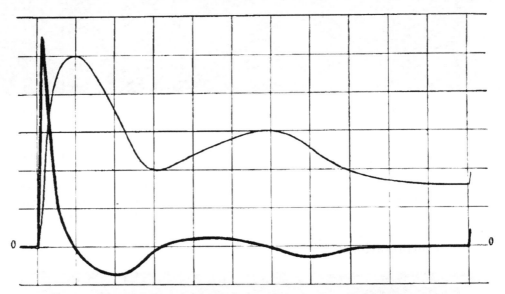

Fig. 118.—The line curve is the first plethysmogram of Fig. 117 enlarged and drawn out. The black curve is the tachygram, constructed graphically by measuring the degree of inclination of the different sections of the plethysmogram. (Luciani.)

have assumed had it been recorded on a drum rotating at double speed. From the plethysmogram thus transformed we have graphically constructed the tachygram represented by the black line of Fig. 118, which has a very similar course to that of the tachygram recorded by Chauveau and Lortet with the haemo-dromograph (Fig. 114). It must be noted, however, that the tachygram thus derived from the plethysmogram does not give absolute values of oscillations in velocity, and that the abscissa oo corresponds not to zero velocity but to the moments in which the volume of the forearm was unvaried, because the arterial inflow at that moment balanced the venous outflow.

In order graphically to transform plethysmograms into tachygrams, the ordinates of which represent the inclination of the different sections of the first curve, the following method must be adopted. At any point P of the plethysmogram draw the tangent to the curve ; measure the trigonometric

tangent of the angle which this makes with the positive direction of the
axis of the abscissa, and then erect upon the point of the axis of the abscissa
corresponding to P an ordinate proportional to the measured trigonometric
tangent. Fick has given a very practical method of determining these
tangents.

XII. Having thus analysed the principal phenomena relating
to circulatory pressure and velocity, it is necessary to consider a
scheme for combining them synthetically. With this object Fig.
119 shows in a single diagram the most important facts of the
circulation in the arteries, veins, and capillaries. In the arteries

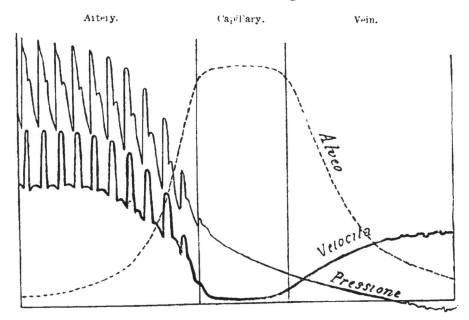

Fig. 119.—Synthetic diagram of progressive variations in area of blood current, pressure, and
velocity, in the three main sections of the systemic circulation. (Gad and Fredericq.) The
schema does not show the respiratory and vasomotor oscillations of pressure and velocity.

the circulatory area (represented by the total section of the vessels)
increases slowly at first from the aorta to the small arteries, and
then rapidly from the small arteries to the capillaries. Both the
pressure and the velocity curves exhibit the same general course.
The pulse and the cardiac oscillations of velocity in the arteries
diminish slowly from the aorta to the capillary threshold.

In the capillaries, where the circulatory area becomes
maximal, pressure continues to diminish slowly, and velocity
becomes minimal and constant.

In the veins the area again decreases, rapidly at first, then
more slowly to the mouth of the venae cavae, where, however, it
is more extensive than at the aortic orifice: pressure decreases
constantly, becoming negative in the intrathoracic veins: velocity,
on the other hand, increases more slowly from the farthest

capillaries to the venae cavae, where, however, it is lower than in the aorta. The intra- and extra-thoracic veins nearest the heart show gentle pulsatile oscillations, either of pressure or velocity, which coincide with the presystole and systole of the right heart.

If we consider the great velocity with which the wave movements, produced by the intermittent outflow of blood from the heart, are propagated through the arteries, it is evident that they have no connection with the mean velocity of the circulation, *i.e.* with the time required by a drop of blood or a corpuscle to traverse the whole vascular circuit and return to its starting-point. "Unda non est materia progrediens, sed forma materiae progrediens." In this expressive sentence E. H. Weber does not deny that the passage of the sphygmic wave through the arteries is accompanied by an acceleration of the flow, and is thus an adjunct to the circulatory movements; he only intended to make a sharp distinction between the average velocity with which the blood streams through the vessels and the rate of transmission of the pulse wave, which is essentially *a form propagated in a fluid.*

In order to measure (at least approximately) the duration of the entire circulation, E. Hering (1829) invented a method which consisted in the injection of a harmless and easily recognisable substance into the jugular vein of an animal, after which a sample of blood was taken from the jugular vein on the opposite side at intervals of five seconds (as marked by a metronome), and tested for the injected substance. He selected ferrocyanide of potash, since its presence, even in minimal quantities, can be detected by an iron salt, in the presence of which Prussian blue is formed. The results which he obtained on the horse were confirmed at a later time by Vierordt (1858), and applied to other animals, by a method which was a little more exact in regard to measuring the intervals between the extraction of the different samples of blood.

It was found from the best of Hering's experiments on horses that the blood required 26·2 secs. (on an average of nineteen experiments) to pass through the entire circulation from one jugular vein to the other. This path from one jugular to the other is one of the shortest that a drop of blood can take, in order to return to its starting-point after traversing the entire system. If, on the other hand, the ferrocyanide is injected into a crural vein, and the blood from the crural vein on the other side tested, the path is considerably longer, and more time is required. Vierordt's work shows, however, that the time difference between these two paths is very small, so that the blood in the larger arterial and venous vessels circulates very rapidly, any marked delay first occurring in the capillaries and the smallest vessels.

The discovery that the average time of circulation varies among the different mammals, and that it is shorter in small than in larger animals, is certainly among the most important results of

Vierordt's many observations. When, further, we compare the time of circulation with the number of heart-beats required to complete it, we arrive, according to Vierordt's experimental data, at the fact that twenty-six to twenty-nine pulsations are necessary in every animal, independent of the mass of its body, to drive the blood through the whole circulation from one jugular to the other. This is seen from the following table :—

Animal.	Time of Circulation in seconds.	Pulse Frequency per minute.	Number of Pulsations in One Circulation.
Rabbit	7·46	220	26·1
Goat	14·14	110	26·0
Dog	16·7	96	26·7
Horse (Hering) . .	31·5	55	28·8

As regards the time of the circulation in man, Vierordt thinks it probably stands midway between that of the dog and the horse, *i.e.* he estimates it = 27·1 secs., which with a pulse-frequency of 72 per minute corresponds to 27·7 heart-beats.

These data for the circulation time obtained by the methods of Hering and Vierordt express not the mean velocity with which the blood circulates in the vessels, but rather the maximal velocity, *i.e.* that of the axial lines of the fluid flowing through the vessels (see p. 189). V. Kries (1887) accordingly proposed to reduce Vierordt's figures by half, to obtain the value of the average velocity of the circulation. By the laws of hydrodynamics, the mean velocity of a fluid traversing a tube must be equal to half the greatest velocity of the axial current. Tigerstedt, however, pointed out that the theory of the passage of fluids was only applicable to the capillaries on the assumption that the stream of fluid is free from solid particles, which depress the value of the maximal velocity in the axial current. We know that the erythrocytes which move in the axial current are so large that they almost fill the capillary lumen, hence the mean velocity in the blood capillaries must certainly be somewhat more than half the maximal velocity. Still it can be positively affirmed that the average time of circulation must be less than that given by Hering's method.

BIBLIOGRAPHY

In addition to Bibliography at the end of Chap. VII. (p. 231) see :—

E. H. u. W. WEBER. Wellenlehre auf Versuche gegründet. Leipzig, 1825.— Observationes anat. et phys. Lipsiae, 1825.—Ber. d. sächs. Gesell. d. Wissenschaften, 1850.—Arch. f. Anat. und Physiol., 1851-1853.

VOLKMANN. Die Hämodynamik. Leipzig, 1850.

DONDERS. Physiologie des Menschen. Leipzig, 1859.

A. FICK. Medicinische Physik. 2nd ed. Braunschweig, 1866.

LANDOIS. Lehre vom Arterienpuls. Berlin, 1872.

MAREY. Traveaux du lab. Paris, 1875-1878.

MOENS. Die Pulscurve. Leiden, 1878.

A. MOSSO. Ricerche sfigmografiche, R. Accad. delle scienze di Torino, 1878. R. Accad. dei Lincei, 1887.

GRASHEY. Die Wellenbewegung elastischer Röhren. Leipzig, 1881.

A. FICK. Die Druckcurve und die Geschwindigkeitscurve in der A. radialis des Menschen. Würzburg, 1886.

VON KRIES. Studien zur Pulslehre. Freiburg, 1891.

A. MOSSO. Sphygmomanomètre pour mesurer la pression du sang chez l'homme. Arch. ital. de biologie, 1895.

HÜRTHLE. Über eine Methode zur Registrierung des arteriellen Blutdrucks beim Menschen. Deutsche med. Wochenschr., 1896. Beschreibung einer registrierenden Stromuhr. Pflügers Arch., xcvii., 1903.

RIVA-ROCCI. Un Nuovo Sfigmomanometro. Gazzetta medica di Torino, 1896-97.

M. L. PATRIZI. Il Progredire dell' onda sfigmica nel sonno fisiologico. Arch. ital. de biol., xxxvii., 1897.

DUCCESCHI. Un Nuovo Metodo di sfigmografia. Arch. di fisiol. del Fano, i., 1904.

TSCHUEWSKY. Über Druck, Geschwindigkeit und Widerstand in der Strombahn der Art. carotis ecc. Pflügers Arch., xcvii., 1907.

Recent English Literature :—

J. H. M'CURDY. The Effect of Maximum Muscular Work on Blood Pressure, Amer. Journ. of Physiol., 1901, v. 95.

L. HILL. On the Residual Pressures in the Vascular System when the Circulation is arrested. Journ. of Physiol., 1902, xxviii. 122.

R. BURTON-OPITZ. Muscular Contraction and the Venous Blood-Flow. Amer. Journ. of Physiol., 1903, ix. 161.

R. BURTON-OPITZ. Venous Pressure. Amer. Journ. of Physiol., 1903, ix. 198.

O. H. BROWN and C. C. GUTHRIE. The Effects of Intravenous Injections of Bone-Marrow Extracts upon Blood Pressure. Amer. Journ. of Physiol., 1905, xiv. 328.

P. M. DAWSON. The Lateral "Blood Pressures" at Different Points of the Arterial Tree. Amer. Journ. of Physiol., 1905-6, xv. 244.

T. LEWIS. The Influence of the Venae Comites on the Pulse Tracing, with special reference to Valsalva's Experiment and Dicrotism ; a note on Anacrotism. Journ. of Physiol., 1906, xxxiv. 391.

T. LEWIS. The Factors influencing the Prominence of the Dicrotic Wave. Journ. of Physiol., 1906, xxxiv. 414.

O. RIDDLE and S. A. MATTEWS. The Blood Pressures of Birds and their Modification by Drugs. Amer. Journ. of Physiol., 1907, xix. 108.

T. LEWIS. Studies of the Relationship between Respiration and Blood Pressure. P. i. and ii. Journ. of Physiol., 1908, xxxvii. 213, 233.

E. C. SCHNEIDER and C. A. HEDBLOM. Blood Pressure, with special reference to High Altitudes. Amer. Journ. of Physiol., 1908, xxiii. 90.

CHAPTER IX

PHYSIOLOGY OF CARDIAC MUSCLE AND NERVES

CONTENTS. —1. Intrinsic processes by which cardiac rhythm is determined and regulated. 2. Extrinsic chemical conditions of cardiac activity. 3. Effects of ligation and section on different parts of the heart. 4. Automatic or reflex activity of heart. 5. Myogenic or neurogenic origin of cardiac rhythm. 6. Evidence for these conflicting theories. 7. Special mode in which cardiac muscle reacts to external stimuli. 8. Regulation of cardiac rhythm by nervous system: inhibitory or diastolic nerves. 9. Accelerator or systolic nerves. 10. Theory of anabolic action of diastolic nerves and katabolic action of systolic nerves. 11. Afferent nerves of heart or other parts of the body which influence cardiac rhythm. 12. Nerve-centres for cardiac nerves; their tonic excitability, and theory of regulation of cardiac rhythm. Bibliography.

THE mechanical functions of the heart and vessels, as discussed in the last two chapters, are modified by a variety of oscillations or changes. Between certain limits these changes not only come within the scope of normal vital activity, but also satisfy the physiological necessity for adapting both the general velocity of circulation, and the distribution of blood in the several parts of the body, to the different external conditions and temporary needs of the whole organism, or of its several organs or tissues.

The physiological changes in the activity of the heart consist in increased or diminished frequency or force of its beats; the physiological changes in the activity of the vessels consist in their dilatation or constriction (particularly in the small arteries), as determined by the expansion or contraction of the muscle cells of which they are constructed.

Even to the lay mind, it is obvious that these modifications and adaptations of the activity of the heart and vessels depend essentially on the nervous system, which is the supreme regulator of all important vital functions. From the fact that the heart responds to the psychical emotions by various modifications of its activity, sprang the old Aristotelian belief that it is the seat of the soul—a belief still surviving in popular ideas and expressions. The fact that the emotions readily produce blushing and pallor of the countenance shows that the nervous system is capable, independent of the circulatory centre, of modifying the blood supply to the several vascular regions.

With the object of determining the limits of this regulatory activity of the nervous system as exactly as possible, we shall in the next two chapters discuss the better ascertained and more important facts of human physiology, with respect to the physiological conditions that underlie the activity of the heart and vessels.

I. As shown in Chapter VII., the mechanical activity of the heart is due to the regular sequence of three different states in its muscles—contraction, expansion, and rest. In order to obtain a clear idea of the origin, succession, and propagation of these three states in the different segments of cardiac muscle, we must return to this subject and attentively study the exposed heart of the living frog or tortoise (Fig. 120).

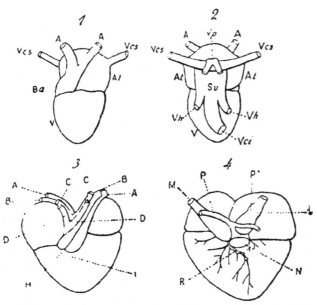

On cutting the fraenum, which attaches the posterior wall of the ventricle to the dorsal surface of the pericardium, and lifting up the heart, we see that the contraction commences along the venae cavae, and spreads from these to the sinus venosus in which they unite.

From the sinus venosus, which opens into the right auricle, the contraction spreads to the two auricles; from the

Fig. 120.—1 and 2, Anterior and posterior aspects of frog's heart. At, Auricles; V, ventricle; A, A, rami of aorta; Ba, aortic bulb; Sv, sinus venosus; Vci, vena cava inferior; Vcs, vena cava superior; Vp, pulmonary vein; Vh, hepatic vein. 3 and 4, Anterior and posterior aspects of tortoise heart. A, A', Pulmonary arteries; B, B', left and right aorta; D, D', left and right subclavian arteries; H, hemi-annulus of bulb; I, auriculoventricular groove; P, P', pulmonary veins; M, L, left and right superior vena cava; N, inferior vena cava; R, coronary vein.

two auricles it passes to the ventricle; and from the ventricle, lastly, to the bulbus arteriosus, which contracts actively in the frog, as first noted by Spallanzani. The contraction or systole of the heart thus takes the form of a wave, which originates in the afferent vessels and passes to the heart, where it spreads peristaltically from auricles to ventricle, leaving the heart by the afferent vessels.

It should, however, be noted as a fact of great importance that the peristaltic wave of contraction does not proceed uniformly, but undergoes a delay or block at the junction between the sinus and the auricles, the auricles and the ventricle, and, lastly, at that between the ventricle and the bulbus arteriosus. It therefore follows that when the auricles begin to contract, the sinus begins to expand; when the ventricle enters systole, the auricles are commencing diastole; when, lastly, the systole of the bulbus arteriosus begins, the ventricle is entering diastole. The two active phases (systole and diastole) are followed by the state of rest or functional pause, which in the same way appears earlier in the sinus than in the auricles, and in the auricles than in the ventricle, with the resting phase of which the cardiac cycle or revolution is complete.

These phenomena, which are easily detected on the frog or the tortoise, are in complete agreement with those which can be observed under greater difficulties in warm-blooded animals. In these, too (as we have seen), the wave of contraction arises in the large veins, which, as they have no sinus venosus, open directly into the auricle: from the auricles it is propagated peristaltically to the ventricles, where it is arrested, since these have no contractile bulbi arteriosi. In warm-blooded animals, too, the wave of contraction encounters a block, or momentary delay, at the passage from auricles to ventricles, so that the diastole of the auricles coincides with the commencement of ventricular systole, a necessary condition for the perfect functioning of the cardiac pump.

From these fundamental phenomena arise all the complex problems relating to the physiological conditions of the cardiac functions. On what does the rhythmical action of the heart depend? What are the external chemical conditions indispensable to its activity? Is its rhythm of a reflex nature, dependent on extrinsic conditions or stimuli, or is it automatic in character, dependent on intrinsic conditions or stimuli within the heart? Is it a function of the nervous system, or simply a property pertaining to the cells of cardiac muscle? Is the peristaltic contraction wave propagated by way of the nerves or by the muscle cells? Why does the wave of contraction arise in the venous paths that lead to the heart: and on what do the blocks or brief delays, to which it is subjected on passing from one segment of the heart to the other, and which are of such great importance to its mechanical functions, depend? These are the fundamental problems which have to be examined.

METHODS OF STUDYING CARDIAC MOVEMENT

Cardiac movement must be studied either on the exposed heart *in situ*, or on the fully isolated heart. The frog's heart isolated from the body is capable, provided it be protected from drying in a moist chamber, of continuing its normal activity for some time (several days), and thus represents the most accessible object for the study of cardiac movements. For this reason the methods employed in the graphic registration of these movements were especially contrived for the frog's heart. Observations of the surviving heart of warm-blooded animals are, on the contrary, impossible, except under certain special conditions, and acquaintance with these conditions is one of the most recent acquisitions of scientific technique.

A. Cold-Blooded Animals. In order to obtain graphic tracings of the cardiac movements in the frog or any other cold-blooded animal, three different methods may be employed. Of these there are various forms, the most important being :—

(a) *Tonographic Methods.*— These consist essentially in the use of a small mercury manometer, which records the oscillations of the internal pressure of the frog's heart in relation to the phases of its activity. The apparatus represented by Fig. 121 fulfils all requirements for studying the mode in which the activity of the heart exhausts itself, when excised from the animal, filled with a nutrient fluid, and exposed to constant diastolic pressure at a given temperature. The heart is tied to a simple cannula (Fig. 122, A) introduced into the cavity of the ventricle through an opening in the sinus venosus. Owing to its structure, it is easy to study the effect of successive ligatures applied at different heights of the auricles, when the heart is fixed in the tonographic apparatus. Since the same nutrient fluid leaves the heart at each systole and re-enters it at each diastole, the renewal of the solution can only be effected slowly by diffusion through the supernatant fluid, and filtration through the vessel walls.

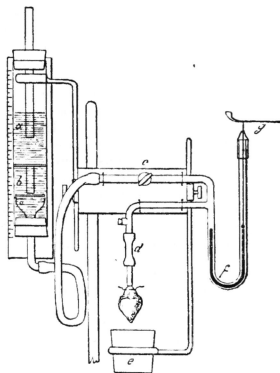

Fig. 121.—Luciani's tonographic apparatus for recording the beats of the heart, when isolated and attached to cannula at different heights of the auricles (semi schematic). *a*, Reservoir of serum or other nutrient fluid, closed by Mariotte's method so as to keep the filling and pressure of the heart constant ; *b*, valvular apparatus, closed during systole ; *c*, tap for interrupting communication between the reservoir and the heart ; *d*, cannula to which the heart is tied, fixed to apparatus ; *e*, small vessel full of serum, which can be raised during the experiment, so as to bathe the whole of the outside of the heart ; *f*, small mercury manometer, provided with float, which records the beats of the heart on the revolving cylinder with a glass pen.

This is a great drawback when the heart is to be kept for any length of time under constant and normal conditions of nutrition. Under these circumstances it is necessary to replace the simple cannula by the two-way cannula of Kronecker, figured in 122, B. An improvement on Kronecker's apparatus is that of Williams (Fig. 123). This provides for the circulation of the nutritive solution, by the complete separation of the fluid which enters, from that which leaves, the heart, by means of two valves for its entrance and exit. If the frog's heart is to be attached to the apparatus by a cannula introduced into the ventricle through the aortic bulb, it is necessary to supplement Kronecker's irrigation cannula by a very fine connecting tube, as shown in Fig. 122 C.

The tonographic method introduced by Oehrwall (1896) is much simpler By this it is possible to obtain simultaneous tracings of the activity of the right auricle and the ventricle of the frog. No artificial valves are required to separate the vessel containing the nutrient solution from the tonographic apparatus, since the auriculo-ventricular valves of the heart itself are utilised for the purpose. As shown in Fig. 124, the heart is attached to two cannulae, one of which is tied to the aorta so that the valve is unable to perform its function, the other to the sinus. The two cannulae communicate on the one hand with the vessel containing the serum or nutritive solution, on the other with two separate elastic tonographs similar to small Marey's capsules, which record the oscillations of pressure in the right auricle and ventricle as transmitted by the air. When disconnected from the reservoir by applying a couple of pressure forceps at the points indicated in the figure, the heart is made to beat in presence of a small quantity of fluid which circulates continuously. When, on the other hand, the forceps are unclamped, so as to open communication with the reservoir, the whole of the fluid present is perfused through the heart. In the first case the curves recorded by the two tonographs are naturally more ample, because they represent the total pressure developed within the heart; in the second case they are less ample, because the lateral pressure is recorded.

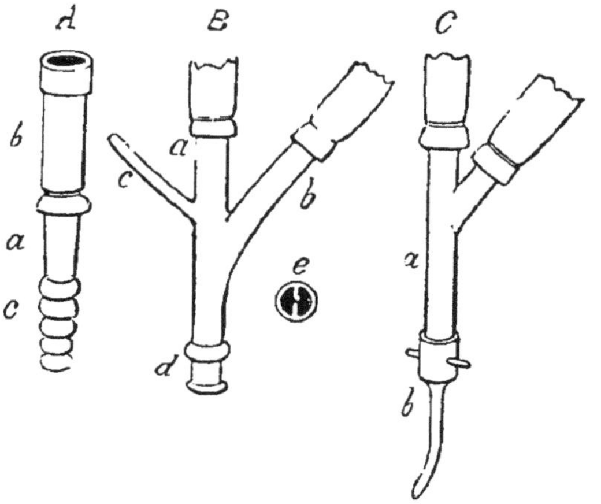

(b) *Plethysmographic Methods.* —These aim at recording the variations in the volume of the heart during the pulsatory cycle. They have been applied in various ways to the heart of the frog or the tortoise by François-Franck, Roy, Gaskell, and Williams. As shown in Fig. 123, plethysmograms of the frog's heart are most simply obtained by a slight modification in Williams' apparatus, the heart being placed in a small closed cylinder empty or filled with oil, and connected with a Marey's tympanum.

FIG. 122. —*A*, Simple cannula (Luciani) for frog's heart, natural size. Consists of glass tube *a*, joined to rubber tube *b*, which connects it with the manometer, and has various metal rings (*c*) at the end, 2 mm. apart, by which ligatures can be applied to the heart at equal distances. *B*, Two-way cannula (Kronecker) composed entirely of metal divided into two arms, *c*, *'*, which unite externally into one arm *d*, divided internally by a septum as shown in section at . The arm *a* is connected with the chamber for the serum; the arm *b* with the recording manometer. The metal wire *e* serves as electrode, in the electrical stimulation of the heart. The fluid expelled by the heart at each systole is partially turned out, so that fresh serum enters the heart at each diastole. *C*, Cannula adopted in Williams' apparatus. The same two-way cannula, as above, with the addition of a small, simple metal cannula *b*, which is introduced into the ventricle by the bulbus aortae.

(c) *Myographic or Cardiographic Methods.*—By these we can record the modifications in the external form of the heart, produced by cardiac systole or diastole. These methods have been applied in a variety of ways. A light lever may be placed directly upon the ventricle, or two levers, one on the ventricle, the other on the auricles, when the magnified movements due to changes in form of the heart (Marey's double myograph for heart of frog and tortoise) can be read off. An ingenious modification of this method is represented in Fig. 125 (Marey's *pince myographique*). Gaskell introduced a method of suspension with which he obtained interesting results. It consisted in fixing the heart at the auriculo-ventricular groove by a screw-clamp, which could be easily adjusted. The apex of the ventricle and tip of the auricle are attached by silk threads to very light levers, placed respectively above and below the heart, which are pulled upward or downward during systole, and record the magnified movement on a revolving cylinder.

Engelmann's suspension method (Fig. 126) is simpler as well as more reliable. The cardiograms which it records (independent of the differences in form and amplitude due to modifications in loading and length of lever) always exhibit marked anatricrotism, *i.e.* the ascending curve rises to the summit in three shoulders, and falls rapidly in a single line, as shown on Fig. 127. With a signal, made by a writing lever, worked with the finger, the moment at which the systole and diastole of the sinus (*Ss Sd*), the systole and diastole of the auricles (*As Ad*), the systole and diastole of the ventricle (*Vs Vd*), and the systole and diastole of the bulbus arteriosus (*Bs Bd*) commence can

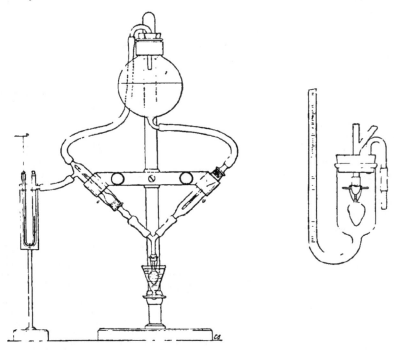

Fig. 123.—*Left:* Williams' tonograph for recording movements of frog's heart; excised and attached to cannula, inserted into the ventricle by the bulbus aortae (semi-schematic). A reservoir of serum, *s*, communicates from below with the cardiac cavity by the valve *c*, which opens in diastole and closes in systole. A second valve *c*, which opens in systole and closes in diastole, leads the serum back to the reservoir *s*. The manometer is put in communication with the heart by means of an arm of the second valvular apparatus, and traces on the revolving cylinder the lateral pressure of the fluid coming from the heart. *Right:* Portion of Williams' apparatus substituted for the little cup that encloses the heart when it is desired to see the changes of volume during the beats. If the small chamber containing the heart is left empty, and the end of the curved arm of the manometer connected with a highly sensitive Marey's tambour, the apparatus is converted into a cardiac plethysmograph.

be accurately enough determined. The result of these experiments (according to Engelmann) is that, generally speaking, the movements *Vs* and *Vd* are the only ones of which the commencement is clearly traced in the cardiogram. The beginning of *Vs* coincides with the beginning of the second rapid rise, and of *Vd* with that of the rapid descent from the summit of the curve. By using the signal, however, it is possible (taking the average of a good number of experiments) approximately to determine the other periods of the pulsatory cycle, and to estimate their duration in hundredths of a second. (Engelmann, "Observations et expériences sur le cœur suspendu," *Arch. Neerlandaises*. vol. xxvi.)

B. Warm-Blooded Animals.—The methods employed for the graphic registration of oscillations of pressure and volume of the heart *in situ*, were discussed in the chapter. Changes in form may be recorded by the method of multiple suspension from writing levers, attached by threads to different parts of the heart (François-Franck, Knoll). Various methods have

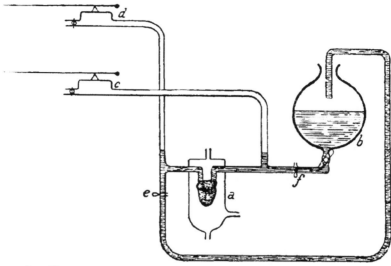

Fig. 124.—Oehrwall's tonograph. *a*, Glass bulb to cover outside of heart; *b*, reservoir of nutrient fluid; *c*, tonograph for right auricle; *d*, tonograph for ventricle; *e, f*, clips for altering communication with reservoir.

been adopted in the study of the mammalian heart, independent of any cerebrospinal nervous influence and of the systemic circulation, with the object of more or less completely isolating the cardio-pulmonary circulation

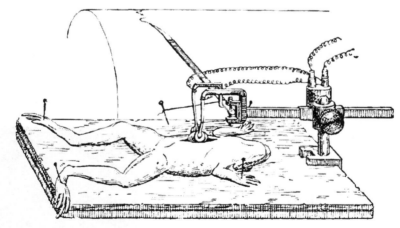

Fig. 125.—Marey's myograph for recording movements of frog's heart *in situ*. This is a sort of clip formed of two spoons supported by two curved arms at right angles, one fixed, the other movable. The latter carries a horizontal lever, provided at the end with a point, writing on a smoked cylinder. The movable spoon, which is displaced at each systole, is brought back to its original position at each diastole by a fine rubber thread, fixed by a pin to the board on which the frog is fastened. Both spoons are connected with wires, by which various kinds of electrical stimuli can be transmitted to the heart. The exact moment of stimulation is recorded in the cylinder by a Depréz signal.

(Newell, Martin, H. E. Hering, Hédon and Arrous, and others). Langendorff (1895) was the first who succeeded by the method of direct transfusion through the coronary arteries in keeping the mammalian heart alive for any considerable time, when completely isolated and removed from the body (under which conditions, without special treatment, it speedily ceases to beat. By means of a cannula tied to the aorta, in the direction of the heart, he caused blood or other nutrient solutions to circulate at a temperature of 38° C. under a pressure corresponding to the normal pressure of the aorta. The fluid keeps the semilunar valves closed, circulating through the coronary system of the heart, and flowing out again through the opening in the right auricle. The cardiac cavity remains empty. A heart thus artificially fed is capable of continuing its activity almost normally for many hours. The graphic record of its movements can be taken by means of suspension, or (after occluding the veins of the right auricle) by a manometer applied to the pulmonary artery (Siewert, 1904).

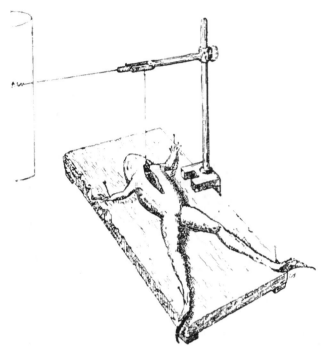

FIG. 126.—Engelmann's myograph for recording beats of frog's heart *in situ*, when suspended from the apex by a thread connected with a highly sensitive lever. The apparatus is a two-armed lever, one arm of which is attached to a fine silk thread, the other to a long straw or strip of aluminium, which magnifies the movements of the writing point on a smoked surface. At the end of the thread is a fine glass hook, with sharp point, which is inserted into the tip of the apex, after cutting the fraenum by which the two layers of the pericardium are united dorsally.

II. The fact that it is possible to keep the isolated heart of different animals alive for a comparatively long period has been used as the starting-point for a series of researches on the nutritive medium, or external chemical conditions, necessary to its survival.

This work has familiarised us with the so-called physiological solutions, which are artificial nutrient fluids, capable (at least for a certain time) of replacing the blood, since they contain all the elements necessary for sustaining the life of the heart. The importance of this subject exceeds the limits of the present chapter, for it may logically be concluded that artificial fluids which

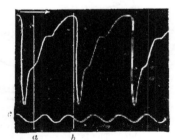

FIG. 127.—Cardiograms taken from frog by Engelmann's method. *a*, Commencement of ventricular systole (*Vs*); *b*, commencement of diastole (*Vd*); *c*, curves of a tuning-fork which vibrates 10 times per second.

are capable of sustaining the vitality of the excised heart will also maintain the vitality of other organs or isolated tissues, or are, at any rate, innocuous to the body as a whole, when introduced into the circulation.

We should, *a priori*, expect the best effects to result from those solutions which in their chemical composition most closely resemble the complex constitution of blood—the natural food of all the tissues. In practice, however, this is the case only to a limited extent.

A point much discussed by the various investigators has been the importance of oxygen in these physiological solutions. No one, however, now doubts that it represents an element indispensable to the survival of the heart.

Von Humboldt (1797) was the first to emphasise the vivifying power of oxygen in the excised heart of the frog. Following his initiative, Castell (1854) made a systematic series of researches in the same direction. He found that a frog's heart placed in a moist chamber at 16-20 R. went on beating for three hours in ordinary air, for twelve hours in the presence of oxygen, for about one hour in presence of hydrogen or nitrogen, for a few minutes only in presence of carbonic acid.

In our own researches on the excised frog's heart (1873), connected with a manometer, and filled with serum of pig or rabbit, we observed that the frequency and force of the beats augmented each time the serum already used was reinforced by fresh oxygenated serum; the rhythm slowed down and weakened when the heart was made to float in oil. The vivifying action of oxygen on the frog's heart was confirmed by Rossbach and Klug.

Langendorff (1884) experimented with the asphyxiated heart, and noted that it absorbed oxygen with great rapidity, so that the blood introduced into it suddenly assumed a venous hue.

Yeo (1885) made the reduction of oxyhaemoglobin by the frog's heart the subject of a methodical research. He found that this reduction increased with the work done by the heart. Heffter and Albanese confirmed the fact that the presence of oxygen is indispensable to the maintenance of cardiac activity.

The most exact and minute researches on asphyxia and the revivification of the excised frog's heart are, however, due to Oehrwall (1893-97). He studied the mode of onset and the duration of asphyxia in the frog's heart filled with blood or serum, through which a solution of sodium chloride or of some indifferent gas was circulated, as well as revival by the substitution of oxygenated for asphyxiated blood, or by the direct action of air and oxygen.

The importance of oxygen to the function of the heart in warmblooded animals was shown by Fano (1889-90) on the embryonic chick's heart, isolated on the second or third day of incubation.

A. Porter (1898) succeeded in keeping the isolated mammalian heart alive for many hours in the presence of blood serum and oxygen under a pressure of two atmospheres. But the same effects may be more simply obtained by the artificial circulation through the coronary system of a physiological solution (to be described below) saturated with oxygen, or even with air. It is essential in both cases that the fluid should not stagnate in the vessels.

Rusch (1898) found that the circulation of serum instead of defibrinated blood necessitated a higher pressure to make it circulate with greater velocity, in order to provide the heart with the quantum of oxygen necessary to its activity.

Other researches on the necessity of oxygen to the survival of the mammalian heart were instituted by Strecker (1900), and more particularly by Magnus (1902), who was the first to circulate gases instead of fluids through the coronary arteries of the isolated cat's heart. He found, on injecting oxygen, that the heart beat for about an hour. Its arrest is due to the permeability of the vessel walls by gas. He saw that when hydrogen was injected in place of oxygen, the heart continued to beat for about half an hour, while it stopped after a few minutes when carbonic acid was injected. The beneficent action of the circulating hydrogen depends, therefore, upon the elimination of the carbonic acid developed by the heart during its activity; but hydrogen is not sufficient to keep it going for a long time, and the heart ceases to beat after it has exhausted all the oxygen which it holds in loose combination.

Winterstein controlled the importance of oxygen by circulating Ringer's solution, charged sometimes with oxygen, sometimes with nitrogen, through the coronaries of the isolated cat's and rabbit's heart. He came to the following conclusions:

(a) The mammalian heart requires external oxygen to maintain its activity. Its rhythm alters and it soon comes to a standstill, if nitrogen is substituted for oxygen.

(b) If after a definite lapse of time the current of oxygen is re-established, the heart is able to beat again.

(c) It is possible to reproduce the state of asphyxia repeatedly in the same heart, and in the above experiments it was observed that the time necessary for reproducing asphyxial arrest was shorter than that required for its first incidence.

(d) The immediate condition of asphyxial arrest appears to consist in the consumption of internal oxygen that takes place during cardiac activity.

Does the function of free oxygen, as the necessary condition of the rhythmic activity of the heart, consist in the oxidation of the muscular biogen which produces the alternate contractions and expansions of the myocardium, or does it rather lie in the oxidation of the toxic katabolic products that result from the metabolism of the muscle, transforming them into innocuous substances, readily eliminated?

Arguments in favour of this last hypothesis are not wanting, but the first must also be admitted as credible, until it is directly contradicted by experiment.

C. Ludwig (1868) was the first who employed the method of artificial circulation in excised organs, in studying their survival. The primitive physiological solution, consisting of a dilute solution of sodium chloride (0·50-0·75 per cent), was largely used by him and his school as a substitute for defibrinated blood, in experimenting on the metabolism of excised organs. A little serum added to the saline will keep up the vitality of the excised heart of a frog for a very long time.

Kronecker and Stirling (1875), however, found that the beats of a frog's heart tied by the ventricle to a cannula (Bowditch's preparation) were retarded, and its activity brought to a standstill in a short time, when a simple 0·6 per cent solution of NaCl was substituted for the blood or serum. Salt water, therefore, does not in itself contain the whole of the chemical constituents necessary for the maintenance of cardiac activity.

Merunovics (1877) tried the effect of watery solutions made of the ash, or the alcoholic extract of serum, which, he found, maintained cardiac activity better than the simple solution of sodium chloride. He attributed this effect to the beneficial action of the alkaline carbonate.

Stienon (1878), following Merunovics, observed that the difference between the action of the fresh serum and its filtrate, after this had been boiled, consisted in the more limited capacity of the latter to revive a cardiac preparation of which the activity had been reduced to its minimum by prolonged treatment with saline. He also found that neutralisation of the normal alkalinity of the serum with acid diminished its beneficial action on the heart. Lastly, he demonstrated that a solution of sodium chloride rendered alkaline with 0·1 per cent sodium carbonate is capable of restoring the activity of a heart that had previously been arrested by treatment with salt solution. Gaule, later on, found it more useful for this purpose to add a small quantity of soda instead of the carbonate, pointing out that the alkali is neutralised during cardiac activity by the development of carbonic acid, which converts it into the carbonate.

Martius (1882) explained the beneficial action of serum by assigning a greater importance to its organic than to its inorganic constituents, and to serum albumin in particular, assuming that the development of cardiac energy was dependent on the presence of some nutrient matter in the circulating fluid.

Against this positive assumption, however, we must set the work of Ringer, who made a series of experiments to show that the addition of calcic or potassic salts to the NaCl solution effectively prolongs cardiac activity, as has since been confirmed by all who have taken up this subject. Ringer's solution consists of—

        100 c.c. of a 6 per cent solution of NaCl
          1   ,, 1   ,,   ,,   NaHCO₃
          1   ,, 1   ,,   ,,   CaCl₂
        0·75 ,, 1   ,,   ,,   KCl

Locke (1895) showed by new work that the addition of a small quantity of glucose to Ringer's solution rendered it more capable of maintaining cardiac activity.

Göthlin, under Oehrwahl's direction, has recently (1902) carried out some detailed experiments on the chemical conditions of cardiac activity in the excised heart of the frog. He prepared a complex solution of mineral substances, including all those which chemical analysis has shown to be present in blood serum, in the following proportions :—

NaCl	.	. 0·65 per cent.	Cl	. . .	. 0·01 per cent.
NaHCO₃	.	. 0·1 ,,	CaCl₂	.	. 0·0065 ,,
Na₂HPO₄	.	. 0·0009 ,,	NaH₂PO₄	.	. 0·0008 ,,

He found that on replacing the blood by this solution cardiac activity was maintained unaltered for many hours. The proportions in which the different salts enter into solution are by no means unimportant. On substituting Ringer's solution for the above, both rhythm and type of beat were modified. Göthlin further saw, on preparing solutions in which one or other of the constituents predominated (with the object of determining the influence of each upon cardiac activity), that the results indicated all to be more or less necessary to its maximal prolongation.

In a second series of researches he proposed to determine on what the great difference between the survival period of a heart treated with his solution, composed solely of inorganic substances, and that of a heart treated with normal blood, depends. As regards the importance of the erythrocytes and of haemoglobin the fact he discovered is worth noting, that a haemolytic fluid (i.e. one which contains dissolved haemoglobin) is injurious rather than beneficial. He explained the toxic action of this dissolved haemoglobin to consist in its combining with the lime-salts of the serum, so that they are removed from the heart, which requires lime salts electrolytically dissociated in the form of Ca-ions. In fact, he found that the subsequent addition of lime salts renders haemolytic blood innocuous.

In other experiments he found that after weakening the heart with his saline solution, he could restore its activity by perfusing it with a new complex solution consisting half of serum of ox blood, half of the saline solution. He concluded that serum must contain a substance capable of exerting this beneficial action on the heart, and proposed to ascertain experimentally which it was of the numerous organic substances present. He tested glucose, serin, and paraglobulin with negative results.

Baglioni (1905-6) was more fortunate in his experiments on the isolated heart of Selachians. He knew from the previous researches of Städeler and Frerichs, and of v. Schröder, that the blood of these animals is very rich in urea dissolved in the plasma. According to v. Schröder the blood of the *Scyllium* contains on an average 2·61 per cent urea. This facts explains the high values of the molecular concentration of the blood in these fishes, which corresponds to a solution of about 3·5 per cent of NaCl. Straub had already found that a saline solution of this concentration was incapable of keeping the excised heart of these animals alive, even for a short time—an observation contrary to what had been observed on the hearts of frogs and other poikilothermic animals. Baglioni discovered that it is possible to keep the isolated Selachian heart alive for a prolonged period by treating it with a solution containing a definite amount of urea. He found the most effective solution to be one that contained 2 grms. of urea, and 2 grms. of sodium chloride in 100 c.c. of tap water, which invariably yields traces of lime salts. He further tried to determine the specific action of urea, and concluded from his experimental results that it promotes the contraction of the muscle cells, while larger doses arrest the heart in systole. Sodium chloride. on the contrary, promotes expansion of the muscle cells, and large doses cause diastolic arrest.

Lambert (1905) confirmed the favourable action of urea on the frog's heart; Baglioni and Federico 1906 on that of the toad. In these animals, also, urea increases the intensity and duration of the systolic phase.

Analogous observations were made on the isolated heart of warm-blooded animals Gross (1903 carried out a methodical series of experiments on the action of the various components of Ringer's solution, confirming the results already obtained for the frog's heart. The antagonism in the action of potassium and calcium ions was marked. The former exerted a systolic, the latter a diastolic action: in large doses the first arrested the heart in systole, the second in diastole.

Langendorff and his pupils, confirming the necessity of the presence of lime salts, studied the action of dissolved haemoglobin, when they found that only certain mammalian hearts behave like that of the frog. The hearts of cat and dog do not to any marked extent exhibit toxic effects with dissolved haemoglobin, while that of the rabbit behaves like the frog's heart. In explanation of this difference, Langendorff points out that the rabbit's erythrocytes contain a much larger quantity of potassium salts than those of the dog or cat. Supposing that a large amount of potassic salts are diffused in the rabbit's serum along with the haemoglobin, these might exert a toxic action upon the cells of the myocardium. The beneficial effects of adding lime salts to the haemolytic fluid may be explained by the antagonism between the salts of calcium and potassium.

Bachmann (1906), under Oehrwall's direction, carried out a fresh series of researches upon the action on the isolated mammalian heart of the organic nitrogenous substances present in normal blood, adding it in known doses to Locke's solution, and perfusing it by Langendorff's method. He studied the action of urea, of ammonium carbonate, of sodic hippurate, of sodic urate, of creatine, of hypoxanthine, of xanthine, of allantoin. Generally speaking, he found that these substances, in doses approximately equal to their proportions in normal blood, exercised only a slight and parallel action upon the heart, increasing the amplitude of the systole. Some of them further accelerated the frequency of rhythm, in particular urea, which agrees completely with the results of Baglioni.

Special mention must be made of the recent attempts to revive the dead heart of warm-blooded animals. Kuliabko (1901-3) was the first to revive the heart of animals three or four days after death (the bodies being kept meantime in ice), by perfusing the coronaries with Ringer-Locke solution. Seven days after death it was found impossible to revive the normal pulsations of the whole heart: fibrillary contractions could, however, be observed in the auricles. The heart of an infant that had died of pneumonia was made to beat again after twenty hours.

H. E. Hering continued the researches of Kuliabko on the hearts of rabbit, cat, and monkey. In a monkey found dead in the laboratory he succeeded, four and a half hours later, in reviving the heart, left *in situ*. The body was then frozen. On the following day, *i.e.* 24 hours and 32 minutes after the animal had been found dead, the heart was revived for the second time. The carcase was again frozen, and a third revival successfully attempted 53 hours and 43 minutes after.

The same experiments of revival were attempted on the human adult heart. Dencke and Adam succeeded in obtaining pulsations in the heart of a criminal forty-three years old, 13 minutes after his execution.

More recently Hering succeeded, with Ringer's solution alone, in reviving the heart of a young criminal of thirty-five, eleven hours after death, and was able to use it for experiment for three hours. It is interesting to note that both Dencke and Hering assert that they found no difference between the human and other mammalian hearts as regards their reaction to circulating fluids.

III. The most generally noted and recognised fact is that the conditions of rhythmical cardiac activity are located in the heart itself, and are independent of the connections which unite it by the afferent nerves with the cerebrospinal axis. Galen was aware that the excised heart is able to beat for a considerable time. Under favourable conditions of moisture, temperature, irrigation with blood and other nutrient fluids, and in presence of oxygen, the excised heart, not only of cold-blooded animals but of mammals also, may continue its functions for many hours.

The earlier Hallerian doctrine, which saw in this fact a proof of the rhythmic activity of cardiac muscle independent of nerves and nerve-centres, was disallowed after it had been shown by Bichat and J. Müller that the peripheral sympathetic ganglia function as independent centres in the organs of vegetative life, while Remak (1844), Ludwig (1848), and Bidder (1852) discovered a nerve-plexus rich in ganglion cells in the frog's heart.

Remak demonstrated the existence of a conspicuous accumulation of ganglion cells at the mouth of the sinus venosus in the right auricle of the frog's heart. Ludwig described other ganglionic

Fig. 128.—Interauricular septum of frog's heart. (Bidder.) *a*, Muscular fibres; *b*, endocardium; *c*, free border of septum; *d, d*, ventricular walls; *e, f*, right and left branches of cardiac vagus, with partial decussation; *h, h'*, anterior and posterior nerves to septum, with numerous ganglion cells, particularly at points *k, k'*; *l, l'*, ganglia near the auriculo-ventricular border (Bidder's ganglia).

elements in the region of the interauricular septum. Bidder discovered two other masses of ganglion cells near the auriculo-ventricular groove (Fig. 128). Nothing after these discoveries could be more natural than to ascribe the function of excitatory centres of the rhythmic peristaltic movements of the heart to these intracardiac ganglia.

Certain well-known experiments of Stannius (1852) gave fresh sanction to this theory of the intracardial ganglionic centres, although they received various and even contradictory interpretations. In his experiments on the frog's heart Stannius discovered two facts which appeared to be of extreme interest :—

(*a*) When a ligature is applied at any height of the auricle, between the opening of the sinus venosus into the right auricle, and the region nearest the auriculo-ventricular junction, arrest of the heart is, *ipso facto*, produced in all parts below the ligature, while above, in the sinus and the part of the auricle that is not blocked, the rhythm is undisturbed.

(*b*) When a second ligature is applied to the auriculo-ventricular groove in a heart that has been arrested by the first ligature, the ventricle begins to beat again, even though much more slowly than the normal, while the auricles still remain motionless.

Eckhard (1858-60) showed that practically the same results were obtained by making incisions in the frog's heart, as by the method of Stannius. At the same time he denied their supposed constancy, and found a great variety of effect both from ligation and from sections, in accordance with fluctuations of external temperature, and the varying sensitivity of the preparation, and more particularly of the different regions operated on. He confirmed the fact already observed by Heidenhain that the arrest of the heart produced by the ligature or section is not permanent, for the beats invariably recommence after a longer or shorter pause (lasting from a few minutes to an hour).

None of the several hypotheses advanced in explanation of these facts will bear searching criticism. Eckhard accounts for the effect of the first Stannius ligature on the rhythm of the heart by assuming a sort of *næud vital*, represented by Remak's ganglia. To explain the effects of the second ligature, he assumes that it provokes a certain excitation of Bidder's ganglia. Remak's ganglia must function automatically, since the spontaneous movements of the heart cease when their influence is cut out: Bidder's ganglia must be reflex in function, since the stimulus of ligaturing the auriculo-ventricular junction is required to throw them into activity. When, in fact, instead of ligation, an incision is made in this region, which would not have much excitatory effect on Bidder's ganglia, permanent standstill of the ventricle, usually preceded by only 8-10 beats, is produced.

This theory, which involves a specific differentiation of the cardiac ganglia into automatic and reflex, is unsatisfactory. In order to defend it, we must assume that the upper Stannius ligature has, for its sole effect, the physiological exclusion of Remak's automatic ganglia, and that the lower ligature on the contrary causes the reflex excitation of Bidder's ganglia.

We attacked this question in Ludwig's laboratory in 1872, and saw that when the ligature was applied to the frog's heart, after the insertion of a simple cannula, with its point projecting into the ventricle, the same effects were obtained as with the Stannius ligatures. But when the cannula was filled with fresh rabbit's or sheep's serum, by which a certain pressure was exerted on the interior of the frog's heart, it began to beat again vigorously, regardless of the point at which the ligature was applied.   In order to study the course of the heart's action under these conditions we connected

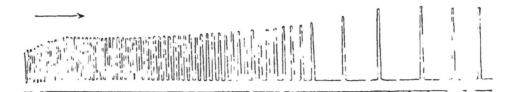

FIG. 129.—*Paroxysm* in form of ascending staircase, shown by frog's heart, filled with sheep's serum, and tied at auriculo-ventricular groove immediately after attachment to tonographic apparatus. (Luciani.)

the cannula with the excised frog's heart to a small recording mercury manometer (Fig. 121), and then obtained the curves of three distinct and quite characteristic phenomena, representing

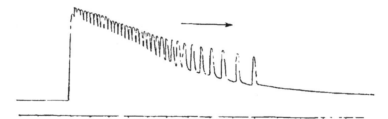

FIG. 130.—*Tetaniform paroxysm* presented by frog's heart already attached to tonographic apparatus, as the effect of a second ligature 2 mm. below the auriculo-ventricular groove. (Luciani.)

three different phases of cardiac activity, which precede the exhaustion of the heart.

The first phenomenon may be termed the "paroxysm"

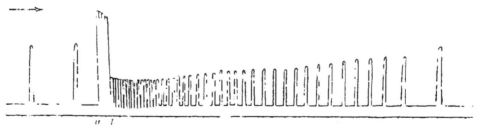

FIG. 131.—*Tetaniform paroxysm* commencing at *a*, after ligature of auricles, converted at *b* into an ascending staircase, by the momentary opening of the valve of the tonographic apparatus. (Luciani.)

(*accesso*), and consists in a sudden increase of cardiac muscular tonus in conjunction with great frequency of beat.   With the progressive diminution of tone the beats become less frequent, but are at the same time more ample in diastole, since the presystolic filling of the ventricle steadily increases.

This fact is shown (owing to the special character of the apparatus) in the curve of Fig. 129 as an ascending staircase, produced by the progressive increase not of systole, but of diastole, in proportion as the tone of the myocardium diminishes. For when a second ligature is applied to the auricles, the heart being already connected with the recording apparatus, the tracing assumes a tetanic form, and the beats, as they become more excursive, rise above a regularly descending line, which is the exact expression of the progressive

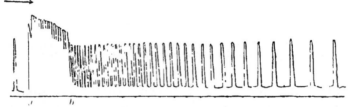

Fig. 132. *Tetaniform paroxysm* commencing at *a* after provisory ligature of auricles; converted at *b* into slightly ascending staircase, the beats becoming less frequent, after removal of ligature. (Luciani.)

decrease in tonicity (Fig. 130). If, after applying the second ligature to the auricle, the valve which separates the heart from the vessel of serum is opened, the beats which accompany the attack assume the form of an ascending staircase, as in Fig. 129, which bears out our interpretation (Fig. 131). Practically the same result is obtained if the ligature is applied soon after the paroxysm has commenced (Fig. 132).

Fig. 133. *Periodic rhythm* shown by frog's heart tied at the auricles, 2 mm. above the auriculo-ventricular groove, filled with rabbit's serum and attached to tonographic apparatus of Fig. 121. (Luciani.) The figure shows four periods of regular increase, both in number of beats in groups and in duration of pause. The divisions along the abscissa represent intervals of 1 second.

The phenomenon of "paroxysm," which shows that the ligature applied at different heights of the auricles (in conjunction with the action of serum and of a certain degree of pressure) invariably acts not merely by separating, but also by contusing and irritating the walls of the heart, seems to us the most direct refutation of the doctrine of the twofold nature of the cardiac ganglia.

When the paroxysm is over, a new phenomenon appears which we have termed periodic rhythm, in which the cardiac pulsations occur, not at regular intervals, but in groups, separated by long pauses (Fig. 133). This strange effect may continue for two or three hours, and usually exhibits a regular course. Often the duration both of the groups and of the succeeding pauses declines regularly; at other times it increases in the primary phase, and declines in the next; other cases again present irregular oscillations with a constant tendency to decrease.

The number of beats in each group has no apparent relation with the duration of the respective pauses. Their frequency varies usually in regular order.

The more typical groups commence with rare contractions that are gradually accelerated, and then again slow down into a long pause. The height of the contractions in each group usually

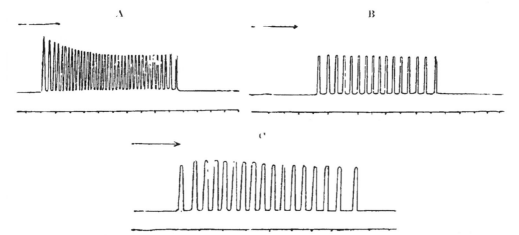

Fig. 134.—Three groups of beats obtained from various frogs' hearts tied at the auricles. (Luciani.) In A the beats form a descending staircase; in B they are approximately the same height; in C the first four beats form an ascending staircase.

forms a descending staircase: more rarely a straight horizontal line; more rarely still, a slightly ascending staircase (Fig. 134).

Our experiments tend to show that the groups are of longer duration, and the intervals between them shorter, when the ligature is nearer the sinus. This fact agrees with Eckhard's conclusions—to the effect that the duration of the pause increases in proportion as the incisions in the heart are made at different heights, from limit of sinus to auriculo-ventricular groove.

The periodic rhythm is an absolutely constant phenomenon when the cannula is attached at any height whatever of the auricles, and given all the other conditions of our method, in re serum, temperature, and pressure. When the ligature falls on the auriculo-ventricular groove, the phenomenon may appear in a rudimentary form, or may be altogether absent. When it falls on the upper limit of the ventricle (1-1·5 mm. below the auriculo-ventricular groove) Bowditch's preparation is obtained, of which we shall speak below. When the paroxysm is over there will in every case be some isolated contractions, after which all spontaneous movement ceases, although the ventricle preserves its reflex excitability, and responds to electrical and mechanical stimuli by strong contractions. When the ligature falls on the junction of the sinus, the periodic grouping of the cardiac contractions is barely and irregularly indicated. When, lastly, it falls on the sinus (1-1·5 mm. above its opening into the right auricle) no trace of periodic grouping is visible.

These facts obviously exclude the hypothesis that the periodic rhythm observed by us during the above experimental conditions depends exclusively on a specific toxic action of the serum, or on asphyxia, due to its non-renewal, as was held by Rossbach Langendorff and others: while they show us just as convincingly, that in the case of our experiments the fundamental determining condition of the phenomenon consists in the physiological exclusion of the sinus venosus effected by the ligature.

They further show that the rhythmical activity of the heart is

FIG. 135.—Crisis of periodic rhythm in frog's heart, tied 3 mm. above the auriculo-ventricular groove, and filled with pig's serum. (Luciani.) Shows gradual dissolution of groups into isolated beats.

most highly developed in the venae cavae and sinus venosus (where lie the conspicuous ganglionic masses described by Remak), after the separation of which the rhythmical impulses probably encounter resistance, and must summate before they can be efficacious. Accordingly, there are long pauses, during which tension is accumulated, and groups of contractions, during which it is discharged again.

In proportion as the activity of the heart exhausts itself the pauses shorten, and the beats in the groups are separated by wider intervals, till eventually all periodic grouping disappears. This is the phenomenon we have termed the "crisis" (crisis), represented by a longer or shorter series of single beats, which become constantly rarer and weaker, until they disappear entirely, as soon as the asphyxia and exhaustion of the heart are complete (Fig. 135).

The crisis indicates that the resistances which determine the periodic rhythm are gradually diminishing, and that the heart is slowly adapting itself to the new conditions produced by the ligature. Renewal of the serum after the crisis has set in does not reinstate the periodic rhythm. This is a striking fact, and in our opinion indicates that the adaptation has been complete.

IV. At the time at which we took up these physiological

studies of the frog's heart there was a great tendency to deny any kind of automaticity, and to regard cardiac rhythm as a simple reflex phenomenon dependent on rhythmic excitation determined by external stimuli. Goltz assumed that systole, by removing the cardiac stimulus (due to the blood and its gases), induced diastole. But this hypothesis disregards the elementary consideration that the excised heart, in which rhythmical filling and emptying is no longer possible, continues to beat vigorously.

Others ascribe a kind of elastic resistance to the heart, alternating with the different phases of its activity. The stimuli, as continuous agents, must develop a certain tension in order to surmount this elastic resistance, before they can produce their effect. When systole is over, resistance rises, and a new discharge can only take place after the latent excitation has overcome the corresponding tension. This schematic representation implies a tacit recognition that the immediate cause of rhythmical activity is a condition intrinsic to the organ. But the *naïveté* of this hypothesis, which predicated a kind of elastic resistance, was shown on the discovery of *periodic rhythm*, which, in its multiple manifestations, its varied course, and its crisis, shows how changeable the internal conditions which determine the activity of the heart may be, when the external conditions remain constant and almost unaltered. "The rhythm of the heart-beats" (as we concluded in 1873) "is the external expression of a corresponding rhythm of the nutritive process which is accomplished within the organ."

Henceforward, no one contested the theory of the automaticity of cardiac action, since it was impossible to invent a hypothesis which explained the many and complex forms of its rhythm by any external stimulus.

The *automatic excitability* of the heart does not of course exclude its *reflex excitability*, and the doctrine of Bidder and Eckhard, who assumed the existence of distinct automatic and reflex mechanisms, must be modified to the effect that the different parts of the heart exhibit different degrees of excitability, whether automatic or reflex.

It can be asserted on the ground of weighty arguments that automatic excitability is most pronounced in the venae cavae and sinus, less in the auricles, and least in the ventricle. The facts already cited showing that (i.) the duration of cardiac arrest, after applying ligatures or sections to the heart by the methods of Stannius and Eckhard, becomes increasingly greater, the lower these are placed on the auricles between the orifice of the sinus and the auriculo-ventricular groove; (ii.) the periodic groups become constantly smaller and the pauses longer with physiological separation, as in our method, combined with the action of serum and of pressure; (iii.) the arrest of cardiac activity by exhaustion due to whatever means, which takes place in different parts of the organ at different times, *i.e.* first in the ventricle, then in the auricles, lastly in the sinus and the venae cavae,—all go to prove that automaticity in the various parts of the heart decreases gradually from sinus to auricles, from auricles to ventricle. To these facts, as determined on the heart of the frog, we may add those observed by MacWilliam on the fish's heart. When it is divided into segments each of these continues to beat, but each with its own proper rhythm—the more slowly in proportion as the segment is farther away from the veins opening into the auricles.

In mammals, again, similar phenomena may be observed. By an ingenious operative method Tigerstedt succeeded in the rabbit in completely separating the auricles from the ventricles without interrupting the circulation, and found that the latter continued to beat, although the rhythm was markedly slower.

Porter, on extending the experiments with artificial perfusion through the coronary system, found that the rhythm persisted even in isolated sections of the ventricles connected with the rest of the heart by a single branch of the coronary artery.

It may therefore, generally speaking, be concluded that every segment of the heart, whether in poikilothermic or in homothermic animals, is endowed with rhythmical automatic excitability, which decreases from the sinus venosus downwards, from the mouths of the venae cavae to the auricles, from the auricles to the ventricles,

Other experiments show that the rhythmical activity of the more automatic determines the rhythm of the less automatic segments. Gaskell found that changes of temperature localised at the sinus in the frog's heart modified the frequency of the beats of the whole heart, as if the heart had been warmed or cooled *in toto*. Adam experimented by the same method on the heart of cat and rabbit. He saw that when an area between the mouth of the two venae cavae near the lowest segment of the wall of the right auricle was warmed or cooled, the frequency of the beats of the whole heart was modified. No effect was produced on varying the temperature of the venae cavae or pulmonary veins, of the two auricular appendages, or the walls of the left auricle. It is, therefore, evident that the sinus venosus in cold-blooded animals and the orifice of the venae cavae as indicated by Adam on the mammalian heart, represent the most automatic parts, in which the pulsatory cycle is initiated, and on which the frequency of rhythm of the entire heart depends.

When automatic excitability is played out, reflex excitability usually persists for some time ; when the heart is stimulated either by a localised mechanical shock or by an induction shock, it reacts with a beat or a series of beats, which are either transmitted to the other segments of the heart, or remain circumscribed in the segment stimulated.

When reflex excitability is extinguished, the reaction to

external stimuli ceases in the various segments, in the same order in which the automatic excitability disappeared; first, the ventricle becomes inexcitable, next the auricles, and shortly after the sinus venosus. On the basis of these facts it may be sustained that the two forms of excitability are in direct reciprocal relation, and that the segments most excitable to internal stimuli are also the most excitable to external stimuli.

V. Does the falling excitability (automatic and reflex) from sinus venosus (or mouth of venae cavae) to auricles, from auricles to ventricles, which determines cardiac rhythm, depend on the varying number and arrangement of the ganglion cells in the different segments of the heart, since these have the property of generating rhythmical impulses which are then transmitted to the muscle cells, provoking contraction in the form of a peristaltic wave; or is it independent of the intracardiac nervous elements, and inherent in the muscle cells of the myocardium? For a long time the first doctrine was very generally admitted. Two special phenomena were adduced in its support which from their simplicity appeared to be direct evidence :—

(*a*) The lower two-thirds of the apex of the frog's ventricle, which shows no nerve-cells under the microscope, invariably ceases to beat automatically when separated by an incision or ligature from the other parts of the heart, which are provided with nerve elements (Stannard, Eckhard and others).

(*b*) Circumscribed excitation of any part of the frog's heart and its integuments always produces a contraction that commences in the auricles, and not at the point directly stimulated (Kürschner, Budge, Pagliani).

The first phenomenon seemed to be a direct proof of the neurogenic origin of automatic excitability, and the second a direct proof of the neurogenic origin of reflex excitability. Subsequently, however, the supposed constancy and affirmative character of both was disputed.

Ranvier and Engelmann observed rhythmical pulsations under the microscope in fragments of the adult heart in which it was impossible to detect any trace of nervous elements. The apex of the ventricle, again, when excised and lightly attached to a cannula will, after a pause (if conveniently distended and irrigated with a nutrient fluid), begin to beat spontaneously, and continue to do so for a long time, although the rhythm may be slower than usual. This proves that even if this part has no ganglia, it also has an inherent automatic capacity, although to a much smaller extent than the rest of the heart. It should be added that this masked excitability is a characteristic peculiar to the ventricle of the adult frog. That of the tortoise, on the contrary, although it has no nerve-cells, will beat for a considerable time after it has been isolated (Gaskell).

Some trustworthy observers, on the other hand, have contradicted the statements of Kürschner, Budge, and Pagliani, and hold that the reaction of the heart to a circumscribed stimulus invariably commences in the part directly excited, whence it is propagated either in the peristaltic or in the anti-peristaltic form, *i.e.* from auricles to ventricle, or from ventricle to auricles.

On the theory of the myogenic origin of the rhythmic activity of the heart in all animals, both in the embryonic and the adult state, this rhythmicity must be an inherent property of the muscle cells, independent of the agency of the nervous system (whether extra- or intra-cardiac), which thus fulfils simply a secondary function, regulatory and trophic. Many workers have contributed to the elaboration and stability of this view, among them Engelmann in Germany (1893-97), Gaskell in England (1882-87), and Fano in Italy (1885-90).

Some of the experimental arguments on which the myogenic hypothesis was founded have been disproved by more recent investigations carried out with better technical methods, which show the presence of nerve-cells in points of the heart at which their non-existence had previously appeared certain. The following arguments of the myogenists, however, seem incontestable :—

(*a*) The automatic movements of the embryonic heart begin before the presence of ganglion cells can be demonstrated under the microscope. In the chick, for instance, the heart begins to beat thirty-six hours after incubation, while the ganglion cells are only formed after six days (His, jun.); the human heart begins to beat three weeks after gestation (Pflüger), while the nervous elements only appear at the commencement of the fifth week (His, jun.). The ganglia or cardiac nerves are not formed *in situ* by the differentiation of the muscle cells of which the cardiac tube is composed, but enter the heart from outside, from the cerebrospinal and sympathetic systems, penetrating along the veins in the lower vertebrates (fishes, frogs), along the arteries in the higher vertebrates (birds, mammals)—(His and Romberg).

(*b*) In studying the cardiac function of the excised embryonic heart of the chick on the second or third day of development, Fano succeeded by the photographic registration of its movements in demonstrating that the beats of the primitive cardiac tube differ in no essentials from those of the adult heart. It exhibits a rhythm in the form of a peristaltic movement that passes from the auricular to the ventricular segment of the tube. The first portion is more resistant, the second is more easily exhausted. If divided by a transverse section, the first continues to beat, the second stops. Longitudinal or oblique sections of the cardiac tube show that the segment nearest the venous end is the first to contract, and from it the contractile wave is propagated towards the arterial extremity. Toxic or indifferent gases first arrest the beats of the ventricular, then those of the auricular portion. On sub-stituting air or oxygen for the said gases, shortly after the beats have been arrested, they are seen to reappear, first in the auricular, subsequently in the ventricular section. In short, the embryonic heart of the chick, which has no nerve elements, exhibits like the adult heart a decrease of automaticity from the venous to the arterial end (Fig. 136).

(c) No less interesting are the observations of Fano in regard to the mode in which the rhythm-ical automatic activity of the same embryonic heart becomes exhausted. When isolated and exposed to favourable conditions of moisture and temperature, it continues to beat for a time which usually exceeds one hour, and may reach a maximum of two or three. But in the last stage o its life, rhythmical is transformed into periodic activity, as repre-sented by groups of beats separated by long pauses, in complete agree-ment with the phenomenon dis-covered by us on the adult heart of the frog. As in that, so in the embryonic heart, the periodic rhythm gradually resolves itself into an irregular series of single beats, which become constantly weaker and less frequent until they vanish altogether. The auricular or venous segment of the heart not only beats a good deal longer than the ventricular segment, but it exhibits the periodic grouping of beats much later. After the automatic rhythm

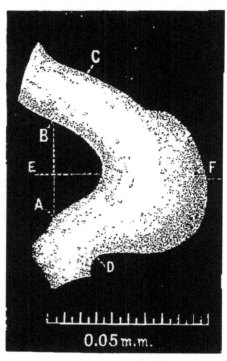

Fig. 136. Chick's heart on third day of in-cubation. (Fano.) *AD*, venous extremity, from which the auricles develop; *BC*, arterial end, from which the bulbi arteriosi develop; *EF*, median line of ventricular portion; *AB*, concave line or lesser curva-ture of heart; *DFC*, convex line, or greater curvature of heart. Each of the divisions indicated below the figure corresponds to 0·05 mm., and the whole line to 1 mm.

ceases, reflex excitability continues for some time. Since these effects appear in a part entirely devoid of nervous elements, they can only be due to automatic or reflex excitability of the embryonic muscle cells.

(d) On repeating the same observations and experiments on the chick's heart in the second half of its development, *i.e.* on the eleventh day of incubation, when there is no essential morphological difference between it and the adult heart of vertebrates, Bottazzi obtained the same results as those recorded by Fano for the first hours of incubation. In that stage of development also automaticity declines from sinus to auricles, from auricles to ventricles. Functional exhaustion is again preceded by the phenomenon of periodic rhythm, or crisis. similar to that described by us for the adult frog's heart.

(c) We have seen that it is possible to revive the rabbit's heart five days after death, by the artificial circulation through the coronary arteries of suitable nutrient fluids, at a given temperature and pressure (Kuliabko). Now it has been found by experiments on the vitality of the peripheral ganglionic elements in general, that they survive suppression of circulation very imperfectly in comparison with the conducting nerve fibres, and more particularly with the muscle cells. Langendorff demonstrated loss of excitability in the ciliary ganglion immediately after bleeding and death from asphyxia of an animal, and showed that the pre-ganglionic fibres ceased to influence the pupil long before the post-ganglionic. H. E. Hering confirmed this fact (1903), but noted that the excitability of the vagus, and still more of the sympathetic, for the heart, persisted for a considerable time after the death of the animal. He further observed that when the cells of the superior cervical ganglion had ceased to function it was impossible to revive it by perfusion with Ringer's solution, which, however, can restore vagus excitability six hours after the death of the animal, and that of the accelerator fibres after a much longer period (fifty-three hours). If, now, the intracardiac behave like the other sympathetic ganglia, it is evident that the rhythm of the heart, which may be re-established by Ringer's solution as much as six days after death, cannot be due to the ganglia, but must derive from the automatic recovery of the muscle cells.

The absolute and unconditional value of some of the arguments for the myogenic theory of cardiac rhythm is challenged by the work of Bethe (1903), who adopted an improved technique, based on the staining of nerve elements by methylene blue. According to these observations there is not in the whole body of the frog a muscle richer in nerve fibres than the heart. A fine network of fibrils from the minutest ganglion cells invests the muscular sheath of the entire myocardium, including the apex of the ventricle. Bethe asserts that the muscles of the auricle in the frog are completely separated from those of the ventricle, just as these last are separated from the muscles of the aortic bulb. The nervous reticulum of the auricles again does not seem to be in direct continuation with that of the ventricle, but is connected with it exclusively, or at least to a great extent, by means of Bidder's ganglia, which, as we have seen, lie in the auriculo-ventricular groove.

On these histological grounds, Bethe ranges himself among the supporters of the neurogenic theory, alleging that while the nervous reticulum of the heart is not the sole incentive to its rhythmic automaticity, it does represent the conducting element of excitation.

The most important and convincing arguments in favour of the neurogenic theory of cardiac rhythm were, however, adduced by Carlson (1904-5).

He directed all his observations to the invertebrate heart, in which, from the phylogenetic point of view, the automatic activity of the muscle cells should reach their highest development.

One of the strongest arguments adduced by Engelmann in favour of the myogenic theory, was the non-existence of nerves and ganglion cells in the adult heart of many of the *Invertebrata* (molluscs, arthropods, tunicates, lower crustaceans). He reasoned from the observations of A. Brandt, C. Eckhard, M. Foster and Dew Smith, W. Biedermann and Ransom. Carlson, however, noticed that these negative results do not hold for all invertebrates. In a great many molluscs and arthropods the heart is visibly invested with nerve-cells and fibres, while, according to Hunter,

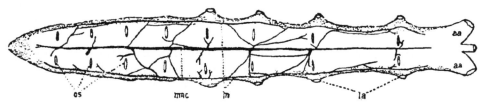

Fig. 137.—Heart and cardiac nerves of *Limulus polyphemus*. (Carlson.) *aa*, Anterior arteries; *la*, lateral arteries; *la*, lateral nerves; *mgc*, median ganglionic chain; *os*, ostii or afferent stomata, each pair of which corresponds to one of the segments into which the *Limulus* heart is divided.

these elements also exist in certain tunicates, *e.g.* in *Molgula.* Carlson worked on the heart of an invertebrate, *Limulus polyphemus* (an arachnid, according to others a crustacean), the American "horse-shoe crab." The heart of this animal (which in the best-developed specimens may be as much as 10-15 cm. long) is in the form of an elongated sac, divided into segments by arterial rami which originate in a double lateral series (Fig. 137). During systole this heart contracts simultaneously in its entire length, or else the wave of contraction is peristaltically propagated with such velocity that the eye is incapable of following its progression. The nerve plexus by which the heart is invested is disposed above the ectocardium in three principal trunks, the median of which may be regarded as an extended nervous ganglion, mixed with nerve fibres, while the two lateral nerves, and the branches by which these are connected with the median ganglion, contain no nerve fibres. In this case, therefore, it is comparatively easy to separate the nervous elements without injuring the muscular walls of the heart, which is impossible in any other animal.

By a technique as simple as it is conclusive, Carlson has

shown that the conduction of excitability and co-ordination of the cardiac movements of *Limulus* depend on the median ganglion cord. When this is removed the beats cease entirely, while the intact heart, when exposed, may continue to beat regularly for many hours. On dividing the cord at any point, the beats become a-synchronous in the several segments, and continue so for an indefinite time. When, on the other hand, the muscle is divided transversely at any point along the heart, while the ganglion cord is spared, there is no longer any appreciable disturbance of co-ordination in the pulsations. If a single node of the ganglion cord is extirpated, the heart ceases to beat in the corresponding muscular segment, while it continues to beat in the rest.

The ganglion cord of *Limulus* is the centre not only for the automatic activity of the heart, but for its reflex activity as well. It receives the moderator and accelerator nerves, which modify the cardiac beats acting not directly on the muscle cells, but reflexly or through the ganglion. When this has been excised, and the beats of the heart have ceased, rhythmical activity is not restored on exciting the lateral nerves; tetanic contractions are, however, obtained.

Lastly, certain cardiac poisons (atropine, nicotine) act on the *Limulus* heart as on that of vertebrates, paralysing the activity of the inhibitory nerve fibres which reach it from without.

There can be no doubt as to the accuracy of Carlson's experiments, or the theoretical conclusions which result from them. As the supporters of the myogenic theory emphasise particularly the automatic rhythmical activity of the embryonic heart and that of certain invertebrates in which nervous elements are wanting; so the supporters of the neurogenic theory may invoke the *Limulus* heart as direct evidence and proof that its automatic and reflex excitability, the conduction and the co-ordination of excitations, depend exclusively on the ganglion cells which it contains.

Without venturing on any general conclusion, and assuming that the results obtained from *Limulus* are applicable to the heart of vertebrates also, it is only fair to admit unhesitatingly that the neurogenic theory seems more probable since Carlson's discovery than the myogenic. Its definite and unconditional acceptance for the heart of every animal could only be possible if, with better methods of research, it were discovered that both the embryonic heart of mammals, and the heart of all invertebrates, possess ganglionic elements that have so far evaded detection.

VI. The elements which constitute the vertebrate myocardium are not perfectly comparable with those of either striated or smooth muscle. They are neither composed of fibres, nor of fusiform fibro-cells; but consist of nucleated cells of prismatic form, which usually bifurcate into two broad short processes, and exhibit a rather dark striation. Each cell is joined at its extremity to other similar cells by means of little protoplasmic bridges (Przewoski), and a series of such cells constitutes a cardiac fibre, which never has a sarcolemma, and is joined by the processes, as above, to other adjacent fibres, making with them a kind of network. At certain points, more particularly beneath the endocardium, are muscle cells that are non-striated, or striated only in the outer layers, with no striae at the nucleus (Purkinje). These represent cells which are less well developed and more embryonic in character (Fig. 138).

Given this structure of the elements of the myocardium, it is easy on the myogenic theory to see how the contraction wave which arises in the more automatic muscle cells of the venae cavae and sinus venosus must be propagated in a peristaltic form from cell to cell, independent of the nervous system. Each cell being in simple protoplasmic continuity with all the rest, the entire myocardium may, from a physiological point of view, be regarded as a united

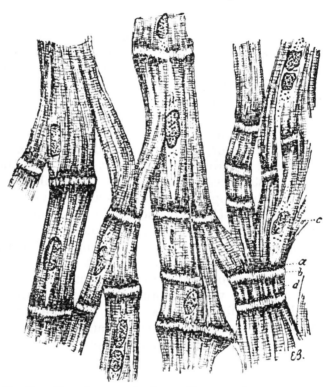

FIG. 138.—Muscular network of normal heart of adult man. (Przewoski.) *a*, Terminal granular layer; *b*, filiform protoplasmic processes, stretched between the muscle cells; *c*, nuclei of these cells; *d*, bundle of primitive muscle fibrils.

mass of hollow muscle. We must now briefly enumerate the most important experimental facts by which this theory is supported.

As early as 1874 A. Fick showed that any excitation due to stimulation of a circumscribed area of the cardiac muscular mass was propagated in every direction. Engelmann almost simultaneously confirmed this fact, and further showed that the contraction can be propagated in a ventricle divided into zigzags by incisions, from one section to another.

Porter (1899) established a similar fact for the heart of mammals, irrigated with defibrinated blood circulated through the coronary arteries, at 36° C. After cutting across the mass of the ventricle, in such a way that the segments above and below were united only by means of little muscular bridges and the rami of the coronaries, synchronous contractions were found to persist throughout the ventricular mass. These facts, which appeared incompatible with nervous conduction, have, since Bethe's work on the neuro-ganglionic system diffused throughout the frog's myocardium, and that of Berkley on the mammalian myocardium, lost all evidential value, since they can be explained by the conduction of excitation through the fibrillary nervous network.

Gaskell, to exclude the intervention of nerves and ganglia in the transmission of cardiac excitation, divided on the tortoise the large nerve trunks that supply the ventricle, and on the frog excised the interauricular septum with all its nerve trunks, and found that the peristaltic propagation of beats from auricle to ventricle was not interrupted. Analogous experiments with the same results were carried out at a later time on the mammalian heart by Krehl, in collaboration with Romberg. These experiments, however, cannot be adduced in favour of the theory of myogenic conduction, since it has been demonstrated by the latest histological methods that the whole myocardium is pervaded by minute ganglionic elements and nerve fibrils.

Either on the hypothesis of myogenic, or on that of neurogenic conduction, it is difficult to explain the fact of the brief arrests or delayed transmission of the contraction wave at the points at which it passes from one segment to the other of the heart, i.e. at the junction between the sinus and the auricles, the auricles and ventricle, the ventricle and the arterial bulb.

It was formerly assumed, on the strength of the early anatomical researches, that each of these parts of the heart possessed a perfectly distinct system of muscle fibres. For the heart of man and other mammals, in particular, Donders admitted as a well-established fact that there was complete interruption of the muscular walls corresponding with the auriculo-ventricular groove, and he used this to account, on the neurogenic theory, for the perfect a-synchronism between the systole of the auricles and that of the ventricles. More recent and exact observations have proved the existence of muscle bridges, which connect the different parts of the heart, and form a united myocardium.

As early as the end of 1876 Paladino, in the heart of man and various other vertebrates, demonstrated the presence of muscular fasciculi extending uninterruptedly from auricles to ventricles. In 1883, Gaskell demonstrated the same for the hearts of frog and tortoise, and these observations were subsequently confirmed by Stanley-Kent (1892-94), by His, jun., and by Engelmann, for the heart of other vertebrates also.

According to the recent and very minute researches of Tawara (1905) on the human heart, this connecting system of auriculo-ventricular fibres forms a diffuse and complex muscular ramification, which continues uninterruptedly from auricles to ventricles. From this system a short bundle of muscle goes out at the back to the coronary sinus, where it joins the ordinary muscles of the auricle. Another bundle runs inwards from the muscular system, towards the muscles of the ventricle, and bifurcates at the two walls of the septum. At the base these two branches break up into a number of small bundles, some of which enter the musculi papillari, while others spread over the whole internal surface of the endocardium, passing either to the apex or the base of the ventricles. Throughout its course the auriculo-ventricular bundle is separated by connective tissues from the cardiac muscle proper, and connects with the fibres of the ventricle by its terminal branches only.

It would be interesting to study the effects on cardiac rhythm of interrupting the conduction of excitation along this system of muscle fibres, which passes uninterruptedly from auricles to ventricles. Some physiologists have attempted the experiment on the isolated surviving

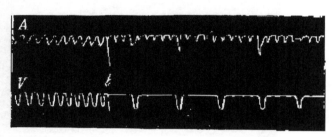

Fig. 139.—Tracing of beats of auricle (A) and ventricle (B) of small, isolated dog's heart. At *l* a thread was tied round the bundle of His, after which a decided allorhythmia of the two cardiac segments is apparent. (Humblet.)

heart of mammalia: *e.g.* His, jun., Graupner, Erlanger, and especially H. E. Hering. Gentle compression of the principal bundles increases the interval between presystole and systole, without altering their normal sequence. Stronger compression produces the allorhythmia, in which 2, 3, or 4 presystoles correspond with a single systole (Fig. 139). Marked and sudden compression when the cardiac rhythm is very frequent and intense may produce a longer or shorter arrest in systole, after which the ventricles begin to beat with a rhythm of their own, independent of that of the auricles. The same results occur when the conductivity of the auriculo-ventricular bundle is impaired by cooling, while the excitability of the auricles is simultaneously raised by warming.

The experiments which most definitely bring out the importance of this bundle as the bridge across which the wave of contraction passes from auricles to ventricles, are those of H. E. Hering (1905) on the dog's heart. He kills the animal, and then revives the heart (without isolating it from the body), perfusing Ringer's physiological solution from the aorta through the coronaries. While the heart is still motionless, he divides the auriculo-ventricular bundle by a comparatively small incision in the septum (across the right auricle). Each time the incision into the bundle of His is complete (as can subsequently be ascertained anatomically) a sharp functional dissociation between the beats of the auricles and those of the ventricles, a true allorhythmia, appears when the cardiac cycle recommences. Hering studied this effect on ten dogs' hearts, with results as follows :—

(*a*) The ventricles beat more slowly than the auricles (Fig. 140).

(*b*) The wave of contraction is neither transmitted from the auricles to the ventricles, nor *vice versa*, whether it be spontaneous, or determined by external artificial stimuli.

(*c*) Both auricles and ventricles possess independent automatic activity.

From these experimental data Hering deduces a new argument in favour of myogenic conduction, adopting the ideas previously

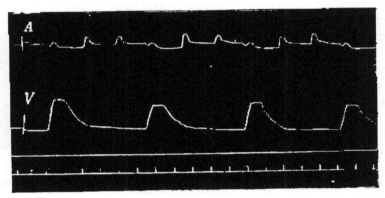

FIG. 140. Tracing of beats of auricle (*A*) and ventricle (*V*) in a dog's heart, in which the bundle of His had been cut. Time in seconds. (H. E. Hering.)

brought forward by Gaskell in connection with the amphibian heart.

According to Gaskell, communicating fibres between the sinus and auricles, and the auricles and ventricle, present certain morphological peculiarities in which they approximate to embryonic cardiac fibres. These less differentiated fibres, which in arrangement and structure resemble those of the primitive cardiac sheath, have also from the physiological point of view preserved a more embryonic character, since they are endowed with a far higher degree of automatism, and probably (according to Gaskell) conduct the excitation from cell to cell far more slowly. This is sufficient to explain in the simplest possible manner, why the contraction wave arising in the sinus is not of uniform velocity, but is delayed at the limits of the several segments, breaking up into contractions of sinus, auricles, ventricle, and bulbus arteriosus.

The highly developed automatic excitability of the muscle cells of the venae cavae and sinus explains why these parts govern the rhythm of all the remaining segments of the heart, where automatic activity is slower and weaker. Gaskell observed (as above) that with localised warming of the sino-auricular and ventricular segments, acceleration of cardiac rhythm resulted in the first case only. He therefore concluded that when the heart is functioning *as a whole*, the rhythm proper to the less automatic segments remains latent under normal conditions, and that the more frequent and powerful rhythm of the more automatic segments governs the movements of the entire heart. This is the reason why under normal conditions the contraction wave always travels in the peristaltic direction from sinus to auricles, from auricles to ventricle, from ventricle to bulbus arteriosus.

With this view we must again contrast the latest results of microscopic work, both on the frog's heart (Bethe), and on the muscular bundle of His in the mammalian heart, where there is found to be an exceptional abundance of nerve elements (Hofmann).

H. E. Hering has recently (1907) modified his previous opinions, calling attention to other experimental data, which he thinks are better explained on the neurogenic theory. These are as follows :—

(*a*) In the adult mammalian heart there is a segment which, when isolated from the rest, is incapable of reacting automatically. This is the auricular appendage of the right auricle. It now appears from microscopic researches that this particular part has no ganglionic nerve elements.

(*b*) Under certain conditions it can be demonstrated that the automaticity of the mammalian heart, and its capacity for reacting to artificial stimuli, are properties independent of one another. It is possible for a heart in diastolic or systolic arrest to be more excitable to artificial external, than to automatic internal stimuli, and *vice versa*.

(*c*) A small incision in the region of the orifice of the venae cavae, or a single induction shock of minimum intensity in the right auricle, may suspend the automatism of the auricular region of the heart for a considerable period.

(*d*) Lastly, Hering has recently discovered that a mammalian heart arrested from any cause whatsoever, is capable of recommencing its beats in consequence of the stimulation of the accelerator nerve. He holds that these facts are better explained on the theory of a nervous, than on that of a muscular automaticity in the adult mammalian heart.

VII. It can be demonstrated independently of the neurogenic or myogenic theory of rhythm that cardiac muscle differs from ordinary skeletal muscle in its peculiar physiological characteristics. Bowditch (1870) was the first to study in Ludwig's laboratory the phenomena exhibited by the apex of the heart (attached to a simple cannula filled with serum, and connected with a recording manometer), when excited by various agencies.

He found that the apex-beats called out at regular intervals by induction shocks did not increase in intensity with increased strength of stimulus, as is the case with normal muscle. When an induction current, no matter of what intensity, is strong enough to provoke a contraction, this is invariably maximal, *i.e.* as strong as can be obtained from the heart at the given moment ("all or nothing," Law of Bowditch). This fact, which was fully confirmed by the observations of Luciani, Kronecker, and Stirling, proves that the contraction of cardiac muscle depends essentially upon its inner conditions, and to a much less degree upon the external stimulus, as if the effect of the latter was limited to enabling the muscle to serve up a spontaneous contraction, of which it would not have been capable without such a stimulus.

This view is justified by other phenomena elucidated by Bowditch. When cardiac muscle is stimulated with weak induction shocks, the reaction sometimes occurs and sometimes fails (*stimolazioni fallaci*). If the strength of stimulus is increased, or the interval between each is diminished, the number of effective

Fig. 141.—Bowditch's ascending staircase from frog's heart ligatured at the auricles, with a series of induction shocks thrown in at intervals of 4″. (Luciani.) The tracing shows a gradual increase of both systolic and diastolic excursions.

shocks increases also. If the current is still further strengthened, there will be a response to every stimulus (*stimolazioni infallibili*). After a long series of regular contractions a weaker current is seen to produce the same effect. Hence a strength of current which is at first uncertain (*fallace*) becomes certain (*infallibile*) after a sequence of shocks. These facts prove that the excitability of cardiac muscle to external stimuli is very variable, and oscillates from one moment to another, and that the contractions are capable of determining the said oscillations of excitability.

On experimenting with frogs' hearts, ligatured at the auricles, we obtained the same results with Bowditch's method of electrical stimulation as he discovered for the apex of the heart.

Another phenomenon that can be observed on experimenting either with the apex or the auricular ligature, is the so-called *Bowditch staircase*. After complete rest for 5 to 10 minutes, rhythmical excitation with induction shocks of uniform strength, thrown in at intervals of 4 to 6 seconds, produces a series of contractions, which steadily increase in height up to a certain maximum. We were able to demonstrate that Bowditch's staircase expresses not merely an increment in systole, but an increment in diastole also. This means that the prolonged rest produces a certain inertia in the heart, associated with exaggeration of tonus, and that the electrical stimuli arouse the heart from this state, when it gradually recovers its activity, systolic as well as diastolic Fig. 141).

With regard to the tonicity of cardiac muscle, *i.e.* the intermediate state between systole and diastole, at the pause, Fano discovered an interesting phenomenon on the heart of the tortoise (*Emys europea*). If one auricle of this animal is connected by a thread with a writing lever, its spontaneous beats complete them-

A
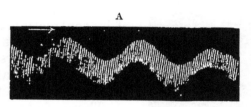

B
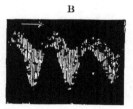

Fig. 142.—A and B. Myograms from auricle of tortoise heart (*Emys europea*), obtained by suspension method; showing two different forms of rhythmical oscillation of auricular tone. (Fano.)

selves above a line of rhythmical oscillating tonicity. These automatic oscillations of tone in the auricle are of varying intensity, and comprise a larger or smaller number of beats (Fig. 142, A and B). If the rhythm of the two auricles is recorded simultaneously, it will be seen that while the beats are perfectly synchronous, the oscillations in tone of the two auricles are quite independent as regards intensity and frequency. When the heart is exhausted the oscillations in tone are the first to disappear. On

C
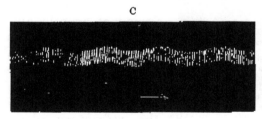

D
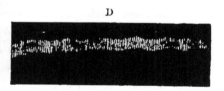

C, Oscillations of auricular tone in toad's heart (*Bufo viridis*) (Bottazzi).
D, The same from heart of *Rana esculenta*.

exciting the vagi, the tonic oscillations increase, while the beats are arrested. These facts led Fano to suggest that the rhythm of tonicity may be due to the contraction and expansion of a protoplasmic substance, other than that which determines the rhythm of the beats.

Bottazzi observed automatic oscillations in tonus both in the auricles of the amphibian heart (Fig. 142, C and D) and also on the sinus venosus, even when they were bloodless. Since he found the same phenomenon in the oesophagus of amphibia and of the chick embryo, and Ducceschi has noted it in the stomach of the dog (organs which consist of muscle cells that are very rich in

sarcoplasm), he thinks the oscillations in tonicity are probably due
to the contractions and expansions of the sarcoplasm, and the
ordinary and more frequent beats to the doubly refractive substance
of these elements.

The oscillations of excitability in cardiac muscle recorded by
Bowditch with electrical stimuli were determined more exactly by
the later work of Kronecker and Stirling.
They showed that the
heart becomes inexcit-
able during the time
of its contraction, and
that if cooled this in-
excitability persists
for some time after
the beat is completed.

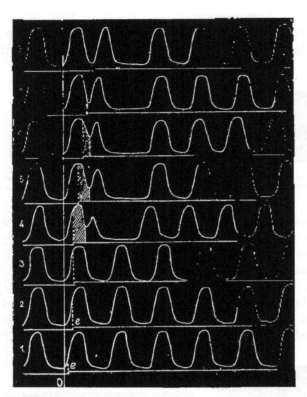

Fig. 143.—Myograms of frog's ventricle, obtained by Marey with
apparatus of Fig. 126, and reduced one-half by photography.
Shows effect of excitation by break of induction current, at
various moments of the cardiac cycle. The line O indicates
the commencement of all the beats, during which the
shock is sent in. In 1, 2, and 3 the heart is refractory to
the stimulus. From 4 to 8 the heart reacts by an extra
systole, by a delay or lost time which is progressively less,
as shown by the sections shaded obliquely to make them more
conspicuous. The extra-systoles increase in height from 4
to 8, each being followed by a compensatory pause. At *a*,
the line marked by the electric signal, the break induction
shocks were thrown in.

These facts were
confirmed by Marey,
who analysed the
phenomenon of peri-
odic inexcitability to
electrical stimuli in
the automatically
beating heart, and
termed it the refrac-
tory phase of the
cardiac cycle. It
corresponds with the
period of systole, and
its duration varies
with that of the
stimuli and other
extrinsic conditions.
With weak stimuli
the refractory phase
persists throughout
the systole: with
stronger stimuli it is
limited to the first
period of systole, or obliterated altogether. Warming shortens
or suppresses it; cooling prolongs it. Each forced or extra-
systole is more ample in proportion as it appears later after
the spontaneous systole that preceded it. The extrasystole is
followed by a resting period longer than that which usually occurs
between two systoles (compensatory pause), by which the temporary
disturbance of cardiac rhythm is adjusted (Fig. 143).

Later observers, who, after Marey, studied the compensatory

pause which succeeds the extrasystole, attributed it to the intrinsic nervous system of the heart, because in experiments with the apex, where there were supposed to be no ganglia, the extrasystole appeared, but not the compensatory pause observed upon the intact heart supplied with ganglia (Dastre, Marcacci, Gley, Keiser). Subsequently, however, Engelmann showed that the compensatory pause can be obtained at the apex also, previous observers having failed to detect it because they employed a tetanising current as stimulus, instead of single make or break shocks. He demonstrated that the compensatory pause may fail in the entire ventricle also, with the constant current. Bottazzi, on the other hand, observed the compensatory pause on the embryonic heart of the chick, which excluded the possibility of its being essentially conditioned by the nervous elements.

It has frequently been noted, on stimulating the heart at the sino-auricular junction, that not only is it possible to obtain an extrasystole with weak currents that would be ineffectual beyond these limits, but that a series of rhythmical beats, of greater frequency than the normal, may also occur (Langendorff, Keiser). This was explained by the presence of ganglion cells in these parts. But in view of Gaskell's discovery that it is just these parts which contain the more embryonic muscle cells, endowed with a marked automatic rhythm, the difference observed in the response may obviously depend rather upon these muscular elements than upon the ganglia.

The refractory phase of the cardiac cycle accounts for the regular alternation of systole and diastole, and explains why it is difficult to produce a true tetanus of the heart by means of a tetanising current, i.e. to fuse a number of contractions into a single very marked and persistent one, as in the case of ordinary muscle (Kronecker and Stirling).

The direct action of tetanising currents upon the surface of the mammalian heart produces the strange effect termed by Ludwig and Hoffa (1849) *delirium cordis*. This is a wholly unco-ordinated activity of cardiac muscle, in which it contracts at isolated points, and simultaneously relaxes at others, so that the mechanical work of the heart becomes impossible. Co-ordinated activity may be resumed after a delirium lasting for several minutes, but only when the current has not been unduly strong, nor the stimulation too prolonged. The origin of this phenomenon has been variously explained. MacWilliam held it to be independent of nervous influences, and merely the effect of direct excitation and altered conduction in the muscle cells. Kronecker, on the contrary, interprets *delirium cordis* as the functional disturbance of a nervous centre of co-ordination for cardiac movements, situated in the upper third of the interventricular septum. He showed that in the dog, and frequently in the rabbit also, it was only necessary to thrust a needle into this spot in order to produce a fatal delirium of the heart, while any number of punctures at other points of the ventricle had no effect on the co-ordinated contractions. The trend of recent evidence in favour of the neurogenic theory (which has always been upheld by Kronecker for the heart of mammalia also) increases the presumption for this interesting hypothesis of a co-ordinating, ganglionic centre for cardiac rhythm.

VIII. Admitting that the rhythmicity of the heart depends on the automatic and reflex excitability of its intrinsic ganglion system, it follows by exclusion that the extracardiac nerve plexus through which the heart is brought into relation with the cerebrospinal axis can merely exert a regulatory function upon the rhythm, modifying it in accordance with varying external circumstances and the temporary needs of the body. We must now investigate the nature of this regulation of cardiac movements is exercised by the nervous system.

At the Congress of Italian Naturalists at Naples (September

Fig. 144.—Inhibitory effect of electrical excitation of frog's vagus. (Waller.) The period of stimulation is marked on the abscissa by an electric signal. At the close of excitation the beats become larger.

1845) the brothers Weber communicated the results of certain experiments which they had undertaken on the effect of stimulating the vagus by tetanising induction currents. To their surprise they obtained neither acceleration nor reinforcement of the beats of the heart, but found they were slowed, or arrested in diastole. Stimulation of the intact vagus or its peripheral trunk produced the same result in all classes of vertebrates (Fig. 144). In the frog the excitation of the nerve centres from the optic lobes to the tip of the calamus scriptorius had the same effect. This was a discovery of capital importance, which cleared the way for a vast number of other observations. Budge discovered the same facts, independent of the Webers, and almost at the same moment, but declared himself unable to decide whether the arrest of the heart was due to a cardiac tetanus, as he was then inclined to believe, or to a temporary paralysis of the heart (for which he subsequently concluded on becoming acquainted with the Webers' communication).

Three different views have been advanced in explanation of this phenomenon : that of the Webers, who regarded the vagus nerves as the restrainers of the heart; that of Budge, which was immediately accepted by Schiff and at a later time by Moleschott, to the effect that the vagi were motor nerves, easily exhausted by electrical stimuli; and, lastly, that of Brown-Séquard, who held the vagus to be a vasomotor nerve of the coronary system. Budge's view was soon found to be untenable, since even the weakest currents retard or arrest the movements of the heart. Still easier was it to overthrow Brown-Séquard's hypothesis, seeing that ligation of the coronary arteries does not arrest the heart, and in the frog's heart, which has no cardiac vessels, the vagus still produces the same effect. Only the Webers' theory, therefore, remains, and the object of later researches has merely been to determine the mode and mechanism by which the retardation or inhibition of the beats is effected in vagus stimulation. The most important results of these observations are briefly stated as follows:—

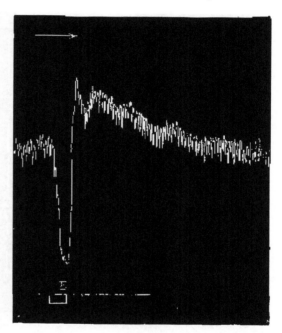

FIG. 145.—Depressor effect of strong excitation of vagus in dog. (Morat.) The period of stimulation is marked at E on the abscissa. The carotid is connected with Ludwig's kymograph.

In warm-blooded animals the standstill brought about by the vagus never lasts more than a minute. If the curve of arterial pressure is registered during vagus excitation by Ludwig's kymograph, a more or less rapid depression may be observed, according as arrest (Fig. 145), or merely slowing of the beats (Fig. 146), is obtained. The inhibitory action is more pronounced in mammals than in birds, where as a rule there is only delay (Claude Bernard), or arrest of a few seconds (Wagner, Meyer). In the poikilothermic vertebrates, on the other hand, the standstill is more pronounced than in mammals.

Cardiac arrest by vagus stimulation has repeatedly been determined on man. Henle obtained it in 1852 on a decapitated criminal, whose right auricle was still beating (*ultima moriens*): Czermak, Thanhoffer, Concato, Malerba, Wasilewsky, Cardarelli obtained it by compression or friction of the neck along the course of the vagus and the carotids. This is an *experimentum periculosum*, since it may produce disquieting systems of syncope (Thanhoffer).

The latent period of vagus excitation is comparatively long, the effect being usually manifested only after a heart-beat (Schiff, Pflüger and others), as shown in Figs. 144, 145, 146.

Excitation by a single induction shock has little effect: constant currents usually produce retardation only: tetanising induction currents are the most effective (Donders, Heidenhain, etc.

Stronger currents produce a more obvious and prolonged inhibition: minimal currents always produce delay, never acceleration of rhythm, contrary to the observations of Moleschott (v. Bezold, Pflüger, Rosenthal, etc. The frequency of the induction

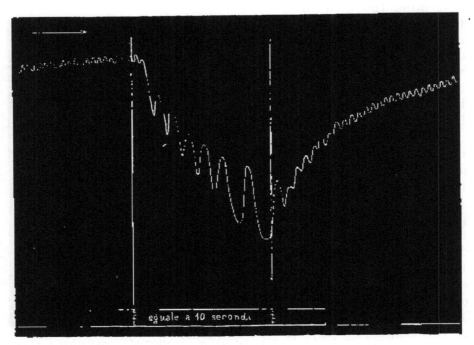

Fig. 146. Depressor effect of moderate excitation of frog's vagus. (Tigerstedt.) The two vertical lines indicate the duration of stimulation. Carotid connected with Ludwig's kymograph.

shock tells more than intensity of the stimulus (Legros and Onimus.

A difference in the inhibitory action of the two vagi has often been observed, particularly in amphibia (Meyer, Gaskell, Mac-William, Wesley Mills, Tarchanoff. In the rabbit the right vagus is often more effective than the left (Masoin). The same has been found in the horse and dog (Arloing and Tripier, and also in man (Czermak).

When on cessation of the arrest produced by the stimulation of one vagus the other is at once excited, an effect similar to the first is produced, without any resting period, if the first nerve had not been unduly fatigued (Tarchanoff, Eckhard, MacWilliam and others).

Besides the modifications of rhythm 'Engelmann's chronotropic effects) it is important to consider the changes produced by vagus excitation on the amplitude of the beats, or more exactly, on the degree of systolic contraction and diastolic expansion 'inotropic effect).

Coats was the first 1869) to note that the excitation of the vagus obstructed systole and favoured diastole. He found by exact observations, carried out in Ludwig's laboratory on the frog's heart *in situ*, connected with a recording manometer, that vagus stimulation, without moderating the rhythm, not infrequently diminished systolic contraction and augmented the diastolic expansion. It was on these and other

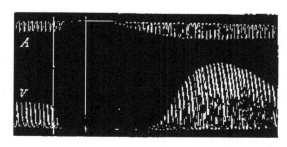

FIG. 147. Myographic tracing of frog's heart : A, Auricles, V, ventricle, with method of double suspension. (Gaskell.) Electrical excitation of the vagus in section between the two vertical lines. Shows arrest of beats, both in auricle and ventricle, which continues after the close of stimulation ; the beats subsequently recommence, and become rapidly larger than they were before stimulation.

phenomena observed in the dog, in relation to the aspiration of the heart, which increases during vagus excitation, that we in 1871 based the first principles of our theory of active diastole see Chap. VII. 8 .

Coats's results were fully confirmed and better worked out in 1882 by Heidenhain and Gaskell. The former found, on stimu-

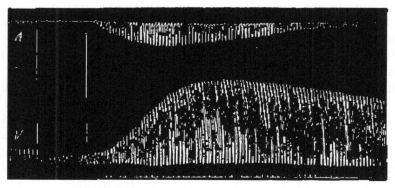

FIG. 148.—Myographic tracing of frog's heart as in preceding figure. (Gaskell.) In this case, vagus stimulation does not arrest the beats, nor retard them, but diminishes their amplitude.

lating the vagus with induction shocks thrown in at intervals of two to five seconds, that the systoles almost disappeared without diminishing in frequency.

Gaskell found that vagus arrest only occurs in the frog when the heart is well nourished, and fails to come off when it is slightly fatigued. Figs. 147 and 148 represent two curves obtained by

Gaskell, from the frog's heart, in which the inotropic negative effects of vagus stimulation on the auricles and the ventricle are simultaneously recorded. The greater diastolic relaxation produced by the vagus is not necessarily associated with diminished frequency and height of systole, since it occurs also when vagus stimulation produces no change either in frequency or intensity of the contractions. This fact, which has been substantially confirmed for mammalia by the researches of MacWilliam, Johannson and Tigerstedt, François-Franck, and especially by Stefani (Chap. VII. 8) completely justifies us in applying the term of diastolic nerves to the vagi. We shall presently consider the nature of the process by which the vagus actively incites the cardiac diastole.

In addition to producing negative chronotropic and inotropic effects, the stimulation of the vagus can also impede the conduction of the contraction wave, or, in Engelmann's nomenclature, can produce negative dromotropic effects.

Nuël found in the frog, on recording the contractions of the auricle and ventricle separately, by means of writing levers connected to those parts of the heart by threads, that vagus excitation acts more easily on the auricle than on the ventricle. Gaskell, on the other hand, has frequently observed the opposite effect, i.e. that the ventricular contractions almost disappeared, while the auricular contractions increased. In the land tortoise, he failed to establish any action of the vagus on the ventricle, while the contractions of the auricles were much reduced, without any slowing of rhythm. Wesley Mills again found in certain amphibia, reptiles, and fishes that the effect of the vagus was greater on the auricles than on the ventricle; MacWilliam, however, found the opposite on other animals. We cannot at present give any explanation of these phenomena.

Other facts, on the contrary, show clearly that vagus excitation diminishes conduction of excitation from one segment of the heart to another. Gaskell noted in tortoises that stimulation of the right vagus had no effect on the beats of the sinus venosus, while it brought the auricles and ventricle to a complete standstill. In mammalia, MacWilliam observed cases in which the auricles beat with a more frequent rhythm than the ventricles: the excitation was not propagated from the first to the second segment, although the excitability of the ventricles was undiminished. Bayliss and Starling finally discovered a method by which it is easy to show that the stimulation of the vagus produces negative dromotropic effects. They induced an artificial rhythm of the heart by direct excitation of the auricles three to four times per second, and then found that a gentle excitation of the vagus sufficed to reduce the number of ventricle beats to half the number of those of the auricle, or even stopped them for a short time, while the auricle beats continued.

Some observers have stated that during the arrest of cardiac movements produced by vagus stimulation the heart becomes inexcitable to direct artificial stimuli (Schiff, Eckhard, Mill). MacWilliam, on the other hand, observed that when, in mammals, vagus excitation produces not arrest, but pronounced weakening of the systole (negative inotropic effect), the value of the threshold of excitation, or least minimal efficacious stimulus applied directly to the auricles, rises, i.e. the excitability of the myocardium is lessened.   Engelmann found, on the contrary, in the frog's heart that during the inotropic negative effects due to stimulation of the vagus, excitability of the auricles to direct stimuli may remain unaltered, and even sometimes be augmented, which he terms the positive bathmotropic effect.   Engelmann, however, admits (experimenting always with the frog's heart) a great variety in the results of his researches.   The most frequent case is the association of negative inotropic with negative bathmotropic effects ; but other cases are to hand of simultaneous positive bathmotropic and positive inotropic effects.   At other times vague excitation gives rise now to inotropic and now to bathmotropic actions.

On the strength of this last fact more particularly, Engelmann holds that the changes of excitability in cardiac muscle (bathmotropic influence) are of a primary nature independent of the simultaneous inotropic influences.   This opinion is, however, contradicted by H. E. Hering, who holds the bathmotropic effects to be secondary and dependent on changes in the duration of the systole.

IX. The discovery that the heart receives accelerator or systolic branches of the sympathetic in addition to the inhibitory or diastolic fibres of the vagus was made in 1862 by V. Bezold, and worked out more accurately by Bevor (1866).   On dividing the two vagi and cervical sympathetics in rabbit, excitation of the medulla oblongata and cervical cord produced a rise of blood pressure, with acceleration of cardiac rhythm.   On repeating the same experiment after dividing the cord between the first and second vertebra (with the object of cutting out the influence of the bulbar vaso-motor centre of Ludwig and Thiry), acceleration was obtained without rise of pressure.   There must accordingly be accelerator nerve fibres running from the cervical cord through the rami communicantes of the sympathetic to the heart.   Von Bezold afterwards demonstrated that these accelerator fibres pass through the last cervical ganglion, and thence to the heart.

The brothers Cyon obtained the same results in 1866, on dividing the splanchnics instead of the cord ; and further observed that when the first thoracic ganglion was destroyed, there was no longer acceleration of cardiac rhythm.

Schmiedeberg (1870) detected the presence of accelerator fibres in the frog also, running with the vagus ; after a mild dose of atropine or nicotine, stimulation of these nerves no longer causes inhibition, but only acceleration of rhythm. Heidenhain (1882) and Gaskell (1884) subsequently showed that the accelerator fibres are derived from the sympathetic, and unite with the latter immediately after the vagus leaves the cranium (Fig. 149).

In 1871 Schmiedeberg, with Ludwig, studied the topography

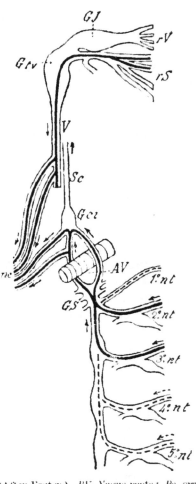

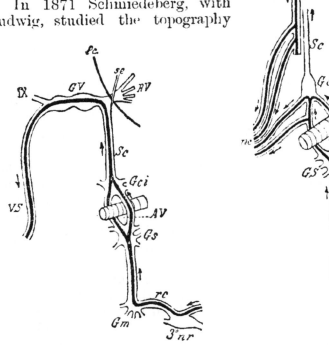

FIG. 149.—*Left*. Diagram of frog's cardiac nerves. (After Foster.) *RV*, Vagus roots; *Pe*, cranial wall; *GV*, vagus ganglion; *IX*, glosso-pharyngeal; *VS*, vago-sympathetic; *se*, cervical sympathetic, which unites with vagus ganglion; *sc*, sympathetic branch which traverses the cranium and gives off fibres to the Gasserian ganglion; *Gci*, first sympathetic ganglion receiving fibres from first spinal nerve; *AV*, annulus of Vieussens traversed by subclavian artery; *Gs*, second sympathetic ganglion receiving fibres from second spinal nerve; *Gm*, third sympathetic ganglion, which receives fibres from third spinal nerves, *3'nr*, via ramus communicans, *rc*. The direction of the arrows indicates direction, first ascending, then descending, in which the excitation of the cardiac fibres by the vago-spinal nerves is transmitted to the heart.

FIG. 150.—*Right*. Diagram of cardiac nerves in dog. (After Foster.) The upper portion of the figure represents the inhibitory fibres, the lower part the accelerators; *rV*, roots of vagus; *rS*, roots of spinal accessory, the internal roots of which, shown by black line, run in the trunk of the vagus, *V*; *GJ*, jugular ganglion; *Gtv*, ganglion of vagus trunk; *V*, trunk of vagus united with cervical sympathetic to form vago-sympathetic nerve; *Sc*, cervical sympathetic; *Gci*, inferior cervical ganglion; *AV*, annulus of Vieussens traversed by subclavian artery; *GS*, stellate or first thoracic ganglion; *nc*, cardiac nerves, of which the two upper branches come from the accessory or spinal, and the two lower from the first to the fifth thoracic nerves (particularly from second and third, as shown by black lines), the fibres of which ascend by rami communicantes to the stellate ganglion and from the loop of Vieussens. The direction of the arrows indicates the direction, first ascending, then descending, in which the activity of the cardiac nerves travels to the heart.

of the cardiac plexus in the dog, and distinguished the inhibitory from the accelerator fibres (Fig. 150).

The inhibitory fibres arise in the accessory or eleventh cranial nerve.   After extirpation of this nerve in the dog, and lapse of sufficient time for the peripheral fibres running with the vagus to degenerate, vagus stimulation produces no effect upon the heart, as was shown by Waller in 1856, and subsequently confirmed by Schiff, Heidenhain, and François-Franck.   Giannuzzi, however, found that vagus excitation still produced a slight moderator effect fourteen days after extirpation of the accessory nerve, which he ascribed to certain fibres belonging to the vagus itself, with the same function as those of the accessory.

The accelerator fibres unite the lower cervical with the first thoracic (or stellate) ganglion.   They, too, emerge from the cord (according to Stricker, in the first six thoracic nerves), and pass by the rami communicantes to the sympathetic system.   Albertoni and Bufalini found the third dorsal nerve particularly effective

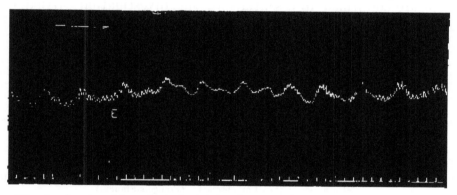

Fig. 151.—Acceleration of heart-beats by brief excitation at E of the two branches of the nerve that form the annulus of Vieussens, in curarised dog.   (Doyon.)   Carotid connected with Ludwig's kymograph.

(Fig. 151).   The cervical trunk of the vagus also seems to contain some accelerator fibres, as shown by the action of atropin (Rutherford).

The functional character of the accelerator fibres was studied by Heidenhain and Gaskell on poikilothermic, and by Schmiedeberg, Bowditch, Baxt, Boehm, François-Franck, E. Voit, and Roy and Adami more particularly on warm-blooded animals.   Their results may be summarised as follows:—

Excitation of the accelerators manifests itself after a rather long latent period, which may amount to two seconds.   The maximum of acceleration (positive chronotropic effect) first appears after ten or more seconds.   The effect of a brief excitation is therefore shown when it is over, as an after-effect.   This lasts for a considerable time, exceeding two seconds.   The duration of acceleration depends on the length of stimulus, since the accelerators are hard to fatigue, even with an excitation lasting for two minutes.

The acceleration may rise from 7 per cent to a maximal 70 per cent, according to the prevailing frequency of rhythm. The difference in effect depends principally on the frequency of rhythm previous to excitation. The maximum of acceleration is not increased when the accelerators on both sides are excited simultaneously. The duration of the after-effect is in proportion with the duration of the stimulus.

The positive inotropic and dromotropic effects must be distinguished from acceleration or positive chronotropic effects. Heidenhain and Gaskell observed on the frog that stimulation of the sympathetic fibres increases the height of systole and shortens diastole by raising the tonicity of cardiac muscle (inotropic effect); the capacity of the latter to transmit the excitation from one segment to the next (dromotropic effect) also increases; the effects from every point of view are antagonistic to those of the vagus. These facts are confirmed in essentials by the investigation carried out

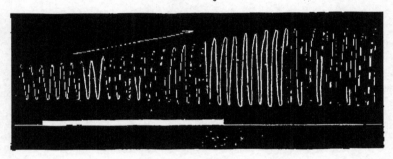

FIG. 152.—Augmentation of ventricle beats of dog after electrical tetanisation of first left accelerator nerve, as traced on abscissa. (François-Franck.)

with various experimental methods on mammals by François-Franck, Roy and Adami, Bayliss and Starling. They appear to justify the physiological name of *systolic* nerves given by us to the cardiac branches of the sympathetic, in opposition to the *diastolic* nerves or cardiac fibres of the vagus (Fig. 152).

When these two nerves (which seem to be antagonistic in function) are excited simultaneously, the effects are not algebraically summed up and cancelled, but both are expressed,—first those proper to the vagus, then those from the sympathetic. This remarkable fact was discovered on the dog by Baxt (1875) in Ludwig's laboratory. It can also be observed when the vagus is excited with minimal induction currents, and the sympathetic with strong currents to produce maximal effect (Fig. 153). The probable interpretation, according to Baxt, is that the two kinds of nerve fibres act upon the heart at two different points. During the excitation of the diastolic nerve the fibres of the systolic nerve cannot act, the excitability of the cardiac muscle being modified; they will confine themselves to storing up the latent excitability in the ganglion, to appear as an after-effect at the close of

stimulation.   It should, however, be stated that the experimental
data of Baxt, and his interpretation, have to some extent been
corrected by the subsequent work of Meltzer (1897), Reid Hunt
(1897), and Engelmann (1900); who demonstrated that the effects
consequent on the simultaneous stimulation of the two distinct
cardiac nerves are more varied and complex than was supposed by
Baxt, and that the chrono- and isotropic may be complicated by
dromotropic effects.

X. After defining cardiac inhibition due to stimulation of the
vagus as a diastolic effect, in so far as it favours diastole and

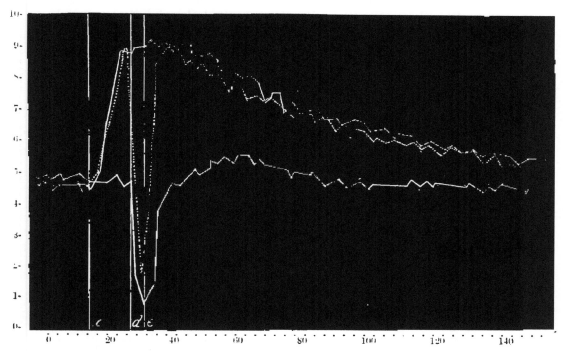

FIG. 153.— Diagram representing frequency of cardiac beats after excitation of vagus (continuous
broad line), accelerator nerves (continuous thin line), and of both nerves (dotted line).
(Baxt.)   The stimulation of the accelerators lasts from *a* to *e*, (16"), that of the vagus from *d*
to *e* (4"), and commences 12" later.   Time marked in seconds on the abscissa ; number of beats
occurring in each 2" shown on areas of ordinates

obstructs systole, and the acceleration due to the sympathetic as a
systolic effect, in so far as it favours systole and obstructs diastole,
we still have no definite idea of the inner mechanism of these
phenomena.   As, according to the supporters of the myogenic
doctrine, the automatic rhythm of the heart is a property independent of the nervous system, inherent in the muscle cells of the
myocardium, it is logical to assume that the two kinds of nerve
which influence the heart from without determine opposite results,
inasmuch as they alter the metabolism of the muscle cells—which
underlies automaticity in an opposite direction.   This was
established by Gaskell (1887) in his important discovery of the

electrical phenomena that accompany the inhibitory processes, and are the converse of those concomitant with the accelerator processes.

The intact and the resting heart are iso-electric. When any point of the walls is injured, or excited, by any cause, that point becomes galvanometrically negative in relation to the intact, or inactive, parts: and on connecting the injured, or active, point with any other intact, or inactive, point, a current known as the *demarcation*, or *action*, *current* passes through the galvanometer (Hermann).

Now Gaskell has shown that if the heart of a tortoise is arrested by the upper Stannius ligature, and the tip of the auricle killed with hot water, then on leading off the demarcation current to the galvanometer, and exciting one of the branches of the vagus (running with one of the coronary veins from the sinus venosus to the auriculo-ventricular groove), a positive variation, *i.e.* an increase of the demarcation current, is apparent. Since this effect cannot be due to increased (galvanometric) negativity of the dead point, we must assume that it is the result of augmented (galvanometric) positivity of the intact part. We must therefore conclude that excitation of the vagus in a resting heart produces modifications of its metabolism, expressed in an electrical variation, opposed to that which occurs in the contraction of cardiac muscle.

According to Gaskell, the altered metabolism produced by vagus excitation consists in an increase of reparatory or *anabolic* processes: while the stimulation of the sympathetic fibres accelerates the disintegrative or *katabolic* processes. The action of the vagus is therefore diastolic because it promotes anabolic processes, while that of the sympathetic is systolic because it promotes the katabolic processes. The probability of this theory is attested by the fact that vagus excitation is followed by a phase of increased activity as its after-effect, showing that the cardiac muscle is strengthened, not weakened, while, on the other hand, excitation of the sympathetic is followed by breaking-down, consumption, and exhaustion of the myocardium (Gaskell). The anabolic action of the vagus is, as we have seen, associated with diminished reflex excitability of the cardiac muscle (negative bathmotropic effects), so that the latter on direct stimulation no longer reacts by a contraction, save when the stimulus is excessive. This fact explains the mechanism of active diastole, as determined by the vagus: it is the effect of the lowered excitability of the myocardium, by which systole is hindered, and diastolic expansion of the muscle cells promoted.

Other facts described at different times by various authors harmonise with Gaskell's theory (which Fano was the first to bring forward in Italy). Panum and Giannuzzi observed on the rabbit that weak stimulation reinforced a previously weakened cardiac activity. Traube noticed that on interruption of artificial respiration in curarised animals, the heart beat longer when the vagi were intact than when they had been previously divided. Brown-Séquard found on bleeding two rabbits, in one of which the vagus had previously been excited, in the other not, that asphyxia and eventual arrest of the heart were produced more rapidly in the second than in the first. Konow and Stenbeck stated that the rabbit's heart *in situ*, but completely isolated from the central nervous system, beat for a shorter time, in consequence of asphyxia, than when the vagi were left intact and the spinal cord destroyed.

Lastly, the anabolic action of the vagus was confirmed by the nutritional disturbances that occur in cardiac muscle some time after the division of these nerves. Eichhorst observed in birds, and Wasilieff in rabbits, that the division of the vagi resulted in a certain degree of fatty degeneration of the myocardium. The results obtained by Fantino and Timofeew were, however, more convincing. The former confined himself to cutting one vagus, so that the operated animal remained alive for a longer period. After killing this animal he found nothing remarkable at the *post mortem*, except the atrophy and non-fatty degeneration of the muscle cells, localised in various regions, according as the right or left vagus had been divided. Timofeew divided the right vagus below the recurrens, and the left eight days later. The animal only survived the second operation three to five days. Death ensued from *adynamia cordis*, owing to degeneration of the cardiac muscle, induced by the failure of the anabolic action of the vagus.

The value of these positive data cannot be impaired by the negative results obtained on the frog by Bidder and Klug, since the metabolism of these animals is so sluggish, that they could survive inanition for many months.

XI. We must next investigate the processes by which the systolic and diastolic nerves of the heart regulate the cardiac rhythm. It has long been known that the heart sends information to the nerve centres of all modifications in its functions, but the study of its afferent nerves is more recent. While investigating the physiological function of the different branches of the cardiac plexus in the rabbit (1886) Ludwig and Cyon discovered a branch, which they termed the depressor nerve. It arises, as shown in Fig. 154, from two roots. Its division produces no change in cardiac rhythm, which proves that it is not in tonic excitation. Stimulation of its peripheral end has no effect, showing that it contains no afferent fibres. Excitation of the central end lowers arterial blood pressure, and simultaneously retards the beats of the heart. After division of the vagi this last effect is abolished, while the first remains. The slowing of the rhythm must therefore be a vagus reflex, and the arterial depression a reflex by way of the vaso-dilators. The depression of blood pressure continues after cutting out both vagi and the ganglion stellatum. Accordingly, it cannot depend on the centrifugal nerves of the cardiac plexus. After dividing the splanchnic nerve the depressor effect is much less. The vascular dilatation must, therefore, take place largely in the vessels controlled by this nerve, and only in a minor degree in other vessels.

These results were confirmed and extended by various observers on the cat, horse, dog, and pig. In poikilothermic animals no separate depressor nerves could be discovered.

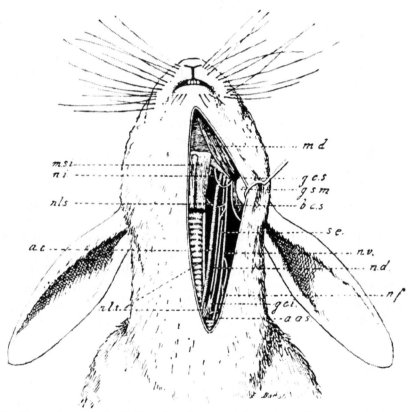

Fig. 154.—Exposed nerves of rabbit's neck. (Doyon and Morat.) *ac*, Vagus nerve; *nd*, depressor nerve, arising above in two branches, one given off from the vagus trunk, the other from the superior laryngeal; *nls*, superior laryngeal nerve; *nli*, inferior or recurrent laryngeal nerve; *bes*, external branch of spinal nerve; *ni*, hypoglossal; *gcs*, superior cervical ganglion; *sc*, cervical sympathetic; *gci*, inferior cervical ganglion; *ac*, carotid artery; *aas*, axillary ganglion; *md*, digastric muscle; *msi*, stylo-hyoid muscle.

Attempts were made to determine the exact peripheral distribution of the depressor nerve. Wooldridge and Kazem-Beck believed that its fibres entered the walls of the ventricle; more recently Köster and Tschermak (1902) discovered that its nerve-endings lay in the wall of the aorta.

It is highly probable that the depressor (which, as we have said, is not in tonic excitation) is only excited when the pressure in the aorta becomes excessive, and obstructs the systolic evacuation of the heart. The vessels then dilate, pressure falls, and the resistance which the heart has to overcome is reduced. The retarded rhythm tends to the same result.

Some interesting experiments of Sewal and Steiner illustrate this theory. On ligaturing the two carotids they observed a rise of arterial pressure, which was obviously nervous in origin, since it failed when the vagi had previously been divided. When, on the contrary, the depressors alone had been cut before ligaturing the carotids, a much greater pressor effect was obtained than with the intact depressors. They concluded that the depressors are highly sensitive to any increase of mechanical resistance presented to the functions of the heart.

In studying blood pressure during asphyxia, Konow and Stenbeck saw that it was far more irregular when the depressors had been previously divided than when they were left intact, a proof of their importance in the regulation of the circulation.

Direct proof that the rise in aortic pressure stimulates the depressors, independent of cardiac influence, was obtained by Köster and Tschermak (1902). They showed that even in the isolated heart the passive distension of the walls of the aorta, on filling it rapidly with artificial fluid, produced stimulation of the depressors, as exhibited in a negative variation (action current) of the demarcation current led off from two points of the nerve.

Spallitta and Consiglio endeavoured to ascertain whether the depressor fibres run with the vagus or the accessory. After dividing the ramus internus of the accessory, they found that excitation of the depressors produced a fall of blood pressure, but no slowing of cardiac rhythm. The depressors accordingly contain two kinds of fibres : one set cause reflex dilatation of the vessels, and belong to the vagus : the other reflexly excites the inhibitory centre of cardiac rhythm, and runs in the accessory. Mirto and Pusateri confirmed these results by histological methods. After intracranial section of the roots of the accessory nerve they found degenerated fibres in the depressor.

The afferent fibres from the heart are incapable of conveying clear or conscious sensations. This was shown by Harvey's experiments on the exposed heart of Viscount Montgomery. The indefinite *malaise* complained of in the cardiac region by cardiopaths (v. Ziemssen) may result from compression of the sensory nerves beyond the heart. Although incapable of arousing conscious sensations, the centripetal cardiac nerves are able reflexly to produce more or less diffuse movements of the skeletal muscles. Budge, Goltz, Gurboki, on pinching the heart in rabbit and frog, obtained these reflex movements, which failed when the vagi had been divided.

Even such afferent fibres of the vagus as do not belong to the heart reflexly modify cardiac rhythm. If the central end of one divided vagus is stimulated while the other is intact, a delayed rhythm is obtained, which does not appear after cutting the other vagus (v. Bezold, Drechsfeld, Aubert and Roever, etc.). The various pulmonary branches of the vagus were stimulated, according to Hering, by insufflating the lungs with open thorax, producing acceleration of cardiac rhythm, which is absent with division of the cervical vagi. The acceleration of pulse which Sommerbrodt observed in man after screaming, singing, coughing, inhaling of compressed air, is due to the same cause, i.e. to abnormal rise of bronchial pressure.

Central excitation of the superior laryngeal, as also stimulation of the laryngeal mucosa above the vocal cords, produces arrest or slowing of the heart-beat with intact vagi (François-Franck). This does not occur with centripetal excitation of the inferior laryngeal, or on stimulation of the laryngeal mucosa below the vocal cords.

On exciting the abdominal sympathetic by repeated taps of moderate strength on the belly wall, slight inhibitory phenomena are readily obtained on the frog (Goltz).

The sensory branches of the posterior spinal roots have a double reflex action on the heart, either a slowing (Cl. Bernard, François-Franck), or an acceleration of rhythm (Asp). Central excitation of the sciatic plexus by mechanical stimuli provokes inhibition, by electrical stimuli, acceleration. The muscular nerves also produce opposite effects : the same thing produces inhibition with a strong stimulus, acceleration with a weaker one. When chemically excited (e.g. by inhalation of chloroform), the sensory fibres of the trigeminus readily induce slowing and even arrest of the heart, and syncope, which has a great practical significance. The nerves of the special senses also act in this twofold way upon the heart.

XII. The afferent nerves of the heart affect the efferent through centres which determine the reflex effects.

The centre of the diastolic nerves is in the bulb or medulla oblongata (E. Weber, Budge). In the frog it extends from the optic lobes to the tip of the calamus scriptorius. In the rabbit it is apparently confined to the bulb (François-Franck). In the cat there is about half-way up the rhomboid sinus, a point at which excitation by a needle produces arrest or slowing of the heart (Laborde).

The centre for the systolic nerves has up to the present not been exactly located. The whole upper section of the cervical cord reacts by acceleration of cardiac rhythm.

Although the paths are not yet exactly determined, it must be remembered that the cardiac centres are in connection with the cortical and subcortical centres of the brain. The influence of psychical states upon the heart is undeniable : some people even have the faculty of voluntarily influencing their heart-beats.

It is probable that under normal conditions the cardiac

centres are in continuous slight excitation, on which depends the tone of the vagi, exhibited in the acceleration of the beats, on simple division of that nerve, or administration of atropin. This effect does not appear when section of the vagus is preceded by division of the cervical cord (Bernstein). Acceleration is also obtained after dividing the splanchnic nerve (Asp), due not to the lowering of blood pressure, which usually produces the opposite effect, but to the depression of vagal tonus. In the newborn, tonicity seems to be wanting in the vagus till after the second week, since in kittens neither section of the vagus nor exhibition of atropine causes acceleration of pulse (Soltmann).

It is possible that the systolic nerves and centres also have normally a certain tonicity, although subordinate to the diastolic nerves. After extirpation of the lower cervical and stellate ganglia on both sides, there is, when the vagi are divided, a marked acceleration of rhythm (Tschirjew, Stricker, and Wagner). With intact vagi, a permanent slowing of beat can be obtained on dividing the accelerators (Timofeew).

The tone of the cardiac centres and nerves may be *automatic* or *reflex*, or as is most probable, *automatic and reflex* in character. It is known that the frequency of cardiac rhythm normally stands in inverse ratio to the height of the average arterial blood pressure, *i.e.* that rise of blood pressure produces lowering of pulse frequency and *vice versa*. After section of the vagi this ratio is no longer so distinct and constant, showing that the blood-pressure regulates the tone of the cardiac nerve centres, those of the vagus in particular, directly or reflexly.

BIBLIOGRAPHY

In addition to previous Bibliographies, see also : -
Fundamental Memoirs *in re* Physiology of Cardiac Muscle and Intracardiac Nervous System : —

STANNIUS. Arch. f. Anat. u. Physiol., 1852.
ECKHARD. Beiträge zur Anat. und Physiol. (Giessen, 1858-60. Experimentelle Physiol. des Nervensystems. Giessen, 1866.
GOLTZ. Arch. für path. Anat., 1860-62.
BOWDITCH. Ber. d. sächs. Ges. d. Wiss., 1871.
LUCIANI. Ber. d. sächs. Ges d. Wiss., 1873. Edizione italiana, Rivista clinica di Bologna, 1873.
KRONECKER und STIRLING. Beiträge zur Anat. und Physiol., 1874.
MAREY. Compt. rend., 1879.
GASKELL. Arch. de physiol. normale et pathologique par Brown-Séquard, 1888.
FANO. Lo Sperimentale, 1885. Archivio per le scienze mediche, 1890. Archives ital. de biologie, 1888.
ENGELMANN. Arch. néerlandaises, 1893-97. Arch. f. Anat. u. Physiol., 1902.
KRONECKER. Zeitschrift für Biologie, 1897.
BOTTAZZI. Pubblicazioni del R. Istituto di Studi superiori di Firenze, 1897.
H. E. HERING. Pflügers Arch. lxxxvi., 1901 ; cxv., 1906 ; cxvi., 1907.
A. J. CARLSON. American Journal of Physiology, xii., 1905.
F. B. HOFMANN. Nagel's Handbuch der Physiol. i., 1905.
M. HUMBLET. Arch. intern. de Physiol., 1904, i.
E. VON CYON. Die Nerven des Herzens. Berlin, 1907.

Physiology of Intracardiac Nerves and Centres that control the Functions of the
  Heart :—

E. WEBER. Annali universali di medicina di Omodei, 1845. Handwörterbuch der
  Physiol., 1846.
BUDGE. Handwörterbuch der Physiol., 1846.
SCHIFF. Arch. f. phys. Heilkunde, 1849.
v. BEZOLD. Untersuchungen über die Innervation des Herzens. Leipzig, 1863.
LUDWIG und CYON. Ber. d. sächs. Ger. d. Wiss., 1866.
COATS. Ber. d. sächs. Ges. d. Wiss., 1869.
SCHMIEDEBERG. Ber. d. sächs. Ges. d. Wiss., 1870.
BAXT. Arch. f. Anat. u. Physiol., 1877.
HEIDENHAIN. Arch. f. d. ges. Physiol., 1882.
GASKELL. Philosophical Transactions, 1882. Journal of Physiol., 1882-87.
  Beiträge zur Physiol., C. Ludwig gewidmet. Leipzig, 1887.
FRANÇOIS-FRANCK. Travaux du laboratoire de Marey. 1880.
PAWLOW. Arch. f. Anat. u. Physiol., 1887.

Chemical Conditions essential to the Survival of the Isolated Heart :

H. OEHRWALL. Arch. f. Anat. u. Physiol., 1893. Skandin. Arch. vii., 1897.
G. I. GÖTHLIN. Skandin. Arch. f. Physiol. xii., 1902.
H. WINTERSTEIN. Zeitsch. f. allgem. Physiol. iv., 1904.
O. LANGENDORFF. Arch. f. Anat. und Physiol., 1884. Pflügers Arch., 1895, lxi.;
  1899, lxxviii. Herzmuskel und intrakardiale Innervation. Ergebnisse der
  Physiol., 1. Jahrg., 2. Abt. (322 other works cited). Neuere Untersuchungen
  über die Ursache des Herzschlages, Ibidem, 1905 73 other recent works
  cited).
S. BAGLIONI. Zeitsch. f. allgem. Physiol. vi., 1907.
LOCKE and ROSENHEIM. Journal of Physiology, xxxvi., 1907.
E. L. BACKMAN. Festschrift f. O. Hammarsten, 1906.

Recent English Literature :—

E. C. WALDEN. Comparison of the Effect of certain Inorganic Solutions and
  Solutions containing Serum Albumin on the Rhythmic Contractility of the
  Frog's Heart. Amer. Journ. of Physiol., 1900, iii. 123.
J. A. MACWILLIAM. Further Researches on the Physiology of the Mammalian
  Heart, Part I. On the Influence of Chloroform upon the Rate of the Heart-
  beat, etc., etc. Journ. of Physiol., 1899-1900, xxv. 233.
A. W. CADMAN. The Position of the Respiratory and Cardio-inhibitory Fibres in
  the Rootlets of the 9th, 10th, and 11th Cranial Nerves. Journ. of Physiol.,
  1900-1901, xxvi. 42.
T. G. BRODIE and A. E. RUSSELL. On Reflex Cardiac Inhibition. Journ. of
  Physiol., 1900-1901, xxvi. 92.
D. J. LINGLE. The Action of certain Ions on Ventricular Muscle. Amer.
  Journ. of Physiol., 1901, iv. 265.
W. H. HOWELL. An Analysis of the Influence of the Sodium, Potassium, and
  Calcium Salts of the Blood on the Automatic Contractions of Heart Muscle.
  Amer. Journ. of Physiol., 1902, vi. 181.
D. J. LINGLE. The Importance of Sodium Chloride in Heart Activity. Amer.
  Journ. of Physiol., 1903, viii. 75.
R. S. WOODWORTH. Maximal Contraction, Staircase Contraction, Refractory
  Period and Compensatory Pause of the Heart. Amer. Journ of Physiol.,
  1903, viii. 213.
E. G. MARTIN. An Experimental Study of the Rhythmic Activity of Isolated
  Strips of the Heart-muscle. Amer. Journ. of Physiol., 1904, xi. 103.
E. G. MARTIN. The Inhibitory Influence of Potassium Chloride on the Heart,
  and the Effect of Variations of Temperature upon this Inhibition and the
  Vagus Inhibition. Amer. Journ. of Physiol., 1904, xi. 370.
A. J. CARLSON. Contribution to the Physiology of the Heart of the California
  Hagfish (Bdellostoma Dombeyi). Zeitschr. f. allgem. Physiol., 1904, iv. 259.
A. J. CARLSON. The Nervous Origin of the Heart-beat in Limulus, and the
  Nervous Nature of Co-ordination or Conduction in the Heart. Amer. Journ.
  of Physiol., 1905, xii. 67.

A. J. Carlson. Further Evidence of the Nervous Origin of the Heart-beat in *Limulus*. Amer. Journ. of Physiol., 1905, xii. 471.

S. R. Benedict. The Rôle of certain Ions in Rhythmic Heart Activity. Amer. Journ. of Physiol., 1905, xiii. 192.

A. J. Carlson. The Nature of Cardiac Inhibition, with special reference to the Heart of *Limulus*. Amer. Journ. of Physiol., 1905, xiii. 217.

A. J. Carlson. Comparative Physiology of the Invertebrate Heart. Part II. Amer. Journ. of Physiol., 1905, xiii. 396; Part III. *ibid.*, 1905, xiv. 16; Part IV. *ibid.* 1905-6, xv. 127; Parts V., VI., VII., VIII., *ibid.*, 1906, xvi. 47, 67, 85, 100.

W. H. Howell and W. W. Duke. Experiments on the Isolated Mammalian Heart to show the Relation of the Inorganic Salts to the Action of the Accelerator and Inhibitory Nerves. Journ. of Physiol., 1906-7, xxxv. 131.

A. J. Carlson. Comparative Physiology of the Invertebrate Heart. Part IX. Zeitschr. f. allgem. Physiol., 1907, vi. 287.

W. T. Porter. Studies in the Physiology of Muscle. Observations on the Tonus of Heart Muscle. Amer. Journ. of Physiol., 1905-6, xv. 1.

T. Sollmann. The Revival of the Excised Mammalian Heart by Perfusion with Oil. Amer. Journ. of Physiol., 1905-6, xv. 121.

A. J. Carlson. On the Mechanism of Co-ordination and Conduction in the Heart, with special reference to the Heart of *Limulus*. Amer. Journ. of Physiol., 1905-6, xv. 99.

W. H. Howell. Vagus Inhibition of the Heart in its Relation to the Inorganic Salts of the Blood. Amer. Journ. of Physiol., 1905-6, xv. 280.

J. Erlanger. Further Studies on the Physiology of Heart Block. Amer. Journ. of Physiol., 1906, xvi. 160.

A. J. Carlson. On the Chemical Conditions for the Heart Activity, with special reference to the Heart of *Limulus*. Amer. Journ. of Physiol., 1906. xvi. 378.

F. S. Locke and O. Rosenheim. Contribution to the Physiology of the Isolated Heart. The Consumption of Dextrose by Cardiac Muscle. Journ. of Physiol., 1907-8. xxxvi. 205.

C. C. Guthrie and F. H. Pike. The Relation of the Activity of the Excised Mammalian Heart to Pressure in the Coronary Vessels and to its Nutrition. Amer. Journ. of Physiol., 1907, xviii. 14.

H. E. Eggers. The Rhythm of the Turtle's Sinus Venosus in Isotonic Solutions of Non-electrolytes. Amer. Journ of Physiol., 1907, xviii. 64.

A. J. Carlson. On the Mechanism of Refractory Period in the Heart. Amer. Journ. of Physiol., 1907, xviii. 71.

A. D. Hirschfelder and J. A. E. Eyster. Extrasystoles in the Mammalian Heart. Amer. Journ. of Physiol., 1907, xviii. 222.

J. Erlanger and J. R. Blackman. A Study on Relative Rhythmicity and Conductivity in various Regions of the Auricles of the Mammalian Heart. Amer. Journ. of Physiol., 1907, xix. 125.

D. R. Hooker. May Reflex Cardiac Acceleration occur independently of the Cardio-inhibitory Centre? Amer. Journ. of Physiol., 1907, xix. 417.

T. G. Brodie and W. C. Cullis. An Apparatus for the Perfusion of the Isolated Mammalian Heart. Journ. of Physiol., 1908, xxxvii. 337.

G. N. Stewart. Some Observations on the Behaviour of the Automatic Respiratory and Cardiac Mechanisms after Complete and Partial Isolation from Extrinsic Nerve Impulses. Amer. Journ. of Physiol., 1907-8, xx. 407.

A. J. Carlson. The Conductivity produced in the Non-conducting Myocardium of *Limulus* by Sodium Chloride in Isotonic Solution. Amer. Journ. of Physiol., 1908, xxi. 11.

A. J. Carlson. A Note on the Refractory State of the Non-automatic Heart Muscle of the *Limulus*. Amer. Journ. of Physiol., 1908, xxi. 19.

A. J. Carlson and W. J. Meek. On the Mechanism of the Embryonic Heart Rhythm in *Limulus*. Amer. Journ. of Physiol., 1908, xxi. 1.

W. H. Howell and W. W. Duke. The Effect of Vagus Inhibition on the Output of Potassium from the Heart. Amer. Journ. of Physiol., 1908,

W. J. MEEK. The Relative Resistance of the Heart Ganglia, the Intrinsic Nerve Plexus, and the Heart Muscle to the Action of Drugs. Amer. Journ. of Physiol., 1908, xxi. 230.

W. H. SCHULTZ. Studies in Heart Muscle. The Refractory Period and the Period of Varying Irritability. Amer. Journ. of Physiol., 1908, xxii. 133.

A. J. CARLSON. Comparative Physiology of the Invertebrate Heart. Part X. Amer. Journ. of Physiol., 1908, xxii. 353.

H. J. B. FRY. The Influence of the Visceral Nerves upon the Heart in Cephalopods. Journ. of Physiol., 1909-10, xxxix. 184.

J. ERLANGER. Can Functional Union be re-established between the Mammalian Auricles and Ventricles after Destruction of a Segment of the Auriculo-Ventricular Bundle ? Amer. Journ. of Physiol., 1909, xxiv. 375.

CHAPTER X

PHYSIOLOGY OF VASCULAR MUSCLE AND NERVES

SUMMARY.—1. Discovery of vasomotor nerves. 2. Vascular tone and its rhythmic and a-rhythmical variations, as depending essentially upon the automatic and reflex excitability of the smooth muscle cells. 3. Theory of vaso-constrictor nerves. 4. Theory of vaso-dilator nerves. 5. Vascular reflexes. 6. Bulbar vaso-constrictor centre. 7. Spinal and cerebral centres for vaso-constrictor nerves. 8. Centres for vaso-dilator nerves. Bibliography.

THE preceding chapter on the physiology of cardiac muscle and the cardiac nerves will facilitate our investigation of the physiology of the muscle cells and nerves with which the walls of the blood-vessels are provided. As we shall see, there is an exact analogy between the physiological phenomena in both cases.

I. After Haller, Spallanzani, Magendie, and Poiseuille had demonstrated the possibility of the circulation of the blood, in virtue simply of the heart's activity as a force-pump, and the physical elasticity of the blood-vessels, the older theories as to the importance to the circulation of the muscle cells and vascular nerve fibre were disregarded and almost forgotten. At the commencement of the last century, however, certain normal and pathological phenomena, which directly contradicted the purely mechanical theory, again attracted the attention of physicians and physiologists. Among these are: abnormal conditions of temperature and nutrition in paralysed limbs, circulatory changes (blushes and pallor) due to emotional states or to neuralgia, hyperaemia, and congestion at the seat of inflammation, pneumonia after section of the vagi, panophthalmia on dividing the trigeminal, failure of erection of penis, when the spinal nerves have been divided, and so on.

The precursors of the physiology of the active movements of the vessels included E. H. Weber (1831), Henle (1840), Stilling (1840), Valentin and Schiff (1844), who adumbrated not a few of the facts and theories which subsequently received experimental confirmation.

In 1851 Claude Bernard discovered and described the phenomena that occur in the vessels of the rabbit's ear, on

341

division of the cervical sympathetic, after which the notion of vascular nerves became familiar. Cl. Bernard was more struck by the marked rise of temperature in all parts supplied by the sympathetic than by the dilatation of the vessels, so much so that in 1852 he gave an erroneous interpretation of the same, declaring the sympathetic to be a thermal nerve. Shortly afterwards, however, Brown-Séquard completed the discovery by describing the converse phenomena that occur in the vessels of the ear, when the peripheral end of the divided nerve is excited by an electrical stimulus. This he rightly interpreted as meaning that the primary effects were dilatation and constriction of the vessels, the secondary effects, the warming or cooling of the parts supplied; and he gave the name of vaso-constrictors to the rami auriculares of the cervical sympathetic system. A. Waller almost simultaneously confirmed these same facts and their significance, without knowing of Brown-Séquard's publication.

In 1854, M. Schiff, observing the vessels of the rabbit's ear by transmitted light, described an irregular succession of contractions and dilatations, which are much slower than the rhythm of the heart, and quite independent of it. Owing to these undulations, the flow of blood through the ear alternately diminishes and increases (*ischaemia* and *hyperaemia*), with a consequent fall and rise of its temperature, blood pressure, and volume.

In 1856 he showed indirectly that besides the vaso-constrictors, vaso-dilators are also present in the cervical sympathetic, so that the rhythm, which he detected in the vessels of the ear, must be regarded as the result of the alternate functional predominance of one or other kind of vasomotor nerve. He found when the animal was artificially warmed some days after dividing the cervical sympathetic, or was forced to take violent movements, or infected with a septic or toxic fever, that the vessels of the ear on the normal side showed much greater vascular dilatation, hyperaemia and heating than those on the operated side, a fact which led Schiff to the conclusion that the former were under the control of dilator nerves, which in the second case had been divided.

Schiff's view was brilliantly confirmed in 1858 by Claude Bernard, who discovered the effect produced in the vessels of the submaxillary gland of the dog, by electrical stimulation of that branch of the facial nerve which traverses the tympanic cavity, joins the lingual branch of the trigeminal, and then under the name of chorda tympani passes partly into the tongue, partly to the submaxillary and sublingual glands. That the chorda tympani contains vaso-dilator fibres is shown by the fact that its stimulation produces marked hyperaemia of all the vessels of the submaxillary gland, associated with such marked acceleration of the blood-stream that the flow through the glands has scarcely

time to acquire the characteristics of venous blood, while the
pulse wave of the arteries passes beyond the capillaries, and
reaches the small veins (Fig. 155).

There are, accordingly, *constrictor* and *dilator* nerves to the
blood-vessels : the former correspond to the systolic, the latter to
the diastolic, nerves of the heart. Vascular rhythm and tonicity
are analogous to cardiac rhythm and tonicity. Just as the
innervation of the heart regulates the circulation as a whole, so
the innervation of the vessels regulates the circulation in the
several vascular regions. The same questions as were examined

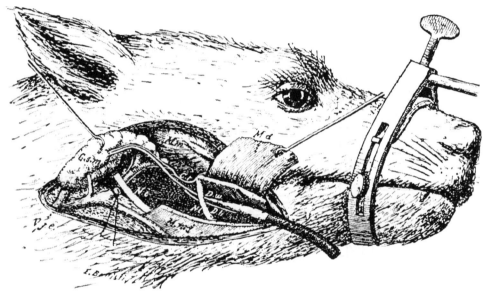

Fig. 155.—Operative procedure for exposing submaxillary gland, duct, nerves and vessels.
(Cl. Bernard.) *Gsm*, Submaxillary gland : *Dw*, Wharton's duct, into which a glass cannula is
inserted to draw off the saliva secreted by the gland ; *Db*, Bertholin's duct to sublingual ;
N7, lingual nerve ; *Ct*, chorda tympani, running to gland along with excretory duct ; *C*, carotid
accompanied by small nerve branches of sympathetic *ss* ; *Vje*, external jugular vein ; *V*,
efferent vein from gland ; *Ni*, hypoglossal nerve ; *Md*, anterior half of digastric muscle, lifted
by hook ; *Mmj*, mylo-hyoid muscle, cut so as to expose the lingual nerve, and excretory ducts
beneath it ; *Mv*, masseter muscles.

and discussed in studying the active movements of the heart
crop up in the study of the active movements of the vessels.
We must therefore consider separately the rhythm and the tone
of the vessels, the vaso-constrictors, and the vaso-dilators, in the
better-known vascular regions.

II. The slow rhythm of dilatation and constriction, as first
described by Schiff for the vessels of the rabbit's ear, is no isolated
phenomenon. It was observed by Wharton Jones in the vessels of
the bat's wing, by Saviotti on the frog's peritoneal arteries, by
Riegel in the small mesenteric arteries and web of the same
animal. In this category must also be included the long irregular
waves "of the third order," which are independent of cardiac rhythm
and respiratory movements, and were first noted in blood-pressure

curves by Traube and Hering. Lastly (1875), Mosso found with his plethysmograph (Fig. 156) that the volume of the human forearm exhibits the same long and irregular oscillations, which can only be interpreted as the effects of a peculiar rhythm of alternate contractions and dilatations of the vessels of the limb. Von Basch

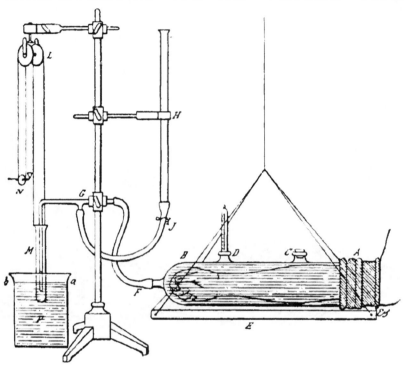

FIG. 156.—Mosso's plethysmograph, for recording slow variations in volume of vessels of forearm (diagram). A, B, glass cylinder to receive the forearm, closed by rubber band; this rests on the board E, which is suspended from the ceiling by a wire; C, opening closed with a cork, through which the cylinder can be filled with lukewarm water; D, opening through which a thermometer is passed, showing temperature of water; F, G, tube through which the cylinder containing the forearm communicates with the small cylinder M, which floats above the level of the fluid a, b, contained in large vessel P; N, lead weight carrying the pen to write on moving cylinder of kymograph, which counterpoises M, with which it is connected by two silk threads passing over the double pulley L; H, J, burette that can be raised or lowered in adding or changing the water in the float. The instrument works as follows: when the vessels of the forearm contract, an amount of water corresponding with the diminution in volume is aspirated from the float M to the cylinder A, B; this raises the float and depresses the counterpoise N, which records the diminution of volume on the revolving cylinder. When, on the contrary, the vessels of the forearm dilate, a quantity of water in the cylinder A, B is driven out into M, so that it sinks, and N is raised, recording the increase of volume. To avoid positive or negative pressure above the forearm immersed in the cylinder A, B, care must be taken that its upper level is at the same level a, b as the water contained in the receiver P where M is floating.

(1876) confirmed Mosso's facts with a weighing plethysmograph, which gives more relative values than Mosso's apparatus. From all these observations it appears probable that the autochthonous rhythm of the vessels is common to many other vascular tracts that have not yet been fully examined (Figs. 157 and 158).

It must not, however, be assumed that rhythmical activity is continuous and constant in all vascular regions: in most cases, indeed, the microscopic study of transparent vascular tracts shows no alteration in the diameters of the vessels, which may remain for a considerable time in the state intermediate between excessive dilatation and excessive constriction, which is commonly known as tonus or tonic contraction of the vessels.

Vascular rhythm, being much slower and less regular, does not correspond with the *functional* rhythm of the heart, *i.e.* with the alternation of cardiac systole and diastole. On the other hand, it does correspond, and is in strict analogy, with the *tonic* rhythm discovered by Fano in the walls of the tortoise auricle, and results from the alternate contraction and expansion of the sarcoplasm of the smooth spindle-shaped muscle cells of the tunica media, particularly in the small arteries.

The tone and rhythmical activity of the veins is obscure, and has been little studied; their muscular cells are few in number, and vary considerably in different regions and tissues. The veins of the bones and brain have no contractile elements: the veins of the portal system are highly muscular It is only at the extreme ends of the venae cavae and pulmonary veins, where they open into the auricles, that, in addition to a perhaps slowly varying tonus, we find any rapid and fairly regular rhythmicalactivity,such as gives rise to the systolic and diastolic rhythm of the heart.

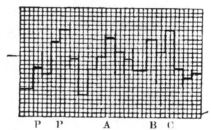

Fig. 157.—Tracings obtained with plethysmograph of Fig. 156. (Mosso.) The revolving drum is moved on a short distance at each minute, so that the writing point traces a horizontal line. The variations in volume that occur during the minute in which the drum is stationary are indicated by vertical lines, which show the extent of the oscillations in volume during that period. In this case each cm. in height from the ordinate corresponds to 2 c.c. of blood. At P, P the subject replied to questions put by the experimenter. At A he raised his left hand to rub his nose, at B to rub his ear. At C he heard the sound of an electric bell.

The autochthonous activity of the vessels, whether tonic or rhythmic, resembles that of the heart, in being *automatic, i.e.* independent of external stimuli acting on the muscle cells. This conclusion is reached, not merely by analogy, which in this instance is of great value, but also by direct observation, from which every unbiased observer must perceive that the oscillations of tone in the vessels of the rabbit's ear are independent of changes in external conditions. It is uncertain whether the tonic and rhythmic activity of the vessels is, like that of the heart, an inherent property of the muscle cells, as claimed by the myogenists, or whether it is brought about by the peripheral ganglia and nerve fibres which are particularly abundant in the walls of the arteries, where they form a delicate plexus round the smooth muscle cells. Experience shows that the neuro-paralytic hyperaemia and rise of temperature consequent on the division of all the nerves of the limb does not persist, but disappears gradually, so that after some days the paralysed limb is more ischaemic and cooler than the healthy limb on the opposite side (Goltz and others). This means that the muscle cells, or peripheral ganglionic elements, may, independent of the nerve centres, acquire a degree of tonic contraction in excess of the normal. On the other hand we know that even excised organs, *e.g.* the dog's kidney, artificially circulated, exhibit with the

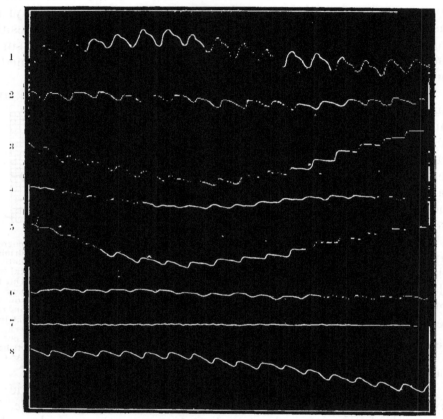

Fig. 158.—Plethysmogram of forearm, obtained by connecting the cylinder, A. B, of plethysmograph with a Marey's writing tambour. (Mosso.) The rotating drum moves at uniform speed. The experiment was performed in an iron room, where the air could be compressed to various measurable pressures. Each tracing, in addition to the plethysmograms of the pulse, shows the slow oscillations in volume of the forearm which depend on the oscillations of vascular tone. 1, Tracing made before compression of air; 2, at 100 mm. Hg compression; 3, at 100 mm. Hg; 4, at 80 mm. Hg; 5 at 50 mm. Hg; 6, at ordinary barometric pressure; 7, two minutes after return to ordinary barometric pressure; 8, a quarter of an hour later.

plethysmographic method constant irregular oscillations of volume, which obviously depend on oscillations of tone in the renal vessels (Mosso, 1874).

A similar effect was noted by Bernstein in the amputated paw of the dog. So, too, the work of Bayliss (1901), on the reaction of certain blood-vessels to changes of blood pressure, shows that the vascular muscles are capable of altering their tone independent of the nervous system. Bayliss found on recording the changes in volume of the hind limb of an animal, completely separated from the central nervous system by the plethysmograph, that artificial depression of blood pressure—caused by compression of the abdominal aorta, or by stimulating the peripheral trunk of the vagus, or depressor nerve—produced an initial shrinkage of volume. Even during the fall of blood pressure, however, there was a gradual return to the earlier volume, while after normal pressure was restored there was a marked increase in volume, a proof that the vessels reacted to the fall of blood pressure by a definite dilatation. Artificial rise of blood pressure (e.g. from stimulation of the splanchnic, produced constriction of the vessels of the limb.

The muscular coat of the vessels (like the muscular wall of the heart) is automatically active both in constriction and in dilatation—the former caused by the shortening, the latter by the lengthening or expansion of the sarcoplasm of the spindle-shaped muscle cells. This hypothesis, which found little favour when we propounded it in 1871-73, as the logical deduction from Weber's theory of muscular elasticity, is now, on the strength of recent work on the automatic rhythmicity of the cardiac muscle cells (that of Gaskell and Engelmann in particular), not only unopposed, but even included, in many modern text-books. "We have repeatedly insisted" (says Foster [1]) "that the relaxation of a muscular fibre is as much a complex vital process, is as truly the result of the metabolism of the muscular substance, as the contraction itself: and there is *a priori* no reason why a nervous impulse should not govern the former as it does the latter."

Vascular tonicity and its slow rhythmical oscillations (Fig. 158) are probably inherent properties of the smooth muscle cells and the vascular nerves that direct and regulate them, since they exert a double and opposite influence, katabolic and anabolic, upon the metabolism of muscle. The vaso-constrictors function by promoting the dissimilatory processes; the vaso-dilators, on the contrary, by favouring the assimilatory processes of cellular sarcoplasm. The first are therefore katabolic, the second anabolic nerves to the vessels. The active movements of the vessels are thus regulated by mechanisms perfectly analogous to those which govern the active movements of the heart.

III. It is known, on the strength of numerous experiments, that every vascular region is supplied with *vaso-constrictor nerves*. This is plain on recapitulating the most important heads of the copious literature of the subject.

The great splanchnic nerve contains numerous constrictor fibres which supply the most extended area, since it controls the blood-vessels of the greater portion of the abdominal viscera. Ludwig and Cyon (1866), v. Bezold and Bever (1867), found

[1] *Text-Book of Physiology*, Part I. p. 313, 5th ed., 1888.

that division of this nerve produced a marked fall of lateral pressure in the aorta, while stimulation of the peripheral end of the divided nerve raised the pressure above that which obtained before section. On investigating the state of the visceral vessels after section. marked congestion was observed in the venous portal system, with distinct hyperaemia of the small vessels of the mesentery, intestinal canal, and renal parenchyma. These effects are more pronounced in the rabbit than in the dog (Asp), apparently because in herbivores the gastric canal is much longer than in carnivores.

The constrictor fibres of the splanchnic run to the coeliac plexus, and thence to the stomach, intestines, and kidneys. Excitation of the splanchnic on one side only causes the vessels of both kidneys to contract (Cohnheim and Roy).

The constrictor fibres of the hepatic vessels also emerge from the splanchnic, and pass to the coeliac plexus, and thence to the liver, along the bile-duct and hepatic artery (Vulpian). The vaso-constrictors of the spleen come from the left splanchnic, and perhaps also from the right (Roy).

It is known from other observations that the great splanchnic does not contain all the vaso-constrictor fibres of the abdominal viscera. The lesser splanchnic has fibres of the same character (Asp), and the abdominal branches of the vagus also appear to contain vaso-constrictors for the spleen (Oehl).

Next to the great splanchnic, the vaso-constrictor nerve which supplies the most extended tract is certainly the cervical sympathetic, which not only regulates tonicity in the vessels of the ear, as discovered by Claude Bernard, but also exerts its constrictor function on all other external and internal vessels of the head, as appears from the investigations of several observers.

It was plain from the work of Budge and Waller (1853) that the constrictor fibres of the cervical sympathetic did not arise in the ganglia situated along its course, but in the anterior roots of the spinal nerves, whence they emerged by the rami communicantes. The constrictor fibres run principally with the vessels round which they form a plexus; but they are partly associated with the cerebral nerves, leaving them again later, to join the vessels. Thus the hypoglossal and lingual branches of the trigeminal contain vaso-constrictor fibres for the tongue (Vulpian). The facial nerve, again, contains many fibres of the same kind, so that division of this nerve is followed by a rise of temperature in the whole face (Cl. Bernard). These vaso-constrictor fibres do not originate in the centres of the cerebral nerves, seeing that destruction of these centres produces no sign of vascular paralysis. They probably emerge from the sympathetic.

It is, however, possible that besides the constrictor fibres from the sympathetic, the vessels of the head are affected by other constrictor fibres, the origin of which is not yet determined. Thus, *e.g.*, the vessels of the ear also receive constrictors from the second and third nerves of the cervical plexus (Schiff, Lovèn, etc.).

The vaso-constrictors of the limbs run principally to the cutaneous vessels, the vessels of the muscles being less well supplied with motor nerves (Sadler, Hafiz, Grützner and Heidenhain, and others).

The vaso-constrictors of the fore-limbs originate in the anterior roots of the median tract of the thoracic cord (third to seventh nerves), join the sympathetic, and unite at the first thoracic ganglion with the ramifications of the brachial plexus. The cervical roots which contribute to the formation of this plexus contain no vaso-constrictor fibres (Cl. Bernard, Cyon, etc.). Some of these fibres accompany the vessels of the limb directly, without joining the branches of the brachial plexus (Vulpian).

The vaso-constrictors of the lower limbs have been more studied. They emerge, not from the roots of the lower segment of the cord, but from the thoracic tract and upper segment of the lumbar cord, particularly from the eleventh, twelfth, and thirteenth dorsal, and the first and second lumbar nerves (Bayliss and Bradford). They pass by the rami communicantes to the thoracic and abdominal sympathetic, then, for the most part, joining the great nerve trunks to the limbs, the sciatic especially; while a few only accompany the vessels of the limbs direct from the abdominal ganglia.

It is clear from the consensus of observations on the vaso-constrictors in different regions that they originate principally in the anterior roots of the dorsal tract of the cord, pass by way of the rami communicantes to the ganglion sympathetic system, and thence run directly or indirectly to the vessels, where they form a fine plexus round the muscular tunica media. Their excitability is less, and their latent period longer than that of the motor nerves to the skeletal muscles, and they are constantly in a certain state of activity, on which the tone of the vessels depends. Section of these nerves accordingly produces vascular atony and subsequent hyperaemia, while excitation of the peripheral cord produces constriction or vascular hypertonia and subsequent ischaemia.

What modifications in local blood pressure and velocity of circulation are produced by such hyperaemia or ischaemia? Little was known definitely before Dastre and Morat published their observations on the horse. They employed two sphygmoscopes, one applied to the facial artery, the other to the facial vein of the animal. They found that ligation or section of the cervical sympathetic caused a fall of blood pressure in the artery, and a rise in the vein (local circulatory delay). Stimulation of the nerve, on the contrary, produced rise of arterial and fall of venous pressure (local acceleration of circulation), followed by the contrary phenomenon, viz. fall of arterial and rise of venous pressure, greater than that which occurs on simple division of the nerve (local circulatory delay) in consequence of fatigue (Fig. 159).

The fact of vascular ultra-dilatation is very interesting, as it implies that strong and persistent excitation of the nerve exhausts the peripheral ganglia, and thus depresses the tone which these maintain in the vessels even after the nerve has been divided.

IV. Since 1874, the theory of *vaso-dilator nerves* has been much developed. Next to Bernard's discovery of the vaso-dilator fibres contained in the chorda tympani (referred to above), the discovery of the nervi erigentes of the penis by Eckhardt 1863 demands special mention. These nerves are

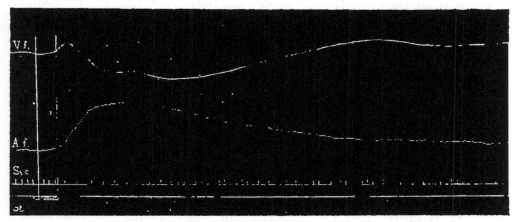

FIG. 159. Effect on arterial and venous pressure in facial vessels of electrically exciting the peripheral trunk of horse's cervical sympathetic. (Dastre and Morat.) *Af*, tracing of blood pressure in peripheral trunk of facial artery ; *Vf*, of facial vein. The excitation took place at the part between the two vertical lines, marked on abscissa by an electric signal separate from that which shows the time in seconds. The tracings show that stimulation of the sympathetic is followed by a rise of arterial and fall of venous pressure (preceded by temporary rise due to increased outflow), which is succeeded by the opposite effect, *i.e.* fall of arterial, and rise of venous pressure, due to extra-dilatation of vessels.

branches from the sacral plexus, which, when peripherally stimulated, cause erectile swelling of the corpora cavernosa, due not to obstruction of the venous outflow, but to increased arterial influx, owing to active dilatation of the helicine arteries. These two discoveries, however, remained isolated for more than a decade, and Goltz (1874) was the first to suggest that the dilators, like the constrictors, were distributed to every vascular region, the difficulty of experimental proof arising from the fact that they nearly always run jointly with the constrictor fibres, which by their prevailing influence on the tone of the vessels mask the antagonistic action of the dilators.

For this reason it cannot be decided whether the dilator nerves are, like the constrictors, in tonic activity ; section of the chorda tympani or nervi erigentes produced no perceptible constriction of the vessels to which they are distributed.

There has been much discussion as to whether the sciatic trunk contains vaso-dilator fibres. Goltz and others noted, as the primary effect of dividing the nerve, the atonic dilatation of the vessels in the limb, exhibited principally in the increased temperature of the paw; while the primary effect of peripheral stimulation is vascular constriction, shown chiefly in the cooling of the same—as also by increased blood pressure in the small arteries of large animals (Fig. 160). Shortly after the section of the sciatic, however, the paralysed limb cools off gradually, till at the end of a few days it is colder than the healthy leg, probably because the peripheral ganglia are capable, even when separated from the spinal centres, of recovering their vascular tone until it exceeds the normal. If, when this effect has been produced, the divided

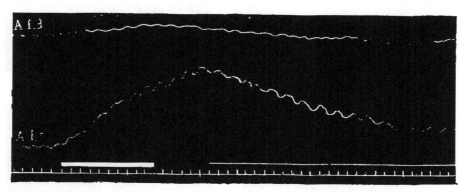

Fig. 160.- Effect upon smallest arteries of posterior extremity of exciting peripheral trunk of left sciatic in horse. (Morat.) $A. f, d$, pressure in central trunk of right femoral artery; A, f, s, pressure in peripheral trunk of left femoral artery. Two electric signals record the time in seconds, and the duration of excitation by a tetanising current on the abscissa. Shows that the constriction of the small arteries of a posterior limb hardly increases the central pressure in the femoral of the other limb, while the peripheral pressure in the femoral of the same side, which anastomoses with the small contracting arteries, is conspicuously increased.

sciatic is again exposed and excited mechanically at the peripheral end, the temperature of the paw rises considerably and exceeds that of the normal side. This shows the presence of dilator fibres in the sciatic, which retain their excitability for a longer time after section than the vaso-constrictors. These results of Goltz were essentially confirmed by the subsequent observations of Ostroumoff, Heidenhain and Grützner, Kendall and Luchsinger, and others.

In 1876 v. Frey in Ludwig's laboratory took up Cl. Bernard's studies on the vascular nerves of the submaxillary gland, and determined the amount of blood which flows out of the chief vein of the glands in the time-unit, when the dilators in the chorda tympani, or the constrictors of the carotid branches of the sympathetic, are separately stimulated; or, lastly, when both kinds of nerves are excited simultaneously. The separate stimulation of the two nerves showed that the dilators have a much longer after-effect, and are more quickly tired than the constrictors. Simultaneous stimulation showed the functional predominance of the constrictors over the dilators, of which, however, the excitation is manifested by an after-effect—in agreement with Baxt's experiments on the cardiac nerves. When, on the contrary, the constrictors are stimulated with a weak, and the dilators with a strong, current, the latter predominate.

Certain experiments of Lepine, and later on of Bernstein,

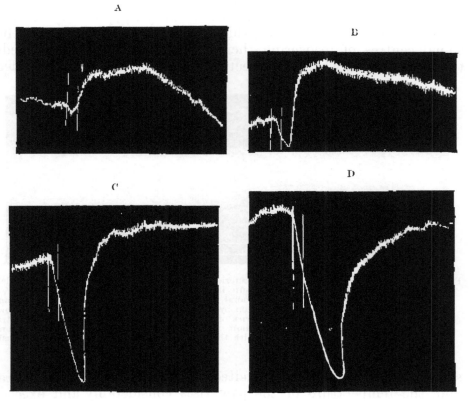

FIG. 161. Plethysmograms of hind-limb of cat during electrical excitation of divided sciatic, by induction shocks of varying frequency. (Bowditch and Warren.) The sciatic was excited in the intervals comprised between the two vertical lines—15′. At A, with 1 shock at each second, a slight vascular contraction, followed by marked dilatation, was obtained. At B, with 4 shocks at each second, the contraction was larger, with a larger succeeding vascular dilatation. At C, with 16 shocks per second, there was marked contraction with very small dilatation. At D, with 64 shocks per second, there was a very marked contraction, with no subsequent vascular dilatation.

indicate that the atonic or hypertonic state of the vessels previous to electrical excitation of their respective nerves leads to the preponderance of the constrictors over the dilators, and *vice versa*. They found, namely, that the stimulation of the sciatic produced constriction or dilatation of the vessels, according as the extremities had previously been warmed or cooled with hot or cold water.

Ostroumoff further showed that a different rhythm, or a varying intensity of electrical excitation, led to the predominance of one or other kind of vascular nerve. The *dilators* are more readily excitable to currents of slow rhythm or low intensity; the *constrictors*, on the other hand, to tetanising currents, *i.e.* currents of high frequency, or great intensity. These results were strikingly developed and confirmed in the experiments of Bowditch and Warren on the cat by the plethysmograph method, in which the oscillations of volume in the hind-limbs were recorded during the excitation of the sciatic by currents of high or low frequency and intensity. The plethysmograms of Figs. 161 and 162 are so plain as to need no description.

On the other hand, Piotrowski was unable on the dog to obtain the same results as Bowditch and Warren. On stimulating the sciatic with varying frequencies, he constantly observed a diminution and never an increase in the volume of the limb.

The two kinds of vascular nerves, which run together in the peripheral nervous system, may take a separate course at a higher point and leave the cord at different places. This was shown by

A   B   C

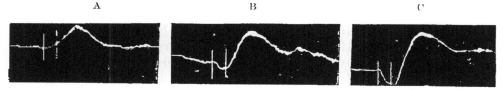

Fig. 162.—Plethysmograms of hind-limb of cat during electrical excitation of divided sciatic, by induction shocks of equal frequency (1 per second), and equal duration (20″), but of varying strength. (Bowditch and Warren.) At A, with strength of shock 100, primary dilatation of vessels of limb; at B, with strength of shock 150, more pronounced dilatation preceded by temporary contraction; at C, with strength of shock 200, still more marked dilatation, preceded by greater vascular constriction.

Dastre and Morat, who, on exciting the thoracic sympathetic immediately above the diaphragm, constantly obtained dilatation of the vessels in the lower limbs, while on exciting the abdominal sympathetic or sciatic they were constricted.

Yet more interesting is another fact discovered by the same authors, which plainly shows that the two kinds of vascular nerves, running in a single nerve trunk, may supply quite distinct regions at the periphery. On repeating the stimulation of the cervical sympathetic (which forms with the vagus a single trunk, known as the vago-sympathetic) on a curarised dog, they observed blanching in the skin of the ear and mucosa of the tongue, epiglottis, tonsils, and soft palate on the side excited, with the simultaneous flushing of the mucosa of the lips, gums, cheeks, hard palate, and nasal mucosa on the same side. The effect is particularly striking on comparison with the other side, and on contrasting the ischaemic and hyperaemic parts. At the close of excitation the differences gradually disappear, until the several parts regain their normal colouring. The entire effect is due to the sympathetic alone, and not to the vagus, since it appears when the sympathetic is excited above or below its union with the vagus, or when the latter has been divided above the point of junction.

It thus appears that while the vaso-dilators almost always run with the vaso-constrictors, their presence in the several nerve-trunks can be detected, either by the physiologically distinct character of their activity, or by their different course, their central origin, and their morphologically distinct peripheral distribution.

The data at present before us in regard to the course and central origin of the vaso-dilators to the different regions are less complete than those relating to the vaso-constrictors.

The dilators contained in the cervical sympathetic were traced by Dastre and Morat into the two branches of the Annulus of Vieussens, the rami communicantes to the second to fifth spinal nerves, and the anterior roots of the same. The majority unite on their way to the periphery with the trigeminal, by an anastomosis between the superior cervical and Gasserian ganglions. For after section of the first branch of the trigeminal in the pterygoid-maxillary groove, the vascular dilatation resulting from stimulation of the cervical sympathetic appears only to a minimal degree in the regions above indicated. On the other hand, with excitation of the trigeminal, after division and degeneration of the cervical sympathetic, dilatation of the facial vessels is obtained. This shows that the dilator fibres of this nerve cannot all emerge by the sympathetic and be of spinal origin ; others accompany the trigeminus from its roots and are cerebral in origin. According to Carlson (1907) the cervical sympathetic carries both vaso-dilators and vaso-constrictors to the cat's submaxillary gland. This fact had been overlooked by preceding investigators (Heidenhain, Langley, Bayliss), who speak only of vaso-constrictor fibres to the salivary gland in the cervical sympathetic. This is due to their observations having been made upon the dog (and other mammals), in which the constrictors probably preponderate in the cervical sympathetic, so that on stimulating the nerve the constrictor effect alone is apparent.

According to Langley, the dilators of the fore-limb originate in the thoracic nerves (5th-8th pairs). The greater proportion of the dilators to the hind-limbs run in the sciatic, a very few in the crural. The work of Ostroumoff and others shows that these do not arise in the sacral, but in the lumbar roots (2nd-4th pairs), passing thence by the rami communicantes to the abdominal sympathetic (and in a minority to the thoracic sympathetic) before they unite with the sciatic. According to the observations of Stricker, subsequently confirmed by Cossy, Vulpian, and others, they do not arise like all other motor nerves in the anterior roots alone, but also in the posterior roots of the fourth to fifth lumbar pairs. This is the only well-proved exception to Bell's law (see vol. iii.)

The recent work of Bayliss (1901) on the origin of the vaso-dilator nerves has confirmed and completed Stricker's observations, although it is partly contradictory of the conclusions just enumerated. Electrical, chemical, thermal, and above all mechanical stimulation of the peripheral trunk of the divided posterior roots of the fifth, sixth, and seventh lumbar, and the first sacral nerves, determine on the dog a pronounced vaso-dilatation of the hind-limb. A similar dilatation of the fore-limb is exhibited on stimulating the posterior roots of the sixth, seventh, and eighth cervical and first thoracic nerves. The dilator fibres of the hind-limbs do not run with the abdominal sympathetic, but enter the lumbo-sacral plexus direct. They degenerate after extirpation of the spinal ganglia, but do not degenerate when the posterior roots are cut between the cord and the spinal ganglia. They thus behave in a manner perfectly analogous to all other nerve-fibres emerging from the posterior roots, which have their trophic centres in the spinal ganglia. Lastly, it has not been demonstrated that the hind-limbs receive any vaso-dilator fibres other than those which run in the posterior spinal roots.

Till quite recently little was known of the dilator fibres to the visceral vessels. Bradford, on methodically stimulating the several pairs of spinal nerves with low frequency currents, found that the eleventh, twelfth, and thirteenth dorsal pairs at least, in addition to the constrictor fibres, contain numerous dilator fibres to the renal vessels, these being, on the contrary, very few in the other dorsal pairs, and altogether absent in the lumbar pairs. On experimenting by the same method with the splanchnic, the most important of the vaso-constrictor nerves, he found that it also contains vaso-dilator fibres, which probably serve the intestines.

After Eckhard's discovery of the nervi erigentes (1863) they were at a later period studied by Gaskell (1887) and Morat (1890), with the object more particularly of determining their origin. It was found that stimulation of the anterior roots of the second and third sacral nerves in rabbit, and first and second sacral nerves in the dog, caused almost as pronounced an erection of the penis as the stimulation of the nervi erigentes. Stimulation of the posterior roots never produces the slightest trace of erection.

These are the most important experimental data in regard to the origin and course of the vaso-dilators.

V. The vascular nerves, like the cardiac nerves, are capable of *reflex excitation*, i.e. they can be stimulated by the afferent nerves to the centres. As in the heart there are afferent nerves which act reflexly upon the heart itself, so in the vessels we must assume the existence of afferent nerves, capable of acting reflexly on the vessels. This was first demonstrated by Heger (1887). In the curarised dog or rabbit he injected nicotine or silver nitrate, peripherally, by the crural artery, and simultaneously recorded the lateral pressure of the aorta after ligaturing the crural vein. Directly after the injection he observed either an instantaneous fall of blood pressure, or a fall preceded by a rise. Heger referred this reflex phenomenon to the action of the capillary walls, since neither pressor nor depressor effects appeared, when the injected substance was localised in the artery or vein. The reflex also occurs when the hind-limb is only connected by the sciatic to the rest of the body.

Spallitta and Consiglio, in Marcacci's laboratory, extended and completed the observations of Heger. According to the Italian workers, excitation of the sensory nerves to the internal surface of the blood-vessels, by chemical agents, constantly produces not merely rise of blood pressure, but also slowing of heart-beat with increased amplitude of pulse. Since excitation of the sensory nerves of the heart, or, according to the latest researches, of the aorta, produces a depressor effect, antagonistic, *i.e.* to that of the afferent nerves to the peripheral vessels, it seems logical to conclude that under normal conditions also the two kinds of sensory nerves exert an opposite action on the circulation. The sensory nerves of the heart or aorta prevent undue filling or overloading of the heart; the sensory nerves of the peripheral vessels obviate undue filling and distension of the vessels.

Since it is proved that vascular reflexes may be excited by afferent fibres in the walls of the vessels themselves, it is probable that they play a part in the physiological regulation of blood pressure. On the other hand, the tone of the vessels can be reflexly influenced by any centripetal nerve. Localised vascular reflexes usually cause the vessels to widen, but at other times they are first narrowed, and subsequently, as an after-effect, become wider. This means that the stimulation of the afferent nerves is transmitted either by the vaso-dilators, or by the vaso-constrictors, or lastly, by both kinds of nerves. The inconstant or totally negative results of a number of experiments find their probable explanation in the partial or total inhibition of the effect. Only a few examples can here be cited.

If the nerves of taste are excited by sapid substances, there is not only a reflex secretion of saliva, but also a marked dilatation of the vessels innervated by the chorda tympani (Claude Bernard). Central excitation of the posterior auricular nerve usually produces dilatation of the vessels of the rabbit's ear : often, however, this is preceded or followed by vaso-constriction (Snellen and Lovén). On stimulating the nerve in the dorsum of the dog's paw, dilatation of the saphenous artery is obtained ; on exciting the infra-orbital, or mental (labial) nerve, there is dilatation of the external maxillary artery (Lovén). Central excitation of the sciatic, the vagus, or the posterior spinal roots, usually produces reflex constriction of the kidney vessels : on the other hand, dilatation of the same vessels is obtained when the posterior roots of the eleventh and twelfth dorsal nerves are stimulated, because in that case the excitation is conveyed by the anterior roots of the same, which, as we have seen, contain dilator fibres (Bradford).

The vascular reflexes may extend from one side to the other of the body. On central excitation of the sciatic, the paw on the opposite side becomes warmer (Masius and Vanlair): stimulation of the nasal mucosa dilates the vessels of the whole head, but more decidedly on the excited side (François-Franck).

The vascular reflexes in man have also been investigated. When one hand is dipped into cold water, the vessels of the other hand contract (Brown-Séquard). On electrical excitation of one limb the vessels of the opposite side contract (Maragliano).

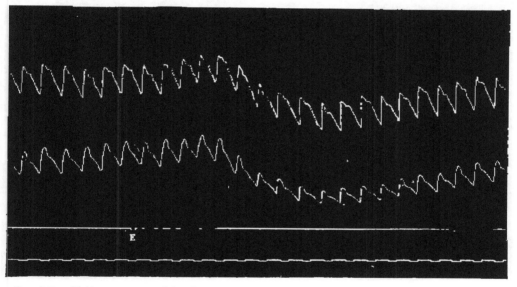

FIG. 163. — Plethysmograms of hand (M) and foot (P) recorded from healthy subject in recumbent and motionless posture. (Fano.) The abscissa S, traced with a Deprez signal, indicates at E the moment of electrical excitation of the skin. The line D is traced by a tuning-fork vibrating at 10 vibrations per second.

Fano has also experimented on the vascular reflexes of man, using an air plethysmograph, by which he was able to record simultaneously the pulse and the changes in volume of the hand and foot. He came to the following conclusions: the reaction time of the vessels is always very long: it oscillates between two and seven seconds, according to the conditions in which the subject of the experiment is placed, and the part of the body stimulated. The vascular constriction consequent on a stimulus is always more pronounced in sleep than in waking. The reaction time is longer in sleep than in waking. The reaction always occurs, independent of the point of stimulation, first in the upper and then in the lower extremities. In the latter, however, the constriction is more persistent (Fig. 163).

Patrizi instituted numerous plethysmographic researches with the object of determining the exact vasomotor reflex tissues in the arms, legs, and brain of man, when awake, when asleep, and under various other conditions. Besides confirming certain general laws for reflexes, in the vascular regions, Patrizi found that the vascular reflex times, which are fairly equal in the waking state, for the arms and legs, with a slight advantage on the side of the upper limbs, undergo in the latter a considerable delay in sleep, whereas the reflex time for the lower limbs remains constant. During sleep the reflexes are most delayed in the cerebral vessels.

Patrizi and Cavani also detected a right- and left-handed

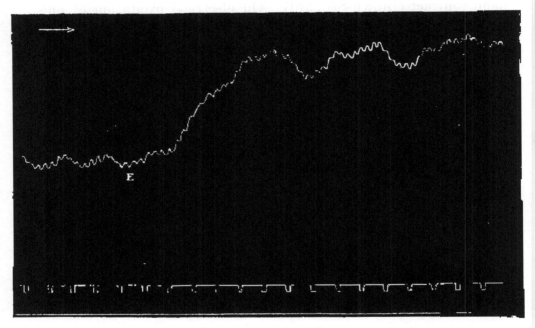

Fig. 164.—Reflex pressure effect on excitation of rabbit's skin at E. (Tigerstedt.) Carotid connected with Ludwig's kymograph. Time tracing from an electric signal, along the abscissa, in seconds.

vasomotor asymmetry in man, to which they attributed a more rapid and pronounced vasomotor reaction, in one as against the other half of the body.

This superiority of vasomotor functions usually obtains in that half of the body which shows itself most capable of muscular force. The time gained in the vascular reflexes in the favoured half of the body may amount almost to one second.

In all probability the vasomotor asymmetry is due to the greater permeability of the nerve paths in the better exercised limb, which does not exclude the possible influence of the varying sensory excitability in the two halves of the body, and in the two corresponding sides of the brain.

These reflexes not infrequently occur in the vascular regions

most remote from the afferent nerves stimulated. The visceral
vessels innervated by the splanchnic readily respond to the reflex
action of any sensory nerve, for the most part by contracting,
sometimes by dilating. Stimulation of the sciatic also constricts
the vessels of the tongue (Vulpian); excitation of the brachial
nerve dilates the vessels of the ear (Lovén). This last effect may
be seen on the rabbit, whatever the sensory nerve stimulated, but
the dilatation is usually preceded by vaso-constriction (Eckhard).

When the vascular reflexes are not confined to any circumscribed area, but extend to a wider region, they cause a general

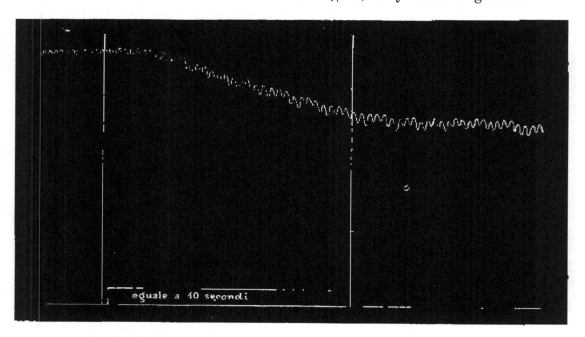

FIG. 165.—Reflex lowering of arterial pressure, from electrical excitation of depressor
nerve of rabbit, in period comprised between two vertical lines. (Tigerstedt.)

modification in blood pressure, usually expressed in an abnormal
rise, sometimes in a fall of pressure.

The reflex pressor effects of exciting the sensory nerves, already
noted by Magendie, were clearly worked out for the first time by
von Bezold (1863), and were subsequently extended by a number
of other experimenters.

They follow particularly on the stimulation of the posterior
spinal roots, the vagus, the trigeminus, the sciatic, the greater and
lesser splanchnic, the cutaneous and muscular nerves, the nerves of
the special senses (Fig. 164). The rise of blood pressure varies with
the nerve excited, and also with the intensity and nature of the
stimulus. The state of the animal prior to stimulation also has
great influence on the intensity of the pressor effect. In the
normal animal, *e.g.*, acoustic stimuli induce a considerable rise of

arterial pressure, which varies with the pitch, strength, and timbre
of the sound, whereas in curarised animals the rise is hardly
perceptible (Dogiel). Lastly, both the number of sensory nerves,
and the extent of the area stimulated, have great influence on the
degree of pressor effect. For instance, on exciting a limited area
of the skin with strong chemical stimuli, with boiling water, or
red-hot iron, little or no rise of pressure is obtained; on the other
hand, slight contact, tickling, or blowing of extended areas of the
skin, raises the arterial pressure to nearly double the normal
(Heidenhain and Grützner).

We saw in the preceding chapter that the central excitation of
the depressor nerves of Ludwig and Cyon invariably produces a

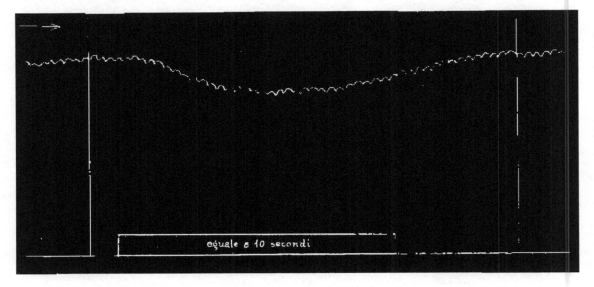

eguale a 10 secondi

Fig. 166. —Reflex lowering of arterial pressure of rabbit from electrical excitation of
centripetal muscular nerve, in period comprised by vertical lines. (Tigerstedt.)

marked reflex fall of arterial pressure (Fig. 165). The afferent
nerves to the muscles also constantly produce a similar effect on
blood pressure (Fig. 166).

Few other afferent nerves are capable of producing reflex
depressor effects. The glosso-pharyngeal usually, but not invariably,
lowers blood pressure (Knoll). With mechanical stimulation of
the rectal and vaginal mucosa, especially on touching the anus
and vaginal orifice, a primary fall of aortic pressure may be
observed on the curarised dog (Belfield). But if the stimulation
of the mucosa is pushed to deeper parts, the depression is less,
and may even be replaced by a pressor effect. Mechanical stimulation of the skeletal muscles, again, may produce a depressor effect
(Kleen).

We saw that the fall of arterial pressure consequent on excitation of the depressors is due principally to the vaso-dilator fibres

of the splanchnic nerve, partly to other dilator nerves, since, when the splanchnics are divided, the depressor part is not entirely abolished. It has, however, been established that the depressors do not exert their reflex dilator action upon all the vascular regions, and that the vessels of the ear, face, adjacent mucosae, and perhaps of the skin in general, are constricted during stimulation of the depressors (Dastre and Morat).

The reflex pressor effects on excitation of the sensory nerves are chiefly due to the vaso-constrictor fibres of the splanchnics, because when these nerves are divided, they are much reduced. But even in these cases vaso-constriction is not the only reflex effect, since it can be shown that while the internal visceral vessels contract, the cutaneous vessels dilate. This fact, which indicates a certain antagonism between the deep and the superficial vessels of the body, was demonstrated by Heidenhain in measurements of the temperature of the skin and of the deep-lying portions of the body during excitation of the sensory nerves.

The antagonism between the cutaneous and visceral vessels is even more apparent in the asphyxia produced by suspension of artificial respiration in curarised animals. While the cutaneous vessels of ear, face, and extremities dilate, those of the viscera (intestine, spleen, kidneys, uterus) contract. The pressure effect results from the predominance of vaso-constriction in the visceral vessels over dilatation of the superficial vessels (Dastre and Morat). It is highly probable, although definite experimental evidence is wanting, that this dilatation is active, and not the passive effect of the constriction of the deep vessels.

We must not, however, take this supposed antagonism between the deep and the superficial vessels in too absolute a sense, since the fact that in vascular reflexes constriction of the one and dilatation of the other occurs is not constant. Heidenhain, indeed, observed with strong electrical excitation of the medulla oblongata that there was a pressor effect greater than that of asphyxia or any kind of reflex stimulation, which was determined not merely by constriction of the internal vessels, but by that of the cutaneous and muscular vessels also.

VI. The vascular reflexes, *i.e.* the excitatory processes transmitted from the centripetal or afferent to the centrifugal or efferent nerves (the constrictors or dilators of the vessels), are necessarily carried out by means of the centres in the cerebrospinal system, from which the vascular nerves arise. The capacity of the peripheral ganglia of the sympathetic system to function as centres for reflex processes (in so far as reflex is taken in the restricted sense of a transformation of afferent into efferent influences) has not yet been demonstrated, even if it cannot be *a priori* excluded.

We have seen that the greater part, if not the whole, of the vaso-constrictor fibres arise from the anterior roots of the nerves in the median or thoracic section of the cord, which is therefore the principal seat of the *apparent origin* of these fibres. Next arises the question as to the *centres*, *i.e.* the *real origins* of the same. Other special questions are associated with these. Is there in the central nervous system one single vasomotor centre, or are there several centres? If several, are they unified in their functions, and associated so as to form one single system, or can they function independently one of another? Are there controlling centres of general circulation on which the tone of the whole vascular system depends, and controlling centres of local circulation, on which the vascular tone of this or that organ or tissue depends? Generally speaking, it must be admitted that we are not yet in a position to give a clear and exhaustive answer to these different questions, particularly to that of the precise localisation of the vascular centres. We must confine ourselves to the more fundamental and better established data, and to drawing from these such conclusions as are legitimate in the present state of our knowledge.

As early as 1855, shortly after the discovery of the vaso-constrictors, M. Schiff suggested, in view of the effects of transversely dividing the cord at different heights, that these nerves might have their centre in the bulb or medulla oblongata. In 1859 Cl. Bernard observed a considerable fall in blood pressure after division of the cervical cord, but he did not pursue the subject, and von Bezold next took it up in 1863. He found in curarised animals that stimulation of the cervical cord produced such an increase in arterial pressure that it becomes seven times greater than it was immediately after section of the cord. This marked rise of pressure, which was associated with a pronounced acceleration of cardiac rhythm, was referred by him to increased activity of the heart, without taking into consideration the intervention of vascular nerves.

A year after the publication of von Bezold's theory, Ludwig and Thiry showed it to be erroneous, emphasising the fact that during excitation of the cervical cord the small arteries throughout almost the entire body are constricted, which causes the pressor effect. For, on exciting the cervical cord, a maximal rise of aortic pressure is obtained, even after the whole of the cardiac nerves have been divided. The fall after section is therefore the effect of paralytic atony of the vessels; the rise of pressure during excitation is the effect of vascular hypertony; there must therefore exist in the bulb, *i.e.* above the divided and excited cord, a vaso-constrictor centre, which exerts a constant tonic action upon all the small arteries.

Contemporaneously with Ludwig and Thiry, Goltz, by certain experiments on the frog, showed the importance of vascular tone to the circulation. After destruction of the central nervous system, there is a marked dilatation of the visceral vessels, particularly of the veins, in consequence of which nearly the whole of the blood collects in those vessels, while the remaining parts of the body are much impoverished. On exposing the beating heart, he saw that it was almost bloodless, since very little blood reached it during diastole, and therefore very little could be expelled into the aorta during systole. It follows that vascular tonicity is an indispensable condition of the circulation, and that not merely the arteries, but the veins as well, possess a tone that is dependent on the central nervous system in general.

The bulbar centre for the vaso-constrictors was more exactly localised and determined in the subsequent investigations of Owsjannikow (1871) and Dittmar (1873), in Ludwig's laboratory. Starting from the fact that central excitation of the sciatic in curarised dogs and rabbits, even after separation of spinal bulb from brain by a transverse section, reflexly produces a perceptible increase in arterial blood-pressure, they endeavoured to define the region of the bulb in which this reflex occurred. With this object Owsjannikow made successive cross-sections from above downwards at different heights of the medulla, and examined both the depressor effect of each section, and the reflex pressor effect on exciting the sciatic. The upper limit of the vascular centre lies at the level of that section after which there is a fall in aortic pressure, and a diminution in the height of the reflex rise of pressure; the lower limit is at that section after which aortic pressure reaches its minimum, and no longer rises on excitation of the sciatic. By pursuing this method, with the guidance of the above data, he decided that the bulbar vasomotor centre in the rabbit is about 4 mm. high; its upper limit is 1-2 mm. below the corpora quadrigemina, its lower limit 4 mm. above the point of the calamus scriptorius. Since longitudinal section of the bulb in the median line produces no perceptible fall in aortic pressure, he concludes that the centre is not in the median line, but consists of two centres situated at either side of the bulb.

Dittmar, who practically confirmed the results of Owsjannikow in regard to the longitudinal extension of the bulbar vascular centre, went on to establish its limits in the two other dimensions, by the same method of systematic sections. He discovered that in each half of the bulb there is a small prismatic space, on destroying which the reflex vascular constriction is abolished. In this area a nucleus of grey matter is visible under the microscope, described by Clarke as the antero-lateral nucleus, in the rabbit.

The main results of Ludwig's pupils were subsequently confirmed by Heidenhain, Berkowitsch, Latschenberger, and Deahna.

VII. After Ludwig's School had investigated the bulbar vaso-constrictor centres, and had shown that after destroying their function it was no longer possible to obtain reflex vaso-constriction on exciting the sciatic, the opinion generally held was that the cord contained no other centre capable of influencing the tone of the vessels independent of that in the spinal bulb, and that this was probably the only true vasomotor centre. Very soon, however, other experimental observations came to light which showed the fallacy of this view, and led to the opinion that there were secondary vaso-constrictor centres along almost the whole of the cord, which were able to function after the principal bulbar centre had been cut out.

Goltz was the first to propose this theory (1864-74). He found in the frog that the vascular atony was far from complete after extirpation of the entire brain, including the bulb, and became so only after destruction of the spinal cord. He further observed in dogs that when the cervico-dorsal tract was cut off by division from the lumbo-sacral, and the animal kept alive until the vascular atonia of the hind-limbs had disappeared, this atonia was reproduced on destroying the lumbar cord. He concluded that the restoration of vascular tone after section of the cord was due to the presence of vasomotor centres in the lumbar medulla.

When cut off from the bulb, the spinal vasomotor centres are also capable of reflexly constricting the vessels, and of raising arterial pressure, when excited, as was first shown by Schlesinger (1874) in dogs and rabbits, after he had increased the excitability of the cord by injecting minute doses of strychnine. This fact was subsequently confirmed by many observers.

In curarised animals, when the cord is separated from the spinal bulb, the asphyxia produced by cessation of artificial respiration suffices to cause vascular constriction, as was first demonstrated by Kowalewsky and Adamük (1868). Since this effect depends on excitation of the spinal centres, it follows that, after destruction of the cord, asphyxia no longer exercises any pressor action (Schlesinger, Luchsinger, Konow, and Stenbeck).

The spinal centres for the vaso-constrictors lie not only in the lumbo-sacral region (Goltz), but also in the dorsal tract (Vulpian and Kabierscki). On the other hand, they appear not to exist, or to be very scanty, in the cervical tract, since aortic pressure is not affected by section of the cervical cord at any height, after the bulbar centre has been cut off (Stricker).

The vaso-constrictors in the bundles of the cord for the most part run directly, and only follow the crossed paths to a minor extent (Brown-Séquard and Schiff), as appears from the effects of hemisection of the cord. They are chiefly mingled with the sensory and motor fibres to the skeletal muscles which make up the lateral bundles (Dittmar), as shown by the effects of partial section in different segments of the cord.

Nothing certain is known about the anatomical and functional relations which exist between the spinal vasomotor centres and the bulbar centre. Certain comparative experiments of Kowalewsky and Adamük, Luchsinger, and others on the vascular effects consequent on asphyxia in animals with intact and others with divided cord lead, however, to the conjecture that the spinal vaso-constrictor centres are less excitable than the bulbar centre. For in curarised animals, when the bulb is cut off from the cord, the rise of arterial pressure at the close of artificial respiration begins and reaches its maximum, much later than in animals with intact spinal cord. This leads to the view that the normal tone of the vascular centre, and its rhythmical or a-rhythmical, automatic or reflex oscillations, depend principally, if not exclusively, upon the bulbar centre, which, in consequence of its greater excitability, reacts more quickly to all stimuli, extrinsic or intrinsic.

Just as there are vaso-constrictor centres below the ruling bulbar centre, so it seems logical also to assume the existence of vaso-constrictor centres above the bulb, i.e. in the brain. But the experiments adduced in this connection give no convincing evidence in favour of such a hypothesis, since they are susceptible of various interpretations. Excitation of the cerebral peduncles in curarised animals is followed by a pressor effect (Budge); on stabbing the anterior or posterior corpora quadrigemina, vaso-constriction followed by dilatation is obtained (Eckhard): if the corpora striata or the internal capsule are electrically stimulated, there is rise of arterial pressure (Danilewsky and Stricker); when the cortex, particularly in the region of the so-called motor zone, is electrically excited, a more or less distinct pressor effect ensues, even if no epileptic fit is set up (Danilewsky, Bochefontaine, Richet, François-Franck and others). These phenomena may be explained in the sense that there are no true vaso-constrictor centres in the cerebrum, but only simple nerve paths, which throw the bulbar vasomotor centres into activity, like the afferent peripheral nerves. The effects of lesions in these parts, however, seem to witness more than those of stimulation to the presence of true vaso-constrictor centres in the brain.

After circumscribed extirpation of certain points upon the cerebral cortex in the region of the motor zone, a marked and fairly protracted rise of temperature in the hind-limbs has been observed (Eulenburg and Landois); in clinical paralysis from a variety of central lesions the same effect may be observed in the paralysed limbs, as well as ecchymosis in different organs, notably in the lungs and joints (Charcot and others).

VIII. We have fewer data in regard to the localisation of the vaso-dilator centres in the several parts of the central nervous system. It seems highly probable, however, that they are no less widely distributed than the vaso-constrictor centres, and that there is in the bulb, along with the controlling centre which normally regulates the constriction of the vessels, another controlling centre which regulates their relaxation, so that the slow oscillations of vascular tonicity should be regarded as the effects of the alternating functional predominance of one or other of the two opposing bulbar vasomotor centres. The few data relating to this subject may be briefly summarised.

The rapid and infallible effect of central excitation of the depressor nerves, which is antagonistic to the effect consequent on central stimulation of the sciatic or other large nerve trunks, in itself makes the existence of a controlling vaso-dilator centre highly probable (Ludwig and Cyon). It has so far proved impossible to demonstrate that it is situated in the medulla. Certain experiments of Laffont (1880) are, however, of interest in this connection. He observed as the effect of puncturing the floor of the fourth ventricle, an active dilatation of the hepatic vessels, which would therefore seem to depend not on the destruction, but on the stimulation of the centre. On the following day stimulation of the depressors in the same animal failed to produce the customary fall of blood pressure, probably in consequence of paralysis due to the after-effects of the puncture in the bulbar vaso-dilator centre.

The following experimental results prove the existence of vaso-dilator centres in the cord as well. In dogs that have survived transverse division of the spinal cord at the level of the last dorsal vertebra, mechanical stimulation of the penis is able to evoke erection. After destruction of the lumbar cord this effect is abolished (Goltz). In the same dog, with divided cord, the central excitation of one sciatic produces active dilatation of the paw on the opposite side (Goltz, Masius and Vanlair, Ustimowitsch and others). When the cervical cord is excited, aortic pressure falls (Johannson); there is dilatation of the vessels of the ears, cheeks, and corresponding mucosa (Dastre and Morat); of the vessels of the mesentery and intestinal walls (Vulpian): and of those of the penis (Eckhard). After division of the cord at the level of the first or second dorsal vertebrae, central excitation of the brachial plexus causes a fall in aortic pressure (Smirnow).

Again, the existence of cerebral vaso-dilator centres is rendered probable by the fact that electrical stimulation of the cortex at certain points, particularly of the parietal lobe, produces not a rise but a fall of pressure in the aorta (Bochefontaine, Stricker, Bechterew, and Mislawsky). These are probably the centres whose activity causes the sudden blush that accompanies psychical emotions.

In 1893 Bayliss, after describing various experimental results on vascular reflexes, put forward the hypothesis that " the vasomotor centre consists of a constrictor and a dilator part, the depressor nerve acting in an inhibitory manner on the former and in an exciting manner on the latter, while pressor nerves act in an opposite way on both." Considerable support is given to this view by his recent work (1908) on the reciprocal innervation in vasomotor reflexes. It appears that in depressor reflexes there is, along with inhibition of tone in the vaso-constrictor centres, an excitation of vaso-dilator centres. Corresponding effects, although more difficult to demonstrate, take place in the pressor reflexes. The action of strychnine upon the vasomotor centres affords a strict analogy with its action as demonstrated by Sherrington in the case of the reflexes to voluntary muscle, *i.e.* conversion of the inhibitory phase of all vascular reflexes into an excitation. The depressor nerves cause a rise of blood-pressure under full doses of the alkaloid by exciting the constrictor centre with the same mechanism that normally inhibits it.

BIBLIOGRAPHY

In addition to the copious information contained in the general and special treatises referred to in previous chapters, the student may consult the following monographs and memoirs :—

M. SCHIFF. Untersuchungen zur Physiologie des Nervensystems. Frankfurt a. M., 1855. Lehrbuch der Physiol., I. Jahr., 1859. Recueil des mémoires physiologiques. Lausanne, 1194.
CL. BERNARD. Leçons sur la physiologie du système nerveux. Paris, 1858.
ECKHARD. Beiträge zur Anat. und Physiol. 1863.
LUDWIG und THIRY. Sitz. Ber. d. kais. Akad. d. Wiss., 1864.
LUDWIG und CYON. Ber. d. sächs. Gesellsch. d. Wiss., 1866.
LOVÉN. Ber. d. sächs. Gesellsch. d. Wiss., 1866.
V. BEZOLD und BEVER. Untersuchungen aus dem Laborat. in Würzburg, 1867.
BROWN-SÉQUARD. Leçons sur les nerfs vaso-moteurs. Paris, 1872.
MOSSO. Ber. d. sächs. Gesellsch. d. Wiss., 1874.
GOLTZ. Arch. f. path. Anat., 1864. Arch. f. d. ges. Physiol., 1874-75.
VULPIAN. Leçons sur l'appareil vaso-moteur, 1875.
HEIDENHAIN und GRÜTZNER. Arch. f. d. ges. Physiol., 1877.
GASKELL. Journal of Anat. and Physiol., 1887.
DASTRE et MORAT. Recherches sur le système nerveux vaso-moteur. Paris, 1884.
STRICKER. Medicin. Jahrbücher, 1886.
PATRIZI. Arch. ital. de biologie., xxviii. 1897.
CAVANI. Ibidem, vol. xxxix., 1903.
PIOTROWSKI. Arch. f. d. ges. Physiol., 55, 1894.
BAYLISS. Journal of Physiol., Bd. 26, 1901.
ASHER. Die Innervation der Gefässe. Ergebnisse der Physiologie, I, 2. 1902. (Sixty-eight memoirs are cited in this review.)
BAYLISS. Die Innervation der Gefässe. Ergebnisse der Physiologie, V, 1906. (Seventy-four memoirs are cited in this article, which is the continuation of the preceding.)

Recent English Literature : -

W. T. PORTER and H. G. BEYER. The Influence of the Depressor Nerve to the Vasomotor Centre. Amer. Journ. of Physiol., 1901, iv. 283-299.
W. M. BAYLISS. On the Origin from the Spinal Cord of the Vaso-dilator Fibres of the Hind-limb and on the Nature of these Fibres. Journ. of Physiol., 1900-1901, xxvi. 173-209.

W. Hunter. On the Presence of Nerve-fibres in the Cerebral Vessels. Journ. of Physiol., 1900-1901, xxvi. 465-469.

W. M. Bayliss. On the Local Reactions of the Arterial Wall to Changes of Internal Pressure. Journ. of Physiol., 1902, xxviii. 220-231.

S. J. and Clara Meltzer. A Study of the Vasomotor Nerves of the Rabbit's Ear contained in the Third Cervical and in the Cervical Sympathetic Nerves. Amer. Journ. of Physiol., 1903, ix. 57-68.

W. E. Dixon and T. G. Brodie. Contributions to the Physiology of the Lungs. Part II. On the Innervation of the Pulmonary Blood-vessels ; and some Observations on the Action of Suprarenal Extract. Journ. of Physiol., 1904, xxx. 476-502.

A. J. Carlson. Vaso-dilator Fibres to the Submaxillary Gland in the Cervical Sympathetic of the Cat. Amer. Journ. of Physiol., 1907, xix. 408-416.

W. T. Porter, H. K. Marks, and J. B. Swift. The Relation of Afferent Impulses to Fatigue of the Vasomotor Centre. Amer. Journ. of Physiol., 1907-1908, xx. 444-450.

W. T. Porter and H. K. Marks. The Effects of Haemorrhage upon the Vaso-motor Reflexes. Amer. Journ. of Physiol., 1908, xxi. 460-465.

W. M. Bayliss. On Reciprocal Innervation in Vasomotor Reflexes and the Action of Strychnine and of Chloroform thereon. Proc. Roy. Soc., 1908, lxxx. series B, pp. 339-375.

W. M. Bayliss. The Excitation of Vaso-dilator Nerve-fibres in Depressor Reflexes. Journ. of Physiol., 1908, xxxvii. 264-277.

W. T. Porter and R. Richardson. A Comparative Study of the Vasomotor Reflexes. Amer. Journ. of Physiol., 1908-1909, xxiii. 131-140.

T. Sollman and J. D. Pilcher. The Reactions of the Vasomotor Centre to Sciatic Stimulation and to Curare. Amer. Journ. of Physiol., 1910, xxvi. 233-259.

CHAPTER XI

CHEMISTRY AND PHYSICS OF RESPIRATORY EXCHANGES

CONTENTS.—Early notions of the importance of respiration (Aristotle, Galen, Leonardo da Vinci, van Helmont, Boyle, Hook, Fracassati, Lower, Mayow). 2. Modern doctrines (Black, Bergmann, Priestley, Lavoisier). 3. Theory of gas exchanges in the lungs and tissues (Lagrange and Spallanzani, W. Edwards). 4. Extraction of gases from the blood (Magnus, L. Meyer, Hoppe-Seyler, Ludwig, Pflüger). 5. Varying content of arterial, venous, and asphyxiated blood. 6. State of the oxygen in the blood. 7. State of the carbonic acid in the blood. 8. Tension of gases in venous and arterial blood and in inspired and expired air ; theory of pulmonary gas exchange by diffusion and by secretory processes. 9. Theory of gas exchanges in the tissues. 10. The respiratory quotient and its variations. Bibliography.

JUST as the Circulation provides for the exchange of fluid materials between the blood and the tissues, so Respiration provides for the exchange of gaseous materials between the environment and the blood, and between the blood and the tissues.

We have already seen that the function of respiration is common to all living beings (see Chap. II. 4 ; Chap. III. 3). Even Pasteur's anaërobes develop carbonic acid, utilising the oxygen which is combined with the organic substances, and by its means producing exothermic reactions, such, i.e., as the liberation of energy in the form of heat. They thus fulfil the function of respiration, albeit in a different way from other living beings, so that it cannot be said that they do not breathe. The vast majority of living creatures, however, respire free oxygen : the simplest organisms directly ; those which have circulating blood, indirectly, i.e. through the oxygen of the blood. Among these last we distinguish external respiration, or the gas exchanges between the environment and the blood, from internal respiration, or the gas exchanges between the blood and the tissues. By means of the first, the venous blood in the lungs and gills is rendered arterial ; by the second, the arterial blood in the capillaries of the aortic system or greater circulation is rendered venous.

I. The phenomena of respiration first received a scientific explanation in modern times, although they arise in physiological processes that have a first claim on the attention of mankind.

The need of breathing is, as a fact of common experience, imperative; we begin to breathe when we begin to live, we cease to breathe when we die.

Aristotle (354 B.C.) remarked that all mammals, including the whales which live in water, breathe air, and that fishes, molluscs, and crustaceans breathe the water in which they live. Both air and water serve to refrigerate them, *i.e.* to temper the innate heat. He notices that the warmer animals breathe more intensely, and explains this on the supposition that they had a greater need of refrigeration—a confusion of effect and cause. Animals in closed vessels perished, according to Aristotle, because they warm their environment, and can no longer cool themselves by respiration.

Herophilus and Erasistratus, the leaders of the Alexandrian School (300 B.C.), had a more physiological notion of respiratory phenomena. They described a systole and a diastole of the lungs (expiratory and inspiratory movements), which permitted the pneuma to penetrate into the arteries, whence it was conducted to the different parts of the body in order to vivify, that is, to warm them. It was, however, Galen (see Chap. VI. 2) who first grasped the chemical function of respiration, since he assumed that the vital spirit was absorbed in the pulmonary diastole, while the fuliginous vapours were expelled along with the water vapour in the pulmonary systole.

With Galen, therefore, as we shall see, begins the experimental study of the mechanics of respiration. His ideas prevailed unchanged during the Middle Ages. Servetus' book, *Restitutio Christianismi*, was the last echo—stifled in the flames kindled by the Catholics of Vienna and the Calvinists of Geneva.

Leonardo da Vinci's conception of the respiratory function (1452-1519) was far superior to Galen's in accuracy and lucidity. Leonardo was one of the most universal geniuses the human race has ever seen, inasmuch as he combined with the eminent gifts of an artist the experimental instinct and divining power of the man of science, in the most modern sense of the word. In the scientific aphorisms published after his death there is a brilliant study on the nature of a candle flame, which is a complex physical and chemical problem. In this study, among other admirable observations, he affirms that " the flame first disposes of the material that is to nourish it · *i.e.* reduces to the gaseous state the combustible matter of the candle), and then feeds itself on the same . . . where the air is not fitted to maintain the flame (*i.e.* where the air has been consumed by the flame), no flame can live, neither any terrestrial nor aerial animal . . . where flame cannot live, no animal that breathes can sustain existence" (*Codice Atlantico*, folio 170, fasc. XXIII. p. 963).

These words, besides being an inspired conception of the analogy between the phenomena of combustion and of respiration, convey an experimental fact of the highest importance, although Leonardo adduces no evidence.

The first real discovery in the field of experimental chemistry was made by Jean Baptiste van Helmont (born at Brussels, 1577; d. 1644), noblest of the experimental alchemists, precursor of Priestley and Lavoisier, the founders of modern chemistry. He found that on burning coal and in the fermentation of wine, a gas which he called *gas silvestre* escaped, which is incapable of maintaining a flame, and produces asphyxia and death in animals. This gas may develop in the heart of the earth, as in the famous Grotta del Cane near Naples; it bubbles up in certain mineral waters, as at Spa, and can also be evolved from the calcareous concrements formed in the crab's stomach (the so-called "crab's eyes") by dissolving them in vinegar. In short, van Helmont's *gas silvestre* is nothing else than the carbonic acid of modern chemists. Haller used this discovery of the Belgian alchemist to refute the Aristotelian theory of respiration which Cesalpinus and Harvey had sought to resuscitate.

In the year 1670 another distinguished philosopher and investigator, Robert Boyle (1626-1691), the leader of the group of scientific men who formed the nucleus of the Royal Society, proved, with the help of the pneumatic machine introduced by the Magdeburg physicist, von Guericke, that not only do all land animals perish in a vacuum, but all water animals as well, showing that these equally require the air which is dissolved in the water they inhabit. He concluded from many experiments that the air contains a vital substance—thus adumbrating the oxygen of modern chemistry, which enters into the phenomena of combustion, respiration, and fermentation. He also confirmed, experimentally, the fact already advanced by Leonardo da Vinci and van Helmont, to the effect that the air becomes unbreathable through respiration —not because it gets heated, but because it suffers chemical change.

Robert Hook, friend and contemporary of Boyle, pointed out the need of incessant renewal of the air in the lungs for the maintenance of life. Vesalius had noticed, a hundred years previously, that in order to prolong the life of a dog after opening of the thorax and consequent retractation of the lungs, it was only necessary to inflate them rhythmically with air; but he brought forward no conclusions of importance in regard to the physiology of respiration. Hook perfected the method of artificial respiration in the dog with opened thorax by rhythmically blowing air from a bellows into the lungs, or by continuous insufflation after making an opening on the surface of each lung. In both cases he saw that the animal could be kept alive for a prolonged period, and only died when the air stagnated in the lungs from cessation of the rhythmical or continuous ventilation. He concluded that the significance of respiration lay in the renewal of the pulmonary air and not in the alternate expansion and contraction of the lungs, as was believed by certain iatro-mechanicians.

The ancients were undoubtedly aware of the difference in colour between arterial and venous blood. It was perhaps owing to this difference that they termed the pulmonary artery *vein,* and the pulmonary veins *arteries.* It was also known to the older surgeons that the clot formed from the blood extracted by bleeding exhibits the scarlet colour of arterial blood in the upper layers, and the darker colour of venous blood in the deeper layers. In 1665 it was discovered by Fracassati, a famous physician of Bologna, that the florid colour of the superficial layer of the clot was produced by the action of the air, and that it sufficed to invert the clot for the darker layers, which had been in contact with the walls of the vessel containing it, to assume the same hue as the arterial blood.

This was confirmed by Lower (1669), another friend and collaborator of Boyle, who at the same time discovered a further weighty fact : he observed, namely, that when artificial respiration was used with the opened thorax, the venous blood became arterial, not in the heart, but in the lungs, while the reduced blood of the lungs also became venous if artificial respiration was interrupted.

So far nothing positive was known about the chemical processes that take place in respiration, and the analogy between respiration and combustion was merely guessed at, not proven.

The pioneer in the chemistry of the air and the doctrines of respiration, combustion, and oxidation of metals was John Mayow (1640-1679). In a series of original experiments published at Oxford when he was twenty-eight, he expressed his conviction that the air was not a simple body but a mixture of at least two different gases or " spirits," one of which (termed by him *spiritus nitro-aëreus* or *igneo-aëreus*) is competent to support life by passing into the blood during respiration, and rendering it florid and able to ferment and develop heat. It is this same vital gas which combines with burning bodies, generates acids, and rusts iron. The air that remains after the consumption of the *spiritus nitro-aëreus* is inadequate for life, for combustion, for the rusting of metals. The experiments by which Mayow was led to these remarkable results, which virtually involved the discovery of oxygen and nitrogen, consisted chiefly in the introduction of small animals and lighted candles into a closed vessel over water. He noted the diminution of the volume of air in consequence of respiration and combustion, and the cessation of life and of combustion after a certain time, due not to the accumulation of fumes, but to the consumption of the igneo-aëreal particles. Unfortunately this genius, who antedated the greatest discovery of the chemistry of the air by a century, died at the age of thirty-three, a few years after the publication of his early experiments. The great importance of his unfinished work was overlooked, and it hardly had any influence upon the progress of physiology.

II. Before Mayow's notions of the composition of the air could be regarded as a definite achievement, it was necessary to perfect the methods of investigating the chemical study of gases, more especially the art of manipulating them like solid or fluid bodies. Many workers contributed to the building up of this technique, in particular Hales (1678-1761), who was the promoter of the so-called pneumatic chemistry, by inventing the method of collecting gases in an inverted test-tube, suspended in a vessel of water or mercury into which the gas was passed by means of bent tubes. By this method, known as the *eudiometric*, Joseph Black, Professor at Glasgow in 1757, again isolated and studied the properties of that gas which van Helmont termed *gas silvestre*, to which Black gave the name of "fixed air." He showed experimentally that it was a product of the respiration of man and other animals. On blowing through lime water or a solution of caustic alkali, he saw that the lime was precipitated and the alkali was rendered mild. Bergmann of Stockholm subsequently (1772) continued Black's investigations on "fixed air," which he termed "aëreal acid," finding it, though in small quantities, in the atmosphere. Black and Bergmann, in these weighty experiments, were the immediate precursors of Priestley and Lavoisier, who are usually accredited with the prestige of being the founders of modern chemistry.

Priestley (1733-1804) eagerly pursued the researches of his predecessors; in 1772 he experimented with the object of seeing whether it were possible to restore the vital properties of air that had deteriorated in consequence of animal respiration and combustion, and after many fruitless experiments he discovered that plants thrive in this air and renew it for purposes of animal life and combustion. In 1775 he discovered that red precipitate of mercury on calcination developed a gas which was exceedingly favourable for combustion and animal respiration; this (in accordance with Stahl's doctrine which then predominated) he termed dephlogisticated air, *i.e.* air free from the imaginary principle known as *phlogiston*. This was the same gas that Mayow called nitro-aëreal or igneo-aëreal, and which Priestley succeeded in obtaining pure, and isolated from the other atmospheric gases. By various other processes he also isolated the irrespirable gas obtained from air, after burning coal or sulphur, and dissolving the products of combustion in water. He studied the properties of this and called it phlogistic air, *i.e.* air charged with phlogiston. Lastly, in continuation of the experiments above described, of Fracassati and Lower (the results of which had been confirmed by Cigna and Hewson in 1773), Priestley showed that the dephlogisticated air which he had discovered was essential for the conversion of venous into arterial blood, and that the blood, even through an animal membrane, makes normal air irrespirable and unable to support combustion, by converting it into phlogistic air.

After Priestley's discoveries it remained for Lavoisier (born in Paris, 1743; infamously guillotined March 8, 1794) to earn the glory of rearing a solid and complete edifice on their basis, both as regards the chemical composition of the air, and the phenomena of combustion and respiration.

In order to refute the cumbrous doctrine of Stahl's phlogiston, it was only necessary for Lavoisier to employ the balance, and to show that the so called earths or metallic oxides are heavier than metals. Stahl's theory presupposed that metals, when converted into oxides, lost their phlogiston, and therefore lost in weight, the oxides on conversion into metals becoming phlogistic and therefore gaining in weight. Lavoisier (1776) established that the air is not a simple fluid which robs the igneous principle from animals and gives it up to plants, but a mixture of two fluids, one inadequate to support life, which he termed azote, the other eminently respirable, which he called oxygen. The former corresponds with Priestley's phlogistic, the latter with his dephlogisticated air.

In 1780 Lavoisier discovered the chemical composition of van Helmont's *gas silvestre* (the "fixed air" of Black) and showed it to be the result of the combination of carbon with oxygen in definite proportions. He succeeded in correlating the formation of carbonic acid gas in expired air with the synchronous consumption of oxygen, and conceived of pulmonary respiration as a phenomenon of combustion, in which, under the influence of life, the oxygen combines with the carbon exhaled from the body, and becomes the principal source of the internal heat generated by the animal. Nor was this all; by means of the balance he showed that the amount of oxygen consumed in the respiratory work of animals is greater than that contained in the carbonic acid given off. The recent discovery of the chemical composition of water, made by Cavendish (1781), and soon after confirmed by Lavoisier, enabled him to account for this fact and to complete his theory of the chemistry of respiration, which he conceived as a double combustion, from which are formed carbonic acid and water. He made this deduction from repeated experiments, which enabled him to conclude that "respiration is a slow combustion of carbon and hydrogen, perfectly similar to that which occurs in a burning lamp; and from this point of view animals which breathe are true combustible bodies that burn and are consumed."

In 1789 Lavoisier published with Séguin a large number of researches that are of fundamental importance to the theory of respiration. The two experimenters noted that the intensity of respiratory combustion does not vary essentially, whether the animal breathes pure oxygen or a mixture of fifteen parts nitrogen and one of oxygen ; that during respiration the nitrogen does not sensibly increase nor diminish, and may without injury be substituted for hydrogen, which also behaves as an indifferent gas ; that during digestion and the muscular movements the intensity of respiratory combustion increases ; that lastly, the consumption of oxygen in man increases sensibly when the external temperature is lowered.

As regards the seat of respiratory combustion, Lavoisier was less happy than in his previous researches, for he asserted with Séguin that it took place in the lungs, where the oxygen of the air encountered the combustible material, represented by a hydro-carbonous fluid. This hypothesis, which makes the lungs the seat of respiratory combustion, was open to grave objections. It was observed that the temperature of the lungs is no higher than that of the other internal organs, making it dubious whether heat could spread thence to the rest of the body. Starting from this fact, Lagrange (born at Turin, 1736 ; died 1813), one of the most illustrious of mathematicians, was the first to rectify Lavoisier's error. He maintained the hypothesis that only gas exchanges take place in the lungs, in which the blood circulating through them yields its carbonic acid to the air and absorbs oxygen from it ; and that respiratory combustion is accomplished in every part of the body to which the blood circulates.

III. The earliest experimental proofs of the theory of internal or tissue respiration, as foreshadowed by Lagrange, were given by Lazzaro Spallanzani (1729-1799), who claims an important place in the history of the chemistry of respiration. In a long series of comparative studies on the respiration of a great number of animals, terrestrial, aquatic, vertebrate, and invertebrate, he extended the doctrine of Lavoisier, proving that oxygen is in every case essential to life, and that in all it is absorbed by the organs of respiration (lungs, gills, trachea, skin) and carried to the circulation, where it determines the vitality of the tissues by entering into combination with them.

Further, by ingenious experiments on snails he showed that excretion of carbonic acid is independent of absorption of oxygen, since it remains almost always constant, even when these creatures are enclosed in tubes, plunged in a mercury bath, and filled either with water that has been boiled and deprived of gases by the air-pump, or with nitrogen or hydrogen.

The *Memorie su la respirazione* is the posthumous work of the Abbé Spallanzani, and contains only a few of his observations. After his death the protocols of his experiments were confided to his friend the Genevese scientist and librarian, Jean Sénébier, who extracted from them the materials for a work entitled *Rapport de l'air avec les êtres organisés* (Geneva, 1807). This is a valuable collection of experimental facts, showing how much of the progress of our science is due to this illustrious physiologist. Undeniably, however, it lacks that concise method and critical elaboration which it would have received had the author been able to complete his own work.

The subsequent researches of William Edwards (born in Jamaica, 1776; died Versailles, 1842) were on the lines of Spallanzani's most important experiments. On bringing frogs, whose lungs had been emptied by compression of the flanks, under a bell-jar of hydrogen immersed in mercury, Edwards observed that the animal in the space of a few hours developed an amount of carbonic acid almost equal to the volume of its body. Similar results were obtained from experiments on fish, which breathe through their gills. In order to prove that the same fact holds for mammals, which die as soon as they are deprived of oxygen, he took newborn animals, which have a longer resistance to asphyxia, and showed that when immersed in an atmosphere of hydrogen, they continue to exhale carbonic acid. These facts are only the confirmation and generalisation of those enunciated twenty-five years earlier by Spallanzani; but Edwards deduced from them more clearly and explicitly the erroneous nature of Lavoisier's theory of pulmonary combustion, and the proof of Lagrange's theory of pulmonary gas exchanges. Carbonic acid (as he approximately concluded) is exhaled from the body independent of the entrance of oxygen into the lungs and its absorption by the blood. It is probably derived from the tissues, and may be already formed and dissolved in the venous blood, from which it is exhaled on circulating through the pulmonary vessels.

Collard de Martigny (1830), Johannes Müller (1835), Bischoff (1837), Marchand (1844), with improved and varied methods of experiment, obtained the same results as Spallanzani and Edwards.

IV. The theory of external respiration as a gaseous exchange between the air contained in the pulmonary alveoli and the blood gases circulating in the pulmonary capillaries, and the theory of internal respiration in the sense of a gaseous exchange between the blood gases circulating in the aortic capillaries and those produced by the living elements of all the tissues, received a solid experimental basis from the researches on the quality and quantity of the gases contained in the blood, and the inter-comparison of the gases extracted from arterial and those extracted from venous or asphyxial blood.

When in 1824 Edwards published his essay, *The Influence of Physical Agents on Life,* in which the theory of the respiratory gas exchanges was clearly formulated, some scanty data existed in support of the hypothesis that the blood was the vehicle of these exchanges, and held in solution or loose combination both the oxygen and the carbonic acid. The blood gases were first extracted with the vacuum pump by Boyle and Mayow; Humphry Davy (1803) was the first to extract them by the method of warming, and to recognise that arterial blood contains little carbonic acid and much oxygen.

Priestley (1776), Fontana (1804), Nasse (1816), Brande (1818), Vauquelin (1820) and others were able either by the method of simple diffusion, by bringing the blood into contact with indifferent gases such as hydrogen and nitrogen, or by agitating the blood with the said gases or passing them through it, to determine the fact that it holds both oxygen and carbonic acid in solution. These results, obtained with somewhat loose methods, were, however, contested by other distinguished physiologists, so that John Davy, Johannes Müller, Gmelin, Tiedemann and others agreed in denying the presence of free gases in the blood, while Vogel, Nasse, Scudamore, Th. Bischof, Collard de Martigny, and van Enschut maintained that carbonic acid was not found in the blood in a state of solution.

It was Magnus (1837), Professor of Physics at Berlin, who put an end to this uncertainty, and performed his experiments on the gases of the blood with the scientific method that was indispensable to make his results convincing. He extracted the gases of the blood by means of the Torricellian vacuum, with an ingenious apparatus which as it were combined the mercury pump and the pneumatic machine. As the result of his analysis, he stated that both arterial and venous blood contain not only carbonic acid, but oxygen and nitrogen as well, and that carbonic acid preponderates in venous, oxygen in arterial blood. He was the first who attempted to account for the mechanism of the pulmonary gas exchanges, considered as an effect of simple diffusion, according to the physical law formulated by J. Dalton in 1805.

In 1857, however, Lothar Meyer demonstrated that the amount of oxygen liberated from the blood does not increase proportionally with the lowering of pressure, as it should according to Dalton's law, and that it is only when the pressure acting on the blood is reduced to $\frac{1}{50}$ that the oxygen of the blood begins to dissociate. On combining the vacuum method of extracting the blood gases with the method of heating to 40 C. blood that had been extracted and diluted with a quantity of water previously boiled and deprived of its gases, he completed and partially rectified the conclusions of Magnus.

While approximately true, Meyer's data were not yet entirely accurate, as was shown by the succeeding work of Hoppe-Seyler (1854), Ludwig (1858), and Pflüger (1865). They introduced interesting improvements in technique, with the object of obtaining the maximal quantity of gases that can be extracted from a given quantity of arterial, venous, or asphyxial blood. In order, as briefly as possible, to condense the more important conclusions arrived at in the actual state of science, we must pass from the historical exposition of the subject to a summary of the experimental data.

Laws of Absorption and Diffusion of Blood. In order to understand what follows in regard to the mechanism of respiratory gas exchanges, it is necessary to recapitulate certain physical laws which are closely bound up with this process.

Since gases have no definite shape like solids, nor definite volume like liquids, and since the molecules which constitute them have the property of mutual repulsion, so, when two gases that do not enter into chemical combination, are brought into contact, they promptly expand one into the other, until they form a uniform mixture independent of their different densities. This phenomenon is called the diffusion of gases.

The force with which the molecules of the gases tend to expand in a space, and by means of which they exert uniform pressure in every direction, is called the tension of gases. Obviously, the greater the number of gaseous molecules brought together in a confined space, the greater will be the pressure. It follows that the tension of a gas is inversely proportional to its volume (Mariotte's law).

Again, when two gases are separated by a porous septum, there is reciprocal diffusion, but the velocity with which the molecules of each diffuse across the septum varies according to their densities; the lighter gases, such as H and CH_2, diffuse more rapidly than Cl and CO, which are heavier. It may be said approximately, with Graham, that the rate at which gases traverse the pores of the septum is inversely proportional to the square root of their densities.

There is a marked attraction between gases and particles of solid porous bodies, whereby the former are attracted and condensed between the pores of the latter. Thus, for example, 1 vol. of boxwood charcoal may condense at 12 C., and at ordinary barometric pressure, 35 vols. of CO_2, 9·4 vols. of O_2, 7·4 vols. N, 1·75 vols. H_2. This process is termed the absorption of gases by solid bodies, and is invariably accompanied by evolution of heat in ratio with the energy with which the absorption proceeds. Non-porous bodies, too, are capable of condensing, if not of absorbing on their surface, a layer of the gases with which they may be brought into contact.

More important for us is the absorption of gases by liquids. In this connection it has been found that the volume of a gas absorbed by a liquid is independent of its pressure. Since, however, the density of a gas is proportional to the pressure under which it is placed, and since its weight is equal to the product of volume × density (Boyle, 1662; Mariotte, 1679), it follows that the weight of gas absorbed by a liquid is proportional to the pressure, although its volume remains the same (Dalton-Henry law). Hence the gas must be regarded as physically absorbed by the liquid, whence it can be recovered in quantities proportional by weight to the lowering of pressure to which it is subjected. When, therefore, the pressure is reduced to zero by the Torricellian vacuum, the liquid can be deprived of all the gases which it has absorbed.

The absorption coefficient of a liquid for a gas is the figure which indicates that volume of gas which at 0 C. and 760 mm. Hg pressure, is absorbed by the unit volume of the liquid (Bunsen).

Temperature has great influence on coefficients of absorption. A liquid absorbs less gas, in proportion as its temperature is higher, and at boiling-point there is no longer any absorption. It is therefore sufficient, in order to extract the gases absorbed by any liquid, to heat it to boiling-point.

The degree in which different liquids absorb the same gas, and in which the different gases are absorbed by the same liquid, varies considerably. One volume of distilled water is capable of absorbing :—

C.	N.	O_2.	CO_2.	Air.
0	0·020	0·041	1·797	0·025
5	0·018	0·036	1·500	0·022
15	0·015	0·030	1·002	0·018
37	0·012	0·025	0·530	0·015

Indifferent salts which are incapable of combining chemically with gases, lower the absorption coefficients in watery solutions in proportion to their concentrations.

In the body it is always with gaseous mixtures in the fluids of the tissues, and never with isolated gases, that we have to deal. We must, therefore, investigate the absorption of gas mixtures by liquids. Since gases exert no reciprocal pressure, one volume of liquid may absorb several gases successively or simultaneously, in different volumes, according to the respective coefficients of absorption, and each gas absorbed is at a tension proportional with the volume that it occupies in the mixture of absorbed gases. Bunsen gave to this the name of partial pressure, because it represents the pressure in mm. Hg, which each gas would exert in the surrounding atmosphere, if there were neither absorption nor emission of gas on the part of the liquid. Since, e.g., the average pressure of atmospheric air is 760 mm. Hg, and it consists in round numbers of 21 vols. per cent O_2 and 79 vols. per cent N, the partial pressure of the oxygen absorption will be equal to 0·21 : 760 = 160 mm. Hg, and the partial pressure at which the absorption of N occurs is equal to 0·79 × 760 = 600 mm. Hg.

During absorption each gas of the mixture diffuses in the liquid in an amount proportional to the difference in concentration of the adjacent layers, as Graham shows for other substances in solution. Diffusion ceases and absorption is complete when in all layers of the liquid, and in the atmosphere with which it is in relation, complete equilibrium of tension for each of the gases contained in the atmosphere, or dissolved in the liquid, is established.

The rate of diffusion of a gas through a layer of liquid stands in direct ratio with the solubility coefficient of the gas, and in inverse ratio with the square root of its density. So that, e.g., although the diffusion rate of the molecules of H_2 is greater than that of the molecules of CO_2, the latter being more soluble in water than the former, more CO_2 than H_2 passes through a layer of liquid in a given time.

Generally speaking, the velocity of diffusion of a gas in a liquid is very low (Duncan and Hoppe-Seyler, 1894). They found that at ordinary barometric pressure and mean temperature, atmospheric air penetrates extremely slowly into a given quantity of water closed on all sides, save at the top where the air enters. After fourteen days of contact, absorption in the lower layers of the column of water was still incomplete.

V. The most important conclusions from the work carried out under the directions of Ludwig and Pflüger confirm the fact already determined by Magnus, to the effect that the amount of gas that can be extracted from arterial blood differs considerably from that of venous blood.

From the average of twelve analyses performed by Pflüger with the rapid method, it appears that the arterial blood of the dog contains 22·6 vols. per cent of oxygen (at 0 C. and 760 mm. Hg), 34·3 per cent of carbonic acid, and 1·8 per cent of nitrogen.

According to an analysis of Setschenow, human arterial blood contains 21·6 vols. per cent oxygen, 40·3 per cent carbonic acid, 1·5 per cent nitrogen. Some analyses of the blood of herbivores (sheep, rabbit) made by Sezelkow and Walter give 10·7-13·2 vols. per cent oxygen, 34-45 per cent carbonic acid, 1·8-2·1 per cent nitrogen.

The gas content of venous blood is more variable, according to analysis, since it depends on the circulatory velocity and activity of metabolism in the several tissues traversed. At present we have only analyses of the blood of the right heart, in which the reduced venous blood from the whole aortic capillary system meets and mingles. On the average of numerous analyses given in the tables of Zuntz, the venous blood of the dog contains 7·15 vols. per cent oxygen less than the arterial blood, 8·2 vols. per cent more carbonic acid, and much the same quantity of nitrogen, as arterial blood.

After asphyxia pushed so far as to kill the animal, the oxygen does not disappear from the whole of the blood, while the carbonic acid increases considerably. From a number of analyses of asphyxial blood made by Setschenow, Holmgren and others, it appears to contain 0·96 vols. per cent oxygen and 49·53 per cent carbonic acid: i.e. there is a deficit of 17·3 vols. per cent oxygen and 10·43 per cent excess carbonic acid, as compared with normal arterial blood, according to the values obtained by the said authors.

Method of Extracting Gases from the Blood. — The various forms of apparatus adopted, after Magnus, for the mechanical extraction of gases from the blood, are those of Hoppe-Seyler, Ludwig, Lothar Meyer, A. Schmidt, Pflüger, etc. They are all based essentially upon the Torricellian vacuum, and aim at liberating the gases dissolved in the fluids or held in loose combination. The most perfect form for the rapid and complete extraction of gases is that of Pflüger, as represented in Fig. 167.

It consists of three principal parts: the bulb *A* which receives the blood direct from the artery or vein; the tube for absorption of the water vapour to dry the extracted gases *B*; the mercury pump *CD* for aspiration and the reverse, *i.e.* production of the Torricellian vacuum, and expulsion of the gases extracted into the eudiometer tube for analysis.

The details of construction of the apparatus are so plain on the diagram that a minute description is superfluous.

The bulb *C* is first connected with the tube *H* by turning the 3-way tap *G*. The vessel *D* is then raised by the handle *L*, so that the whole of bulb *C*, with which *D* communicates by means of the strong rubber band *F* and the glass tube *E*, is filled with mercury. When *C* is full, communication with *H* is closed by a quarter turn of the tap *G*, and opened to the tube connected with the desiccating apparatus *B*, and also with the double bulb *A*, after opening the tap *P*. The vacuum is then started in the apparatus by lowering the vessel *D* by means of the handle *L*, on which all the mercury passes from *C* into *D*, and air rushes in from *A* and *B* to *C*. The tap

G is then brought back to its first position by a quarter turn, so that C is now connected with H and no longer with A and B, while the vessel D is once more raised, driving the air out of C, which fills with mercury. Frequent repetition of this process (of turning the tap G, alternately with raising and lowering of the vessel D of the mercury pump) produces a perfect vacuum throughout the apparatus, which occurs at the exact moment at which the

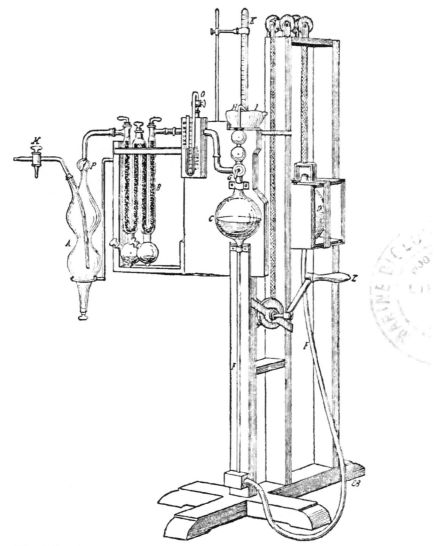

Fig. 167.—Pflüger's apparatus for extraction of blood gases. (Explanation in text.)

mercury of the manometer O, attached to the tube that connects C with B, falls to zero. The steadiness or oscillations of the manometer column show whether the apparatus is air-tight or not.

After making a perfect vacuum, the pointed upper end of the bulb A is connected with the cannula previously introduced into the blood-vessel (carotid or jugular). The 2-way tap M is turned so as to fill the connecting tube with blood which drives the air out, after which another quarter turn of the same tap lets the blood flow in the required quantity into the bulb A.

Directly the blood rushes into the vacuum it froths up, owing to the liberation of the gases. The froth collects in the upper part of the bulb, and cannot pass through the minute aperture of the cock P. In order to promote and complete the extraction of the gases, a cylinder of water heated to about 60 C. may be applied to the exterior of A. The gases liberated from the blood pass into the absorption tube B (which contains concentrated sulphuric acid in its lower end, and bits of dried pumice-stone saturated with the same acid along its length) and lose their water vapour, so that only dried gases reach the vessel C and are ready for chemical analysis.

The amount of blood run into the apparatus is next determined. Since the total capacity of the receiver is known, the amount of water still required to fill it at the end of the experiment is subtracted—the difference representing the volume of the blood employed. The determination is more exact if the amount of water absorbed in the tube B is calculated by weighing B before and after the experiment.

For quantitative determination of the gases extracted from the given amount of blood, they must be allowed to pass from the holder C into the eudiometer tube K, which is filled with mercury and inverted over the mercury trough I. This is easily done by making connection between C and K by the tap G through H, closing the connection between C and B, and raising the vessel D by the handle L, so that C acts as a pressure-pump. Frequent repetition of this process drives all the extracted gases into the eudiometer.

To determine the volume of the CO_2, a pellet of caustic potash, moistened at the surface and fused at the end to a platinum wire, is introduced into the eudiometer. When all the carbonic acid is converted into potassium carbonate, the pellet is removed by cautiously withdrawing the platinum wire. The diminution in volume of the gas in the eudiometer gives the volume of CO_2 extracted from the blood.

The volumetric determination of the O_2 is effected in a similar way by introducing a pellet of phosphorus on a platinum wire, or a ball of filter-paper saturated with a solution of pyrogallic acid in caustic potash, which greedily absorbs oxygen. After the ball has been removed, the further diminution of gas in the eudiometer shows the volume of O_2 extracted from the blood.

The volume of gas remaining in the eudiometer after the absorption of CO_2 and O_2 consists of nitrogen.

VI. Some notion of the quantity of the gases that can be extracted from the blood is a necessary premiss to determining the state in which they are found, whether free, or in simple physical solution, or in chemical combination.

As regards oxygen, it may be argued from the large amount contained in the blood that it cannot be merely in a state of solution. As a matter of fact the coefficient of absorption of water for oxygen stands at a rather low figure; at 0 C. and 760 mm. Hg, of an atmosphere of pure oxygen, not more than 4 vols. per cent are absorbed, hence from the air (in which the partial pressure of oxygen is five times less) under 1 vol. per cent is absorbed. On raising the temperature of the water to that of the body, the coefficient of absorption for oxygen is still further lowered. It is also lowered considerably if the water is replaced by a watery solution isotonic with blood plasma. Obviously, therefore, the 22 vols. of oxygen contained in arterial blood must, to a large extent, be in a state of chemical combination (Liebig, 1851 ; L. Meyer and Fernet, 1857). We know, in fact, that the oxygen absorbed by the blood is in loose combination with the haemoglobin of the erythrocytes, which gives rise to the formation of oxyhaemoglobin (Hoppe-Seyler, 1864 ; see Chap. IV. 7).

The proof of this fact, one of capital importance in the physiology of the respiratory exchanges, is that a watery solution of 14 per cent pure haemoglobin (which corresponds to the normal haemoglobin content of the blood) is capable of absorbing and chemically fixing as much oxygen as an equal volume of blood, and

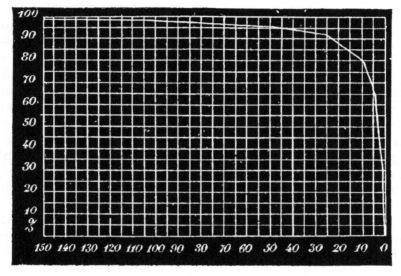

Fig. 168.—Curve to show percentage variations of oxyhaemoglobin in a solution of 14 per cent blood-pigment, with variations of partial pressure of the atmospheric oxygen with which it comes in contact. (Hufner.) Quantity of oxyhaemoglobin in $\frac{1}{100}$ along axis of ordinates ; partial pressure of oxygen in mm. Hg, along axis of abscissa.

by means of the Torricellian vacuum it is possible to extract as much oxygen from the same solution as from blood.

It was fundamental to the conception of oxygen absorption in the blood, to determine to what point the quantity that combines with haemoglobin depends on its partial pressure in the atmosphere. Bohr (1885) and Hüfner (1888) made a number of experiments with this object. The method consisted in placing a given quantity of defibrinated blood, or better, of 14 per cent solution of pure haemoglobin (which, as we have said, corresponds with the haemoglobin content of the blood) in contact either with normal air, or with artificial air containing a considerably less amount of oxygen per cent ; and then shaking it. It is then determined how much oxygen combines with, or is dissociated from, the haemoglobin on a rise or fall of its partial pressure in the mixture of gases Hüfner's results are clearly expressed in the diagram (Fig. 168), which represents the curve of dissociation of oxygen and haemoglobin, in proportion with the fall of partial pressure in the mixture of gases. The curve shows that at the partial pressure of 150 mm. Hg (which is a little lower than that of the oxygen of normal air) almost the whole of the haemoglobin (about 98 per cent) combines with the oxygen : that the dissociation proceeds very slowly till a partial pressure of 50 mm. (which corresponds to about a third of the partial pressure of the oxygen of normal air) is reached ; and that it only becomes rapid at a partial pressure of 25 – 10 - 5 mm. Hg. These results show that the blood, in consequence of the chemical affinity of haemoglobin for oxygen, is able to provide itself with an abundant supply, even when the organism is breathing an atmosphere very poor in this gas ; while, on the other hand, the absorption of oxygen in the blood cannot rise far above the normal, even when the organism is made to respire an atmosphere of pure oxygen.

A proof of this great independence of the absorption of the oxygen of the blood from its partial pressure in the atmosphere is shown in the fact that mammals do not exhibit any visible disturbance of respiratory function when they are made to breathe an artificial atmosphere three times richer, or one-half poorer in oxygen than the normal air ; and it is only when the partial pressure of oxygen falls below this limit that the respiratory movements are progressively accelerated, and death from lack of oxygen only occurs when the partial pressure of O_2 is lowered to ·3·5 mm. Hg (W. Müller, P. Bert).

On examining in dogs how the oxygen content of arterial blood varies with the progressive rarefaction of the atmospheric air respired, it was found that it remains normal up to a total pressure of 410 mm. Hg : that it diminishes slightly at a pressure 378-365 mm. (= about half an atmosphere) : and that it is only at a total pressure of 300 mm. that any conspicuous diminution of oxygen can be observed in arterial blood (Fränkel and Geppert). These facts agree with the observations made during aërostatic ascents, which show that respiratory disturbances only begin at a height of 5000 meters (= 400 mm. Hg). On the other hand, it has been observed on the high plains of the Andes that men and animals can live as well at 4000 metres altitude as at the level of the sea.

Not quite the whole of the oxygen is in chemical combination with haemoglobin ; a small fraction of it (0·1-0·2 vols. per cent) is normally held in solution in the plasma. This quantity is, however, less, under normal conditions, than what can be absorbed by an equal volume of distilled water at the same temperature. It may vary according to the Henry-Dalton law, i.e. the volume of oxygen dissolved in the plasma is proportional to its tension. In proportion as the tissue elements absorb the oxygen of the plasma, and the tension lessens, there must necessarily be dissociation of the haemoglobin of the erythrocytes from the oxygen, which diffuses in the plasma to re-establish equilibrium between the tension of the oxygen in the plasma and the corpuscles.

VII. The carbonic acid of the blood is also for the most part in chemical combination, and to a minimal extent in solution. This is proved by the fact that the coefficient of absorption of this gas in water, at 37° C., is about 0·57, while on the other hand we have seen that arterial blood only contains 34 and venous blood 42 vols. per cent. Unlike oxygen, however, which enters into combination only with haemoglobin, carbonic acid unites chemically with many substances, both of the plasma and of the corpuscles.

Among the substances capable of holding the carbonic acid of the blood in readily dissociable forms, great stress was formerly laid upon sodium carbonate, which as a base (see p. 132) abounds in the ash of plasma. The phenomena of electrolytic dissociation of the solutions of this salt have, however, demonstrated that it can only be of very secondary importance in the chemical combination of the carbonic acid of the plasma, by converting it into bi-carbonate. In fact, according to the researches of Bohr, a very dilute solution of 0·15 per cent sodium carbonate becomes almost saturated at a pressure of only 10 mm. Hg of carbonic acid, while on raising the pressure to 120 mm. there is no appreciable increase in the amount fixed or dissolved. Hence it is evident that sodium carbonate is incapable of fixing more than a minimal amount of the carbonic acid of the blood.

The alkaline phosphates of plasma, which are capable of conversion into acid phosphates by association with carbonic acid, were again erroneously credited with too much importance (Fernet). We saw in fact (p. 139) that the main part of the phosphoric anhydride found in the ash of plasma is derived from combustion of the lecithin and nucleo-albumins, and that normal plasma contains only the merest trace of sodic phosphate (Sertoli).

On the other hand, according to the observations of Setschenow and Torup, maximal importance in the fixation of carbonic acid must be assigned to the globulins of the serum, which, by acting as weak acids, are able to combine with the alkalies of the blood. When the tension of carbonic acid increases, the globulins of the alkalies are dissociated, and combine with the carbonic acid to form carbonates; when, on the contrary, the tension of carbonic acid falls the globulins are again associated with the alkalies, leaving the CO_2 in the free state.

Since carbonic acid is also found in the corpuscles of the blood in a readily dissociable form, it is probable that the combinations of the globulins with the alkalies exercise the same office in the corpuscles as in the plasma, in the dissociation of carbonic acid. It should, however, be noted that the absorption of the latter, as effected by the corpuscles, is, in comparison with absorption in the

serum, dependent to a much greater extent on the partial pressure
of the CO_2.   According to Bohr, this fact depends on the capacity
of the haemoglobin to unite chemically not only with the oxygen,
but also with the carbonic acid.   He further showed that this last
combination is in no way obstructed by the simultaneous combination with oxygen; which leads us to suppose that the two gases
are fixed in two different portions of the haemoglobin molecule, *i.e.*
the oxygen in the iron-containing portion of the colouring matter,
the carbonic acid in the protein residue (Fig. 169).

   According to Fredericq the non-coagulated venous blood of the
horse is capable of absorbing 71·4 vols. per cent of carbonic acid,
while the mass of corpuscles from the same animal only absorbs

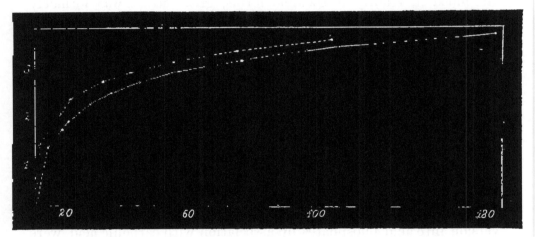

Fig. 169.—Curve of absorption of CO_2, by 1·76 per cent solution of haemoglobin (dotted line), and
   by one of 3·8 per cent (unbroken line) in relation to progressive increase of pressure. (Bohr.) The
   pressure (in mm. Hg) is recorded along the axis of the abscissae ; the amount of CO_2 (in c.c.)
   absorbed by 1 grm. haemoglobin, along the axis of the ordinates.

49·6 vols. per cent.   It follows that the amount of CO_2 fixed by the
plasma is greatly in excess of that fixed by the corpuscles.

   The carbonic acid of the serum, according to the unanimous
results of Fredericq, Zuntz, and Alex. Schmidt, is about 86 per
cent of that contained in the whole of the blood.   It is possible,
however, that in the process of defibrination, part of the carbonic
acid of the corpuscles may pass into the serum, and that under
normal conditions the gas content of the blood is divided in
different proportions between the corpuscles and the plasma.
Certain experiments of Hamburger show, indeed, that by merely
changing the amount of gases in the blood, some individual substances may pass from the plasma to the corpuscles, and from
the corpuscles to the plasma.

   Another notable fact is, that by means of the Torricellian
vacuum, it is possible to extract from the blood the whole of the
carbonic acid which it holds in combination (Setschenow).   From

serum, on the contrary, with the simple vacuum, it is only possible to extract one part, and the addition of a weak acid is required to extract the residue, which is more stably combined, and is present in the blood to the amount of 5-9 vols. per cent (Pflüger). The fact that this portion also is turned out, *in vacuo*, in the presence of corpuscles, without adding acid, suggests that the corpuscles contain substances that function as acids, and that these are diffused into the plasma during the action of the vacuum, or that the sodic carbonate of the plasma penetrates to the corpuscles. Among the acids of the corpuscles the first place must be given to phosphoric anhydride, which they contain in larger quantities than the plasma: besides which the oxyhaemoglobin functions as an acid, as was demonstrated by Preyer, since it is capable of liberating carbonic acid from its sodium combinations *in vacuo*.

In regard to nitrogen and argon, we must confine ourselves to saying that these gases are found in the blood in amounts differing little from those in which they are absorbed and dissolved by watery fluids in the presence of atmospheric air. According to Regnard and Schloesing, about 0·04 vol. per cent of the 2 vols. per cent of indifferent gases extracted from the blood are argon. The opinion held by some that a small amount of free nitrogen is developed during the oxidative processes of the nitrogenous substances of the tissues, and is subsequently poured into the blood, has not at present been confirmed by any incontrovertible evidence. Regnault and Reiset found a slight increase of nitrogen in expired as compared with inspired air. So, too, the nitrogen extractible from venous blood is always somewhat greater than that which can be extracted from arterial blood. Pettenkofer and Voit gave an adequate explanation of these facts, on the assumption that they depend on the swallowing of air with the food, and on the absorption of the nitrogen contained in the gases of the intestines.

VIII. Since both oxygen and carbonic acid are thus found in the blood in the form of readily dissociable combinations (in relation to variations of partial pressure), it is natural to conclude that the gas exchanges which take place incessantly between the blood circulating through the capillaries of the lungs and the air contained in the pulmonary alveoli (external respiration) are accomplished by a simple physical process of diffusion, regulated by Dalton's law. They depend, *i.e.*, on the difference of the partial pressures of the said gases as contained in the fluid and gaseous media, separated by permeable septa or membranes, formed by the walls of the capillaries and the epithelial cells that line the alveoli.

The scientific demonstration of this theory involved a series of researches, directed to the separate determination of the partial pressures of the two gases in venous and in arterial blood, in order to compare them with those of inspired and expired air.

In order to determine the *tension* or *partial pressure* of the O_2 or CO_2 of the air (at 0° C., and mean pressure of 760 mm. Hg) it is sufficient to know

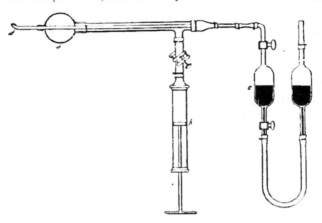

FIG. 170.—Pflüger's pulmonary catheter, modified by Ludwig.

its percentage composition. Since inspired air contains 20·96 per cent of O_2 and 0·03 per cent of CO_2, the partial pressure of the $O_2 = 159\cdot3$ mm. Hg, and that of the $CO_2 = 0\cdot228$ mm. Hg. To determine the tension of the gases of expired air, whether emitted from the trachea, or at a deeper level where it bifurcates with the bronchi, it is sufficient to determine the percentage composition of the O_2 and CO_2 in the air obtained during expiration by an air-pump attached to a simple sound, the end of which can be introduced more or less deeply into the respiratory passages.

It is, on the contrary, difficult to determine exactly the tension of the O_2 and CO_2 of the circulating blood, venous or arterial. Indirect methods have to be employed for this purpose.

Pflüger and Wolffberg, to determine the tension of O_2 and CO_2 in venous blood circulating in the pulmonary capillaries, devised the method of sounding the lung by a very simple instrument, which they called the pulmonary catheter (Fig. 170). It consists of two elastic tubes, the finer of which is inserted into the larger. The first has an open end, intended to communicate with one of the bronchi, from which air can be aspirated by means of the Torricellian vacuum at the other end. The second is closed, and terminates in a thin rubber balloon, which can be easily inflated by a small bellows.

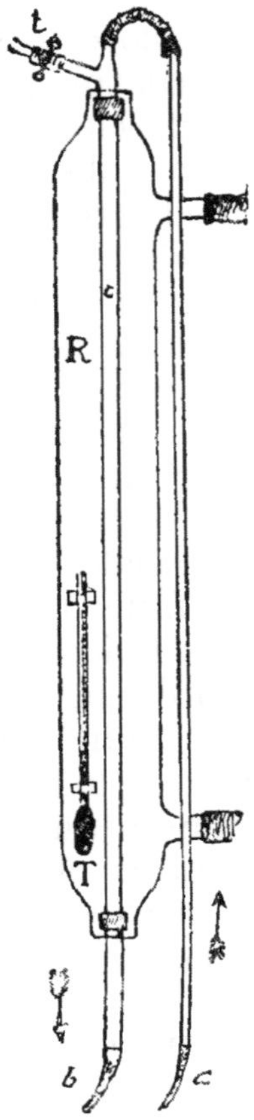

Having opened the trachea of a dog, the sound is introduced into the bronchus leading to the inferior left lobe of the lung; the small terminal vesicle of the external tube is then inflated, so that it hermetically seals the bronchus into which it is introduced, and makes the corresponding lobe of the lung impervious to external air, which does not appreciably disturb the respiratory movements of the animal. After four to five minutes the air contained within the blocked lobe of the lung

FIG. 171.—Fredericq's aerotonometer. The blood, which is rendered incoagulable with peptone, rises from the carotid in tube *a*; spreads over surface of larger tube *c*, where, by diffusion, it is brought into equilibrium of tension with the mixture of gases therein contained; and returns by the jugular vein into the animal by tube *b*. Tube *c* is covered with a large tube *R*, within which water at the temperature of the animal's body is kept continuously circulating. The small lateral tube *t* introduces the artificial mixture of gases into tube *c* at the commencement of the experiment. The thermometer T regulates temperature of water circulating in *R* during the experiment.

is again in equilibrium with the tension of the gases of the venous blood circulating in it. The air is then aspirated from the sound, and its percentage composition determined by Bunsen's method.

The values found for the CO_2 and O_2 tension indirectly indicate the tension of these gases in the venous blood circulating in the capillaries of the lungs.

The tension of the O_2 and CO_2 of arterial blood is determined by means of the so-called aerotonometers. The simplest form is that of Fredericq, represented in Fig. 171. It consists of a glass tube, filled with a gaseous mixture of known composition (10 per cent of O_2, 5 per cent CO_2, and the rest N), along the internal surface of which there is a constant flow of blood from the carotid artery. During its passage through the tube, the tensions of the blood-gases and of the artificial mixture of gases are equilibrated.

By making the blood incoagulable through previous injection of propeptone or albumose, and returning to the circulation by the jugular vein the blood that left by the carotid, the experiment can be prolonged for a considerable time (an hour or more), so as to be certain of having established equilibrium of tension between the gases of the arterial blood and those contained in the aerotonometer. The blood that flows through the instrument is maintained at body temperature by means of an external glass jacket in which water is circulated at the required temperature. When the experiment is completed, the percentage composition of the mixture of gases in the aerotonometer is calculated by the usual method, and the values obtained express the partial pressure of the O_2 and CO_2 of arterial blood.

The experiments on the tension of the respiratory gases have not led to uniform results: they vary greatly even in the same animals under slightly different conditions.

The following table gives the average values cited by F. Schenck and A. Gürber in their *Text-Book of Human Physiology* (1897), which all relate to experiments carried out on dogs :—

At 0 C. and 760 mm. Hg.	Inspired Air.	Expired Air.	Arterial Blood.	Venous Blood.
	mm. Hg.	mm. Hg.	mm. Hg.	mm. Hg.
Oxygen . .	150	122	29·6	21·0
Carbonic Acid .	0·3	30	22·0	41·0

These data coincide perfectly with the theory which holds the respiratory gas exchanges to be the effects of simple diffusion, which causes the gases to pass from the point of greater to that of less tension. In fact the tension of O_2 is seen to diminish from inspired to expired air, and from that to arterial blood; and the tension of CO_2 diminishes from venous blood to that of expired air, and thence to that of inspired air. The oxygen must therefore be absorbed by diffusion from the respiratory passages into the arterial blood, while the carbonic acid must be exhaled by diffusion from the venous blood into the respiratory passages.

The results of Bohr's subsequent experiments do not, however, agree with this theory. With one of his special aerotonometers he determined the tension of the gases in the circulating arterial blood, and that of the expired air at the tracheal bifurcation. He repeatedly found that the partial pressure of the carbonic acid of the blood was less, and that of the oxygen greater, than the respective partial pressures of the two gases in expired air.

In some of Bohr's experiments, for instance, the partial pressure of the O_2 and CO_2 varies as follows :—

O_2 of arterial blood	= 100-144 mm. Hg.	
O_2 of expired air, at tracheal bifurcation .	. 95-130	,,
CO_2 of arterial blood	. = 17- 30	,,
CO_2 of expired air, at tracheal bifurcation	. 35- 41	,,

Against these results of Bohr, the objection that he did not allow sufficient time for equilibrium of tension to be established between the gases of the arterial blood and the artificial air contained in the aerotonometer, has no weight, because in this air, before the entrance of the arterial blood, the partial pressure of the O_2 was less, and that of the CO_2 was greater, than after the experiment. On the basis of these facts, which are opposed to the theory of diffusion as the sole determinant of pulmonary gas exchanges, Bohr puts forward the hypothesis that the walls of the pulmonary alveoli function as a secreting gland, and that the cells that line them are capable of actively absorbing oxygen and exhaling carbonic acid, even against the laws of the diffusion of gases.

Fredericq in his latest work does not accept Bohr's conclusions. He invariably finds the tension of oxygen in the arterial blood to be less, and that of carbonic acid greater, than the respective tensions of the two gases in alveolar air. But this (as Tigerstedt has pointed out) does not contradict the phenomena observed by Bohr. One single fact, determined under valid experimental conditions to be irreconcilable with the exclusive theory of diffusion, gives legitimate reason to suspect that other forces intervene in the production of gas exchanges, and are capable of accelerating the effects of diffusion, and even of acting in opposition to its laws. The study of this interesting question deserves to be pursued without prejudice, the more so as Bohr has discovered another fact that appears to be of the utmost importance. After collecting and analysing the gases contained in the swim-bladder of certain fishes caught at a great depth, he found them to contain as much as 80 per cent oxygen. On puncturing and emptying the swim-bladder, he found that it filled anew with oxygen, but only on condition that the nerve plexuses leading to it were spared. Once this fact is admitted, the legitimate conclusion must be that the cells lining the swim-bladder (which may be regarded as a modified lung) function as glandular elements secreting oxygen under the influence of the nervous system, and contrary to the laws of diffusion ; just as the salivary cells, in obedience to nervous impulses, secrete saliva in defiance of a counter-pressure greater than that of the arterial blood circulating in the gland (Ludwig).

Haldane and Smith (1896) investigated the tension of oxygen in the pulmonary blood by a method applicable to man. The method is based on the fact already demonstrated by Haldane in 1895, that with simultaneous action of oxygen and carbonic oxide on the blood, the amount of the carbonic oxide fixed by the blood is proportional to the oxygen tension, so that it is possible from the degree of absorption of carbonic oxide in the blood to calculate the tension of the oxygen present. If a man or other animal is made to breathe a gaseous mixture containing a small quantity (exactly determined) of CO for a time long enough to make the carbonic oxide content constant in the blood (measuring it at intervals by small samples of blood taken from the subject), it is possible from the degree, thus measured, of fixation of CO by the blood, to calculate the O_2 tension that prevails in the pulmonary blood. It results from these experiments that the O_2 tension in the blood of a man's lungs amounts to 26·2 hundredths of an atmosphere equal to 200 mm. Hg, a figure that is inexplicable on the hypothesis of simple gas diffusion as the cause of the absorption of oxygen in the lung. Identical results were obtained from experiments on birds and mice (1897), by means of which these authors were also able to show how want of oxygen acted as a stimulus to the active absorption of this gas by the pulmonary epithelium.

With regard to the process of the elimination of CO_2 from the lungs in the air of the pulmonary alveoli, Grandis (1900) called attention to a new factor which had till then escaped the notice of physiologists.

It is known that in addition to CO_2, a considerable amount of water-vapour is eliminated by the expired air from the blood plasma circulating through the lung (according to Loewy, alveolar air contains about 6 per cent of aqueous vapour). The blood accordingly undergoes a temporary increase of concentration during its passage through the lungs, which, by raising the CO_2 tension, must facilitate its expulsion into the alveolar air. Grandis confirmed the importance of this fact by certain experiments in vitro, in which he artificially increased the concentration of the blood, by adding strong solutions of sodium chloride and sugar, with the effect of a prompt rise of tension in the gases of the blood.

On the ground of these experiments he thinks it probable that in living animals also the greater concentration of the blood, on evaporation of the water in the pulmonary alveoli, must facilitate the expulsion of CO_2. The experiments of Grandis, however, show that the greater concentration of the blood raises the tension, not only of the CO_2, but also of the O_2, and thus can have no appreciable value as a factor in the pulmonary gas exchanges—seeing that if on the one hand it facilitates the elimination of CO_2 from the blood, it checks the absorption of O_2 on the other.

Another question indirectly connected with the nature of the pulmonary gas exchanges, is that which refers to the influence which is, or can be, exercised upon them by the nervous system.

At the end of 1892, Henriques demonstrated experimentally in rabbits and dogs that stimulation of both vagi might cause variations in the respiratory gas exchanges of the lungs. These experiments were taken up by Maar in 1902, and extended both to cold-blooded animals (tortoises) and to the warm-blooded (rabbit). He endeavoured to define the precise effect of section and artificial stimulation of the vagus and sympathetic upon the pulmonary gas exchanges. The experiments on cold-blooded animals led to the conclusion that absorption of oxygen by the lungs was under the influence of the nervous system, the vagus containing both nerve fibres that increase the absorption of oxygen, and also other fibres that diminish it. The former run to the lung of the opposite side, the latter to that of the same side. It was found impossible to establish any direct influence of the sympathetic on respiratory pulmonary exchanges, nor did the experiments on warm-blooded animals lead to any definite or concordant results. The demonstration of a *direct* influence of the nervous system on the pulmonary gas exchanges tells in favour of Bohr's theory.

In speaking of recent work on this subject, mention must be made of Krogh (1904), who studied the cutaneous and pulmonary respiration of the frog, and came to the conclusion that cutaneous respiration (which serves especially for elimination of carbonic acid) is independent of the nervous system, and can be explained on purely physical grounds (gaseous diffusion), while pulmonary respiration (which particularly controls the absorption of oxygen) is, on the contrary, effected principally by secretory processes of the epithelium, and is regulated by the nervous system.

On the other hand, Loewy and Zuntz in their latest publication (1904) still contend that the laws of diffusion adequately account for the gas exchanges between the alveolar air and the blood. They determined the velocity with which carbonic acid traverses an excised frog's lung, and from this, taking into account the varying thickness of the pulmonary walls, deduced the conditions of gas diffusion in the human lung. They conclude that the conditions of diffusion for the passage of oxygen from the pulmonary alveoli to the blood, and thence to the tissues, are so favourable that they ensure more than sufficient absorption of oxygen, even in the most extreme cases of rarefaction of air compatible with life.

IX. We know very little as yet about the physico-chemical processes which complete the gas exchanges between the blood circulating in the aortic capillaries, and the living cells of the tissues, by the agency of the interstitial lymph (*internal respiration*).

It was formerly supposed that the transformation of arterial into venous blood took place within the capillaries. But there are well-ascertained facts which prove the blood, when extracted and kept at body temperature, not to be the seat of any very energetic oxidative phenomena. The oxygen it contains gradually disappears, *i.e.* drawn arterial blood slowly becomes venous. On the other hand, circulating arterial blood is known not to become venous along the entire course of the aortic system, but only when it is passing through the capillaries. This fact was explained on the hypothesis that the intermediate products of tissue consumption, which reach the arterial blood by the capillaries, consisted of reducing substances, *i.e.* are avid of oxygen, which they rapidly subtract from the oxyhaemoglobin. This supposition is no longer admissible, since it has been demonstrated that only the erythrocytes, not the blood plasma, nor the lymph of asphyxiated animals (in which there must be an accumulation of many reducing substances), are capable of chemically combining with oxygen. Neither the blood plasma, then, nor the lymph, contain reducing substances, since the latter do not pass into these fluids, but arise in the living cells of the tissues which breathe in virtue of their metabolism, *i.e.* they take up oxygen and give off carbonic acid. It is therefore evident that the tissues are the seat of internal respiration, and if the blood also breathes, however slowly, this is in virtue of the mass of corpuscles which it contains, and by which it functions as a tissue.

Many direct proofs might be adduced as to the correctness of this theory. When fragments of living tissue, particularly of muscle, are dissolved in drawn arterial blood or in a solution of oxyhaemoglobin, a rapid reduction follows, by which the oxyhaemoglobin is promptly converted into haemoglobin in that portion of the fluid which immediately surrounds the fragments (Hoppe-Seyler). If benzylic alcohol or salicylic aldehyde are added to the arterial blood drawn from the vessels, it does not oxidise to any appreciable extent; if, on the other hand, this blood, *plus* one of the above substances, is circulated in the vessels of organs recently extracted from a living animal (kidney or lung), considerable quantities of benzoic or salicylic acid are at once produced by oxidation (Schmiedeberg). The oxidation performed by the isolated surviving organ seems due to the action of special enzymes contained within the cells of the tissues (Schmiedeberg, Jacquet, Buchner).

All tissues breathe (Paul Bert), but it is particularly in muscle that the oxidising processes acquire a greater degree of intensity, and have been most studied. Active muscle breathes in excess of resting muscle. Blood coming from the vein of a tetanised muscle is dark in colour, and contains a minimal amount of oxyhaemoglobin : while the blood which comes from a muscle that is resting, or paralysed by section of its motor nerve, presents the normal characters of venous blood, in which—as we have seen—the oxygen content may exceed 15 vols. per cent of the blood.

Again, when muscle is placed under conditions that prevent it from absorbing oxygen, *e.g.* when it is brought into an atmosphere of hydrogen or nitrogen, it continues to give off carbonic acid, and for a certain time is capable of contracting (Hermann, see p. 68). It would thus seem that muscle must be allowed the property of taking up and storing oxygen in such a condition that it cannot be removed by simple lowering of pressure. The oxygen required for the formation of carbonic acid, given off by muscle in the presence of nitrogen and hydrogen, is certainly derived from that previously stored up and fixed in a compound similar to, but more stable than, that into which it enters with haemoglobin, and which has been wrongly termed *intermolecular oxygen*.

According to recent work of Verworn, Baglioni, and H. Winterstein (1900-1907), the tissue whose vitality is most strictly associated with the action of free oxygen is the central nervous system. Baglioni, *e.g.*, found on isolating the frog's spinal cord from the body after cutting out the circulation, and taking as the index of its activity the reflex movements of a posterior limb, connected with the cord by the sciatic nerve, that the reflex activity of the cord is in strict ratio with the O_2 tension of the surrounding atmosphere. If placed in a moist chamber, through which nitrogen is passed without a trace of oxygen, such a spinal cord at a temperature of 15-20° C. ceases to exhibit reflexes after half to three-quarters of an hour. If it is then suddenly brought back into the presence of oxygen, it recovers its vitality. On the other hand, Baglioni succeeded in keeping alive the isolated spinal cord of amphibia for a comparatively long period (forty-eight hours and more) by placing it in a warm chamber through which pure oxygen was circulated. This specifically high demand of the central nervous system for oxygen explains the fact that in all cases of asphyxia or lack of oxygen in the blood, the first tissue that feels the toxic effects, and ceases its activities, is the central nervous system (cerebral cortex, spinal cord : see p. 70). We shall return to this subject in Vol. III., in treating of the physiology of the nervous system.

Moleschott enunciated the hypothesis that the oxygen passing from the blood to the tissues is utilised in the constructive processes, *i.e.* it enters into the most complex substances of the tissues, which then, on splitting up, generate carbonic acid. Cl. Bernard also admits that "the oxygen combines in some way with the tissues so as to constitute a provision for use when the animal is unable to procure it from without." He based this assumption particularly on the fact that muscle absorbs more oxygen during rest, and spends more during activity, as though it accumulated reserves to expend lavishly when need arises. Nothing definite is known, however, as to the nature of the probable combinations formed by oxygen with the different materials for building up muscles and other tissues, or of the intermediate anabolic and katabolic forms, through which it passes in combining with carbon into carbonic acid. "The whole mystery of life," says Foster, "lies hidden in the story of that progress, and for the present we must be content with simply knowing the beginning and the end."

We know that carbonic acid is one of the ultimate products of the katabolic processes, and that the variations in the amount formed and eliminated by the tissues are, as Fano says, an expression "of corresponding changes in the course of the destructive processes. The assimilated oxygen on the contrary enters, at least in part, into the molecular structure of our tissues, is included in the series of synthetic processes, and may partially be considered as an element which contributes to the anabolic or constructive processes." We shall return to this argument in treating of the metabolism or material exchanges of the body as a whole.

In regard to this subject of the respiratory gas exchanges between the blood and the tissues, the facts observed by Pflüger and Strassburg, to the effect that the lymph, serous fluids, and certain secretions (bile, urine, saliva, milk) formed within the living tissues contain merely a trace of oxygen, and a comparatively large amount of carbonic acid, are very remarkable. These authors conclude that O_2 tension is low or practically *nil* in the tissues, while the CO_2 tension on the contrary is high.

The high tension of carbonic acid that prevails, according to recent researches, in living tissues is of especial significance, because it facilitates the dissociation of oxygen from oxyhaemoglobin, and thus places at the disposal of the tissues the maximum possible amount of the oxygen received from the blood. Bohr, Hasselbalch, and Krogh (1904) found that on bringing dog's blood, *in vitro*, at 38° C. into the presence, simultaneously, of O_2 at low tension (5 mm. Hg), and of CO_2 at various tensions, the blood absorbs a less degree of O_2 than when it is in presence of O_2 alone, and that the decrease in absorption is proportional to the amount of CO_2 simultaneously present. This influence is much less felt if the O_2 tension is progressively raised, as is clearly shown on the diagram (Fig. 172).

The physiological value of this fact will be readily appreciated.

Since the tension of the carbonic acid constantly increases with the passage of the blood into the aortic capillaries, this must facilitate the dissociation of oxygen, and increase its concentration in the blood plasma, so that it can be easily absorbed by the endothelia of the capillaries and the tissue cells. The increase in tension of the carbonic acid partly compensates for the diminished concentration of oxygen in the plasma due to its consumption by the tissues. This regulation is of especial importance in asphyxia, when the oxygen of the blood is much attenuated.

On the other hand the high tension of carbonic acid in the pulmonary capillaries does not in any way diminish the absorption

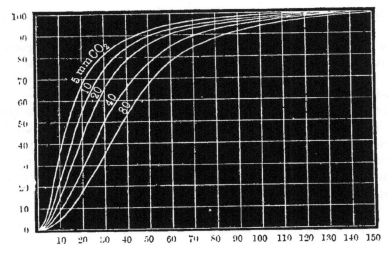

FIG. 172.—Curve showing influence of varying quantity of CO_2 on absorption of oxygen at different pressures, from defibrinated dog's blood at 38° C. (Bohr, Hasselbalch, and Krogh). The percentage amount of oxygen absorbed is marked on the axes of the ordinates; the different pressures of oxygen in mm. H_g, on the axes of the abscissa, while the different pressures of CO_2 acting simultaneously in the pressure of blood, are indicated above the respective curves.

of oxygen, for which, as has been shown, the influence of carbonic acid becomes negligible in the presence of high oxygen tensions.

This fact suffices to explain on a simple process of diffusion the gas exchanges between the blood and the tissues, by which the latter continually absorb oxygen and give off carbonic acid, converting arterial into venous blood. The data in regard to external respiration, do not, however, preclude the probability that the physical laws of diffusion may, in the case of internal respiration also, be modified by the activity of the cells which build up the walls of the capillaries.

X. We have seen that Lavoisier conceived of respiratory chemistry as a slow double combustion of carbon and hydrogen by which are formed carbonic acid and water. He was the first to show that the amount of O_2 absorbed exceeds that of the CO_2 exhaled, from which fact he deduced the formation of water.

The gas exchanges of respiration are, however, more complicated, as is readily seen on examining the changes induced in external air by animal respiration.

Expired air, in comparison with inspired air, presents the following differences :

(*a*) It contains 5 vols. per cent less of oxygen (according to Vierordt 16·033 vols. per cent instead of 20·95 vols. per cent).

(*b*) It contains a considerable amount of carbonic acid (from 3·3-5·5 vols. per cent, according to Vierordt).

(*c*) According to Regnault and Reiset, and Seegen and Nowak, expired air contains a slight excess of nitrogen, but whether this is a waste product from the tissues owing to decomposition of protein is doubtful, as already stated; more probably it comes from absorption in the blood of the excess nitrogen contained in the intestinal gases.

(*d*) It contains traces of free hydrogen, of marsh gas, of ammonia, and of other gases of hitherto unknown composition. It is certain that these substances arise partly from the absorption of intestinal gases, partly from exhalations of putrefactive excreta that clog the skin and integuments (Hermann, 1883), partly from pulmonary exhalations which when collected and condensed in sterilised water, and inoculated subcutaneously, have a toxic action (Brown-Séquard and D'Arsonval). Formanek has recently (1900) occupied himself exclusively with the question of the toxicity of expired air. He found that air passed by the method of Brown-Séquard and D'Arsonval through cages of animals contained a really toxic substance, which was identified with ammonia. This ammonia was not, however, derived from the expired air, but from the decomposition of urine and faeces within the cages. When this source of impurity was eliminated, expired air was obtained which had no toxic action. Formanek concluded that no toxic substances were developed in the lungs of man and other healthy animals. The sense of malaise which sensitive persons experience in crowded rooms must arise reflexly, from disturbance of thermal regulation, or the respiration of foul-smelling substances.

(*e*) The expired air is saturated or nearly so with the aqueous vapour exhaled along the respiratory passages.

(*f*) It is partly deprived of the dust, and the germs or sporules that are never absent from inspired air, and which are arrested all along the respiratory tract by the moisture of its walls —these being clothed with vibratile epithelia, whose function is to expel them, along with the mucus secreted by the muciparous cells.

(*g*) Its temperature is approximately that of the body (35-36° C.), consequently its volume when it issues from the respiratory passages exceeds that of the inspired air, to which the aqueous vapour with which it is saturated also contributes. When the expired air is again reduced to the temperature and degree of moisture of that inspired, it presents in relation to the latter a slight diminution of volume, as first noted by Lavoisier (1777).

The chemical composition of expired air varies between sufficiently wide limits, not merely in different classes and species of animals, but also in the same individual under different external and internal conditions, according to the frequency and depth of the respiratory movements. The slower and deeper these are, the greater will be the output of carbonic acid and intake of oxygen. The first portions of air given off in a respiratory act, which come from the more superficial bronchial passages, contain less carbon dioxide and more oxygen, in comparison with the later portions of expired air, which come from the deeper bronchial tubes and the alveoli.

It is obvious that the more perfect the pulmonary ventilation consequent on the deepest respiratory acts, the more rapid and abundant will be the gas exchanges, and therewith the emission of carbonic acid and absorption of oxygen in the time unit. Experience, however, shows that increased pulmonary ventilation does not merely increase the gas exchanges, which would be a temporary effect, but also increases the formation of carbonic acid, i.e. the absolute quantity which is expelled in the unit of time. This phenomenon depends on the fact that increased pulmonary ventilation exacts more work from the respiratory muscles, and naturally determines an increase of combustion and thus of carbonic acid production.

When a known volume of oxygen is converted by combustion into carbonic acid, the original volume of gas is not altered. Since, however, in respiration the volume of oxygen absorbed exceeds that of carbonic acid exhaled, it follows that a greater or less amount of oxygen must be applied to other oxidative purposes. Among these, besides the combustion of hydrogen by which water is formed, must be reckoned the combustion of sulphur to form sulphates, and of phosphorus, which forms phosphates.

The ratio between the volume of carbonic acid exhaled and the volume of oxygen absorbed is known as the respiratory quotient. This quotient, expressed by the formula $\frac{CO_2}{O_2}$, is generally lower than 1, and varies considerably in the different classes of animals, and even in the same individual, according to the nature of his food.

In the combustion of the different food-stuffs outside the body a different quantity of oxygen is required according to the different chemical constitution of their molecules. Thus, each molecule of the substances comprised in the carbo-hydrate group contains oxygen enough to convert the whole of the hydrogen into water. Accordingly for their complete combustion the only oxygen required is that necessary for conversion of the carbon into carbonic acid. Hence the volume of CO_2 formed is perfectly equal to the volume of O_2 consumed, the quotient $\frac{CO_2}{O_2} = 1$.

For the perfect combustion of fats and proteins, on the contrary, more O_2 is required, since in their molecules there is not enough O_2 to convert all the H_2 into water. The quotient $\frac{CO_2}{O_2}$ is therefore less than 1. In the complete combustion of fats, the quotient $= 0.71$; in the complete combustion of proteins $= 0.78$.

It follows that if the substances introduced as food were oxidised exclusively within the body, the respiratory quotient in a pure carbohydrate diet would be $= 1$, in a fatty diet $= 0.71$, in a protein diet $= 0.78$. But since not only do the food-substances introduced into the body share in its oxidative processes, but the various tissue-forming substances also take part, it seldom happens that the respiratory quotient rises to 1, i.e. for the most part it is represented by a variable proper fraction. It is only under special circumstances that the respiratory quotient may temporarily attain the value of 1, or even exceed it, as when fats are formed from carbohydrates in the body, or when there is a rapid diminution in the oxygen content of inspired air (Rosenthal, 1902). An apparent increase of the quotient may appear in certain birds in whose crop there is fermentation of the food stored there, with production of CO_2.

It is a very interesting fact that the respiratory quotient oscillates with the substances that predominate in the food: in a diet mainly composed of starch the value rises to 0.9; in a diet that is chiefly fatty it drops to 0.55: while lastly, in a diet mainly consisting of meat it attains an intermediate value of 0.7-0.65. In an ordinary mixed diet the respiratory quotient is about 0.8.

When we consider the metabolism or material exchanges of the body as a whole, we shall examine the importance of these and other facts relating to the oscillations of the respiratory quotient; we shall discuss the different methods employed for animals, or man, in the study of the absolute magnitude of the respiratory gas exchanges; we shall see that this magnitude changes with age, sex, constitution, external temperature, work or rest, the different hours of the day or night, etc. These investigations obviously exceed the limits of the physiology of the respiratory apparatus, and involves the functioning of the body as a whole.

BIBLIOGRAPHY

ARISTOTLE. Historia animalium, ed. Didotiana.

CLAUDIUS GALENUS. De usu partium corporis humani.

VAN HELMONT. Ortus medicinae, ed. Amsterdam, 1664.

ROBERT BOYLE. Nova experimenta pneumatica de respiratione. Genevae, 1680.

ROBERT HOOK. Philos. Trans., 1667, vol. i.

C. FRACASSATI. De lingua et cerebro. Bononiae, 1665.

R. LOWER. Tractatus de corde : item de motu, colore et transfusione sanguinis. Lugduni Bat., 1669.

JOHN MAYOW. Tractatus quinque medico-physici, quorum primus agit de sal nitro et spiritu nitro-aereo, secundus de respiratione, tertius de respiratione foetus in utero et ovo, quartus de motu musculari, et cet. Oxonii, 1674.

JOSEPH BLACK. Lectures on the Elements of Chemistry, delivered in the University of Edinburgh, 1803, 3 vols.

BERGMANN. Mémoires de l'Académie de Stockholm, 1775. Opuscula physica et chimica. vol. i., 1788.

JOSEPH PRIESTLEY. Observations on Different Kinds of Air. Philos. Trans., 1772, lxii.

LAVOISIER. Mém. de l'Acad. des Sc., 1774-77.

LAVOISIER and LAPLACE. Mém. de l'Acad. des Sc., 1780.

LAVOISIER and SEGUIN. Mém. de l'Acad. des Sc., 1789.

SPALLANZANI. Memorie su la respirazione. Opera postuma. Milano, 1803. French trans by Sénébier. Geneva, 1803.

SÉNÉBIER. Rapport de l'air avec les êtres organisés, 3 vols. Geneva, 1807.

W. EDWARDS. De l'influence des agents physiques sur la vie, 1824.

GUSTAV MAGNUS. Über die im Blute enthaltenen Gase, Sauerstoff, Stickstoff, und Kohlensäure. Ann. d. Physik, xl., 1837.

LOTHAR MEYER. Die Gase des Blutes. Göttingen, 1857.

F. HOPPE-SEYLER. Beitr. z. Kenn. d. Konstitution d. Blutes. Med. Chem. Unters., 1866-68.

G. HÜFNER. Über die Quantität Sauerstoff, welche 1 Gramm Hämoglobin zu binden vermag. Zeitschrift phys. Chem., 1877. Neue Versuche über die Tension des Sauerstoffes in Blute und in Oxyhämoglobinlösungen. Zeitschrift phys. Chem., 1888.

P. BERT. La Pression barométrique. Recherches de phys. exp. Paris, 1888.

N. ZUNTZ. Blutgase und resp. Gaswechsel. Hermann's Handbuch d. Physiol., iv. Leipzig, 1882.

FRAENKEL and GEPPERT. Über die Wirkungen der verdünnten Luft auf den Organismus. Berlin, 1883.

CHRISTIAN BOHR. Experimentelle Untersuchungen über die Sauerstoffaufnahme des Blutfarbstoffes. Kopenhagen, 1885. Über die Lungenatmung, Skandinavisches Archiv f. Physiol., i., ii., 1891-93. Blutgase und respiratorischer Gaswechsel, in Handbuch der Physiologie des Menschen, von W. Nagel, i., 1905.

HALDANE and SMITH. The Oxygen Tension of Arterial Blood. Journ. of Physiol., xx., 1896. The Absorption of Oxygen by the Lungs, ibidem, xxii., 1897-98.

A. KROGH. On the Cutaneous and Pulmonary Respiration of the Frog, etc. Skandin. Archiv f. Physiol., xv., 1904.

LOEWY and ZUNTZ. Über den Mechanismus der Sauerstoffversorgung des Körpers. Archiv f. Anat. u. Physiol., xv., 1904.

A. JAQUET. Der respiratorische Gaswechsel. Ergebnisse der Physiol., ii., 1.

Recent English Literature : —

J. BARCROFT. The Gaseous Metabolism of the Submaxillary Gland. Part I. On Methods, with a Description of an Apparatus for Gas Analysis. Journ. of Physiol., 1899-1900, xxv. 265-282.

J. HALDANE. The Ferricyanide Method of determining the Oxygen Capacity of Blood. Journ of Physiol., 1899-1900, xxv. 295-302.

J. HALDANE and J. L. SMITH. The Mass and Oxygen Capacity of the Blood in Man. Journ. of Physiol., 1899-1900, xxv. 331-343.

J. BARCROFT and J. S. HALDANE. A Method of estimating the Oxygen and Carbonic Acid in Small Quantities of Blood. Journ. of Physiol., 1902, xxviii. 232-240.

W. M. FLETCHER. The Influence of Oxygen upon the Survival Respiration of Muscle. Journ. of Physiol., 1902, xxviii. 354-359 and 474-498.

L. HILL and J. J. R. MACLEOD. The Influence of Compressed Air and Oxygen on the Gases of the Blood. Journ. of Physiol., 1903, xxix. 382-387 and 492-510.

J. BARCROFT and T. G. BRODIE. The Gaseous Metabolism of the Kidney. Journ. of Physiol., 1905, xxxii. 18-27, and 1905-1906, xxxiii. 52-68.

E. G. MARTIN. A Study of the Absorption and Consumption of Oxygen in Heart Tissue. Amer. Journ. of Physiol., 1905-1906, xv. 303-320.

H. H. NEWMAN. On the Respiration of the Heart, with Special Reference to the Heart of Limulus. Amer. Journ. of Physiol., 1905-1906, xv. 371-386.

H. M. VERNON. The Conditions of Tissue Respiration. Journ. of Physiol., 1906-1907, xxxv. 53-87, and 1907-1908, xxxvi. 81-92.

J. BARCROFT and W. E. DIXON. The Gaseous Metabolism of the Mammalian Heart. Journ. of Physiol., 1906-1907, xxxv. 182-204.

W. A. OSBORNE. The Haldane-Smith Method of estimating the Oxygen Tension of the Arterial Blood. Journ. of Physiol., 1907-1908, xxxvi. 48-61.

J. BARCROFT. Differential Method of Blood-Gas Analysis. Journ. of Physiol., 1908, xxxvii. 12-24.

J. BARCROFT and M. CAMIS. The Dissociation Curve of Blood. Journ. of Physiol., 1909-10, xxxix. 118-142.

J. BARCROFT and FF. ROBERTS. The Dissociation Curve of Haemoglobin. Journ. of Physiol., 1909-10, xxxix. 143-148.

J. BARCROFT and W. O. R. KING. The Effect of Temperature on the Dissociation Curve of Blood. Journ. of Physiol., 1909-10, xxxix. 374-384.

J. BARCROFT and FF. ROBERTS. Improvements in the Technique of Blood-Gas Analysis. Journ. of Physiol., 1909-10, xxxix. 429-437.

CHAPTER XII

MECHANICS OF RESPIRATION

SUMMARY.—1. Historical. 2. Glandular structure of the lungs. 3. Conditions of the lungs and other viscera within the thorax ; passive movements due to variations in the negative thoracic pressure. 4. The thoracic cavity : changes of form and dimensions with inspiratory and expiratory movements. 5. Muscular mechanism of inspiratory and expiratory movements. 6. Normal and forced respiration. 7. Accessory or concomitant respiratory movements. 8. Ventilation or renewal of pulmonary air (spirometry), and respiratory pressure in the air-passages (pneumatometry). 9. Respiratory displacement of the lungs, and acoustic phenomena of percussion and auscultation. 10. Respiratory variations of intra-thoracic and intra-abdominal pressure. 11. Respiratory variations of pressure in the vena cava. 12. Respiratory variations of aortic pressure. 13. Effect of respiratory mechanics on the circulation of the blood. 14. Special forms of respiratory movements. Bibliography.

IN order that the respiratory gas exchanges may be adequate for the needs of ordinary life, it is essential that the air contained in the alveoli of the lungs should be constantly renewed. A slow but continuous replacement of alveolar air occurs by diffusion with the air contained in the respiratory tract, which is, as we have seen, persistently richer in oxygen and poorer in carbonic acid, from the small to the large bronchi, and from these to the trachea. This renewal by diffusion is facilitated by the gentle impacts given to the lungs by the rhythmical movements of the heart (cardio-pneumatic movements, as discussed in Chap. VII. 10). During the physiological lethargy of hibernating animals, and in the profound cataleptic state of apparent death produced under certain morbid conditions, or by hypnotic influences, such as are employed by the Indian fakirs, this occult and silent renewal of the pulmonary air may suffice to maintain life for a long time, since the physiological need of respiration is extraordinarily reduced. But under normal conditions there is a crying want for more energetic replacement of the air by a real pulmonary ventilation, produced by the alternate rhythmical expansion and retraction of the thorax, in which the lungs are hermetically enclosed—these organs being eminently elastic, and yet capable of passively following the thorax when it acts as a suction and a pressure pump.

I. The simplest and most fundamental experiments on the

mechanics of respiration are those of Galen (A.D. 131-203). He was the first to assert that the lungs passively followed the movements of the thorax, but he assumed that there was a layer of air between the pulmonary walls and the thorax.

Oribasus (A.D. 360) was the first who noticed the collapse of the lung in double pneumothorax, and Vesalius (as we have seen, p. 371) the first who employed artificial respiration by a bellows inserted into the opened thorax to maintain life.

Malpighi 1661 first described the structure of the lungs. Alfonso Borelli 1679, first formulated a complete theory of the mechanism of pulmonary ventilation. To Haller (1780) belongs, however, the merit of explicitly denying that the pleural cavity contains air—a notion which many clung to, producing not a little confusion of ideas. He further asserted the absolute passivity of the movements of the lungs, which some of the earlier physiologists regarded as the *primum morens* of pulmonary ventilation, while others after him (Rudolph, 1821 : Laennec, 1819) still believed, on the strength of fallacious or wrongly interpreted observations, that the lungs were capable of active movements independent of the thorax.

The exact determination of the muscular mechanisms that govern the alternate acts of inspiration and expiration, and the right appreciation of their functional value in normal (eupnoea) and abnormal (dyspnoea) respiratory rhythm, is still the subject of innumerable controversies, as we shall see in the course of the present chapter.

II. We must leave the full description of the structure of the lungs and air-passages, *i.e.* the trachea, and the large and small bronchi which lead to the alveoli (where, as we have seen, the gas exchanges between air and blood are carried on), to text-books of anatomy and histology ; it is sufficient here to remark that from the physiological point of view they may be regarded as large branching glands lined with mucosa, in which the ramified bronchial tubes represent the excretory canals, and the infundibuli divided by internal septa into alveoli, or terminal air-cells of somewhat polygonal form, the secreting glands. These air-cells are lined with a single layer of cells, which are characterised by their reduction to thin laminae, some nucleated, others non-nucleated, which accounts for their secretory activity being reduced to a minimum, as suggested tentatively in the previous chapter, or entirely wanting, as held by the great majority of physiologists. In immediate contact with the alveolar epithelium is the network of pulmonary capillaries, with exceedingly fine meshes, in the centre of which lies the denser and nucleated part of the epithelial cells, while the more attenuated marginal cells, which are reduced to a delicate lamella, invest the surface of the capillaries facing the alveoli, so that the capillary network and the epithelium which lines them internally form but a single layer.

Each infundibulum is surrounded by connective tissue, rich in elastic fibres, and containing blood and lymph vessels. A certain number of infundibuli, with their respective bronchioles, interconnected by connective and elastic tissue, and by larger vessels, make up the pulmonary lobules, provided in their turn with lobular bronchi, which arise from the junction of the bronchioles. A number of these lobules, united by the said tissues, by still larger vessels, and by lobar bronchi, form the pulmonary lobes which in conjunction make the lung.

The structure of the respiratory passages changes gradually from bronchioles to lobular bronchi, from these to the lobar bronchi, from the larger bronchi to the trachea. We must confine ourselves to stating that the bronchioles are lined with a single layer of cubical, non-ciliated, epithelial cells, surrounded with a thin sheath of connective and elastic tissue, sparsely provided with smooth muscle fibres. The epithelium of the lobular bronchi is cylindrical and ciliated, and the tube consists of an external sheath of connective tissue, rich in elastic fibres and concentrically arranged smooth muscle cells. In the interlobular and lobular bronchi the tube is more muscular and somewhat rigid, because the coat of elastic and connective tissue, found on the outside of the circular muscular layer, contains small irregularly distributed plates of hyaline cartilage. These cartilage plates become larger in the direction from medium to greater bronchi, while the transverse layer of muscle diminishes. The mucosa thickens from small to large bronchi. The epithelium is stratified (three or more layers of cells : between the cylindrical ciliated cells mucous goblet cells are occasionally visible. Beneath the epithelium is a reticulated adenoid tissue with thin elastic fibres, and on the outside a compact and conspicuous elastic layer, formed of the predominantly longitudinal fibres, which are arranged in a network, in which are many small mucoid and acinous glands, opening into the lumen of the bronchus by small ducts that pierce the elastic layer, reticulated tissue, and epithelium. The mucous secretion of the goblet cells and small glands intercepts the solid particles introduced with the air, while the cilia drive the mucus with the agglutinated particles towards the trachea and larynx.

The tracheal tube is much more rigid, since the elastic sheath is more external and tougher, and contains rings of hyaline cartilage, interrupted at the back and completed by bundles of smooth muscle fibres, stretched transversely across the ends of the cartilage, while a few other muscle bundles run longitudinally outside the former. The tracheal mucosa is not essentially different from that of the greater bronchi, and contains more mucous glands. The strong elastic layer adjusts the mucosa to the longitudinal alterations of the tube, keeping it tense and smooth. The smooth muscle cells found along the air-passages, and most abundantly in the smallest bronchi, are able, according to the degree of their tonus, to alter the lumen of the canal as required.

III. The lungs of the foetus are void of air (atelectatic, and therefore sink in the test known as *docimasia hydrostatica*) when immersed in water. The first respiratory movements which occur after birth expand the alveoli of the lungs and fill them with air, and lungs removed from any individual who has already breathed float on the surface of water in *docimasia hydrostatica*, because the elastic retraction they undergo when the thorax is opened is not strong enough to expel all the air from the alveoli. This is because the capillary bronchi or bronchioles (which, as we have seen, contain no cartilaginous platelets such as give a certain rigidity to the larger bronchi) collapse, and hinder the complete expulsion of the alveolar air. The lungs of a new-born infant, which has already breathed, may after a certain time become atelectatic again by the reabsorption of the air which they contain. From the same cause the lungs of a man or other animal become atelectatic in a few hours, if the pleural cavity has been opened on one side.

The form and volume of the atelectatic foetal lungs correspond exactly with the form and volume of the thoracic cavity in which they are enclosed. They are in perfect elastic equilibrium, since on opening the thorax they do not retract, and if a mercury or water manometer is connected with the trachea so as to measure the intrathoracic pressure (Donders), it is found to be equal to atmospheric pressure, the manometer showing no movement on opening of the thoracic wall (Bernstein).

These conditions gradually alter during extra-uterine life. As the thorax grows more rapidly than the lungs, these are thrown into a state of increasing elastic tension, in proportion as the difference between the capacity of the thorax and the volume of the lungs increases, when they are respectively in the normal position of equilibrium. This can easily be determined by Donders' method on the bodies of persons of different ages, provided they did not die of pulmonary diseases. If a manometer is connected with the trachea of a dead new-born infant, that had breathed, the lungs do not retract, and the column of mercury does not rise, on opening both pleural cavities; the same conditions, therefore, persist after birth as in the foetal atelectatic lung (Hermann). When, on the contrary, the same experiment is repeated on the body of an adult, the lungs retract more or less according to age, by elastic recoil, till they are in equilibrium with a column of mercury of 5-7·5 mm. Accordingly, in the cadaveric, or the passive respiratory position of the adult thorax, it is the atmospheric pressure which acts within the pulmonary air-passages, and cannot act upon the surface of the lungs (these being hermetically enclosed in the thoracic cavity, formed mainly of rigid walls), that determines the passive distension as well as the elastic tension of the same, and the negative pressure within the thoracic cavity in the expiratory position.

Normally the thoracic cavity is completely filled by the lungs, which adapt themselves perfectly to its conformation. The two layers, visceral and parietal, of the pleura, are in immediate contact, separated only by the thinnest stratum of lymph, which facilitates the gliding of one over the other. The pleural cavities are potential only; under morbid conditions they are formed by the liquid or solid exudation that is poured out between the two layers; or by a unilateral or bilateral, external or internal, aperture in the same. The rapid death by asphyxia in double pneumothorax shows the passivity of the lung movements, owing to which ventilation or renewal of the air essential to the life of the animal ceases. When, however, from the partial or complete occlusion of the opening, the air cannot freely enter or leave the pleural cavities, the lungs are still able to distend; this explains why in many cases of perforation of the thorax the respiratory gas exchanges are not profoundly modified.

Besides the lungs, the thoracic cavity also contains the heart with the large venous and arterial trunks, which, as hollow organs, indirectly feel the effects of the atmospheric pressure acting directly upon the extrathoracic vessels that communicate with the heart. Intrathoracic negative pressure accordingly determines not merely the distension of the lungs, but also that of the heart and intrathoracic vessels, in proportion with their capacity for dilatation. The thick-walled ventricles of the heart, and the arteries, which are always under strong internal pressure, feel little or no effect from the negative intrathoracic pressure; the auricles and large trunks, on the contrary, which have thin walls, and are not distended by positive internal pressure, suffer a certain degree of expansion, by which the lumen is widened, and the course of the blood from the extrathoracic to the intrathoracic veins facilitated.

The oesophagus, as a hollow intrathoracic organ communicating with the exterior, should dilate to a certain extent in consequence of the negative pressure that obtains within the thorax; its cavity, however, is potential, and is only formed when the canal is traversed by foreign bodies, such as food. Under ordinary conditions the walls of the oesophagus are in contact, so that the lumen is obliterated, and the negative intrathoracic pressure, far from aspirating air into the canal, only makes the walls adhere more closely, in consequence of the atmospheric pressure exerted externally upon its intrathoracic portion. But if a hollow sound is passed through the oesophagus, it is converted into an intrathoracic cavity communicating with the exterior, and subject, like the lungs, to all the changes of intrathoracic pressure (Luciani). The method of automatic registration of variations of intrathoracic pressure by the oesophageal sound, which we introduced into the experimental technique of physiology in 1877, is based on this fact.

In conclusion it must be noted that the negative intrathoracic pressure also affects the soft movable portions of the walls of the thorax, more particularly the *diaphragm*, by which its floor is separated from the abdominal cavity and the intercostal spaces. The former, as well as the latter, are during the expiratory position of rest, and in the dead body, curved or bent towards the thorax, where pressure is negative, while they are subjected externally to atmospheric pressure.

IV. Let us now consider the changes in form and dimensions exhibited by the thorax during the alternate movements of expansion (inspiration) and contraction (expiration), which compose the respiratory rhythm.

During inspiration the whole thoracic cavity dilates more or less, in its several diameters, in proportion to the intensity of contraction and the number of muscles which come into play.

The dilatation of all the horizontal diameters of the thorax is the effect of the raising of the ribs, which, with the vertebral column, with which

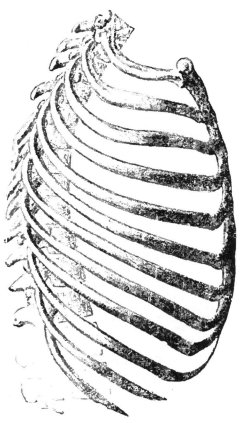

Fig. 173.— Right half of thoracic skeleton. (Spaltenholtz.)

they articulate posteriorly, and the cartilaginous prolongations and the sternum, to which they are united anteriorly, form the skeleton or rigid system of the thorax.

The ribs, to the number of twelve on each side, constitute a series of long, slender, arched bones, which start from the dorsal vertebrae to extend outwards and forwards. They slant obliquely from above downwards, so that their points of posterior articulation are a little above the anterior end, which is united with the sternum by means of the cartilaginous prolongations, directly (first seven ribs) and indirectly (eighth, ninth, tenth ribs). The two last ribs are loose, and are of less importance in the respiratory mechanism (Fig. 173).

By means of a double articulation with two vertebral bodies and with a transverse process, each rib is able to rotate round an approximately horizontal axis, which passes along its neck, and forms a greater or lesser angle with the horizontal plane. The axes of rotation of the two corresponding ribs are convergent in front, and decussate, forming angles that decrease, according to Volkmann, from the first to the tenth rib (from 125°-88°). It follows that in the upward rotation of the ribs, the point of the costal arch which rises most, corresponds not with the anterior end of the rib, but with a lateral point of the costal convexity, through which passes a tangent parallel to the axis of rotation, as shown in Fig. 174. And since the angle formed by the anterior crossing of

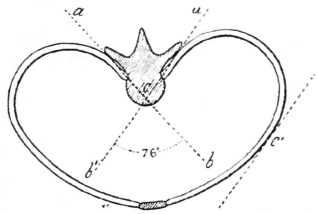

the axes of rotation diminishes from above downwards, the point of maximal rise for the different ribs in inspiration is displaced and pushed more towards the side, in proportion with the descent from the first to the tenth rib.

The increase in oblique, transverse, and antero-posterior diameter also varies

FIG. 174.—Horizontal projection of costal ring formed by 5th ribs. (Luciani.) *ab* and *a'b'* are the two axes of rotation of the double costo-vertebral articulation, which cross, forming in this case an angle of 76°. The tangent *c*, parallel to *a'b'*, shows the point of greatest elevation of the arch in inspiration.

in the different costal hoops, becoming greater in proportion to the inclination of the ribs, and to their length and curvature.

With the rise and forward inclination of the ribs the sternum is also displaced, describing an arc of a circle from above downwards, and from behind forwards, in the vertical sagittal plane of the thorax. Since this forward and upward displacement of the sternum is least at its upper, and greatest at its lower end, it follows that the different sections of the sternum must bend a little towards each other, and the costal cartilages make a slight revolution round their longitudinal axes.

In consequence of the inclination of the ribs and their elasticity, the curvature increases when they rise to an approximately horizontal position; on the other hand, at the junctions of their anterior ends with the cartilages, the curvature becomes slightly flattened, which induces a certain widening of the intercostal spaces, proportional to the degree of their inclinations and respiratory elevation. According to Ebner, this dilatation is not perceptible in the two first intercostal spaces, owing to the low inclination of the first ribs and the minimal rise of the upper end of the sternum.

The inspiratory dilatation of the vertical diameter of the thorax is not directly visible from without, as it is produced by the descent of the diaphragm, but it may be estimated from the rise in the upper end of the abdominal wall, owing to the displacement of the viscera that occupy the diaphragmatic concavity.

The inspiratory muscular contractions which displace the bones of the thorax from the position of equilibrium are opposed by various resistances, due to the weight of the parts to be lifted, the elasticity of the costo-vertebral ligaments of the costal cartilages and bones, and lastly to the elastic resistance of the lungs which produces negative intrathoracic pressure, and the elastic resistance of the gases in the alimentary canal which work against the downward movement of the diaphragm. It follows that when the inspiratory and dilating mechanisms of the thorax cease to work, the bones of the thoracic cavity return spontaneously to the mean position of equilibrium, either from gravity or from the elastic reaction of the ligaments, cartilages, ribs, and lungs, as well as of the stomach and in-

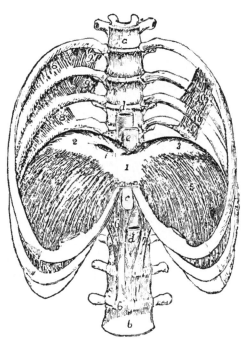

Fig. 175.—Lower half of thorax with four lumbar vertebrae. (Luschka.) Diaphragm seen from the front ; a, 6th dorsal vertebra ; b, 4th lumbar vertebra ; c, ensiform process ; d, d', aorta, which enters diaphragm by special aperture ; e, oesophagus ; f, aperture in tendon of diaphragm for passage of vena cava inferior ; 1, 2, 3, trilobate expansions of tendinous centre ; 4, 5, costal portions, right and left, of diaphragm muscle ; 6, 7, right and left crura of diaphragm ; 8, 8, internal intercostal muscles, which are absent near the vertebral column, where it joins the external intercostals ; 9, 9, 10, 10, subcostal muscles of left side.

testines. We shall, however, see that the movements of expiration, or retraction of the thorax, are always aided by expiratory muscular contractions, which tend not only to bring the bones of the thoracic cavity back into the position of equilibrium, but to force them beyond this position by giving the ribs a twist from above downwards, till in the forced or dyspnoeic respiration they reach the maximal constriction of the thorax and diminution of its several diameters.

V. Of the inspiratory muscles the diaphragm (Fig. 175) is of the first importance, owing to its conspicuous action. By the contraction of its muscular fibres, which converge towards the trilobate tendinous centre, the convexity towards the thoracic cavity diminishes, pushing the abdominal viscera downwards. According to Hasse (1880), during maximal inspiration the right lobe of the tendinous centre descends 2·5 cm., the left lobe 2 cm., and the central lobe about 1 cm. The muscle fibres inserted in the cartilages of the six last ribs contribute to the elevation and expansion of the lower ribs, since they are directed almost vertically upwards, the vault of the diaphragm being supported by the abdominal viscera (Duchenne). The anterior muscle fibres, which run more horizontally towards the tendinous centre, oppose a certain resistance to the forward displacement of the sternum. This may be the reason why the sternum is bent in patients who have suffered a long time from asthma (Thane). Nor is the action of the diaphragm confined to increasing the vertical diameter of the thorax with inspiration, as all admit. It also (by aiding the elevation and expansion of the false ribs) assists the dilatation of the transverse diameter of the base of the thorax, and modifies the amplification of the sagittal diameter at the level of the lower end of the sternum, effects which are less well known and are usually overlooked.

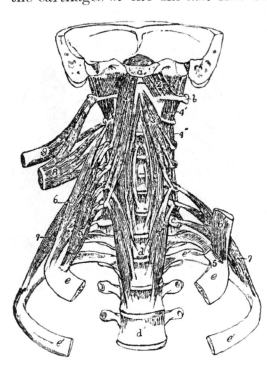

Fig. 176.—Deep and prevertebral muscles of neck. (Allen Thomson.) *a*, Superficial section of basilar process ; *b*, transverse process of atlas ; *c*, transverse process of 7th cervical vertebra ; *d*, *d'*, bodies of 1st and 4th dorsal vertebra ; *e*, *e'*, 1st and 2nd ribs ; 1, 2, rectus capitis anterior major and minor ; 3, 3', 3'', median, upper and lower part of musculus longus colli ; 4, 4', 4'', M. intertransversales ; 5, 5' scalenus anterior and its insertion on 1st rib ; 6, 6' scalenus medius, and insertion on 2nd rib ; 7, scalenus posterior ; 8, posterior part of levator scapulae ; 9, splenius colli.

Other inspiratory muscles are the three scaleni (Fig. 176), which exert traction on the first two ribs, and thus elevate and maintain the entire thoracic wall (Duchenne).

The M. levatores costarum longi et breves, twelve on each side, are able from their insertion in the immediate vicinity of the costo-vertebral articulations to produce an extensive elevation in the anterior ends of the ribs on gentle contraction (Traube, Rosenthal). The inspiratory action of the M. serratus posticus superior is also evident.

Since the direction of the fibres in the M. levatores costarum and the M. intercostales externa (Figs. 177 and 178) coincide, it is natural to regard these also as inspiratory muscles.

The function of the intercostal muscles, external as well as internal, has, however, been a subject of endless controversy, beginning with the lively polemic between Haller and Hamberger, and lasting into our own day. The most varying and opposite points of view have found strong supporters. Setting aside the opinion of Galen and Bartholin, who reckoned the external intercostals to be expiratory, and the internals inspiratory; and the view of van Helmont, Arantius and others who denied any

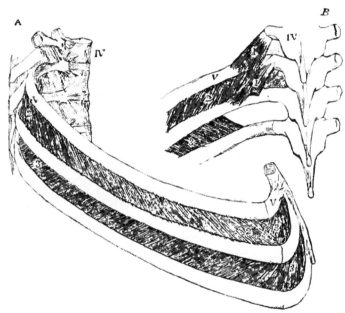

Fig. 177.—Intercostal muscles of 5th and 6th spaces. (Allen Thomson.) A, Side-view; B, back-view; IV, 4th dorsal vertebra; V, 5th rib and cartilage; 1, 1, M. levatores costarum longi et breves; 2, 2, M. intercostales externa; 3, 3, M. intercostales interni, as shown by removal of externi in lower intercostal space. In A there are no external intercostals in the intercartilaginous spaces; in B there are no internal intercostals near the vertebral column.

active function whatever to the intercostal muscles, and regarded them merely as the complement of the thoracic wall, as well as the opposite view of Mayow, Magendie, Burdach, etc., who held both externals and internals to be alternately inspiratory and expiratory in function : there remain four other aspects of the question, which are defended with conflicting arguments by distinguished physiologists, and are set forth in modern text-books :—

(a) Both external and internal intercostal muscles are *inspiratory* (Borelli, Senac, Boerhaave, Winslow, Haller, Cuvier, Duchenne).

(b) Both kinds of muscles are *expiratory* (Vesalius, Diemer-Brock, Sabatier, Beau and Maissiat, Longet).

(*c*) The *external* intercostals are *inspiratory*, the *internal* are *expiratory*, with the exception of the intercartilaginous portions (Spigel, Vesling, Bayle, and Hamberger, Hutchinson, A. Fick, Martin, and Hartwell).

(*d*) The intercostals are of *no great importance* in regard to the movements of the ribs: they serve rather to regulate tension

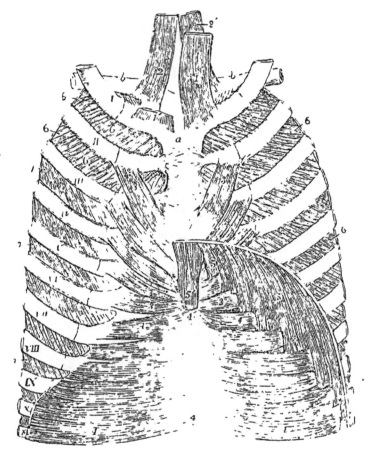

FIG. 178.— Deep muscles of anterior wall of thorax, seen from behind. (Allen Thomson.) *a*, Posterior part of manubrium sterni; *b*, *b*, clavicle; i-ix, anterior part of ribs and cartilages; 1, 1', M. sterno-thyroidei; 2, 2', M. sterno-hyoidei; 3, 3', M. triangulares sterni; 4, 4, upper part of transverse muscles of abdomen which meet at 4' 4' of linea alba posterior; 5, insertions of diaphragm on lower ribs, crossing fascia of transverse muscles; 5' bundles of diaphragm inserted into ensiform process; 6, 6', intercostales interni; 7, 7, 7, intercostales externi, exposed by removal of interni.

in the intercostal spaces, and to reinforce them during inspiration, impeding their retraction by the increased negative intrathoracic pressure (Henle, Meissner, Brücke, von Ebner, Landois).

Criticism of these several theories would necessitate a prolonged dissertation, disproportionate to the true importance of the arguments and the scope of this text-book. Here we can only summarise the facts that appear of most importance, and may determine our choice among so many opinions.

It is incontrovertible that the direction of the fibres in the external intercostals between two ribs is identical with that of the levatores costarum, and that the shortening of any one fibre can only occur, notwithstanding the extension of the intercostal space, when both ribs are raised. On the other hand, it is a fact that the fibres of the internal interosseous intercostals, which run in the opposite direction, can only shorten when the intercostal spaces are reduced by the lowering of the ribs. The tenability of this view is apparent if we expose the intercostal muscles of the thorax of a dead body, and imitate the inspiratory process, by drawing the sternum upwards with a hook, introduced through a hole in the manubrium. It will then be seen that as the intercostal spaces widen, the *external* intercostal muscles relax, and the *internal* interosseous intercostals contract: this shows that during life the insertions of the external intercostals come together during inspiration, and those of the internal intercostals separate.

Since the muscles shorten actively during their contraction, and are passively elongated by the action of the antagonists, it follows that the external intercostals must be *inspiratory* and the internal intercostals *expiratory*. Hamberger's schema and machine (1751), however imperfect and inadequate as an exact reproduction of the physiological process, still serves to elucidate the mechanics of this fact (Fig. 179). When the ribs *ac* and *bd* pass into the inspiratory position *ag* and *bf*, the

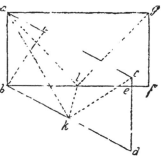

Fig. 179. Hamberger's schema to demonstrate the functional antagonism of internal and external intercostals (reproduced from Fig. 2 of his dissertation).

intercostal space dilates (*bh*<*ab*): the sternum *gf* moves away from the vertebral column *ab* (*bf*>*be*): the fibres of the external intercostals *ak* shorten (*ak*>*al*), and those of the internal intercostals *ck* lengthen (*ck*<*lg*). The reverse occurs when the system passes from the inspiratory position *a b g f* to the expiratory position *a b c d*.

In regard to the inspiratory function of the intercartilaginous muscles which form the anterior prolongation of the internal intercostals, Hamberger's explanation is less convincing, but it is intelligible by the help of the following schema (Fig. 180). When the ribs are curved, they may be regarded as rods bent at an angle *acd* and *bef*, in which the articular points *c* and *e* represent the symphysis between the bony and cartilaginous parts on which the traction is exerted. During inspiration the fibres of the intercartilaginous muscles, which have the direction *gh*, move the sternum *df* away from the vertebral column *ab*, like the fibres of the external intercostals, which run in the direction *kl*. During this double action the angles *c* and *e* must get blunted, because the

muscles of the upper intercostal spaces work simultaneously, and
the entire thorax is slightly elevated by the contraction of the
scaleni. It follows that both the external intercostals and the
intercartilaginous muscles are active in the inspiratory position,
although they have an opposite course ($gh > g'h'$, $kl > k'l'$). This
view of Hamberger's was better illustrated at a later time by
Hutchinson (1852).

It is supported as regards the inspiratory action of the external
intercostals by direct observations on the living. These muscles
have been observed on animals to become tense, and to harden and
thicken during inspiration, while during expiration they relax and
flatten (Antonio Marcacci, 1843; Duchenne, 1866; Rosenthal,

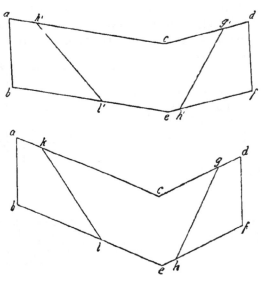

1882). When in the dog
or cat a section of the _in-
ternal_ intercostal muscle is
exposed by carefully cutting
away the _external_ intercostal
that covers it, so that both
intercostal muscles, the external and internal of one
or two adjacent intercostal
spaces, can be simultane-
ously observed, an alternate
contraction of their fibres
can be detected — those of
the external intercostals
being active during in-
spiration, and those of the
internal intercostals during
expiration (Ant. Marcacci).
At a later time this was
confirmed by graphic records,
which showed that the

Fig. 180.—Schema to demonstrate that the function
of the internal intercartilaginous intercostals is
identical with that of the external interosseous
intercostals.

internal interosseal intercostals contract _alternately_ with the
diaphragm, and therefore have an expiratory action (Newell-Martin
and Hartwell, 1879).

The experiments with localised electrical stimulation, which
proved to Duchenne and others that there was always a narrowing
of the intercostal space and elevation of the lower above the upper
rib, either when the external intercostals alone are stimulated, or
when the internal are excited as well, does not contradict the
above facts, since normally, in inspiration, all the external intercostals contract synergically, the thorax being lifted and supported
by the scaleni, which must necessarily cause distension of the
intercostal spaces.

The function of the intercartilaginous muscles, again, has been
experimentally confirmed. R. du Bois-Reymond and P. Masoin

found in dogs, cats, and rabbits that with forced respiration
the intercartilaginous muscles contract synchronously with the
diaphragm, *i.e.* are inspiratory, which was confirmed later on by
Bergendall and Bergmann. R. Fick
(1897) made an exhaustive investigation of the subject, both
critically and by means of vivisections on dogs, and came to the
same conclusion.

Besides the internal interosseous intercostals, all the muscles
contained in the depth of the abdominal wall act as inspiratory by
compressing the abdominal viscera,
thus pushing the diaphragm upwards and the lower ribs down-
wards.   Such   are   the   rectal
abdominal, the oblique external
and internal, and also the transverse muscles.

The instruments used in measuring
the different diameters of the thorax,
and the variations which these undergo
during normal and forced respiration,
are known as *thoracometers*.   That of
Sibson, represented in Fig. 181, is the
most generally used, and is easy to
apply.

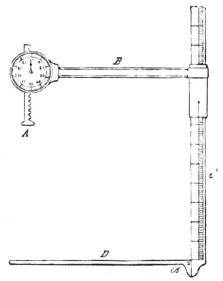

FIG. 181. — Sibson's Thoracometer. Two
metal rods at a right angle, D is applied
to vertebral column, and B (which runs
along the graduated scale C) carries at
its extremity a toothed rod A, provided
with a button to be applied to the
sternum. This moves an index, which
shows the excursions, magnified on a
dial.

If this instrument is reduced to the form of a measuring compass
(callipers), the limb A, which runs in a cogged wheel, and moves the
indicator of the dial, being replaced by a capsule covered with a rubber
membrane, kept taut by an elastic spring, and provided with a button, the

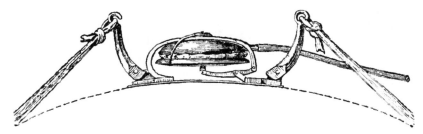

FIG. 182.—Marey's Pneumograph (latest model). Flexible steel plate, curved by the traction of
two arms of a lever joined at the circumference of the thorax by a silk band. The curve of the
plate is shown by a lever attached to the centre of the elastic membrane of an exploring
tambour. This records the pneumogram inversely upon a revolving drum, *i.e.* the descending
line corresponds with the inspiratory dilatation of the thorax, and the ascending line with
its expiratory retraction.

respiratory variations of any given thoracic diameter can be registered on a
revolving cylinder.

This is the model on which the thoracograph of Bert and of Fick, and
the stethograph of Burdon-Sanderson are constructed.

Marey's pneumograph (Fig. 182), of which there are various types, makes regular and measurable tracings of the variations of the thoracic circum-ference. It is one of the instruments most employed for clinical purposes.

Rosenthal's phrenograph is used to obtain exact tracings of the excursions of the diaphragm. It consists in a spatula-shaped lever, applied, after making an opening in the median line of the epigastrium, to the concave vault of the diaphragm. A simpler method is that which introduces a flat elastic rubber bag between the diaphragm and the abdominal organs, which is compressed when the diaphragm contracts, and decompressed on its relaxation, these effects being transmitted to a Marey's writing tympanum (Foster). This method records not only the movements of the diaphragm, but also the alternate contractions of the abdominal muscles. The simplest method, which involves no vivisection, and is therefore applicable to man, consists in applying the button of an exploring tympanum, or of Vierordt's sphygmo-graph, or of Burdon-Sander-son's cardiograph (Fig. 107, p. 267) to any point of the epigastrium. In man (who, as we shall see, breathes with-out active intervention of the abdominal muscles) this method yields fairly satis-factory results.

VI. After defining the inspiratory and expiratory muscular mechanisms, on which depend the rhyth-mical expansion and contraction of the thor-acic cavity, we next have to determine which of these intervene and have a preponderating action during normal respiration, and which come into play in forced or dyspnoeic respiratory rhythm.

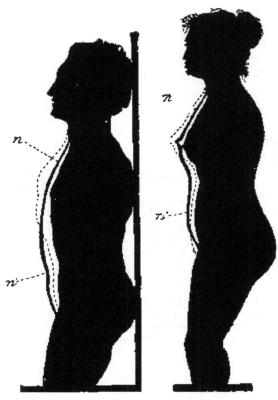

Fig. 183. — Diagram of variations of antero-posterior diameter of thorax and abdomen in the two sexes during normal breathing and forced respiration. (Hutchinson.) (Explanation in text.)

Even in ordinary quiet breathing two types of respiratory movements can be distinguished, the *abdominal* and the *costal*: in the former the activity of the diaphragm is the more pro-nounced, in the latter that of the external intercostals, or generally speaking, of the muscles by which the ribs are elevated.

According to Hutchinson's observations (1852), a man's breathing is always abdominal, a woman's costal. By drawing on a flat plane the outline of the shadows projected by two persons of different sex, at the several moments of normal or forced respiratory movements, he obtained the diagrams of Fig. 183, which illustrate very effectively the two types of respiration.

During inspiration and quiet expiration, the anterior profile of the thorax and abdomen oscillate between the limits of the boundaries of the black line *nn'*. It will be seen that this tract is deepest in man at the level of the epigastrium, and in woman at the upper region of the mammae. The excursion of the thoracic-abdominal profile of maximal inspiration reaches the dotted line in the two figures, and in maximal expiration it falls to the outline of the same. It will be seen that during forced respiration there is no longer the marked difference observed in quiet breathing, between the variations of the sagittal diameter of the thorax in man and woman. In both there is maximal costal dilatation and forward displacement of the sternum during forced inspiration, and maximal abdominal retraction in forced expiration.

According to Hutchinson, the difference between the normal types of respiration in man and woman is not the effect of stays, because this type of breathing is seen in girls who have never worn them. Apparently it is a secondary sexual character, formed in the course of phylogenesis as the effect of pregnancy, which necessarily develops costal respiration, increasing intra-abdominal pressure, and confining the action of the diaphragm. Many, however, hold that the thoracic type of respiration is an effect of the corset or ceinture (Beau and Maissiat, Walsche, Sibson , and A. D. Waller has put forward the same opinion, adducing the fact that women of savage races, like the males, exhibit abdominal respiration.

As regards the abdominal type of respiration in the male sex, it is desirable to correct an error that is widespread even in modern text-books, to the effect that the diaphragm exerts a preponderating influence over all the other inspiratory muscles. A. Fick (1866) remarked that inspiratory movements can be produced on oneself, with a little practice, by throwing the diaphragm only into action. This is most easily effected by associating the idea of pressing the contents of the abdomen with the act of inspiration. During this purely diaphragmatic inspiration, the transverse and antero-posterior diameters of the thorax undergo hardly any change, save near the base, where they are slightly enlarged, although less than in normal costal breathing. Fick affirms that only the sagittal diameter near the ensiform process increases, and that the transverse diameter near the last ribs diminishes: but we have been unable on ourselves to verify this last assertion. We have always found that pure diaphragmatic breathing is far more fatiguing than normal respiration, the proof being that man as well as woman normally breathes more with the whole of the external intercostal muscles, which elevate and extend the ribs, than with the diaphragm.

If we assume with Donders that the external surface of the thoracic cavity covers some 20 dcm., and that this surface on an average increases only some 2·5 mm. on every side by the action of the external intercostals, this still, according to Fick, yields a volume increase of 500 c.c., which corresponds to the average volume of normally inspired air. According, therefore, to Fick's calculations, the diaphragm hardly takes any part in normal inspiration, or at most the tonicity of its fibres is augmented, in order to check any upward aspiration during the widening of the thorax.

This theory is evidently exaggerated, and does not harmonise with the fact that in the quiet breathing of man the maximal excursion of the sagittal diameter is observed to correspond with the epigastrium (Fig. 183), which can only result from the inspiratory activity of the diaphragm. The fact, however, remains

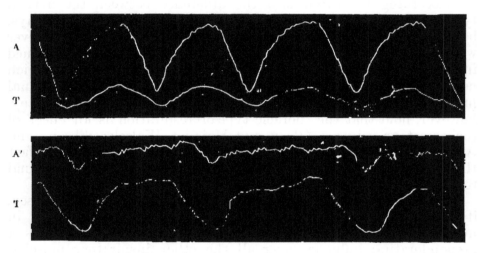

Fig. 184.—Thoracic and abdominal pneumograms during waking (T and A) and sleep (T' A'). (A. Mosso.) The curves are reversed, T and T' being traced with Marey's pneumograph, A A' with Vierordt's sphygmographic lever applied near the umbilicus.

that the function of the diaphragm is normally far less important than that of the external intercostals taken as a whole. Hultkrantz has recently shown that in an individual who takes in on an average 490 c.c. of air, 320 c.c. are to be referred to thoracic dilatation, and only 170 c.c. to the depression of the diaphragm.

Again, it appears from certain curves of thoracic and abdominal respiration which Mosso recorded simultaneously in the waking and the sleeping states, that the characteristic abdominal type of human respiration in the waking state disappears in sleep, during which the activity of the intercostals increases, while that of the diaphragm is reduced to a minimum (Fig. 184).

As regards the question whether during normal quiet breathing the external intercostals only come into play by the raising of the ribs, or whether the scaleni and levatores costarum breves et longi are also involved, opinions are much divided, and no positive facts can be adduced on either side.

On the other hand, it is clear that in forced respiration the action of all these muscles is reinforced by that of other accessory muscles, whose ordinary office is not to assist the dilatation of the thorax. Such are the sterno-cleido-mastoid, the pectoralis major and minor, the trapezius, serratus and extensors of the vertebral column. Further, those muscles intervene actively which serve to lower the larynx and widen the glottis, as well as the muscles of the palate, fauces, and dilators of the nostrils.

Another question which is difficult to solve, and as to which opinions are divided, is whether in normal quiet breathing expiration takes place *passively* by simple elastic reaction, or is *actively* promoted by the interosseous portion of the internal intercostals, triangularis sterni, and serratus posticus inferior. The great majority of writers, headed by Donders, adopt the first view; Fick's arguments in favour of the second seem to us, however, to carry a certain weight. He showed that with a little practice, active expiration can be performed voluntarily without throwing the abdominal muscles into any kind of tension. This is easy by concentrating the attention in expiration on dropping the upper ribs and shoulders, and not breathing the air out forcibly, which would throw the abdominal muscles into contraction. If during this intentionally thoracic expiration a water manometer is connected with the oral cavity, the meniscus can be seen to rise 4-5 cm., which gives a clear idea of the force exerted by the thoracic muscles, and, according to Fick, proves the expiratory action of the internal intercostals, as to which there has been so much discussion. That these do take part even in normal respiratory rhythm is shown by the fact that the expiratory act can be voluntarily interrupted at any moment, which certainly depends on voluntary inhibition of the expiratory muscles already in action, and not upon the entry of the antagonistic inspiratory muscles, about which we know very little.

Another cogent argument in favour of this theory seems to us to lie in the tracings of normal human respiration, recorded by Marey's pneumograph (Fig. 185). Neither the inspiratory nor the expiratory excursions constantly reach the same abscissae, as though drawn between two parallel lines; but they are now more, now less, extensive, according as in the different breathings the contraction of the antagonistic muscles in individual respirations was more or less intense.

To this it may be added that in dogs (Luciani, 1877) expiration under normal conditions is always active, owing to the intervention of the abdominal muscles, the contraction of which normally prevails over the alternating contractions of the diaphragm, in relation to intra-abdominal pressure, which, as we shall see, rises during expiration and sinks during inspiration. This fact increases the probability that in man also the normal expiratory movements are active, even if this be due to participation of the internal intercostals, and not of the abdominal muscles.

The most convincing evidence for the *active* character of expiration under normal conditions also was, however, furnished by Aducco (1887). From a series of ingenious experiments performed on men and dogs, he adduced the following facts, which show as a whole that in the expiratory process the contraction of certain muscles co-operates with the elastic reaction of the lungs, thorax, abdominal walls, and intestinal gases :—

(*a*) Normal expiration, being favoured by many passive factors, has in the waking state a longer duration than inspiration, which meets with corresponding resistance from these same factors.

(*b*) Expiration proceeds quite regularly, even when some of its principal passive factors are excluded, *e.g.* after the abdominal and

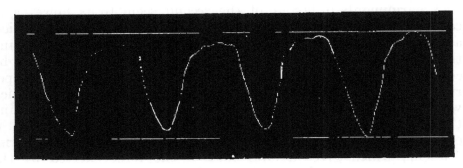

Fig. 185.—Pneumograms taken with Marey's pneumograph during normal, quiet breathing. The lower abscissa is at the level of the dead point of the deepest inspirations : the higher abscissa at the dead point of the more active expirations.

thoracic cavities have been widely opened to exclude the elastic reaction of the intestinal gases and distended lungs.

(*c*) When to the passive factors of expiration is added a force which works in the same direction (a rubber sheath compressing the thorax, a weight placed on the thorax), the time relations between the two acts of respiration is very little altered.

(*d*) With artificial expiration on the dead body, when only passive factors can come into play, a given weight is invariably less displaced by the thoracic walls than in normal expiration.

(*e*) Given two expirations of equal strength, one made by the living animal, the other artificially induced on a dead body of the same, the positive tracheal pressure developed by the latter is lower.

(*f*) If during sleep, thoracic and abdominal pneumograms are taken on a person breathing through Müller's water-valves, and the pressure raised in the expiratory valve by adding a little water, the curve (Fig. 186) shows that while thoracic expiration undergoes little change in its course and duration, abdominal respiration becomes slower in the middle of its period. This slowing is the proof that in quiet breathing the abdominal muscles do not in any way function as expiratory factors. On the other hand, the absence of any effects of increased expiratory resistance in the pneumograms of the thorax proves that the thoracic expiratory muscles come actively into play, so that they readily overcome this resistance. Thus, then, "thoracic expiration, even when accomplished under conditions of perfect rest, as is the case in sleep, is an active process."

VII. The respiratory movements, of which we have so far treated, directly determine the alternate filling and emptying with air of the lungs—inspiration and expiration. Besides these respiratory movements in the strict sense of the word, there are others, which affect the air-passages beyond the bronchial tubes and the thorax, and indirectly favour pulmonary ventilation. These

Fig. 186.—Thoracic and abdominal pneumograms recorded (with two exploring button tambours) during quiet sleep of an individual breathing with a mask through Müller's water-valve. (Aducco.) At T and A, the inspiratory and expiratory valves offer least resistance. At T' and A' the expiratory valve offers higher resistance owing to addition of a little water. The effect of this greater resistance is seen in the descending expiratory line of the abdominal tracing.

are known as accessory or concomitant respiratory movements. Some of them are purely passive in character, i.e. they represent simple secondary effects of the respiratory movements proper: such are the movements of the larynx and trachea, which in inspiration are drawn down by the expansion of the lungs and fall of the diaphragm, rising again with the succeeding expiration. Others, however, and it is these which must now be mentioned briefly, are of an active character, due to the contraction of certain special muscles.

In the first place, we must consider the respiratory movements of the laryngeal muscles proper, which produce inspiratory dilatation and expiratory constriction of the glottis. On some animals, particularly dogs, these movements may be regularly observed, while in men their presence in quiet breathing is much disputed, since there seems rather to be a permanent widening of the glottis. In a certain percentage of cases (16 per cent, according to Semon) these movements are, however, perceptible in man during quiet breathing.

Next to the respiratory movements of the vocal cords come those of the nostrils, which are essentially analogous with the first, and also appear regularly in man, in a certain number of cases, while in some animals (*e.g.* rabbit) they are never wanting, and in others (*e.g.* the horse) they play a very important part, paralysis of the corresponding muscles being apt to produce suffocation. They consist in the expansion of the nostrils, coincident with inspiration (or more accurately, commencing just before the phase of inspiration proper), and a subsequent constric-

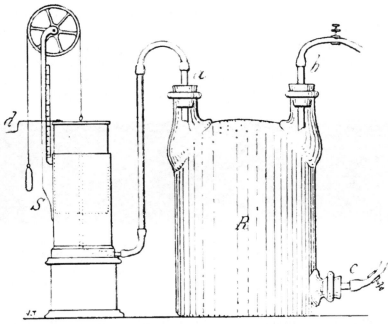

Fig. 187.—Apparatus for registering respiratory movements of an animal by the oscillations of pressure in the respiratory passages. *S*, Hutchinson's spirometer, to which is attached a small metal pointer *d* which records the oscillations of pressure in the animal's trachea upon the smoked drum; *R*, large receiver from which the animal breathes, connected by *a* to spirometer, by *b* to the trachea. The tube *c* permits more or less rapid renewal of air in receiver, according as the lumen is more or less constricted.

tion, which coincides more or less exactly with the expiratory phase.

In forced respiration (dyspnoea) these concomitant respiratory movements occur, as we have seen, to an exaggerated degree, even in individuals in whom they are not observed in normal quiet respiration. Other movements are then associated with them, *e.g.* foaming at the mouth, protrusion of the tongue, etc., etc., showing that the object is to give free access of air to the respiratory passages.

VIII. Ventilation or the renewal of the pulmonary air, effected by the alternate movements of dilatation and contraction of the thorax, varies in proportion to the varying intensity of these movements. The name of *tidal air* is given to the volume of air which enters and leaves the pulmonary air-passages during a normal inspiration and expiration. It can be measured by a well-calibrated and graduated glass bell, which Hutchinson (1860) termed a *spirometer* (Fig. 187). A properly constructed gasometer, which offers minimal resistance to the passage of the air, can be substituted (Mosso).

The amount of tidal air varies, according to Vierordt, between 367 and 699 c.c. in an adult. The average generally taken is 500 c.c. With an average frequency of 16 respirations per minute, the amplitude of pulmonary ventilation (Rosenthal's respiratory capacity) amounts therefore to 8000 c.c. This amount increases in proportion as the respirations are more intense and deeper. Hutchinson gave the name of *complementary* air to that amount which, after a normal respiration, may still be breathed in by a maximal inspiration; of *reserve* air to that which may be expelled after a normal expiration by a maximal expiration; and, lastly, he termed the sum of tidal, complementary, and reserve air obtained on following a maximal inspiration by a maximal expiration, the *vital capacity*. The values of the determinations (by means of spirometers) of the volumes of these different measures of air, vary considerably in experiments undertaken on different individuals. According to Haeser's observations, the mean vital capacity of Germans is 3222 c.c.; of English (who are taller on an average), 3772 c.c. The vital capacity is affected not only by stature, but also by volume of trunk, body, weight, age, sex, profession or trade, condition of digestion or inanition, etc.

In order to avoid a gross error in spirometry, it is necessary, as v. Hoesslin pointed out, to breathe into a receiver warmed to body temperature (by heating the bottom or walls of the spirometer, or filling it with warm water). Thus with a spirometer warmed to 37° C. the vital capacity amounted to 2850 c.c., while with the spirometer at 6° C. it was only 2375 c.c., a difference of 16·5 per cent.

The air left in the lungs after a maximal expiration is termed the *residual air*. It can be determined on the living by the methods of H. Davy and Grehant, which consist, after making a maximal expiration, in breathing for a certain time from a rubber balloon containing a known quantity of hydrogen. When it is supposed that all the residual air has mixed with the hydrogen, the percentage analysis of the air in the balloon is taken, and the value of the residual air is then found by an easy calculation. In different experiments these observers found it to be 1230-1640 c.c. On an average it can be assumed that the residual air is equal to half the vital capacity (Gad).

It appears from the total of spirometric observations that in each normal respiratory cycle or revolution only a portion of the air in the lungs can be renewed, which part may be taken as corresponding to $\frac{1}{6}$-$\frac{1}{4}$.

If in the course of a series of normal quiet breathings a single inspiration of hydrogen is made, and a sample of the air collected from each succeeding expiration, to ascertain which no longer contains any trace of hydrogen, the result is, approximately, that after 6-8 cycles the whole air of the lungs is renewed; after that time every trace of hydrogen in the expired air vanishes (Grehant).

During the entrance of air into the lungs the pressure in the air-passages becomes negative; the pressure during the exit of air from the lungs, on the contrary, is positive. In order to estimate these variations of intrapulmonary pressure it is only necessary to connect a mercury manometer with one nostril, while the mouth is kept closed, and to breathe with the other nostril (Donders). It will be seen that in quiet breathing the mercury column falls 1 mm. during inspiration and rises 2-3 mm. in expiration. These oscillations are increased in forced respiration.

To ascertain the maximal values of negative and positive intrapulmonary pressure, obtained by exerting all available inspiratory and expiratory forces, it is only necessary, starting from zero pressure, to close the mouth and the open nostril, and then to make the maximal inspiratory or expiratory effort. According to Donders, the maximal negative inspiratory pressure is on an average $= -57$ mm. Hg (36-74) and the maximal positive expiratory pressure $= +87$ mm. Hg (82-100).

When we consider that on the one hand the inspiratory muscles have to overcome great resistances in order to dilate the thorax and the extensible organs which it contains, and on the other the expiratory muscles are assisted in their action by the same conditions which hinder the action of the former, we must (notwithstanding that the manometric value of the pulmonary pressure indicates a greater effect of the expiratory than of the inspiratory muscles) assume that the latter develop a distinctly greater amount of energy than the former.

The oscillations of pressure along the respiratory tract may be used in man as in other animals for recording tracings of respiratory movements. The simplest method is to introduce one end of a tube into the nasal cavity or the mouth, and to attach the other to a Marey's tambour. With animals it is more convenient to insert a two-way cannula into the trachea, one arm of which communicates freely with the external air, while the other is connected by a rubber junction with the tambour. By constricting or distending the lumen of the tube through which the animal breathes, a greater or less fraction of the oscillations of pressure in the tracheal air can be recorded on the registering apparatus.

A better and more exact method is that of making the animal breathe into a very large vessel, communicating on the one hand with the trachea, on the other with a writing tambour (Bert), or with a small and very sensitive spirometer provided with a writing point that records the excursions on the rotating cylinder (Tigerstedt), as shown in Fig. 187. The chamber in which the animal breathes must be entirely shut off when it is desired to trace the progressive alterations in the respiratory movements due to asphyxia (Luciani); otherwise it communicates with the outer air by a more or less open tube, which allows the air within the bottle to be renewed when required (Tigerstedt). In that case, however, the oscillations in the tracing are not proportional with those of the intrapulmonary pressure.

The same effect may be obtained when the animal is breathing free air, while enclosed within a hermetically sealed glass cylinder (Knoll). A tube tied in the trachea, or fitting closely over the mouth and nostrils of the animal, passes through one wall of the box and communicates with the external air. The internal air of the box is connected by means of a second tube with a recording tambour, and traces, like a plethysmograph, the variations in the total volume of the animal, corresponding to the inspiratory and expiratory movements. The simplest application of this method is that of Bernstein, represented in Fig. 188.

IX. In proportion as the negative intrathoracic pressure increases or diminishes in consequence of the inspiratory and expiratory movements, the lungs dilate and retract with the air that penetrates through the glottis to the pulmonary passages, where equilibrium of air pressure is restored.

Both in dilatation and in retraction of the lungs the two layers of the pleura, visceral and parietal, remain, as we have said in constant contact. At the

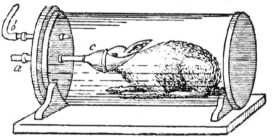

Fig. 188.—Bernstein's pneumoplethysmograph or spirograph. Hermetically sealed glass cylinder, in which the animal breathes the external air freely from the mask c and tube a. The rubber tube b, communicating with the inside of the cylinder, is connected with a Marey's tambour and writing-lever.

same time they glide one over the other, because the cavity of the thorax, owing to the action of the respiratory muscles, does not dilate and contract equally in all its diameters, but undergoes perceptible changes of form, particularly at the base, so that the lungs (which must passively follow the excursions of the thorax) also change their form in order to adapt themselves to the new shape of the thoracic cavity (Donders).

The most immovable part of the lungs, which undergo the least displacement, are the roots, the apices, the posterior border, and that portion of their external surface which underlies the lateral parts of the vertebral column: the most mobile are those farthest removed from the fixed parts, i.e. their inferior and anterior borders, and the median surfaces. The movement of the pleural layers, therefore, takes place specially in the longitudinal direction from above downwards, and in the transverse direction from behind forwards.

Under normal conditions this movement can be distinguished by percussion, which yields a clear, full sound in every part of the thoracic wall beneath which there is pulmonary substance, and a dull sound where there are viscera which contain no air. The lower border extends in normal expiration from the sternal margin on both sides almost to the insertion of the sixth rib, in the axillary line almost to the upper border of the seventh (Fig. 189). The anterior margin of the left lung, in ordinary expiration, reaches the line that goes from the median point of the insertion of the fourth rib to the insertion of the sixth (see line *l'l''*).

In deep inspiration the inferior borders of the lungs pass beyond the sixth and reach the seventh rib (see line *mn*); posteriorly they reach the eleventh; the anterior margin of the left lung comes forward to the line *ii'*.

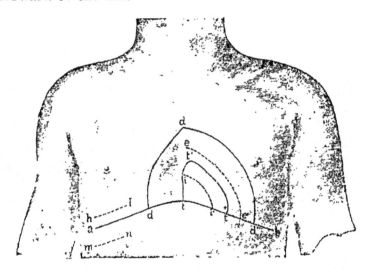

F . 189. Displacement of pulmonary borders in respiratory movements. (Landois.) The line *all* indicates the lower border of the lungs when all the respiratory muscles are at rest. The line *mn* indicates the right pulmonary border in deep inspiration; *hl* in deep expiration. The triangle *tt't''* corresponds with area of *absolute* dulness of heart when thorax is at rest. In deep inspirations this area is reduced to the small triangle *t ii'* owing to advance of internal border of left lung; in deep expiration, on the contrary, the triangle extends to *tee'* by the retraction of this border. The line *dd'd''* limits the area of *relative* dulness of heart, the heart being separated from the thoracic wall by a thin sheet of lung.

In very energetic expiration the lower borders of the lungs rise to the line *hl*; the anterior margin of the left lung protrudes as far as the line *ee'*.

In *pleuritis exudativa*, when the pleural layers become roughened on the surface, their friction during the respiratory movements gives rise to a characteristic murmur of friction, which the physician uses in diagnosis.

With direct auscultation, and with the stethoscope, a murmur is heard on inspiration throughout the whole extent of the lungs, which is known as the vesicular murmur, because it depends on the dilatations of the alveoli and the friction of the air that traverses the bronchioles. The murmur is rougher in children up to the age of twelve, because the pulmonary infundibuli are about ½ smaller than in adults.   In expiration a weak and quiet murmur is heard.

In auscultating along the larger respiratory passages (larynx, trachea, great bronchi), both in inspiration and in expiration a harsh murmur is heard, sharp and clear, resembling the guttural German *ch*, which is known as the bronchial murmur.   This is perceptible not merely in the neck, along the larynx and trachea, but also in the thorax between the two shoulder-blades at the level of the fourth dorsal vertebra, the point at which the bronchi bifurcate.   It is a little more accentuated on the right side, because the right bronchus is of greater calibre and is stronger as a rule in expiration than in inspiration.   In the other parts of the thorax the bronchial murmur is imperceptible, being covered by the vesicular murmur.   But it is heard distinctly in certain parts of the pulmonary area, when the alveoli are atelectatic or infiltrated.   In pneumonia, accordingly, the area of lung that has become impervious to air, or *hepatised*, can be determined

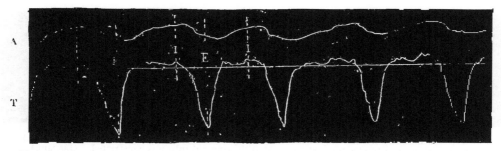

Fig. 190.—Respiratory oscillations of intrathoracic pressure (T) and intra-abdominal pressure (A in anaesthetised dog.   (Luciani.)

from the extent of the region in which the bronchial murmur is abnormally audible.

X. As above stated it is not only the lungs, but also the heart and blood-vessels that feel the effects of the changes in pressure determined by respiratory rhythm.

To obtain an exact knowledge of these effects it is necessary first to study the oscillations of intrathoracic and intra-abdominal pressure in the two periods of the respiratory cycle or revolution. This is most simply effected by the method of the oesophageal or rectal sound, in conjunction with Marey's recording tambour (Luciani, 1878 : Rosenthal, 1880 .

The tracings of Fig. 190, which we obtained by this method from an anaesthetised dog, are highly instructive, since they show that the respiratory oscillations of pressure within the thorax and abdomen are not coincident but interfering.   While intrathoracic pressure falls during inspiration and rises in expiration, intra-abdominal pressure rises in the first period of inspiration and falls in the second, and falls in the first period of expiration and rises again in the second. To interpret these facts it is necessary to assume that the diaphragm intervenes actively only in the first period of inspiration, and that the abdominal muscles intervene actively only in the second period of expiration. This agrees with what was stated above as to the relative inspiratory importance of the external intercostal muscles, and the constantly active character of the expiratory movements.

The respiratory oscillations of pressure in the two great body cavities are the more ample, or extensive, in proportion as the entrance and exit of air from the pulmonary passages, which tends to compensate them and to re-establish equilibrium, is more difficult. This fact can be experimentally verified by recording the tracings of intra-abdominal pressure in a tracheotomised animal, and observing how the respiratory curves are modified when the lumen of the tube attached to the tracheal cannula is constricted. Fig. 191 shows that the effect consists more particularly in a conspicuous exaggeration of the inspiratory acts, which become deeper

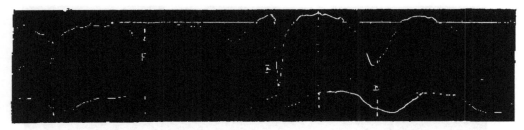

FIG. 191. —Respiratory oscillations of intrathoracic pressure (T) and intra-abdominal pressure (A) in anaesthetised and tracheotomised dog. At B the tracheal tube was constricted. (Luciam.)

and longer. Expiratory activity is also exaggerated, but in a less degree, and with reference solely to intensity and not to duration. The interference of the two curves, intrathoracic and intra-abdominal, persists.

The determination in the different higher animals, and in man, of the absolute values of the respiratory oscillations of intrathoracic and intra-abdominal pressure has not been fully worked out. We have only the few data obtained on the rabbit from Adamkiewicz and Jacobson, and those of Rosenthal, which show that in this animal, in normal inspiration, the pressure falls to − 40 mm. water (= − 3 mm. Hg), and that in the most intense inspirations, with closed trachea, the negative pressure may amount to − 250 mm. water (= − 20 mm. Hg).

More recently certain observers (Ewald, Einthoven, Aron, van der Brugh) have succeeded by means of a special apparatus (without causing pneumothorax) in introducing into the pleural cavity a cannula attached to a manometer, and thus directly measuring the pressure of the pleural cavity. Einthoven and his pupil, van der Brugh, found during expiration a negative pleural pressure equal to – 80, during inspiration equal to – 102 mm. of water.

The simplest method for recording the oscillations of intrathoracic pressure in animals is to introduce into the oesophagus, after previous oesophagotomy, an elastic sound, or hollow metal tube, covered at one end with a fine rubber membrane, which is connected with a writing tambour, after ligation of the oesophagus (Fig. 192). This last operation is necessary to ensure the perfect occlusion of the oesophagus above the exploring sound, while beneath it the tonicity of the cardiac orifice is sufficient to guarantee closure, save at the moment of deglutition, which rarely occurs in the narcotised animal. The imperfect closure of the oesophagus, after introducing the sound by the mouth or nostril,

FIG. 192.—Luciani's oesophageal explorer. Elastic sound, covered at the end with fine rubber sheath.

makes it difficult to obtain these oscillations of intrathoracic pressure in man (Rosenthal). It might be possible to remove this inconvenience by the expedient employed by Pflüger and Ludwig in their pulmonary catheter (Fig. 170, p. 388).

Bert's method may be employed for recording the intra-abdominal pressures. This consists in the introduction into the rectum of a glass tube, fixed against the anal sphincters by a kind of pessary to make it air-tight, and connected with a water manometer and writing tambour (Fig. 193, A). The inter-vention of a manometer is, however, superfluous, and no special contrivance is required to ensure closure of the anal orifice, which was sufficiently guaranteed by the tonic contraction of the sphincters. The same object can be effected by the introduction of a short length of urethral catheter of large diameter, perforated in several places, and provided at the ends and centre with three circular ridges formed of rubber rings, over which is drawn a thin membrane (Luciani). This method is applicable to man, and is invariably successful, so long as the precaution is taken of emptying the intestine of the faeces accumulated at the lower end (Fig. 193, B).

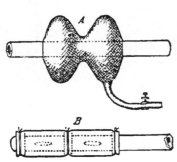

FIG. 193.—Rectal explorers—Bert (A) and Luciani (B). A, Glass tube, open at the end, which is introduced into the rectum and plugged in anal aperture by inflation of a hollow elastic pessary joined to the tube. B, Elastic or metal sound, with two lateral openings, fitted with three rubber rings, covered with a small fine sheath.

XI. Whatever the absolute values of these oscillations of pressure in the two body cavities determined by respiratory rhythm, it is evident that they must have a considerable influence on the centripetal course of the blood in the veins, and be an effective aid to the circulation as controlled by the heart.

This physiological doctrine is fairly ancient. Valsalva (1760) and Haller (1766) seem to have been the first who observed on man the swelling and emptying of the jugular vein coincident with expiration and inspiration. David Barry (1825), from the aspiration of coloured fluid along a tube fastened centrally in the jugular, formed an exaggerated notion of the functional importance of inspiratory thoracic aspiration. Wedemeyer (1828) repeated the same experiments with more discretion. Poiseuille (1831) applied his haemodynamometer to the veins, and attempted to reduce to figures the force of the aspiration exerted in the inspiratory act, and to establish at what distance from the thorax its influence ceases. With the discovery of Ludwig's Kymograph (1847) began the series of researches by the graphic method, which were directed to the more exact determination of the influence of respiratory mechanics upon blood pressure in the veins and arteries (see p. 242).

In Fig. 194 we have a very clear representation of the intra-thoracic respiratory curves and the simultaneous curves of blood pressure in the vena cava superior. Apart from the secondary oscillations which depend on cardiac rhythm (see Chap. VII. 10), it will be seen that the respiratory curves follow the same course, and coincide with them, apart from a slight delay which the curve of venous pressure exhibits in relation to that of intrathoracic

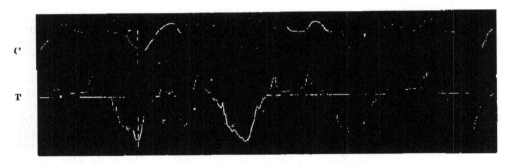

Fig. 194. — Respiratory oscillations of intrathoracic pressure (T) and pressure in vena cava superior (C) in anaesthetised and tracheotomised dog. (Luciani.) T, taken with oesophageal explorer ; C, with water manometer both connected to Marey's recording tambours.

pressure, which is probably dependent upon the presence of the water manometer. It may therefore be concluded that the negative pressure of the intrathoracic wave suffers diminution during the inspiratory act, so that the velocity with which the blood flows from the extrathoracic into the intrathoracic vein and the heart, increases proportionately. The opposite occurs during the ex-piratory act.

When the effects of the respiratory movements are exaggerated by constriction of the lumen of the tracheal tube, the respiratory curves become more extensive, whether they are transmitted from the oesophageal sound or from the vena cava superior (Fig. 195).

The impulse given to the venous circulation by the inspiratory movement is not counterbalanced by the opposite effect of the expiratory movement. Expirations are, in fact, always somewhat slower than inspirations : further, intrathoracic pressure always remains negative even during the ordinary expiratory acts, so that

it invariably favours the centripetal course of the blood in the
veins: lastly, the effects of the respiratory undulations of intra-
abdominal pressure must also be taken into consideration. They
are always favourable to the course of the venous blood, especially
when the expirations are assisted by the active intervention of
the abdominal muscles, as, according to our experiences, occurs
constantly in the dog.

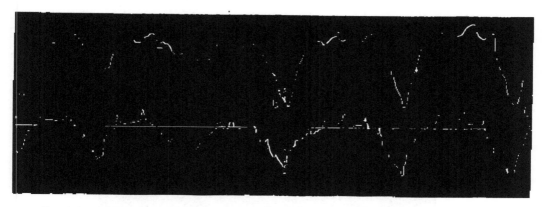

FIG. 195. Continuation of last figure. At B the tube connected with the trachea was slightly
constricted.

Fig. 196 is highly instructive, because it shows that the
respiratory undulations of pressure in the vena cava inferior are
approximately coincident with, and present the same course as,
those simultaneously traced by the superior vena cava This

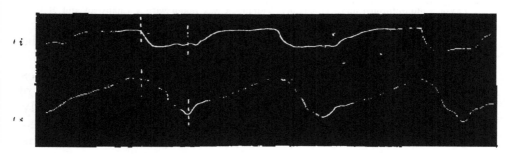

FIG. 196 – Respiratory oscillations of pressure in vena cava superior (Cs) and vena cava inferior
(Ci) in chloroformed dog. (Luciani.) In Ci the descending inspiratory line exhibits a pause
due to action of diaphragm, which is not seen in Cs.

proves the active intervention of the abdominal muscles, which
during expiration produce a pressor effect upon the inferior vena
cava, while the action of the diaphragm during inspiration is only
capable of reducing the depressor effect due to the relaxation of
the abdominal muscles.

XII. The influence exerted by the respiratory movements
upon the pressure and centrifugal course of the blood in the
arteries must necessarily be the opposite of that which it exerts

upon the veins. It should, however, be remembered that the arteries are not subject in the same degree as the veins to the effects of the oscillations of intrathoracic and intra-abdominal pressure. The walls of the arteries are in fact more robust, less yielding, and are under high pressure. They are more liable to the effects of the functional modifications of the heart induced by the respiratory movements than to the direct consequence of these movements.

Generally speaking, physiologists in investigating the respiratory waves of arterial blood-pressure have arrived at sufficiently disparate results. This appears to us to be due less to fallacies in the observations or to the method employed, than to the varying effects of the respiratory mechanism upon arterial pressure, according to the form and intensity of respiratory rhythm. This may be extremely frequent and superficial, or extremely infrequent and deep: and between these two extremes

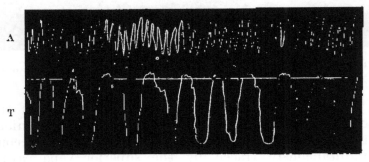

FIG. 197.— Respiratory oscillations of intrathoracic pressure (T) and pressure in carotid artery (A) in a chloroformed dog. (Luciani.) Tracing A was taken with a Chauveau and Marey's sphygmoscope.

many gradations of form may be observed, between which the normal type represents the centre of the scale.

With extreme frequency of respiration, arterial pressure does not undergo any sensible modification, because the effects of inspiration are obliterated by those of expiration, which rapidly succeed them. But when the respiratory rhythm is not excessively frequent, and is very intense, the respiratory undulations do appear on the tracings of arterial pressure, and may suffer the same delay, and coincide approximately with the waves of intrathoracic pressure. This is apparent in the tracings of Fig. 197, registered on a chloroformed dog, which in ten seconds gave nine profound respirations and thirty-nine cardiac beats. It will be seen that arterial pressure rises at each expiration, and falls with each inspiration. It is highly probable that these results depend essentially upon exaggerated expiratory activity of the abdominal muscles, which obstructs the arterial blood-stream flowing to the abdomen by compression of the capillaries, thus producing indirect rise of pressure in the intrathoracic arteries,

similar to that which constantly occurs when the abdominal wall
is compressed by the hand along the course of the aorta.

When the respiratory rhythm begins to assume its normal
form, in respect of frequency and intensity, its influence on
arterial blood pressure diminishes proportionally till it entirely or
almost disappears, as seen in the tracings of Fig. 198. A similar
result was obtained by Marey, who explained it by the antagonistic
influence exerted by the movements of the diaphragm on the

Fig. 198.—Respiratory oscillations of pressure in vena cava superior (cs) compared with tracing
of pressure in carotid artery (Jc) in chloroformed dog. (Luciani.)

pressure of the thoracic and abdominal cavities. This interpretation does not seem to us correct, when we consider on the one
hand the secondary part played by the diaphragm in respiratory
mechanics, and on the other the strong and constant expiratory
activity of the abdominal muscles as observed in the dog. It
suffices, in order to explain the small or negative effect of ordinary
respiratory rhythm on arterial pressure, to admit that normally

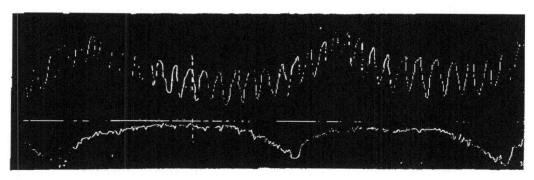

Fig. 199.—Tracing of intrathoracic pressure (Tc) and carotid (Cc) in non-anaesthetised dog of
medium size, showing slight trembling particularly in expiration. (Luciani.)

the respiratory movements are accomplished slowly and quite
gradually, and that the abdominal muscles either act moderately
during expiration (dog), or remain completely inactive (man).

When the respiratory rhythm becomes very slow and deep,
a marked interference is perceived between the respiratory waves
of intrathoracic pressure and the respiratory curves of arterial
pressure. This phenomenon was first illustrated by Einbrodt
1860, in an excellent publication from Ludwig's laboratory.
The tracings of Fig. 199 show the phenomenon in the most

classical form in which it has ever been recorded. At the first moment of expiration the arterial pressure rises, falling in the second period; in the first period of inspiration it continues to fall, and then rises at the second. Arterial pressure therefore reaches its maximum in the first period of expiration, and its minimum in the first period of inspiration.

In explanation of this fact Einbrodt assumes that the inspiratory fall of intrathoracic pressure, by determining an acceleration of the venous current, favours the diastolic refilling of the heart, which is followed by a larger systolic outflow, raising arterial pressure. This increase is maximal during the first period of expiration, either on account of the previous excess filling of the heart, or from the expiratory increase of intrathoracic pressure, which favours the centrifugal course in the arteries and the systolic action of the heart. In the second period of expiration the arterial pressure falls owing to retardation of the venous current in the blood, which diminishes the diastolic refilling and systolic emptying of the heart.

This theory is inadequate, because it takes no account of the pressor influence of the abdominal muscles, which is capable of raising arterial pressure during expiration, by compressing the capillaries of the vessels belonging to the intra-abdominal aortic system.

Funcke and Latschemberger 1877 held the fundamental cause of the phenomenon to lie in the changes of capacity in the capillary pulmonary system, effected by the alternate dilatation and retraction of the lungs, the respiratory oscillations of pressure in the thoracic cavity being only of secondary importance. They found in fact that in curarised rabbits, during artificial respirations by the bellows, with open thorax, there were still respiratory oscillations of carotid pressure. They explained this fact by admitting that when the alveoli of the lung dilate (whether from positive tracheal, or from negative pleural pressure) the capillary network which they contain must become stretched, with a consequent elongation and constriction of the vascular lumen, resulting in a considerable diminution in their capacity. The opposite changes must occur at each expiratory retraction of the pulmonary alveoli, which increases the capacity of the capillary rete. Given these effects of the respiratory movements, they must not merely influence the course of the blood in the lesser circulation, but must also act indirectly upon the pressure of the aortic system, which is fed from the pulmonary blood. The inspiratory increase in pressure would depend upon the expulsion of the blood from the compressed pulmonary capillary system into the left heart; the expiratory fall of pressure, on the retention of the blood in the newly dilated capillaries of the lungs.

This theory, if not wholly unfounded, is at any rate very

exaggerated.   The respiratory oscillations of arterial pressure
are not obtained with open thorax, unless the rhythmical
pulmonary dilatation with the bellows is grossly exaggerated.
The same authors constantly observed that the respiratory waves
of arterial pressure obtained with closed thorax in the curarised
rabbit, with a medium degree of rhythmical insufflation, became
notably weaker, or even disappeared altogether, when the pleural
cavity was scarcely yet open, and it was only on increasing the
insufflations that they could be made to reappear, or resume their
former level.

This fact shows the predominating importance of the oscillations of intrathoracic and intra-abdominal pressure, as causal
factors in the respiratory arterial undulations.

Heinricius and Kronecker (1888), taking up Einbrodt's experiments, showed that whatever impeded the cardiac diastole lowered

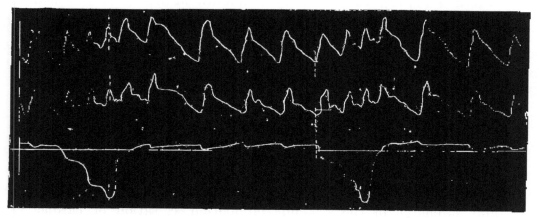

FIG. 200   Tracings of intrathoracic pressure (*T.*), pressure in crural artery (*A. c*), and in carotid
artery (*A. c.*) in anaesthetised dog with cut phrenics.   (Luciani.)

arterial pressure, and whatever facilitated and aided the former
increased the latter.   The influence of the respiratory movements
of the filling and emptying of the heart would thus be the fundamental condition of the respiratory waves of arterial pressure.
" Regular respiration," according to these authors, " produces a
salutary massage of the heart."

In order adequately to interpret the arterial respiratory wave,
the influence which respiratory rhythm, when sufficiently pronounced, can exert on cardiac rhythm must also be taken into
account.   When the vagi are highly excitable, cardiac acceleration may frequently be observed in inspiration, and a delay in
expiration.   The tracings in Fig. 200 give a striking example of
this phenomenon.   Since this effect disappears after section of
the vagi, Einbrodt correctly takes it to be the effect of a reflex
rhythmical excitation of the bulbar centre of the cardiac vagi
during the expiratory acts.

XIII. It is easy from the above to deduce the beneficial influence of the respiratory mechanism upon the circulation of the blood (and lymph), as shown more particularly in the aspiration exerted by the thorax during inspiration, which accelerates the centripetal current, and increases the filling of the heart. This inspiratory influence cannot be eliminated by the contrary effects of the expiratory movements, particularly when the abdominal muscles intervene actively, as has constantly been verified on certain animals.

Some observers, however, particularly Filippo Pacini in Italy, have exaggerated the importance of the respiratory mechanism on the circulation of the blood, contending that a drowned person whose cardiac movements have practically ceased, can be brought back to life merely by artificial respiration. The untenability of this view is shown by two classical experiments, one devised by Valsalva (1740), the other by Johannes Müller (1838), which consist in determining what influence can be exerted by the respiratory movements on the circulation, under conditions in which the respiratory oscillations of intrathoracic and intra-abdominal pressure are in a position to exert maximal influence upon the course of the blood, or more accurately upon the entrance and exit of the blood from the thoracic cavity.

If the glottis is closed after a deep inspiration, and a strenuous and prolonged expiratory effort is then made, such pressure can be exerted on the heart and intrathoracic vessels that the movements and flow of the blood are temporarily arrested (Valsalva). Pronounced swelling of the veins, visible principally in those of the neck and face, evacuation of the vessels in the pulmonary system, and surcharge of the systemic circulation, cessation of cardiac sounds, and disappearance of the arterial pulse, can all be witnessed (E. H. Weber, Donders).

If instead of a forced expiration, the glottis is closed, and a prolonged inspiratory movement made, the heart and all the intra-thoracic vessels fill to such an extent that the arterial pulsations cease, owing to the surcharge of the lesser, and comparative evacuation of the greater circulation (J. Müller).

These experiments cannot be performed without a certain amount of risk, particularly to individuals who are no longer young, and whose cardio-vascular system is no longer vigorous and functioning normally. They may, however, be conveniently reproduced on an artificial schema which represents the thoracic cavity, lungs, heart, and related vessels, as shown in Fig. 201.

The results of these researches show that the respiratory movements are only favourable to the circulation of the blood when they are performed quietly, in a normal manner and with open glottis, so as not to disturb cardiac activity, or compress or dilate the heart to any extent. It is then seen (as can readily be confirmed on the schema) that the inspiratory movements assist the venous (and lymphatic) current, and favour the diastolic filling of the heart, while the expiratory movements facilitate the arterial current and systolic evacuation of the heart.

XIV. The rhythmical respiratory movements suffer various modifications, in abnormal or unusual conditions, or to satisfy various temporary needs or occurrences, or, lastly, as the motor expression of special sentiments of pleasure or pain, fatigue, ennui,

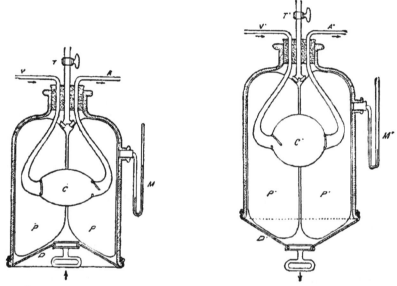

Fig. 201.—Schema to demonstrate effect of strong positive and negative intrathoracic pressures upon heart and blood-stream. (Landois.) D, D′, stout elastic membrane which closes the floor of a bell-jar, and can be pushed up or down by a handle, to imitate expiration and inspiration. P, P, and P′ P′, two thin rubber balloons, to imitate the lungs, communicating with a central tube, representing the trachea, which passes through the centre of the bell-glass, with tap *r* to simulate the glottis. CC′, a rubber ball, to represent the heart, communicating on one side with the tube V, V′, which represents the afferent vessels of the heart (provided with a valve that opens in inspiration and closes in expiration), on the other with the tube A, A′, representing the efferent artery (with valve that closes in inspiration and opens in expiration). When *r* is closed, the manometer M shows a marked diminution of pressure, with dilatation of heart and lungs, in inspiration; in expiration it shows marked increase of pressure, while the heart and lungs retract.

sleep, etc. The principal forms may be briefly summarised as an appendix to the mechanics of respiration.

When there are mechanical impediments to the thoracic or abdominal respiratory movements, *e.g.* plaster bandages applied to the chest or epigastrium, the activity of the diaphragm or the levator muscles to the ribs, respectively, is exaggerated, and the rhythm becomes deeper and slower.

When the respiratory movements cause or increase pains in the thorax or abdomen, respiratory rhythm becomes more frequent and superficial.

Where there is morbid stenosis of the air-passages, the respirations become deeper and less frequent. In pneumonia or pleurisy, with effusions into the pleural cavity, both frequency and depth of rhythm are accentuated.

Both secretions and exudations along the air-passages, as also foreign bodies, solid, liquid, or gaseous, which penetrate them, readily produce a reflex cough. This consists in loud, expiratory efforts, which produce enforced opening of the previously closed glottis, and by means of which the irritant is expelled. Coughing may be voluntary, and even when the cough is involuntary, it can be moderated and even inhibited by the will.

The presence of mucus, of foreign bodies, or of substances which irritate the nasal mucosa, may give rise to sneezing, which consists in one or more sudden and noisy expirations through the nasal passages, preceded by profound inspirations. In sneezing, the glottis is always open, the posterior nares are constricted by the rise of the soft palate, the mouth is seldom open. It is invariably a reflex act, which can only be imitated imperfectly by the will; it can, however, be voluntarily modified. The use of snuff makes the nasal mucosa insensitive after a few days, and suppresses sneezing.

Noisy crying, such as is frequent in childhood and youth, as the expression of physical and moral pain, consists in short and spasmodic inspirations, followed by prolonged expirations, with constricted glottis, relaxed muscles of face and jaw, simultaneous flow of tears and emission of high, inarticulate, laryngeal sounds. Sometimes it is associated with sobbing, which consists in repeated contractions of the diaphragm, producing sudden closure of the vocal cords, with a characteristic and quite involuntary sound.

Noisy laughter, the expression of sudden pleasant and un-expected sensations, or of hysteria, consists in short and rapidly succeeding expiratory efforts through the vocal cords, which are now brought close, and now separated, producing high, clear, and inarticulate tones, with trembling of the soft palate. The mouth is generally open, and the facial muscles contract in a characteristic manner. Laughter can easily be imitated at will, and to a certain extent can be voluntarily suppressed or moderated.

Yawning, the external expression of ennui, drowsiness, hunger, consists in a long, deep inspiration, in which many of the accessory inspiratory muscles participate, while the mouth, fauces, and glottis open convulsively. Inspiration is followed by a shorter expiration, and the two acts are accompanied by prolonged characteristic sounds, and by a general stretching of the arms and trunk. It is always an involuntary modification of breathing easily imitated by the will.

BIBLIOGRAPHY

A. BORELLI.   De motu animalium, 1713.

A. HALLER.   De respiratione, 1746.

G. E. HAMBERGER.   Dissertatio de respirationis mechanismo et usu genuino. Jenae, 1748.

BEAU et MAISSIAT.   Arch. gén. de méd., 1842, iii. série, t. xv.

ANT. MARCACCI.   Sul meccanismo dei moti del petto.   Pisa, 1843.

VIERORDT.   Art. Respiration, in Wagner's Handwörterb. ii., 1844.

SIBSON.   Phil. Trans., 1846.

HUTCHINSON.   Art. Thorax, in Todd's Cyclopaedia, 1852.

VIERORDT und LUDWIG.   Arch. f. phys. Heilk., 1855.

DUCHENNE.   Mouvements de la respiration.   Paris, 1866.

L. LUCIANI.   Archivio per le scienze mediche.   Torino, 1877.

A. MOSSO.   Archivio per le scienze mediche.   Torino, 1878.

WALDENBURG.   Zeitschr. f. klin. Med., 1876.

MARTIN und HARTWELL.   Journ. of Physiol., ii., 1879.

ROSENTHAL.   Handbuch d. Physiol. von Hermann, iv. 1882.

BERNSTEIN.   Arch. f. d. ges. Physiol. xxviii., 1882, xxxiv., 1884.

HERMANN.   Arch. f. d. ges. Physiol. xxx., 1882, xxxv., 1884.

A. FICK.   Festschrift des Vereins f. Naturkunde zu Cassel, 1886.

V. ADUCCO.   Atti della R. Accademia delle scienze di Torino, xxii., 1887.

G. HEINRICIUS und H. KRONECKER.   XIV. Abhandl. d. math. phys. Klasse der Königs. Sach. Gesellsch. d. Wissensch., 1888. (At the end of this monograph there is a list of the publications down to 1888 "über den Einfluss der Respirations-bewegungen auf den Blutlauf im Aortensystem.")

R. FICK.   Über die Atemmuskeln.   Arch. f. Anat., 1897, Supp. vol.

R. DU BOIS-REYMOND.   Mechanik der Atmung.   Ergebnisse der Physiol., I. Jahrg., 2 Abt., 1902 (review of the subject).

Recent English Literature : -

F. H. BARTLETT.   On the Variations of Blood Pressure during the Breathing of Rarefied Air.   Amer. Journ. of Physiol., 1904, x. 149-163.

M. P. FITZGERALD and J. S. HALDANE.   The Normal Alveolar Carbonic Acid Pressure in Man.   Journ. of Physiol., 1905, xxxii. 486-494.

C. C. GUTHRIE and F. H. PIKE.   The Effect of Changes in Blood-Pressure on Respiratory Movements.   Amer. Journ. of Physiol., 1906, xvi. 475-482.

C. C. GUTHRIE and F. H. PIKE.   Further Observations on the Relation between Blood Pressure and Respiratory Movements.   Amer. Journ. of Physiol., 1907-1908, xx. 451-456.

J. F. HALLS DALLY.   A Contribution to the Study of the Mechanism of Respiration, with especial reference to the Action of the Vertebral Column and Diaphragm. Proc. Roy. Soc., 1908, lxxx. B. 182-187.

L. HILL and M. FLACK.   The Effect of Excess of Carbon Dioxide and of Want of Oxygen upon the Respiration and the Circulation.   Journ. of Physiol., 1908, xxxvii. 77-111.

A. E. BOYCOTT and J. S. HALDANE.   The Effects of Low Atmospheric Pressures on Respiration.   Journ. of Physiol., 1908, xxxvii. 355-377.

R. O. WARD.   Alveolar Air on Monte Rosa.   Journ. of Physiol., 1908, xxxvii. 378-389.

J. S. HALDANE and E. P. POULTON.   The Effects of Want of Oxygen on Respiration.   Journ. of Physiol., 1908, xxxvii. 390-407.

CHAPTER XIII

THE NERVOUS CONTROL OF RESPIRATORY RHYTHM

CONTENTS.—1. Motor nerves to respiratory muscles and smooth muscle cells of bronchi. 2. Bulbar respiratory centres and their localisation. 3. Spinal respiratory centres. 4. Cerebral respiratory centres. 5. Each of these centres results from the association of an inspiratory and an expiratory centre, which function rhythmically and alternately. 6. Automatic regulation of normal respiratory rhythm, by afferent pulmonary fibres of vagus. 7. Influence exerted on respiratory rhythm *via* the cerebral tracts and sensory nerves in general. 8. Phenomena consequent on the separation of the bulb from the brain and spinal cord. 9. Dyspnoea and its different forms. 10. Eupnoea or normal quiet respiration. 11. Experimental apnoea from artificial respiration with the bellows. 12. Foetal apnoea, and the analogous forms of experimental apnoea that can be produced in the adult. 13. Voluntary, as compared with experimental apnoea. 14. Apnoea produced by continuous ventilation in birds. 15. Periodic respiration, or Cheyne-Stokes phenomenon. 16. Physiological theory of respiratory rhythm. Bibliography.

THE previous chapter shows that the respiratory processes are highly complex, owing to the number of muscles, anatomically very distinct, and even remote from each other, which co-operate in them. Their efficacy in determining the rhythmical dilatation and constriction of the thoracic cavity, and consequent pulmonary ventilation, which are indispensable to life, is entirely due to co-ordination, *i.e.* to the harmonious association and sequence of the contractions of the individual inspiratory and expiratory muscles. If, for example, the external intercostals were to contract before the scaleni, or if the diaphragm became active along with the internal intercostals, no adequate renewal of pulmonary air would be obtained except with a useless expenditure of energy.

Since the rhythmical activity of respiration results from the co-ordinated functions of many and very distinct muscles, it cannot be founded (as that of the heart may possibly be), on a physiological property inherent in the muscles, but must necessarily depend (as the facts prove clearly) upon the rhythmical co-ordinating function of complex nervous processes, which are the subject of the present chapter.

I. The nervous mechanisms on which the respiratory rhythm depends are as follows :—

(*a*) Motor nerves to the individual muscles which take part in the inspiratory or expiratory movements ;

(*b*) A central organ, or, better, a complex of nerve centres, interassociated, and constituting a small system;

(*c* Afferent nerves capable of modifying, directly or indirectly, the activity of the said centres.

The motor nerves to the muscles, which normally determine inspiratory expansion and expiratory retraction of the thorax, all arise in the anterior roots of the spinal nerves. The motor nerves to the scaleni emerge from the cervical tract, more exactly from the second to the seventh nerves, and thus form the cervical and brachial plexus, from which the branches to the muscles are given off. The phrenic nerves which serve the diaphragm take origin specially in the fourth cervicals, but are reinforced by fibres from the third and also from the fifth pairs. The levatores costarum longi et breves, the external and internal intercostals, and the abdominal muscles receive nerves from the thoracic pairs of the spinal cord: and, in particular, the rami posteriores of the dorsal nerves serve the levatores costarum: the intercostal nerves, the muscles of the same name; and the internal or anterior branches of the intercostals, the muscles of the abdomen, which also receive fibres derived from the first lumbar pair.

Physiological proof of these morphological data is afforded by the following experiments. A transverse section through the spinal cord below the exit of the last intercostal nerve leaves all respiratory movements entirely unaffected, while a cross-section in the thoracic cord paralyses all the respiratory muscles, the nerves of which arise below the section. When the lower part of the cervical cord is transversely divided, *i.e.* above the first intercostal and below the exit of the fifth cervical nerves, all the motor muscles of the ribs are paralysed (with the partial exception of the first two, which are raised by the scaleni) so that the respiratory movements are effected almost exclusively by the rhythmical activity of the diaphragm (Fig. 86, p. 229). If the results of this operation are compared with those following the section of the phrenic nerves (Fig. 202), they show the extreme functional importance of the intercostal as compared with the diaphragmatic muscles—paralysis of the latter being in no way dangerous to the life of the animal, save in the case of young rabbits, in which the thorax is not sufficiently rigid, nor the thoracic muscles sufficiently developed, to allow of ready compensation for the failure of the diaphragm. These observations are confirmed by those made on the human subject, which show that after paralysis of the diaphragm the respirations become somewhat more frequent, but are accomplished solely by the muscles to the ribs with no active co-operation of accessory muscles.

When the section through the cord is made above the exit of the third cervical nerves, as far as the apex of the calamus scriptorius, all the respiratory muscles properly so-called are paralysed, including those of the diaphragm, and only the rhythmical movements of the glottis and the muscles of the lips and nose persist, which, as we have seen, not infrequently accompany the rhythmical movements of the thorax. These muscles are served by nerves, which emerge from the medulla oblongata ; the muscles of the lips and nose receive branches from the facial nerve, and the muscles of the larynx are innervated by branches of the vagus (the crico-thyroid muscle from the superior laryngeal, and the rest of the laryngeal muscles from the inferior laryngeal).

The vagus also provides the motor nerves to the smooth muscles of the bronchial tubes. This was first demonstrated by Longet (1842); it was subsequently contested, and finally confirmed by the later experiments of Bert, Schiff, Gerlach and others. The fact that stimulation of the peripheral trunk in certain kinds of animals reduces the volume of the lung, which can only be due to the contraction of the smooth muscles of the bronchi, is very

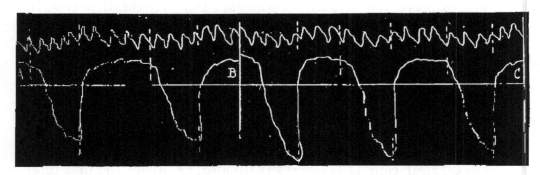

Fig. 202. Effect of dividing phrenics in dog. (Luciani.) To, intrathoracic pressure ; Ca, carotid pressure. A-B, previous to section of phrenic ; B-C, after section. The tracing shows that both inspiratory and expiratory movements are exaggerated after section.

striking. Roy, with Brown, and Sandmann claimed to have also discovered dilator bronchial fibres in the vagus, the action of which is expressed by pulmonary dilatation, when the peripheral end of the vagus is excited with strong currents. It is not improbable that the presence of these dilator fibres in many cases weakens or nullifies the effect of the simultaneous excitation of the constrictor fibres, which would account for the negative result obtained by some observers.

Division of the vagi in the horse causes a considerable increase of volume in the lung, a proof that the constrictor fibres of the bronchi in these animals are in constant or tonic excitation. In dogs, on the contrary, section of the vagi produces a scarcely perceptible dilatation of the lung, showing that there is only weak tonic excitation.

According to some interesting observations of Fano and Fasola, the lungs of the marsh tortoise are capable of very extensive active movements, due partly to the smooth muscle cells which are innervated by the vagus, partly to the striated fibres derived from the muscles of the diaphragm, which penetrate the parenchyma of the lungs, to invest the large alveoli, and are innervated from the spinal nerves. When the vagus is stimulated in the neck of this animal, a curve of slow prolonged contraction is obtained from the lung, exactly similar to that served up by smooth muscle. When, on the other hand, the spinal cord is excited, a rapid pulmonary contraction results, which is evidently due to the striated muscles.

The physiological function of the smooth muscles of the bronchi, and of the constrictor and dilator nerves which serve them, is not yet fully explained. It seems obvious that they give greater resistance to the bronchial walls, and reinforce this resistance by their contraction, when the negative intrathoracic pressure falls too low, during forced inspiration. Probably the development of the pulmonary emphysema is promoted by atony, or by the paresis or paralysis of the smooth muscles.

II. As a whole the central mechanisms, from which the several motor nerves to the respiratory muscles receive their rhythmical impulses, must be excessively complicated, seeing that the co-ordination of the inspiratory and expiratory movements, i.e. the harmonious and synergic contraction of the muscles which alternately expand and contract the thorax, depend upon them. The immediate centres for the motor respiratory nerves must, however, be distinguished from the true controlling and co-ordinating respiratory centre. The former lie in the cervico-dorsal tract of the spinal cord, and are formed from the grey matter of the anterior horns, which contains the nerve cells of which the nerves to the respiratory muscles are the prolongation ; the second is situated in the medulla oblongata, and has probably no direct influence upon the muscles, but is confined to exciting and regulating the functions of the former.

When the brain is extirpated to the level of a plane which passes along the inferior limit of the pons, or when a section is made at the level of this plane, it will be seen that after temporary disturbance the animal continues to breathe spontaneously, in a regular and perfectly co-ordinated manner. This experiment proves that the co-ordinating centre for the respiratory movements does not lie higher than the spinal bulb. When, on the contrary, the bulb is divided from the cervical cord at the apex of the calamus scriptorius by a transverse section, the respiratory movements ipso facto come to a standstill. This proves that the respiratory centre lies within that section of the bulb which is situated between the two planes of division indicated.

Which portion of the bulb is it, however, which represents the respiratory centre? The experiments directed towards the localisation of this centre have a very involved history, which must be recapitulated in its principal headings. Galen already knew that a section through the highest part of the cord produced the immediate death of the animal. "Perspicuum est, quod si post primam aut secundam vertebram, aut in ipso spinalis medullae principio sectionem ducas, repente animal corrumpitur" (*De anat. administr.* lib. viii. cap. ix.).

This experiment was successfully repeated in 1760 by Lorry, and perfected in 1811 by Legallois, who at a later time showed experimentally on the rabbit that "respiration depends upon a very circumscribed region of the medulla oblongata, which is situated at a short distance from the occipital sulcus, and near the origin of the eighth or pneumo-gastric nerves."

A few years later (1842) Flourens took up these experiments of Legallois, and endeavoured to localise the respiratory centre more exactly, but he added nothing substantial to the results of Legallois. In a subsequent communication (1851) he defined as *point, ou næud vital* a very minute tract of grey matter, the size of a pin's head, lying in the median line towards the tip of the calamus scriptorius, ablation of which infallibly led to the immediate death of the animal.

It was, however, shown by Volkmann (1842), Longet (1847), and M. Schiff (1858) that the respiratory centre is a double organ, which can be divided by a median longitudinal section down the sinus rhomboidalis into two halves, without causing arrest of respiration by the section. After these publications Flourens also (1859) recognised that the *næud vital* is double, and that in order to destroy life "a transverse section of 5 mm. is required, passing through the centre of the V. of grey matter in the medulla oblongata," *i.e.* half way up the beak of the calamus scriptorius.

Longet, and even more definitely Schiff, endeavoured to show that the true respiratory centre is located in the large nucleus of grey matter in the alae cinereae, which lies in the lower part of the bulb, external to the nucleus of the hypoglossus, beneath the floor of the fourth ventricle, and that the paths by which the impulse is conducted thence to the spinal cord run in the lateral bundles, unilateral section of which, at the lower level of the bulb, or at the level of the second and third cervical vertebrae, suffices to produce respiratory paralysis of the muscles of the same side (Schiff's *respiratory hemiplegia*). The animal may survive this operation for weeks and months, and active movements of respiration never reappear on the operated side (1854).

This last fact suffices to refute Brown-Séquard, who in 1858 denied the existence of a bulbar respiratory centre. In his opinion, the sudden death of the animal after lesion of the bulb was the effect, not of paralysis or deficiency, but of traumatic excitation of an inhibitory centre or the paths for the respiratory movements.

If this were correct, the respiratory hemiplegia consequent on unilateral division of the lateral bundles in the upper cervical region would disappear after a short time. It is, however, true that with great care the whole of the so-called *nœud vital* of Flourens, as also, according to Schiff, the whole internal or median half of the ala cinerea can be destroyed, without producing permanent arrest of respiration. It is only when the external half of the ala cinerea is separated from the central grey matter that respiration on the corresponding side is abolished for ever.

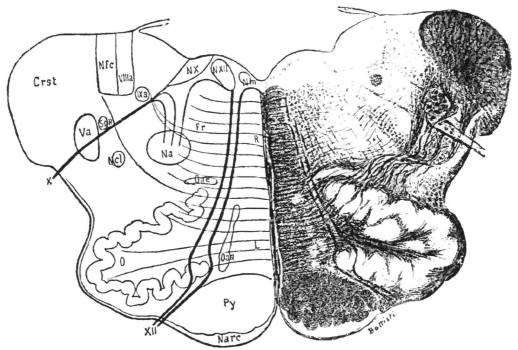

FIG. 203.—Section of spinal bulb in man at level of exit of vagus and hypoglossal nerves—from the section. (Luciana.) *Crt*, Rectiform body ; *Nfc*, nucleus of funiculus cuneatus ; *VIIIa*, ascending root of auditory nerve ; *NX*, nucleus of vagus, which appears as ala cinerea at surface of rhomboidal sinus ; *NXII*, nucleus of hypoglossal ; *Na*, median nucleus (or nucleus of funiculus teres) ; *IXa*, ascending root of glosso-pharyngeal (or funiculus solitarius) ; *Fr*, formatio reticularis ; *R*, raphe ; *SaR*, substantia gelatinosa Rolandi ; *Va*, ascending root of trigeminal ; *X*, vagus ; *Na*, nucleus ambiguus ; *Oae*, accessory external olive ; *Oaa*, accessory anterior olive ; *O*, olive ; *XII*, hypoglossal ; *L*, fillet ; *Py*, pyramidal bundle ; *Narc*, arciform nucleus.

From these facts (which were confirmed in the last years of his life by Schiff, and by his pupil Girard) we must conclude that the most indispensable part of the respiratory centre lies within the outer half of the ala cinerea, bordering on the median limit of the restiform body, *i.e.* external to the dorsal or sensory nucleus of the vagus and glosso-pharyngeal, along with the solitary bundle, and the dorsal and distal portion of the formatio reticularis (Fig. 203).

In the year 1873 Gierke, under Heidenhain's direction, carried out a series of experiments with a view to determining more exactly in which section of the bulb lesions brought about a sudden respiratory standstill. He carefully located the site of the bulbar lesions inflicted during the life of the animal, by microscopic examination of the hardened and stained preparations. He found that the arrest of the respiratory movements was invariably determined by the division, or at any rate the injury, of the solitary bundle, which he regarded as the respiratory centre proper, since it consists of a column of small multipolar nerve cells, mingled with nerve fibres.

Gierke's results do not contradict those of Schiff, since it is impossible to divide the solitary bundle without at the same time destroying the external, deep section of the dorsal nucleus of the vagus or the nerve fibres descending from it. It is only the interpretation of the results that differs.

In 1892 Gad and Marinesco published a series of interesting experiments on the slow and gradual destruction of the floor of the fourth ventricle by the method of repeated punctiform cauterisation by fine glass rods, rounded and heated at the end, which avoided haemorrhage, traction, and pressure on the adjacent parts. By these experiments, undertaken with the utmost precaution, they were able to destroy not only Flourens' *nœud vital* at the apex of the calamus scriptorius, but also the external portion of the ala cinerea, including the solitary bundle, without finally bringing respiration to a standstill. They frequently noted respiratory disturbances and even arrest, due to excitation of inhibitory paths, which soon passed off, and permitted them to proceed cautiously with the cauterisation. Only when the lesion was prolonged deep into the formatio reticularis was there final arrest of respiration. In addition to the respiratory tracts, descending to the spinal centres, the formatio reticularis contains a number of cells, which, although few in number, and not grouped into a nucleus, may very well as a whole represent the respiratory centre. At the same time it is not necessary to destroy the whole of this formation to obtain immediate arrest of respiration.

With Deiters, Gad distinguished that part of the formatio reticularis, which lies medially to the root of the hypoglossus and extends to the raphe, from the lateral part which lies outside this root. In rabbit it is only necessary to injure this last segment deeply enough, in order to produce permanent arrest of the respiratory movements. In the cat, on the other hand, the same result is obtained by cauterising the part which lies between the root of the hypoglossus and the raphe. In any case, whatever segment of the formatio reticularis is destroyed, it suffices, if not to bring about total arrest of the respiration, invariably to produce a considerable weakening in respiratory energy. It is therefore probable that the whole of the formatio reticularis (which as a unit includes a much more extensive segment of the bulb than the *nœud vital* of Flourens) constitutes the bulbar centre of respiration. Evidence for this theory is given, according to Gad, in the fact that very circumscribed electrical excitation by means of fine needles, varnished as far as the points, and thrust into the parts of the formatio reticularis which lie above and beneath those parts whose destruction produces respiratory arrest, provokes only an acceleration of respiratory rhythm, and not a tetanus of the inspiratory muscles, as occurs when the respiratory tracts in the lateral bundles of the cervical cord are excited.

Whatever the extension of the true bulbar respiratory centre, it is certain that the symmetry of the respiratory movements on the two sides of the thorax depends on the intrabulbar commissural fibres, which unite the two lateral halves of the respiratory centre; and that the descending paths, which unite the bulbar centre with the spinal centres of the respiratory muscles, and run directly, without decussating, in the lateral bundles and in the highest portion of the cervical region, are probably located in the processus reticularis, which lies between the anterior and posterior horns of the grey matter of the cord.

III. We have already seen that Brown-Séquard, in 1858, denied the existence of a bulbar respiratory centre, and interpreted the results of Flourens' experiments as inhibitory phenomena, by which the rhythmic activity of the spinal centres, the sole cause of the respiratory movements, were suspended. The successful destruction of the so-called *nœud vital* without abolishing respiration seemed to justify his opinion. Now, however, we know that the *nœud vital* does not constitute the whole of the bulbar respiratory centre, which is much more extensive, and apparently comprises the entire formatio reticularis.

In 1880 Langendorff attempted to resuscitate the doctrine of Brown-Séquard, in Germany, on the strength of an interesting fact discovered in 1874 by P. Rokitansky. He saw that in young rabbits it is possible for a certain time to revive the respiratory movements suppressed by separation of the bulb from the spinal cord, after suspending artificial respiration and slightly strychninising the animal, to increase the excitability of the cord. Schroff confirmed this in 1875, adding that in order to reinstate some respiratory movements in animals with divided bulb, without employing strychnine, it was only necessary to avoid cooling during artificial respiration by keeping the animal in a warm chamber. Langendorff (1880 further found, after dividing the bulb, that natural respiration was reinstated for a considerable time in newborn puppies and kittens without resorting to adventitious aids other than artificial respiration. Since it is well known that in the newborn, as in the lower animals, the functions of the spinal cord exhibit a far greater degree of autonomy and independence of the higher centres than in the adult, Wertheimer (in 1886) endeavoured in France to repeat the same experiments on adult animals by prolonging artificial respiration for ¾-2 hours after section of the bulb, in order to give time for the supposed traumatic inhibition to pass off. He observed that at the close of artificial respiration the animals made certain movements of the thorax. abdomen, and limbs, which produced a kind of pulmonary ventilation, and kept them alive for a considerable time, even in some cases for three-quarters of an hour.

On the whole, no definite conclusions as to the independence of the spinal respiratory functions from the bulb can be deduced from these experiments. There is no proof that the movements of thorax and abdomen observed under the above conditions after division of the bulb, are co-ordinated like normal inspirations and expirations; in fact, it appears from Wertheimer's own observations that they are irregular and inco-ordinate. Often they are simple active abdominal expirations, followed by passive inspirations; at other times the inspirations are associated with repeated expirations, which cancel their mechanical effects, and look like double or triple inspirations. Very frequently the thoracic and abdominal movements are associated with other movements of the limbs, tail, and vertebral column, due to spread of excitation from the spinal centres. The long survival period in animals with divided cord may also be due to the marked fall of temperature, caused by the prolonged artificial respiration by which the animals are reduced to the poikilothermic or hibernating condition, in which they are able to survive for a long time with minimal renewal of pulmonary air.

Langendorff endeavoured to sustain his theory of there being only an inhibitory and regulatory centre for respiratory movements in the bulb—their activity being due solely to the spinal centres—by showing that mechanical, electrical, and chemical stimulation of the floor of the fourth ventricle, in chloralised rabbits, induced phenomena of respiratory arrest, which ceased with the excitation.

On the other hand Kronecker and Marckwald (1887-89), on repeating the experiments with rabbits in which the spinal bulb was separated from the cerebrum, obtained quite opposite results. Respiration was accelerated by electrical stimulation of the bulb, which also caused respiratory movements, intercalated between those made by the animal. This was confirmed by Aducco (1889) on intact and non-anaesthetised dogs, both with electrical excitation of the sinus rhomboidalis (Fig. 204`, and with its chemical excitation by a crystal of sodium chloride.

The effects of applying cocaine to the bulb, as determined by Aducco's experiments, are even more striking. When, e.g., cocaine hydrochloride (either in the form of crystals, or as a powder mixed

with vaseline; is applied to the floor of the fourth ventricle, it is
seen after a few seconds or minutes, according to the rapidity of
absorption, that all respiratory movements cease and the thorax is
fixed in the cadaveric posture.   This paralysis of the respiratory
movements is preceded by a brief period of excitation, in which
the inspiratory movements are exaggerated.   Quite different effects
are obtained on the heart, the beats being accelerated directly after
the application of the poison, as after section of the vagi, or intoxication with atropine, an effect that persists after the respiratory
standstill.   When the cocaine hydrochloride is applied in the form
of an ointment, so that the poison is more slowly and gradually

A

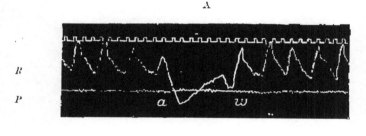

B

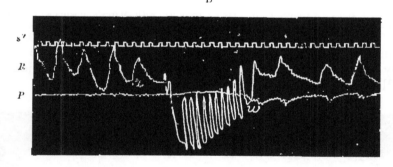

Fig. 204. Effects of weak (A) and medium (B) electrical excitation of spinal bulb in dog.
(Aducco.) Excitation from *a* to *w*. R, Respirations recorded with Marey's pneumograph; P.
arterial pressure traced with Marey's metal manometer ; ", seconds. The inspiratory effects
are seen on both tracings.

absorbed, different phases of modification may be distinguished in
the respiratory and cardiac movements.   Fig. 205 shows the
curves of normal respiration and heart-beat in the dog ; there are
four respirations and eighteen heart-beats in 20 seconds.   One
minute after applying the cocaine to the floor of the fourth
ventricle the curve of Fig. 206 is obtained, which shows five less
ample respirations and three beats in 20 seconds.   Nine minutes
after applying the poison the form of respiration is entirely altered
(Fig. 207) and has become quite slow.   The line of rest of the
thorax corresponds with the extreme inspiratory position, which
is due, not to an inspiratory tetanus, but to the fact that the expirations only are active, while the inspirations are passive, *i.e.* they
represent the elastic recoil of the thorax to the position of

equilibrium at the close of expiration. The acceleration of the cardiac movements persists; thirty-eight beats may be counted in 20 seconds. Ten minutes from the commencement of the

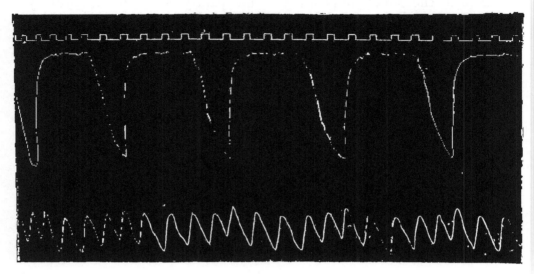

Fig. 205.—Normal tracings of respiration (R) and carotid pulse (P) in a dog after exposing the rhomboidal sinus. (Aducco.) R, Tracing recorded with Marey's pneumograph; P, with Marey's metal manometer; s'', with Deprez signal.

experiment the active expirations also cease, and the animal quickly succumbs to asphyxia, unless artificial respiration with the bellows is resorted to.

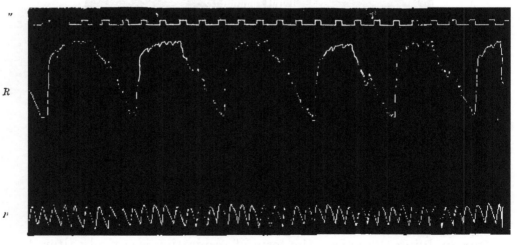

Fig. 206.—Same as preceding, one minute after applying 0·5 grm. cocaine ointment to floor of 4th ventricle. (Aducco.)

The paralysing action of cocaine on the bulbar centres was confirmed by Aducco with the addition of a highly characteristic group of effects: enormous dilatation of pupil, insensibility of conjunctiva, immobility of pupil, inertia and flaccidity of tongue and muscles of jaw, suppression of salivary secretions, marked fall of temperature, inhibition of swallowing reflexes, failure to vomit after injection of apomorphine: lastly, suspension of any kind of reaction from the cocainised bulbar substance to electrical stimuli, however strong.   The possibility that under these conditions there can be paralysis of the spinal, as well as the bulbar centres, owing to spread of the poison, seems to be excluded by the rate at which complete arrest of respiratory movements may occur (less than 20 seconds), as well as by phenomena which prove that the excitability of the spinal centres is maintained—*e.g.* rhythmical contraction and relaxation of the sphincter on introduction of the finger into the rectum.

These results led Aducco to the important conclusion that a true motor centre exists in the bulb, besides the inhibitory centre

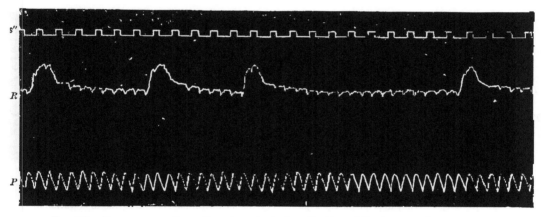

Fig. 207.—Same as preceding, after nine minutes' application of the drug. (Aducco.) Tracing R shows the active and passive inspirations.   Followed by complete arrest of respiration.

to the heart, and that both are paralysed by the local action of cocaine.   The paralysis of the cardiac inhibitory centre (formed as we have seen by the nuclei of origin of the accessory) causes acceleration of the beats; paralysis of the respiratory centre (constituted in all probability by the formatio reticularis) causes arrest of respiratory movements.   Hence it is the bulbar respiratory centre that sends co-ordinated rhythmical impulses to the spinal centres of the respiratory muscles.   These last centres are, therefore, incapable of any rhythmical activity, independent of that of the bulbar centre.   If under certain conditions (as in the experiments of Langendorff, Wertheimer and others) they show activity independent of the bulb, this activity is not co-ordinated, and is conditioned by the peripheral or central stimuli, of which we have still to study the mechanism.

The simplest, clearest, and most incontrovertible proof of the absolute dependence of the spinal centres of the respiratory muscles upon the controlling bulbar centre appears, however, in the fact that permanent respiratory hemiplegia ensues on unilateral section of the upper cervical cord (Fig. 208). Schiff rightly directed attention to this fact in his last work on the respiratory centre (1894), in order to refute the old doctrine of Brown-Séquard as tentatively revived by Langendorff and Wertheimer.

It is, however, still uncertain whether we should, with Langendorff, admit the existence of another autonomous inhibitory centre for respiratory movements, along with the controlling centre in the bulb. Landergreen's studies on the circulatory and respiratory phenomena in asphyxia (1897), those of Prevost and Stern on the final respirations (1906), and, lastly, those of Mosso on the asphyxial pause, contain no conclusive arguments for or against the theory of an inhibitory, respiratory, bulbar centre.

Patrizi and Franchini, on the ground of certain peculiarities of

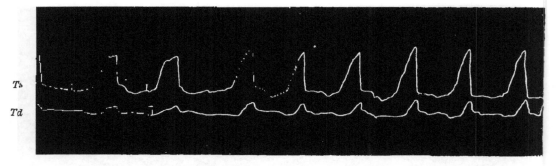

FIG. 208.—Pneumograms of most convex part of right (*Is*) and left (*Id*) half of thorax in young hound, operated on three weeks previously by hemisection of cord at level of highest cervical tract. (M. Schiff.) The slight respiratory movements of the right half of the thorax are passive, . . . they depend on the aspiration of the mediastinum to the left due to elevation of sternum.

respiratory arrest from centripetal excitation of the vagus (1906-7), are inclined to admit Langendorff's contention. The question is a difficult and complex one, and will require extensive experimental researches before we can hope for its solution.

IV. It is doubtful whether the bulbar respiratory centre, and the spinal respiratory centres scattered along the cervico-dorsal tract of the spinal cord, really represent the whole of the central nervous mechanisms which take an active part in bringing about the mechanical processes of respiration. In all probability, we must, in addition to the bulbar and spinal centres, also admit the existence of true respiratory centres in the brain.

We know that the respiratory mechanism can be modified in a variety of ways, both by voluntary impulses and by simple psychical emotions. A practised singer has such perfect control over his own respiratory movements that in expelling the air from his lungs he is able to produce the finest shades of tone during expiration. Again in conversation, and still more in oratory, the necessity for breathing is relieved by devices very far from ordinary. The inspirations are taken at rare intervals, and are deep and quickly completed; they occur at irregular intervals, and at moments when the phonetic pauses are effective in expression; the expirations, on the contrary, are prolonged and often very powerful, since the expired air is employed wholly in the service of phonetic expression. So, too, in sucking, swallowing, vomiting, defaecation, and parturition, the mechanics of respiration (as we shall see elsewhere) assume different forms and attitudes. Laughing, crying, sobbing, yawning, represent so many typical expressions of feeling, which all, as we have seen, consist essentially in special forms of the respiratory movements. Fear, joy, expectation, preoccupation, are states of mind continually associated with respiratory changes, which are conspicuous enough, even if less characteristic than the preceding. The direct control of the will is only exerted upon the respiratory movements under quite special conditions—*e.g.* we hold our breath when we know the air to be foul or stagnant, when we dive into water, or under other similar conditions.

All these psychical modifications of the respiratory rhythm are governed by impulses emanating from the cerebral cortex, particularly from that region known as the motor area. When this tract is stimulated electrically in the dog or cat, the respiratory movements are visibly accelerated or retarded, which depends less on the seat than on the intensity of stimulation. According to François-Franck, strong stimuli retard the respiratory processes; weak stimuli accelerate them.

The sub-cortical centres are also capable of modifying respiratory rhythm. On exciting the surface of a section, at the level of the anterior and posterior corpora quadrigemina, Martin and Booker obtained unmistakable inspiratory effects. Christiani found the same on exciting the floor of the third ventricle. When, on the other hand, he excited the grey matter, at the entrance of the Sylvian Aqueduct, he obtained expiratory effects.

These different parts of the brain (and probably others not yet investigated because less accessible) affect the respiratory movements, in so far as they are capable of modifying the rhythmical activity of the bulbar respiratory centre, with which they are connected by means of special descending nerve tracts. Evidence for this is afforded in the fact that the clean division of brain from bulb at the level of the upper limit of the pons, has, as we have seen, only a transient effect on respiratory rhythm. This shows that even under normal conditions the cerebral respiratory centres take no active part in modifying the impulses sent out from the bulbar centre. We shall, however, see under what abnormal circumstances the influence of the cerebral respiratory centres is functionally apparent in its full importance.

The complete nervous system on which the respiratory mechanism depends may thus be divided into three sections: the *bulbar*, the *spinal*, and the *cerebral* respiratory centres. From the first emanate the rhythmical impulses to thoracic-abdominal movements on which the activity of the spinal respiratory centres which pass the impulses on to the muscles depends; but the rhythmical activity of the bulbar centres is in its turn regulated, and may be modified in a number of ways, by the cerebral respiratory centres.

V. In order to form a more adequate conception of the mode in which these highly complicated systems function, it must be remembered that we understand by the term respiratory centres an accumulation of central mechanisms, which are capable of a double and antagonistic action —one inspiratory, which dilates the thorax, the other expiratory, which contracts it. As we have seen in the preceding chapter, both forms of movement are *active* and are brought about under normal conditions by the contraction of antagonist muscles; we cannot regard expiration as the simple effect of inhibition acting upon the inspiratory centres, but must further assume the existence of *true expiratory centres*. The concept respiratory centre thus implies the association of two centres, which have an opposite function in respect of pulmonary ventilation, and can, therefore, under normal conditions, only function rhythmically and alternately.

Not only must we recognise the existence of expiratory centres as distinct from inspiratory centres; on the ground of irrefutable observations we must further admit that these centres, while normally associated in their rhythmical and alternating functions, are yet capable under abnormal conditions, particularly the influence of certain poisons, of functioning independent of each other. That the inspiratory centres may, under special circumstances, alone be active will readily be admitted by all (and these form the vast majority) who hold that, normally, inspirations alone are active. But it is also possible to demonstrate that under various other conditions the converse holds good, the expirations only being active, while the inspirations are passive. In these cases the inspiratory centres do not function, and the expiratory centres alone perform their work. Inspiration is effected by the elastic recoil of the thoracic walls, which are pushed below their resting position.

Aducco succeeded in collecting certain observations and recording them graphically enough to establish this fact, which as a contribution to the theory of the centres that control the mechanics of respiration is of no small importance. The curves of Fig. 209 were recorded by two tambours with exploring buttons applied to the sternum and the linea alba abdominis respectively their movements being transmitted to two other tambours writing

on a revolving drum) from a tracheotomised dog which had 3
grms. of chloral hydrate injected in several doses into its jugular
vein.   Under these conditions there are seen to be a few active
abdominal expirations, in which one very energetic and one
shallow effort alternate with tolerable regularity.   All the

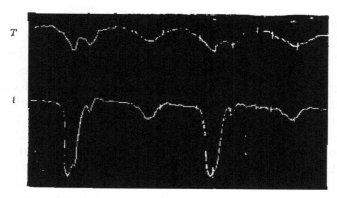

FIG. 209.—Thoracic (T) and abdominal (A) pneumograms obtained from two exploring button
tambours on a dog, after intravenous injection of 8 grms. chloral hydrate.   (Aducco.) The
descending curves of A correspond to active abdominal expirations.   The slight movements
of T are passive.

respiratory processes depend upon these rhythmical abdominal
respirations which pull upon the thoracic walls, on which the
traction of the rectal abdominal muscles follows passively.   In
this case, therefore, the
chloral succeeds (tempor-
arily at least) in paralysing the rhythmic activity
of the thoracic inspiratory
and expiratory centres,
while maintaining and
even increasing the action
of the expiratory centres
for the abdominal muscles.

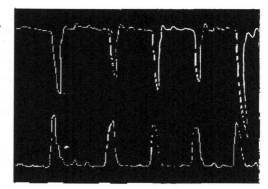

FIG. 210.—Tracings as in last figure.   From dog after
intravenous injection of 5 grms. of chloral hydrate.
(Aducco.) The descending lines of tracing T coincide
with active thoracic expirations, followed immediately
by the ascending lines of passive inspiration. The
inverse abdominal movements (A) are passive.

    In other cases (in which
the specific mechanism of
action is unknown) the
chloral paralyses both the
inspiratory and expiratory
abdominal centres, and
increases the rhythmical
activity of the thoracic expiratory centres. The curves of Fig. 210 were
taken from a tracheotomised dog, after injecting 5 grms. of chloral
hydrate into the jugular vein.   It will be seen that the resting
position of the thorax coincides with the end of inspiration and
commencement of expiration ; between the first and second there is
a pause, after which a marked depression of the thorax occurs, which

produces a passive rise of the abdominal wall, and thus drives the air out of the trachea. Active thoracic expiration is immediately succeeded by passive inspiration, in which the thorax rises again, and the abdomen falls.

These exceptional phenomena, with the cause of which we are unacquainted, and which accordingly cannot be determined experimentally, have no physiological significance other than that of showing the existence of an expiratory centre, which can function separately when the inspiratory centre is put out of court. Moreover, these and other facts investigated by Aducco show that in the dog forced expiration is no functional unity, effected always in the same way, and by the help of the same mechanism. It may be carried out by the walls of the thorax or by the walls of the abdomen. In the abdomen itself, according to Aducco, it is possible to separate two expiratory mechanisms—the interior recti, and the lateral muscles. These different expiratory mechanisms (thoracic, and anterior and lateral abdominal) may function simultaneously or synchronously — or simultaneously and a-synchronously,—or lastly, separately from one another.

Other similar phenomena, noted incidentally by various authors (Hering and Breuer, Luciani, Stefani, and Sighicelli, &c.), but which Mosso (1878-1885) specially emphasised, show that the inspiratory centre, too, may be regarded as an aggregate of centres, which, although they normally function harmoniously, while each retains a certain degree of autonomy and independence, may yet, under certain indefinable conditions, come into play at different times, act with unequal intensity, and even be capable of functioning separately. According to Mosso, we must at any rate accept a facial, a thoracic, and a diaphragmatic centre for inspiration, since on comparing the simultaneous tracings from the three different groups of muscles, a-synchronisms or different intensities of action can be detected at different times upon the same individual. The most striking fact of this kind is that in sleep respiration is essentially costal, since (as shown in another connection, Fig. 184, p. 418) the diaphragm is virtually inactive. In the death-agony, on the contrary, the opposite prevails; only the diaphragm is active, while the intercostal muscles are paralysed. We must conclude that in sleep the thoracic and diaphragmatic inspirations coincide, the first, however, outlasting the second : at other times thoracic inspiration precedes the diaphragmatic.

From these and other similar facts Mosso concluded that " the earlier conception of a single respiratory centre must be abandoned ; the respiratory movements of the facial muscles, diaphragm, thorax, and abdomen have their specific nerve centres, which function autonomously." Schiff, in his last work (1894), criticised this attempted decentralisation of respiratory innervation. According to him the special centres of the spinal cord, on which depend the contractions of the different groups of muscles that serve in respiration, are not true respiratory centres, since they are not perfectly autonomous, and require a co-ordinating centre in the bulb, which is the sole organ on which respiratory stimuli act, and is alone capable of elaborating them so as to throw the spinal centres into activity.   He opposes the theory of decentralisation by one of centralisation.   The difference between the two theories seems, however, to lie in the name rather than in the conception. In our opinion the real problem (which has so far remained unanswered) is the more exact definition of the nature of the co-ordinating function of the bulbar respiratory centre.   Do the various modes of functional association and succession of the several muscles or groups of respiratory muscles depend exclusively on this ; or do the respective spinal centres also co-operate actively ; or (at the least) is the varying degree of excitability of these centres at the given moment in which they receive the impulses from the bulbar centre, of account ?

Nothing definite, again, is known as to the localisation of the supposed subordinate inspiratory and expiratory centres.   We only know that in both categories we must distinguish between the centres of the cerebral, bulbar, and spinal segments, which enormously complicates the problem of their localisation.

VI. In view of the well-established fact that under normal vital conditions, with the senses and all the mental emotions at rest, the respiratory movements are completed involuntarily, in consequence of rhythmically alternating impulses, from the inspiratory and expiratory bulbar centres, the question arises whether these impulses are automatic or reflex in character, i.e., whether they are the effects of rhythmical changes intrinsic to the centres, or depend upon rhythmic or continuous stimuli, coming to them from without ?   In order to determine this point, which is of fundamental importance, we must first of all examine how they are affected by the various afferent nerves, with which they are in direct anatomical and physiological relation.   Among these in the first place is the Vagus.

The cervical trunk of every vagus nerve contains afferent fibres coming from the lung, and passing to the bulbar respiratory centre.   From the terminal ramifications of these fibres in the lungs, rhythmical excitations pass to the centres, and are capable of throwing them into activity, or considerably modifying their intrinsic energy.   This is clear from the experimental researches of Rufus of Ephesus, Galen, and Legallois (1812).

When the trunk of one vagus is suddenly divided in the neck, while the animal breathes air regularly from a large closed cylinder, connected with a Marey's writing tambour, which registers the oscillations of tracheal pressure, the respiratory type changes *ipso facto* ; the breathing becomes more excursive and less frequent, without previous suspension of respiration, or gradual alteration in the transition from one type to another. The same effect appears after cutting the second vagus, but in a more accentuated form: immediately after section the breaths become extremely dyspnœic and infrequent. In rabbit these effects are less marked than in the dog, as appears from the curves of Fig. 211 (Luciani, 1879).

According to Gad (1880) these results are not simply the expression of cutting out the vagus action on the respiratory centres, since in dividing the nerve mechanical stimulation from the operation is inevitable, as well as excitation from the demarcation current set up in the injured trunk. He proposed to nullify

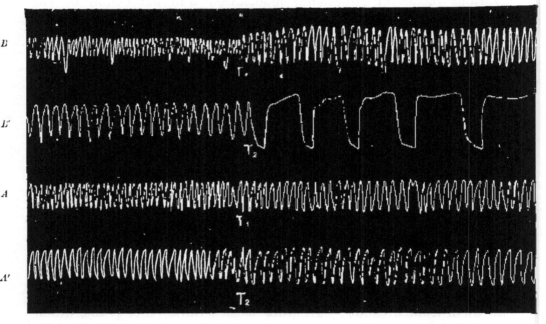

Fig. 211.—Effects of vagus section on respiratory rhythm on rabbits (AA') and dogs (BB'). (Luciani.) The right vagi were cut at T_1, the left at T_2. In A and A' a large rabbit breathed from a closed vessel, containing 12 litres of air, communicating with a writing tambour. In B, B' a small dog breathed from a receiver of 30 litres air.

the function of the vagus, by lifting it over a metal rod cooled below zero, when the nerve would freeze suddenly at the point of contact, and lose its conductivity, without producing excitation. The results obtained with this more elegant method, however, differed little from our own results with simple division, apart from the fact that the inspirations alone became more ample, while the expirations were maintained at the same height as before, or even fell below it, as shown by Fig. 203. Even this difference was only shown in the rabbit; in the dog both inspirations and expirations were increased.

These effects, which follow directly on the abolition of vagus influence upon the respiratory centres, are not associated with any conspicuous changes in the amplitude of respiration, or degree of pulmonary ventilation in the time-unit. According to Gad, after freezing the vagi the amplitude of respiration undergoes a slight diminution; according to Lindhagen, on the contrary (in agreement with our own observations), it remains almost unaltered; this means that the increased depth of the respirations almost perfectly compensates for the diminution in frequency.

From these facts we may deduce the important conclusion that the vagi reflexly exert a marked regulatory influence upon the respiratory centres. The respiratory type witnessed after suppression of this influence is, as justly remarked by Gad, very ill-adapted for its purpose, since the respiratory effort is considerably greater, while its utility, as represented by the respiratory volume, is not increased, and may even be diminished. It is in fact from the ratio between force and effective utility that we must judge of the degree of adaptation. If with intact vagi the

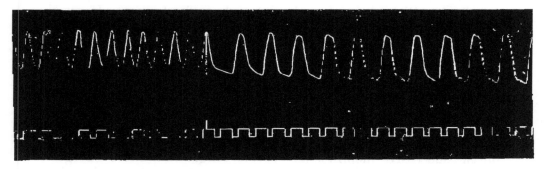

Fig. 212.—Effect of freezing the vagus on respiratory rhythm of rabbit. (Lindhagen.) The rabbit breathes from receiver of Fig. 187 (p. 422). The vertical line marks the moment at which the vagi were frozen. The lower tracing marks seconds.

play of the respiratory muscles is modified, this obviously means that they reflexly regulate the respiratory rhythm in such a way that the same effect is obtained with far less effort, and with minimum expenditure of energy.

In 1868 Hering and Breuer, in an important series of experiments, attempted to elucidate the mechanism of this regulation of the respiratory processes by the vagi. They found on animals that any dilatation of the lungs, produced no matter by what means, checked the inspiratory and promoted the expiratory act; whatever, on the contrary, caused contraction of the lungs, inhibited expiration and determined inspiration. After vagotomy, these effects ceased altogether; the respiratory rhythm assumed the type described above, which undergoes no modification with reference to the state of contraction or dilatation into which the lungs are artificially thrown. The results of Hering and Breuer may be recapitulated the better to define their effects, and bring out their importance :—

(*a*) If on a tracheotomised rabbit, with intact vagi, breathing normally, rhythmical insufflations (positive ventilation) or rhythmical aspirations of air (negative ventilation) are made through the tracheal cannula, so that in the first case rhythmical dilatation, and in the second, rhythmical retraction of the lungs, is produced, it will be seen that the animal reacts to each insufflation by an expiration, as plainly shown by the constriction of the nasal pinnae, and to each aspiration of air by an inspiration, as evidenced by the widening of the nostrils. If the insufflations or aspirations are retarded or accelerated, the animal adapts its respiration to the required rhythm by making the opposite movement, *i.e.* it reacts with an expiration to each dilatation, with an inspiration to each contraction of the lungs. This harmony between natural and artificial respiration ceases absolutely after section of the vagi.

(*b*) If the rubber ring attached to the tracheal cannula of an animal (with intact vagi and regular respiration) is constricted or occluded at the moment at which expiration ceases and inspiration sets in, it will be seen that the latter lasts far longer. If, on the contrary, the trachea is constricted or occluded at the close of an inspiration and commencement of an expiration, the animal is seen to extend its expirations and remain longer in the expiratory posture. These effects cease after section of the vagus.

(*c*) When a ventilating apparatus is attached to the tracheal cannula of a dog or rabbit, which favours inspiration and hinders expiration, so that the extent of pulmonary distension increases at each inspiratory act, it is seen that the expiratory acts consequent on the successive inspirations become longer and more energetic, until the tetanic force of the expiratory abdominal muscles ejects the ventilating apparatus from the cannula.

(*d*) If in an animal with normal respiration, double pneumo-thorax is suddenly produced by opening the two pleural cavities, the vagi being intact, a deep and prolonged inspiration follows—a true inspiratory tetanus.

(*e*) Similar facts are met with clinically, when in consequence of any kind of morbid condition the expiratory retraction or inspiratory dilatation of the lungs encounters some obstacle. In the first case (*e.g.* in pulmonary emphysema) expiration, in the second (*e.g.* stenosis of the larynx or trachea, plural or peri-cardial effusions, etc.) inspiration, is prolonged.

In the year 1888 Stefani and Sighicelli (in continuation of the researches of Hering and Breuer) endeavoured to determine what changes in respiratory rhythm occurred when a rabbit was made to pass rapidly from breathing air under normal pressure to respiration at higher or lower pressures, so that the lungs became passively dilated or contracted. The method consisted in applying a T-cannula with a three-way tap to the animal's trachea. One of the outer branches of this cannula communicated freely with the external air, the other was connected with a receiver containing more or less condensed or rarefied air. A turn of the tap was sufficient instantly to change the connection of the lungs from atmospheric to rarefied or condensed air.

The results obtained by this method do not seem substantially to contradict those of Hering and Breuer. The transition from free to compressed air provokes a short or prolonged expiration, according as the rise of pressure causes marked or slight expansion of the lungs. Transition from free to condensed air induces an inspiration more or less deep or prolonged, according as the diminution of pressure evokes a slight or pronounced contraction of the lungs.

On the strength of the facts enumerated above, Hering and Breuer propounded the so-called *theory of the automatic regulation of respiration*, which consists in the assumption that the respiratory movements comprise a respiratory mechanism in themselves, regulated by the centripetal fibres of the pulmonary vagi, since these excite the inspiratory centres when the lungs contract, and the expiratory centres when the lungs expand. In this way, the inspiratory state of the lungs reflexly cuts off inspiration and promotes expiration, and the expiratory state reflexly inhibits expiration and effects inspiration. Two different kinds of afferent fibres must be distinguished in the pulmonary vagi—those excited by the dilated and those excited by the contracted state of the lungs; the former are in relation with the expiratory centres, the latter with the inspiratory.

The explanation offered by Stefani is somewhat different.

He holds that the inspiratory fibres are stimulated, not by pulmonary retraction but by the fall of pressure in the alveoli, and that the expiratory fibres are excited, not by pulmonary expansion, but by rise of pressure in the alveoli. These small modifications explain why in cases of stenosis of the air-passages the breaths are deep and infrequent (dyspnoea), and why in cases of restriction of the respiratory tract there are frequent and superficial respirations (tachypnoea). For in the first case, both inspiratory depression and expiratory rise of intrapulmonary pressure must be greater, owing to the greater difficulty encountered by the air in penetrating or leaving the respiratory passages. In the second series of cases the conditions are exactly opposite, so that the excitation of both kinds of vagus fibres is shorter and weaker.

Confirmation for this theory of automatic regulation by the afferent fibres of the pulmonary vagus has been sought in the study of the phenomena consequent on exciting the central ends of the divided vagi. Owing, however, to the presence of the two antagonistic kinds of fibres in the vagus, the effects of its central excitation are not constant, but vary with the nature and intensity of the stimuli, so that the action now of the inspiratory, now of the expiratory fibres preponderates.

As early as 1847 it was remarked by Traube, and later on by Rosenthal, that electrical excitation of the central end of a vagus cut in the cervical region caused excitation of the inspiratory centres, as shown by acceleration of rhythm, and with stronger stimuli by an inspiratory tetanus (Fig. 213). This proves that the vagus trunk contains centripetal fibres which on excitation act on the inspiratory centres by acceleration of their rhythmical

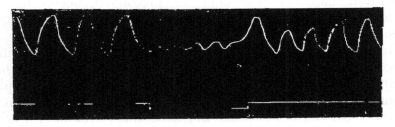

FIG. 213.- Inspiratory effects of electrical excitation of central trunk of vagus in rabbit (Fredericq). The period of excitation is marked on the abscissa. The tracing shows the respiratory oscillations of pulmonary pressure.

impulses. This result, however, is not constant; it is only necessary to alter the strength of the exciting current in order to produce a diametrically opposite effect, i.e. slowing of rhythm, with preponderating expirations, and also expiratory tetanus. This contrary effect proves that the vagus contains other afferent fibres which act on the expiratory centres. If these are rarely manifested with electrical excitation of the central end of the

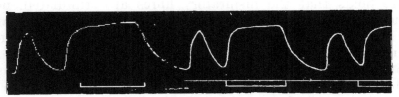

FIG. 214.—Expiratory effects of electrical excitation of central trunk of vagus in chloralised rabbit (Fredericq). The period of excitation is marked on the abscissa. Each stimulation is followed by a respiratory arrest.

vagus, it is because the antagonistically working fibres preponderate. Chemical excitation of the central end of the vagus, however, causes reflexes of a predominating expiratory nature (Gad). When the animal is poisoned with strong doses of chloral hydrate, which, as we have seen, weakens the activity of the inspiratory centres, the centripetal expiratory fibres of the vagus come into play. For under these conditions electrical stimulation of the central end of the vagus nerve is invariably followed by an expiratory tetanus, as appears from the researches of L. Fredericq and Wagner (Fig. 214).

According to Patrizi and Franchini, the diaphragmatic arrest on stimulation of the central trunks of the vagus is not invariably (in profoundly anaesthetised animals) the effect of predominance of the excitatory muscles, but may be merely an inhibitory suspension. Whatever the phase in which the diaphragm is overtaken by the appropriately graduated stimulation of the vagus, it becomes immobilised without change of tone (level of record., and completes its movement at the close of the inhibitory respiratory effect, resuming it from the point at which it had been interrupted. They do not deny that excitation of the vagus may, at a certain point, produce respiratory movements, since they more than once had occasion to verify that particular result; but they do affirm that the respiratory arrest on centripetal stimulation of the vagus is not seldom a merely inhibitory phenomenon.

Treves 1905) also admits that the effects of faradisation of the central end of the vagus are inhibitory in character. After eliminating the action of the principal expiratory muscles by ligature of the cord at a point below the origin of the phrenic nerve, he found that section of the vagus was followed by more intense respirations, and sometimes by a prolonged inspiratory tetanus, interrupted only by passive expirations, which became more and more frequent, and irregular in their rhythm and amplitude. Under these conditions the excitation of the central end of the vagus had a constant inhibitory effect, reducing the depth of the inspiratory act, and the frequency of respiration may be augmented or diminished according to the more or less pronounced tetanic character of the respiration after section of the vagus.

VII. Besides the pulmonary fibres of the vagus, other influences may affect the rhythmical impulses of the bulbar respiratory centres. These may emanate from the cerebral centres, or from the periphery of the centripetal nerves in general, and particularly of the sensory nerves, with which the mucosa of the nasal, buccal, pharyngeal, laryngeal and tracheal air-passages are provided.

The afferent influences from the cerebral centres to the bulbar centres of respiration are conspicuous after section of the vagi. The respiratory type, which, as we have seen (Fig. 211), follows immediately on this operation, depends on and is specially maintained by the active intervention of the cerebral centres, in lieu of the missing regulatory influence of the vagi. To prove this, it is only necessary to compare the effects of separation of brain from bulb in animals with intact and with divided vagi. In the former, as we know, the normal respiratory type is not greatly modified after a transitory disturbance due to the traumatic effects of the operation; in the latter, on the contrary, extraordinary changes in the mode of respiration ensue. The respiratory movements succeed each other with marked retardation; the inspirations become deeper and are followed by long pauses (inspiratory tetanus); the expirations are rapid, with active intervention of the abdominal muscles, and are followed by brief pauses; at the same time the normal rhythm, *i.e.* the regular succession of inspirations and expirations, remains unaltered. These effects may vary in intensity, and inspiratory tetanus is sometimes absent, in accordance probably with the varying degree of operative traumatism and consequent haemorrhage. But in all cases the amplitude of respiration or pulmonary ventilation in the unit of time is diminished by about one-half, so that the animal no long time after succumbs to asphyxia.

These striking results, as disclosed by the researches of Marckwald in Kronecker's laboratory (1887), and confirmed in essentials by Loewy in Zuntz' laboratory (1888), show the great importance assumed by the functions of the centres and afferent nerve-paths from brain to spinal bulb in pulmonary respiration, when the vagi, which normally regulate respiratory rhythm, are cut off. While, however, the afferent vagus tracts to the bulbar respiratory centres are able perfectly to compensate the deficit in the cerebral paths, these last are only partially able to compensate for the failure of the vagus. The effects of double deficiency show that the whole of the other afferent paths to the respiratory centres which remain intact, after section of the vagi and separation of the brain from the bulb, are incapable of influencing the said centres so as to provide the respiratory movements essential for adequate pulmonary ventilation.

Among these afferent nerve-paths, special mention must be made of the trigeminus, to which the nasal mucosa owes its sensibility; the superior and inferior laryngeal branches of the vagus, which contain the sensory fibres to the laryngeal and tracheal mucosa; and the glosso-pharyngeal, which serves the specific sensibility of the tongue and pharynx. All these paths are in special relation with the expiratory centres, and their stimulation, whether at the peripheral ending or along their course, almost invariably produces expiratory effects.

We know how readily sneezing is induced by chemical excitation of the nasal mucosa. Its electrical stimulation produces expiratory arrest (Hering and Kratschmer). Expiratory standstill, or a true expiratory tetanus, can also be elicited by stimulation of the endings of the trigeminus, which are distributed to the skin of the face, if a large surface is excited, *e.g.* if the animal's head is dipped into water.

Coughing is produced by the stimulus of foreign bodies upon the mucosa of the larynx and windpipe, transmitted more particularly by the afferent paths of the superior and inferior laryngeals. Gentle electrical stimulation of the superior laryngeal produces a retarded respiration, with prolonged expiratory pauses. With a stronger stimulus the expirations become very vigorous, and assume the form of expiratory tetanus (Rosenthal).

The effects of stimulating the glosso-pharyngeal are less constant. Apparently this determines respiratory standstill in the phase of the respiration that obtained prior to excitation. Few experiments, however, have been made on this point.

In any case these afferent nerve fibres, situated along the air-passages, which when stimulated have a moderating action on the respiratory processes, or a decisively active expiratory influence, do not function under ordinary conditions of life, since they have normally no tonicity, and are not therefore capable, like the pulmonary fibres of the vagus, of exerting a constant influence upon the bulbar centres. Cocainisation of the nasal mucosa (Marckwald), and bilateral intracranial section of the trigeminus (Loewy), effect no permanent alteration in respiratory rhythm. On a rabbit operated on in this way successive vagotomy produces no more pronounced effect than when the operation is performed on an intact rabbit. The paths of the trigeminus do not, therefore, normally exert any regulatory control upon the respiratory impulses sent out from the centres.

The same may be affirmed of the afferent paths of the glosso-pharyngeal and superior and inferior laryngeals, section of which produces no permanent modification of respiratory rhythm.

All other centripetal paths, which lead directly or indirectly, from above or from below, to the respiratory centres, and which under normal conditions do not influence the respiratory mechanism, may, when artificially excited, or under certain fortuitous conditions, produce modifications in respiration.

Stimulation of the olfactory nerve by odoriferous substances may give rise now to inspiratory and now to expiratory effects, according to the acuteness of the sensations evoked, and their pleasant or unpleasant character. Electrical excitation of the optic and auditory nerves regularly produces acceleration of rhythm, with reinforcement of inspirations. The sensory nerves to the skin, when slightly stimulated, excite inspiratory effects; with painful stimulation, they exaggerate and prolong the expiratory acts. The phrenic nerves also contain afferent fibres, which when excited behave like the cutaneous nerves. So, too, the centripetal nerves of the sympathetic system are able reflexly to modify respiratory rhythm. According to Pflüger, excitation of the splanchnic invariably produces respiratory effects, which do not occur on exciting other rami of the sympathetic.

The majority of these reflexes are of no essential importance to the theory of the nervous mechanisms that normally and continuously regulate the respiratory rhythm. On the other hand, a special importance in the auto-regulation of respirations attaches to another group of reflexes, which till now have been little considered by physiologists, *i.e.* those reflexes determined by the impulses which originate in the afferent nerves to the respiratory muscles.

In speaking of concomitant respiratory movements (p. 421) we said that in many animals each inspiratory act is accompanied by active dilatation of the glottis and nostrils, while constriction of these apertures accompanies each act of expiration. R. du Bois - Reymond and Katzenstein (1901) observed in dogs that these movements of the glottis may appear also in double pneumothorax, or when the lungs are retracted. Under these conditions they noted that the passive compression of the thorax (expiratory position) determined a constriction, while the elastic return to the inspiratory position determined active dilatation of the glottis. From this they inferred that these effects depend on changes in the position of the thorax. In all probability this is an example of co-ordination of reflexes by way of the sensory muscular and tendinous innervation, which, as we shall see in Vol. III., has been worked out by Sherrington for locomotor movements.

The two authors named above have indicated another fact of great importance to the theory of central respiratory innervation. They described the concomitant respiratory movements of the vocal cords with intact thorax during the movements of the diaphragm determined by excitation of the phrenic in the neck. Under these conditions they saw that the tetanic stimulation of one or both phrenics determined movements of adduction in the vocal cords. The contraction of the diaphragm preceded by an appreciable interval the closure of the glottis, which lasted as long as the stimulation of the phrenic. They interpreted these reflexes as due to excitation of the pulmonary fibres of the vagus, which tallies with the auto-regulatory theory of Hering and Breuer.

Mislawsky (1892) also communicated to the International Physiological Congress at Turin, a reflex action of quite similar character, as established by the work of his pupil Luria. Excitation of the tendinous centre of the diaphragm determines expiratory arrest of the thorax. Stimulation of the peripheral trunk of the phrenic nerve has the same effect. Here, again, as in the case of R. du Bois - Reymond and Katzenstein, we have an inspiratory act (contraction of the diaphragm) determining reflexly an expiratory act (adduction and closure of the vocal cords, expiratory position of thorax). Mislawsky, too, holds that these reflexes are completed by way of the pulmonary vagi. As a matter of fact they disappear after section of the vagi.

Baglioni (1903) in his study of the same reflexes took into consideration the afferent nerve paths, which, as we have seen, run in the phrenic nerves along with the afferent fibres.

In order to study the reciprocal and opposite action of the two respiratory phases (inspiration and expiration) he uses a prolonged contraction of the rabbit's diaphragm, produced by direct faradisation of the diaphragm itself, exposed by means of a large aperture in the thorax, artificial respiration being temporarily suspended.

He noted that when the contraction of the diaphragm had hardly begun the nostrils became fully dilated, as in every normal act of inspiration. Almost at once, however, if the tetanic contraction of the diaphragm was kept up, the nostrils became constricted nearly to complete closure, and remained in that position during the whole period of the contraction.

On bilateral section of the phrenic in the neck this reflex disappeared completely. Accordingly it originates in the contracted diaphragm, and determines secondarily the closure of the nostrils, which, as we have seen above, is a purely expiratory act. "Hence," concludes Baglioni, "we have here a respiratory reflex of essentially the same character as those respiratory reflexes on which Hering and Breuer based their theory of auto-regulation, but with this difference, that here the afferent impulse travels not by the pulmonary vagus but by the centripetal fibres of the phrenic."

Recently (1907) Baglioni has emphasised the importance he attaches to these respiratory reflexes, which must be determined by the two respiratory phases, the inspiratory muscles by their contraction exciting the centres, and thus reflexly determining the contraction of the expiratory muscles, and *vice versa*.

VIII. From all that has been said above, we may deduce the following conclusions, which are of fundamental importance to the theory of respiratory innervation : —

" Normal respiratory rhythm (*eupnœa*), which is the best adapted to produce with minimum expenditure of energy that degree of pulmonary ventilation which suffices for the chemical needs of the organism, is essentially conditioned by the activity of the centripetal fibres of the pulmonary branches of the vagus, which are in direct relation with the bulbar centres. It persists after the separation of the spinal bulb from the brain.

b) It is the function of the pulmonary fibres of the vagus to maintain the lungs in that state of average dilatation which obtains when all the respiratory muscles are inactive. They are excited on the one hand by the rise of pulmonary pressure and of the inspiratory dilatation of the lungs, which reflexly determine the act of expiration, just as the fall of pulmonary pressure and the expiratory retraction of the lungs reflexly determine the act of inspiration.

c) When the auto-regulation of respiration by means of the vagi is suppressed, an abnormal type of respiratory rhythm appears.

which, although it provides for a degree of pulmonary ventilation sufficient to maintain life, must yet be termed dyspnoeic, since it is not obtained without useless expenditure of muscular energy. Under these conditions it seems to us probable that a vicarious self-regulation comes into play, due to the rhythmical and alternate excitation of the sensory paths to the inspiratory and expiratory muscles.

(d) The dyspnoeic respiration, consequent on section of the vagi, is largely maintained by the active intervention of the cerebral respiratory centres which tend to compensate the deficiency of the vagus. When, indeed, the influence of the descending cerebral tracts is also cut off, respiration becomes far more highly dyspnoeic, and is inadequate for the needs of existence, although rhythm, i.e. the alternation of inspiratory and expiratory acts, still persists.

(e) All the other centripetal nerves, which are capable of reflexly influencing the respiratory mechanism, are normally inactive, since their occlusion produces no apparent change in respiration, and they are inadequate, after the vagi and afferent cerebral paths to the bulb have been cut out, to compensate the deficiency and substitute their own functions.

It would be a mistake to conclude from these facts as a whole that the rhythmically alternating impulses which emanate from the inspiratory and expiratory centres localised in the spinal bulb are merely reflex acts determined by stimulation of the said afferent nerve tracts. As a matter of fact, we have seen that respiratory rhythm, even when the spinal bulb is cut off from the brain and section of the vagi, persists in a highly energetic form, although it is inadequate for physiological requirements. If, after these two operations, we proceed to a third, in which the cervical cord is bisected at the level of the exit of the fourth pair of cervical nerves, from which the fibres of the phrenic emerge, the thoracic abdominal respiratory rhythm persists, though it is represented almost exclusively by the energetic rhythmical contractions of the diaphragm (Rosenthal). Lastly, if the spinal bulb is suddenly and completely isolated by another transverse cut below the tip of the calamus scriptorius all thoracic movement ceases, but the facial, nasal, and laryngeal movements that accompany the movements of respiration continue. That is to say, the respiratory centres persist in their rhythmical functions, although these can only find expression in the few motor paths that remain (Rosenthal).

Since, however, we know that the sensory tracts which are still connected with the bulb under these conditions of isolation are able reflexly to provoke rhythmic and alternate excitation, it would be rash to conclude from these data that the respiratory rhythm of the bulbar centres is automatic in character, i.e. entirely independent of external stimuli. It is also legitimate to suspect that the rhythmical activity of the isolated bulb may be maintained by irritation from the sections and the external agents acting on the surface of these sections. We must now turn to a striking series of facts which show that the rhythmical activity of the respiratory centres is influenced in great measure, besides the afferent stimuli by the nerve paths, by the condition of the blood and lymph that are circulating in them, *i.e.* by the nature of the medium which bathes the nervous elements of which they are constituted.

IX. Under all the varied circumstances, natural or experimental, in which there is an abnormal rise of venosity of the blood in consequence of the diminished gaseous exchanges between the environment and the organism, *dyspnoea* is produced. *i.e.* increased intensity and frequency of the respiratory rhythm. This occurs regularly :

(*a*) When the animal (or man) is forced to breathe an atmosphere surcharged with carbonic acid :

(*b*) Or an atmosphere poor in oxygen and rich in indifferent gases ;

(*c*) When under any morbid conditions (pneumonia, pleuritic effusions, pneumothorax) the alveolar respiratory surface is abnormally diminished ;

(*d*) When owing to uncompensated organic lesions of the heart there is an abnormal retardation of circulation ;

(*e* When, lastly, owing to profuse haemorrhage, or copious bleeding, the mass of blood in circulation is largely diminished.

Since the respiratory movements are destined by the ventilation of the lung to provide for the normal gas exchanges between the atmosphere and the blood, and indirectly between the blood and the tissues, these facts show that the amplitude of the respiratory movements, *i.e.* the degree of pulmonary ventilation, increases with the need for increased elimination of CO_2 and O_2 absorption. Accordingly, there is a certain degree of adaptation between the gas exchanges and the respiratory activity, which implies that either the carbonic acid, or other waste products of the tissues avid of oxygen, act as direct stimuli to the respiratory centres, or at least modify their metabolism so as to increase their rhythmical and alternate function.

The theory of adaptation between the need for air and the respiratory magnitude of ventilation is confirmed by the fact that there is exaggerated activity of the respiratory centres, and therefore of the depth and frequency of respiration, whenever the organic processes of combustion, *i.e.* the consumption of oxygen and production of carbonic acid, are increased. The most classical example of this fact is, under normal conditions, the dyspnoea developed in consequence of intense muscular work. The influence exercised by work upon the respiration of the muscular tissues and the combustion which takes place within them is enormous. To form an idea of it we must consider the variations per time unit of the quantity of carbonic acid given off in different states of the muscle. According to Gad, the same individual gave off in one minute from the lungs:—

During sleep . . . . 0·38 grms. of CO_2
During the waking state and horizontal position . 0·57 ,,
In walking . . . . 1·42 ,,
In more rapid walking . . . . . 2·03 ,,
In climbing . . . . 3·83 ,,

It will be noted that in the work of climbing ten times as much carbonic acid is eliminated as in sleep. The need of breathing, therefore, increases proportionately, and is amply satisfied by the dyspnoea which provides for the due elimination of the excess CO_2 formed, and absorption of the excess O_2 consumed.

Analysis of the blood gases of animals which are dyspnoeic in consequence of muscular work show, however, that both carbonic acid and oxygen are present there in normal quantities. According to the elegant researches of Geppert and Zuntz (1888), the oxygen is somewhat increased and the carbonic acid considerably diminished below the normal. There is thus a certain adaptation between the need of air and the pulmonary ventilation, but it is not strictly commensurate with the chemical requirements of our tissues. The dyspnoea of muscular work exceeds the limit of strict necessity, i.e. there is a superfluous increase of the respiratory activity which cannot be explained either by the increase of CO_2, or by the diminution of O_2 in the blood. Since the effect of energetic muscular work is to diminish the alkalinity of the blood, it has been supposed (in order to account for the increased activity of the respiratory centres) that the muscles during their activity develop an acid product of consumption, different from carbonic acid, which is capable of exciting the respiratory centres (Curt Seehman). It is possible that this product may be lactic acid, which is developed and poured out into the blood by the muscles during their activity (Spiro), and which is found, e.g., in the urine of soldiers after a long and fatiguing march, or gymnastic exercises (Colasanti).

But in explaining the superfluous increase of respiratory activity in the dyspnoea of muscular fatigue, we must also take into consideration the increased temperature of the blood, which is necessarily associated with the increased combustion of the muscular tissues, and which in itself is capable of provoking a dyspnoeic acceleration of respiratory rhythm to which the name of *tachypnoea, polypnoea,* or *thermal dyspnoea,* characterised by very rapid and superficial respirations, with increased tone of the inspiratory centres, has been given.

The simplest case of tachypnoea occurs in dogs, under perfectly normal conditions, during the hottest days of summer. The accelerated rhythm, which causes an abundant evaporation of water, is, in this case, a protection against an abnormal rise in temperature of the blood, rather than against the accumulation of carbonic acid there (Richet). The thermal excitation of the cutaneous nerves is probably in this case the sole condition acting reflexly upon the bulbar centres, so as to determine tachypnoea (Gad .

Under all other contingencies in which there is already an abnormal rise in the temperature of the blood, as in fever due to any cause, the phenomenon of dyspnoea is much more complex: but one of the fundamental conditions that determines it is certainly the abnormal rise of excitability in the centres, due to the heightened temperature of the blood that circulates in them. Goldstein demonstrated this in 1872 in Fick's laboratory. In order to avoid rise of general temperature in the animal, he surrounded the carotids with two little metal sheaths, with double walls, within which he circulated water warmed so as to produce febrile temperature in the pharynx, while the rectal temperature remained steady. There was at once a rhythmical acceleration of respiration (tachypnoea, in the animal, due solely to the heating of the blood circulating in the head, which raised the excitability of the bulbar centres (particularly of the inspiratory centres . In fact, under these conditions it was found impossible to produce apnoea which we shall discuss elsewhere) with artificial respiration.

In face of these facts it seems indubitable that the pulmonary ventilation, determined by the dyspnoea due to muscular fatigue, which is excessive as regards the chemical needs of the tissues, may and should be explained, at least partly, as an effect of the increased excitability of the bulb, consequent on increased temperature of the blood. The genesis of febrile dyspnoea is highly similar.

Jappelli has recently (1906), from his experiments on man and other animals (dog, rabbit, pigeon), demonstrated a fact which tends to explain many forms of polypnoea in muscular work (running, jumping, etc. in a different way to those heretofore considered, *i.e.* independent of the chemical or thermal changes in the blood which irrigates the respiratory centres. He saw that there is in the respiratory nerve centre a distinct tendency to synchronise its rhythmical and alternate impulses with the external rhythmical impulses, which are eventually transmitted to the central nervous system *via* the sensory nerves. If, *e.g.*, in a dog breathing normally, the central end of the sciatic is rhythmically excited with weak induced currents of varying frequency (40-80 per minute , it will be seen after a longer or shorter latent period that the respiratory rhythm is modified, becoming more frequent and perfectly synchronous with the rhythm of the artificial stimuli. Again, the polypnoea induced in man by rhythmical exercises which impart considerable vertical oscillations to the torso (running, jumping), is characterised by a tendency to synchronisation between the respiratory phases and the rhythm of rise or fall of the centre of gravity. These rhythmical movements of running or jumping must, therefore, determine afferent nerve impulses to whose rhythm the respiratory centre tends to adjust the rhythm of its own proper activity. And since the rhythm of the afferent nerve impulses is in these cases more frequent than the rhythm of normal respiration, dyspnoea ensues as the direct effect.

This theory also explains certain peculiarities of the said dyspnoea; for example, the fact of its rapid onset, at the very beginning of the running and jumping, *i.e.* before it is possible to assume any production of toxic substances or rise of temperature, such as are invoked in the preceding theories. So, too, its immediate disappearance, sometimes at the very moment the exercise is over. On this theory, again, it is easy to explain the other fact known to professional athletes, to wit, that properly trained runners are able to hold out for a long time without experiencing dyspnoea.

"We can also understand" (adds Jappelli) "what the importance of learning how to take breath in running may be. How, if this were determined by the quantity of blood circulating in the capillary network of the bulb (deficit of O_2, increase of CO_2), could it be modified by a physical education? The polypnoea of running is, however, mainly a luxus-respiration, an effect of synchronisation, which represents a useless expenditure of energy, and which, once the exigencies of the respiratory exchanges are satisfied, may be modified for the sake of avoiding fatigue. The education of respiratory rhythm in a runner therefore amounts to developing in him an inhibitory cerebral faculty, so that he moderates the frequency of his respiration, opposing the tendency towards synchronisation with the movements of the lower limbs."

X. Let us now examine whether in normal quiet respiration (eupnoea) the respiratory activity is commensurate with the quantity of oxygen required by the tissues, and the carbonic acid which they exhale; or if in this case also, as in the dyspnoea of muscular work, the renewal of pulmonary air is in excess of what is required, the nervous mechanisms of the respiratory rhythm being to a certain extent independent of the gaseous content of the blood circulating in them.

Rosenthal in 1862 espoused the first theory on the strength of a number of experiments, more particularly the phenomenon of experimental apnoea, of which he may be termed the discoverer, and which we shall consider below. His theory, broadly speaking, found general acceptance, and Pflüger gave it the authority of his name in 1868.

A. Mosso was the first who, in 1885, pointed to some quite evident facts which, according to him, show that " the number and extent of the respiratory movements are not always in close relation with the respiration of the tissues and the blood, while they are directly proportional with the need for supply of oxygen or elimination of carbonic acid." He gave the name of *extra-* or *luxus-respiration* to the excess renewal of air in the lungs, such as normally occurs and is not, strictly speaking, necessary to the organism.

Some of the facts which he brings forward do not really appear to stand in close relation with the theory of luxus-consumption. Such, *e.g.,* are the well-known fact that respiration is profoundly modified by simple nervous activity (emotions, intellectual work) quite independent of the degree of venosity of the blood : that dogs after running frequently pass from deep respiration (dyspnoea) to quick and superficial breathing (tachypnoea) as if the register were suddenly changed without apparent reason ; again, that in sleep, both in man and other animals, temporary disturbances of a purely nervous character may be observed in the regularity of the rhythm. All these effects confirm what we said above as to the influence exerted by the nervous system upon the regulation, and more particularly the mode of distribution of the work of the respiratory muscles, and have nothing to do with the capacity for pulmonary ventilation, which may continue practically unchanged in the time-unit under very dissimilar and even opposite forms of respiratory rhythm (Rosenthal .

Another fact brought forward by Mosso is more significant, *i.e.* that we can voluntarily reduce to about one-half the amount of air inspired, without inconvenience, for a considerable period (10-15 minutes). At the same time this would only bear on the theory of luxus-respiration, if it could be proved that breathing, when voluntarily restrained for so long a time, would not be followed by a compensatory dyspnoea.

Lastly, we attach great importance to the observations made by Mosso during his Alpine excursions, which show that at a level of 3000 metres much less air is breathed than at sea-level : hence at sea-level the amount of air respired far exceeds the needs of the organism. In proportion as one ascends, the superfluous or luxus-respiration diminishes owing to the rarefaction of the air. These high altitude effects do not, however, appear to be constant, which as we shall see impairs their cogency for luxus-respiration in the plains.

According to Mosso, luxus-respiration (which we may shortly designate *eupnoea*) is profitable to the organism, because it makes the regulating factors less complex. It is clear that if the ordinary respiratory mechanism were not, within certain limits, independent of the chemical needs of the body, or the gas content of the blood, then " at every change of the barometer (some of which are enormous, every man and every animal would have suddenly to alter both frequency and depth of respiration, in order to equalise the changes in the atmosphere " (Mosso, 1898).

Here, however, we touch upon new problems, which demand solution. For if we accept this theory of eupnoea, it may be asked: " What are the external factors causing this excess of pulmonary ventilation ? If in the dyspnoea from hard muscular work, pulmonary ventilation increases to oppose the increased venosity of the blood, and if this effect exceeds the immediate requirement, must not the same effect occur in eupnoea, and the venosity of the blood diminish to such an extent that it would in a short time become inadequate to maintain the activity of the centres ? If, in order to explain the dyspnoea of work, we are obliged to invoke the presence of a (probably acid) waste product of muscle in the blood, capable of sur-exciting the respiratory centres, are we not equally obliged to admit that an analogous product may be acting in eupnoea, stimulating the activity of the centres, and raising the respiratory capacity (by about one-half) beyond the immediate need ?

Again, how does the chemistry of respiration alter at high altitudes where luxus-respiration ceases ?

According to the analyses of blood gases made on the dog by Fränkel and Geppert (1883) to test the effect of varying barometric pressures, in air rarefied to a pressure of 410 mm. the O_2 and CO_2 content of arterial blood is not perceptibly altered : and at a pressure of 198 mm. the loss of gases from the blood is still extremely small (1 part O_2 and 1·65 part CO_2). Mosso attributes great importance to this relatively minute diminution of the CO_2 of the blood. He believes it to represent a state of the blood contrary to that which prevails in asphyxia, and proposes to call it acapnia, holding it to be one of the causes of mountain sickness. This conclusion seems to us to be premature and hazardous. We admit that acapnia, or the abnormal diminution of CO_2 in the blood, can only be regarded as the effect of two opposite processes, either, i.e., of a diminished production of CO_2, as in sleep, or of its augmented excretion, as in artificial or forced voluntary respiration. Now neither the one nor the other condition of acapnia is fulfilled in respiration at a high altitude above sea-level. From the experiments undertaken by Mosso upon three soldiers, after they had rested, so as to exclude the effects of muscular fatigue, it appeared that " no important modification in the elimination of CO_2 and the volume of respired air can be detected at high altitudes." This proves that even in rarefied air " the organism requires its normal supply of oxygen," *i.e.* it consumes the same amount, and therefore eliminates the same quantity of carbonic acid. It may be noted in passing that these facts contradict the preceding data on which Mosso rests his theory of luxus-respiration.

Recently (1906) Zuntz, Loewy, F. Müller, and Caspari, in the course of their numerous researches on the physiological action of climate at high altitudes and of alpine excursions on man, have enumerated a series of observations and data which directly contradict the theory of acapnia. They found, as a matter of fact, that there is in the majority of cases a progressive diminution of CO_2 tension in the lungs in proportion with the altitude. Thus, *e.g.*, while the tension of the pulmonary CO_2 was in Zuntz, at a barometric pressure of 715 mm., 38·5 mm., at a barometric pressure of 689·9 mm. it fell to 32·6, becoming 27·2 at 439·3 mm. barometric pressure. It is, however, true that there is a simultaneous increase of respiratory intensity, *i.e.* an augmentation of pulmonary ventilation.

The diminished pulmonary tension of the CO_2 would thus be a secondary effect of increased ventilation, which in its turn depends upon the diminution of the oxygen in the respired air.

They further note that not every individual presents the same diminution of CO_2 tension in respect of altitude. In one person, *e.g.*, no diminution in CO_2 tension was noted, and yet he was one of those who suffered most from mountain sickness. Others, on the contrary, who exhibited the said diminution, were exempt from sickness.

In order, at least to some extent, to clear up this uncertainty as to the theory of eupnoea, and the better to define the nature of the relations existing between the chemistry and the mechanics of respiration, *i.e.* between the gas content of the blood and the capacity of pulmonary ventilation, it will be well diligently to examine the various conditions under which it is possible to observe the phenomenon of apnoea.

XI. If the rhythmic and alternate activity of the respiratory centres is strictly bound up with the quantity of oxygen and carbonic acid of the blood that is circulating through them, it should be suspended when the venosity of the blood is artificially reduced, so as to render pulmonary ventilation useless. The name of *apnoea* has been given to such suspension of the respiratory movements when they have become temporarily superfluous.

Hook (1667) (see p. 371) was the first to observe it, but he formulated no conclusion as regards the process by which the respiratory centres enter into rhythmic activity. The first to study apnoea by making it the basis of the doctrine of respiratory rhythm was, as we have stated, Rosenthal (1862). His work was taken up and enlarged by Pflüger (1868).

We have seen that when artificial respiration with the bellows is performed on any animal, the lungs being rhythmically dilated in proportion as the normal limits are transcended, the animal, owing to the auto-regulation set up by the vagus, reacts to each insufflation by a respiratory movement. After a few insufflations, however, these reactions diminish, and soon cease altogether. If artificial respiration is now suspended, the animal remains for a few seconds, half a minute at the outside, without breathing, it has become *apnoeic*. To Rosenthal this phenomenon of apnoea appeared to be an *experimentum crucis* in favour of the doctrine which subordinates the respiratory movements to the degree of venosity of the blood. When there is a relative augmentation of CO_2, and a relative diminution of O_2, there is in the time unit a corresponding augmentation in the respiratory capacity. The latter then depends upon, and is in strict ratio with, the venosity of the blood. The vagi, according to Rosenthal, only distribute the work of the respiratory muscles in various ways, since it remains approximately the same after section of these nerves.

But the forced apnoea of artificial respiration is by no means so simple a phenomenon as was assumed by Rosenthal; indeed it is highly complex. It can be easily demonstrated that it depends not so much on the diminished venosity of the blood, as on an inhibition or reflex paralysis of the rhythmical activity of the centres, determined by mechanical excitation of the centripetal pulmonary branches of the vagi. Brown-Séquard (1877) was the first who brought forward this opinion, founding it on the fact (subsequently confirmed by all experimenters) that apnoea is entirely absent or lasts for a few seconds only, when forced respiration is employed after section of the vagi. It is therefore conditional on the integrity of those nerves.

On the other hand, there are not wanting facts which show that the diminished venosity of the blood is of secondary importance in determining apnoea. In 1865 Thiry noticed that he was able to produce apnoea even when air mixed with half its bulk of some indifferent gas, such as hydrogen, was insufflated. It was subsequently found by Fredericq, Gad, and Knoll that in order to produce apnoea, it is not necessary to insufflate with pure air, but that provided the vagi are intact, repeated insufflation with the same air (which becomes more and more charged with carbonic acid and poorer and poorer in oxygen) suffices to produce the phenomenon. Knoll further observed that after prolonged pulmonary ventilation, the apnoeic state is persistent even when the blood becomes blackish, *i.e.*, has assumed the character of asphyxial blood. On exposing the heart in a rabbit, by removal of the sternum, without opening the pleura (which is possible in this animal owing to the persistence and bulk of the thymus) and inducing apnoea by energetic artificial respiration, Gad observed that the right auricle preserves the usual venous colour, while the left auricle is at first of a bright arterial scarlet, and then grows darker during the course of the apnoea, a process which usually ceases only when the colour of the left auricle has become much darker than the normal. This shows that the mechanical action of artificial respiration with the bellows causes by means of the vagi a diminution of excitability in the respiratory centres. In fact a highly venous blood, which under normal conditions would determine a rise of excitability in the rhythmical activity of the centres, is unable, after vigorous artificial respiration, to interrupt the apnoea.

From these facts as a whole we may conclude that the apnoea obtained with artificial respiration is the result of a certain ratio between the venosity of the blood and the excitability of the respiratory centres. Since it is thus possible to obtain apnoea even when the venosity of the blood, far from being reduced, has exceeded the normal limits : since, on the other hand, it does not appear after section of the vagi, *i.e.*, when the moderating influence exerted by these nerves upon the excitability of the bulbar centres when mechanically stimulated, is eliminated,—it follows that the said apnoea must depend principally upon the reduced excitability of the respiratory centres.

Miescher proposes to give the name of *true apnoea* to that which is determined by the diminished venosity of the blood, and *spurious apnoea* to that which depends on the diminished excitability of the respiratory centres. Before accepting this distinction, we must inquire whether there is any true apnoea in Miescher's sense, and whether it is possible to produce it artificially in man or other animals.

XII. Let us in the first place consider the phenomenon of *foetal apnoea*. We know that under normal conditions, so long as it is contained within the uterus, the foetus performs no respiratory movements ; it is apnoeic. The placental circulation provides for the exchange of gases necessary to the internal respiration of the foetal tissues. The umbilical arteries conduct the blood that has become venous in these tissues to the placenta, and the umbilical veins reconduct the blood which has become arterial by gas exchanges with the maternal blood, to the foetus. The transformation of arterial into venous blood is, however, but little accentuated in the foetus. According to Zweifel and Zuntz, the colour of the blood in the umbilical arteries differs little from that of the umbilical veins, showing that the foetus consumes little oxygen, and gives off little carbonic acid. Enclosed within the maternal womb, immersed in a tepid bath, it has no need to provide for its own calorification ; the muscles and digestive glands are in almost complete repose ; the heart is the only foetal organ that functions with any activity, and consumes a certain amount of energy (Pflüger). At the seventh month the foetus is perfectly vitalised, so that its respiratory apparatus is even at that time fully developed and ready to function. If, then, during the last two months of pregnancy no respiratory acts are performed under normal conditions, we may say that it is in a state of apnoea, because having every aptitude for breathing, it does not breathe.

At the end of 1858 Schwarz enunciated the doctrine that foetal apnoea depends on the fact of the apnoeicity of foetal blood in relation to the low excitability of the respiratory centres. The foetus does not breathe, because the physiological cravings of its tissues are amply provided for by the utero-placental gas exchanges, but we must also admit that the excitability of its respiratory centres is lower than in those of the mother, the activity of which is maintained by blood of the same degree of venosity as that which circulates in the foetus.

The first respiratory act of the foetus is accomplished when any cause whatsoever compresses the vessels of the umbilical cord, or impedes access of the maternal arterial blood by the placenta. This may occur even within the uterus, as Vesalius pointed out in 1542. Under these conditions, if the interruption to the gas exchange persists, the foetus may perish, asphyxiated within the uterus. But if the venosity of the foetal blood develops slowly, as when the mother is slowly dying, the foetal respiratory centres gradually lose their excitability before ever they have become active.

Under normal conditions the foetus begins to breathe when in consequence of the expulsory act of parturition or detachment from the placenta, the venosity of the foetal blood increases so rapidly as to dispel the torpor of the respiratory centres. In many cases, however, when by long travail the excitability of the respiratory centres has become abnormally weakened, the high venosity of the blood is not sufficient in itself to provoke the first acts of respiration (asphyxial foetus). In such cases it is necessary to start respiratory activity by employing accessory stimuli, mechanical, thermal, or electrical (cold air, cold bath, slaps, electrical shocks).

Under conditions of normal excitability of the foetal respiratory centres, the rapid increase of venosity in the blood suffices to cut short the intra-uterine apnoea at the moment of birth, as is demonstrated by numerous authentic observations upon foetuses that are still wrapt in their integuments, and sufficiently protected from the cold of the air, and which yet begin to breathe at the simple interruption of the placental circulation, or ligature of the umbilical cord. It is easy to repeat this demonstration on the foetuses of rabbits or guinea-pigs (Engström). In the foetuses of dogs taken from the uterus with the integuments intact, respiration, on the contrary, does not begin regularly until the integuments are lacerated (Pflüger). In this case, then, besides the interruption of the placental circulation, the action of the external air is required to start pulmonary respiration.

No one can miss the analogy between foetal apnoea and that which can be provoked on adult animals by artificial respiration with the bellows. Both the one and the other are due to a certain relation between the venosity of the blood and the excitability of the respiratory centres ; neither the one nor the other depends upon an absolute reduction in the venosity of the blood, but rather upon the low excitability of the respiratory centres.

Under all circumstances in which there is an abnormal diminution in the excitability of the respiratory centres, or where such conditions are produced experimentally, it is easy to obtain a longer or shorter period of apnoea, by circulating through the respiratory centres a blood that under ordinary conditions is adequate for the maintenance of respiratory rhythm.

In the rabbit, ligature of the two vertebral arteries and of one carotid produces no conspicuous change in the respiratory mechanism. But if the second carotid is compressed, with arrest of the cerebral circulation, there will at once be a marked dyspnoea, followed by epileptiform convulsions, and then by a pronounced delay in the respiratory rhythm, owing to the exhaustion of the centres (Kussmaul and Tenner). If free course be then given to the flow of blood through the carotid, there will instantly be a period of apnoea, due to the fact that the stimulation of the centres by the venosity of the blood diminishes rapidly, while their excitability is slowly re-established (Gad).

A similar explanation holds good for the apnoea produced immediately after transfusion of blood or even of a simple isotonic solution of sodium chloride in an animal which had previously been bled copiously, so as to produce asphyxial dyspnoea, and successive debilitation and retardation of respiratory movements, owing to exhaustion of bulbar excitability (Gad).

Similar to this is the apnoea from vigorous stimulation of one peripheral trunk of the vagus, which determines a prolonged suspension of the beats of the heart. During this inhibition of the cardiac systole arterial pressure falls enormously (as we have seen), in consequence of which there is a marked diminution in the arterial afflux to the vessels that irrigate the bulbar respiratory centres. This determines so pronounced a dyspnoea as, on the one hand, to subtract all the CO_2 from the blood in the pulmonary vessels, and on the other, to produce a certain degree of fatigue in the said centres. When the cardiac beats are re-established and the pulmonary blood, strongly arterialised, flows on to irrigate the brain, a characteristic suspension of the respiratory rhythm ensues, because the blood is apnoeic in relation to the somewhat depressed excitability of the centres (Meyer). Neither, then, is this any " true apnoea " in Miescher's sense due, i.e., to the positively apnoeic character of the blood, even if we allow that the diminished excitability of the bulbar centres is not the main determinant of the phenomenon.

XIII. Voluntary apnoea, *i.e.* the temporary suspension of respiratory rhythm that we can produce upon ourselves by a voluntary effort, is a phenomenon entirely different from the cases of apnoea which we have been examining. It depends upon a voluntary inhibition of the rhythmical activity of the bulbar respiratory centres, transmitted by the descending paths from the so-called motor zones of the cerebral cortex. When the voluntary suspension of respiration is preceded by a certain number of profound or dyspnoeic respirations it may last for a very considerable time. Neither in the one case nor the other, however, is the duration of this voluntary apnoea in ratio with the vital capacity of the lungs, nor with the anaemic or plethoric habit, nor with the body-weight and mass of the tissues in the individual experimented on (Mosso). We may therefore conclude that the resistance to asphyxia is a phenomenon essentially connected with the individual degree of excitability of the nerve centres, and is to a certain point independent of the composition of the blood, or the sum of the stimuli acting *ab extrinseco* on these centres.

In order to form a clear notion of the main objective differences between voluntary apnoea and the apnoea of artificial respiration, we need only compare the tracings which show how respiratory rhythm is picked up in the one case and in the other at the close of the apnoeic period.

The tracings of Fig. 215 are reproduced from a series of researches which we made at Bologna in 1874: they represent the mode in which experimental apnoea in dogs and rabbits ceases before and after section of the vagi. They show that with intact vagi the respirations do not immediately resume their normal type when the period of apnoea is over, but return by a slow increase in both inspiratory and expiratory excursions. After section of the vagi, when the pulmonary ventilation has been sufficiently prolonged, it is not possible to produce an apnoea lasting more than a few seconds; but the resumption of respiratory rhythm only differs from the preceding by a more rapid increase, so that the animal more promptly resumes its ordinary rhythm.

We do not yet know how far the increment consequent on experimental apnoea depends upon the growing venosity of the blood, and progressive restoration of excitability in the bulbar centres. But it is easy to show that now one and now the other condition predominates.

It is a fact that the venosity of the blood is diminished during apnoea, not so much in consequence of increased oxygen, as because the carbonic acid which it contains is diminished (P. Hering). On comparing the quantity of gases extracted from the same

animal before and during experimental apnoea, Ewald found that
the O_2 content of the arterial blood was hardly increased (+ 0·1,
+ 0·9 per cent) while that of the venous blood was considerably
reduced ; hence after apnoea the blood, as a whole, is poorer in

A

A

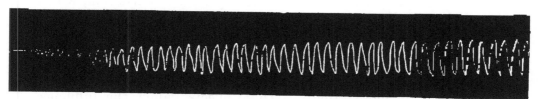

B

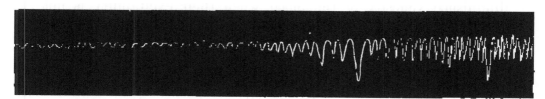

B'

Fig. 215.—Increase of respirations after cessation of the apnoea produced with artificial respiration,
before and after section of vagi, in rabbit and dog. (Luciani.) A, A Adult rabbit, tracheotomised and given artificial respiration with the bellows ; A, respiratory tracing consequent
on apnoea, the trachea being connected with a receiver of 12 litres air, which in its turn communicates with a Marey's writing tambour ; A', the same, after section of both vagi.
B and B', Puppies of 3·800 kgrms. anaesthetised with 2 c.c. laudanum injected into a vein,
tracheotomy and artificial respiration with bellows ; B, respiratory tracing after apnoea, the
trachea being joined to a receiver of 30 litres air, communicating with a writing tambour ;
B', the same, after cutting second left vagus.

oxygen. On the other hand, the CO_2 of the arterial blood
diminished by more than half, while that of the venous blood
increased. This fact is readily explained on the assumption
that forced pulmonary respiration, by compressing the alveolar

capillaries, moderates the circulation in the lungs, thus lessening the work of the heart, and lowering the pressure of the aortic system. The blood in the systemic circulation, during ventilation with the bellows, remains longer in contact with the tissues, so that it loses more oxygen and gains more carbonic acid; in the lesser circulation, on the contrary, it remains longer in contact with the pulmonary air, so that it gains a little more oxygen and loses much more carbonic acid. When the forced respiration ceases a blood much less venous than usual flows to the brain, which partly determines the apnoea and gradual establishment of respiratory rhythm, in proportion as the blood circulating in the bulb regains its normal degree of venosity.

On the other hand, it is clear that the mechanical stimulation of the pulmonary ending of the vagi by forced ventilation, which is capable of depressing the rhythmic excitability of the bulbar respiratory centres to a very marked extent, must also contribute to the production of apnoea and the succeeding increase in respiratory rhythm. In fact, under the influence of the vagi, the apnoea is cut short and practically disappears, while the successive increment in rhythm occurs more rapidly. These effects gauge the influence exerted on the rhythmical functions of the centres by the diminished venosity of the blood, when their excitability is not altered in any way by the mechanical action of forced ventilation.

If we contrast these analyses of experimental with that of voluntary apnoea it is at once evident that the two phenomena are the effects of entirely different processes. Fig. 216 shows that voluntary apnoea, when not preceded by a voluntary dyspnoea, is followed, not by increase, but by diminution in the inspiratory and expiratory excursions, i.e. by a brief compensatory dyspnoea, which ceases when the venosity of the blood (which has increased progressively during the suspension of respiration) returns little by little to the normal state on the resumption of rhythmical activity.

When, on the contrary, the voluntary suspension of breathing is preceded (as in Fig. 217) by four forced inspirations, the period of apnoea is longer, and is also followed by a diminution, though less pronounced than the preceding. This confirms the statement that exaggerated ventilation diminishes the venosity of the blood, and depresses the excitability of the centres, through the vagi. If under these circumstances the apnoea is not succeeded by an increment this is because the resumption of respiration is retarded by the action of the will, which inhibits the rhythmical activity of the bulbar respiratory centres, via the descending paths from the brain.

Neander (1902) carried out upon himself a number of researches on the respiratory pause consequent on deep voluntary inspirations. He differed from Mosso in not prolonging the apnoeic period to the utmost by means of voluntary inhibition. On the contrary, he tried as far as possible to eliminate this factor, turning his attention away from the respiratory acts, so that they should be as independent as possible of mental influences.

The results of his researches differ from those above described, inasmuch as the apnoeic period is followed not by a measure of compensatory dyspnoea, but by the opposite phenomenon, *i.e.* an increment in the inspirations similar to that exhibited by an animal after the apnoea from artificial respiration with the bellows.

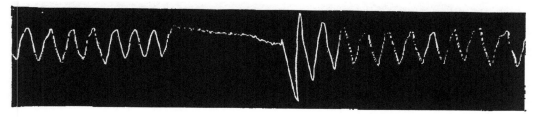

Fig. 216.— Compensatory dyspnoea, consequent on period of voluntary apnoea in man. (Mosso.) Tracing recorded with Marey's pneumograph.

From his observations, as a whole, Xeander draws the conclusion that the apnoea which he studied must be looked upon as a combination of true and spurious apnoea. He found, in fact, that its duration is in ratio with the percentage quantity of the oxygen of the expired air. On the other hand, it starts as a spurious apnoea deriving from fatigue of the centres, since a deep inspiration

Fig. 217.—Voluntary apnoea in man, preceded by four forced inspirations, and followed by a scarcely visible decrement. (Mosso.)

of pure hydrogen equally determines a marked pause, although of brief duration. The prolongation of the pause consequent on a series of deep inspirations must be considered as the effect of greater central fatigue combined with diminished venosity of the blood, which becomes normal again during the increment of the succeeding respirations.

XIV. Let us see if it is possible to obtain a true apnoea in Miescher's sense by substituting gentle continuous ventilation of the lungs for forced rhythmical ventilation, in order as far as possible to avoid the mechanical excitation of the pulmonary vagus endings. This is easy in birds, whose lungs, as we know, communicate *via* the bronchi both with the bony chambers, and with the diaphragmatic, axillary, and abdominal air-sacs. These last are highly developed; on opening the body they are conspicuous, and when they are pierced, and the walls of the abdomen held apart by a blepharostat, the air from a gasometer, blown through the trachea (under a gentle, regular, and continuous pressure), escapes by the ventral opening.

Bieletzsky (1881) was the first to attempt this experiment.

Fig. 218.—Gradual transition from normal respiration to apnoea, with continuous pulmonary ventilation in turkey. (Luciani and Bordoni.) Ventilation commences at V at a pressure of 1 mm. Hg. Tracing recorded with a tambour with exploring lever applied to sternum, connected with a tambour with writing lever.

He stated that he obtained perfect apnoea lasting for the whole time of the inflation. But he made very few experiments; and worse, he stopped half-way, omitting the most important part of the research, *i.e.* that of seeing what effect was produced by continuous inflation after the section of the vagi at the neck.

We resumed these experiments with Bordoni at Florence (1888). The following are the most striking of our results, the full value of which, in regard to a general theory of respiratory

Fig. 219.—Continuation of previous tracing during prolonged period of apnoea. At point C ventilation ceases, and there is a gradual return to normal respiration.

rhythm, can be appreciated now that we have made a physiological analysis of the various forms of apnoea.

(*a*) In turkeys, continuous ventilation with intact vagi constantly produces the apnoeic state. When air is insufflated with Waldenburg's gasometric apparatus, at a pressure of 4-5 mm. Hg, apnoea is instantaneously produced; at a pressure of 2-3 mm. Hg the transition from normal respiration to apnoea occurs, with a distinct decrease in the respiratory acts, which is of brief duration; finally, at a pressure of 1-1·5 mm. Hg the decrease previous to apnoea is very gradual and prolonged (Fig. 218). The return to normal respiration at the close of insufflation is invariably preceded by an increase in the respiratory movements (Fig. 219).

(*b*) In pigeons also the apnoea is constant. At a pressure of 1-2 mm. Hg expiratory arrest is instantaneous (Fig. 220, A), at other times it is preceded by a gradual decrease (Fig. 220, B). The return to normal respiration is also preceded by an increase, as in the turkey (Fig. 221).

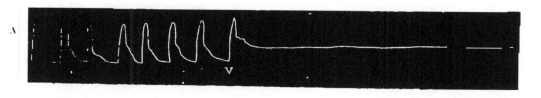

FIG. 220.—Apnoea from continuous ventilation in pigeons. (Luciani and Bordoni.) A, Instantaneous transition from normal breathing to apnoea, as soon as ventilation commences at V. B shows transition from normal respiration to apnoea, after ventilation had commenced at point V.

(*c*) In fowls, apnoea is fairly difficult to obtain, no matter at what pressure the pulmonary ventilation is effected. Generally speaking, it is invariably incomplete, and respirations of an extremely limited character can always be detected, showing persistence of rhythmical activity in the centres (Fig. 222, A).

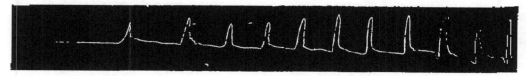

FIG. 221.— Gradual and delayed return of normal respiration after prolonged period of apnoea in pigeons. (Luciani and Bordoni.)

Here also the return to the normal is preceded by an increase (Fig. 222, B).

(*d*) The apnoea of birds from continuous ventilation is, like that of mammals (Berns), immediately interrupted by the insufflation of a minute quantity of carbonic acid, as also by the momentary closing of the ventral aperture, or of the inflating tube, or by excitation of the vagi in the neck (Fig. 223).

(*e*) When pulmonary ventilation is effected with pure oxygen instead of air, at a pressure of 1 mm. Hg, complete apnoea is never produced in pigeons (Fig. 224, A): at a pressure of 2 mm. Hg apnoea is produced suddenly or with a short decrease; but the resumption of respiration is preceded almost invariably by general movements of the animal, without the gentle and regular increase that always succeeds the apnoea produced by air (Fig. 224, B). Often the return occurs with periodic respiration, which soon dies away, and is replaced by the ordinary rhythm (Fig. 224, C).

(*f*) After section of the vagi, complete and persistent apnoea can no longer be obtained in birds, either by inflation with air, or

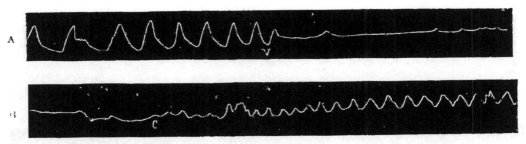

Fig. 222.—Effects of continuous pulmonary ventilation in fowls. (Luciani and Bordoni.) A, Incomplete apnoea after ventilation commencing at V; B gradual return to normal respiration, after insufflation ceases, at C.

with oxygen, no matter at what pressure the ventilation is effected. Respiration becomes weakened to a very marked extent in pigeons, and to a less degree in turkeys and fowls (Fig. 225, A, B, C). If the vagi are divided during apnoea, it will usually persist for a certain time, owing perhaps to the effect of operative traumatism. Sometimes, however, the respiratory movements are reinstated immediately after section of one vagus (Fig. 226).

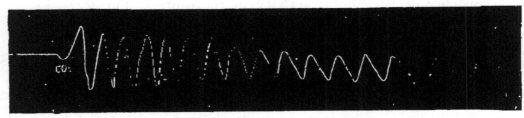

Fig. 223.—Effect of passing a small amount of CO_2 through the respiratory passages, during apnoea from continuous ventilation in turkeys. (Luciani and Bordoni.)

Most of the interpretations of respiratory rhythm suggested from Rosenthal onwards (Pflüger, Hering, Rosenbach, Burkart, Marekwald, Gad, etc.) start with the fundamental concept that not only nutrition, but also functional activity, is maintained in the respiratory centres by the blood circulating in them, which, when normally constituted, acts as an external stimulus, *i.e.* it contains stimulating factors such as carbonic acid or the other products of tissue consumption. This general theory is always based on the apnoea which inevitably sets in when these stimulating matters have to any considerable extent been

FIG. 224.—Effect in pigeons of continuous pulmonary ventilation with oxygen (Luciani and Bordoni.) A, ventilation with oxygen (V-Chat pressure of 1 mm. Hg; B, ventilation with oxygen at pressure of 2 mm. Hg; C, ventilation with oxygen at pressure of 2 mm. Hg.

removed from the blood, so that it no longer acts as an effective stimulus.

The analysis of the different cases of respiratory rhythm which we have so far been examining rather lead us, on the other hand, to the conclusion that no apnoea is exclusively determined by the diminished venosity of the blood. Even the apnoea of birds produced by continuous ventilation, which Miescher considered the most typical case of true apnoea, is, according to our results, a complex effect, essentially determined by a vagus reflex. Indeed, when the pressure by which pulmonary ventilation is effected is strong enough, it is instantaneously produced, without any gradual diminution of the respiratory acts, *i.e.* before any decarbonisation of blood can have taken place. Accordingly, it must depend essentially on reflex excitation by the centripetal

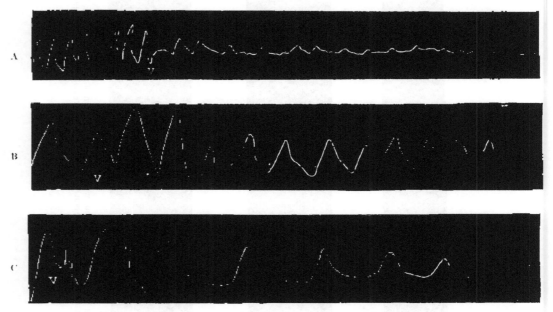

Fig. 225.— Effect of continuous ventilation after section of vagi in birds. (Luciani and Bordoni.) A, In pigeon ; B, in turkey ; C, in fowl. In all three tracings the insufflation of air commences at V.

paths from the lungs and air-sacs, in which the air is normally but little regenerated, and which, accordingly, are highly sensitive to the passage of air, even at low pressures.

In fowls apnoea is hard to obtain, perhaps because their air-sacs are less sensitive to the mechanical action of air. Striking evidence of this theory is afforded by the fact that after section of the vagi it was no longer possible to obtain complete apnoea in any of the birds experimented on. The decarbonisation of the blood reduces the respiratory processes considerably, but it does not suppress them, which upsets the usually accepted theory that respiratory rhythm is maintained by the external stimuli of the blood or interstitial lymph, circulating in the centres.

No less interesting (although of doubtful significance) is the

fact that with intact vagi it is not possible to obtain complete
apnoea, when continuous ventilation is made
with pure oxygen instead of air. Is it possible
that oxygen lowers the tone or paralyses the
afferent fibres of the vagi, so that the respiratory
centres resume partial or total independence of
their rhythmical and alternate messages? Or
does oxygen perhaps excite the peripheral
extremities of these nerves to such an extent
as to throw into reflex activity other centres,
which in functioning counteract the inhibitory
messages to the centres of respiration? The
general movements and restlessness of the
animal on ventilation with oxygen, rather tends
to support this second hypothesis At all
events this curious phenomenon is a fresh
argument towards showing that the decarbonisation of blood and its marked arterialisation
is not enough to check the rhythmical and
alternate activity of the respiratory centres.

Rhythmical and alternate activity! That
is to say, rhythmical activity of the inspiratory centres, alternating with rhythmical
activity of the expiratory centres, even in
apnoea, even during the quiet expiration of
sleep! This fact—which, as we have seen, was
clearly demonstrated by Aducco—excludes the
assumption that the mechanical activity of
respiration depends upon any kind of external
stimulus. So that it does not appear to us
possible, in explaining the alternate activity of
two centres that are antagonistic in action, to
invoke as a causal factor an external stimulus
of any kind whatsoever, acting continuously
upon these centres.

We can only conclude that the activity of
the said respiratory centres depends essentially
upon the special intrinsic organisation of the
elements of which they are composed.

These elements are not merely endowed
with reflex excitability, i.e. are thrown into
excitation by simple external stimuli, coming
to them in the form of nervous vibrations
from the periphery of the centripetal nerves,
or as the chemical products of tissue con-
sumption acting directly upon those tissues; but they also possess
automatic excitability properly so-called, i.e. they are capable of

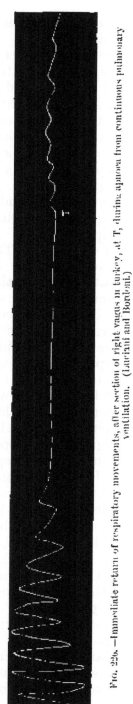

FIG. 256.—Immediate return of respiratory movements, after section of right vagus in turkey, at T, during apnoea from continuous pulmonary ventilation. (Lacciani and Bordoni.)

reacting to internal stimuli, by intrinsic variations in their metabolism.

This logical deduction from a long series of premisses appears at first sight to be contradicted by some of Fredericq's latest experiments (1901). He claims to have obtained true apnoea upon dogs, by eliminating (with the simple reduction of the carbonic acid of the blood circulating in the centres certain mechanical causes that act through the afferent paths of the pulmonary vagi.

The experimental method which he employed for this purpose is extremely ingenious, although not easy to carry out. It consists in establishing between two dogs the so-called crossed cephalic circulation. It is necessary to connect the carotids of the animals by glass cannulae and rubber tubes (after ligaturing the vertebral arteries, and rendering the blood incoagulable by injections of pro-peptone) so that the central end of the carotid in one and the peripheral end of the carotid in the other are brought together, and *vice versa*. The blood being circulated in this new system, it follows that the brain of the first animal is irrigated by the greater part of the blood derived from the heart of the other animal, and *vice versa*.

Under these conditions, Fredericq observed that the artificial increase and reduction of venosity in the blood of one of the dogs affected the respiratory centres of the other, which exhibited dyspnoea or apnoea respectively. If, *e.g.*, the trachea was compressed in dog A so as to produce asphyxia in that animal, the blood surcharged with waste products, on reaching the brain of dog B, determined a violent dyspnoea, while dog A continued to breathe quietly, or showed a slight inclination to apnoea, its centre being irrigated with blood from B which was highly arterial, in consequence of the dyspnoeic respiration of the latter.

If, on the contrary, profound artificial respiration with the bellows is performed on dog B, perfect apnoea is seen on dog A, which, according to Fredericq, can only depend upon the reduced venosity of the blood circulating in its respiratory centres from the heart of B, all abnormal mechanical action of the lungs being thus eliminated in A (Fig. 227).

On determining with the aerotonometer the state of the gases in the blood of dog A during artificial respiration, Fredericq found a slight rise in the percentage content of oxygen, and conversely a marked reduction (by more than half, in the percentage of carbonic dioxide. From this he concluded that the apnoea that obtains during crossed cephalic circulation is exclusively determined by diminished tension in the carbonic acid of the blood. Have we here, for the first time, evidence of a true apnoea, in Miescher's sense, determined by the state which Mosso calls acapnia?

On carefully considering the experimental conditions of Fredericq's method it becomes apparent that he is far from

having demonstrated that the respiratory acts are normally determined by the carbonic acid circulating in the centres. Baglioni
and Winterstein aptly pointed out that in Fredericq's experiment
the vagi were left intact. Now, when the excitability of the
respiratory centres is altered, it is quite conceivable that the
excitations of the pulmonary terminations of the vagi, which
normally exert a reflex control over the acts of respiration, may
determine an inhibition of the centres, and thus produce spurious
apnoea. That in Fredericq's cases the excitability of the centres
was enormously depressed may be inferred from the narcosis (due
to the morphin or chlorotorm administered, the operations
necessary to produce the crossed circulation in the brain, the
diminished blood-supply to the brain (ligature of vertebral

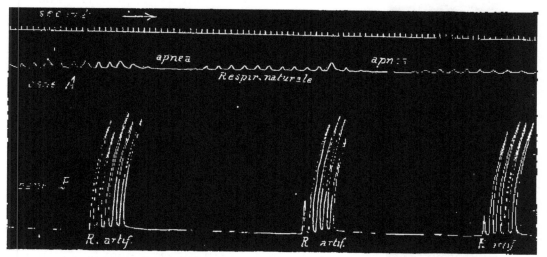

Fig. 227.—Pneumograms obtained from two Knoll's pneumographs in two dogs (A and B) during
experimental crossed circulation. (Fredericq.) The blood from trunk of B circulates in head of
A; that from trunk A in head B. Each application of artificial respiration in B produces a
short period of apnoea in A.

arteries), and lastly, the general intoxication of the centres due
to the injection of pro-peptone, which induces a quasi-comatose
state. It is also conceivable that under such conditions the sum
of the excitations which reach the bulbar centres continuously
by the afferent paths of the pulmonary vagi, the muscles, fascia,
tendons, determine a brief inhibition of the respiratory movements.
We say brief, because Fredericq has not demonstrated that prolonged artificial respiration in dog B determines any apnoeic state
of corresponding duration in dog A.

The tracings of Fig. 227, on the other hand, demonstrate that
in two repeated experiments five strong pulmonary insufflations
on dog B determine a suspension of respiration in dog A lasting
8-10 seconds, after which natural respiration re-commences very
feebly, in accordance with the depressed excitability of the centres.

XV. Just as the phenomenon of periodic cardiac rhythm supplied the most direct argument in favour of the theory of the automatic functions of the heart, so that of periodic respiration, or, at least, of certain forms which it may assume, gives us direct evidence of the automaticity of the respiratory centres.

Periodic respiration, in its most classic form, as first described by the English physicians Cheyne and Stokes (1816-1854), consists in an alternation of apnoea and dyspnoea, of pauses and groups. Each group of respirations shows a rise and successive fall of intensity as well as frequency. The first and last respirations are minimal or at any rate quite shallow, while the central respirations are deep or highly dyspnoeic. Each group may reach a maximum of 20-30 respirations. The duration of the pauses may be equal to, less than, or greater than that of the groups : but it is always above 40-50."

These classical cases of periodic grouping of the respiratory acts are rare, and are usually met with in serious disease of the brain and heart, in the comatose period of certain acute infections, and in the later pre-agonic stage of various diseases. A typical case of Cheyne-Stokes breathing is that observed by Gibson (Fig. 228) in a man suffering from chronic renal disease of the kidneys. Less intense forms, on the contrary, in which the groups are represented by a few respirations and the pauses give intermittency for a few seconds (Fig. 229 A) are tolerably frequent. The pauses may even be absent, when the periodicity of breathing is reduced to the rise and fall in intensity of the respiratory acts, which succeed with a certain rhythm, with no positive distinction of groups and pauses (Fig. 229, B).

The most important thing to note in all these forms of periodic respiration is that the duration of the pauses is not in any relation with the duration or number of the respirations in the groups. Of great significance, again, is the fact that the form of the groups may vary considerably ; sometimes they exhibit an increment and decrement (Fig. 230): at other times an increment alone (Fig. 230); at others a decrement alone (Fig. 231): at others again the respirations of the group all exhibit much the same intensity.

A

B

Fig. 229.—Periodic respiration observed in man at high altitudes. (Mosso.) A, Tracing obtained with Marey's pneumograph on Mosso himself when awake, at 3620 metres. B, Tracing taken during light sleep from watchman at the Regina Margherita hut, 4500 m.

Periodic respiration is not essentially a morbid phenomenon. It invariably accompanies the lethargy of hibernating animals (Mosso, Fano, Langendorff, Patrizi): is sometimes seen in the sleep

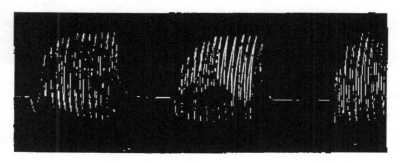

Fig. 230.—Periodic respiration in man. (A. D. Waller.) The rotating cylinder moves slowly. The signal marks minutes on abscissa.

of healthy individuals, particularly in old people and children (Mosso); often at high altitudes (2500-4500 m. above sea-level); it is observed conspicuously in sleep (Fig. 231), and in a less degree in waking (Egli-Sinclair, Mosso).

A number of attempts have been made to evoke experimental

periodic respiration in man or other animals. Flourens (1842) accidentally observed periodic respiration in an animal on which, after extirpating the brain, the two vagi had been divided. M. Schiff 1859) described the same phenomenon in mammals after copious haemorrhage and pressure exerted upon the medulla oblongata.

Traube (1871, induced periodic respiration in cases of heart

FIG. 231. Periodic respiration observed on U. Mosso during sleep, 4560 metres.

disease by hypodermic injection of morphia, and increased it by the same means in patients who already exhibited the phenomenon.

In 1874 we obtained the same effect in dogs, by giving them intravenous injections of laudanum and subsequent artificial respiration sufficient to produce apnoea (Fig. 232).

Filehne and Heidenhain (1874) simultaneously obtained it in dogs and rabbits with intravenous injections of chloral hydrate.

FIG. 232.- Periodic respiration in dog anaesthetised by intravenous injection of 5 c.c. laudanum. Tracheotomy was performed after previous production of apnoea by artificial respiration with the bellows. (Luciani.) The tracing was obtained by connecting the tracheal tube with a receiver containing 30 litres of air, joined to a writing tambour.

Cuffer 1878), who had noticed the frequent coincidence of the respiratory phenomenon with interstitial nephritis, succeeded in provoking it in dogs by intravenous injections of creatine and ammonium carbonate. Smirow (1884) obtained it in dogs with inhalations of sulphuretted hydrogen; Langendorff (1881) with injections of muscarine and digitaline; Bordoni (1886) with injections of scillaine and gelsemine, on frogs and toads.

After discovering the cardiac phenomenon in the frog (1872-1873, in Ludwig's laboratory) we attacked the experimental study of the respiratory phenomenon, with the object of verifying whether the two effects (which present such a marked analogy) had a common origin. Since the cardiac effect is instantly and conspicuously obtained upon the isolated heart perfused with serum, when the most automatic part of the frog's heart is cut off by a ligature, we inquired whether the respiratory effect would be produced, on transversely dividing the spinal bulb in the rabbit, above the origin of the vagus nerves, so as to separate its highest segment from the respiratory centres. These investigations (carried out like the former in Ludwig's laboratory) were long and laborious, because not always successful. Sometimes we obtained respiratory standstill, immediately or soon after the section. At other times there was no radical modification of respiratory rhythm, which (although it became irregular and progressively slow and shallow till death occurred) never presented the peculiar grouping characteristic of Cheyne-Stokes breathing.

Fig. 233.—Periodic respiration in rabbit, after transverse section of bulb at level of visible apex of alae cinereae. (M. Marckwald.) Tracing taken with phrenograph. The ascending curves correspond with the contractions of the diaphragm.

But in other more fortunate cases it did appear in the form of groups, which exhibited no increment but merely a rapid decrement followed by the pause. The number of respirations in the successive groups increased or diminished somewhat irregularly; at the same time the pauses became now longer, now shorter than the groups. In the most successful experiment, however, we were able to watch the tendency of the groups to become gradually smaller, and of the pauses to shorten, till the crisis of the phenomenon set in, when the groups resolved themselves into a series of staccato respirations separated by long pauses, and progressively decreasing till death ensues. The varying position of the section on the bulb, and the different degrees of the consequent hæmorrhage, appear to us sufficient to account for the difference in results.

Marckwald (1888) obtained precisely similar results in Kronecker's laboratory on separating the medulla oblongata from the rest of the brain at a level above the respiratory centres of the rabbit. When the section falls at the level of the apex of the alae cinereae, respiration immediately becomes periodical. After long pauses groups of three, four, or five respirations occur, which decrease in depth (Fig. 233). On dividing the medulla at a higher point, periodic respiration may sometimes be observed when pressure is exerted on the respiratory centres by the extravasation of blood in the neighbourhood of the alae cinereae. On removing the clot ordinary respiration is reinstated. Sometimes, after section of the bulb, respiration will at first be normal and subsequently become periodic, perhaps owing to the exposure of the bulb to air. In conclusion—no essential difference from the results we published eight years previously.

In 1874, on studying the course of asphyxia in narcotised and tracheotomised dogs, with intact or divided vagi, making them breathe into a large closed receiver, which transmitted the respiratory movements to a writing tambour, we not infrequently observed, in the final moments before the death of the animal, the formation of a series of small groups consisting of two respirations, the first being somewhat deeper than the second, separated by pauses occupying a period about three times as great as that of the groups (tracings similar to that of Fig. 231). So that the mode in which the vitality of the respiratory centres dies out in asphyxia recalls the *modus moriendi* of the frog's heart, when excised and filled with serum that is never regenerated (see Chap. IX. 3).

In 1880 Sokolow and Luchsinger published their ingenious researches on the respiratory phenomenon observed in the frog, during asphyxia of the centres from ligature of the aorta, and during the resumption of activity when the ligature has been removed. They noticed that in the first case the number of respirations in the successive groups diminishes, while the subsequent pauses are prolonged; in the second case the opposite occurs, *i.e.* the groups become progressively larger and the pauses shorter until normal rhythmical respiration is resumed. We have no information as to the form of the groups, the authors not having employed the graphic method.

The important researches of Fano, carried out in our laboratory at Florence in 1883, on the periodic respiration of tortoises, agree perfectly with those of Sokolow and Luchsinger, although they grew out of a side issue. After excising the heart of a big land tortoise he saw that the animal continued to breathe, no longer rhythmically, but in groups separated by long pauses. Periodic respiration (though of a highly irregular character in regard to number of respirations and duration of groups and pauses) is very frequently observed, both in land and water tortoises, during the winter lethargy. In the majority of groups the respirations present much the same amplitude, and none of them exhibit the characteristic rise and fall of the classical Cheyne-Stokes phenomenon (Fig. 234).

On trephining the carapace of such an animal, opening the pericardium and ligaturing the pulmonary artery and the two aortae with a single thread, so as to arrest the circulation, the respiratory phenomenon continues: the pauses lengthen, the groups shorten, so that the periodicity of the rhythm becomes more marked.

When these hibernating tortoises are made to breathe indifferent gases such as nitrogen and hydrogen, instead of air or pure oxygen, the periodic respiration continues to be of the same character: dyspnoea is entirely absent, while the number of respirations in the time unit becomes much less. Respiration with indifferent gases may be kept up for a long time, without cessation of life in the animal. Thus, *e.g.*, a tortoise continued to breathe for two days in an atmosphere of pure nitrogen.

None the less, protracted respiration of asphyxial or toxic gases, such as carbonic acid and carbon monoxide, does suppress

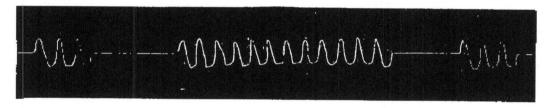

Fig. 234.—Periodic respiration in hibernating tortoise. (Fano.) Pneumograms obtained by letting animal breathe from small receiver, connected with a writing tambour.

periodic respiration in the hibernating tortoise. In certain cases carbonic acid produces an inclination to dyspnoea, but only of brief duration. In all cases, whether suddenly or after a short time, the pauses become longer, the groups of respirations less frequent and smaller, until they die out. A water tortoise breathed 18 litres of carbon monoxide for 36 hours. It was removed from the apparatus after its breathing had ceased for about an hour: yet it was still alive, and after a little time began to breathe again and to move spontaneously. When killed and dissected it showed the most unmistakable signs of carbon monoxide poisoning.

When a hibernating tortoise is chloroformed, there is a rapid and progressive diminution in the groups of respirations till absolute standstill of the respiratory centres is obtained. Chloroform, the "reagent for vital excitability," as it was termed by Cl. Bernard, attacks the innermost conditions of the activity of the nerve-centres, removing from the respiratory centres in a short time their capacity to liberate the energy which they accumulate by the accustomed paths.

XVI. Periodic respiration is a physio-pathological phenomenon intimately connected with the difficult problem of the nature of the normal rhythmical functions of the respiratory centres. The first to perceive the importance of this point was Traube, to whose initiative is due the harvest of literature on this interesting subject, which we have briefly summarised.

In 1879 we drew up an exhaustive refutation of Traube's doctrine, and of the more complicated theory opposed to it by Filehne in 1874, showing the absolute inadequacy of these hypotheses to account for the whole of the experimental data, and the great variety of clinical forms, which the respiratory phenomenon may assume. We showed that it was impossible, in face of the proved facts, to solve the problem by the postulate usually admitted and defended, to the effect that the capacity and functional activity of the central mechanisms of respiratory rhythm are always in direct and immediate dependence upon *extrinsic* conditions of stimulation and nutrition: *i.e.* in other words, that the said centres merely transform what at any given moment they receive, in the same degree and with the same rhythm at which they receive it. The experimental evidence shows that there is, between the external action and the reaction, a whole, complex, chemico-molecular, *internal* process, of which we are aware in virtue of its results, but as to the laws of which we are entirely ignorant.

The obvious facts on which we have insisted amply suffice to prove that there is no ratio between the duration and the degree of pulmonary ventilation represented by the *groups* and the duration of the *pauses*: that the form of the groups may vary greatly and in opposite ways that are not comparable *inter se*; that periodic respiration may be observed even where no gas exchanges between the atmosphere and the blood are possible —all these clearly demonstrate the fundamentally automatic character of the function of the bulbar respiratory centres. "The different forms that may be assumed by the respiratory rhythm, including those of periodic grouping, are merely the external expression of corresponding modes of oscillation in the nutritional processes, which are carried on within the depths of the respiratory centres" (Luciani, 1879).

Normally, however, these centres, in addition to an *automatic excitability*, are provided with a most delicate *reflex excitability*, which enables them immediately to react even to the slightest external stimulus, thus giving rise to profound modifications in the form and rhythm of the automatic excitability as dependent upon the internal impulses. Our task is now to determine (as precisely as possible) what are the relations of co-existence of these two forms of excitability, both in normal conditions, and under exceptional or abnormal conditions, of the respiratory centres.

The normal respiratory rhythm of man and other homothermic animals in general is essentially conditioned by the reflex activity of the centres. In eupnoea it is the established auto-regulation of the vagi that predominates, *i.e.* the mode in which the air that passes rhythmically through the lungs in a certain time is distributed, depends on the rhythmical and alternate impulses that reach the centres from the peripheral extremities of the pulmonary vagi. The proof of this lies in the fact that normally the nervous and muscular mechanisms of the thoracic movements are always active; inspirations alternate with expirations without pause or intermediate rest (cf. tracings of Figs. 184, 185, 186, on pp. 418, 420, 421), as if the excitation passed from the inspiratory to the expiratory centres, and *vice versa*, by an uninterrupted reciprocal, intercentral transmission, and with a delay that just

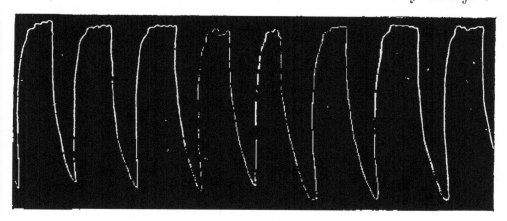

Fig. 235.— Thoracic respiration of a soldier, recorded with Marey's pneumograph at 4560 metres. (A. Mosso.)

suffices for the two antagonistic movements to succeed without coincidence.

Under certain special conditions, however, this perfect eupnoea fails, probably in consequence of a diminished sensibility of the afferent fibres of the vagi, which renders the impulse transmitted to the inspiratory centres from the expiratory position of the lungs *nil* or inadequate. In this case there is between the end of expiration and the commencement of inspiration a more or less prolonged pause. This phenomenon, which we believe to be not uncommon in clinical cases, was recorded graphically by Mosso in two robust soldiers during rest upon the High Alps (4560 m. above sea-level), as shown in the tracing of Fig. 235. We do not interpret this as meaning that at high altitudes one breathes less, since it is shown elsewhere that "at high altitudes no important modifications in the output of carbonic acid and the intake of inspired air occurs." Until the contrary is proved, we hold it logical to assume that the phenomenon described depends upon a paretic state of the vagus, determined by the altitude. In this case the eupnoea is no longer perfect, and the inspiratory acts are no longer determined by the nervous vibrations that ascend by the afferent paths of the vagus to the centres, but by a certain degree of venosity acquired by the blood circulating in them during the expiratory pause.

While the intermittent excitations *via* the centripetal nerve-paths determine particularly the *frequency* of rhythm, i.e. the distribution of the total air that passes through the lungs in the time unit, the chemical excitation produced by the venosity of the blood especially determines the *intensity* of the rhythm, i.e. the total quantity of air breathed in the time unit. The theory of dyspnoea agrees perfectly with this conclusion. In dyspnoea, in general, and particularly in that determined by the increased production of carbonic acid, the reflex excitability of the centres comes into play, and causes automatic excitability to become latent by adapting the respiratory rhythm to the chemical needs of the organism.

As in apnoea and dyspnoea the factor of the central excitations determined by the amount of the external stimuli predominates, so in tachypnoea and apnoea the factor of increased, or diminished, excitability predominates, owing to which the centres become more sensitive, or refractory, to the action of the said stimuli.

But the excitability of the centres whether automatic or reflex is an oscillating quantity, which follows closely, and is, so to speak, modelled on all the vicissitudes of the intimate metabolic processes. Each explosion of energy that accompanies a katabolic disruption determines a relative degree of resistance in the centres to external and internal stimuli; each accumulation of energy, determined by an anabolic construction, increases their susceptibility to the same. Further, these respiratory tracings show not merely the rhythmic and alternate activity of the antagonistic respiratory muscles, but they sometimes, particularly after the action of certain poisons, exhibit slow positive and negative oscillations in the tone of the said muscles, which recall the oscillations of tone in the auricles, as described by Fano, and in the vessels, as described by Schiff and by Traube and Hering. This is well illustrated in the tracing of Fig. 236, registered by Mosso from a rabbit intoxicated with piridine. Under normal conditions these oscillations in the tone of the respiratory muscles are absent, but occasionally they become visible in sleep as in Fig. 237. These slow oscillations in the tone of the muscles are the external expression of the corresponding oscillations of excitability (automatic and reflex) in the respiratory centres.

As soon as these oscillations of excitability of the centres are exaggerated, the phenomenon of Cheyne-Stokes breathing sets in. The *pauses* depend essentially upon the depression of excitability below the threshold, at which the external and internal stimuli are inadequate to throw the central organs into excitation; the *groups* appear when, owing to rise of excitability, the external and internal stimuli again become effective (Luciani, 1879). The same theory of periodic respiration was formulated almost simultaneously by Rosenbach (1880); by Sokolow and Luchsinger

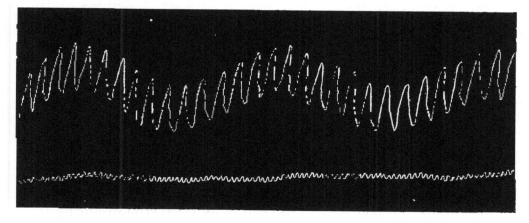

Fig. 256.—Oscillations of tone in respiratory muscles in rabbit poisoned with piridine. (Mosso.) R. respirations recorded with a Marey's tambour applied to xiphoid process. P, tracing of blood pressure in carotid, recorded simultaneously with a mercury manometer. The pronounced oscillations of respiration are seen not to be associated with perceptible alterations of blood pressure.

(1880), who endeavoured to reinforce it by ingenious marshalling of the facts; by Langendorff and Siebert (1881), who confirmed and developed the work of their predecessors: lastly, by A. Mosso (1885), who resumed and consolidated it by new observations.

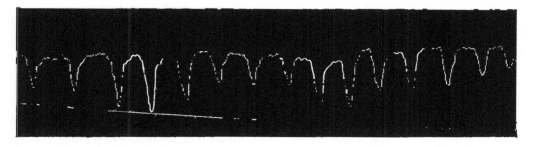

Fig. 257.—Thoracic respiration in sleep of robust subject, recorded with Marey's pneumograph; shows periodic oscillations of both inspiratory and expiratory excursions. (A. Mosso.)

Zuntz (1882) correctly pointed out the great analogy between the classical phenomenon of Cheyne-Stokes respiration and the alternation of sleep and waking. Sleep corresponds with the *pause*, the waking state with the *group*. Just as complete awakening is preceded by an ascending phase of waking up, and sleep is preceded by a descending phase of drowsiness, so the Cheyne-Stokes phenomenon shows increase and decrease.

Mosso has pointed out other yet more convincing analogies from clinical observation. In sleep the pupils contract, the eyes rotate inward and upward; in the waking state the pupils dilate, the eyes rotate outward (Fontana). Just so in periodic respiration, when the pause commences, the pupils retract, the eyes converge inwards and upwards; when the group commences, the pupil dilates, the eyes look forward (Leube). At the beginning of the pause some patients are drowsy and become insensible; at the beginning of the group they are restless, and again suffer pain (Leube, Merkel). Certain subjects close their eyes at the termination of the group, at the commencement of the pause, and in the midst of it, and open them again at the commencement of the group or soon after (Fräntzel, Hein, Kaufmann). In more serious cases the stupor and unconsciousness are continuous throughout the Cheyne-Stokes breathing; in other cases consciousness returns, partly at any rate during the groups; in others, lastly, the respiratory phenomenon takes place in the awakening state. These are differences of intensity, shades and gradations of one fundamentally identical process, which explains why the patient now reacts and now fails to respond to external stimuli during the periodic pause. "The pause," writes Mosso, "always implies a more or less serious drowsiness of the nerve centres," which is as much to say, in more exact and strictly physiological language, that during the pauses the respiratory centres suffer a negative variation in their excitability. *Reflex* excitability, *automatic* excitability, or *reflex and automatic* excitability together? The answer to this important question necessitates some consideration.

Let us consider the extremes. In many cases, whether clinical or experimental, of periodic respiration, the reflex excitability of the centres is maintained. Sometimes it is sufficient to invite the patient to breathe, or to excite him with acoustic, luminous, thermal or painful stimuli, during the pause, in order immediately to cut it short, and obtain respiratory movements (Biot, Saloz, Murri, Bordone). In rabbits with divided bulb which breathe periodically, faradisation of the centres, with strong and infrequent break shocks, will produce respiratory movements, either during the groups or during the pauses (Kronecker and Marckwald). These facts do not, as some maintain, contradict the theory that periodic respiration depends essentially upon periodic oscillations in the excitability of the centres, because the substitution of artificial for natural stimuli probably involves disturbance of the whole of the intimate and delicate metabolic process on which the periodic grouping of the central impulses that determine Cheyne-Stokes respiration depends; but it has certainly been demonstrated that the reflex excitability of the centres, though reduced, is not suspended, during the pauses in these cases. Accordingly, it must be assumed that the periodic quantitative variation in the external stimuli acting on the centres, can and must co-operate with the functional intermittence characteristic of these centres, owing to the alternations of groups and pauses.

The other extreme cases of periodic respiration are the experiments of Sokolow and Luchsinger, and of Langendorff and Siebert on the frog, and more particularly those so admirably carried out by Fano on the tortoise. In these cases the reflex excitability of the centres (particularly the capacity of reacting to the stimulus of the blood) is not merely lessened, but is entirely suspended. Here, then, periodic respiration is a more simple phenomenon: when reflex excitability is suspended, the automatic excitability of the centres dominates the stage completely, and the grouping of the respirations is the external expression or record of the special mode in which the energy accumulated within them— in consequence of the slow processes of metabolism—is liberated and developed, until it is finally exhausted. The importance of the facts adduced by Fano consists not in any refutation of the theory formulated by us in 1879, which is left untouched because it deals with an essentially distinct order of phenomena: but in its demonstration that the two forms of excitability with which the elements of the respiratory centres are endowed do not suffer from the vicissitudes of metabolism in the same degree, since in poikilothermic animals, under certain special conditions, reflex activity may be entirely suspended, or profoundly depressed, while automatic excitability persists and is manifested by characteristic upward and downward fluctuations.

This lengthy chapter has been exclusively devoted to the nervous factors of the *respiratory mechanism*. But a further series of important facts shows that the *chemical* respiratory activity of the tissues is also dominated by the nervous system, which may excite or moderate it, and even cause the value of the respiratory quotient, *i.e.* the ratio between the oxygen absorbed and the carbonic acid given off, to oscillate.

We shall consider this interesting subject, which exceeds the limits of the physiology of the respiratory apparatus, in due time, along with the metabolism, or material exchanges, of the body as a whole.

BIBLIOGRAPHY

The following monographs and memoirs are most frequently quoted from the copious literature of this subject :—

FLOURENS. Recherches expérimentales sur les propriétés et les fonctions du système nerveux. Paris, 1842.

BROWN-SÉQUARD. Journal de physiologie, i., 1858.

M. SCHIFF. Lehrbuch der Physiol., 1858-59. Gesam. Beiträge zur Physiol., i. Lausanne, 1894.

ROSENTHAL. Die Atembewegungen und ihre Beziehungen zum Nervus vagus. Berlin, 1892. Hermann's Handbuch d. Physiol., iv. Leipzig, 1882.

HERING and BREUER. Sitzungsber. d. Wiener Akademie, lvii., ii., 1868.

PFLÜGER. Archiv f. d. ges. Physiol., i., 1868.

TRAUBE. Gesammelte Beiträge, ii. Berlin, 1871.

EWALD. Archiv f. d. ges. Physiol., vii., 1873.

GIERKE. Archiv f. d. ges. Physiol., vii., 1873.

LUCIANI. Lo Sperimentale. Firenze, 1879.

SOKOLOW and LUCHSINGER. Pflüger's Arch., xxiii., 1880.

LANGENDORFF and SIEBERT. Du Bois-Reymond's Arch. f. Physiol., 1881.

GAD. Du Bois-Reymond's Arch. f. Pysiol., 1880-81-85-86.

FANO. Lo Sperimentale. Firenze, 1883-84-86.

MIESCHER. Du Bois Reymond's Arch. f. Physiol., 1885.

MOSSO. R. Accademia dei Lincei. Roma, 1885. Fisiologia dell' uomo sulle Alpi. Milano, 1898.

ZUNTZ and GEPPERT. Pflüger's Arch., xxxviii., 1886.

MARCKWALD. Zeitschrift für Biologie, 1887. (Contains summary of publications to that date.)

BORDONI. Lo Sperimentale. Firenze, 1888.

STEFANI and SIGHICELLI. Lo Sperimentale. Firenze, 1888.

ADUCCO. Annali di freniatria e scienze affini. Torino, 1889.

GAD and MARINESCO. Du Bois-Reymond's Arch., 1893.

GIBSON, G. A. Cheyne-Stokes Respiration, 1882.

LEWANDOWSKY. Du Bois-Reymond's Arch., 1896.

FREDERICQ. Arch. d. Biol., 1900-1.

NEANDER. Skandin. Arch. f. Physiol., ii., 1902.

BAGLIONI. Centralbl. f. Physiol., 1903. Zur Analyse der Reflexfunktion, Wiesbaden, 1907.

BORUTTAU. Ergebnisse der Physiol., i. and iii., 2, 1902, 1904.

N. ZUNTZ, A. LOEWY, F. MÜLLER, W. CASPARI. Höhenklima und Bergwanderungen, 1906. Bong & Co.

Recent English Literature : -

W. J. GIES and S. J. MELTZER. Studies on the Influence of Artificial Respiration upon Strychnine Spasms and Respiratory Movements. Amer. Journ. of Physiol., 1903, ix. 1-25.

W. E. DIXON and T. G. BRODIE. Contributions to the Physiology of the Lungs. Part I. The Bronchial Muscles, their Innervation and the Action of Drugs upon them. Journ. of Physiol., 1903, xxix. 97-173.

I. H. HYDE. Localisation of the Respiratory Centre in the Skate. Amer. Journ. of Physiol., 1904, x. 236-258.

J. S. HALDANE and J. G. PRIESTLEY. The Regulation of the Lung Ventilation. Journ. of Physiol., 1905, xxxii. 225-266.

I. H. HYDE. A Reflex Respiratory Centre. Amer. Journ. of Physiol., 1906, xvi. 368-377.

G. N. STEWART and F. H. PIKE. Resuscitation of the Respiratory and other Bulbar Nervous Mechanism with Special Reference to the Question of their Automaticity. Amer. Journ. of Physiol., 1907, xix. 328-359.

G. N. STEWART and F. H. PIKE. Further Observations on the Resuscitation of the Respiratory Nervous Mechanism. Amer. Journ. of Physiol., 1907-8, xx. 61-73.

G. N. STEWART. Some Observations on the Behaviour of the Automatic Respiratory and Cardiac Mechanisms, etc. Amer. Journ. of Physiol., 1907-8, xx. 407-438.

C. G. DOUGLAS and J. S. HALDANE. The Causes of Periodic or Cheyne-Stokes Breathing. Journ. of Physiol., 1909, xxxviii. 401-419.]

C. G. DOUGLAS and J. S. HALDANE. The Regulation of Normal Breathing. Journ. of Physiol., 1909, 420-440.

CHAPTER XIV

THE LYMPH, AND INTERCHANGES BETWEEN THE BLOOD AND THE TISSUES

CONTENTS.—1. Structure of lymphatic vascular system, lymph spaces, sinuses and cavities. 2. Origin; physical, morphological and chemical characteristics; qualitative and quantitative variations of lymph. 3. Lymphatic circulation, and the various mechanical factors by which it is determined. 4. Formation of lymph from the blood capillaries, and the so-called lymphagogues. 5. Secretory theory of Heidenhain, and transudation theory of Cohnheim. 6. Formation and modification of lymph by the tissues. 7. Lymphoid tissue, follicles and lymphatic glands. 8. Bone marrow. 9. The thymus. 10. The spleen. Bibliography.

No less important than the gas exchanges between the blood and the tissues, to the life of the cells of which the latter consist, is the exchange of solid matters in which the blood yields to the tissues the substances necessary to their nutrition and restoration (histogenic substances), and the tissues yield to the blood the products of their elaboration, transformation, or consumption (histolytic substances, anabolic and katabolic.)

The nutritive, like the respiratory, exchanges are almost invariably accomplished by means of the lymph, which is the true internal medium in which the elements of the tissues live. Hence the study of the nutritive exchanges includes the study of the lymph: of the functions of the lacunar and vascular system which contain it: of the functions of the tissues and organs which more particularly contribute to its formation and modifications; of the mechanical factors that are constantly setting it in motion and renewing it, driving it out into the blood torrent. All these will be discussed in the present chapter.

I. The Lymphatic System, discovered by Aselli, Pecquet, Rudbeck, Bartholin, in the first half of the seventeenth century (see Chap. VI. 6), is one of the most extended and most important in the body. It embraces, not only the vessels, follicles, and lymphatic glands, but also the whole of the connective tissues, and the system of lacunae or interstitial spaces which exist in every part of the body, particularly where there are more or less loosely constituted connective tissues. Even the large serous cavities, such as the peritoneum, the pleura, the pericardium, the meninges, and, generally speaking, the whole of the serous sheaths that invest the organs, form part of the lymphatic system in the widest sense of the word.

As regards the morphological questions, many of them very complicated and much disputed, that arise over this system, we must refer to treatises on anatomy and histology. Here we can only summarise the general notions that are most intimately connected with physiological problems.

From the structural point of view, we may distinguish in the lymphatic system : the lymph vessels properly so-called, the lymphatic capillaries, the parenchymatous lymph spaces, the large lymphatic or serous cavities.

(*a*) The lymphatic vessels constitute a rich system of canals

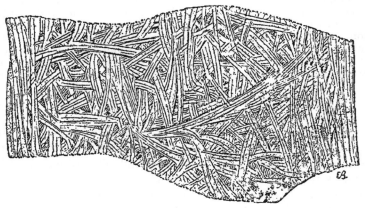

Fig. 238.—Supravalvular swelling of lymphatic in cat's mesentery, treated with silver nitrate. (Ranvier.) The smooth muscular fibres which surround the vessel interlace in various directions at the seat of the swelling.

which are very similar in the structure of their walls to the veins, and like them are richly provided with valves, which open centripetally and close in a centrifugal direction. These are specially abundant in the small lymphatic vessels, *e.g.* in those of the mesentery. Above each valve the vessel is somewhat dilated, so that when there are many valves the vessel assumes a moniliform or beaded appearance. The muscle cells in the tunica media of the vessel walls are for the most part arranged in a circular direction ; but at the supravalvular points of dilation they run in various directions, so as to form a network (Fig. 238). Like the blood-vessels, the lymphatics lie in a bed of connective tissue, and gradually unite into vessels which become increasingly larger, until they finally converge (in man and in the higher vertebrates) into two principal channels : the thoracic duct, which opens by an orifice provided with valves into the left subclavian vein ; and the right lymphatic trunk, which opens into the right subclavian vein. The lymphatics from the right side of the head and neck, right arm and lung, right side of thorax, and heart, and part of the upper surface of the liver, unite in the right lymphatic trunk; all the other lymph vessels, including those which come from the intestines (known as lacteals, because during the absorption of the digestive products of alimentation they conduct the chyle, which has a milky aspect', lead into the thoracic duct.

In this union of the lymphatics into ever-widening channels, their diameter does not increase as rapidly as that of the veins; moreover, they often form plexuses which anastomose among themselves; while, lastly, they enter all along their course into special relations with the so-called lymphatic glands which, from a schematic point of view, may be considered as analogous in structure to the rete mirabile of the blood-vessels, and which retard the flow of the lymph along the vessels that conduct it.

(b) The lymph capillaries are simpler in structure than the lymphatic vessels properly so-called. They consist of a simple membranous coat, the exceedingly delicate structure of which, when stained with silver nitrate, shows flat plates with characteristic wavy outlines interlacing one with another (Fig. 239). They have no valves, but are usually larger in calibre than the smallest of the lymphatics, and distinctly larger than the blood capillaries.

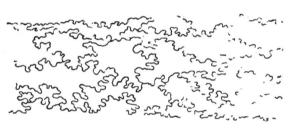

Fig. 239.—Epithelioid platelets of lymphatic capillaries from rabbit's intestine, treated with silver nitrate. (Ranvier.)

They are irregular in form, and anastomose among themselves so as to form a species of network, with uneven meshes and very varied form. This lymphatic rete, irregularly excavated from the connective tissue which supports it, opens or communicates freely with the lymph vessels, which, although smaller than the capillaries, have a more regular course, are clothed with fusiform epithelial cells of less sinuous outline, and are provided with valves.

To form a clear conception of the difference in form, arrangement, and proportions of the blood and the lymphatic capillary network, Fig. 240, in which the two capillary retes are injected with contrasting stains, may be studied.

From the physiological point of view it is important to note the special relation of the lymphatics and the blood-vessels in particular parts of the body, e.g. the central nervous system, the parenchyma of the liver, the bone tissues. In these regions the smallest arterial and venous blood-vessels are enveloped with lymphatic sheaths, just as the heart is invested by the pericardium and the viscera by the peritoneum (perivascular lymphatics, Fig.

241. It can be shown by the method of double staining with silver nitrate and carmine that there is a perivascular lymphatic space between the peripheral layer of the sheath and that which adheres to the surface of the blood-vessels; that slender connecting filaments or lamellae pass between the two layers; that the wavy epithelioid plaques of the external layer are continued on to the

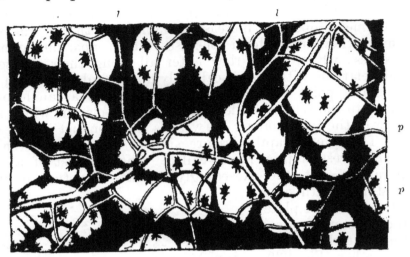

Fig. 240.—Frog's interdigital membrane, with injected blood and lymph vessels. (Ranvier.) ss, Network of blood capillaries; ll, network of lymph capillaries; pp, pigment cells. Magnification, 50 diameters.

internal layer, and also invest the connecting lamellae. Where the blood-vessels are much increased in size, they perforate the lymphatic sheath, and the two kinds of vessels run distinct from, but alongside, one another. In certain of the lower animals,

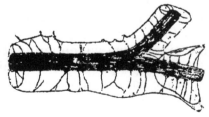

Fig. 241.—(Left.) Artery of frog's mesentery, enclosed in perivascular lymphatic, which is stained with silver nitrate, to show the outlines of epithelioid cells. (Klein.)

Fig. 242.—(Right.) Aorta of tortoise, enclosed in large perivascular lymphatic. (Gegenbaur.) Numerous filaments of connective tissue are seen, connecting the blood-vessel with the lymphatic

however, e.g. in the frog, the larger vessels are also surrounded by lymphatic sheaths, as also the aorta in the tortoise (Figs. 241, 242). Rusconi (1845) was the first to describe the perivascular lymphatic sheath.

(c) Outside the lymph capillaries also, in every part of the body, and more particularly where there is loose connective tissue, a labyrinth of lacunae or interstices of the most varied forms and dimensions, which are generally known as lymphatic spaces, because they are full of lymph, may be observed. Again, the tissues devoid of blood-vessels, like the cornea and the cartilages, are provided with minute lacunar canaliculi, to which the lymphatic humour necessary to cell nutrition penetrates. These parenchymatous lymph spaces cannot be considered as lymph capillaries, because they are not invested with the characteristic epithelioid lining, which forms the true wall of the latter. They represent a diffuse system of lacunae, interstitial to the cells of the various tissues, which, according to Bichat's doctrine, is generally regarded as the origin of the vascular lymphatic system, i.e. of that provided with characteristic walls. In many invertebrates the lacunar system, which has no proper wall, is the only one that co-exists with the blood vascular system: so that we may logically regard the lymphatic vascular system as a perfecting, a canalisation or successive centralising, of the primary lacunar or interstitial system (Milne Edwards .

We know that the lymph spaces communicate freely with the lymph capillaries properly so-called, because a fluid stain such as Prussian blue, when injected into the meshes of the subcutaneous connective tissue by means of a syringe, penetrates to the interior of the lymphatics, particularly if the oedematous swelling that forms at the point of injection is compressed by the finger, so as to increase the tension of the distended lacunar spaces and facilitate the penetration of the coloured fluid by the natural way of communication with the lymphatics.

(d. Besides the minute parenchymatous lymph spaces and sinuses, the lymphatic capillaries and vessels communicate freely with the serous cavity of the peritoneum, pleura, pericardium, tunica vaginalis of the testicles, sub-arachnoid spaces, chambers of the eye, membranous labyrinth of the ear, etc. So that these larger and smaller cavities, which normally contain lymphatic effusions, are, with regard to the system of lymphatic vessels, in the same relation as the minute parenchymatous lymph spaces. The researches of Recklinghausen, of Ludwig and Schweigger-Seydel, of Dogiel, of Ranvier and others, have shown this theory, as previously enunciated by Mascagni, to be correct. It is easy with Prussian blue to inject the lymphatic rete of the centre of the diaphragm in a rabbit recently killed by bleeding and hung head downwards, on pouring the stain into the abdominal cavity of the diaphragm and assisting its penetration to the lymphatic rete of the tendinous centre by means of artificial respiration with the bellows (Fig. 243). On treating the excised diaphragm of a rabbit with silver nitrate (1 in 300), the impregnation of the tendinous tissue and epithelioid investment of the two faces, pleural and peritoneal, reveals its structure and special disposition. On the pleural surface the system of lymphatic vessels is shown in the form of

arborisations with anastomosing trunks, the extreme branches of
which form parallel canaliculi, corresponding to intertendinous
clefts (Fig. 244).

The black lines of intercellular impregnation are clearer and
more delicate on the peritoneal face where there are large polygonal
cells, with here and there small islands of lesser and rounded cells :
these are the lymph cells which invest the orifice and walls of the
small canals that bring the peritoneal cavity into direct communication with the lymphatic rete of the tendinous centre (Fig. 245).

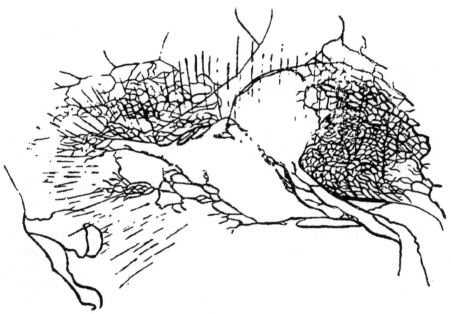

FIG. 243.　Rabbit's diaphragm, viewed from abdominal surface, with lymphatic rete injected with
　　　　Prussian blue.　(C. Ludwig and Schweigger-Seydel.)　The figure is somewhat reduced.

According to Ranvier there is no need to invoke the existence of
intercellular stomata to explain the ready penetration of coloured
fluids or solid particles from the peritoneal cavity to the lymphatic
plexus, since the small cells which occupy the orifices of the aforesaid canaliculi do not completely occlude them.　Still the retroperitoneal membrane of the frog, which forms the wall of the
cisterna lymphatica major in these animals, has, according to
Schweigger-Seydel and Dogiel and Ranvier himself, true stomata
or apertures surrounded by epithelial cells which are somewhat
differentiated and communicate freely with the peritoneal cavity
(Fig. 246).

It is very probable that there is direct communication, similar to that which has been described in detail for the peritoneal cavity and lymphatic capillary network of the tendinous centre of the diaphragm, in all the other serous cavities of the body. Bizzozero

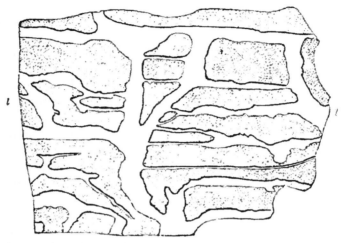

FIG. 244.—Central tendon of rabbit's diaphragm treated with silver nitrate, viewed from pleural surface. (Ranvier.) *l, l,* Lymphatic vessels in form of clear spaces anastomosing with one another, and united by almost parallel intertendinous clefts. Magnification of 20 diameters.

and Salvioli described the communicating canaliculi between the lymphatic of the parietal pleura and the pleural cavity.

Other writers admit free communication, in the form of small

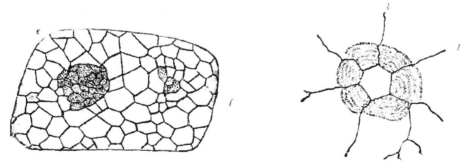

FIG. 245.—(Left.) Central tendon of rabbit's diaphragm, treated with silver nitrate, seen from peritoneal surface. (Ranvier.) *f,* Intertendinous lymphatic cleft; *e,* epithelioid investing cells, forming at certain places along the lymph canaliculae islands of small, somewhat granulated cells, which surround a stoma that is not always visible.

FIG. 246.—(Right.) Epithelioid platelet from frog's retroperitoneal membrane, treated with silver nitrate, viewed from peritoneal surface. (Ranvier.) *l, l,* Intercellular lines of platelets which surround an aperture or stoma communicating with lymphatic canaliculi.

pores or canaliculi, with the lymphatic rete in the free walls of certain mucosae, such as the bronchial and nasal mucosa. The interstitial adenoid tissue of the lungs is rich in lymph canals, which form a large irregular lymphatic meshwork round the bronchi, pulmonary lobules and blood-vessels. When animals are made to breathe pigmented fluids by means of a spray, the pigments penetrate by tiny pores through the epithelial cells of the mucosa (Klein).

This theory is reinforced by the extraordinary rate at which fluids and also blood are absorbed when injected into the trachea of living animals. Nothnagel found blood-corpuscles in the interstitial lymph spaces of the lungs barely 3-5 minutes after injection.

II. The lymph contained in the lymphatic system, as briefly described above, comes from three different sources:—

a) The blood, which, by the network of blood capillaries to the various tissues, constantly pours into the lymph spaces the materials required for the nutrition of the tissue cells.

b) The living elements of the tissues, which continually give off to the same system, both the products of their synthetic or anabolic processes, destined for use by other tissues and organs, and the products of their analytic or katabolic processes, destined to be eliminated from the body.

c) The food-stuffs introduced, and more or less modified or digested in the alimentary canal, known as a whole by the name of *chyle*, which is periodically absorbed by the lymphatic roots of the intestinal villi. On the strength of this threefold origin we may theoretically distinguish between blood lymph, tissue lymph, and lymph of the digestive apparatus or chyle. Leaving aside for the moment the chyle, the formation and absorption of which will be discussed elsewhere, we will consider the constituents of lymph properly so-called (of the blood and tissues), which is constantly being formed and poured out into the lymphatic lacunar spaces. Since the demand for nutritive materials in the different tissues and organs is quantitatively and qualitatively very different, and since, on the other hand, each tissue and organ is the seat of specific anabolic and katabolic processes, it follows necessarily that the lymph in the lacunar system of the different organs must differ in consistency and composition.

Up to the present however, we possess very few analytical data in regard to the differences presented by the lymph coming from the different organs, nearly all these differences being much attenuated, or even obliterated, in the lymph collected from the larger vessels, into which alone it is possible to introduce a cannula. In examining the general characters and chemical composition of lymph, it is almost always collected, as it flows, from a cannula introduced into the thoracic duct of a fasting dog, which yields the whole of the chemical constituents from the several lymphs (coming by the lymphatic channels to the different tissues of the organs) that have not been consumed by the tissues, nor absorbed by the blood-vessels. In collecting lymph from animals of small bulk rabbits, cats, etc., the thoracic fistula (direct method) may be replaced by an indirect method, i.e. the fistula of the jugular or, as Jappelli advises, of the subclavian.

The lymph which flows from the fistula of the thoracic duct is a watery, slightly opalescent fluid, with a specific weight of 1012-1022, less viscous than blood; when left to itself it coagulates slowly, forming a more tenuous and less copious fibrin reticulum than that which forms in the blood. A small quantity of peptone injected into the veins makes it incoagulable, although the blood remains coagulable (Shore).

When examined under the microscope it presents a certain number of leucocytes precisely similar to those of the blood, varying in size from 5 μ to 10 μ. The smaller and younger leucocytes predominate in the lymph, the larger and adult specimens in the blood; but the total quantity contained in 1 c.mm. of lymph, though it varies considerably in different animals and in the same animal under different circumstances, seems not far removed from that of the leucocytes in the blood.

A certain number of erythrocytes are also constantly present in lymph, even when precautions are taken to avoid any admixture with blood, or when the lymph which is moving through the lymphatics of a living animal is examined. The lymph being almost or wholly deprived of oxygen, the erythrocytes give a brownish colour to the fluid; but on contact with air, owing to the transformation of the haemoglobin into oxyhaemoglobin, they assume a clear red hue, which tinges the surface of the clot. It is probable that some of these are not formed locally, but come by diapedesis from the blood capillaries. So far as is known at present there are no blood-platelets in lymph (Chap. IV. 9, p. 118).

The plasma of lymph contains all the essential constituents of blood plasma: but the quantitative relations are a little different. In particular it has been pointed out that lymph plasma, as compared with that of blood, is poor in protein, which has been partly absorbed by the tissues: on the other hand, it is richer in water and alkaline salts, so that its reaction is generally more alkaline than that of blood plasma. For the rest, the chemical composition of lymph varies considerably. According to the most reliable of the existing analyses, the percentage quantity of water varies from 93·5-95·8: the total solid residue is much less than that of blood, varying from 4·2-6·5; the protein varies from 3·5-4·3, fibrin from 0·04-0·06: generally speaking, the protein content diminishes owing to the muscular movements, and increases in proportion with rest and sleep. The neutral fats, soaps, cholesterin and lecithin are scanty in lymph 0·4-0·9 per cent; when it sometimes looks turbid and highly opalescent this is due not to fats but to protein compounds in a special state of aggregation. It also contains a small quantity of sugar (dextrose). Some observers have also found a considerable amount of urea. The ash of lymph, like that of blood serum, oscillates from 0·7-0·8 per cent, and contains an excessive amount of sodium chloride, from the lymph flowing from the thoracic duct in dog. Hammarsten was unable to extract more than traces of oxygen and 37-53 per cent of carbonic acid, i.e. a quantity greater than that contained in arterial and less than that which can be extracted from venous blood.

This last fact shows that part of the carbonic acid developed by the tissues is directly absorbed by the blood capillaries and veins, both in the lymph spaces and in the lymph capillaries. So, too, we must remember that many of the solid products of the tissues are directly absorbed by the blood-vessels, and that the lymph contains only such substances turned out by the blood as are not taken up by the tissues (blood-lymph) and such products of the tissues as are not directly absorbed by the blood-vessels (tissue-lymph). The lymph spaces and capillaries thus represent an internal medium in which the reciprocal exchange of materials between blood and tissues takes place : and the lymph vessels, properly so-called, represent a drainage system which slowly, by long and circuitous paths. reconducts all the residual matters, both from blood- and tissue-lymph, left over from the direct exchanges in the lymph spaces and capillaries, to the circulatory torrent. In view of this it is evident that the quantity of lymph that flows through the thoracic duct in the time-unit cannot be taken as a measure of the total amount of lymph poured into the blood day by day. According to Heidenhain, the average amount of lymph flowing in 24 hours from the thoracic duct of a dog that weighs 10 kgrms. is about 640 c.c. Noel Paton, from the thoracic duct of a patient who weighed 60 kgrms., obtained about 1 c.c. of lymph per minute, i.e. 1440 c.c. in 24 hours. From a woman, Munk and Rosenstein obtained a quantity varying between 1200 and 2280 c.c. *per diem*.

It is possible also to collect lymph from different parts of the body by introducing a small cannula into the larger lymphatic trunks of the upper and lower limbs, the liver, and the intestine. The lymph from the limbs is similar to that flowing from the thoracic duct of a fasting animal, but it contains a smaller amount of solids (2-4 per cent). On the other hand, the lymph from the liver contains more solids (6-7 per cent), even in the fasting animal. That coming from the intestine during inanition exhibits an amount of solids intermediate to the above. For the rest, both the composition and the quantity of these various lymphs differ considerably according to circumstances, especially in regard to the degree of functional activity in the tissues and organs whence they are taken.

The large serous cavities of the peritoneum, pleura, pericardium, tunica vaginalis of testicles, etc., normally contain only a small quantity of lymphatic effusion, sufficient to lubricate the walls. But under abnormal conditions, particularly with mechanical obstruction of the venous circulation, and with marked delay in the circulation, however produced, it is possible to collect large quantities of fluid from these cavities, which differs considerably in composition from the lymph obtained from the thoracic duct. It has a low specific gravity 1008-1015; contains a minimum amount of proteins 2·2-7·3 per cent); is almost free of corpuscles: does not, generally speaking, coagulate spontaneously, but since it contains fibrinogen, coagulates on the addition of thrombin, or fluids which contain it see Chap. V. 6).

Bainbridge, Asher, Mendel and Hooker noted that, under given experimental conditions, the flow of lymph from the cannula inserted in the thoracic duct continues for a not inconsiderable time after death. Jappelli and D'Errico have recently demonstrated that a *post-mortem* flow of lymph occurs in every case, but is especially persistent when the death of the animal occurs instantaneously 'electrocution) and without haemorrhage. According to the same authors small quantities of *post-mortem* lymph are constantly obtained from the cervical and brachial trunks as well. It is, however, mainly, though not exclusively, visceral in origin.

Post-mortem lymph differs essentially in its characteristics from the normal by :—

a Its osmotic pressure, which gradually increases up to and beyond that of normal blood :

b Its gradually decreasing electrical conductivity :

c Its increased viscosity and greater content of solids ;

d Peculiar changes in the velocity of outflow ;

e Its appearance, now more haematoid, now more chylous, always more turbid.

These researches of D'Errico and Jappelli show plainly that *post-mortem* lymph is not pre-formed lymph. Hence it becomes necessary to admit that the processes of lymphagenesis, whatever these may be, continue for some time after death. Nor should this be surprising when we reflect that after somatic death there is no instantaneous abolition of all the haemodynamic, osmotic, cellular, and other factors which are invoked in explaining the formation of lymph in the living animal.

III. The lymph contained in the lymphatic system is in continual movement from the roots to the large trunks, like the blood in the veins into which these empty themselves. This is proved by the fact that ligation of a lymphatic trunk produces filling and swelling below and comparative evacuation above, as in the veins; and that the valves in the lymphatics as in the veins impede the centrifugal course of the fluids within them. With direct microscopic observation of the mesenteric lymphatics of small mammals, again, it is possible to follow the slow centripetal movements of the lymph by the motion of the leucocytes which it contains.

In this movement of the lymph, as in the analogous case of the blood, we have to determine the mechanical factors by which it is produced, its velocity and pressure, and its variations under given conditions.

It is a fact that the lymphatic vessels are under a certain degree of tension, *i.e.* they support a certain amount of pressure which dilates them (Ludwig and Noll). In a lymphatic of the horse's neck, the pressure is 10-20 mm. of water (Weiss). Since fluids moving in a tube always proceed from higher to lower pressure, we must assume (even if it cannot be directly proved) that the pressure is maximal at the roots of the lymphatics ; that it gradually falls from the branches to the lymphatic vessels ; that, lastly, it is minimal at the point at which the thoracic duct opens into the left subclavian, and the right lymphatic trunk into the right subclavian. *A priori* the velocity of movement of the lymph should decrease from the greater trunks to the more peripheral branches in proportion as the area of the current-bed widens. Experimentally, however, it is found that even in the larger lymphatic vessels, *e.g.* the lymphatic trunk of the horse's neck, the velocity of movement is very low ; according to Weiss it equals 250-300 mm. per minute.

What is the origin of the *vis a tergo* which produces the centripetal movement of the lymph, and is sufficient in man to overcome the force of gravity from the extreme end of the lower limbs to the height of the venous vessels of the neck ? In the frog and other amphibia, reptiles and fishes, the lymph hearts which beat rhythmically, and which, by their muscular structure and function, present many analogies with the blood heart, are undoubtedly of great importance to the lymph flow. The frog is provided with four lymph hearts : the two (posterior) sacral hearts situated at the sides of the coccyx, being covered only by a delicate aponeurosis and by the skin, can be seen beating even before they are dissected ; the two (anterior) axillary hearts are covered by the scapula. The sacral hearts carry away the lymph from the lymphatics that accompany the sciatic vein ; the axillary hearts that of the vessels coming from the head and anterior limbs. In other amphibia, reptiles and fishes, there are only two lymph hearts. Without entering into their mode of functioning, we can see that since the frog is poorly provided with regular lymphatic vessels, and in compensation has a copious supply of large sinuses and lymph sacs, the four hearts represent so many pumps necessary for promoting the flow of lymph from the said sacs and sinuses.

There are no lymph hearts in man and other mammals; the walls of the lymph vessels are, however, provided (as above stated) with muscular elements, which interlace above the valves in various directions (Fig. 238) in such a manner as to suggest that they may, by their rhythmical contraction, function as minute hearts (Foster). No direct observations exist to confirm this theory. On the other hand, there are certain data which indicate that some of the lymphatic vessels, under given conditions, are capable of rhythmical and peristaltic contractions and dilatations in the direction of the current. Arnold Heller observed under the microscope, in the mesentery of a guinea-pig anaesthetised with chloral hydrate, that the lymphatics successively contracted and relaxed (on an average six times a minute) in the peristaltic direction from the periphery to the centre. This observation is unsupported, and, generally speaking, it must be held that the muscle cells of the lymphatic walls behave passively, like those of the blood-vessels, in regard to the normal lymph current.

Pursuing the line of strict analogy between blood-vessels and lymphatics, it may also be stated that the muscle cells of the lymphatics have an automatically oscillating tonus, which may be modified or regulated by the influence of special vascular nerves. The recent work of Gley and Camus (1894-1895) has made it possible, in the physiology of the lymphatic vessels, to define accurately certain fundamental ideas as to the dilator and constrictor functions of the nerves which influence the muscle cells of the receptaculum chyli and the thoracic duct. After successfully overcoming some serious technical difficulties, these two experimenters succeeded in registering on dogs the pressure in the receptaculum, when reduced to a closed cavity, communicating below by a cannula with a receiver filled with physiological saline, kept at low and constant pressure; above, it communicated by a second cannula inserted into the thoracic duct with a small water manometer, provided with a float and a lever writing on a smoked cylinder. Fig. 247 gives a clear idea of the method.

FIG. 247.—Receptaculum chyle in dog, injected and slightly distended, viewed from posterior surface. (Camus and Gley. The aorta and its branches are seen at the back; i.i, lower cannula; c.s, upper cannula.

The results arrived at by Gley and Camus can be summed up in a few words :—

(*a*) The left splanchnic nerve contains dilator fibres and also constrictor fibres to the receptaculum. As the electrical excitation of the nerve trunk almost always produces depressor effects, we must conclude either that the constrictor fibres are not very numerous in the part of the nerve which is stimulated, or that they are much less excitable than the dilator fibres.

(*b*) The motor nerves to the thoracic duct run in the thoracic part of the sympathetic chain. Here also there are dilator and constrictor fibres, and the activity of the former outweighs that of the latter.

(*c*) It is also possible, reflexly, by exciting a sensory nerve to determine dilator effects upon the receptaculum and thoracic duct. If, *e.g.*, one sciatic is ligatured, alternate constriction and dilatation will be observed in place of the former constant tonus. On exciting the central end of a divided sciatic, there is invariably a dilator effect. On the other hand, asphyxia on cessation of artificial respiration determines contraction of the thoracic duct similar to that exhibited by the stomach, bladder, uterus, bile duct, etc.

These observations show the importance of the muscle cells and motor nerves of the lymphatic vessels, in so far as they are capable of altering their lumen, and can thus facilitate or hinder the centripetal movement of the lymph. If these active vascular movements were more energetic, rhythmical, and peristaltic or progressive from the branches to the lymphatic trunks, it is evident—in view of the function of the many valves with which the lymphatic system is furnished—that they would have the same effect as the heart-beats, and would represent a form of propulsion adequate to account for the lymphatic circulation. But this view has no experimental basis, nor does it harmonise with the theory of the venous circulation, which depends essentially upon the *vis a tergo* developed by the cardiac rhythm.

According to Ludwig the lymphatic circulation depends essentially on the *vis a tergo* due to the pressure on the lymph that fills the parenchymatous lymph spaces, which in its turn depends on the pressure under which the blood circulates in the capillaries. Thus the lymph circulation is also, in last resort, the effect of the force of the heart. The lymph represents a transudate from the blood through the fine membrane constituted by the capillary walls, by a process of *filtration* which depends on the difference of pressure between the blood circulating in the capillaries and the lymph poured out into the spaces. This theory will be analysed below. For the moment it is enough to say that it is correct, in so far as it assumes the lymph circulation to be due to the *vis a tergo* caused by the pressure on the lymph in the lacunar system ; but it is inadequate, in so far as it holds the lymph to be merely a product of simple filtration. The pumping of the heart promotes the flow of lymph, not merely by favouring filtration through the capillaries, but by another simpler mechanism. At each systolic efflux the whole arterial tree is dilated by the passage of the pulse wave, in consequence of which the whole of the perivascular lymphatics immediately receive an impulse to centripetal evacuation of the lymph which they contain. Since it is shown from plethysmographic observations that the total volume of the body is increased at each beat transmitted from the heart, it may logically be admitted that the lymphatics which run separate from, and independent of, the blood-vessels must, at each pulsation of the arteries, be sensible of a pressor effect which favours the movement of the lymph.

More important, however, and certainly better demonstrated, is the influence exerted on the lymph circulation by the active and passive movements of the skeletal muscles. If a cannula is introduced into the principal lymphatic vessel from the lower extremity of a large dog, no flow of lymph will be perceived so long as the muscles of the limb are relaxed and motionless. As soon, however, as active movements are excited in the limb, or alternate passive movements of flexion and extension are performed on it, the flow of lymph through the cannula becomes suddenly active. This fact shows that the muscular movements compress the lymphatics and empty them in the centripetal direction, because the valves prevent movement of the lymph, as of venous blood, in a centrifugal direction. The rise of the lymph in the lower limbs is principally effected by this mechanism.

On the other hand, the respiratory mechanism exerts a preponderating influence on the movements of the lymph in the visceral lymphatics. The lymphatic, like the venous, current is continuously affected by the normally negative pressure of the thorax, by which the lymph is aspirated, like the venous blood, from the extrathoracic to the intrathoracic vessels. This negative thoracic pressure increases during inspiration, and the positive abdominal pressure increases during active expiration. These two factors accelerate the flow of lymph, particularly in the visceral lymphatics and thoracic duct, and propel it to the mouths of the two subclavian veins, where it mixes with the venous blood.

IV. The exact determination of the mechanism which effects the formation of lymph is one of the most complex problems in physiology, and has been much discussed of late years since Heidenhain (1891) opposed to the *mechanical theory of filtration* (a relic of the ancient doctrine of Bartholin and Mascagni, to which Ludwig and his School endeavoured to give an experimental basis) his *secretory theory*, in which he asserts that the formation of lymph is essentially the effect of the activity of the living cells which form the walls of the blood capillaries. For better orientation in this difficult and complex subject we will tabulate the different groups of facts brought forward and consider them separately.

A consensus of experimental results shows that increased pressure in the blood capillaries is followed by increased formation of lymph :—

(a) We know from the works of Emminghaus that the occlusion of the veins in one limb not only increases the current flowing through the cannula inserted into the lymphatic of that limb, but considerably modifies the constitution of the lymph, so that it becomes richer in erythrocytes and poorer in dissolved solids. This fact is in agreement with clinical observation, which shows that in cardiac failure, hepatic cirrhosis, thrombosis of the veins, and in fact in every case in which there is obstruction or local interruption to the venous circulation, with consequent increase of pressure in the capillaries, the lymph transudes through these so freely that oedema, i.e. stagnation or accumulation of lymph in the tissue spaces, results.

(b) Both Heidenhain and Starling obtained the same results as Emminghaus after ligaturing the portal vein in the dog. The marked rise of intra-capillary pressure in the intestine increased the flow of lymph from the cannula in the thoracic duct four to five times, with diminution of colloids and increase of red blood-corpuscles.

(c) On obstructing the vena cava inferior above the diaphragm there is a marked fall of arterial pressure, in consequence of which the viscera become anaemic, while there is still an acceleration of lymph-flow greater than that which occurs after ligation of the portal vein. The lymph does not contain more blood, but becomes richer in solids, while at the same time clearer and less coagulable. These results of Heidenhain were controlled by Starling, who demonstrated that in the above experiments the lymph was derived from the lymphatics of the liver and not of the intestines, as Heidenhain believed. In fact, after the occlusion of the vena cava, pressure increased below the point where the block occurred, producing a corresponding rise of pressure in the hepatic capillaries : on the other hand, the pressure in the portal vein diminished (as shown by the blanching of the intestines) in consequence of the marked fall of aortic pressure.

(d) On occluding the thoracic aorta (by introducing from the right carotid a catheter ending in a rubber balloon which could be inflated by the injection of water), Heidenhain observed that arterial pressure below the point obstructed could fall to zero, while the lymph current might continue for 1 to 2 hours longer, although with diminished velocity and progressive reduction.

The composition of the lymph also changed, since it became turbid and whitish, not from increase in the fats and leucocytes, but owing to a kind of partial precipitation of the proteins. This turbidity does not always persist; sometimes it ceases after 15 to 30 minutes. In any case the percentage content of solids in the lymph increases, even after it has become clear. Lastly, the lymph, while of greater density, becomes less coagulable during the occlusion of the aorta. On repeating this experiment Starling saw that the pressure in the inferior vena cava is not altered, and may even rise slightly under the conditions described, while that in the aortic system is greatly reduced. The lymph that continues to flow after the occlusion of the aorta can therefore only come from the lymphatics of the liver. Indeed, on ligaturing the latter, he found that the entire flow of lymph from the thoracic duct was arrested.

According to Heidenhain these phenomena cannot all be interpreted on the mechanical theory of filtration; according to Starling, on the other hand, since they demonstrate that the increase of lymph flow is invariably associated with a corresponding increase of pressure in certain capillary regions, they are cogent arguments for the importance of filtration in the formation of lymph. The various changes in constitution and concentration presented by the lymph from the different regions have still, however, to be explained.

It will be observed that in all the experiments referred to, the increase of pressure in the blood capillaries is due to a block in the venous circulation, which is accompanied either by abnormal retardation or by venous stasis. This fact never occurs under physiological conditions. It may be conjectured that the walls of the blood-vessels are altered by the long stagnation of the venous blood, that they become more permeable, more sensitive to changes in pressor effects, and permit an abnormal filtration of lymph, to which they do not lend themselves under normal conditions. We cannot, therefore, from these facts deduce a physiological theory of the normal formation of lymph by a process of simple filtration. Physiologically, capillary pressure only varies in consequence of slow oscillations in tone of the small arteries, which are provided with strong muscles. When these dilate, capillary pressure rises, because, owing to diminished resistance, a larger amount of the impulsive force of the heart is transmitted to the capillaries; but, in addition to the rise of pressure, the velocity of circulation through the capillary network rises also, so that its walls are bathed in a blood that undergoes rapid and constant renewal. In order to establish the significance of filtration in the formation of lymph under physiological conditions, it must also be shown that a simple rise in arterial and capillary pressure, with unimpeded venous flow, constantly produces increase in the lymphatic current. The following are the facts which bear upon this proposition :--

(*a*) When in a dog all the cervical and brachial nerves to an anterior limb are divided so as to paralyse all motor nerves to the muscles as well as the vessels, and the cervical cord is stimulated electrically so as to produce contraction of all the vessels of the body except those of this limb, there is necessarily a marked efflux of blood with increased arterial and capillary pressure in all the vessels of the paralysed limb. Nevertheless the quantity of lymph flowing with the aid of the passive, rhythmical movements of the limb from the cannula inserted into its lymphatic trunk does not show the slightest augmentation, but rather tends to diminish gradually, as it did previous to stimulation of the spinal cord (Ludwig and Paschutin).

(*b*) When the so-called chorda tympani is excited there is a conspicuous dilatation of the small arteries of the submaxillary gland, associated with increase of pressure and acceleration of the blood-flow through the capillaries (Chap. X. 1, p. 341). These effects are certainly associated with increased formation of lymph, which pours into the glandular lymphatic spaces, and (as we shall see, Vol. II. Chap. II.) is immediately utilised by the gland cells for the formation of an abundant salivary secretion (Ludwig), so that it does not accumulate in the glandular lymphatics. If, before exciting the chorda tympani, the animal is slightly atropinised, the vessels of the gland will equally dilate, and capillary pressure rises as before; but the salivary secretion does not occur, nor is there any increased formation of lymph, since it does not accumulate in the connective-tissue spaces of the gland, nor does the flow of lymph from the glandular lymphatics increase (Heidenhain). To interpret this effect we must remember that atropine paralyses the activity of the *secretory* nerves, leaving the vasodilator fibres of the chorda tympani untouched. Mere arterial dilatation and rise of pressure and circulatory velocity in the capillaries of the gland are not enough to provoke increased formation of lymph, such as does, on the other hand, occur when the secretory activity of the gland cells are excited.

These facts are obviously irreconcilable with the theory that a primary importance must be assigned to the mechanical process of filtration in the physiological formation of lymph. They prove that when the increased pressure in the blood capillaries is associated with acceleration, instead of with slowing or stasis of the circulatory current, no increased formation of lymph takes place.

Another important series of experimental observations shows that the lymph current may increase conspicuously, independent of any marked rise in pressure in the blood capillaries :—

(*a*) Certain chemical substances, when injected into the blood, induce a considerable increase in the formation of lymph, and were therefore termed *lymphagogues* by Heidenhain. Such are commercial peptone, extracts of crab's muscle, of the head or body of leeches, the body of river mussels, the intestine or liver of dog, egg albumin, curare, and (according to D' Errico) gelatin. All these substances produce the same effect as regards flow of lymph from the thoracic duct: immediately after the injection of the lymphagogue into the vein, the lymph current increases as much as four times, and the effect may last for over an hour. The lymph becomes richer in proteins; it subsequently becomes turbid, then clears again: its coagulability diminishes or disappears. This increase in the lymphatic current coincides with a slight fall of arterial pressure, associated with acceleration of cardiac rhythm. Starling holds that under these conditions also the lymph derives principally from the liver, and is therefore more concentrated: and that if the portal lymphatics are ligatured there is no longer any lymphagogic action after injection. Pugliese, however, has shown that extract of crab's muscle and curare produce a marked increase of lymph in the front limb of the dog as well, with a sensible increase in its content of solids. Increased lymph formation cannot therefore be considered as a phenomenon localised in the hepatic capillaries.

(*b*) As against these lymphagogues which increase the lymph that is derived from the *blood* Heidenhain ranges a second class of substances, which are lymphagogues because they increase the lymph that comes from the *tissues*. Such are sugar, urea, sodium chloride, and other crystalloid substances when injected in sufficient quantities into the blood. They soon leave the blood, abstracting large quantities of water from the tissues, which is partly reabsorbed by the blood, partly goes to swell the lymphatic current. The flow is accelerated; the lymph becomes momentarily turbid, and is reddish; presently it coagulates slowly, although it contains many crystalloids: it is conspicuously poor in colloids. The composition of the blood changes in consequence: the water increases, and the relative quantity of erythrocytes and haemoglobin is lessened. The increase in the lymph stream is usually associated with a slight rise of arterial pressure, proportionate in each case to the quantity of lymph produced.

The lymphagogues of the second series accordingly produce changes in the blood and lymph of an opposite character to those observed with lymphagogues of the first series. Their antagonistic action is also shown by the fact that the latter do not excite urinary secretion, while the former do, so that the acceleration of the lymph stream is parallel to the excretion of urine.

V. These facts, as demonstrated by Heidenhain, were confirmed by successive experimenters; but they have given rise to various interpretations. Heidenhain made them the basis of his secretory theory. Cohnheim had already on several occasions expressed the idea that the vessel walls must be something more than a simple passive filter. Following out this idea, Heidenhain affirmed that the lymphagogic effects of the double series of substances above indicated should be considered as proving that the epithelioid cells which constitute the walls of the blood capillaries are to be considered as secretory cells analogous to gland cells, capable, i.e., of separating certain substances from the blood, and of pouring them into the system of lymph spaces with a brisk displacement of water, to provide for the various and specific nutritive needs of the different tissues and organs. Heidenhain alleges that certain secretory organs, such as the udder of the milch cow, are capable of yielding 25 litres of milk *per diem*, containing 42·5 grms. of lime. Since the lymph poured into the thoracic duct does not contain more than 0·18 per thousand grams, 236 litres of lymph would be required to provide the gland cells with all the lime needed for the production of the milk, on the hypothesis that they derive all the materials required for their function from the lymph as such. If, on the other hand, we assume secretory activity on the part of the cells forming the capillary walls, it is easy to explain how, with slight translocation of water, they are able to supply the gland with all the material required. Seeing that each organ or tissue must obtain its specific nutritive materials from the lymph, it is assumed that they pour out specific products into the lymph, which excite the secretory activity of the capillary walls, and thus provoke secretion of those substances which the organ requires.

It cannot be denied that this theory of Heidenhain is a very bold one. Not because (as one of our younger physiologists maintains, it diverges from the principle of the mechanical interpretation of functional processes—the admission of one secretion within the body more or less could not sensibly modify the general trend of science ; but because Heidenhain, prior to formulating his secretory theory, did not examine fundamentally to what point the process of lymph formation could be interpreted by the aid of the physical laws at present known to us.

To the secretory theory, W. Cohnstein, in a series of interesting papers (1893-1896`, opposes what he terms the *transudation theory*, according to which the formation of lymph is due to two well-determined physical processes: *filtration*, which depends on the difference of pressure between the two liquids separated by a permeable membrane, represented by the capillary walls ; and *diffusion*, due to the different chemical constitution of the two fluids. The lymph contained in the extra-capillary lymph spaces is during life the subject of continuous changes, produced by the metabolic activity of the parenchymal cells, which draw from it the substances required for their nutrition, and pour out the progressive and retrogressive products of their elaboration. Accordingly, chemical differences between the lymph and the blood plasma of the capillaries are constantly arising, and promote a continuous diffusion current from the blood to the lymph. In the above example of the mammary gland it is conceivable that its secretory epithelia, by constantly subtracting lime from the lymph, set up a persistent diffusion current, by which fresh lime passes continually from the blood to the lymph by way of the capillary walls. That this diffusion current may be rapid enough to provide for the chemical needs of the several tissues will be readily understood on considering the extraordinary rapidity of respiratory gas exchanges, arterial being transformed into venous blood in the time during which the capillaries are traversed. Cohnstein also quotes the researches of v. Brasol (1884) and of Klikowicz (1886), which prove that sugar and salts injected into the blood in concentrated solutions pass in a few moments from the blood to the tissues, and thence drive out into the blood such quantities of fluid as considerably to increase the blood pressure and diminish the relative quantity of haemoglobin from 30-60 per cent. These facts show that simple processes of diffusion in the body can sufficiently account for the rapid transport of considerable quantities of solid matters from the blood to the tissues. Undoubtedly the same may occur in the normal formation of lymph when diffusion is aided by filtration.

There is no necessity to resort to any mechanism other than that of diffusion and filtration to explain the effects of the lymphagogues of Heidenhain's second category. Since these increase the concentration of the blood, much water passes from the tissues into the blood to re-establish iso-tonicity, or equilibrium of osmotic pressure, which raises the pressure in the capillaries and favours filtration, and therewith the lymph stream, along with which the injected substance passes out of the blood. Heidenhain observed that the lymphagogic action of crystalloids was proportional to their power of attracting water, which again, according to v. Limbeck, is proportional to their diuretic action.

More controversy arises as to the interpretation of the effects of lymphagogues of the first category. Since the increase in the lymph current cannot be explained by a rise in intra-capillary pressure, which, on the contrary, falls, Starling holds that these substances, which are toxic to the heart, muscles, and leucocytes, are also toxic to the epithelioid cells of the capillary walls, by chemically altering them and rendering them more permeable, so that the normal pressure is sufficient to cause increased filtration. Cohnstein, on the other hand, maintains that the lymphagogic action of these substances must be interpreted as the effect of diminution of the endosmotic equivalent of the blood, and consequent diminution in the quantity of water that passes by diffusion from the lymph spaces into the blood capillaries. We know that peptone, extract of crab's muscle, etc., alter the composition of the blood, making it more permeable and rendering it incoagulable; but Cohnstein has demonstrated experimentally that it undergoes such modifications in its chemical constitution as to reduce its endosmotic equivalent very considerably, this being the reason why the amount of lymph increases, and with it the lymphatic current.

The doctrine of transudation (which results from a combination of the process of filtration with that of diffusion) is thus adequate to explain all the phenomena of the formation of lymph under various experimental conditions, and to render the hypothesis of the secretory functions of the capillary cells superfluous. Of course this theory does not exclude the possibility that these cells may under abnormal conditions suffer chemical or physical changes which induce modifications in the normal formation of lymph, since both filtration and diffusion are known to depend upon the constitution of the permeable animal membranes. In a word, it is not denied that the living cells of the capillary walls are the seat of incessant changes corresponding with the degree and kind of their metabolism. What is denied, as being superfluous and non-proven, is that they fulfil a *secretory* function properly so-called, and that the substances secreted from the blood in the lymphatic spaces differ specifically according to the specific needs of the several tissues and organs.

The latest work on this subject by Lazarus Barlow, Hamburger, and Asher tends to show that the rôle of filtration in lymphagenesis must be less than that of the osmotic processes (diffusion), while the relative permeability of the cells of the individual tissues is undoubtedly of importance (Ellinger). Asher and his pupils, in particular, have studied the influence of the activity of cell metabolism in the several tissues on the formation of lymph.

Another series of experimental observations, made recently by Carlson, Greer, and Luckhardt (1907-10), is of some interest in the problem of the mechanism of lymph formation. Here we can only state briefly that in a large number of experiments (seventeen horses and five dogs the chloride content of the lymph was found higher than that of the blood serum; this statement is confirmed by the fact that lymph is a better electrical conductor than serum. A ten per cent increase in the NaCl content of a physiological saline solution causes an increase in the electrical conductivity which is comparable to the increased conductivity of the lymph over the serum (Luckhardt). These facts do not agree with any mechanical theory of lymph formation, whether the filtration or the osmosis theory. According to the former, the quantitative salt content of both lymph and serum ought to be the same; according to the latter it ought to be maintained constant.

Pugliese (1901) investigated the influence of the vasomotor

centres on the formation of lymph. On cutting the medulla oblongata, or blocking its blood-supply in dogs by means of artificial emboli, he noted a rise in the amount, and fall in the concentration, of the lymph flowing from the thoracic duct. Under these conditions, also, the intravenous injection of curare, bile, and urea determined an increase of lymph, which with the two first substances becomes more concentrated, with urea, on the contrary, less concentrated than the normal. Peptone in dogs with a paralysed vasomotor centre exhibits a much less intense lymphagogic action than the normal. The lymphagogic action of caffein disappears entirely, while sodium chloride preserves its action of lymphagogic potency.

VI. All that we have been considering refers exclusively to what Heidenhain calls *blood-lymph*. We must now examine the so-called *tissue-lymph*, and the organs which more particularly concur in forming and modifying it.

We have seen that lymph cannot be considered as a simple residue of blood plasma, unappropriated by the tissue cells. Part, at least, of the chemical products formed by these cells is poured into the lymph spaces, and modifies and renders more complex the lymph turned out of the blood capillaries. Theoretically, it is undeniable that the lymph from different organs and tissues must have a different composition. The work of Heidenhain, completed and partly rectified by Starling, gives confirmatory evidence of this. The lymph coming from the limbs regularly contains a lower percentage of proteins than that from the intestine, and the latter contains a larger amount of proteins than that from the liver. It appears improbable that this difference depends—as supposed by Starling—on the normal differences in permeability of the blood capillaries in different areas. It is more logical to admit that the three kinds of lymphs are dissimilar because, coming from different tissues, they are modified in various ways by the elaboration products of the same.

The quantity of lymph, again as was justly observed by Asher and Barbera—may and must depend on the degree of functional activity of the tissue cells. When the work of an organ increases, the quantity of dissimilation products increases also, and with it the quantity of lymph poured into the lymphatic spaces; on the other hand, this increase in the products eliminated by the organ may, since it modifies the difference in osmotic pressure between blood and lymph, determine an increase in the transudation of plasma through the blood capillaries. Experimental data in support of this theory are not wanting. Stimulation of the lingual branch of the trigeminus causes a marked accumulation of lymph, with consequent oedema in the corresponding half of the tongue. This phenomenon was first observed by Ostroumoff, and was subsequently confirmed and developed by Marcacci (1883. It is only necessary to tetanise the lingual nerves for a long time, and with brief interruptions, in order to produce conspicuous tumefaction of the half of the tongue corresponding to the side stimulated, associated with dilatation of the arterial and venous vessels. Marcacci has shown that the effect depends principally upon the pronounced formation and accumulation of lymph (oedema), rather than on hyperaemia. After protracted tetanisation of the lingual nerve, he saw not only that the lymphatics of the tongue dilated, but also that a large lymphatic gland which is in direct relation with them, and lies near the submaxillary gland, swelled and increased in weight. Since, as has been seen, the rise of arterial pressure is not of itself enough to determine any great increase of filtration through the capillaries, we hold that the effect depends on the extension of nerve influence in this case to the lymph-forming elements of the lingual tissue, which, when excited, pour a more copious flow of lymph into the lymphatic spaces. The same thing is seen on exciting the chorda tympani, which innervates the submaxillary gland, but with the difference that in this case the lymph which is more abundantly formed does not, after transformation into the saliva of the glandular cells, flow back into the lymphatic system, but is canalised in the excretory ducts of the gland.

All tissues that are in relation with the lymphatic system are more or less lymphagenic in a wide sense, i.e. they pour into the lymphatic system and thence into the blood system a part at least of their elaboration or waste products, thereby contributing to the formation of the lymph or modification of its composition. Among these, more particularly, are the so-called lymphoid tissues in general, the follicles and glands attached to the lymphatics, the red bone-marrow, the thymus, and the spleen.

VII. Lymphoid (or Adenoid) Tissue is the name given to such tissues as consist essentially of branching cells and fibres of connective tissue which are so interconnected as to constitute a network with very fine meshes, within which the leucocytes are enclosed in great numbers. Diffuse in form, with no circumscribed boundaries, the lymphoid tissue is found in the mucosa of the respiratory passages, throughout the intestinal tract, in the marrow of bones, etc. In the sharply-defined form of rounded nodules the size of a small pin's head, lymphoid tissue appears in the so-called solitary follicles, which are found in large numbers in the intestinal mucosa, especially in its lower part. Each follicle consists of an adenoid rete, with very fine and regular meshes, filled with leucocytes. The meshes are larger, and the leucocytes less crowded, at the centre and periphery of the nodule, as shown in Fig. 248. At the surface, where the follicle projects into the intestine, the villi are usually absent. and the crypts of Lieberkuhn are found at its circumference. One or more arterioles penetrate into the nodule,

and break up into a capillary network which subsequently reforms
into one or more venules. Round the nodule there is a space or
lymphatic sinus filled with lymph, interrupted by afferent and
efferent blood-vessels and filaments of connective tissue, which
unite the tissue of the adenoid serosa with the surrounding
connective tissue. The lymph sinus and the blood-vessels and
connective-tissue bridges are clothed with epithelioid plates, as
shown by the silver nitrate reaction.

The leucocytes implanted in the adenoid rete are usually
smaller than those of the blood, owing to the paucity of protoplasm
around the nucleus. Many of them, lying within the central

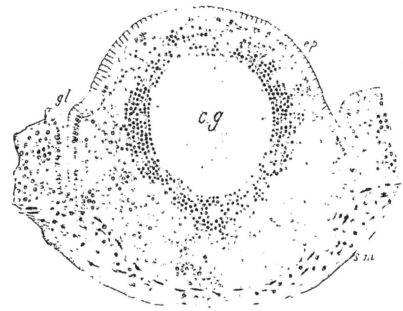

FIG. 248. Solitary follicle from large intestine of man. (Bohm.) *ep*, Intestinal epithelium; *gl*, Lieberkuhn's crypt; *c.g*, germinal centre; *m*, sub-mucous tissue.

mass of the follicle, are in the stage of mitotic division, so that
Flemming gave the name of *centrum germinativum* to the mid-
point of the follicle, at which there is a continuous multiplication
of leucocytes. In proportion as new leucocytes are formed at the
centre, the adult leucocytes which lie at the peripheral part of
the follicle are driven towards the lymphatic sinus, where they
are caught up in the general lymph current. The *vis a tergo* that
drives them out of the meshes of the adenoid rete is no doubt
due to the lymph which transudes from the network of the
blood capillaries in the follicle, and increases the tissue tension.
The lymph which is thus formed, while it serves as food for the
leucocytes, is modified by the products of their metabolism. It is
probable that a proportion of these products passes by diffusion
into the interior of the blood-vessels, so that the blood, on

traversing the follicles, yields up some materials and acquires others.

The so-called Peyer's Patches, of an oblong oval form, which are found to the number of 20-30 in the small intestine (particularly in the ileum), consist of groups of the solitary follicles, so that they are also termed agminated follicles. Each patch in man consists of 50-100 follicles, arranged in one plane, which lie immediately beneath the intestinal epithelium, and dip down so far into the submucosa that they interrupt the muscular layer. From the physiological standpoint they differ in no essential from the solitary follicles.

A more complex structure attaches to the lymphatic glands, numerous and widely distributed bodies which lie along the

Fig. 249. Vertical section of dog's lymphatic gland, the afferent lymphatics injected with Prussian blue stained with picrocarmine. (Klein.) c, Capsule, showing a lymph vessel cut transversely, communicating with cortical sinuses; a, lymph follicles of cortex surrounded by lymph sinuses, and separated by trabeculae; b, medullary portion of gland, showing reticular adenoid tissue and lymphatic sinuses injected with blue. Magnification of 25 diameters.

course of the lymphatic vessels. They differ in size, and are for the most part bean-shaped or kidney-shaped, with a concavity which is called the hilum of the lymphatic gland, whence issue the efferent lymphatics, while the afferent vessels enter on the convex side. The arterial and venous blood-vessels enter and leave respectively at the hilum. Each ganglion is invested with a capsule composed of two layers, the outer of which consists of loose connective tissue, and the interior of more compact connective tissue with numerous smooth muscle cells. From this internal capsular layer septa, or trabeculae, of the same connective and muscular character as the capsule, run out, and pass to the hilum, where they divide the cortical part of the gland into various compartments known as alveoli. On joining the internal or medullary part of the gland the trabecular tissue divides into finer strands interconnecting in every direction, and forming an open network which divides the medulla into a number of spaces, much smaller than the alveoli, that communicate freely among themselves to form a labyrinth. The capsule and cortical trabeculae and the network of medullary septa make up the skeleton or supporting tissue of the lymphatic gland (see Fig. 249).

Each alveolus of the cortex is occupied by adenoid tissue rich in leucocytes, in structure very similar to a solitary follicle, and therefore known as an alveolar follicle. This is separated from the walls of the alveoli (represented by the capsule and trabeculae) by a lymph sinus, which merely differs from that surrounding a solitary follicle by the fact that its lumen is traversed by a larger amount of reticulated tissue (Fig. 250). The medullary spaces, too, are occupied by follicular substance in the form of ramified and anastomosing cords known as the medullary cords. These also are surrounded by lymph sinuses throughout their course. As the adenoid tissue of the cortical follicles continues in the medulla as the medullary cords, so the circumfollicular lymph sinuses continue in the spaces which surround the medullary cords. In the hilum of the gland the whole of the lymph sinuses collect into a terminal sinus, which

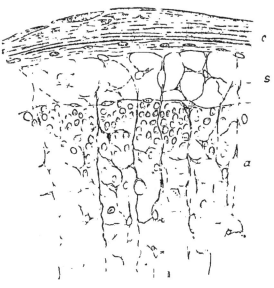

Fig. 250. Cortical section of lymphatic gland of man. through capsule, cortical sinus, and peripheral portion of a follicle. Many of the lymphocytes have been removed by the shaking. (Klein.) c, Capsule composed of external fibrous stratum, and internal layer of flat, nucleated corpuscles of connective tissue; s, circumfollicular lymph sinus, containing large meshed reticulum of ramified connective-tissue cells; a, adenoid tissue of a follicle, composed of network with finer and more compact meshes. Magnification, 350 diameters.

communicates with the efferent lymphatics. The afferent lymphatics, after forming a plexus between the two layers of the capsule, communicate with the perifollicular lymph sinuses. Like the lymph sinuses of the solitary follicle, those of the glands are invested with epithelioid platelets as shown by the silver nitrate reaction.

The small arteries which penetrate into the hilum of the gland ramify along the trabecular skeleton, here and there giving off branches that traverse the sinuses and plunge into the adenoid tissue, where they are resolved into a capillary network that extends to the medullary cords and the follicles contained in the alveoli. The small veins that arise from the capillary rete also cross the sinuses and enter the trabeculae, leaving eventually by the hilum.

The leucocytes which fill the meshes of the adenoid tissue, both of the follicles and of the medullary cords, differ in no way from those of the solitary follicles of the intestine. The follicles of the alveolar glands also show a germinative centre, where many leucocytes are seen in process of mitotic division (Fig. 251). Mitosis can also be seen in the medullary cords, though less freely.

The preceding description of the functions of the solitary and

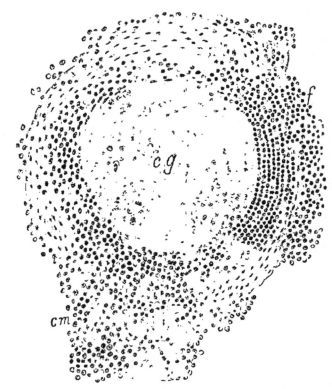

Fig. 251.— Alveolar follicle with adjacent medullary cord of a lymphatic gland, in man. (Böhm.) *f*, Follicle; *cm*, medullary cord; *cg*, germinal centre in which many leucocytes are seen undergoing mitosis.

agminated follicles applies perfectly to the lymphatic glands as well. We may regard the former as simple terminal lymphapoietic organs, which are found sparsely disseminated at the roots of the lymphatic system: and the latter as complex lymphapoietic organs, intercalated along the course of the lymphatic vessels, and therefore, unlike the former, provided with afferent and efferent vessels.

After the microscopic work that has been done on the lymphatic glands under various physiological and pathological conditions, there can be no doubt that the leucocytes that subsequently pass into the lymph and blood are generated and multiply in these organs. The most convincing experimental evidence is that given by Brücke. In carnivorous animals the lymphatic glands of the mesentery are all collected into a large semilunar mass known as the "pancreas of Asellius," which lies at the root of the mesentery. If a little lymph is collected from the lymphatics of a cat's mesentery, fed on a diet as free from fats as possible, the fluid is clear and contains hardly any corpuscles. If the lymph of the efferent lymphatic of the so-called pancreas of Asellius is examined at the same time, it is seen to be opalescent, and contains a great number of leucocytes. Further, we have unmistakable pathological evidence of the formation of leucocytes in the lymphatic glands, since hyperplasia of the lymphatic glands is associated with *leucaemia*, that is, an extraordinary increase of the leucocytes in the blood.

The mechanism of the escape of leucocytes from the adenoid tissues where they are generated and develop, is rather more complicated in the lymphatic gland than it is in the solitary follicle. It is certain that the smooth muscle fibres of the capsule and trabeculae have here an important function, whether in promoting the lymph stream through the glandular sinuses, or in driving the leucocytes out of the adenoid rete and propelling them into the efferent lymphatics. For when these muscular elements contract (as can be experimentally brought about by electrical excitation of the ganglion), the capsule and the trabeculae exert pressure directly on the circumfollicular sinuses and indirectly upon the whole parenchyma of the gland, so that all the lymphatics are emptied like a squeezed-out sponge through the efferent lymphatics. When, on the contrary, the muscle cells relax, the lymph sinuses swell up again, and are filled with lymph (Brücke).

In addition to this lymphapoietic function, we may reasonably hold that adenoid tissues in general are the seat of an exchange of materials between the blood and the lymph. We are unable to gauge the physiological importance of this exchange, which may be enormous, since it is impossible to examine the phenomena of absolute deficiency of the lymphatic glands, which are able to act vicariously and supplement each other. It is further probable that many of the katabolic products poured out by the tissues into the lymph stream, which if directly reabsorbed into the blood would exercise a toxic action, are rendered innocuous and even beneficial to the organism by the specific activity of the numerous lymphatic glands through which they pass before rejoining the blood. To give an experimental basis to this hypothesis, Asher and Barbéra studied on the dog the effect on arterial pressure and pulse frequency, of injecting into the central end of the carotid either defibrinated lymph from the head or neck (obtained by continuous centripetal massage of those parts, so that it remained as short a time as possible in the lymphatic glands), or defibrinated arterial, or lastly venous blood from the same animal. They showed that it was only after injection of the lymph that decided modifications appeared in the curves of arterial pressure and pulse frequency. The lymph obtained by continuous massage thus contains specific substances that do not exist in the arterial and venous blood of the same animal. It is therefore probable that these are destroyed and modified in the adenoid tissue of the lymphatic glands (in consequence, as it seems to us, of the metabolism of the leucocytes accumulated there in large quantities). Gabritschewski also put forward the suggestion that the leucocytes absorb certain substances noxious to the body by transforming them into innocuous substances, a phenomenon to which he gives the name of *pinocytosis*.

We must also assign a protective function, in the mechanical sense, to the lymphatic glands, owing to their labyrinthine structure, by which they function as filters to arrest, or at any rate retard, the entrance into the blood of many pathogenic microbes. This is proved by the fact that in miners, and also in tobacco smokers, the reticulated tissue of the bronchial glands is impregnated with pigment due to the particles of carbon introduced into the bronchi with the inspired air.

VIII. Among the lymphoid tissues Bone Marrow has acquired a capital importance, ever since in 1865 Bizzozero in Italy and Neumann in Germany discovered its haemapoietic functions. Three different varieties of marrow can be distinguished : red marrow, yellow marrow, and gelatinous marrow. The red marrow is found in the spongy strata of the flat bones and proximal epiphyses of the long bones of the extremities (Neumann). Yellow marrow is found in the adult in the distal epiphyses of the long bones of the limbs, and is the result of infiltration and fatty degeneration of the red marrow, which gradually increases with growth and old age. In consequence of fasting, and in various morbid states with general emaciation, the yellow is transformed into gelatinous marrow, but does not lose its capacity for reconversion into yellow, taking up fresh supplies of fat.

Special interest attaches to the red marrow, which presents a spongy mass, supported by reticular adenoid tissue (which, as already stated, consists of fixed and ramified connective-tissue cells and a rich plexus of branching blood-vessels). The nutrient arteries that enter the bones divide at once into a number of branches, which resolve themselves into a capillary network ; this passes into a system of venous lacunae partly or wholly wanting in organised walls, in which the blood moves very slowly ; out of this lacunar or cavernous rete arise the small veins by which the blood flows out. It is notable that the veins that occur within the medullary tissue are wholly deprived of valves, while those that issue from the bone are furnished with an extraordinary number of them.

The cells contained in the lacunar system of the marrow are quite characteristic of this tissue. Among them four principal kinds can be distinguished: leucocytes, megacaryocytes (giant cells), erythroblasts, erythrocytes.

The *leucocytes* of bone marrow comprise many varieties, which

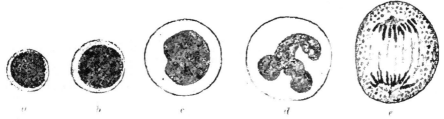

Fig. 252.—Leucocytes from dog's bone marrow, dry preparation. *a, b,* Young leucocytes, or lymphocytes, with giant nuclei and little cytoplasm; *c, d,* medullary cells or adult leucocytes with reniform and polymorphous nuclei; *e,* leucocytes undergoing mitotic division.

probably represent different states of development of a single cellular type, since there are always numerous transitional forms from the one to the other variety. The differences lie in the dimensions, form of nucleus, and character of cytoplasm. The youngest (lymphocytes) are the smallest, owing particularly to the paucity of protoplasm around the nucleus; the disc-shaped nucleus is rich in chromatin. The more adult (medullary cells) are larger, with a reniform polymorphous, sometimes multiple nucleus, poor in chromatin. These are not found in normal circulating blood, only in states of leucaemia (Fig. 252).

Howell's *megacaryocytes* were discovered in 1869 by Bizzozero, who called them giant cells with a budding central

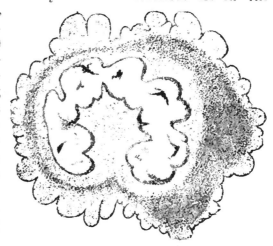

Fig. 253.—Megacaryocyte of bone marrow, in which a large horseshoe nucleus can be distinguished from the cytoplasm, divided into three concentric zones. (Heidenhain.)

nucleus. They have an average diameter of 25-45 μ. Their nucleus is very variable in form, often horseshoe-shaped. Heidenhain distinguishes several types or varieties according to the different degree of differentiation of the cytoplasm, which is sometimes arranged in three concentric zones (Fig. 253). Bizzozero had already suggested that the giant cells were derived from the leucocytes of bone marrow, since there is a whole series of forms

intermediate between the two.   The leucocytic origin of the giant
cells is nowadays admitted by every one, although the process by
which the one form of cell passes into the other is still unknown.

    The *erythrocytes*, or *nucleated red corpuscles*, were described
in 1868 by Bizzozero and Neumann, who recognised that they

FIG. 254.—Erythroblasts and erythrocytes from bone marrow of dog, dry preparation. *a, b, c,*
    Erythroblasts with more or less developed and excentric nucleus ; *d,* erythroblasts in mitotic
    division ; *e, f,* erythrocytes apparently destitute of nucleus.

contained haemoglobin.   Among them may be distinguished
young forms, adults, and those undergoing mitotic division.   They
can easily be differentiated from the lymphocytes of the same size,
not only by the haemoglobin which they contain, but also by the

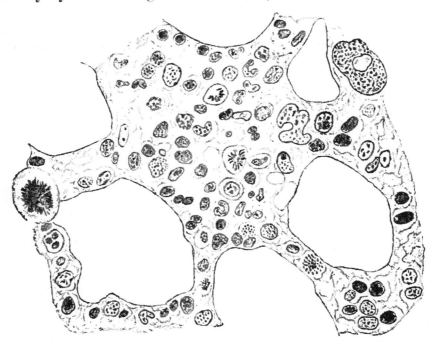

FIG. 255.—Preparation of human bone marrow, showing the various migratory cells, implanted in
    the lacunae of an adenoid tissue, leaving large irregular spaces here and there, which are
    occupied by adipose tissue.   (Böhm and v. Davidoff.)

different reaction of their cytoplasm to certain stains.   Erythroblasts never in their different stages of development present any
cytoplasmic granulation, such as stains with indulin (Trambusti).
In their constitution as in their size, the erythroblasts exactly
resemble the apparently non-nucleated erythrocytes of the blood,
which are found mingled with the nucleated cells of bone marrow.

Fig. 255 gives an idea of the mode in which these multiple elements are connected and intermingled in the areolar tissue of human bone marrow.

From what has been said, the great functional importance of bone marrow will readily be admitted. The red marrow, like all other lymphoid tissues, certainly contributes to lymphapoiesis, owing to its content of leucocytes at various stages of development. Since the different varieties of leucocytes differ in chemical constitution — inasmuch as they show granulations that stain differently with special pigments—it is not improbable (as suggested by Trambusti) that their specific metabolism may serve for special functions, of which, however, we are at present entirely ignorant.

It is more interesting to consider the functions of the mega-

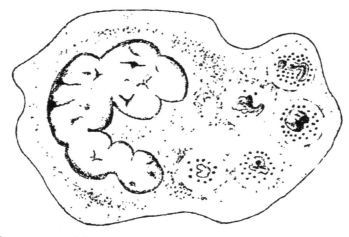

FIG. 256.—Megacaryocyte of bone marrow, with resting nucleus and finely granular cytoplasm, differentiated into three layers and containing five leucocytes in process of digestion. (Trambusti.)

caryocytes, on which much work has been done. The cytoplasm of some of these (particularly in the first stages of acute infections experimentally produced in animals) often contains corpuscles, which in their characteristics in no way differ from common leucocytes (Fig. 256). They were at first regarded as leucocytes in process of formation by endogenous mitosis, or gemmation of the nucleus of giant cells. Later researches have shown, however, that they are worn-out leucocytes in process of degeneration, which are actively absorbed by the giant cells, and are destined to be digested by them. It is possible under the microscope to follow the different phases of digestive necrosis of the ingested leucocytes, by means of double staining with safranin and indulin (Trambusti). These observations exclude the suggestion of Heidenhain, that in cases in which leucocytes are included in giant cells the former are the active invaders, and the latter the passive victims doomed to destruction. Other observations, moreover, show that when the giant cells exhibit signs of necrosis, they never contain leucocytes, as would be the case if Heidenhain's interpretation were true. It is evident, therefore, that the megacaryocytes fulfil a phagocytic function within the body, which probably serves to free the lymphapoietic organs from the leucocytes that are dead or in process of dissolution (van der Stricht).

P. Foà (1899) has recently investigated the experimental conditions under which it is possible to obtain the phenomenon of phagocytosis upon a large scale with these megacaryocytes. He found it appeared vigorously in inanition, extensive burning of the skin, and with intravenous injections of lecithin, milk, and bacterial proteins, especially in gravid or very young rabbits of 700-800 grams. in weight. Under all these conditions the megacaryocytes were seen to contain numerous polymorphous leucocytes within their protoplasm, some of which had already undergone protoplasmic dissolution and nuclear fragmentation, on the way to their complete disappearance. At the same time, the protoplasm of the megacaryocytes was seen to undergo alteration and disruption, and their nucleus shrank, and passed free into the circulatory torrent, where it blocked the capillaries of the lungs and was finally disintegrated. These two phenomena : destruction of leucocytes by the megacaryocytes, and embolism of pulmonary capillaries by the liberated nuclei of the giant cells, are always combined, and may be noted in a lesser degree under normal conditions as well, particularly during pregnancy. In pathological states the phenomenon is exaggerated, and indicates destruction of leucocytes that are no longer capable of functioning.

Other notable facts show that the megacaryocytes exert an important secretory function in regard to the regeneration of the blood. In fact, after repeated bleeding of the rabbit, their number conspicuously increases (van der Stricht, Bambeke, Heidenhain). The external zone of their cytoplasm (which stains less readily) exhibits bud-like protuberances, which increase in volume, and become clearer in consequence of the increasing amount of fluid imbibed by the delicate reticulum (Fig. 253). At a later stage the said buds fuse one into the other, and form large clear vesicles, in which it is no longer possible to distinguish the protoplasmic network. When the intracellular tension of the secretory product has reached its maximum, the fluid pours out, and the distended protoplasmic reticulum contracts again to form a new external stratum of cytoplasm. It should be noted that the bone marrow of rabbits which have been freely bled seldom exhibits leucocytes ingested by giant cells, showing that under these conditions the secretory function of the latter predominates.

We are ignorant of the precise physiological destination of the products elaborated in the giant cells. But from the very important fact discovered by van der Stricht to the effect that in a case of progressive pernicious anaemia there was complete absence of giant cells in the bone marrow, it may be assumed that they are useful to the production of erythrocytes.

The simultaneous presence in bone marrow of erythroblasts (nucleated embryonic red corpuscles) and erythrocytes (adult red corpuscles with no visible nuclei) shows beyond doubt that it is the seat of an active formation of the latter which are found in the blood in large numbers. After repeated bleeding the haematopoietic function of the bone marrow is conspicuously increased. The number of haematoblasts undergoing mitotic division increases; even that part of the marrow of the long bones which is normally inactive assumes a haematopoietic function (Orth, Litten, Foà and Pellacani, Bizzozero and Salvioli). Under these conditions a large number of nucleated red corpuscles enter the circulatory torrent (Erb).

Alterations in bone marrow can also be observed in many diseases in which there is marked alteration of the corpuscles (leucaemia, pernicious anaemia, typhoid, smallpox).

According to Danilewski and Selenski the subcutaneous or intraperitoneal injection of watery extracts of bone and splenic marrow produces a considerable increase in the number of erythrocytes (up to 50 per cent) and the haemaglobin content (up to 40 per cent) of the blood of rabbits and dogs. This effect was confirmed by Fowler in regard to extract of bone marrow.

It was formerly admitted (Bizzozero), and is still retained by some authors (Paladino), that erythrocytes arise from direct transformation of leucocytes. This theory, for which there is no experimental evidence, is now being given up. The only well-established fact is that the erythrocytes increase by mitotic division.

On the other hand it is certain that adult erythrocytes are derived from embryonic haematoblasts. The blood of the human foetus at the fourth month contains only nucleated red corpuscles; at the end of the ninth month these have become very rare. After that they are completely replaced by erythrocytes with no perceptible nucleus. How does the disappearance of the embryonic nucleus of the mammalian erythrocyte come about? Rindfleisch asserts that there is active extrusion of the nucleus: the haematoblast is deformed into the shape of a bell or watch-glass, the vertex of which, containing the nucleus, is finally disrupted. The bi-concavity of the erythrocytes is a vestige of this enucleation, which may be regarded as a kind of autocastration. The majority of observers hold more simply that the embryonic nucleus atrophies gradually, and ends by disappearing. If, however, this view were well founded we ought to find a number of transitional forms intermediate between the erythroblast and the eventual erythrocyte, whereas, on the contrary, every one admits that the transitory forms are rarely met with. The question must, therefore, be regarded as unsolved.

Petrone (1898-99) thought he had demonstrated that, while apparently deprived of nuclei, the erythrocytes, when subjected to the action of special reagents, contain a body which has all the cytological and chemical characters of the nucleus. In order to see this it is only necessary to make an extract of living blood with a 1 in 4000 solution of osmic acid. In successful preparations the erythrocytes are seen under the microscope to be in good preservation, perfectly globular (no longer bi-concave), with a homogeneous content. At the centre, or more or less at one side, they exhibit a body with wavy or dentate outline, in which a fine filamentous-granular structure may be detected. This alone stains electively with nuclear stains, while the rest of the erythrocyte stains with protoplasmatic dyes (Fig. 257). According to Petrone the supposed nucleus of the circulating erythrocytes is almost always in a state of complete rest, although he thinks it premature to say that it is entirely lacking in germinative activity. He thinks it probable that this depends upon the comparatively short life

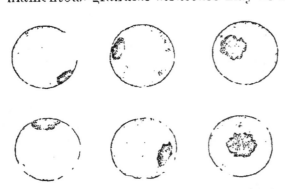

Fig. 257. Erythrocytes of healthy man, showing the more or less central or excentric corpuscles which Petrone holds to be permanent nuclei. From blood immersed in 1:4000 osmic acid, subsequently treated with baths of picric acid, and then stained with formic haematoxylin and aurantia.

of the erythrocyte, and the predominance of a special iron-carrying haemoglobinogenic function which he attributes to it.

The work of Negri (1900), however, invalidates Petrone's conclusion that the part of the protoplasm which is shown up by his method of staining can really be interpreted as the nucleus of the erythrocytes. Negri found that this characteristic body can always be demonstrated, on using Petrone's method, in the true nucleated erythrocytes as well, independent of the nucleus proper, both in the blood of the mammalian embryos and in the blood of such adult animals as normally contain nucleated corpuscles (birds and amphibia).

IX. Among the lymphoid organs we must also include the Thymus, which consists of a collection of closed follicles, separated by septa or trabeculae of connective tissue. The section of a lobe of the thymus shows under a small magnification a cortical and a medullary substance, which recalls the structure of the lymphatic glands (Fig. 258). The reticulated adenoid tissue and a rich network of blood capillaries support it, with finer meshes in the cortical part and wider meshes in the medulla. The cellular elements of the reticulum are collected more abundantly in the former than in the latter. The arrangement and relations of the lymphatic vessels in the thymus are still imperfectly determined.

The thymus begins to develop in the earliest periods of embryonic life. In man the development is rapid between the third and ninth months. It is, however, a fallacy to hold that the thymus is exclusively a foetal organ, because it continues, though slowly, to grow after birth, up to the second year of life; it remains stationary till the tenth year, after which it gradually atrophies and undergoes fatty degeneration. The process of involution is not unusually much retarded: it is found, for example,

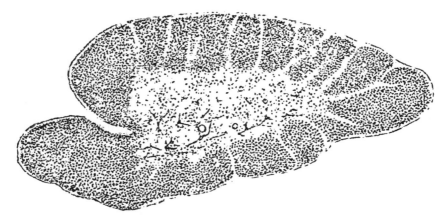

Fig. 258. — Section of lobule of child's thymus. (Böhm and v. Davidoff.) The hilum and cortical substance are seen in distinct follicles, separated by delicate trabeculae, while the medullary substance is formed by an adenoid tissue with larger meshes.

at the age of twenty-five; even at an advanced age the thymus has been found well developed.

From the fact that in reptiles and amphibia which have no lymphatic glands the thymus is a persistent organ, functioning during the whole of life, we may conjecture that its functions are very similar to those of the lymph glands.

That we must ascribe to it a lymphapoietic function is shown by the fact that the majority of the cells contained in its follicles are represented by lymphocytes of varying magnitude, some of which may be seen undergoing mitotic division. Whether it also has a haemopoietic function is less certain, although some have distinguished among the thymus cells nucleated red corpuscles, i.e. erythroblasts proper, such as are observed in bone marrow.

Recent physiological work on the effect of total or partial extirpation of the thymus, performed on puppies and chickens at different stages of development, and particularly on frogs, has brought to light some very interesting phenomena, which indicate, however indefinitely and incompletely, the functional importance of this organ.

Restelli (1845) was the first who attempted extirpation of the thymus on lambs, dogs, and calves, without, however, obtaining any practical results. Friedleben (1858) resumed the experiments with better success. He succeeded in keeping alive several dogs on which he had operated by excising the thymus alone, or the thymus and spleen together. He did not, however, pay much attention to the age of the animals on which he was experimenting, nor did he undertake comparative experiments under perfectly comparable conditions. In the animals deprived of their thymus he noted increase of water in the blood (hydraemia), increase of leucocytes (leucocythaemia), and diminution of erythrocytes (oligo-erythaemia); conspicuous reduction in the carbonic acid given off in the time unit; general trophic disturbances, particularly in the bony, and also in other tissues. He concluded that the thymus is not an organ indispensable to life, although it is highly important shortly after birth, since during the development of the body it promotes nutrition, formation of the blood, and also, therefore, of the tissues. Nothing was added to these results in a short paper published by Langerhans and Savaliew (1893).

At the International Medical Congress in Rome (1894) Tarulli and Lo Monaco communicated the first results of their experiments as performed in our laboratory, which were subsequently completed and published in a larger memoir.

By means of the Thoma-Zeiss method, they confirmed the fact already stated by Friedleben, to the effect that dogs deprived of their thymus exhibited a more or less pronounced state of anaemia, consisting in a diminution of erythrocytes and increase of leuco-cytes. They added, however, that this was only a temporary effect, and that two or three months after the operation the number of blood-corpuscles became almost equal to that of the normal dogs born in the same litter.

Puppies deprived of their thymus are stunted in growth, weigh less, and have more flaccid muscles than the control animals. The difference is especially conspicuous a month or a month and a half after the operation : later on it dies out gradually, and cannot be detected after about three months. The hair differs both in length and pigmentation in puppies with and without a thymus. Gener-ally speaking the coat of the latter is rougher, without the normal gloss and resistance, and yields to the slightest pressure. Sometimes the bones of the limbs are longer, thinner, and more bowed in puppies with no thymus : sometimes there is an exaggerated development of head at the expense of the rest of the body.

Puppies with no thymus further show reduced resistance and capacity for muscular work ; they seldom leave their bed, and are tired after a few steps; they can hardly drag a weight much lighter than that drawn easily by normal puppies. The difference is very marked even two months after the operation; it then diminishes, and finally disappears. In the first two months after the operation these puppies easily fall ill and die without any particular cause. Nothing abnormal can be detected at the post-mortem, except that the gastro-intestinal mucosa is congested.

The effects of extirpating the thymus in chicks 4 to 5 days old are more apparent. Immediately after the operation they exhibit only the effects of operative traumatism, which soon passes off, so that nothing abnormal is seen the next day. Three to four days after the operation, however, motor disturbances appear, and go on increasing: weakness of limbs, uncertain gait, slight tremors of all the muscles, finally torpor, followed shortly after by death. In 18 operated chicks, 15 died with these symptoms 7 to 8 days after the operation; 2, in which the disturbances were less pronounced, recovered after 10 to 12 days; one only succumbed during the operation.

Of 6 chicks, deprived of the thymus on one side only, one alone (operated on 2 days after birth) perished, the symptoms resembling those of chicks in which both sides were operated on: the others survived, merely exhibiting a slight weakness in the first days after the operation.

In chicks of 10 to 25 days the excision of the thymus, either on one side or on both, produced no perceptible effect.

In the interval between the first and second publications of Tarulli and Lo Monaco, two French experimenters, Abelous and Billard (1896), published their work on the effect of thymus extirpation in the frog, which (as might be anticipated) is more marked than in the case of birds, the thymus in amphibia being a permanent organ, functioning throughout life.

One to two days after the bilateral excision of the thymus, the frog exhibits serious motor disturbances, as shown in progressive muscular debility and incapacity for work, which increases till it amounts to paresis, paralysis, and the death of the animal. It is remarkable that while neuro-muscular activity becomes exhausted, sensibility remains intact, and even increases at first.

Some hours after the operation the copper-green colour of the frog (*Rana esculenta*) changes to a yellowish hue, and the area of black spots is contracted; only the head and limbs escape this discoloration. On the following day this phenomenon is less pronounced; with the onset of the muscular weakness it reappears, and increases steadily till death. Along with the discoloration dystrophic effects begin to appear on the skin in the form of ulcers, zones of necrotic destruction, and subaponeurotic ecchymoses. These changes become more serious the longer the animal survives. The ulcerated surfaces are highly hyperaemic, and bleed at the least touch. These animals may be said to have become haemophilic.

Most frogs at the moment of death exhibit dropsy. Directly the abdomen is opened or the muscles cut through, a colourless or bloody transudate escapes.

The blood from the heart is more watery ; the erythrocytes are changed in form and colour, and are fewer in number, while the leucocytes are increased. The peritoneum, bladder, stomach, intestine, other abdominal viscera, and the cervical region of the cord are all more or less congested.

Undoubtedly death results from functional defect of both lobes of the thymus. It invariably occurs, but after an interval which varies from 3 to 4 days. It ensues equally when the two organs are excised at different times, with a longer or shorter interval between the two operations. After the extirpation of one thymus only nothing abnormal appears save a lessened resistance to fatigue. If the second thymus is exposed 15 to 20 days after, it exhibits a certain degree of hypertrophy. Its excision is rapidly followed by the disturbances above described, and death ensues in a short time.

If the blood or serum from the peritoneal cavity of a frog that is dying from ablation of its thymus glands is injected into a frog that is normal or deprived of one or both thymuses, more or less pronounced disturbances of function will be observed in all, which may produce death even in normal frogs, induce it almost inevitably in frogs with only one thymus, and greatly accelerate it in frogs deprived of both organs. This fact shows that the tissue fluids of the frog entirely deprived of thymus contain energetically toxic substances, and that the fundamental function of the organ consists in the destruction of these, or in rendering them innocuous.

Transplantation or grafting of the excised thymus beneath the skin of the same frog or of another deprived of its thymus, does not inhibit the phenomena of auto-intoxication above described. Abelous and Billard, however, observed a temporary abatement of the phenomena of discoloration. On the other hand, subcutaneous injection of extract of calves' thymus (calves' thymus 20 grms., solution of boric acid 100 grms.) in 1 c.c. doses containing 0·02 grm. of thymus, both in normal frogs and in those which have been partly or wholly deprived of the thymus, produce effects resembling strychnine convulsions, while at the same time cutaneous discoloration ceases, and the normal colour of the skin becomes more pronounced. Accordingly there is a true antagonism between the phenomena of thymus deficiency and those produced by injection of the extract of this organ.

Ver Eecke (1899) also worked on the frog's thymus, coming to conclusions which differed in some respects from those of Abelous and Billard. According to ver Eecke the function of the frog's thymus is subject to periodical oscillations similar to those of bone marrow. He found that the frog's thymus undergoes functional atrophy in winter, and an analogous state can also be observed in summer if the frog is made to fast. The functions of the thymus are thus closely associated with those of the digestive organs. Possibly it further has an antitoxic action. Both during the winter season and in summer, if the animal is made to fast, the thymus is not indispensable to life. Its partial or total excision, whether uni- or bi-lateral, under these conditions has no effect other than to weaken the resistance of the animal to external intoxications.

Basch (1903), after thymus extirpation, noticed alterations in the ossification of the long bones. In animals without a thymus the formation of callosities and union of the fractured bones occurred later than in the normal. The animals operated on eliminated a larger amount of calcium than the control animal, amounting sometimes to five times the quantity.

Svehla (1896-1900), on injecting a watery extract of the thymus of man and other animals (pig, ox, dog) into the circulation, noted in dogs that there was acceleration of pulse and diminution of blood pressure, an effect resembling that of the injection of thyroid and suprarenal extracts. According to the latest experiments, it appears more probable that this action of thymus extract is due not to a specific substance in the thymus— as is the case with the suprarenal capsule—but to the various substances, nucleoproteins in particular, which are dissolved in the water, and are found generally, without exception, in every organ. A similar action has in fact been observed after the injection of extracts of many other organs (Hammarsten).

Cervesato attempted organotherapy with the thymus, starting from the fundamental concept that this organ in man functioned during infancy, and that this may be the reason why infants are less readily attacked by or are even immune from certain diseases. Stoppato describes the results obtained by the administration as a food of raw or undercooked thymus in doses of 29-40 grms. a day, in four cases of infantine atrophy, and in one case of infantine anaemia. In all these he obtained very encouraging results after a two-months' régime : there was marked improvement in the general state of nutrition, with development of body weight and increase of erythrocytes and haemoglobin of the blood. On the other hand, the results obtained from children afflicted with rickets and abdominal scrofula were insignificant, which points to the specific character of the therapeutic action, and therefore to the normal function of the thymus as an organ affecting general metabolism.

X. The Spleen is the largest lymphoid organ, its structure

corresponding to that of the lymphatic glands, thymus, and red bone marrow—which justifies us in assuming that the function of all these organs (apart from their specific differences) is closely allied, so that they are to some extent able to supplement each other, or to act vicariously. Besides its peritoneal sheath the spleen has a capsule, consisting of fibrous elastic and muscular tissue. A number of trabeculae dip into the organ from the inner surface of the capsule, dividing and subdividing, so that the parenchyma is converted into an elastic and contractile network, with large and small meshes, the hollow spaces of which contain the so-called splenic pulp (Fig. 259).

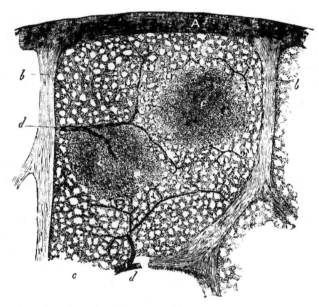

Fig. 259.—Vertical section through a fragment of human spleen, low magnification. (Kölliker.) A, Peritoneal and fibrous capsule; b, b, trabeculae; c, c, Malpighian corpuscles, one of which shows the transverse section, and the other the long section, of an artery; d, injected arterioles; e, splenic pulp.

When the spleen is cut across and squeezed, the pulp escapes, looking like blackish coagulated blood, which after exposure to the air assumes a lighter reddish hue. On examining a thin section of spleen treated with dilute solution of potash under the microscope, the splenic pulp is seen to be contained within the unequal meshes of a lymphoid tissue that supports it, and is composed of fringed connective cells, which ramify and anastomose among themselves, and are in connection with the trabecular tissue (Fig. 260).

The splenic vein and artery are remarkable for their size relative to the volume of the body which they irrigate. After penetrating the hilum to the interior of the spleen by six or more branches, they ramify dendritically, still within the trabeculae,

which cover them with an adventitious lymphoid sheath. In the
small arteries this sheath dilates here and there into grey nodules,
oval or spherical, of various sizes (1-0·36 mm. in diameter), similar
in structure to the solitary follicles of the intestine, and known as

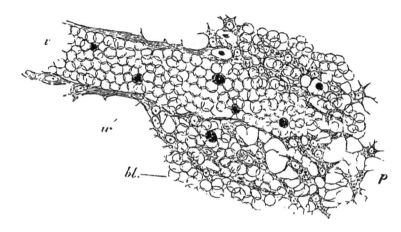

FIG. 260.—Thin section of splenic pulp near the origin of a small vein, highly magnified. (E. A.
Schäfer.) *v*, Venule filled with red and white blood-corpuscles; *bl*, erythrocytes which fill
the interstices of the reticular tissue of the pulp; *p*, branching connective-tissue cells which
form the reticulum containing the pulp.

Malpighian nodules or corpuscles, after their discoverer. These
nodules, for the most part, develop laterally to the small arteries,
from which they receive twigs that irrigate the follicular tissue
(Fig. 261). Under
the high power, each
Malpighian corpuscle
shows a complex reti-
cular structure, by
which they are differ-
entiated from the
homonymous tissue of
the splenic pulp (as
shown in Fig. 262,
which represents a
preparation obtained
by the silver chromate
method).

The small arterial
rami, after leaving the
trabecular tissue and
penetrating the areolar

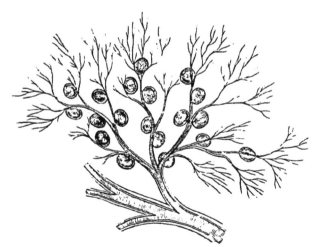

FIG. 261.—Small splenic artery (dog), with many Malpighian
corpuscles attached to the perivascular lymphatic sheath:
magnification of 10 diameters. (Kölliker.)

labyrinthine tissue which contains the pulp, divide into small
feathered tufts of arterioles; they afterwards lose their tubular
form and continue, in the opinion of most histologists, not in
the usual way by a closed capillary network into the veins,

but by opening freely into the labyrinthine spaces of the splenic reticulum. From the same reticulum the roots of the small veins (see Fig. 260) arise by an opposite process and then open into those which course along the trabeculae.

The lymphatics of the spleen form plexuses in the capsule and in the trabeculae. They are not very numerous, and run with the arteries, sometimes surrounding them, to form a plexus. The perivascular adenoid tissue and the follicles composed of the Malpighian nodules communicate with the lymphatic vessels with

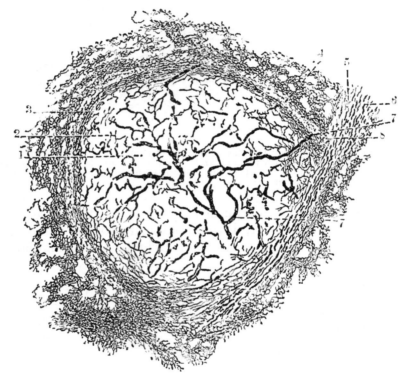

Fig. 262.—Section of Malpighian corpuscle and surrounding tissue of splenic pulp, with injected network of blood capillaries, treated with silver chromate; highly magnified. (Oppel.) 1, Malpighian corpuscle; 2, part of its reticulum; 3, denser reticulum at the edge of the corpuscle; 4, looser tissue external to the former; 5, 6, connective tissue of arterial sheath, to which the corpuscle is adhering; 7, capillaries of corpuscle; 8, reticulum of pulp surrounding the arteriole.

proper walls that run in the tissue of the trabeculae. All the lymphatics issue from the hilum together with the blood-vessels, and then join the lymphatic ganglia of the posterior part of the abdomen.

The nerves of the spleen are derived from the solar plexus; they enter by the hilum along with the vessels. They are certainly in peripheral relation both with the muscle cells of the vessels and with those of the capsule and trabeculae. Their central origin is probably in the bulb and cervical tract of the spinal cord. In order to reach the periphery, the splenic nerves pass by the left splanchnic and semilunar ganglion, from which arises the splenic plexus.

According to the histological researches of Retzius, v. Kölliker, and Fusari, the nerves of the spleen are usually non-medullated and for the most part supply the vascular muscles.

From the above it is evident that the blood which penetrates the spleen by the splenic artery comes into immediate relation with the elements of the splenic pulp contained in the labyrinthine spaces, and that the blood which issues from the spleen by the splenic vein must have traversed the lacunar system.

On examining the mobile elements of the splenic pulp under the microscope, they are seen to consist for the most part of erythrocytes and leucocytes, i.e. of the corpuscles of normal blood, which, owing to the marked circulatory delay within the lacunar system, become concentrated with very little plasma.

Besides the ordinary red and white blood-corpuscles, however,

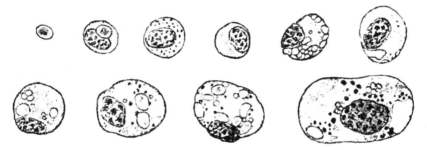

Fig. 263.—Splenic cells of various forms and sizes, containing in their cytoplasm pigment granules, and erythrocytes in process of dissolution, or fragments of already dissolved erythrocytes; magnification of 1200 diameters. (From a dry preparation of F. Müller.)

the splenic pulp contains other elements, similar to those of bone marrow. Megacaryocytes are rare, at least in man; on the other hand, there is an abundance of smaller amoeboid cells (although still twice the size of common leucocytes), many of which exhibit erythrocytes in process of breaking up (globuliferous splenic cells) inside them. There are many intermediate forms between the ordinary leucocytes and the globuliferous cells, all containing in their protoplasm extraneous corpuscles of varying form and magnitude, which represent pigment granules or the detritus of erythrocytes ingested by phagocytes (Kölliker and Ecker; Fig. 263). The plasma, again, in which these amoeboid cells are suspended, contains, in addition to the normal erythrocytes, a certain number of red corpuscles which are at different stages of disruption, and pigment granules derived from the decomposition of haemoglobin.

In the spleen of very young animals, there are constantly present along with the erythrocytes a greater or less number of erythroblasts or nucleated red corpuscles in various stages of development (Funke and Kölliker). In adult animals, too, after repeated bleedings, Bizzozero and Salvioli noted the appearance of haematoblasts, which are absent under ordinary conditions (Neumann).

In view of these facts, and of what has been stated in regard to the functions of bone marrow, we cannot doubt that the spleen is a haemopoietic and haemolytic organ. Its haemopoietic function, as demonstrated by the presence of the erythroblasts, seems to be very active during intra-uterine life, when the bone marrow contains the fewest number of nucleated red corpuscles; it is greatly reduced in the first period of extra-uterine life, when the haemopoietic function of bone marrow increases; it is abolished in adults, in whom bone marrow functions in full activity: lastly, it recurs in adults under circumstances in which the body requires a hurried neo-formation of the cytological elements of the blood.

That the spleen is not an effective haemopoietic organ in adult animals has been conclusively demonstrated by the recent work of Paton, Gulland, and Fowler (1902) on dogs, cats, and rabbits.

These authors employed four different methods of research: (a) comparison of the number of blood-corpuscles present in the splenic artery or carotid with the number of corpuscles present in the splenic vein; (b) determination of the effects on the blood-corpuscles of extirpation of the spleen; (c) measurement of the time it takes in normal and a-splenic animals to regain the normal mass of corpuscles either after haemorrhage or after the action of haemolytic agents; (d) study of the action on haematopoiesis of injections of splenic extract. The following results were obtained: -

In dogs and cats no difference was observed either in the number or character of the erythrocytes in the blood that goes to the spleen, as compared with the blood that flows out from the spleen. It appears, however, that there is a slight reduction in the number of the leucocytes, more particularly in that of the poly-nucleated.

Extirpation of the spleen in dogs, cats, and rabbits has no apparent effect on the number of erythrocytes, nor upon the protein components of the blood plasma (at least in dogs). There appears, however, to be a slight reduction of the eosinophile leucocytes. After haemorrhage in rabbits, and haemolysis in dogs, the normal number of erythrocytes is restored in the same time, both in the control animals and in those which have lost their spleen. Injection of splenic extract does not produce any augmentation in the number of erythrocytes in the rabbit, but they do increase, on the contrary, after injection of extract of red bone marrow.

From the above data the authors conclude that they have not established any fact to prove that the spleen possesses a haemo-poietic function.

The haemolytic function of the spleen may be argued from the numerous phagocytes in various stages of development, the erythrocytes in process of destruction, and the pigment granules contained in the plasma of the splenic pulp. Analysis of the chemical constituents of the spleen, moreover, make it probable that this organ is the seat of highly complex metabolic processes involving the destruction of many corpuscles.

According, however, to the latest work on dogs, cats, and rabbits by Paton and Goodall (1903), it appears that the spleen has no genuine and proper haemolytic function; but that its work is confined to the taking up of erythrocytes that are already dead, and the chemical transformation of their pigment, by storing up the iron, which can then be utilised for the formation of other erythrocytes.

On the other hand, W. Bain (1903), by artificially circulating the isolated spleen and liver of dog, with the object of determining the importance of these two organs in haemolytic processes, came to the conclusion that both spleen and liver, under these conditions of survival, exhibit the property of destroying erythrocytes as well as leucocytes. The spleen acts principally upon the leucocytes, among which it more particularly attacks those with polymorphous nuclei, although a certain quantity of erythrocytes (2·4 per cent) are also destroyed.

Besides the chemical compounds present in these highly vascular organs, there are other special products in the splenic pulp. One of the most important is a ferric albuminate which certainly depends on the chemical changes of the haemoglobin in the erythrocytes broken up by the spleen. The large amount of iron that can be recovered from the spleen has led some observers to consider that it is a storehouse of iron destined to the formation of new haemoglobin.

A series of recent researches by Tedeschi (1899) confirms the fact already admitted by Krüger and Lapicque to the effect that the spleen is an organ rich in iron : that on an average there is less in young than in adult rabbits : and that it seems to diminish again in old age. This excess of iron in the spleen is probably derived from decomposition of the haemoglobin of the erythrocytes broken up in the spleen. This does not, however, forbid the assumption that part at least of these organic iron compounds may serve the erythrocytes that pass through the spleen as materials for the construction of new haemoglobin. Arguments, in fact, are not wanting to show that the haemoglobin contained in the erythrocytes of the venous blood that leaves the spleen is in excess of that contained in the erythrocytes of the arterial blood that enters it : consequently the spleen must take an active part in the formation of haemoglobin and the maturation of the red corpuscles of the blood. This is indicated particularly from the work of Gurwitsch (1893) and Zelensky (1891). The former made 10 minute comparative analyses of the blood of the carotid and splenic vein in dogs: the latter determined on dogs and rabbits the effect of the peritoneal injection of splenic extract. On counting the corpuscles and estimating the haemoglobin with Hüfner's spectro-photometer, before and after injection, there was invariably a marked rise in both, whence the author concluded that "splenic infusion contains the products necessary to the regeneration of the blood."

The lymphoid tissue of the spleen, which consists essentially of Malpighian corpuscles or nodules, is a lymphapoietic or leucocyte-forming organ analogous to the lymph follicles and glands (Virchow). This is plain from the fact that the blood of the splenic vein contains many more leucocytes than the blood of the splenic artery (Kölliker and Hirt, Bizzozero and Salvioli). In the blood of the splenic vein the ratio between the number of the leucocytes and that of the erythrocytes is as $1:60$: in the arterial blood, as $1:2260$. In splenic leucaemia the lymphapoietic function of the spleen is enormously increased, so that it sends out a great quantity of leucocytes into the blood torrent. This fact coincides with a corresponding enlargement of the organ, due to hyperplasia of the lymphoid tissue.

It is to the wealth of leucocytes in the spleen and their special metabolism that we must refer the fact that the chemical compounds of the splenic pulp abound in nuclein and its derivatives, i.e. adenine, xanthine, hypoxanthine, guanine, and uric acid. Lecithin, jecorin, cholesterin, and inosite are also present. The alkaline reaction of the splenic pulp becomes acid after a short time, owing to the development of fatty acids, among which are succinic, formic, acetic, and lactic acid. The constant presence of uric acid in the fresh spleen should be noted, even in these herbivorous animals whose urine does not contain it. Horbaczewski (1889) states that when a fragment of still living spleen is dipped into blood freshly extracted from an animal, it induces the formation of considerable quantities of uric acid. This proves the spleen to be an important, if not the sole, organ in the formation of uric acid, which, as we shall see elsewhere, is derived from the nuclein bases present in large quantities in the splenic pulp.

Since the spleen is a contractile organ, its volume undergoes great variations. Normally it swells during the digestive period, reaching its maximum five hours after meals: it remains turgid for some time, and eventually regains its normal volume. This is the effect of an active hyperaemia analogous to that which is simultaneously exhibited by the mucosa of the alimentary cord, the pancreas, and the other glands attached to the digestive apparatus. This coincidence in hyperaemia points to the probability of the active intervention of the spleen in the chemical phenomena of the digestive secretion. It seems probable, in fact, from the theoretical standpoint that the congested spleen, by means of the nutritive substances freshly absorbed from the digestive apparatus, produces and pours into the blood substances that favour in some way the formation of the enzymes which are the active principles of the gastric (Baccelli) or of the pancreatic juice Schiff, Herzen. We shall return to this point in another connection. It also appears highly probable that the spleen and perhaps the lymphoid organs and tissues in general serve as magazines or reserve stores for the proteins deriving from digestion, and which cannot be immediately utilised by the tissues, just as the liver stores up the carbohydrates that accumulated there, in the form of glycogen. In favour of this hypothesis we have the fact of the marked reduction which the spleen and lymph glands undergo during inanition (Fredericq).

Another important phenomenon observed in clinical practice is the temporary swelling exhibited by the spleen in many of the infective diseases that are accompanied by fever. In malarial fevers the enlargement of the spleen increases constantly, with repeated attacks, until it becomes permanent and may reach considerable proportions, either by the accumulation of the malarial parasites and their products, or, as is probable, by paralysis of all the muscular elements of the organ. We have seen that the lymphatic glands swell by a similar process under similar morbid conditions, and that this process is of great importance in arresting the infective germs, and rendering the toxic substances which they produce innocuous. The spleen may also be regarded as an organ of defence against infective agents, which harmonises perfectly with the fact of the presence of numerous phagocytes contained in the splenic pulp.

The contractility of the spleen has been tested by direct stimulation of the organ, and by excitation of the peripheral nerves that run to it, as also by direct or reflex stimulation of the nerve centres.

If the spleen of an anaesthetised dog is exposed, the contact of the air at first produces a contraction of the organ, which disappears after some time, its surface becoming supple again, and dark red. On then bringing together the electrodes from an induction coil and applying them to any point on the organ, a hollow and blanching will be produced in consequence of local contraction, which drives out the blood. On running the electrodes over the surface of the organ, grooves and white lines of any form desired can be traced (Brücke). The human spleen has less contractility than that of the dog, cat, and many other animals, owing to the smaller number of muscle cells contained in the capsule and the trabeculae: contraction can, however, be determined by the percussion method, after faradisation of the organ through the skin (Botkin).

Roy was able by the plethysmographic method, ingeniously modified and applied to the spleen *in situ*, to study the automatic variations in volume of this organ. He showed that the spleen of dogs and cats presents periodic contractions and expansions lasting in all for about a minute, independent of the slow oscillations of arterial pressure, and therefore of the dilatations and constrictions of the arteries, which must accordingly be referred to the periodic contractions and expansions of the muscle cells of the capsule and trabeculae. The spleen of these animals is therefore a muscular organ which rhythmically expands to receive an increased amount of blood, and rhythmically contracts to expel a considerable part of the blood which it contains, in the direction of the liver. During its expansion the blood which has been driven out into the reticulum of the splenic pulp, and is at rest there, probably undergoes important metabolic changes; during contraction the blood which has suffered these changes, and many of the mobile elements that lodge in the areoli containing the pulp, and the follicular tissue of the Malpighian corpuscles, are driven out through the efferent vessels of the organ.

The muscular activity of the spleen, whether of the muscles of the capsule and trabeculae or of the vessels, is regulated and controlled by the nervous system. A pronounced and more or less rapid contraction of the spleen can be obtained by the electrical excitation of the spinal bulb, the upper cervical cord, left splanchnic, semilunar ganglion, and lastly the nerve plexus to the spleen (Tarchanoff). The same effect can be obtained reflexly by the electrical excitation of a sensory nerve or of the central end of the vagus. The contraction of this organ during asphyxia (as also in strychnine or strong quinine poisoning) is also due to excitation of the nervous system, which governs the muscles of the spleen. Section of the splenic nerves or their paralysis from any cause induces the opposite effects, *i.e.* the passive enlargement of the organ.

According to Bulgak (1877), the reflex and motor centres for the muscles of the spleen lie in the cord between the first and fourth cervical vertebra, while lower down, as far as the eleventh dorsal vertebra, there are only the afferent and efferent nerve fibres to the spleen. Schäfer and Moore substantially confirmed these results.

In view of the marked difference in volume which the spleen exhibits owing merely to fluctuation in the amount of blood that collects in it, certain physiologists, including Brücke, have looked upon it as a diverticulum capable of modifying or influencing the circulation of the other abdominal organs, notably the stomach and the liver, in various ways. This idea is founded on the anatomical fact that the splenic artery and the gastric and hepatic coronaries are three branches of one trunk, the coeliac artery, and that in proportion, as the inflow of blood through the splenic artery is easy or difficult, the blood supply to the stomach and liver must diminish or increase. Drosdoff and Botschet-schkaroff saw by direct observation that the contraction of the spleen induces increased blood supply to the liver. On stimulating the previously divided nerves of the splenic plexus, and thus producing a marked contraction of the spleen, the amount of blood that flows from a puncture previously made on the surface of the liver is conspicuously increased.

Little has been added to these positive data in regard to the various physiological functions of the spleen, from the results of the recent methodical researches on the consequences of its extirpation. Galen and Pliny were already aware that the spleen can be excised without danger to the animal. The first splenectomy performed on man was by Zaccarelli, in 1549. Morgagni mentions a woman whose spleen was removed in consequence of its protrusion from an abdominal wound, and who survived the operation for five years, and subsequently became a mother.

Innumerable experiments have been made in this direction, and there is probably no physiologist who has not successfully attempted the extirpation of the spleen at various times, either on dogs or rabbits. After the introduction of antiseptics, many surgeons performed the operation on man with a therapeutic object. Its want of success in cases of leucaemia, of amyloid degeneration, and of circulatory stasis in the organ is no evidence that the spleen is essential to human life, while the many successful operations (66 per cent, according to Vulpius) in cases of wandering spleen, simple hypertrophy, suppuration, cysts, sarcomata, etc., show, on the contrary, that it is possible to survive splenectomy with no ill consequences, provided other serious lesions are not present.

Not merely can animals resist splenectomy, but it has been demonstrated by the experiments of Tizzoni (1884) on rabbits, of Kurlow (1862) on guinea-pigs, of Dastre (1893) on young puppies, kittens, guinea-pigs, and mice that this operation neither perceptibly retards development, nor does it impair the reproductive capacity.

On counting the blood-corpuscles before and after splenectomy in dogs (Emelianow, 1893), rabbits, and goats (Vulpius, 1894), a relative diminution of erythrocytes and increase of leucocytes has been observed. The same fact has often been noted in regard to man, when splenectomy has been performed, especially in the cases referred to by Credé, Kocher, Severanu, and Czerny. This is the only fact that could be invoked in support of the theory that many leucocytes are transformed into erythrocytes in the spleen, by taking up or forming haemoglobin, with expulsion of the nucleus or its atrophy and reabsorption. We have seen, however, that this theory was contradicted by microscopical observations of the mobile elements of the splenic pulp, among which there are normally no erythroblasts nor other transitional forms between leucocytes and erythrocytes. On the other hand, the observations of Vulpius show that after at most nine weeks after splenectomy it is impossible to recognise any difference between the blood-corpuscles of normal and those of a-splenic animals, showing that the lymphapoietic or haemapoietic function of this organ is readily replaced by either the lymphatic glands or the bone marrow. It is apparently in this sense that we should interpret the more recent negative results obtained by Paton and Gulland, and Fowler, as above cited.

Hypertrophy of the lymphatic glands after splenectomy has been repeatedly observed on animals as well as man: but the effect is not constant, nor is it of long duration, which leads one to suppose that it is the result of the operative procedure. Even without any striking hypertrophy, however, it may be assumed that the lymphatic glands, which are exceedingly numerous, are capable of vicariously assuming the lapsed functions of the spleen.

Bone marrow sometimes seems to contain a large number of haematoblasts after splenectomy (Litten and Orth, Emelianow): in a-splenic rabbits and guinea-pigs it contains more iron than in intact animals of the same age (Tedeschi, 1899. This functional substitution is not, however, always apparent, nor in any case is it indispensable, since in fishes which have no bone, splenectomy is supported without any perceptible alteration of the blood-corpuscles (Pouchet, 1878.

Certain observations exist which tend to show that the functions of the spleen can be partly taken on by the liver. Maggiorani (1862) stated that the weight of the rabbit's liver in splenectomised rabbits exceeded that of intact rabbits by about $\frac{3}{4}$: Montenovesi (1893) describes a clinical case of hypertrophy of the liver consequent on splenectomy: lastly, Tedeschi (1899) has recently shown that the liver of the a-splenic rabbit contains a larger average amount of iron than the liver of intact rabbits, young or old. Still these facts do not seem to us sufficiently conclusive to admit of our assuming that the liver undergoes such modifications as would enable it to resume the haemopoietic functions which it performs during the embryonic life. The increase in volume and weight of the liver after splenectomy, as also the increased wealth of iron, may depend on a more copious blood supply: also, as rightly suggested by Maffucci, on the fact that this organ, after splenectomy for malarial hypertrophy, becomes the principal repository for parasites and malarial pigments.

It has been maintained that the spleen, after total extirpation, is reproduced or regenerated in the form of one or more lesser spleens that did not exist previous to the operation (Vella, Tizzoni). But it was subsequently discovered that there are not seldom nodules of a substance analogous to that of the spleen in its immediate neighbourhood, in the gastro-splenic omentum and great omentum, which represent true accessory or supernumerary spleens, and these after the operation may become more developed (Foà). It has also been demonstrated that if in the act of excising the spleen some of the splenic pulp is scattered in the omentum, it is capable of lodging there and giving rise to the formation of lesser spleens that did not previously exist (Cecchini and Griffini). In no case could the capacity of lymphoid splenic tissue to lodge and reproduce itself be invoked in favour of the theory that the spleen is an organ indispensable to life. Whatever the importance of its functions, they may easily be replaced by the other lymphoid tissues which abound in the body.

Lastly, we must remark that of late years special modifications of the lymphatic glands have been described under the name of haemolymphatic glands (Leydig, Gibbes, Robertson, Drummond, Vincent and Harrison, Weidenreich). They are found along the whole length of the aorta, and are differentiated from the ordinary lymph glands by the fact that no lymphatic vessels can be demonstrated in them. Both sinus and the vessels are filled with blood instead of lymph. According to their histological structure, they must represent a connecting link between the ordinary lymphatic glands and the spleen (Vincent and Harrison). In all probability their function is analogous to that of the other haemopoietic organs (Seemann, 1904).

BIBLIOGRAPHY

L. RANVIER. Traité technique d'histologie. Paris, 1875-82.
E. BRÜCKE. Vorlesungen über Physiologie. Wien, 1885.
C. LUDWIG. Arbeiten aus phys. Anstalt zu Leipzig, 1872, *et seq.*
L. CAMUS and E. GLEY. Archives de physiologie normale et pathologique. Paris, 1894-95.
D N. PATON. Journal of Physiology, 1890.
R. HEIDENHAIN. Arch. f. d. ges. Physiol., xlix., 1891.
E. H. STARLING. Journal of Physiol., xiv., xvi., xix., xxii., 1893-96.
H. J. HAMBURGER. Zeitschrift für Biologie, xii., 1894. Archiv für Physiologie. 1895.
W. COHNSTEIN. Archiv f. d. ges. Physiol., lix., lxiii., 1895-96.
L. ASHER and A. BARBÈRA. Zeitschr. f. Biol., xviii., 1898.
G. BIZZOZERO. Gazzetta medica Lombarda, 1868.
E. NEUMANN. Centralbl. f. med. Wiss., 1868. Archiv f. Heilkunde, x., 1869.
ARNOLD. Virchow's Archiv, xciii., xcvii., 1883-84.
DENYS. La Cellule, ii., v., 1886-89.
VAN DER STRICHT. Arch. de biologie, xii., 1892.
HOWELL. Journal of Morphology, iv., 1890.
TRAMBUSTI. Pubblicazioni del R. Istituto di studi superiori di Firenze, 1896.
P. FOÀ. Ziegler's Beiträge z. path. Anat., xxv., 1899.
ABELOUS and BILLARD. Arch. de physiol. norm. et path., 1896.
L. TARULLI and D. LOMONACO. Bollettino della R. Accademia medica di Roma, xxii., 1896-97.

A. PETRONE. Atti dell' Accademia Gioenia di scienze naturali di Catania, xxi., xiii., 1899.

SCHÄFER and MOORE. Journal of Physiol., 1896.

G. TIZZONI. Archivio per le scienze mediche, viii., 1884.

A. DASTRE. Arch. de phys., 1893.

GURWITSCH. Inaug. Diss. Dorpat, 1893.

SELENSKI. Recueil physiologique par le prof. A. et B. Danilewsky, ii., 1891.

P. EMELIANOW. Arch. de sc. biol. de St-Pétersbourg, ii., 1893.

D. VULPIUS. Beitr. z. klin. Chir., ii., 1894. (With comprehensive bibliography of works on the spleen.)

LAUDENBACH. Arch. de physiol., viii., ix., 1896-97. (Historical review with many quotations from original sources.)

A. TEDESCHI. Journal de physiol. et de pathol. générale, 1 janvier 1899.

Lymphapoiesis : synthetic review :—

ELLINGER. Ergebnisse der Physiologie, 1. i., 1902.

L. ASHER. Biochemisches Zentralbl., iv., 1905.

Haemapoietic organs :—

SEEMANN. Ergebnisse der Physiologie, III. i., 1904.

Recent English Literature :—

SWALE VINCENT. The Question as to Alteration in the Lymphatic and Haemal Glands after Removal of the Spleen. Proc. Physiol. Soc. in Journ. of Physiol., 1899-1900, xxv. pp ii., iv.

L. B. MENDEL and H. C. JACKSON. On Uric Acid Formation after Splenectomy. Amer. Journ. of Physiol., 1900. iv. 163-69.

A MOORE. The Effect of Ions on the Contractions of the Lymph Hearts of the Frog. Amer. Journ. of Physiol., 1901, v. 87-94.

A. MOORE. Are Contractions of the Lymph Hearts of the Frog dependent upon Centres situated in the Spinal Cord? Amer. Journ. of Physiol., 1910, v. 196-8.

F. A. BAINBRIDGE. Observations on the Lymph Flow from the Submaxillary Gland of the Dog. Journ. of Physiol., 1900-1901, xxvi. 79-91.

L. B. MENDEL and D. R. HOOKER. On the Lymphagogic Action of the Strawberry and on Post-mortem Lymph Flow. Amer. Journ. of Physiol., 1902, vii. 380-86.

Wm. STIRLING. Simple Method of demonstrating the Membrane of the Sublingual Lymph-Sac of the Frog. Proc. Physiol. Soc. in Journ. of Physiol., 1901-2, xxvii. p. i.

R. MAGNUS and E. A. SCHÄFER. Does the Vagus contain Motor Fibres for the Spleen? Proc. Physiol. Soc. in Journ. of Physiol., 1901-2, xxvii. p. iii.

D. N. PATON, G. L. GULLAND, and J. S. FOWLER. The Relationship of the Spleen to the Formation of the Blood Corpuscles. Journ. of Physiol., 1902, xxviii. 83-106.

F. A. BAINBRIDGE. On the Formation of Lymph by the Liver. Journ. of Physiol., 1902, xxviii. 204-219.

W. BAIN. The Role of the Liver and Spleen in the Destruction of the Blood Corpuscles. Journ. of Physiol., 1903, xxix. 352-68.

D. N. PATON and A. GOODALL. Contribution to the Physiology of the Thymus. Journ. of Physiol., 1904, xxxi. 49-64.

J. HENDERSON. On the Relationship of the Thymus to the Sexual Organs.—I. Journ. of Physiol., 1904, xxxi. 222-33.

F. A. BAINBRIDGE. The Lymph Flow from the Pancreas. Journ. of Physiol., 1905, xxxii. 1-7.

D. N. PATON. The Relationship of the Thymus to the Sexual Organs—II. Journ. of Physiol., 1905, xxxii. 28-32.

F. A. BAINBRIDGE. The Post-mortem Flow of Lymph. Journ. of Physiol., 1906. xxxiv. 275-81.

A. J. CARLSON, J. R. GREER, and F. C. BECHT. On the Mechanism by which Water is eliminated from the Blood in the Active Salivary Glands. Amer. Journ. of Physiol., 1907, xix. 360-87.

W. T. HUGHES and A. J. CARLSON. Relative Haemolytic Power of Serum and Lymph under Varying Conditions of Lymph Formation. Amer. Journ. of Physiol., 1908, xxi. 236-47.

A. J. CARLSON, J. R. GREER, and A. B. LUCKHARDT. Contributions to the Physiology of Lymph. Amer. Journ. of Physiol., 1908, xxii. 91-103 ; and 104-115 (with Becht).

B. F. DAVIS and A. J. CARLSON. Contribution to the Physiology of Lymph. Notes on the Leucocytes in the Neck Lymph, Thoracic Lymph, and Blood of Normal Dog. Amer. Journ. of Physiol., 1909-10, xxv. 173-89.

A. B. LUCKHARDT. Contributions to the Physiology of Lymph. Amer. Journ. of Physiol., 1909-10, xxv. 345-53.

H. O. LUSSKY. Contributions to the Physiology of Lymph. Amer. Journ. of Physiol., 1909-10, xxv. 354-66.

INDEX OF SUBJECTS

Abdominal respiration, 416
Absorption of gases, 378
Acapnia, 474
Accelerators, heart, 327
Accessorius, nerve, 328
Acid, aceal, 373
  amino-iso-valerianic, 27
  aspartic, 27, 129
  butyric, 37
  caproic, 35
  carbonic, blood, 380, 385, 397
  carbonic, discovery, 373
  carbonic, expired air, 389, 395
  diamino-trioxy-dodecanic, 27
  glutamic, 27
  hippuric, 129
  lactic, plasma, 130
  lactic, urine, 170
  laevulinic, 24
  nucleic, 24, 138
  oleic, 35
  oxalic, 60
  oxypyrrolidine-carboxylic, 27
  palmitic, 35
  a-pyrrolidine-carboxylic, 27
  stearic, 35
  uric, 129, 552
  valerianic, 35
Acid albumin, 23
Actinosphaerium Eichhornii, 74
Adaptation, 19, 63, 65
  of respiration, 469
Adenase, 33
Adenine, 24, 33, 35
Adynamia cordis, 333
Aerobic organisms, 68
Aerotonometer, 385, 490
Afferent nerves, heart, 339
  nerves, respiration, 457, 461
Agminated follicles, 530
Air, alveolar, 390
  complemental, 423
  expired, 397
  inspired, 397
  reserve, 423
  residual, 423
  tidal, 423

Ala cinerea, 445
Alanine, 23, 27
Alanyl-glycine, 23
Alanyl-leucine, 23
Albuminate, ferric, spleen, 551
Albuminoids, 23
Albumoids, 25
Albumose, 23
Alcoholase, 34
Aleuron, 18
Alexines, 154
Alkali albumin, 23
Alkalimetry, blood, 96
"All or nothing," 318
Allonomous metabolism, 87
Allorhythmia cordis, 316
Alveolar air, 390
  pressure, 405
Alveoli, pulmonary, 403
Amoeba, 14
Amoeboid movement, 74
  movement, leucocytes, 115
Amino-acids, 27, 129
Ammonia, plasma, 129
Amylase, 33
Amyloid, 25
Amylopsin, 33
Anabiosis, 66
Anabolism, 43, 46, 57, 68
  vagus, 332
Anaemia, 100
  pernicious, 539
Anaerobic organisms, 68
Anaesthetics, 53
Anelectrolytes, 142
Anhydraemia, 143
Animal gum, 130
Animals, characters, 19, 53
Annulus of Vieussens, 328, 354
Anterolateral nucleus, 363
Anti-coagulants, 124
Anti-kinase, blood, 128, 140
Anti-thrombin, 140
Aorta, pressure, 208
Apex beat, 221
Apnoea, birds, 484
  experimental, 475

Apnoea, foetal, 477
  true and false, 477
  vagi, 479, 488
  voluntary, 480
Arginase, 33
Arginine, 27, 33
Argon, blood, 387
Arteria aspera, 159
  venosa, 159
Arterial pressure, 241, 243, 253
  pressure, pulmonary, 254
  pulse, 263
  tone, 346
Arteries, locomotion, 245, 277
  pressure, 241, 243, 253
  suspension, 245
  tone, 346
  velocity in, 256
Asparagine, 60
Asphyxia, 380, 469
Aspiration, diastolic, 208, 210
  systolic, 208
Assimilation, 86
Atelectasis, 405
Atmosphere, gases, 397
Atmospheric pressure, 72
Atropine, secretion, 522
Auditory nerve, respiration, 465
Auricles, 180
  pressure in, 203
  septum, 299
Auriculo-ventricular bundle, 315
  valves, 192
Auscultation, heart, 196
  lungs, 426
Autolysis, 34
Automatic control, heart, 210
  respiration, 461
Automaticity, heart, 298, 305
  respiration, 457, 480
  vascular rhythm, 343
  vital, 83, 85
Autonomous metabolism, 86
Autosphygmogram, 265
Auxocardia, 186, 215, 226

Bacillus butyricus, 37
Bacteria, metabolism, 61, 65
  nitrifying, 58
Bacteriolysis, 154
Bacterium lacticum, 37
  photometricum, 78
Barometric pressure, blood, 384
  respiration, 471
Barotaxis, 76
Bathmotropism, 327
Benthos, 82
Bilirubin, 109
Biogen hypothesis, 88
Biogenesis, 2
Biology, scope 1

Biomorphosis, 49
Biotonus, 88
Biuret test, 22
Blood, alexines, 154
  alkalimetry, 96
  asphyxia, 380
  bactericidal properties, 154
  buffy coat, 97
  circulation, 157
  coagulation, 97, 132
  corpuscles, 91, 100, 113, 117
  defibrinated, 97
  enzymes, 127
  erythrocytes, 100
  examination, 120
  gases, 132, 379, 384, 388, 474
  immunity, 154
  leucocytes, 113
  lymph, 512
  metabolites, 129
  peptone, 124
  physical properties, 94
  plasma, 123
  platelets, 117
  pressure, 238, 281
  pressure in arteries, 241
  pressure in capillaries, 253
  pressure in veins, 253
  quantity, 98
  reaction, 91
  respiratory rhythm, 490
  specific gravity, 95
  spectra, 110
  stream, 232
  toxicity, 153
  transfusion, 152
  velocity in arteries, 256, 261
  velocity in capillaries, 263, 281
  velocity in veins, 262, 281
  vessels, 343
  viscosity, 151
"Blut-schatten," 106
Bridge, Wheatstone's, 150
Bronchi, 403
Bronchial murmur, 427
  muscle and nerves, 442
Buffy coat, 97
Bulbar centres, respiratory, 450
  vasomotor, 361
Bullous arteriosus, 187
Bundle, auriculo-ventricular, 311
Butyric fermentation, 37

Calcium, coagulation, 136
Canaliculi, lymphatic, 509
Cannula, perfusion, 285, 289
Capacity, vital, 423
Capillaries, blood, 172
  blood, area, 263
  blood, pressure, 253
  blood, velocity in, 263
  lymphatic, 507

Carbohydrates, 36
　in blood, 130
　metabolism, 59
　respiratory quotient, 399
Carbon dioxide, elimination, 391
　of blood, 385
　output, 470
Carboxy-haemoglobin, 110
Cardiac cycle, 205
　ganglia, 299
　muscle and nerves, 285
　nerves, depressor, 360
　nerves, sympathetic, 327
　nerves, vagi, 322
　reflexes, 333
Cardiograms, 223, 268
Cardiograph, 222
Cardio-pneumatic movement, 227
Caseinogen, 23, 40
Casease, 23
Catalases, 34
Catalysators, 31
Catalysis, 31
Catheter, pulmonary, 388
Cell, 8, 13, 16
　chemistry of, 19, 20, 37
　colony, 15
　theory, 12
Cells, giant, 535
　marrow, 538
　splenic, 549
　Traube, 147
Cellulose, 37
Centres, cardiac, 536
　expiratory and inspiratory, 454
　germinal, 529
　nerve, oxygen, 394
　respiratory, bulbar, 443
　respiratory, cerebral, 452, 461
　respiratory, spinal, 451
　splenic, 554
　vasomotor, bulbar, 361
　vasomotor, spinal, 362, 364
Centrifuge, 98
Centrosome, 13
Cerebrin, 35
Chemomorphosis, 49
Chemotaxis, 74
　leucocytes, 178
Chest, cavity, 407
Cheyne-Stokes respiration, 492
Chitin, 37
Chloral, respiration, 455
Chlorophyll, 18, 58
Chloroplasts, 59
Cholesterin, 36, 130
Chondrioderma, 16
Chorda tympani, vasodilatation 350
　tympani, lymph, 522
Chromoproteins, 23
Chronotropism, vagus, 325
Chyle, 512
Chymosin, 33, 128

Circulation, blood, discovery, 157
　dynamics, 233
　intrathoracic pressure, 406, 436
　lymph, 515
　time, 282
Clostridium Pasteurianum, 57
Clupeine, 24
Coagulation, by enzymes, 33
　by heat, 21
　of blood, 97, 132
　of lymph, 513
　of milk, 135
Cocaine, bulb, 450
　protoplasm, 102
Collagen, 23, 25
Colloids, 21
Colpidium colpoda, 66
Complemental air, 423
Concentration, molecular, 141
Conchiolin, 25
Conditions of activity, heart, 292
Conductivity, electrical, plasma, 149
Conjugated proteins, 23
Conservation, of energy, 5
　of matter, 5
Coronary circulation, 210
Corpora Arantii, 187
Corpuscles, blood, 91, 100, 113
　lymph, 513
　Malpighian, 547
　marrow, 535
Crassamentum, 97
Creatine, 35, 129
Creatinine, 35
Crusta phlogistica, 97
Crying, 438
Cryoscopy, 142, 148
Crystalloids, 21
Cube, Schultz, 111
Cycle, cardiac, 180
Cystine, 27
Cystine, 27
Cytoglobulin, 140
Cytoplasm, 13
Cytosine, 24

Darwinism, 47
Death, apparent, 60
Delirium cordis, 321
Denaturation, protein, 21
Depressor nerves, 323, 360
Descent, doctrine of, 8
Desiccation and revival, 60
Deutoplasm, 35
Dextrose, 36
Diamino-trioxy-dodecanic acid, 27
Diapedesis, 115
Diaphragm, 410, 417
Diastases, 33
　blood, 127
Diastole, 180, 208
　active, 208

Diastole, aspiration, 208, 210
  vagal, 325
Dicrotism, 265
Differentiation, 91
Diffusion, gas, 378
Digestion, plant, 54
Dilatator nerves, 350
Dionaea muscipula, 53
Di-saccharides, 37
Dissimilation, 86
Dissociation, ionic, 142
  oxyhaemoglobin, 395, 401
Docimasia hydrostatica, 405
Dromometers, 257
Dromotropism, sympathetic, 330
  vagal, 326
Drosera rotundifolia, 54
Dualism, 6
Duct, thoracic, 506, 512
Dynamics, circulation, 233
Dyspnoea, 403, 468
  compensatory, 480
  febrile, 469
  post-apnoeic, 481
  thermal, 470
  vagotomy, 458, 468
  veno-ity of blood, 469
  voluntary, 482

Ear, vasomotor nerves, 343
Ectoplasm, 17
Eddies, arterial, 189
Effusions, serous, 515
Elastic tubes, flow, 239
Elasticity, blood-vessels, 239
Elastin, 23, 25
Electrical conductivity, 149
  convection, 90
  stimuli, 80
  variations, heart, 332
Electrolytic dissociation, 142
Embryo, heart, 309
Embryology, 3
Emulsions, 21
Enchylema, 17
Endo-enzymes, 34
Endoplasm, 17
Endosmometer, 141
Energy, kinetic and potential, 11
  conservation, 5
Enterokinase, 30
Enzymes, blood, 127
  classification, 31
  properties, 29
Erepsin, 32, 34
Erythroblasts, 535
Erythrocytes, blood, 100, 146
  lymph, 513
  marrow, 535
  nucleated, 536
Eudorina, colony, 15
Eupnoea, 403, 467
Eustachian valve, 182

Evolution, 16
Exchange, gas, 375, 387
Excitability, 44
  heart, 313
Expiration, 419
Expiratory centres, 454
Expired air, 397
Exploring sound, cardiac, 200
  sound, oesophageal, 228, 406, 429
  sound, rectal, 429
Extraction, gas, 377
Extra-systole, 320

Facial nerve, vaso-constriction, 348
Fatigue, 73
Fats, cell, 35
  plasma, 130
  respiratory quotient, 399
Femoral sphygmogram, 270
Ferment, fibrin, 128
Ferments, 21, 39
Ferric albuminate, 551
Fibrin, 97
  ferment, 129, 137
Fibrinogen, 125, 128
Fibrinoglobulin, 135
Fibroin, 25
Filtration, lymph, 521
Fistula, lymphatic, 512
  pericardial, 215
Foetus, apnoea, 477
  lung, 405
Follicles, agminated, 530
  solitary, 529
Formatio reticularis, 445
Frog, heart, 286
  nerves of heart, 328
Fructose, 36
Funaria hygrometrica, 59
Fungi, 57
Funiculus solitarius, 445

Galium aparina, 79
Galvanotaxis, 80
Ganglia, heart, 299
Ganglion, Gasserian, 328, 354
"Gas silvestre," 371
Gases, absorption and diffusion, 378
  atmospheric, 397
  blood, 379, 384, 388
  extraction, 382
  lymph, 514
  plasma, 132
  physics, 378
  protoplasm, 38
  respiratory, 387
Gasometric apparatus, 184
Gelatin, 23
Gelatose, 23
Geomorphosis, 49
Geotaxis, 77
Giant cells, 535
Glands, haemolymphatic, 557

Glands, lymphatic, 530
  submaxillary, 343
Gliadins, 23
Globulins, 23
  serum, 126, 128
Globulose, 23
Glosso-pharyngeal nerve, circulation, 360
  respiration, 465
Glottis, respiration, 421
Glucoproteins, 23, 25
Glucosamine, 27
Glucose, 36
  blood, 130
Glutaminic acid, 27
Glutelins, 23
Glycine, 27
Glycogen, 18, 37
  blood, 120
Glycolysis, blood, 127
Glycoproteins, 23
Glycyl-glycine, 28
Glycyl-tyrosine, 28
Granules, leucocytes, 114
  protoplasm, 17
Gum, animal, 130
Gums, 37

Haemacytometers, 102
Haemapoiesis, medullary, 534, 538
  splenic, 550
Haematin, 108
Haematoblasts, 118
Haematocrite, 104, 148
Haematoidin, 109
Haematoporphyrin, 109
Haemautograph, 265
Haemin, 108
Haemochromogen, 108
Haemolistase, 127
Haemochromograph, 257
Haemodromometers, 257
Haemodynamics, 233
Haemoglobin, 105, 107, 109
  carbon dioxide, 586
  derivatives, 108
  oxygen, 383
Haemoglobinometer, 121
Haemoglobinuria, 153
Haemolymphatic glands, 557
Haemolysis, 105, 143, 154
  splenic, 550
Haemorrhage, 152
Haemotachometer, 274
Heart, anatomy, 182
  apparatus, 287
  automatic regulation, 210
  automatism, 298, 305
  block, 315
  cycle, 180
  delirium of, 321
  embryo, 309
  frog, 286

Heart, ganglia, 299
  impulse, 221
  inhibition, 322
  inhibition, reflex, 336
  intrathoracic pressure, 436
  intrinsic nerves, 299
  invertebrate, 311
  ligature, Stannius, 299
  limulus, 311
  locomotion, 224
  mechanics, 180, 187, 190, 201
  myo- and neurogenic theories, 307, 308, 310
  nerves, accelerator, 327
  nerves, depressor, 333
  nerves, inhibitory, 322
  oxygen, 293
  perfusion, 289
  phases of Luciani, 302
  plethysmograms, 216
  refractory period, 320
  resuscitation, 298
  rhythmicity, 298, 322
  self-steering action 210
  sounds, 196, 198
  staircase, 318
  survival, 298
  tonicity, 319
  tortoise, 286
  urea, 297
  valves, 187, 190
  volume changes, 215
  work, 230
Hearts, lymph, 516
Heat, death, 71
  stimulus, 77
Heliotaxis, 78
Hemiplegia, respiratory, 444, 452
Heredity, 49
Heterogenesis, 52
Hibernation, respiration, 496
High altitudes, blood, 384
Hippuric acid, 129
Histidin, 27
Histogenic substances, 126
Histolytic substances, 93, 126
Histones, 23, 24, 106, 117
History, circulation, 157
  respiration, 369, 402
Hyaloplasm, 17
Hydraemia, 143, 152
Hydrobilirubin, 110
Hydrodynamics, circulation, 232
Hydrogel, 21
Hydrogenase, 34
Hydrolysis, 26, 32
Hydromorphosis, 49
Hydrosol, 21
Hyperaemia, active, 341
  paralytic, 345
Hyperpnoea, 469
Hypoglossal nerve, vasomotors, 318
Hypoxanthine, 24, 35

Ichthulin, 23
Ictus cordis, 222
Idioplasm, 50
Immunity, 154
Impulse, heart, 221
Inanition, 65
Inflammation, 176
Infundibula, lung, 403
Inhibitory centres, heart, 336
  centres, respiration, 452
  nerves, heart, 322
Inorganic constituents, cell, 37
  constituents, serum, 131
Inotropism, heart, 326, 330
Inspiration, 409
Inspiratory centres, 454
  muscles, 409
Intercartilaginous muscles, 411
Intercostal muscles, 411
Intermolecular oxygen, 394
Internal respiration, 375
Intersystole, 201
Intra-abdominal pressure, 427
Intracardiac pressure, 201
Intrapleural pressure, 128
Intrapulmonary pressure 405, 424
Intrathoracic pressure, 406, 427, 436
Inversion, sugars, 37
Invertase, 33
Invertebrate heart, 311
Ions, 32
Ionisation, 142
Iron, haemoglobin, 108
  metabolism, bacteria, 67
  spleen, 551
Ischaemia, active, 342
Isoleucine, 27
Isotony, 142

Jecorin, plasma, 130

Kata-, vide Cata-
Katabolism, 43
Keratin, 25
Kinase, blood, 130
Kinases, 30
Kinetic energy, 44
Knephoplankton, 82
Kymograph, 242

Lactacidase, 31
Lactase, 34
Lacteals, 171
Lactose, 37
Laevulinic acid, 24
Laevulose, 37
Lamarckism, 48
Laryngeal nerves, respiration, 467
Larynx, respiration, 419, 421
Latent life, 65
  systole, 206
Laughter, mechanism 438
Laws of gases, 378

Laws of variation, 48
Lecithin, 35, 130
Leech, coagulation, 124
Leucaemia, 116
Leucine, 27
Leucocytes, blood, 113
  chemistry, 117
  chemotaxis, 116, 178
  coagulation, 138
  diapedesis, 115
  lymph, 513
  marrow, 531
  movement, 115
  narcosis, 178
  origin, 114
  phagocytosis, 115
Leucocytosis, 152
Leuconuclein, 138
Leucyl-glutamic acid, 28
Levatores costarum, 410
Life, minimal, 67
  physical basis, 11
  potential, 65
  pressure, 71
  temperature, 70
Light, a stimulus, 78, 81
Limbs, vasomotor nerves, 349, 354
Limulus, heart, 311
Lipase, 33
  blood, 127
Locomotion, arteries, 277
  heart, 224
Lungs, foetal, 405
  gas exchange, 387
  movements, 426, 412
  structure, 403
  ventilation, 423 484, 487
Luxus respiration, 473
Lymph, 505
  blood-, 512
  cells, 513
  circulation, 515
  composition, 513
  filtration, 521
  formation, 519
  gas, 514
  hearts, 516
  injection of, 533
  liver, 514
  post mortem, 515
  quantity, 514
  secretion, 519
  sources, 512
  tissue-, 512
  transudation, 524
  velocity, 516
Lymphagogues, 523
Lymphatic, canaliculi, 508
  cavities, 514
  fistula, 513
  pressure, 516
  stomata, 510

Lymphatic vessels, 506
Lymphatics, perivascular, 507
Lymphocytes, 114, 513, 529
Lymphoid follicles, 529
  tissue, 528
Lysine, 27

Macrocytes, 101
Maltase, 33
Maltose, 33
Manometer, elastic, 244
  maximum and minimum, 207
  mercury, 244
Marine organisms, 81
Marrow, 534
  cells, 535
  haemapoiesis, 538
  phagocytosis, 537
Materialism, 5
Matter, conservation, 5
  inorganic, organism, 37
  inorganic, serum, 131
Mechanical stimuli, 76
Mechanics, heart, 180
  respiration, 402
Mechanism, protoplasmic, 85
Mechanomorphosis, 49
Medulla oblongata, blood-vessels, 561
  heart, 336
  respiration, 443
Megacaryocytes, 535
Meiocardia, 186, 215
Melanins, 25
Membrane, cell, 13
  semi-permeable, 141
Merotomy, 12
Metabolism, allonomous, 87
  autonomous, 86
  in animals, 42, 61
  in plants, 54
  in saprophytes, 60
  of mineral matter, 62
  splenic, 552
Metabolites, protein, 35, 129
Metaglobulin, 125
Metaprotein, 23
Metazoa, 11
Methaemoglobin, 125
Microcytes, 101
Migratory cells, 175
Milk, clotting, 135
Mimosa pudica, 53
Mineral matter, cell, 37
  matter, metabolism, 62
  matter, serum, 131
Mitral valve, 190
Molecular concentration, 141
Monism, 6
Monosaccharides, 36
Morphology, 2
Mosquitoes, coagulation, 121
Motor nerves, respiration, 441
Mountain sickness, 474

Movements, amoeboid, 16, 74, 117
  arterial, 277
  cardiopneumatic, 227
  pulmonary, 426, 442
Mucoid, serum, 126
Murmurs, bronchial, 427
  cardiac, 198
  vesicular, 427
Muscle, bronchial, 442
  cardiac, 285
  respiration of, 394
  sound of, 197
  vascular, 427
Muscles, expiratory, 419
  inspiratory, 409
  of neck, 410
  of thorax, 412
Muscular dyspnoea, 471
Mutation, 51
Myocardium, 182, 312
  conductivity, 313
  excitability, 313
Myogenic theory, heart, 307
Myosin, 23
Myosinogen, 23
Myxomycetes, protoplasm, 15

Nägelism, 49
Narcosis, leucocytes, 178
Nasal mucosa, respiration, 465
Nasal respiratory movements, 422
Neo-Darwinism, 47
Neo-Lamarckism, 49
Neo-vitalism, 5
Nepenthes, 55
Nerve cells, survival, 310
Nerves, afferent cardiac, 333, 360
  afferent, respiratory, 457
  bronchial, 442
  efferent cardiac, 322, 327
  efferent lymphatic, 517
  efferent, respiratory, 411
  neck, rabbit, 334
  respiratory exchange, 392
  secretory, 522
  submaxillary gland, 343, 522
  vasomotor, 341
Nervi erigentes, 355
Neurogenic theory, heart, 310
Nitrifying bacteria, 57
Nitrogen, 372
  blood, 377, 386
  expired air, 397
Nodulus Arantii, 187
"Nœud vital," 444
Non-electrolytes, 142
Nucleic acid, 24
  acid, coagulation, 138
Nuclein, 23, 35, 49
Nucleohistone, 138
Nucleolus, 39
Nucleoproteins, 23, 24
Nucleus, anterolateral, 363

Nucleus cell, 13
  cell, chemistry, 39
  cell, structure, 19
Nutrition, 64

Occlusion of trachea, 460
Octadecapeptide, 29
Oedema, 520
Oenothera, 52
Oesophageal sound, 429
Olfactory nerves, respiration. 465
Oligocythaemia, 152
Ontogeny, 2, 46
Optic nerve, respiration, 465
Optical activity, protein, 21
Organisms, elementary, 11
  aërobic, 68
  anaërobic, 68
Osazones, 37
Osmotic pressure, blood, 142
  pressure, fish, 145
  pressure, lymph, 515
  pressure, serum, 147
Ovalbumin, 23
Ovomucoid, 126
Oxalates, coagulation, 125
Oxidases, 33
Oxygen, absorption, lung, 389
  blood, 380
  discovery, 372
  expired air, 389, 397
  haemoglobin. 383
  heart, 293
  intermolecular, 394
  life, 68
  nerve centres, 394
Oxyhaemoglobin, 106
  dissociation, 295
Oxyproline, 27
Oxypyrrolidine-carboxylic acid, 27

Palaeontology, 2
Pancreas of Aselli, 533
Panteplankton, 83
Papain, 32, 54
Paracasein, 136
Paraglobulin, 126
Paralysis, 73
Paramoecium, galvanotaxis. 80
  geotaxis, 77
Parasites, 60
Partial pressure, respiration, 389
Patches of Peyer, 530
Pause, cardiac, 180
  respiratory, 199
Pentoses, 24
Pepsin, 32
Peptones, 23
Percussion, lungs, 425
Perfusion, 289
Pericardium, fistula, 209, 215
  pressure, 219

Periodic respiration, 492, 494
Peripheral stream, 189
Perisystole, 180
Perivascular lymphatics, 507
Pernicious anaemia, 539
Peroxidases, 33
Phagocytes, 18, 115, 178, 537
Phaoplankton, 83
Phases, heart, Luciani's, 302
Phenomena, objective and subjective, 6
  psychical, 7
  vital, 1, 12
Phenomenalism, 7
Phenyl-alanine, 27
Phenyl-glucosazone, 37
Phenyl-hydrazine, 37
Phlebograms, 204
Phlogiston, 373
Phlogosin, 178
Phosphates, cell, 48
Phosphoproteins, 23, 24
Phosphorus, reaction, 39
Photomorphosis, 49
Phototaxis, 78
Phrenic nerves, 141
Phrenograph, 416
Phylogeny, 2, 46
Physical basis of life, 11
Physiology, scope, 3
Piezometer, 233
Pigments, 25
"Pince cardiographique," 289
Pinocytosis, 534
Pitot tubes, 234
Plankton. 82
Plants and animals, 53, 55
  insectivorous. 55
Plasma, blood, 123, 142
  carbohydrates, 130
  electrical conductivity, 144, 149
  fats, 130
  gas, 132
  histogenic matter, 93, 126
  histolytic matter, 93
  incoagulable, 124
  inorganic matter, 131
  molecular concentration, 141
  osmotic pressure, 142
  proteins, 125, 126
  viscosity, 151
  lymph, 513
Plasmodium, 113
Plateau, systolic, 206
Platelets, blood, 117
  blood, coagulation, 134
Plethora, 100
Plethysmograms, 216, 279
Plethysmographs, 278, 344
Pleural cavity, 403, 425
Pluralism, 7
Pneumograph, 415
Pneumoplethysmograph, 425
Pneumothorax, 406

Poikilocytes, 101
Polycythaemia, 153
Polypeptides, 23, 28
Polypnoea, 470
Polysaccharides, 37
Post-mortem lymph. 515
Potential energy, 68
Pressure, alveolar, 405, 424
  arterial, 241, 243, 253
  capillary, 253
  intra-abdominal, 427
  intracardiac. 201, 208
  intrathoracic, 406, 427
  lymphatic, 513, 516
  osmotic, 141
  pericardial, 219
Presystole, 180
Pro-enzymes, 30
Proline, 27
Propeptones, 23
Prosthetic group, protein, 24
Protagon, 35
Protamines, 23, 24
Proteins, 20
  classification, 23
  cleavage, 26, 28
  coagulation, 21
  conjugated, 23, 24
  of plasma, 125, 126
  properties, 21
  reactions, 21, 22
  respiratory quotient, 399
  structure, 25
Proteoses, 23
Prothrombin, 137
Protista, 13
Protistology, 3
Protoplasm, 17, 18
  myxomycetes, 15
Protozoa, 11
Pseudopodia, 16
Ptyalin. 33
Pulmonary arterial pressure, 254
  catheter, 388
  circulation, discovery, 160
  epithelium, absorption, 391
  gas exchanges, 387
Pulp, splenic. 547
Pulse, arterial, 263
  cardiac, 221
  negative cardiac. 227
  negative pulmonary, 227
  negative thoracic. 227
  negative venous. 203, 227
  wave, 240, 271
Purine, 24
Pus, 115
Pycnometer, 95
Pyrimidine, 24

Quantity of blood, 99
  of lymph, 514
Quotient. respiratory. 398

Radial sphygmogram, 264
Radiolaria. 11
Reaction of blood, 94
  of lymph, 513
Reactions of carbohydrates, 36
  of proteins, 21
Receptaculum Chyli, 517
Rectal sound. 129
Red blood corpuscles, vide Erythrocytes
Reductase, 34
Reduction, by carbohydrates, 36
Reflexes. cardiac, 336
  respiratory, 464
  vascular, 357
Refractory period, heart, 320
Regeneration, 84
  blood, 152
Reproduction, 43
Reserve air, 423
Residual air, 423
Resistance capacity, 150
Respiration, abdominal, 416
  adaptation, 469
  afferent nerves, 457
  chemistry and physics, 369
  Cheyne-Stokes, 492
  efferent nerves. 441
  external, 376
  internal, 375, 393
  lungs, 472, 473
  mechanics, 402, 433
  nerve centres, 394
  nervous control, 440
  periodic, 492
  rhythm, 437. 440
Respiratory centres, 443, 451, 452, 464
  centres, expiratory, 454
  centres, inhibitory, 452
  exchanges, 379, 392
  hemiplegia, 444
  movements, 416
  pause, 490
  pressures, 429
  quotient. 398
  quotient, carbohydrates. 399
  quotient, fats. 399
  quotient, proteins. 399
Revolution of heart, 180
Rheotaxis, 76
Rhizobium, 58
Rhizopoda, 13
Rhythm, heart, 333
  respiration, 437. 440
  respiration, automaticity. 461
  respiration control, 440
  respiration, periodic, 492
Rhythmicity. heart. 298. 322
Ribs, 408

Saccharomyces cerevisiae, 59, 60
Saccharoses, 37
Salmine, 23
Salts, 57

Salts, heart, 295
Saprophytes, 57, 69
Sarkine, 35
Scalene muscles, 410
Schizomycetes, 57
Sciatic nerve, vaso-constrictors, 351
Sclero-proteins, 23, 25
Scombrine, 24
Scotoplankton, 83
Secretion, and lymph formation, 522
   of lymph, 519
Selection, germinal, 50
   natural, 46
Self-steering action of heart, 210
Semilunar valves, 187
Semipermeable membranes, 141
Sensations, 6, 45
Sensibility, 45
Sensitive plants, 53
Septum, auricular, 299
Serin, 126
Serine, 27
Sero-mucoid, 126
Serous cavities, 514
   effusions, 515
Serum, 97, 127
   ash, 131
   carbohydrates, 130
   conductivity, 150
   enzymes, 127
   fats, 127
   measurement of osmotic pressure, 141, 147
   toxicity, 153
Serum albumin, 126, 128
   globulin, 126
Silkworm, 70
Sinus of Valsalva, 187
   venosus, 286
Skeleton, thoracic, 407
Sleep, 501
Sneezing, 438
Soaps, plasma, 130
Sobbing, 438
Solutions, colloid, 21
   laws of, 141
   normal physiological, 293
Sound, exploring, cardiographic, 200
   exploring, oesophageal, 228, 406, 429
   exploring, rectal, 429
   muscle, 197
Sounds, heart, 196
Spaces, lymphatic, 509
Species, 46
Spectrophotometer, 109
Sphygmograms, analysis, 271
Sphygmographs, 264
Sphygmomanometer, 245
Sphygmoscope, 205
Spinal centres, respiratory, 451
   centres, splenic, 554
   centres, vasomotor, 362, 364

Spiritus igneo-aereus, 372
Spiritus nitro-aereus, 372
Spirograph, 425
Spirometer, 422
Spirostomum, 81
Splanchnic nerves, blood-vessels, 348
   lymph vessels, 518
   respiration, 465
Spleen, 545
   cells, 549
   contractility, 553
   extirpation, 550
   haemapoiesis, 550
   haemolysis, 551
   lymphapoiesis, 552
   metabolism, 552
   nerves, 549
   nerve centres, 554
Spongin, 23, 25
Staircase, heart, 318
Staphylococcus, 178
Starch, 37
Steapsin, 33
Stentor, 14
Sternum, asthma, 410
Stethograph, 415
Stimuli, 73
   chemical, 73
   electrical, 80
   internal, 83
   luminous, 78
   mechanical, 76
   thermal, 77
Stomata, 510
Stromata, erythrocytes, 106
Stromuhr, 257
Sturine, 23
Submaxillary gland, 343
Substances, histogenic and histolytic, 93, 126
Sugars, 36
Sulphates, 38
Sulpho-methaemoglobin, 110
Sulphur, protein, 22
Sulphur metabolism, bacteria, 65
Suppuration, 115, 178
Surface area, capillaries, 263
   thoracic, 417
Survival, heart, 298
   nerve centres, 310
Suspension of artery, 245
   of heart, 290
Suspensions, colloid, 21
Swimming-bladder, gas of, 390
Symbiosis, 58
Sympathetic nerve, blood-vessels, 342
   nerve, heart, 328
Syncytium, 15
System, circulatory, 157, 180
   lymphatic, 505
   respiratory, 369
   vegetative and animal, 92
Systole, 185

Systole, aspiration, 208
  latent, 206
Systolic plateau, 206

Tachograms, 275
Tachypnoea, 461, 470
Tambour, recording, 201
Temperature, and life, 70
Tension of gases, alveolar air, 590
  of gases in atmosphere, 388
  of gases in blood, 388, 389
  of gases in expired air, 389
Tetanus, electrical, 80
  mechanical, 76
  thermal, 77
Thallassicolla, 14
Thermal dyspnoea, 470
  stimuli, 77
Thermomorphosis, 49
Thermotaxis, 78
Thigmotaxis, 76
Thoracic duct, 171
  respiration, 416
Thoracometer, 415
Thorax, skeleton, 407
  surface area, 417
Thrombin, 137
Thrombokinase, 139
Thrombosin, 135
Thrombosis, 133
Thymine, 24
Thymus, 540
  extirpation, 542
  feeding, 545
  structure, 541
Tidal air, 122
Tissue, lymphoid, 528
Tissues, 13
  and lymph, 505
  respiration of, 393
Tone, arterial, 262, 344, 346
Tonicity, heart, 319
Tonograph, heart, 288
Tonometer, arterial, 244, 252
Tortoise, heart, 286
Trachea, 403
Tradescantia, 18
Transfusion, blood, 152
Transplantations, 13
Transudation, lymph, 524
Tricuspid valve, 191
Trypsin, 32
Tryptophane, 27
Tubes, bronchial, 403
  elastic, 239
Types of respiration, 416
Tyrosine, 27

Ultramicroscope, 21
Uracil, 24
Urea, 33, 35
  heart, 297
  plasma, 129

Urease, 33
Uric acid, 129, 552
Urobilin, 109

Vacuoles, cell, 18
Vago-sympathetic trunk, 328, 353
Vagus, apnoea, 479, 488
  cardiac, 218
  cardiac, anabolic action, 332
  cardiac, bathmotropic effect, 327
  cardiac, chronotropic effect, 325
  cardiac, dromotropic effect, 326
  cardiac, inotropic effect, 326
  laryngeal, 464
  pulmonary, afferent fibres, 462
  pulmonary, efferent fibres, 442
  pulmonary, section of, 462
Valve, Eustachian, 182
Valves, cardiac, auriculo-ventricular
    192
  cardiac, semilunar, 187
  veins, 165
Variability of species, 45, 47
Variation, 47
  and Quetelet's law, 48
Vaso-constrictor centres, 361
  nerves, 347
Vaso-dilatator centres, 365
  nerves, 350
Vasomotor centres, 361
  nerves, 341
  nerves, ear, 343
  nerves, head and neck, 348
  nerves, limbs, 349, 354
  reflexes, 357
  viscera, 348
Veins, pressure in, 253
  pulsation, 203
  valves of, 165
  velocity in, 262
Velocity, blood, 174, 263
  in arteries, 256, 261
  in capillaries, 263
  of lymph formation, 523
  in veins, 262
  of lymph, 516
Vena arteriosa, 159
Venosity of blood, dyspnoea, 469
Venous pressure, 253
  pulse, 203
  valves, 165
Ventilation, lungs, 423, 484, 487
Ventricles, pressure in, 201
  structure, 183
  systole and diastole, 185
Vessels, blood, 541
  lacteal, 171
  lymphatic, 506
Vicia faba, 58
Viscosimeter, 151
Viscosity, blood, 151
Vital capacity, 423
Vitalism, 5

Vitellin, 23
Volume, heart, 215
Voluntary apnoea, 180
Vortices, arterial, 189

Water, life, 66
Wave, pulse, 240
  dicrotic, 269
  velocity, 273
Work, heart, 230

Xanthine, 21, 130, 298, 55
Xanthoproteic test, 22

Yawning, 438

Zea mais, 59
Zoospores, 16
Zymase, 30
  blood, 127
Zymogens, 30

INDEX OF AUTHORS

ABDERHALDEN, amino-acids, 26
  physiological chemistry, 39
  proteins, 26
ABELOUS, thymus, 543, 557
ADAM, automatism of heart, 306
  resuscitation of heart, 298
ADAMI, accelerator nerves, 329
  systole, 182
ADAMKIEWICS, intrathoracic pressure,
  427
ADAMS, G. P., phototropism, 90
ADAMUK, vasomotor centres, 365
ADDISON, W., coagulation of blood, 133
  diapedesis, 175
ADUCCO, active expiration, 420, 439
  bulbar centres, 448, 449, 489, 504
  physiology, text-book, 9
  respiratory centres, 454
ALBANESE, oxygen and heart, 293
  viscosity of blood, 151
ALBERTONI, accelerator nerves, 329
  cocaine and protoplasm, 102
  peptone blood, 124
  transfusion, 153
ALBINI, diastolic aspiration, 211
ALBRECHT, active diastole, 214
ARANTIUS, intercostal muscles, 411
  nodule of, 187
ARISTOTLE, respiration, 369, 380
ARLOING, heart, 231
  vagus, 324
ARNOLD, lymphatic organs, 557
ALON, intrathoracic pressure, 427
ARRHENIUS, electric conductivity, 149
  ionisation, 142
  solutions, 142
ARRONET, plasma and corpuscles, 125
ARRONS, isolation of heart, 291
D'ARSONVAL, expired air, 397
ARTHUS, coagulation of blood 136
  lipase of blood, 127
ASELLI, pancreas of, 533
  lymphatic system, 171, 505
ASHER, formation of lymph, 526, 558
  injection of lymph, 533
  innervation of blood-vessels, 367
  post-mortem lymph, 515

ASHER, tissue lymph, 527 557
ASP, cardiac reflexes, 336
  splanchnics, 348
AUBERT, cardiac vagus, 336

BACCELLI, heart-beat, 222
  spleen, 553
BACHMAN, conditions of cardiac activity
  298, 338
BAGLIONI, apnoea, 491
  nerve centres and oxygen, 394
  respiratory reflexes, 466, 504
  urea and heart, 297, 338
BAHR, heart-beat, 225
BAIN, spleen, 551, 558
BAINBRIDGE, post-mortem lymph, 515,
  558
BALDWIN, T. M., development and
  evolution, 63
BALEAN, H., blood, 122
BAMBERGER, heart-beat, 225
BANCROFT, J. W., galvanotaxis, 90
BARBERA, injection of lymph, 533, 557
  tissue lymph, 527, 557
BARCROFT, J., blood gases, 401
  blood, urea, 156
  metabolism, 400, 401
BARKAI, glycolysis in blood, 127
BARRY, mechanics of thoracic move-
  ments, 429
BARTHOLIN, circulation, 166
  formation of lymph, 519
  intercostal muscles, 411
  lymphatic system, 172, 505
BARTLETT, J. H., blood pressure, 459
BASCH, thymus, 545
v. BASCH, plethysmograph, 344
  sphygmomanometer, 245
BATESON, evolution, 62, 63
BAUMANN, E. P., haemorrhage, 156
BAUMGARTEN, auriculo-ventricular
  valves, 192
BAXT, accelerator nerves, 330
  cardiac nerves, 331, 338
BAYLE, respiration, 412
BAYLISS, W. M., acceleration of heart
  330

BAYLISS, W. M., cardiac vagus, 326
  caseinogen, 40
  intracardiac pressure, 201, 207
  systole, 206
  vascular tone, 346, 368
  vaso-constrictors of limbs, 349
  vaso-dilatators of limbs, 354, 367
  vasomotor reflexes, 368
BEALE, coagulation of blood, 133
BEAU, heart-beat, 222
  intercostal muscles, 411, 439
  thoracic respiration, 417
BEAUNIS, physiology, text-book, 9
BECCARI, venous pulse, 203
BECHT, F. C., salivary glands, 558
BECHTEREW, vasomotor centres, 366
BECKMANN, cryoscopy, 148
BEHRING, bacteriolytic functions of
  blood, 154
BELFIELD, vascular reflexes, 360
BELL, law of, 354
v. BENEDEN, centrosome, 13
BENEDIKT, S. R., heart, 339
BERARD, active diastole, 213
  auriculo-ventricular valves, 192
  elasticity of blood-vessels, 239
BERGENDAHL, intercartilaginous
  muscles, 415
BERGMANN, intercartilaginous muscles,
  415
  respiration, 373, 400
BERKELEY, phenomenalism, 7
BERKLEY, myocardium, 314
BERKOWITSCH, vasomotor centres, 363
BERNARD, anaesthetics on animals and
  plants, 53
  blood pressure, 253
  cardiac reflexes, 336
  cardiac vagus, 323
  cervical sympathetic, 341, 348
  chorda tympani, 341, 350, 367
  facial nerve, 348
  general physiology, 89
  haemodiastase, 137
  sensibility and excitability, 45
  tissue respiration, 394
  vaso-constrictors of limbs, 349, 367
  vasomotor centres, 362, 367
  vasomotor reflexes, 356
BERNS, apnoea, 185
BERNSTEIN, cardiac centres, 337
  foetal lungs, 105
  spirograph, 125, 439
  vascular tone, 346
  vasomotor nerves, 352
BERT, atmospheric pressure, 72
  bronchial muscles, 442
  negative pulse, 227
  oxygen of blood, 381, 400
  plants and oxygen, 56
  rectal explorer, 429
  respiratory tracings, 424
  thoracograph, 415

BERT, tissue respiration, 393
BERTOLUS, velocity of blood stream,
  275
BERZELIUS, blood, 91
BETHE, neurogenic theory, 310
BEUTNER, intracardiac pressure, 208
BEVER, accelerators of heart, 327
  splanchnic nerve, 347, 367
BLYER, H. G., vasomotor centre, 367
BLYERINCK, nitrifying bacteria, 58
v. BEZOLD, accelerators of heart, 327
  cardiac vagus, 324, 336, 337
  splanchnic nerve, 347, 367
  vascular reflexes, 359, 367
  vasomotor centres, 362, 367
  water content of organism, 38
BIAL, haemodiastase, 127
BICHAT, animal and vegetable life, 91
  cardiac ganglia, 299
  cardiac diastole, 208
  lymph, 509
BIDDER, cardiac ganglia, 299, 305
  cardiac vagus, 333
BIEDERMANN, invertebrate heart, 311
BIELETZKY, experimental apnoea, 484
BILLARD, thymus, 543, 557
BIOT, periodic respiration, 502
BISCHOFF, quantity of the blood, 99
  respiration, 377
BIZZOZERO, blood-platelets, 118
  coagulation of blood, 134
  giant-cells, 535
  haemorrhage, 152, 539
  lymphatic canaliculi, 511
  marrow, 534, 557
  serous cavities, 511
  spleen, 550, 552
BLACK, respiration, 373, 400
BLACKMAN, J. R., auricular rhythm,
  339
BOCHEFONTAINE, vasomotor centres, 365
BOCKER, respiratory centres, 453
BOERHAAVE, intercostal muscles, 411
BOHM, accelerators of heart, 329
  lymph follicle, 532
  marrow, 536
  solitary follicles, 529
  thymus, 541
BOHR, blood gases, 383, 386, 390, 400
  carbon dioxide and haemoglobin, 386
  oxyhaemoglobin, 395, 396
BORDET, chemotaxis, leucocytes, 75, 178
BORDONI, experimental apnoea, 484
  periodic respiration, 494, 502, 504
BORELLI, intercostal muscles, 403, 411
  respiration, 439
BORUTTAU, nervous mechanism of respiration 501
BOTAZZI, embryonic heart, 309, 321,
  337
  osmotic pressure of blood, 144, 145,
  155
  physiological chemistry, 39

BOTAZZI, tonicity of heart, 319
  viscosity of blood, 151, 155
BOTKIN, spleen, 553
BOTSCHETSCHKAROFF, spleen, 555
BÖTTGER, test for sugar, 36
BOURDON, manometer, 277
BOUSSINGAULT, animals and plants, 55
BOVERI, centrosome, 13
BOWDITCH, cardiac accelerators, 329
  preparation of, 295, 303, 317, 337
  staircase phenomenon, 318
  vasomotor nerves, 352
BOYCOTT, A. E., respiration, 489
BOYLE, law of, 378
  respiration, 371, 378, 400
BRACHET, active diastole, 213
BRADFORD, vascular reflexes, 357
  vaso-constrictors of limbs, 349
  vaso-dilatators of viscera, 355
BRANDE, gas extraction, 377
BRANTLECHT, proteins, 40
v. BRASOL, formation of lymph, 525
BRAUER, centrosome, 13
BREDIG, catalysators, 31, 40
BREFELD, heat, B. Anthracis, 71
BREUER, respiratory rhythm, 459
  inspiratory centres, 456, 503
BRODIE, T. G., bronchial muscle, 504
  heart, 338
  metabolism, 401
  perfusion, 339
  pulmonary vasomotors, 368
  serum injections, 156
BROWN, bronchial nerves, 442
  blood pressure, 245
BROWN, A. E., specific characters, 63
BROWN, O. H., blood pressure, 284
BROWN-SÉQUARD, cardiac vagus, 323, 353
  cervical sympathetic, 342, 367
  experimental apnoea, 476
  respiratory centres, 444, 452, 504
  toxicity of expired air, 397
  vascular reflexes, 357
  vasomotor centres, 364
BRÜCKE, blood plasma, 123
  coagulation of blood, 133
  elementary organisms, 8
  heart, self-steering, 210
  intercostal muscles, 412
  lymphatic glands, 533, 557
  semilunar valves, 187
  spleen, 553
BRÜGH VAN DER, intrathoracic pressure, 427
BUCHANAN, coagulation of blood, 134
BUCHNER, ferments, 30
  tissue respiration, 393
  zymase, 34
BUCHNER, H., alexines, 154
BUDGE, cardiac nerve centres, 336
  cardiac vagus, 322, 335, 337
  cervical sympathetic, 348

BUDGE, neurogenic theory, 307
  vasomotor centres, 365
BUDGETT, galvanotaxis, 80
BUFALINI, heart, accelerators, 329
BUFFON, animals and plants, 1
BUGARSKY, serum, osmotic pressure, 144
BUGLIA, non-coagulable plasma, 124, 155
BUISSON, arterial pulse, 265
  negative pulse, 227
  plethysmograph, 278
BULGAK, spleen centres, 554
BUNGE, blood plasma, separation, 125
  plasma ash, 131
BUNSEN, absorption of gas, 378
  partial pressure, 379
BURCKHARDT, plasma, 126
BURDACH, heart-beat, 222
  intercostal muscles, 411
BURDON-SANDERSON, cardiograph, 267
  sphygmograph, 267
  stethograph, 415
BURKART, expiratory rhythm, 486
BURTON-OPITZ, R., blood, viscosity, 156
  venous flow, 284
  venous pressure, 284
BÜTSCHLI, cell, bacteria, 13
  cell, structure, 17, 19

CADMAN, A. W., cardiac nerve fibres, 338
  respiratory nerve fibres, 335
CAMIS, J., blood, dissociation curve, 401
CAMUS, lymphatic vessels, 517, 557
CATORI, venous valves, 165
CANNANUS, venous valves, 165
CARBONE, coagulation of blood, 155
  fibrin ferment, 128
CARDARELLI, cardiac vagus, 323
CARLILE, heart-beat, 224
  cardiac systole, 186
CARLSON, A. J., haemolytic lymph, 559
  heart, inhibition, 329
  heart, invertebrate, 339, 340
  heart, refractory period, 339
  lymph formation, 526, 559
  neurogenic theory, 311, 337
  salivary glands, 558
  vasomotor nerves, 354, 368
CARNOY, structure of protoplasm, 17
CARPENTER, active diastole, 214
CARSWELL, heart-sounds, 196
CASPARI, acapnia, 475, 501
CASTELL, oxygen and heart, 293
CAVANI, vascular reflexes, 358, 367
CAVAZZANI, E., haemodiastase, 127
  red blood corpuscles, 101
CAVENDISH, composition of water, 374
CECCHINI, splen ectomy, 557
CIRADINI, auxocardia and meiocardia, 186, 227

CERADINI, circulation of blood, 161, 179
   diastolic aspiration, 212
   heart, self-steering, 211
   semilunar valves, 187, 231
CELALSATO, thymus, 545
CESALPINUS, circulation, 163
   respiration, 371
CESARIS DIMEL, red blood-corpuscles,
   101
CHARCOT, vasomotor centres, 365
CHAUVEAU, auriculo-ventricular valves,
   193
   cardiac sound, 201
   haemodromograph, 211, 274
   heart, 231
   heart-beat, 225
   intersystole, 196, 201
   intracardiac pressure, 201, 206
   sphygmoscope, 214
   systolic aspiration, 210
   velocity of blood stream, 274
CHELIUS, plethysmograph, 278
CHEVREUL, blood, 94
CHEYNE, periodic respiration, 492
CHORIOL, active diastole, 213
CHRISTIANI, cerebral respiratory centres,
   153
CHUN, Valdivia expedition, 81
CIAMICIAN, sero-mucoids, 126
CIGNA, respiration, 373
CLARKE, antero-lateral nucleus, 363
CLARKE T. W., sulph-haemoglobin,
   122
COATS, diastole, 209,
   cardiac vagus, 325, 338
COHNHEIM, J., diapedesis, 115, 175
   leucocytes, 115
   lymph formation, 524
   splanchnic nerve, 348
COHNHEIM, O., erepsin, 32, 34
COHNSTEIN, lymph formation, 524, 557
COLASANTI, dyspnoea, 470
   lactic acid in urine, 470
COLL, proteins, 40
COLIN, intracardiac pressure, 208
COLOMBO, blood pressure, 248, 256
COLUMBUS, REALDUS, circulation, 160
CONCATO, cardiac vagus, 323
CONKLIN, E. S., mutation, 63
CONNSTEIN, fats and blood, 127
CONSIGLIO, depressor nerve, 335
   vascular reflexes, 356
COOPER, capillary circulation, 172
CORRIGAN, heart-beat, 222
COSSY, vaso-dilatators, 354
CRAMER, W., protagon, 10
CRAMPTON, H. E., adaptation, 63
CREDI, splenectomy, 555
CULONI, evolution, 52
CUFFER, periodic respiration, 491
CULLIS, W. C., perfusion, 339
CUSANO, arterial pulse, 264
CUSHNY, A. R., heart rhythm, 231

CUVIER, animals and plants, 53
   intercostal muscles, 411
CYON, accelerator nerves, 327, 337
   cardiac nerves, 337
   depressor nerves, 333, 360
   splanchnic nerves, 347
   vaso-constrictor nerves, 349
   vasomotor centres, 366
CZERMACK, cardiac vagus, 224
CZERNY, splenectomy, 555

DAKIN, H. D., oxidation of amino-acids,
   40
   oxidation of fat, 41
DALAND, molecular concentration, 148
DALE, H. H., galvanotaxis, 90
DALLY, J. F. H., diaphragm, 439
DALTON, diffusion of gases, 378
DANILEWSKY, injection of marrow and
   spleen, 539, 558
   vasomotor nerves, 365
DARBISHIRE, A. D., heredity, 63
DARCY, hydrodynamics, 189
DARWIN, doctrine of descent, 46, 62
   insectivorous plants, 53
DASTRE, coagulation of blood, 137
   cervical sympathetic, 349, 353, 367
   extra-systole, 321
   splenectomy, 555, 558
   vascular reflexes, 361
   vasomotor nerves, 353, 366
DAVENPORT, C. D., evolution, 63
v. DAVIDOFF, marrow, 536
   thymus, 541
DAVIS, B. F., lymph, 559
DAVY, H., extraction of gas, 177
   residual air, 423
DAVY, J., blood gases, 377
DAWSON, P. M., blood pressure, 284
DEAHNA, vasomotor centres, 366
DEITERS, formatio reticularis, 446
DELAGE, Y., evolution, 62
DELEZENNE, anti-kinase, 128
   coagulation of blood, 139
DENCKE, resuscitation of heart, 298
DENYS, lymphatic organs, 557
DELITO, evolution, 62
DEW-SMITH, heart of invertebrates, 311
DIEMERBROECK, intercostal muscles, 411
DINEUR, galvanotaxis, 81
DITTMAR, vasomotor centres, 363, 364
DIXON, W. E., bronchial muscle, 504
   heart, 401
   pulmonary vasomotors, 368
DOGIEL, heart-sounds, 197
   serous cavities, 509
   vascular reflexes, 360
   velocity of blood stream, 260
DONDERS, acceleration of heart rhythm,
   181
   auriculo-ventricular groove, 314
   cardiac vagus, 324
   diastolic aspiration, 211

DONDERS, expiration, 419
  intrapulmonary pressure, 105
  human physiology, 231
  lungs during respiration, 425
  mechanics of thoracic movements, 421, 436
  surface of thorax, 417
  waves, 241
DOUGLAS, circulation of blood, 160
DOUGLAS, C. G., Cheyne-Stokes breathing, 504
  quantity of blood, 122
  regulation of respiration, 504
DOYON, accelerators of heart, 327
  lipase of blood, 127
  nerves of neck, rabbit, 334
DRESCHFELD, cardiac vagus, 356
DROSDOFF, spleen, 555
DRUMMOND, haemolymphatic glands, 557
DU BOIS-REYMOND, E., dualism, 6
DU BOIS-REYMOND, R., intercartilaginous muscles, 414
  mechanics of respiration, 439
  respiratory movements, 466
DUCCHESCHI, blood osmotic pressure, 144, 145
  blood plasma, 127
  muscular tone, 319
  sphygmography, 284
DUCHENNE, diaphragm, 410, 450
  intercostal muscles, 411
  scalene muscles, 410
DECLAUX, anaerobic organisms, 69
DUKE, W. W., heart, 339
DUMAS, animals and plants, 55
  blood, 94
DUNCAN, diffusion of gases, 379
DURANTE, thrombosis, 133
DUTROCHET, endosmometer, 141

v. EBNER, intercostal muscles, 412
  intercostal spaces, 409
EBSTEIN, E., diastole, 231
ECKER, spleen, 549
ECKHARD, automaticity of heart, 305, 311
  cardiac vagus, 324, 327
  heart of invertebrates, 311
  nervi erigentes, 350, 355, 367
  neurogenic theory, 307, 357
  vascular reflexes, 359
  vasomotor centre, 365
EDELBERG, coagulation of blood, 138
EDGREN, cardiograms, 224, 231, 268
  heart-sounds, 197
  latent systole, 206
  sphygmograph and sphygmograms, 267
  velocity of pulse wave, 273
EDWARDS, W., respiration, 376, 400
EFCKE ver, thymus, 544
EGGERS, H. E., sinus venosus, 339

EGLI-SINCLAIR, periodic respiration, 493
EHRENBERG, infusoria and temperature, 71
EHRLICH, anaerobic organisms, 69
  examination of blood, 120
  leucocytes, 114
  red blood-corpuscles, 100
EICHHORST, cardiac vagus, 351
EINBRODT, mechanics of respiration and circulation, 433
EINTHOVEN, intrathoracic pressure, 427
ELLINGER, lymph formation, 526, 558
EMILIANOW, splenectomy, 556, 558
EMMINGHAUS, lymph formation, 520
ENGEL, blood, 121
  blood-platelets, 119
  leucocytes, 114
ENGELMANN, active vasodilatation, 347
  auriculo-ventricular bundle, 314
  bacterium photometricum, 78
  cardiac nerves, 325, 351
  cardiogram, 290
  chemotaxis, 74
  compensatory pause, 321
  electrical stimuli, 80
  heart, suspension, 290
  myogenic theory, 308, 314, 337
  oxygen and ciliary movement, 68
ENGSTRÖM, fœtal apnœa, 478
VAN ENSCHUT, blood gases, 377
ERASISTRATUS, arterial pulse, 261
  circulation of blood, 159
  diastole, 208
  lacteals, 171
  respiration, 370
ERL, marrow, 559
ERLANGER, J., auricular rhythm, 339
  auriculo-ventricular bundle, 315
  heart-block, 339
  heart, conduction, 340
D'ERRICO, lymphagogues, 523
  post-mortem lymph, 515
EULENBURG, vasomotor centres, 365
EULER, enzymes and catalysators, 82
EUSTACHIUS, lymphatic system, 171
  valve of, 182
EWALD, experimental apnœa, 481, 504
  intrathoracic pressure, 427
EYKMAN, molecular concentration, 148
EYSTER, J. A. E., extra-systole, 339

FABRICIUS, valves of veins, 165
FAIVRE, blood pressure, 253
  heart beat, 225
FANO, active movements of lungs, 442
  coagulation of blood, 134, 140
  embryonic heart, 309
  histogenic substances of plasma, 127
  metabolism of heart, 332
  myogenic theory, 308, 337
  oscillations of auricular tonicity, 319

FANO, osmotic pressure of blood, 144, 155
  oxygen and heart, 293
  peptone blood, 124
  periodic respiration, 493, 497, 504
  platelets, 118
  sp. gr. of blood, 95
  tissue respiration, 395
  tonicity of heart, 319
  vascular reflexes, 357
FANTINO, cardiac vagus, 333
FARKAS, reaction of blood, 94
FASOLA, active movements of lungs, 442
FEDERICO, urea and heart, 297
FERNET, gases of blood, 383, 385
FICK, A., diaphragm, 417, 439
  diastole, 209, 213
  expiration, 419
  heart beat, 313
  intercostal muscles, 412
  intracardiac pressure, 201
  manometer, 214
  medical physics, 283
  plethysmograph, 278, 281
  pulse, 284
  thoracograph, 415
  work of heart, 230
FICK, R., respiratory muscles, 415, 439
FILEHNE, periodic respiration, 194, 498
FILHOS, active diastole, 213
FISCHER, E., enzymes, 31
  phenyl-glucosazone, 57
  poly-peptides, 28, 39
  proteins, 26, 39
FITZGERALD, M. P., alveolar carbon dioxide, 459
FLACK, M., respiration and circulation, 439
FLEMMING, examination of blood, 120
  lymph follicle, 529
FLETCHER, W. M., oxygen and muscle, 90, 401
FLOURENS, circulation, 162
  nœud vital, 444
  periodic respiration, 494, 503
FLUGGI, bactericidal properties of blood, 154
FOA, marrow, 539
  megacaryocytes, 538, 557
  platelets, 119, 121
  spleen, 557
FODOR, bactericidal properties of blood, 154
FONTANA, extraction of gas, 377
  gas of blood, 377
  sleep, 502
FORMANEK, expired air, 597
FOSTER, M., active vasodilatation, 547
  cardiac nerves, 328
  circulation of blood, 163, 179
  invertebrate heart, 311
  lymphatic circulation, 517
  phrenograph, 416

FOSTER, M., tissue respiration, 395
FOWLER, marrow, 539
  spleen, 550, 556, 558
FRACASSATI, respiration, 372, 400
  thoracic duct, 171
FRANCHINI, inhibitory centres in bulb, 452
  pulmonary vagus, 463
FRANCK, nitrifying bacteria, 58
FRANCOIS-FRANCK, accelerators of heart, 330
  cardiac plethysmograph, 289
  cardiac reflexes, 336
  cardiac vagus, 218, 326, 329, 335, 338
  cardiograms, 223
  centres of cardiac nerves, 336
  heart, suspension, 291
  pericardial fistula, 215
  plethysmograph, 278
  respiratory centres, 453
  vascular reflexes, 357
  vasomotor centres, 365
FRANK, R. T., conductivity of blood, 156
FRANKEL, gas of blood, 384, 400, 474
FRANZEI, periodic respiration, 502
FRASSINETTO, DI, plasma, 127
FREDERICQ, aerotonometer, 388
  apnœa vera, 476, 504
  circulation of blood, 281
  experimental apnœa, 476, 490
  gases of blood, 386, 390
  heart beat, 231
  intracardiac pressure, 203, 210
  latent systole, 210
  œsophageal sphygmograms, 229
  spleen, 553
  stimulation of pulmonary vagus, 462
  systolic aspiration, 203, 210
  venous pulse, 203
FRERICHS, urea in selachii, 297
FRIEND, animal gum, 130
  thrombosis, 133
v. FREY, diastole, 209
  hæmatoidin, 108
  intracardiac pressure, 201
  tonograph, 245
  vasomotor nerves, 351
FRIEDLEBEN, thymus, 542
FRIEDRICH, auriculo-ventricular valves, 192
FROMMAN, structure of protoplasm, 17
FRY, H. J. B., heart, cephalopod, 340
FUNKE, hæmoglobin, 107
  leucocytes, 175
  mechanics of respiration and circulation, 434
  spleen, 549
FUSARI, nerves in spleen, 549

GABRITSCHEWSKI, pinocytosis, 534
GAD, circulation of blood, 281

GAD, elimination of CO_2, 470
experimental apnoea, 477
manometer, 245
platelets, 119
pulmonary vagus, 458, 462
residual air, 423
respiratory centre, 446, 504
respiratory rhythm, blood, 179, 186
tachypnoea, 471
GAGLIO, lactic acid of blood, 131
GALEN, active diastole, 208, 213
arterial pulse, 264
automatism of heart, 299
circulation of blood, 159, 171
"de usu partium," 4, 9, 400
intercostal muscles, 411
mechanics of respiration, 403
pulmonary vagus, 457
respiration, 370
respiratory centres, 444
semilunar valves, 187
spleen, 555
systole and diastole, 180, 208
GALEOTTI, electrical conductivity of serum, 150
electrical conductivity of tissues, 155
GAMGEE, blood, 121
oxyhaemoglobin in magnetic field, 121
GARDELLA, coagulation, 124, 155
GARELLI, molecular weights, 155
GÄRTNER, molecular concentration of blood, 148
tonometer, 252
GASKELL, accelerator nerves, 328
active vasodilatation, 347, 367
auriculo-ventricular bundle, 314, 316, 321
automatism of heart, 306, 338
cardiac plethysmograph, 289
cardiac vagus, 324, 338
heart, electrical variations, 332
heart, suspension, 289
myogenic theory, 307, 314
nervi erigentes, 355, 367
GASSENTI, circulation, 166
GASSER, ganglion of, 328, 354
GAULE, diastole, 208
diastolic aspiration, 212
intracardiac pressure, 207, 212, 214, 220
normal physiological solution, 295
pressure of blood, 254
GAUTHIER, anaerobic organisms, 69
GEGENBAUER, lymphatic vessels, 508
GEPPERT, blood gas, 284, 400, 474
muscular work, 170
respiration 504
GERLACH, bronchial muscle, 442
GIANNUZZI, cardiac vagus, 342
GIBBES, haemolymphatic glands, 557
GIBSON, periodic respiration, 192, 504
GILERKI, respiratory centre, 446, 504
GIES, artificial respiration, 504

GIES, osteomucoid, 40
protagon, 40
GIRARD, respiratory centre, 446
GLEY, cardiac sound, 200
extra-systole, 321
lymphatic vessels, 517, 557
GMELIN, blood gas, 377
GOLDSTEIN, tachypnoea, 471
GOLGI, haemorrhage, 152
GOLTZ, automatism of heart, 305, 337
blood pressure, 254
cardiac vagus, 336
diastole, 209
hyperaemia, paralytic, 315
intracardiac pressure, 208, 214
reflex inhibition of heart, 336
vaso-dilatators, 350, 367
vasomotor centres, 362, 364, 366
GOODALL, spleen, 551
thymus, 558
GÖTHLIN, normal physiological solution, 296, 338
GRAHAM, colloids and crystalloids, 21
diffusion of gases, 373
GRAM, solution of, 103
GRANCHER, leucocytes, 116
GRANDIS, elimination of CO_2, 391
GRASHEY, dicrotic wave, 284
GRASSI, mosquitoes and coagulation, 124
GRAUPNER, auriculo-ventricular bundle, 315
GRAWITZ, blood, 121
GREEN, J. R., lymph formation, 526, 559
salivary glands, 558
GREHANT, residual air, 423
GRIFFINI, spleen, 557
GRISELINI, circulation, 166
GROSS, normal physiological solution, 297
GRUBER, cell, rhizopoda, 13
GRUNMACH, cardiograph, 223
latent systole, 206
velocity of blood stream, 273
GLÜTZNER, vascular reflexes, 360, 367
vaso-constrictors, 349
vaso-dilatators, 351
GRYNS, serum, osmotic pressure, 144
GSCHEIDLEN, quantity of blood, 99
GULDICHT, air pump, 371
GULLAND, spleen, 551, 556, 558
GÜNTHER, circulation of blood, 162
GÜRBER, plasma, mineral matter, 132
respiratory gases, 389
GUREOKI, cardiac vagus, 335
GURWITSCH, spleen, 552, 558
GUTHRIE, C. C., blood pressure, 284
blood pressure and respiration, 439
coronary pressure, 339
red blood-corpuscles, 122

HADLEY, P. B., galvanotaxis, 90
HAECKEL, the cell, 13

HAECKEL, protista, 56
HAESER, vital capacity, 423
HAFIZ, vaso-constrictors, 319
HALDANE, J. S., alveolar CO_2, 439
  barometric pressure and respiration, 439
  blood gases, 391, 400, 401
  Cheyne-Stokes breathing, 504
  haemo-globinometry, 121
  regulation of respiration, 439, 504
HALES, blood pressure, 241
  "pneumatic" chemistry, 373
  velocity of blood in capillaries, 263
HALLER, activity of heart, 299
  auriculo-ventricular valves, 192
  circulation of blood, 160, 164, 167, 172, 341
  diastole, 208
  "elementa physiologiae," 9
  intercostal muscles, 410
  mechanics of respiration, 403
  respiration, 429, 439
HAM, E., blood, 122
HAMBERGER, intercostal muscles, 410, 412, 439
  semilunar valves, 187
HAMBURGER, blood gases, 386
  lymph formation, 526, 584
  molecular concentration, 112, 117
  osmotic pressure and ions, 121, 155
  osmotic pressure of plasma, 143
  osmotic pressure of serum, 114
  semilunar valves, 187
HAMMARSTEN, coagulation of blood, 135
  enzymes, 32
  lymph gases, 514
  nucleoproteins, thymus, 545
  physiological chemistry, 39
  proteins of plasma, 128
  salted plasma, 128
HAMMERSCHLAG, sp. gr. of blood, 95
HANRIOT, lipase of blood, 127
HARDY, colloidal solution, 40
  leucocytes, 113
HARRIS, T. F., proteins, 40
HARRISON, haemolymphatic glands, 557
HARTLEY, P., fat of liver, 41
HARTWELL, intercostal muscles, 412, 414, 439
HARVEY, afferent nerves of heart, 335
  circulation, 166, 169, 171
  diastole, 208
  heart beat, 222, 225
  heart sounds, 196
  rate of blood stream, 259
  respiration, 371
  systole, 182
HARWOOD, W. S., botany, 63
HASLAM, H. C., proteins, 40
HASSE, diaphragm, 410
HASSELBACH, blood gases, 595
HAWK, P. B., blood and muscular work, 122

HAYCRAFT, blood, anti-coagulants, 124
  systole, 186
HAYEM, coagulation of blood, 134
  haemacytometry, 103
  haematoblasts, 100, 118, 121
  haemorrhage, 152
HEDBLOM, C. A., blood pressure, 284
HEDIN, centrifuge, 98
  enzymes in blood, 156
  haematocrite, 104, 121
  molecular concentration, 147
HEDON, isolation of heart, 291
HEFFTER, oxygen and activity of heart, 293
HIGER, P., diapedesis, 179
  vascular reflexes, 355
HEIDENHAIN, accelerators of heart, 328
  cardiac vagus, 218, 324, 325, 329
  formation of lymph, 519, 557
  lymphagogues, 523
  megacaryocytes, 535
  periodic respiration, 491
  quantity of lymph, 514
  respiratory centre, 445
  Stannius heart, 300
  vascular reflexes, 360, 361
  vaso-constrictors, 319
  vaso-dilatators, 351
  vasomotor centres, 363
HEIN, periodic respiration, 502
HEINRICIUS, mechanics of circulation and respiration, 435, 439
HEITZMANN, structure of protoplasm, 17
HELLER, contraction of lymphatics, 517
HELLRIEGEL, nitrifying bacteria, 58
HELMHOLTZ, conservation of energy, 5
  resonators, 197
VAN HELMONT, intercostal muscles, 411
  respiration, 371, 373, 400
HENDERSON, J., thymus, 558
HENDERSON, Y., heart volume, 231
HENLE, blood-vessels, active movements of, 341
  cardiac vagus, 323
  intercostal muscles, 412
  myocardium, 182
HENRIQUES, vagi and gas exchange, 392
HENRY, gas law, 378, 384
HENSEN, plankton, 82
HERBST, quantity of blood, 98
HÉRICOURT, toxicity of blood, 153
HERING, Ed., circulation time, 282
HERING, Ew., automatic control of respiratory rhythm, 459, 503
  blood and respiratory rhythm, 480, 486
  cardiac vagus, 336
  diapedesis, 177
  experimental apnoea, 486
  inspiratory centres, 456
  living matter, metabolism, 86, 89
  oscillations of vascular tone, 500

HERING, Ew., trigeminus and respiration, 464
  Traube-Hering waves, 343
HERING, H. E., auriculo-ventricular bundle, 315, 317, 337
  cardiac nerves, 310
  cardiac vagus, 327
  isolated heart, 291
  resuscitation of heart, 298
HERING, P., blood and respiratory rhythm, 480, 486
HERMANN, demarcation and action currents, 332
  galvanotaxis, 81
  gases of expired air, 397
  lungs of newborn, 405, 459
  oxygen and muscle frog, 68
  physiology, handbook, 9
  tissue respiration, 394
HEROPHILUS, arterial pulse, 264
  lacteals, 171
  respiration, 370
HERTWIG, O., cell and tissues, 39
HERTWIG, R., amoeba, 13
  centersome, 13
HERZEN, spleen, 553
HESSE, myocardium, 182, 190
HEWSON, coagulation, 132, 135
  leucocytes, 93
  respiration, 373
HIELLISHEIM, heart-beat, 225
HILL, L., blood in high barometric pressure, 401
  residual arterial pressure, 284
  respiration and circulation, 439
HIRSCHFELD, platelets, 119
HIRSCHFELDER, A. D., extra-systole, 339
HIRT, spleen, 552
HIS, W., lymphatic system, 179
HIS, jun., auriculo-ventricular bundle, 315
  embryonic heart, 308
HOBER, physical chemistry, 121
VON HOESSLIN, spirometry, 425
HOFER, amoeba, 14
HOFF, VAN 'T, solutions, 141
HOFLA, delirium cordis, 321
HOFFMANN, K., circulation of blood, 170
HOFFMANN, auriculo-ventricular bundle, 317, 337
HOFMEISTER, enzymes, 29
  proteins, 25
HOLMGREN, blood gases, 380
  circulation in capillaries, 173, 178
HOLT, E. B., phototaxis, 90
HOOK, experimental apnoea, 476
  respiration, 371, 400
HOOKER, heart, 339
  post-mortem lymph, 515, 558
HOORWEG, dicrotic wave, 269
HOPKINS, F. G., amino-acids, 40

HOPKINS, F. G., proteins, 40
HOPPE-SEYLER, blood gas, 377, 380, 400
  diffusion of gas, 379
  haemoglobin, 105
  lecithin, 35
  leucocytes, 117
  oxyhaemoglobin, 383
  physiological chemistry, 39
  plasma and corpuscles, 125
  plasma soaps, 130
  proteins, 24
  stromata, 106
  tissue respiration, 393
HORBACZEWSKI, spleen, 552
HORNE, coagulation, 137
HOWELL, W. H., heart, 338, 339
  heart inhibition, 339
  megacaryocytes, 535, 584
  proteins of blood, 156
  vagus action, 339
HUFNER, haemoglobin, 107
  oxygen of blood, 383, 420
  spectro-photometry, 111
HUGHES, W. T., haemolytic lymph, 559
HULIKLANIZ, respiration, 418
HUMBLER, auriculo-ventricular bundle, 315, 337
v. HUMBOLDT, oxygen and heart, 293
HUNT, REID, cardiac nerves, 331
HUNTER, blood, 91
  invertebrate heart, 311
HUNTER, W., cerebral vascular nerves, 368
HÜRTHLE, cardiograph, 222
  dicrotic wave, 269
  haemodromometer, 259, 284
  intracardiac pressure, 201
  latent systole, 206
  manometer, 244
  sphygmomanometer, 250
  viscosity of blood, 151
HUTCHINSON, W. H., sulph-haemoglobin, 122
HUTCHINSON, intercostal muscles, 412, 439
  spirometry, 422, 439
  types of respiration, 416, 439
HYDE, heart, automatic control, 211
  respiratory centre, 504
HYRTL, semilunar valves, 187

INGENHOUSZ, plant metabolism, 54

JACKSON, H. C., splenectomy, 558
JACOBSON, hydrodynamics, 235
  intrathoracic pressure, 427
  plasma, jecorin, 130
  venous pressure, 253
JACQUET, tissue respiration, 395, 400
DE JAGER, diastole, 209, 214
  intracardiac pressure, 207, 214
JAKOWICKI, coagulation of blood, 138

v. JAKSCH, reaction of blood, 96
JAPPELLI, fistula of, 513
  polypnoea, 171
  post-mortem lymph, 515
JENSEN, colpidium colpoda and inanition, 66
  geotaxis, 77
JOHANSSOHN, cardiac vagus, 218, 326
  vasomotor centres, 366
JOLYET, rate of blood stream, 238
JONES, WHARTON, vascular rhythm, 343

KABERSKI, vasomotor centres, 561
KAISER, extrasystole, 321
  heart stimuli, 321
KANTHACK, leucocytes, 113
KATZENSTEIN, respiratory movements, 466
KAUFMANN, periodic respiration, 502
KAYA, R., phospho-proteins, 41
KAZEM-BECK, depressor, 334
KEITH, heart beat, 221
KELLER, hydrostatic pressure, 72
KEMP, G. T., blood-platelets, 121
KENDALL, vasodilatators, 351
KENT, STANLEY, auriculo-ventricular bundle, 314
KEYT, latent systole, 206
  velocity of blood stream, 273
KING, W. O. R., blood, 101
KITASATO, immunisation, 154
KIWISCH, heart beat, 225
KLEEN, vascular reflexes, 360
KLEIN, lymphatics, 509, 530
KLEINENBERG, examination of blood, 120
KLIKOWICZ, formation of lymph, 525
KLUG, automatic control of heart, 211
  cardiac vagus, 333
  oxygen and heart, 293
KNIGHT, geotaxis, 77
KNOLL, cardiograph, 223
  experimental apnoea, 476
  heart, suspension, 291
  pneumoplethysmograph, 125, 191
  vascular reflexes, 360
KOCH, anthrax bacilli, 71
KOCHER, splenectomy, 555
KOCHS, potential life, 67
KOHLRAUSCH, electrical conductivity, 149
v. KÖLLIKER, spleen, 546, 549, 552
KÖNIG, tuning-fork, 6
KONOW, cardiac vagus, 333
  depressor, 335
  vasomotor centres, 364
KÖPPE, molecular concentration of blood, 147, 155
  platelets, 119
KORSCHINSKI, heterogenesis, 52
KOSSEL, histones, 106, 117
  nucleus, 39
  proteins, 25

KOSSEL, proteins of cell, 39
  structure of proteins, 25
KOSTER, depressor, 335
KOWALEWSKI, vasomotor centres, 365
KRATSCHMER, trigeminus and respiration, 464
KREHL, auriculo-ventricular valves, 194
  diastole, 212, 215, 231
  diastolic aspiration, 209
  myocardium, 182, 184
  myogenic theory, 314
von KRIES, capillary pressure, 253
  circulation time, 283
  pulse, 284
KROGH, blood gases, 395
  nervous system and gas exchange, 392, 420
KRONECKER, cannula (perfusion), 288, 337
  co-ordination of heart, 321, 337
  heart muscle, 318, 321
  mechanics of respiration and circulation, 435, 439
  normal physiological solution, 295
  periodic respiration, 495, 502
  red blood-corpuscles, 105
  respiratory centres, 448
  transfusion of blood, 153
KRÜGER, spleen, 551
KRÜSS, spectrophotometer, 112
KÜHNE, chemical stimuli, 73
  electrical stimuli, 80
  reaction of blood, 95
  thermal tetanus, 77
KULIABKO, heart, resuscitation, 298
KURLOW, splenectomy, 555
KÜRSCHNER, activity of heart, 231
  auriculo-ventricular valves, 192
  neurogenic theory, 307
  presystole, 181
KÜSS, auriculo-ventricular valves, 192
KUSSMAUL, asphyxia, 479

LABORDE, cardiac centres, 336
LALANNE, heart sounds, 196
  mechanics of respiration, 403
LAFFONT, vasomotor centres, 366
LAGRANGE, respiration, 375
LAIDLAW, P. P., blood pigments, 122
LAMARCK, biology, 1
  evolution, 48, 65
LAMBERT, urea and heart, 297
LANCISI, automatic control of heart, 211
LANDLEGER EN, asphyxia, 452
LANDOIS, autosphygmogram, 265, 283
  cardio-pneumatic curves, 227
  intercostal muscles, 412
  latent systole, 206
  lungs, movements, 426
  mechanics of respiration and circulation, 437
  pulse, 231
  reaction of blood, 96

LANDOIS, toxicity of serum, 153
transfusion of blood, 153
vasomotor centres, 365
LANGENDORFF, asphyxia and heart, 301
ciliary ganglion, 310
heart, isolation, 291, 338
normal physiological solution, 297
oxygen and heart, 293, 338
periodic respiration, 493, 501, 504
respiratory centres, 447, 451
stimulation of heart, 321
LANGERHANS, thymus, 512
LANGLEY, vaso-dilatators, 354
LAPICQUE, spleen, 551
LAPLACE, respiration, 400
LASSAR, reaction of blood, 96
LATSCHENBERGER, mechanics of respiration and circulation, 431
vasomotor centres, 363
LAUDENBACH, lymphoid organs, 558
LAVOISIER, animal respiration, 54, 374, 400
chemistry of respiration, 396
indestructibility of matter, 5
modern chemistry, 396
volume of expired air, 398
LAZARUS-BARLOW, formation of lymph, 526
LEAVENWORTH, proteins, 40
LEBER, chemotaxis, leucocytes, 178
LEE, F. S., phototaxis, 90
LEEUWENHOEK, anabiosis, 66
capillary circulation, 172
red blood corpuscles, 93
LEFEVRE, systolic aspiration, 210
LEGALLOIS, pulmonary vagus, 457
respiratory centre, 444
LEGROS, cardiac vagus, 324
LEHMANN, blood, 94
quantity of blood, 98
LÉPINE, glycolysis in blood, 127
vasomotors, 352
LEROYENNE, rate of blood stream, 275
LESEM, W. W., protagon, 40
LESSER, transfusion of blood, 153
LEUBE, periodic respiration, 502
LEVENE, P. A., autolysis, 40
edestin, 40
proteose, 40
LEWANDOWSKY, nervous mechanism of respiration, 504
LEWIS, T., heart rhythm, 231
sphygmogram, 284
thoracic movements and blood-pressure, 284
LEYDIG, haemolymphatic glands, 557
LIEBERKÜHN, glands of, 528
leucocytes, 115
LIEBIG, animals and plants, 55
oxygen of blood, 383
LIEBREICH, protagon, 35
reaction of blood, 95
LILIENFELD, coagulation of blood, 136

LILIENFELD, lymphocytes, 117
molybdate test, 59
platelets, 118
LILLIE, R. S., electrical convection, 90
v. LIMBECK, lymphagogues, 525
osmotic pressure of blood, 146
pathology of blood, 155
LINDHAGEN, pulmonary vagus, 459
LINGLE, D. J., heart rhythm, 231
ions and heart, 338
LINNAEUS, animals and plants, 52
immutability of species, 45
LITTEN, marrow, 539
spleen, 556
Lo BIANCO, marine biology, 90
LOCK, R. H., variation, 63
LOCKE, F. S., glucose and heart, 296, 338, 339
normal physiological solution, 296, 338
LOEB, cell theory, 12
galvanotaxis, 80
general physiology, 90
geotaxis, 77
heliotaxis, 79
LOEWY, acapnia, 475, 504
pulmonary gas exchange, 392, 400
respiratory centres, 464
trigeminus and respiration, 465
water of alveolar air, 391
LOMBARD, W. P., heart rhythm, 231
Lo MONACO, thymus, 542, 558
LONGET, bronchial muscle, 412
intercostal muscles, 411
respiratory centre, 444
" Traité de physiologie," 9
LORRY, respiratory centre, 444
LORIET, sphygmograms and tachygrams, 276
LOTSY, doctrine of descent, 62
LOVEN, cervical plexus, 349
negative pulse, 227
vascular reflex, 356, 359, 367
LOWER, auriculo-ventricular valves, 192, 400
respiration, 372, 400
LÖWIT, platelets, 118
LUBARSCH, chemotaxis, leucocytes, 178
LUCHSINGER, periodic respiration, 495, 501, 504
vaso-dilatators, 351
LUCIANI, active vaso-dilatation, 347
active diastole, 208, 214, 231
activity of heart, 300, 337
auriculo-ventricular valves, 194
automaticity, 85
automaticity of heart, 215
automatism of respiratory rhythm, 498, 504
cardiac vagus, 217
excitability and sensibility, 45
experimental apnoea, 480, 484
expiration, 419
haemodromometer, 258

LUCIANI, human bulb, 445
  inanition, 65
  inspiratory centres, 456
  intra-abdominal pressure, 429
  intrathoracic pressure, 407
  intrathoracic and intra-abdominal
    pressures, 231, 427
  leucocytes, 116
  mechanics of respiration and circula-
    tion, 430, 439
  minimal life, 67
  oesophageal sound, 228, 429
  oesophageal sphygmograms, 228
  oxygen and heart, 293
  periodic respiration, 494, 501
  periodic rhythm of heart, 302
  plethysmograms and tachygrams, 280
  pulmonary vagus, 458
  rectal explorer, 429
  red blood-corpuscles, 105
  respiratory movements in asphyxia,
    125, 448
  ribs, 408
  section of phrenics, 435
  semilunar valves, 189
  staircase phenomenon, 318
  tonographic apparatus, 288
  transfusion of blood, 153
LUCKHARDT, A. B., lymph formation,
  526, 559
LUDWIG, accelerated cardiac rhythm,
  181
  accelerators of heart, 327, 338
  auriculo-ventricular valves, 192
  blood pressure, 241, 254
  cardiac ganglia, 299
  cardiac systole, 182, 187
  delirium cordis, 321
  depressor, 353, 360, 367
  formation of lymph, 519
  gases of blood, 367, 377, 379
  glandular secretion, 391
  haemodromometer, 257
  heart beat, 224
  heart sounds, 197
  hydrodynamics, 189
  kymograph, 242
  lymphatic circulation, 518, 522
  lymphatic pressure, 516, 557
  mechanics of respiration, 439
  myocardium, 182
  normal physiological solution, 295
  physiology, text-book, 231
  pulmonary catheter, 588
  recording manometer, 207
  serous cavities, 509
  splanchnic nerve, 347
  vasomotor centres, 347, 362, 366
LUSIN, assimilation of inorganic matter,
  62
LURIA, respiratory reflex, 166
LUSCHKA, thorax, 409
LUSKY, H. O., lymph, 559

LYON, excitation, 90
  geotropism, 90
  rheotropism, 90
LYONET, apparatus of, 173

MAAR, nerves and gas exchange, 592
McCOLLUM, nuclein synthesis, 41
M'CURDY, F. H., blood pressure, 284
MACH, sensations, 6
MACKENZIE, venous pulse, 203
MACLEOD, J. J. R., blood at high
  pressures, 101
MACNALTY, S., heart rhythm, 231
MacWILLIAM, automatism of heart, 306
  cardiac vagus, 326
  chloroform, heart, 338
  delirium cordis, 321
  rigor mortis, heart, 231
MALTECCI, spleen and liver, 556
MAGENDIE, auriculo-ventricular valves,
  196
  cardiac diastole, 213
  circulation, 341
  haemodiastase, 134
  heart sounds, 196
  intercostal muscles, 111
  vascular reflexes, 359
MAGGIORANI, spleen and liver, 556
MAGNUS, G., blood gases, 377, 400
MAGNUS, R., oxygen and heart, 294
  vagus, 555
MAISSIAT, intercostal muscles, 411, 439
  thoracic respiration, 417
MALASSEZ, haemacytometer, 102, 116
  isotonic solution, 143
MALERBA, cardiac vagus, 323
MALFATTI, nucleus, 59
MALPIGHI, capillary circulation, 172
  corpuscles, spleen, 547
  fibrin, 97
  red blood-corpuscles, 93
  structure of lungs, 403
MANCA, osmotic pressure of blood, 146,
  155
MANTEGAZZA, coagulation, 134
MARAGLIANO, vascular reflexes, 357
MARCACCI, ANT., intercostal muscles,
  114, 439
MARCACCI, AUG., extrasystole, 321
  tissue lymph, 527
MARCHAND, respiration, 376
MARCKWALD, blood and respiratory
  rhythm, 494
  periodic respiration, 496, 502, 504
  respiratory centres, 448, 464
  trigeminus and respiration, 465
MAREY, arterial pressure, 241, 248, 433
  cardiac myograph, 291, 337
  cardiograph, 224
  cardiographic sound, 200
  circulation of blood, 231, 284
  diaphragm, 433
  heart beat, 224, 225

MAREY, intracardiac pressure, 201
latent systole, 206
metallic manometer, 244
refractory period, 320, 337
pneumograph, 415
recording tympanum, 201
sphygmograph, 264, 284
sphygmomanometer, 247
sphygmoscope, 205
vascular walls, 241
waves, 241
MARIANNINI, heart beat, 222
MARIETTE, anabiosis, 66
MARIOTTI, gas law, 378
MARINESCO, respiratory centre, 446, 504
MARKS, H. K., vasomotor centres, 368
vasomotor reflexes, 568
MARSHALL, A. K., bionomics, 63
MARTIGNI, COLLARD DE, respiration, 377
MARTIN, cerebrum and respiration, 153
intercostal muscles, 412, 414, 439
isolation of heart, 291
heart, oxygen, 401
MARTIN, E. G., heart, potassium, 338
MARTIUS, normal physiological solution, 295
oesophageal pulsations, 230
MASCAGNI, formation of lymph, 519
serous cavities, 509
MASIUS, vascular reflexes, 357
vasomotor centres, 366
MASOIN, cardiac vagus, 324
inter-cartilaginous muscles, 415
MASSART, chemotaxis, leucocytes, 75, 178
phagocytosis, 116
MATTHEWS, S. A., blood pressure, 284
MATTEO ORFADIO, circulation, 160
MAYER, viscosity of blood, 151
MAYER, J. R., conservation of energy, 5
metabolism of green plants, 55
MAXOW, intercostal muscles, 411
respiration, 372, 377, 400
MECKEL, auriculo-ventricular valves, 192
MEIK, W. J., heart, 339, 340
MEISSNER, intercostal muscles, 412
MELLANBY, J., coagulation, 156
serum, 156
MELTZER, C., vasomotor nerves, 368
MELTZER, S. J., artificial respiration, 504
cardiac nerves, 331
vasomotor, 368
MENDEL, L. B., celestin, 40
lymph, 558
splenectomy, 558
MENDEL, evolution, 52
post-mortem lymph, 515
MENDELEJEFF, periodic system, 20
MENDELSSOHN, thermotaxis, 78

MERKEL, periodic respiration, 502
MERRIMAN, C. V., mutation, 63
MEKUNOWES, normal physiological solution, 295
METSCHNIKOFF, chemotaxis, 75
inflammation, 179
phagocytosis, 18, 115
MEYER, blood gas, 380, 383
cardiac vagus, 324
experimental apnoea, 479
respiration, 377, 400
MICANZIO, circulation, 166
MICHAELIS, fats, blood, 127
MIESCHER, apnoea, true and false, 477, 488, 504
leucocytes, 117
nucleo-proteins, 24, 39
plasma, histogenic substances, 126
MILLER, J. R., galvanotropism, 90
MILLON, protein reaction, 22
MILLS, WESLEY, cardiac vagus, 324, 326
MILNE-EDWARDS, comparative physiology, 9
division of labour, 91
lymphatic system, 509
MINCK, diastolic aspiration, 212
MIRTO, depressor nerve, 335
MISLAWSKI, respiratory reflex, 166
vasomotor centres, 366
MOENS, velocity of pulse wave, 275, 284
waves, 241
MOHL, protoplasm, 11
MOLESCHOTT, cardiac vagus, 322
tissue respiration, 394
MOLISCH, protein reaction, 22
MONILNOVISI, spleen and liver, 556
MONTI, test for phosphorus, 39
MOORE, sugar reaction, 36
MOORE, A., geotropism, 90
lymph hearts, 558
MOORE, B., spleen, 554, 558
MORAT, cardiac vagus, 323
cervical sympathetic, 349, 353, 367
nerves of neck, rabbit, 334
vascular reflexes, 361, 367
vasomotor centres, 366
vasomotor nerves, 351, 353
MORAWITZ, coagulation, 156
thrombokinase, 139
MORGAGNI, spleen, 555
MORGAN, Th. H., evolution, 63
MÖRNER, ovo-mucoid, 126, 129
MOSSO, A., apnoea, 474
asphyxial pause, 452
blood pressure, 255, 284
cardio-pneumograms, 227, 231
diastolic aspiration, 210
inspiratory centres, 456
periodic respiration, 493
plethysmograph and plethysmograms, 275, 344, 367
pulse, 231, 284

Mosso, A., respiration at high altitudes, 172, 499
  luxus respiration, 172
  sphygmomanometer, 284
  thoracic and abdominal respiration, 418, 439
  tidal air, 123
  tonicity of respiratory muscles, 504
  toxicity of heterogeneous blood, 153
  vascular tone, 516
  voluntary apnoea, 480, 483
Mosso, U., periodic respiration 491
  respiration at high altitudes, 474
Mulder, blood, 94
Müller, F., acapnia, 475
  respiration at high altitudes, 504
  splenic cells, 549
Müller, J., blood gases, 376
  cardiac ganglia, 299
  coagulation, 135
  life, 3, 9
  mechanics of respiration and circulation, 436
  physiology, 3, 9
  respiration, 376
  solution of, 104
Müller, W., oxygen of blood, 384
  respiratory valves, 420
Munk, I., lymph, 511
  urea of blood, 129
Mure, de la, locomotion of blood-vessels, 277
Murray, marine biology, 81
Murri, periodic respiration, 502
Myers, W., erythrocytes, 121

Nagel, W., physiology, handbook, 9
Nägeli, adaptation, 65
  evolution, 49, 62
Namias, heart beat, 222
Nasini, solutions, 155
Nasse, blood, 94
  extraction of gas, 377
  glycolysis in blood, 127
Neander, apnoeic respiratory pause, 482, 504
Nega, systolic aspiration, 210
Negri, red blood-corpuscles, 540
Neilson, C. H., enzyme action, 40
  fats, 40
  inversion of starch, 40
Neumann, marrow, 534, 557
  spleen, 550
Neumeister, physiological chemistry, 39
Newman, H. H., heart, 401
Nicolaides, rate of circulation, 260
Nobbe, nitrifying bacteria, 58
Nolf, coagulation, 140
Noll, lymphatic pressure, 516
Noll, F., botany, 62
  heliotaxis, 79
  nitrifying bacteria, 58

Nothnagel, lymphatic vessels, 512
Nowak, expired air, 397
Nufl, cardiac vagus, 526
Nuttall, bactericidal properties of blood, 154

Oehl, abdominal vagi, 348
  cardiac valves, 185, 191
  diastolic aspiration, 212
  luminous stimuli, 78
Oehrwall, oxygen and heart, 293, 338
  tonographic apparatus, 288
Onimus, cardiac vagus, 324
Oppel, spleen, 548
Oppenheimer, ferments, 40
Opitzasus, pneumothorax, 403
Orth, marrow, 539
  spleen, 556
Osborne, T. B., proteins, 40, 41
Osborne, W. A., oxygen tension of blood, 401
Osler, platelets, 118
Ostroumoff, tissue lymph, 527
  vasomotor nerves, 351, 354
Ostwald, catalysis, 31
  energetic monism, 6
  viscosimeter, 151
Otto, glucose of blood, 130
Ovskofi, leucocytes, 114
Owsjannikow, vasomotor centres, 363

Pacini, mechanics of respiration and circulation, 436
  solution of, 103
Packard, A. S., evolution, 63
Pagliani, diastolic aspiration, 210
  neurogenic theory, 308
Paladino, auriculo-ventricular bundle, 314
  auriculo-ventricular valves, 191, 231
  erythroblasts, 539
Panum, cardiac vagus, 332
  transfusion of blood, 153
Pappenheim, platelets, 119
Parchappl, active diastole, 213
  auriculo-ventricular valves, 192
Paschutin, formation of lymph, 522
Pasteur, aerobic and anaerobic organisms, 69, 369
  ferments, 30
Paton, N., lymph, 514, 557
  spleen, 550, 556, 558
  thymus, 558
Patrizi, bulb, inhibitory centres, 452
  periodic respiration, 493
  pulmonary vagus, 463
  rate of pulse wave, 273, 284
  vascular reflexes, 358, 367
Pauly, Darwinism and Lamarckism, 62
Pavy, glycogen of blood, 131
Pawlow, cardiac nerves, 338
  quantity and pressure of blood, 255
Pearl, R., galvanotaxis, 90

PEARSON, K., evolution, 62 63
PECQUER, lymphatic system, 171, 545
PEKELHARING, coagulation, 139
PELLACANI, marrow, 539
PESKIND, S., blood-corpuscles, 121, 122
PETRONE, coagulation, 134
  erythrocytes, 540, 558
PETTENKOFER, nitrogen of blood, 387
PEYER, patches of, 530
PFEFFER, chemotaxis, 75, 178
  osmotic pressure, 141
  vegetable physiology, 62
PFEIFFER, fats of blood, 130
PFLÜGER, animals and plants, 89
  apnoea, 476, 477
  blood gases, 377, 379, 387
  blood and respiratory rhythm, 479,
    486
  cardiac vagus, 324
  embryonic heart, 308
  eupnoea, 472
  living matter, 86, 89
  oxygen and life, 70
  pulmonary catheter, 388
  splanchnic and respiration, 465, 504
  tissue respiration, 86
PICTET, R., cold and life, 71
PIPGEAUX, heart beat, 222
PIRGU, plethysmograph, 278
PIKE, F. H., blood pressure, 439
  heart, 339
  resuscitation of bulb, 504
PILCHER, J. D., vasomotor centre, 368
PILLSBURY, heart rhythm, 231
PIOTROWSKI, vasomotors, 353, 367
PIUTTI, minimal life, 67
PLIMMER, R. H. A., caseinogen, 40
  phosphoproteins, 24, 41
PLINY, splenectomy, 555
PLOSZ, nucleoproteins, 24
  stromata, 106
POISEUILLE, blood pressure, 241
  circulation, 174, 341
  mechanics of thoracic movements, 430
  plethysmograph, 278
PONFIK, transfusion of blood, 153
PORTAL, thoracic duct, 171
PORTER, automatic control of heart, 211
  automatism of heart, 306
  heart, tonus, 339
  intracardiac pressure, 206
  myogenic theory, 313
  oxygen and heart, 293
  vasomotor centre, 367, 368
POSNER, E. R., protagon, 40
  proteins, 40
POTAIN, blood pressure, 246
POUCHET, spleen, 556
POULTON, E. B., bionomics, 63
POULTON, E. P., respiration, 459
PRAXAGORAS, circulation, 162
PREVOST, blood, 94
  terminal respiration, 452

PREYER, analysis, 66
  blood gases, 387
  circulation of blood, 159
  haemin, 108, 121
PRIESTLEY, modern chemistry, 94
  respiration, 373, 377, 400
PRIESTLEY, J. G., respiration, 504
PRZEWOSKI, myocardium, 313
PUGLIESI, formation of lymph, 527
  lymphagogues, 523
PUNNETT, K. C., merism and sex, 63
PURKINJE, myocardium, 313
  systolic aspiration, 210
PUSADRI, depressor, 335

QUINCKE, law of, 48

RABINOWITZ, blood pressure, 246
RANSOM, heart, invertebrates, 311
RANVIER, coagulation, 131
  lymphatic vessels, 505, 557
  myogenic theory, 307
  serous cavities, 509
RAOULT, molecular concentration, 142
  solutions, 141
REEATER, automatic control of heart,
  211
VON RECKLINGHAUSEN, diapedesis, 177
  serous cavities, 509
REGNARD, blood gases, 387
REGNAULT, expired air, 387, 417
RIGOLI, calcium and coagulation, 137
REICHERT, E. T., haemoglobin crystals,
  122
REID, E. W., haemoglobin, 122
REID, myocardium, 183
REISET, expired air, 387, 417
REMAK, cardiac ganglia, 299
  protoplasm, 17
RISTELLI, thymus, 542
RITTGER, L. J., coagulation of blood,
  156
REIZIUS, nerves in spleen, 549
RICHARDS, A. N., elastic tissue, 40
RICHARDSON, R., vasomotor reflexes, 368
RICHET, circulation, 165
  polypnoea, 471
  toxicity of blood, 153
  vasomotor centres, 365
RIDDLE, O., blood pressure, 284
RIEGEL, vascular rhythm, 343
RIGNANO, evolution, 62
RINDFLEISCH, erythroblasts, 539
RINGER, normal physiological solution,
  296
RIOLAN, circulation, 170
  perisystole, 180
RIVA-ROCCI, blood pressure, 253
  sphygmomanometer, 251, 284
RIVE, latent systole, 206
ROAF, H. E., haemoglobin, 156
ROBERTS, Ff., blood gas analysis, 401
  oxyhaemoglobin, 401

ROBERTSON, haemolymphatic glands, 557

ROBERTSON, T. B., infusoria, 90
protein synthesis, 40, 41

ROEVER, cardiac vagus, 336

ROHMANN, glycolysis of blood, 127

RÖHRIG, fats of blood, 130

ROKITANSKI, spinal respiratory centres, 447

ROLLESTON, diastole, 209

ROLLET, hydrodynamics, 235
red blood-corpuscles, 105, 121

ROMBERG, embryonic heart, 308
myogenic theory, 311

ROSENBACH, blood and respiratory rhythm, 186
periodic respiration, 501

ROSENHEIM, glucose and heart, 338, 339
protagon, 11

ROSENSTEIN, quantity of lymph, 514
blood and respiratory rhythm, 176

ROSENTHAL, cardiac vagus, 324
eupnoea, 471
experimental apnoea, 475
general physiology, 90
inspiratory muscles, 410
intercostal muscles, 410, 411
intrathoracic and intra-abdominal pressure, 127
phrenograph, 416
pulmonary vagus, 162, 503
respiratory capacity, 423, 439
respiratory centres, 468
respiratory quotient, 399
superior laryngeal and respiration, 465

ROSS, H. C., leucocytes, 122

ROSSBACH, asphyxia and heart, 304
cardiac vagus, 218
oxygen and heart, 293

ROTH, circulation, 161
Vesalius, 179

ROUANET, heart sounds, 196

ROY, accelerators of heart, 330
blood pressure, 245
bronchio-dilatator fibres, 442
cardiac plethysmograph, 289
cardiac systole, 182
intracardiac pressure, 201
musculi papillares, 202, 213
sp. gr. of blood, 95
splanchnic nerve, 318
spleen, 551

RUDBECK, lymphatic system, 505

RUDINGER, semilunar valves, 187

RUDOLPH, mechanics of respiration 103

RUFFS OF EPHESUS, pulmonary vagus, 457

RUTSCH, oxygen and heart, 294

RUSCONI, perivascular lymphatic, 508

RUSSELL, A. E., heart, inhibition, 338

RUTHERFORD, accelerators of heart, 329

RUYSCH, fibrin, 97

SABATIER, intercostal muscles, 411

SABBATINI, coagulation of blood, 137, 155

SACHS, solution, 58
starch formation, 58

SADLER, vaso-constrictors, 349

SALKOWSKI, autolysis, 34

SALOZ, periodic respiration, 502

SALVIOLI, marrow, 539
serous cavities, 511
spleen, 550, 552

SANDMANN, bronchi, 442

SARPI, venous valves, 165

DI SAUSSURE, plant metabolism, 54

SAVALIEW, thymus, 542

SAVIOTTI, vascular rhythm, 343

SCHÄFER, E. A., blood, 121
physiology, text-book, 9, 12
red blood-corpuscles, 102
spleen, 546, 554, 558
vagus, 558

SCHENCK, cell theory, 12
respiratory gases, 389

SCHENK, H., botany, 62

SCHERER, xanthine bases of plasma, 130

SCHIFF, M., blood-vessels, active movements, 341, 367
bronchial muscles, 442
hemi-section of spinal cord, 452, 503
respiratory centres, 444, 446, 452
spleen, 553
vascular tone, oscillation, 500
vasomotor centres, 362, 364

SCHIFF, cardiac vagus, 322, 327, 329, 337
cervical plexus, 319
periodic respiration, 491
vaso-constrictor nerves, 349

SCHIMPER, botany, 62

SCHLEIDEN, cell theory, 12

SCHLESINGER, vasomotor centres, 364

SCHLÖSING, blood gas, 387

SCHWARZ, pycnometer, 95

SCHMIDT, A., blood, 155
blood gases, 386
coagulation, 134, 135
extraction of gas, 580
salted plasma, 125

SCHMIDT, C., mineral matter of plasma, 131

SCHMIDT-MÜHLHEIM, peptone blood, 124

SCHMIEDEBERG, accelerators, 327, 338
tissue respiration, 393

SCHÖNLEIN, E. C., blood pressure, 284

SCHNEIDER, doctrine of descent, 62

SCHRÖDER, urea and heart, 297

SCHROLL, respiratory centres, 447

SCHULTZE, cube of, 111
heart, 310

SCHULTZE, W. H., cell, 13
chemical stimuli, 73

SCHUITZE, W. H., examination of blood, 120
  leucocytes, 114
  red blood-corpuscles, 101
  structure of protoplasm, 17
  temperature and plant cells, 71
SCHWANN, cell theory, 12
SCHWARTZ, foetal apnoea, 478
SCHWEIGGER-SEYDEL, serous cavities, 509
SCOTT, F. H., phospho-proteins, 24
  phosphorus metabolism, 41
  phosphorus reaction, 39
SCUDAMORE, blood gas, 377
SCZELKOW, blood gas, 380
SÉE, M., auriculo-ventricular valves, 191
SEEGEN, expired air, 397
SEHRMANN, C., muscular work, 470
SEEMANN, haemolymphatic glands, 557, 558
SEGUIN, respiration, 375, 400
SEIFERT, osteomucoid, 40
SELENSKI, marrow and spleen, 589
  spleen, 552, 585
SEMON, laryngeal respiratory movements, 121
SENAC, auriculo-ventricular valves, 192
  circulation, 160
  heart beat, 225
  intercostal muscles, 411
SNEBIER, green plants, 54
  respiration, 375, 400
SERTOLI, blood gas, 385
SERVETUS, circulation, 160
SETSCHENOW, blood gas, 380, 585
SEVERANU, splenectomy, 555
SEWALL, depressor, 335
SHERRINGTON, locomotion and nervous system, 367, 466
SHORE, non-coagulable lymph, 513
SIBSON, thoracic respiration, 417
  thoracometer, 415, 439
SIEBERT, periodic respiration, 501, 504
SIEWERT, isolation of heart, 292
SIGHICELLI, automatic control of respiratory rhythms, 460
  inspiratory centres, 456, 504
SILVIO, Vesalius, 163
SIMON, blood, 94
SKODA, heart beat, 225
SMIRNOW, periodic respiration, 494
  vasomotor centres, 366
SMITH, G., phototropism, 90
SMITH, LORRAINE, oxygen of blood, 391, 400
SNELLEN, vascular reflexes, 356
SOKOLOW, periodic respiration, 495, 501, 504
SOLLMANN, T., resuscitation of heart 339
  vasomotor centre, 368
SOLTMANN, vagal tone, 337
SOMMERBRODT, cardiac vagus, 336

SPALLANZANI, anabiosis, 66
  arterial pulse, 277
  circulation, 341
  circulation in capillaries, 172
  respiration, 375, 400
  science of life, 3
SPALLITTA, depressor, 337
  vascular reflexes, 375
SPALTEHOLZ, thoracic skeleton, 407
SPIGEL, intercostal muscles, 412
SPIRO, muscular work, 470
SPRENGEL, circulation, 165
  diastole, 208
SPRING, active diastole, 213
  presystole, 181
STAEDELER, urea and heart, 297
STAHL, phlogiston, 374
STAHL, E., chemotaxis, 74
  rheotaxis, 76
STANLEY, O. O., blood platelets, 121
STANNIUS, heart, 299, 337
STARLING, accelerators, 330
  cardiac vagus, 326
  intracardiac pressure, 201, 207
  lymph formation, 520, 527, 557
  systolic plateau, 206
STEFFANI, automatic control of respiratory rhythm, 460
  cardiac vagus, 218, 326
  diastole, 209, 231
  respiratory centres, 456, 504
STEINER, arterial pressure, 243
  depressor 335
STENITCK, cardiac vagus, 333
  depressor, 335
  vasomotor centres, 364
STERN, terminal respirations, 452
STEWART, G. N., bulbar centres, 504
  haemolysis, 122, 156
  red blood-corpuscles, 121
STIENON, normal physiological solution, 295
STILLING, active movements of vessels, 341
STIRLING, W., lymph-sac, 558
  myocardium, 318, 321
  normal physiological solution, 295
STOKES, heart-beat, 222
  periodic respiration, 492
STOPPATO, thymus, 545
STRASBURGER, botany, 62
  chondrioderma, 16
  myxomycetes, 15
  phototaxis, 78
  tradescantia, 18
STRASSBURG, tissue respiration, 395
STRAUB, normal physiological solution, 297
STRECKER, oxygen and heart, 294
VAN DER STRICHT, megacaryocytes, 548, 557
STRICKER, accelerators, 329, 337
  vasomotors, 355, 364, 367

SURMAY, auriculo-ventricular valves, 192

SVEHLA, thymus, 545

SWIFT, J. B., vasomotor centre, 368

TAIMA, blood pressure, 245
 heart sounds, 197

TANGL, osmotic pressure of blood, 141

TAPPEINER, quantity and pressure of blood, 255

TARCHANOFF, cardiac vagus, 324
 spleen, 554

TAROZZI, anaerobic organisms, 68

TARULLI, thymus, 542, 558

TAWARA, auriculo-ventricular bundle, 314

TAYLOR, A. E., protamines, 41
 protein synthesis, 40

TEBB, M. C., protagon, 11

TEDESCHI, spleen, 551, 556, 558

TESNER, asphyxia, 479

TERNI VAN DER HELL, cardio-pneumatic curves, 228

TERRY, O. P., galvanotropism, 90

THANE, diaphragm, 410
 sternum, 410

THANHOFFER, cardiac vagus, 323

THEBESIUS, automatic control of heart, 211
 semilunar valves, 187

THIRY, experimental apnoea, 476
 vasomotor centres, 327, 362, 367

THOMAS, diapedesis, 115

THOMA-ZEISS, haemocytometer, 102

THOMPSON, marine biology, 81

THOMSON, ALLEN, heart, 181
 respiratory muscles, 410, 411, 412

TILDEMANN, blood gases, 377

TIGERSTEDT, area of capillary system, 263
  automatism of heart, 306
  blood pressure, 246
  cardiac vagus, 218
  circulation of blood, 161, 231
  circulation time, 283
  haemodromometer, 257
  heart beat, 231
  heart, work, 230
  intersystole, 202
  recording spirometer, 425
  respiratory gases, 390
  semilunar valves, 190
  vascular reflexes, 358
  velocity of blood, 263

TIMOFEEW, accelerators, 337
 cardiac vagus, 323

TISSANDIER, balloon ascent, 72

TIZZONI, splenectomy, 555, 557, 558

TOLLIN, circulation, 160, 166

TORELLE, E., phototaxis, 90

TORRICELLI, hydrodynamics, 233

TORUP, blood gases, 385

TOWLE, E. W., heliotropism, 90

TRAMBUSTI, erythroblasts, 536, 557
 megacaryocytes, 537

TRAUBE, artificial cells, 147
 cardiac vagus, 332
 inspiratory muscles, 410
 oscillations of vascular tone, 500
 periodic respirations, 494, 498, 529
 pulmonary vagus, 462
 vasomotor waves, 344

TRIMBLEY, regeneration, 84

TRIVUS, pulmonary vagus, 463

TREVIRANUS, biology, 1

TRIPIER, cardiac vagus, 324

TROMMER, sugar reaction, 36

TSCHERMAK, depressor, 335

TSCHIRJEW, accelerators, 337

TSHUJEWSKY, velocity of blood stream, 284

TURNER, heart sounds, 196

USTIMOWITSCH, vasomotor centres, 366

VAHLEN, potassium in the cell, 39

VALENTIN, active vascular movement, 341
 velocity, capillaries, 263

VALSALVA, mechanics of thoracic movements, 429, 456
 sinus, 187

VALVERDI, circulation, 161

VAN JAIR, vascular reflexes, 357
 vasomotor centres, 366

VAUQUELIN, extraction of gas, 377

VILLA, splenectomy, 557

VIRNOW, H. M., erepsin, 35
 tissue respiration, 401

VERWORN, biogen hypothesis, 90
 centres and oxygen, 394
 chemical stimuli, 74
 galvanotaxis, 80
 general physiology, 39, 87, 90
 muscle, relaxation, 214
 phenomenalism, 7
 stentor, 15
 thalassicolla, nucleus, 14
 thermotaxis, 78
 thigmotaxis, 76

VESALIUS, artificial respiration, 403
 circulation, 162
 diastole, 208
 foetal apnoea, 478
 intercostal muscles, 411
 semilunar valves, 187

VESLING, circulation, 166
 intercostal muscles, 411

VIAULT, red blood-corpuscles, 105

VIERORDT, auriculo-ventricular valves, 192
 blood pressure, 245
 circulation time, 283
 expired air, 397
 haemocytometry, 102
 haemorrhage, 152

VIFROLDT, haemotachometer, 274
  mechanics of respiration, 459
  spectrophotometer, 111
  sphygmograph, 261
  tidal air, 123
  velocity in capillaries, 263
  work of heart, 233
VIEUSSLNS, auriculo-ventricular valves, 192
  annulus of, 328, 354
VINCENT, haemolymphatic glands, 557, 558
VINCI, LEONARDO DA, respiration, 370
VIOLA, serum, electric conductivity, 150, 155
VIRCHOW, cell theory, 12
  haematoidin, 102
  inflammation, 175
  spleen, 552
VOGEL, blood gases, 377
VOIT, accelerators, 329
  blood gases, 387
  negative pulse, 227
VOLKMANN, blood pressure, 253, 283
  haemodromometer, 257
  haemodynamics, 283
  ribs, 408
  respiratory centres, 444
  velocity in capillaries, 263
  work of heart, 233
VOSS, circulation, 166
DE VRIES, H., molecular concentration, 141
  mutations, 51, 63
  species and varieties, 63
VULPIAN, splanchnic nerves, 348
  vascular reflexes, 359
  vasomotor nerves, 348, 354, 367
VULPIUS, splenectomy, 555, 558

WAGNER, accelerators, 327
  cardiac vagus, 323
  circulation, 171
  pulmonary vagus, 462
WALALUS, circulation, 166
WALDEN, E. C., normal physiological solution, 538
WALDENBURG, blood pressure, 245
  gasometric apparatus, 484
  mechanics of respiration, 439
WALLACE, A. R., Darwinism, 63
WALLER, A., cardiac vagus, 329
  cervical sympathetic, 342, 348
  diapedesis, 175
WALLER, A. D., cardiac vagus, 322
  periodic respiration, 493
  sphygmograms, 266
  thoracic respiration, 417
WALSCHE, thoracic respiration, 417
WALTER, blood gases, 380
WARD, R. O., alveolar air, high altitudes, 439
WARREN, vasomotors, 352

WASILEWSKI, cardiac vagus, 323
WASILIEFF, cardiac vagus, 333
WEBER, E. H., auriculo-ventricular valves, 192
  blood-vessels, active movements, 541
  cardiac centres, 336
  cardiac vagus, 322, 337
  mechanics of respiration, 436
  muscle, elasticity, 547
  quantity of blood, 98
  sphygmographic waves, 210, 282
  velocity in capillaries, 263
  wave theory, 283
WEBER, W., cardiac vagus, 322
  wave theory, 283
WEBSTER, heart sounds, 197
WEDMEYER, mechanics of thoracic movements, 429
WEIDENREICH, haemolymphatic glands, 557
  red blood-corpuscles, 121
WEIGERT, fats in blood, 127
WEISS, lymph, 516
WEISSMANN, heredity, 49, 62
WELCKER, haemoeytometer, 102
  quantity of blood, 99, 121
WELDON, origin of species, 63
WELLS, H. G., autolysis, 40
WENCKEBACH, venous pulse, 203
WERTHEIMER, respiratory centres, 448, 451
WHEATSTONE, bridge of, 150
WILCOCK, E. G., amino-acids, 40
WILLIAMS, heart sounds, 197
WILLIAMS, cardiac vagus, 218
  tonographic apparatus, 288
WILLIS, R., circulation of blood, 179
WINOGRADSKY, nitrification by bacteria, 58
WINSLOW, auriculo-ventricular valves, 192
  intercostal muscles, 111
WINTER, erythrocytes, isotonic solution, 106
  molecular concentration of blood, 143, 155
WINTERSTEIN, nerve centres and oxygen, 394
  heart oxygen, 294, 338
  true apnoea, 491
WINTRICH, heart sounds, 197
WOLFFBERG, pulmonary catheter, 488
WOLLASTON, muscle sound, 197
WOODWORTH, R. S., contraction of heart, 538
WOOLDRIDGE, depressor, 334
WORM-MÜLLER, transfusion of blood, 152
WRIGHT, A. E., bactericidal power of blood, 156
  coagulation of blood, 140, 156

YEO, oxygen and heart, 293

YERKES, R. M., entomostraca and light, 90

ZACCARELLI, splenectomy, 555
ZANETTI, seromucoids, 126, 129
v. ZEILMSSEN, afferent fibres of heart 335
ZUNTZ, acapnia, 475, 504

ZUNTZ, blood gases, 380, 386, 400
 dyspnoea, 470
 foetal blood, 477
 periodic respiration, 501, 504
 pulmonary gas exchange, 392, 400
 reaction of blood, 96
 work of heart, 230
ZWHILE, foetal blood, 477

END OF VOL. I

Lightning Source UK Ltd.
Milton Keynes UK
UKHW03f2053070918
328517UK00003B/262/P